Houghton
Mifflin
Harcourt

# TEXAS SCIENCE
# Fusion

**fusion** [FYOO • zhuhn] a combination of two or more things that releases energy

This **Write-In Student Edition** belongs to

_____

Teacher/Room

_____

# Consulting Authors

## Michael A. DiSpezio

*Global Educator*
North Falmouth, Massachusetts

Michael DiSpezio is a renaissance educator who segued from the research laboratory of a Nobel Prize winner to the K–12 science classroom. He has authored or coauthored numerous textbooks and trade books. For nearly a decade he worked with the JASON Project, under the auspices of the National Geographic Society, where he designed curriculum, wrote lessons, and hosted dozens of studio and location broadcasts. Over the past two decades, DiSpezio has developed supplementary material for organizations and programs that include PBS *Scientific American Frontiers*, *Discover* magazine, and the Discovery Channel. To all his projects, he brings his extensive background in science and his expertise in classroom teaching at the elementary, middle, and high school levels.

## Marjorie Frank

*Science Writer and Content-Area Reading Specialist*
Brooklyn, New York

An educator and linguist by training, a writer and poet by nature, Marjorie Frank has authored and designed a generation of instructional materials in all subject areas, including past HMH Science programs. Her other credits include authoring science issues of an award-winning children's magazine, writing game-based digital assessments, developing blended learning materials for young children, and serving as instructional designer and coauthor of pioneering school-to-work software for a nonprofit organization dedicated to improving reading and math skills for middle and high school learners. In addition, she has served on the adjunct faculty of Hunter, Manhattan, and Brooklyn Colleges, teaching courses in science methods, literacy, and writing.

**Acknowledgments for Covers**

**Front cover:** *fiber optics* ©Dennis O'Clair/Stone/Getty Images; *gecko* ©Pete Orelup/Flickr/Getty Images; *mountain biker* ©Jerome Prevost/TempSport/Corbis; *digital screen* ©Michael Melford/Stone/Getty Images; *Giant's Causeway* ©Rod McLean/Alamy.

**Back cover:** *anemometer* ©Ryan McGinnis/Flickr/Getty Images; *rock formation* ©John Elk III/Alamy; *Mars rover* ©Mark Garlick/Photo Researchers, Inc.; *lava* ©Bruce Omori/epa/Corbis.

## Michael R. Heithaus

*Executive Director, School of Environment, Arts, and Society*
*Associate Professor, Department of Biological Sciences*
Florida International University
North Miami, Florida

Mike Heithaus joined the Florida International University Biology Department in 2003. He has served as Director of the Marine Sciences Program and is now the Executive Director of the School of Environment, Arts, and Society, which brings together the natural and social sciences and humanities to develop solutions to today's environmental challenges. His research focuses on predator-prey interactions and the ecological roles of large marine species including sharks, sea turtles, and marine mammals. His long-term studies include the Shark Bay Ecosystem Project in Western Australia. He also served as a Research Fellow with National Geographic, using remote imaging in his research and hosting a *Crittercam* television series on the National Geographic Channel.

## Donna M. Ogle

*Professor of Reading and Language*
National-Louis University
Chicago, Illinois

Creator of the well-known KWL strategy, Donna Ogle has directed many staff development projects translating theory and research into school practice in schools throughout the United States. She is a past president of the International Reading Association and has served as a consultant on literacy projects worldwide. Her extensive international experience includes coordinating the Reading and Writing for Critical Thinking Project in Eastern Europe and speaking and consulting on projects in several Latin American countries and in Asia. Her books include *Reading Comprehension: Strategies for Independent Learners*; *All Children Read*; and *Literacy for a Democratic Society*.

# Texas Reviewers

**Nigel S. Atkinson, Ph.D.**
*Professor of Neurobiology*
Section of Neurobiology
The University of Texas at Austin
Austin, TX

**Carolyn Barnes, M.Ed.**
Vidor Junior High
Vidor, TX

**Sonal Blumenthal, Ph.D.**
*Science Education Consultant*
Austin, TX

**Hilary Clement Olson, Ph.D.**
*Research Scientist Associate V and Lecturer*
Institute for Geophysics and Department of Petroleum and Geosystems Engineering
The University of Texas at Austin
Austin, TX

**Jennifer Cummings, B.A.**
Bailey Junior High School
Arlington, TX

**Melissa Davis**
Kitty Hawk Middle School
San Antonio, TX

**Jason Hook, B.S.**
Manor Independent School District
San Antonio, TX

**Leslie J McClinton, M.A., B.S.**
Rosemont Middle School
Fort Worth, TX

**David T. Sites, III, M.S. Geology**
Goddard Junior High School
Midland, TX

**Dee Strother, B.S.**
Vidor Junior High School
Vidor, TX

**Gerardo Talamantes, B.S.**
Montwood Middle School
El Paso, TX

**D. E. Winget, Ph.D.**
*Harlan J. Smith Centennial Professor of Astronomy*
*University Distinguished Teaching Professor*
Texas Cosmology Center
Department of Astronomy and McDonald Observatory
The University of Texas at Austin
Austin, TX

**Kim Withers, Ph.D.**
*Associate Research Scientist*
Center for Coastal Studies
Texas A&M University, Corpus Christi
Corpus Christi, TX

**Matthew A. Wood, Ph.D.**
*Professor and Department Head*
Department of Physics & Astronomy
Texas A&M University, Commerce
Commerce, TX

# Content Reviewers

**Arkhat Abzhanov, Ph.D.**
*Associate Professor*
Department of Organismic and
Evolutionary Biology
Harvard University
Cambridge, MA

**Paul D. Asimow, Ph.D.**
*Professor of Geology and
Geochemistry*
Division of Geological and
Planetary Sciences
California Institute of Technology
Pasadena, CA

**Laura K. Baumgartner,
Ph.D.**
*Biology Instructor*
Science Department
Front Range Community College
Longmont, CO

**Eileen M. Cashman, Ph.D.**
*Professor and Department
Chair, Environmental Resources
Engineering
Research Associate, Schatz
Energy Research Center*
Humboldt State University
Arcata, CA

**Wesley N. Colley, Ph.D.**
*Senior Research Analyst*
Center for Modeling, Simulation,
and Analysis
The University of Alabama in
Huntsville
Huntsville, AL

**Joe W. Crim, Ph.D.**
*Professor Emeritus*
Department of Cellular Biology
The University of Georgia
Athens, GA

**Elizabeth A. De Stasio,
Ph.D.**
*Raymond H. Herzog Professor of
Science
Professor of Biology*
Department of Biology
Lawrence University
Appleton, WI

**Julia R. Greer, Ph.D.**
*Assistant Professor of Materials
Science and Mechanics*
Division of Engineering and
Applied Sciences
California Institute of Technology
Pasadena, CA

**John E. Hoover, Ph.D.**
*Professor*
Department of Biology
Millersville University
Millersville, PA

**William H. Ingham, Ph.D.**
*Professor Emeritus*
Department of Physics and
Astronomy
James Madison University
Harrisonburg, VA

**Charles W. Johnson, Ph.D.**
*Associate Professor of Physics,
Division Chair*
Division of Natural Sciences,
Mathematics and Physical
Education
South Georgia College
Douglas, GA

**Tatiana A. Krivosheev,
Ph.D.**
*Associate Professor of Physics*
Department of Natural Sciences
Clayton State University
Morrow, GA

**Joel Leventhal, Ph.D.**
*Emeritus Scientist
(formerly Research Geochemist)*
U.S. Geological Survey
Denver, CO

**Joseph A. McClure, Ph.D.**
*Associate Professor Emeritus*
Department of Physics
Georgetown University
Washington, DC

**Mark B. Moldwin, Ph.D.**
*Professor of Space Sciences*
Department of Atmospheric,
Oceanic and Space Sciences
University of Michigan
Ann Arbor, MI

**Sten Odenwald, Ph.D.**
*Astrophysicist*
Director of SpaceMath@NASA
National Institute of Aerospace
Hampton, VA

**Patricia M. Pauley, Ph.D.**
*Meteorologist, Data Assimilation
Group*
Naval Research Laboratory
Monterey, CA

**Stephen F. Pavkovic, Ph.D.**
*Professor Emeritus*
Department of Chemistry
Loyola University of Chicago
Chicago, IL

**James L. Pazun, Ph.D.**
*Professor and Chair*
Chemistry and Physics
Pfeiffer University
Misenheimer, NC

**L. Jeanne Perry, Ph.D.**
*Director (Retired)*
Protein Expression Technology
Center
Institute for Genomics and
Proteomics
University of California, Los
Angeles
Los Angeles, CA

**Kenneth H. Rubin, Ph.D.**
*Professor*
Department of Geology and
Geophysics
University of Hawaii
Honolulu, HI

**Brandon E. Schwab, Ph.D.**
*Professor and Chair*
Department of Geology
Humboldt State University
Arcata, CA

**Adam D. Woods, Ph.D.**
*Associate Professor*
Department of Geological
Sciences
California State University,
Fullerton
Fullerton, CA

**Natalie Zayas, M.S., Ed.D.**
*Lecturer*
Division of Science and
Environmental Policy
California State University,
Monterey Bay
Seaside, CA

# Teacher Reviewers

**Karen Cavalluzzi, M.Ed.,
NBCT**
Sunny Vale Middle School
Blue Springs, MO

**Katie Demorest,
M.A. Ed. Tech.**
Marshall Middle School
Marshall, MI

**Dave Grabski, M.S. Ed.**
P. J. Jacobs Junior High School
Stevens Point, WI

**Ben Hondorp**
Creekside Middle School
Zeeland, MI

**Mary Larsen**
*Science Instructional Coach*
Helena Public Schools
Helena, MT

**Angie Larson**
Bernard Campbell Middle School
Lee's Summit, MO

**Christy Leier**
Horizon Middle School
Moorhead, MN

**Michele K. Lombard, Ed.D.**
Swanson Middle School
Arlington, VA

**Helen Mihm, NBCT**
Crofton Middle School
Crofton, MD

**Jeff Moravec, Sr., M.S. Ed.**
*Teaching Specialist*
Milwaukee Public Schools
Milwaukee, WI

**Nancy Kawecki Nega,
M.S.T., NBCT, PAESMT**
Churchville Middle School
Elmhurst, IL

**Mark E. Poggensee,
M.S. Ed.**
Elkhorn Middle School
Elkhorn, WI

**Sherry Rich**
Bernard Campbell Middle School
Lee's Summit, MO

**Heather Wares, M.Ed.**
Traverse City West Middle School
Traverse City, MI

**Alexandra Workman,
M.Ed., NBCT**
Thomas Jefferson Middle School
Arlington, VA

# Contents
# in Brief

© Houghton Mifflin Harcourt Publishing Company

# Power up with Texas Science Fusion!

Your program fuses...

**e-Learning and Virtual Labs**

**Labs and Activities**

**Write-In Student Edition**

... *to generate energy for today's science learner — you.*

S.T.E.M. Engineering & Technology

...neering Design Process

### Objectives

- Explain how a need for clean energy has driven a technological solution.
- Describe two examples of wind-powered generators.
- Design a technological solution to a problem.
- Test and modify a prototype to achieve the desired result.

...ills
- Iden...
- Cond...
- Brainsto...ions
- Select a sol...
- ...esign a proto...
- ...ild a prototype
- ...nd evaluate
- ... to improve
- ...te results

#### Bui...

During th... human an... manufactu... easier. How... coal, oil, an... Revolution a... ...ut burning ...aste produc... ...vironment. ...will even... ...lt, we need... un...tand alternative, renewable sou...s of energy.

**1 Brainstorm** What are other possible sources of renewable energy that could be used to power a generator?

...instor... ...r Solution...
...are many s... energy besides fos... ...One of the m...dant renewable ...s is wind. A w...ne is a device that ...ergy from the...turn an axle. The ...g axle can be at...o other equipment ...bs such as pum...er, cutting ...or generating e... To generate ...ty, the axle spin...s around a coiled ...is causes electr...y in the wire. ...electrons produ...tric current. ...rrent is used to...es and ...or electrical ene...ored in

3 Earth's Atmosphere

# e-Learning and Virtual Labs

Digital lessons and virtual labs provide e-learning options for every lesson of ScienceFusion.

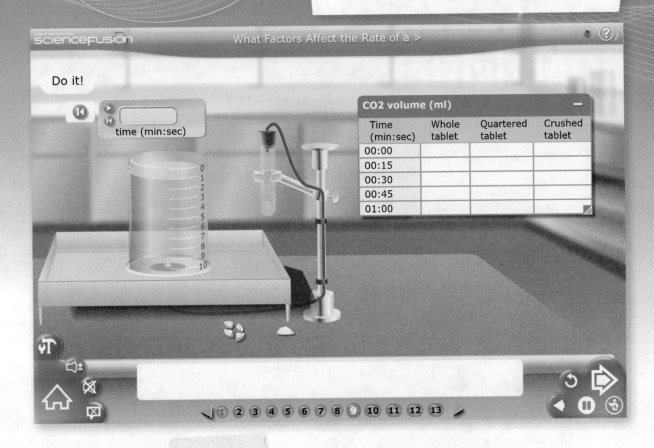

On your own or with a group, explore science concepts in a digital world.

# Continue your science explorations with these online tools:

→ **ScienceSaurus**　　　→ **People in Science**

→ **NSTA SciLinks**　　　→ **Media Gallery**

→ **Video-Based Projects**　→ **Digital Glossary**

# Labs and Activities

ScienceFusion includes lots of exciting hands-on inquiry labs and activities, each one designed to bring science skills and concepts to life and get you involved.

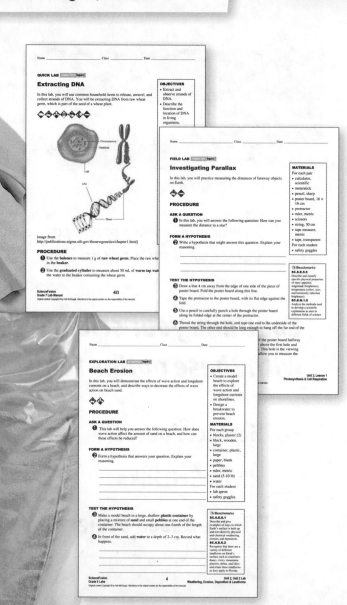

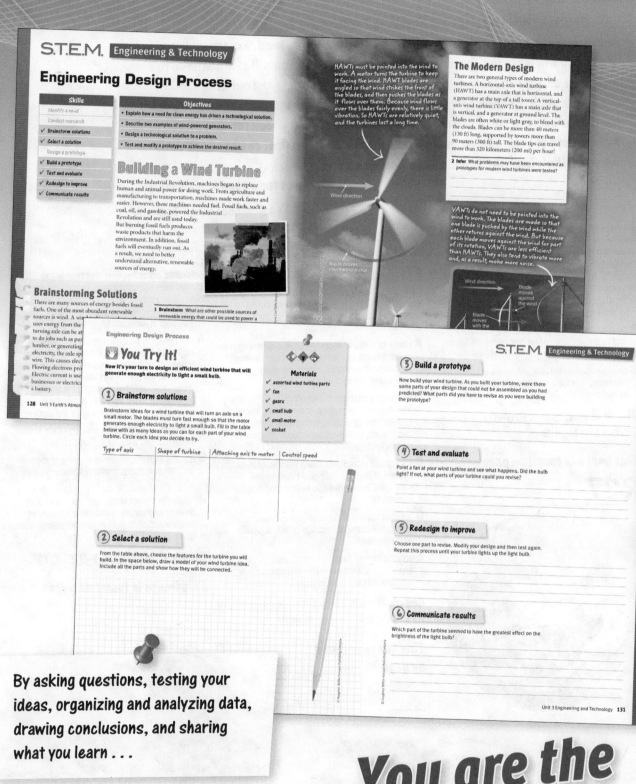

# Engineering Design Process

| Skills |
| --- |
| Identify a need |
| Conduct research |
| ✓ Brainstorm solutions |
| ✓ Select a solution |
| Design a prototype |
| ✓ Build a prototype |
| ✓ Test and evaluate |
| ✓ Redesign to improve |
| ✓ Communicate results |

**Objectives**
- Explain how a need for clean energy has driven a technological solution.
- Describe two examples of wind-powered generators.
- Design a technological solution to a problem.
- Test and modify a prototype to achieve the desired result.

## Building a Wind Turbine

During the Industrial Revolution, machines began to replace human and animal power for doing work. From agriculture and manufacturing to transportation, machines made work faster and easier. However, these machines needed fuel. Fossil fuels, such as coal, oil, and gasoline, powered the Industrial Revolution and are still used today. But burning fossil fuels produces waste products that harm the environment. In addition, fossil fuels will eventually run out. As a result, we need to better understand alternative, renewable sources of energy.

### Brainstorming Solutions

There are many sources of energy besides fossil fuels. One of the most abundant renewable sources is wind. A wind turbine uses energy from the wind to turn. A turning axle can be attached to do jobs such as pumping, cutting lumber, or generating electricity, the axle spins a coil of wire. This causes electrons to flow. Flowing electrons produce electric current. Electric current is used by homes, businesses or electrical energy is stored in a battery.

**1 Brainstorm** What are other possible sources of renewable energy that could be used to power a

HAWTs must be pointed into the wind to work. A motor turns the turbine to keep it facing the wind. HAWT blades are angled so that wind strikes the front of the blades, and then pushes the blades as it flows over them. Because wind flows over the blades fairly evenly, there is little vibration. So HAWTs are relatively quiet, and the turbines last a long time.

Wind direction

Blade moves counterclockwise

### The Modern Design

There are two general types of modern wind turbines. A horizontal-axis wind turbine (HAWT) has a main axle that is horizontal, and a generator at the top of a tall tower. A vertical-axis wind turbine (VAWT) has a main axle that is vertical, and a generator at ground level. The blades are often white or light gray, to blend with the clouds. Blades can be more than 40 meters (130 ft) long, supported by towers more than 90 meters (300 ft) tall. The blade tips can travel more than 320 kilometers (200 mi) per hour!

**2 Infer** What problems may have been encountered as prototypes for modern wind turbines were tested?

VAWTs do not need to be pointed into the wind to work. The blades are made so that one blade is pushed by the wind while the other returns against the wind. But because each blade moves against the wind for part of its rotation, VAWTs are less efficient than HAWTs. They also tend to vibrate more and, as a result, make more noise.

Wind direction
Blade moves against the wind
Blade moves with the

---

Engineering Design Process

## 🖐 You Try It!

Now it's your turn to design an efficient wind turbine that will generate enough electricity to light a small bulb.

### 1 Brainstorm solutions

Brainstorm ideas for a wind turbine that will turn an axle on a small motor. The blades must turn fast enough so that the motor generates enough electricity to light a small bulb. Fill in the table below with as many ideas as you can for each part of your wind turbine. Circle each idea you decide to try.

**Materials**
- ✓ assorted wind turbine parts
- ✓ fan
- ✓ gears
- ✓ small bulb
- ✓ small motor
- ✓ socket

| Type of axis | Shape of turbine | Attaching axis to motor | Control speed |
| --- | --- | --- | --- |
| | | | |

### 2 Select a solution

From the table above, choose the features for the turbine you will build. In the space below, draw a model of your wind turbine idea. Include all the parts and show how they will be connected.

### 3 Build a prototype

Now build your wind turbine. As you built your turbine, were there some parts of your design that could not be assembled as you had predicted? What parts did you have to revise as you were building the prototype?

### 4 Test and evaluate

Point a fan at your wind turbine and see what happens. Did the bulb light? If not, what parts of your turbine could you revise?

### 5 Redesign to improve

Choose one part to revise. Modify your design and then test again. Repeat this process until your turbine lights up the light bulb.

### 6 Communicate results

Which part of the turbine seemed to have the greatest effect on the brightness of the light bulb?

By asking questions, testing your ideas, organizing and analyzing data, drawing conclusions, and sharing what you learn . . .

# You are the scientist!

# Texas Essential Knowledge and Skills

**Dear Students and Families,**

This book and this class are structured around the Texas Essential Knowledge and Skills (TEKS) for Grade 6 Science. As you read, experiment, and study, you will learn the concepts listed on these pages. You will also continue to build your science literacy, which will enrich your life both in and out of school.

Each picture shown below is also found on another page of this book. You can begin your exploration of science this year by looking in the book for that other page, where you can find out more about the picture. The first one has been done for you. (Hint: Look in the units listed for each TEKS.)

Best wishes for a good school year,

The ScienceFusion Team

## TEKS 6.1

**Scientific investigation and reasoning** The student, for at least 40% of instructional time, conducts laboratory and field investigations following safety procedures and environmentally appropriate and ethical practices. The student is expected to:

**A** demonstrate safe practices during laboratory and field investigations as outlined in the Texas Safety Standards; and

**B** practice appropriate use and conservation of resources, including disposal, reuse, or recycling of materials.

**Check it out:** pages R26–R27; Grade 6 Lab Manual

**This image is found on page**

# R27

## TEKS 6.2

**Scientific investigation and reasoning** The student uses scientific inquiry methods during laboratory and field investigations. The student is expected to:

**A** plan and implement comparative and descriptive investigations by making observations, asking well-defined questions, and using appropriate equipment and technology;

**B** design and implement experimental investigations by making observations, asking well-defined questions, formulating testable hypotheses, and using appropriate equipment and technology;

**C** collect and record data using the International System of Units (SI) and qualitative means such as labeled drawings, writing, and graphic organizers;

**D** construct tables and graphs, using repeated trials and means, to organize data and identify patterns; and

**E** analyze data to formulate reasonable explanations, communicate valid conclusions supported by the data, and predict trends.

**Check it out:** Units 1–2; pages R28–R45; Grade 6 Lab Manual

**This image is found on page**

_____

## TEKS 6.3

**Scientific investigation and reasoning** The student uses critical thinking, scientific reasoning, and problem solving to make informed decisions and knows the contributions of relevant scientists. The student is expected to:

**A** in all fields of science, analyze, evaluate, and critique scientific explanations by using empirical evidence, logical reasoning, and experimental and observational testing, including examining all sides of scientific evidence of those scientific explanations, so as to encourage critical thinking by the student;

**B** use models to represent aspects of the natural world such as a model of Earth's layers;

**C** identify advantages and limitations of models such as size, scale, properties, and materials; and

**D** relate the impact of research on scientific thought and society, including the history of science and contributions of scientists as related to the content.

**Check it out:** Units 1–3, 5–8, 10

**This image is found on page**

_____

© Houghton Mifflin Harcourt Publishing Company • Image Credits: (c) ©Martin Shields/Photo Researchers, Inc.; (r) ©Hill Street Studios/Blend Images/Corbis

Answers: 6.2 19; 6.3 90

## TEKS 6.4

**Scientific investigation and reasoning** The student knows how to use a variety of tools and safety equipment to conduct science inquiry. The student is expected to:

**A** use appropriate tools to collect, record, and analyze information, including journals/notebooks, beakers, Petri dishes, meter sticks, graduated cylinders, hot plates, test tubes, triple beam balances, microscopes, thermometers, calculators, computers, timing devices, and other equipment as needed to teach the curriculum; and

**B** use preventative safety equipment, including chemical splash goggles, aprons, and gloves, and be prepared to use emergency safety equipment, including an eye/face wash, a fire blanket, and a fire extinguisher.

**Check it out:** Units 1–2; pages R26–R45; Grade 6 Lab Manual

*This image is found on page*

_____

## TEKS 6.5

**Matter and energy** The student knows the differences between elements and compounds. The student is expected to:

**A** know that an element is a pure substance represented by chemical symbols;

**B** recognize that a limited number of the many known elements comprise the largest portion of solid Earth, living matter, oceans, and the atmosphere;

**C** differentiate between elements and compounds on the most basic level; and

**D** identify the formation of a new substance by using the evidence of a possible chemical change such as production of a gas, change in temperature, production of a precipitate, or color change.

**Check it out:** Unit 3

*This image is found on page*

_____

## TEKS 6.6

**Matter and energy** The student knows matter has physical properties that can be used for classification. The student is expected to:

**A** compare metals, nonmetals, and metalloids using physical properties such as luster, conductivity, or malleability;

**B** calculate density to identify an unknown substance; and

**C** test the physical properties of minerals, including hardness, color, luster, and streak.

**Check it out:** Units 3 and 6

*This image is found on page*

_____

## TEKS 6.7

**Matter and energy** The student knows that some of Earth's energy resources are available on a nearly perpetual basis, while others can be renewed over a relatively short period of time. Some energy resources, once depleted, are essentially nonrenewable. The student is expected to:

**A** research and debate the advantages and disadvantages of using coal, oil, natural gas, nuclear power, biomass, wind, hydropower, geothermal, and solar resources; and

**B** design a logical plan to manage energy resources in the home, school, or community.

**Check it out:** Unit 5

**This image is found on page** _____

## TEKS 6.8

**Force, motion, and energy** The student knows force and motion are related to potential and kinetic energy. The student is expected to:

**A** compare and contrast potential and kinetic energy;

**B** identify and describe the changes in position, direction, and speed of an object when acted upon by unbalanced forces;

**C** calculate average speed using distance and time measurements;

**D** measure and graph changes in motion; and

**E** investigate how inclined planes and pulleys can be used to change the amount of force to move an object.

**Check it out:** Unit 4

**This image is found on page** _____

## TEKS 6.9

**Force, motion, and energy** The student knows that the Law of Conservation of Energy states that energy can neither be created nor destroyed, it just changes form. The student is expected to:

**A** investigate methods of thermal energy transfer, including conduction, convection, and radiation;

**B** verify through investigations that thermal energy moves in a predictable pattern from warmer to cooler until all the substances attain the same temperature such as an ice cube melting; and

**C** demonstrate energy transformations such as energy in a flashlight battery changes from chemical energy to electrical energy to light energy.

**Check it out:** Unit 4

**This image is found on page** _____

Answers: 6.7 288; 6.8 238; 6.9 214

## TEKS 6.10

**Earth and space** The student understands the structure of Earth, the rock cycle, and plate tectonics. The student is expected to:

**A** build a model to illustrate the structural layers of Earth, including the inner core, outer core, mantle, crust, asthenosphere, and lithosphere;

**B** classify rocks as metamorphic, igneous, or sedimentary by the processes of their formation;

**C** identify the major tectonic plates, including Eurasian, African, Indo-Australian, Pacific, North American, and South American; and

**D** describe how plate tectonics causes major geological events such as ocean basins, earthquakes, volcanic eruptions, and mountain building.

**Check it out:** Units 6–7

**This image is found on page**

## TEKS 6.11

**Earth and space** The student understands the organization of our solar system and the relationships among the various bodies that comprise it. The student is expected to:

**A** describe the physical properties, locations, and movements of the Sun, planets, Galilean moons, meteors, asteroids, and comets;

**B** understand that gravity is the force that governs the motion of our solar system; and

**C** describe the history and future of space exploration, including the types of equipment and transportation needed for space travel.

**Check it out:** Units 8–9

**This image is found on page**

## TEKS 6.12

**Organisms and environments** The student knows all organisms are classified into Domains and Kingdoms. Organisms within these taxonomic groups share similar characteristics which allow them to interact with the living and nonliving parts of their ecosystem. The student is expected to:

**A** understand that all organisms are composed of one or more cells;

**B** recognize that the presence of a nucleus determines whether a cell is prokaryotic or eukaryotic;

**C** recognize that the broadest taxonomic classification of living organisms is divided into currently recognized Domains;

**D** identify the basic characteristics of organisms, including prokaryotic or eukaryotic, unicellular or multicellular, autotrophic or heterotrophic, and mode of reproduction, that further classify them in the currently recognized Kingdoms;

**E** describe biotic and abiotic parts of an ecosystem in which organisms interact; and

**F** diagram the levels of organization within an ecosystem, including organism, population, community, and ecosystem.

**Check it out:** Unit 10

**This image is found on page**

# Contents

Scientists get evidence from many types of sources—from laboratory experiments to 10,000-year-old rhinoceros remains!

Building models helps us picture things that are hard to see, like this DNA double-helix shape.

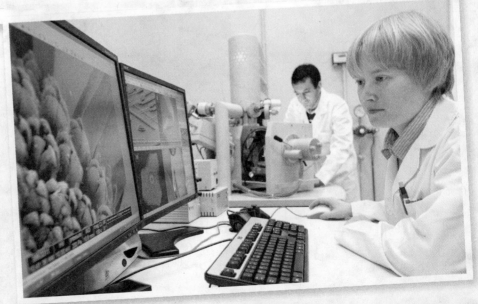

# Contents (continued)

The same particles of matter in our bodies today may once have been a part of a dinosaur or a star!

Which bird has a greater average speed—the diving penguin or the running ostrich?

© Houghton Mifflin Harcourt Publishing Company • Image Credits: (l) ©Specialist Stock/Corbis

# Contents (continued)

Geothermal energy from Earth's interior can be used to produce energy as heat and electricity.

The huge White Cliffs of Dover were formed from the skeletons of organisms, such as the microscopic marine algae shown to the right.

# Contents (continued)

Imagine how hot it must be for rock to melt and flow like water! That's lava for you.

The Pyrenees Mountains, which separate France and Spain, formed when rock layers were squeezed together and pushed upward.

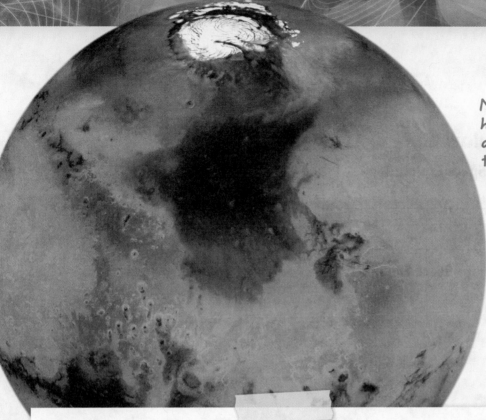

Mars holds the records for having the largest volcano and the largest canyon in the solar system.

# Contents (continued)

Two solid-fuel rockets helped this space shuttle accelerate from 0 to more than 4,828 km/hr in 2 minutes.

Butterfly wings are covered in tiny, colorful scales, which protect the membranes of the wings.

Assignments:

_____
_____
_____
_____
_____
_____
_____
_____
_____
_____
_____
_____
_____
_____
_____
_____
_____
_____
_____
_____
_____
_____
_____
_____
_____
_____
_____
_____
_____
_____
_____
_____

# Safety Preview

Safety is the freedom from danger, injury, or damage. Safety is an important part of every scientific investigation, whether it is in the laboratory or in the field.

## Safety in the Lab

In the laboratory, you are responsible for your own safety and the safety of others. You can help avoid accidents in the lab by keeping these elements of safety in mind:

☐ **Preparation—be sure you understand your materials and your procedure before you start an investigation in the lab.**

☐ **Use proper safety equipment.**

☐ **Follow directions.**

☐ **Keep the lab neat, and clean up when you are finished.**

☐ **Use proper accident procedures, and let your teacher know about an accident immediately, even if it seems minor.**

# Safety in the Field

In the field, you are responsible for your own safety and the safety of others, and also for the organisms and environment in which you are working. You can fulfill these responsibilities by keeping these elements of field safety in mind:

☐ **Preparation—be sure you understand the goal of your fieldwork and the proper way to carry out the investigation before you begin fieldwork.**

☐ **Use proper safety equipment and protective clothing that suits the terrain and the weather.**

☐ **Follow directions.**

☐ **Do not approach or touch wild animals. Do not touch plants unless instructed by your teacher to do so. Leave natural areas as you found them.**

☐ **Stay with your group.**

☐ **Use proper accident procedures, and let your teacher know about a hazard in the environment or an accident immediately, even if it seems minor.**

To find out more about safety, look at these parts of your ScienceFusion program:

**Pages R26–R27 near the end of this book**

**Lab Manual safety pages that you will receive from your teacher**

- Safety Symbols
- Safety in the Laboratory
- Safety in the Field
- Laboratory Techniques
- Student Safety Quiz
- Student Safety Contract

© Houghton Mifflin Harcourt Publishing Company • Image Credits: ©Hero/Corbis

# Strategies for English Language Learners

Are you learning English? You can learn science and English at the same time. You already know a lot about science from the world around you. You can also learn English from the world around you. Your teacher and other students will be happy to help you. Some of the ideas below will help you get ready to learn English. Some ideas will help you learn better in class and while you read. Other ideas will help you remember and use what you learn.

## Get Ready to Learn

You can do these things before you go to science class.

| Get Ready to Learn | |
| --- | --- |
| **Visit Your Classroom and Teacher** | Go to your classroom with other students if you can. Look carefully around the room. <br><br> • Ask your teacher to tell you the names of things you do not know. You can ask, "What is this?" or "Will we use this in class?" or "What does it do?" <br> • Learn how to say and read the names of things you will use in class. <br> • Are there signs on the wall? What do they say? If you do not know, ask your teacher or other students, "What does this say? What does it mean?" <br> • Remember the words on signs. You may see these same words in other places. |
| **Learn Some Science Words** | You will learn a lot of new words in your science class. Some of these new words will be science words. Other new words may not be science words but will still be important to learn. <br><br> • Ask your teacher to say and write some words you need to know. <br> • Ask what the words mean. <br> • Learn how to say and read the words. |
| **Ask Your Teacher for Help with Reading** | Your teacher can help you read your science book. He or she can help you learn new words that you need to know before you read. <br><br> • Your teacher might give you a list of the important words or ideas you will read or a list of questions to answer as you read. <br> • Your teacher might give you a graphic organizer to help you understand what you read. A graphic organizer is a drawing that shows how ideas are connected. |
| **Look at Pictures Before You Read** | Before you read your science book, look at the pictures. It will be easier to read the pages if you already know a little bit from looking at the pictures. <br><br> • As you look at the pictures, think about what you already know. <br> • If there are words with the pictures, read the words. Try to figure out the meaning of the words by what the pictures show. |

| Get Ready to Learn | |
|---|---|
| **Read Before Class** | Your teacher may tell you what he or she will talk about tomorrow. If you read that part of the book today, you will already know some of what the teacher will say. Then it will be easier for you to understand when the teacher talks.<br><br>Before reading a lesson, do the activities on the Lesson Opener. These activities introduce you to some of the words and ideas you will learn in the lesson. 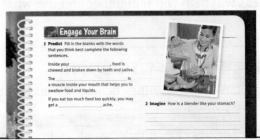 |
| **Start Taking Notes Before Class** | *Taking notes* means writing something to help you remember what you read or hear. Do not write all the words you read or hear. Write just the most important words, or make drawings.<br><br>• It can be hard to take notes when you listen. It is easier if you start your notes before class, when you read your book.<br>• Write down important words that you read, or draw something to help you remember important ideas. Leave lots of space on your paper.<br>• Then, take your notes to class. Use the same paper to take notes when you listen in class. Write more notes in the space you left. |
| **Get Ready to Ask Questions** | You might have questions about what you read before class.<br><br>• First, write down your question or the words that you do not understand. Practice your question.<br>• Bring your question to class. Listen carefully when the teacher talks about the same thing as your question. Your teacher may answer the question.<br>• If you still do not have an answer, raise your hand. Ask the question you wrote and practiced. |
| **Get Ready to Answer Questions** | Learn these question words: *what*, *where*, *when*, *who*, *why*, *how much*, *is it*, *will it*. Learn how to answer questions that use each word.<br><br>• *What:* Tell the name of a thing.<br>• *What will happen, what happened:* Tell how something changes.<br>• *Where:* Tell a place.<br>• *When:* Tell a time (you can also say before or after something).<br>• *Who:* Tell a person. Your teacher might ask, "Who can tell me . . .?" That means, "Do you know the answer?" If you do, raise your hand.<br>• *How much:* Tell an amount.<br>• *Why:* Tell what made something happen, or explain a reason.<br>• *Is it* or *Will it:* Answer yes or no. You can also give a reason for your answer.<br><br>If you do not know the exact words to answer a question, try using words you know to describe your ideas. |

# While You Learn

You can do these things in your science class.

| While You Learn | |
|---|---|
| **Use What You Know** | When you hear or read about something new, think about what you already know.<br><br>If a new word sounds like a word you already know, maybe the two words mean almost the same thing. Maybe you already know something about a new idea. Use what you know to help you understand new words and ideas.<br><br>Some activities in this book help you use what you already know to learn something new. Here are some examples:<br><br>☑ Name one item that you use every day. Describe the natural resources that you think are used to make this item.<br><br>☑ Have you ever been outside and had a gust of wind blow a stack of papers all over the place? If so, you have seen how wind erosion works. In the same way that wind moved your papers, wind moves soil, sand, and rock particles.<br><br>☑ Draw a picture of what you think a scientific investigation might look like.<br><br>Talk to your teacher and classmates about how what you already know relates to what you are learning. |
| **Take Notes During Class** | As you learn new words and ideas in class, listen carefully to your teacher and take notes. The type of notes you take will depend on the topic you are learning about. Here are some suggestions:<br><br>• Write down the main ideas that your teacher explains.<br>• Write down important words and their meanings.<br>• Make lists of characteristics, causes, effects, and examples.<br>• Number the steps in a process.<br>• Draw pictures.<br><br>Put a question mark next to any notes that you do not understand. |

| While You Learn | |
| --- | --- |
| **Understand Instructions** | Instructions tell you how to do something. They are sometimes called *directions*. You need to follow instructions many times in science class. Sometimes your teacher says the instructions. Sometimes you need to read the instructions. |
| | Most instructions have many parts, called *steps*. Sometimes the teacher or book will use numbers (1, 2, 3 . . .) to tell you the order of steps. |
| | Other times, instructions use words. Learn the words that tell you when to do things: *first, then, next, before, after, while, last.* Listen and look for these words in instructions. Use them to help you know when to do things. |
| | You can also use these words to give other people instructions. You can use them to write or tell about something you did. |
| **Learn Some Signal Words** | Signal words are words that show how ideas are connected. Learn the words below, and look for them as you read. |
| | • These signal words show how things are the same or almost the same: *and, also, another, like.* |
| | • These signal words show how things are different: *but, however, although, instead.* |
| | • These signal words show how one thing causes another: *so, because, as a result.* |
| **Look for Different Kinds of Sentences** | There are four main kinds of sentences. They are listed below. Look for these kinds of sentences when you are reading. Listen for them when someone else is speaking. Practice using all types of sentences when you are speaking. |

| Sentence type | Example |
| --- | --- |
| **Statements** end with a period and tell you something. | Differences in air pressure cause wind on Earth. |
| **Commands** tell you to do something. You will see these sentences when there is something for you to do in the book or when you are doing a lab or project. | State what causes wind on Earth. |
| **Questions** end with a question mark. When you are listening, listen for the speaker to pause after they ask a question. The pause gives you time to think about the question or to give an answer to the question. | What causes wind on Earth? |
| **Exclamations** show excitement or surprise and end with an exclamation point. | It is windy outside! |

| | |
|---|---|
| **Get Help If You Do Not Understand** | If you don't understand something that you hear or read, get help. |

- Ask your teacher or another student. Raise your hand and ask in class, or wait until the teacher is done talking.
- If you do not understand a word, try to say the word. Then ask, "What does that word mean?"
- If you do not know how to do something, ask, "How do I do this?"
- If you do not understand an idea or picture, tell what you do know. Then ask about the part you do not understand.

**Answer Questions**

When your teacher asks you a question, you need to answer. Here are some things that can help you:

- Listen carefully to the question. If you do not understand the words, you can ask, "Could you repeat the question?" or "Can you say that more slowly?"
- Listen for the question word. It tells you what kind of answer to give.
- If the teacher is pointing at something, the question is probably about that thing. You can talk about that thing in your answer.
- Remember what the teacher said before the question. The question might be about what the teacher said. Maybe you can use some of the teacher's words in your answer.
- If you do not know an answer, tell the teacher you do not know. You can say, "I don't know" or "I did not understand that very well" or "I don't remember that."

**Talk in Groups**

In science class, you often work with other students. You need to understand what your group should do.

- Read instructions if you have them. You can ask, "Can I have some more time to read?"
- If you do not understand the instructions, you can ask, "Can you help me understand this step?"
- Talk about the instructions after you read. Tell what you can do. Ask the other students what they will do.
- As you work, you can ask your partner for help. You can say, "Can you hold this?" or "What do we do next?"
- Be sure to help your partner. You can ask, "Do you need me to pour that?" or "What can I do to help?"
- If you have an idea, you can say, "I think we should do it this way" or "I have an idea."

## Remember and Use What You Learn

You can do these things to help you learn important science words and ideas. Do them before class, in class, or after class.

| Remember and Use What You Learn | |
| --- | --- |
| **Say It Again (and Again and Again)** | One way to learn new words is to repeat them, or say them many times.<br><br>• First, make sure that you can say the word correctly.<br><br>• Be sure you know what the word means, too. Ask a friend or your teacher if you need to say the word differently or if you do not have the right meaning.<br><br>• When you can say the word correctly and know what it means, say the word several times. With a partner, take turns saying the word and telling each other the meaning.<br><br>• You will remember better if you say the meaning in your own words. You will remember even better if you say your own sentence that uses the word. Try to say a different sentence each time you repeat. |
| **Use Flash Cards** | Flash cards help you learn new words.<br><br>• To make flash cards, use some pieces of paper that are all the same size. What words do you need to learn?<br><br>• Write one word on a piece of paper. Turn the paper over. Write the meaning of the word. Use your own words or draw pictures to help you remember.<br><br>• Write the other words and their meanings on other pieces of paper.<br><br>To use flash cards, look at a word. Say what you think it means. Check the back of the paper for the word's meaning. Do this with all your words.<br><br>• If you get the meaning right, you may not need to look at that card again.<br><br>• If you get some wrong, look at them again and again.<br><br>You can use flash cards alone or with a partner. |
| **Tell Somebody** | Ask a friend or a person in your family to help you learn. Have the person ask you a question. If you need to learn some science words, have him or her ask you what the words mean.<br><br>If you need to remember how something in science works, have the person ask you. Then use your own words to tell what you know from your book or class. Tell the person what the words mean or how something works.<br><br>Answer all the person's questions. Helping that person understand helps you understand and remember too. |

**Make a Picture**

Sometimes a picture can help you remember better than words can. You can draw pictures when you take notes. Draw your own picture, or use a graphic organizer.

There are many different graphic organizers. Here are some examples of graphic organizers used in this book.

A **Venn diagram** shows how two things are the same and how they are different.

- Write how they are different in the two circles.
- Write how they are the same where the two circles come together.

You might be asked to complete a Venn diagram in this book.

*Example:*

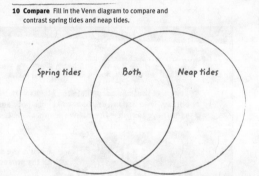

10 **Compare** Fill in the Venn diagram to compare and contrast spring tides and neap tides.

A **concept map** shows how information is connected. Write an important word or idea in the big circle. Draw lines to smaller circles. In the smaller circles, write words that tell more about the idea in the big circle.

*Example:*

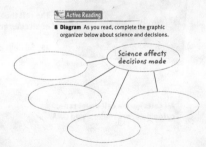

Active Reading

8 **Diagram** As you read, complete the graphic organizer below about science and decisions.

Here are some other types of graphic organizers. You can see examples of these graphic organizers in the Look It Up! section at the end of your book.

- **Content Frame**
- **Combination Notes**
- **Mind Map** and **Main Idea Web**
- **Cause-and-Effect Chart** and **Process Diagram**

## Remember and Use What You Learn

### Summarize

Summarizing can help you remember what you read or hear. A summary includes only the most important ideas.

- You can summarize what you read.
- You can summarize what your teacher says in class.

When you summarize, write or say the most important ideas using your own words. You will remember better if you use your own words.

This book has a Visual Summary at the end of every lesson. The Visual Summary has important pictures and ideas from the lesson. It also has a few questions. Reading the Visual Summary and answering the questions will help you remember better.

*Example:*

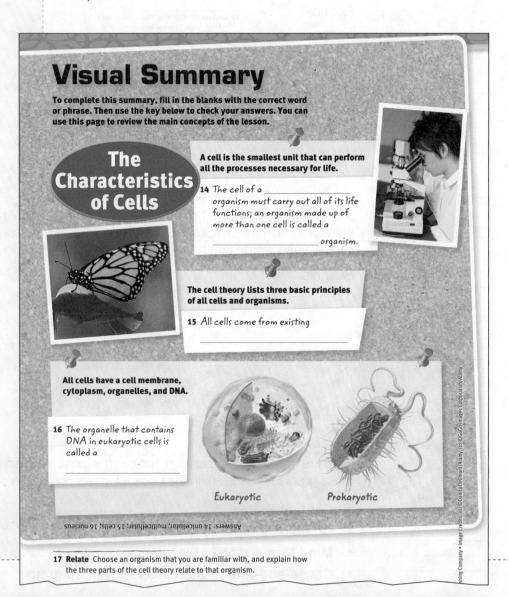

# Visual Summary

To complete this summary, fill in the blanks with the correct word or phrase. Then use the key below to check your answers. You can use this page to review the main concepts of the lesson.

## The Characteristics of Cells

**A cell is the smallest unit that can perform all the processes necessary for life.**

14 The cell of a _____ organism must carry out all of its life functions; an organism made up of more than one cell is called a _____ organism.

**The cell theory lists three basic principles of all cells and organisms.**

15 All cells come from existing _____

**All cells have a cell membrane, cytoplasm, organelles, and DNA.**

16 The organelle that contains DNA in eukaryotic cells is called a _____

Eukaryotic          Prokaryotic

Answers: 14 unicellular, multicellular; 15 cells; 16 nucleus

Image Credits: (tl) ©Danita Delimont/Alamy; (tr) ©GoGo Images Corporation/Alamy

17 **Relate** Choose an organism that you are familiar with, and explain how the three parts of the cell theory relate to that organism.

# UNIT 1
# The Nature of Science

## Big Idea

Scientists use careful observations and clear reasoning to understand processes and patterns in nature.

This false-color satellite image of a crater floor on Mars shows branching rock features that are each several miles across.

## What do you think?

This image was taken by the High Resolution Imaging Science Experiment (HiRISE) camera on NASA's Mars Reconnaissance Orbiter (MRO). How do these observations help scientists understand natural processes on Mars?

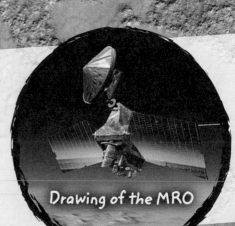

Drawing of the MRO

# Unit 1
# The Nature of Science

## CITIZEN SCIENCE

# Space Travel

In science fiction stories, humans are able to travel across space quickly and easily. In reality, many challenges must be met before humans can take extended spaceflights. New technologies are being developed that may enable humans to live and function in space. Will science catch up to fiction?

This image shows an artist's idea for a future spaceport.

## ① Think About It

What do you know about space travel? Summarize your knowledge of the history of space travel in the space below.

_____

_____

_____

_____

_____

_____

## ② Ask a Question

Would you travel in space aboard a privately owned spacecraft? Explain your answer.

_____

_____

_____

_____

## ③ Make a Plan

**A** Investigate space travel options that are available now. Make notes about your research.

_____

_____

_____

_____

_____

_____

**B** Research the future of private space travel and the possibility of it occurring in your lifetime. Record your findings about current projects and proposals and their timelines.

_____

_____

_____

_____

_____

### Take It Home

**Design and create a poster advertising space travel. Consider the purpose of the trip, the destination, and your target audience. Bring your finished poster to share with the class.**

# Scientific Knowledge

**ESSENTIAL QUESTION**

## What are the types of scientific knowledge?

By the end of this lesson, you should be able to differentiate the methods that scientists use to gain empirical evidence in a variety of scientific fields and explain how this leads to scientific change.

Underwater may seem like an odd place to conduct a science experiment. But scientists often go to faraway places to gather data.

**TEKS** 6.3A in all fields of science, analyze, evaluate, and critique scientific explanations by using empirical evidence, logical reasoning, and experimental and observational testing, including examining all sides of scientific evidence of those scientific explanations, so as to encourage critical thinking by the student

**Lesson Labs**

**Quick Labs**
• Pluto on Trial
• Theory or Claim?

**Exploration Lab**
• Science-Based Commercials

## Engage Your Brain

**1 Predict** Check T or F to show whether you think each statement is true or false.

T   F

☐  ☐  All branches of science have scientific theories.

☐  ☐  A scientist can use only one method to investigate.

☐  ☐  Theories are scientific ideas that have not yet been tested.

☐  ☐  Scientific laws describe what happens in the world.

**2 Synthesize** An aeolipile is a device powered by steam. When heated, water in the bulb produces steam. The bulb rotates as the steam escapes from the nozzles. People were making these devices as long as 2,000 years ago. How do you think they came up with the idea even though they did not have our modern understanding of science?

_____

_____

_____

aeolipile

## Active Reading

**3 Infer** The word *empirical* comes from the Greek word *empeirikos*, meaning "experienced." Based on this information, infer how scientists get empirical evidence.

_____

_____

_____

_____

### Vocabulary Terms

• empirical evidence
• theory
• law

**4 Apply** As you learn the definition of each vocabulary term in this lesson, create your own definition or sketch to help you remember the meaning of the term.

# ...From the **Beginning**

## What is science?

Science is the study of the natural world. Scientists study everything from the deepest parts of the ocean to the objects in outer space. Some scientists study living things. Others study forces such as gravity and magnetism. Name anything you see around you. Chances are, there is a scientist who studies it.

The natural sciences are divided into three areas: biology or life science, geology or Earth science, and physics or physical science. The three areas differ in the subjects they study and the methods they use. Biology is the study of living things. Biologists study everything from the tiniest organisms to human beings. Geology is the study of Earth: what it's made of and the processes that shape it. Physical science is the study of nonliving matter and energy. Chemistry often is included under physical science. A scientist's work sometimes may overlap two or more areas. For example, a biologist often must know chemistry to understand the processes in living things.

Each of the photographs below relates to one of the areas of science in some way. From the captions, can you identify to which area each belongs?

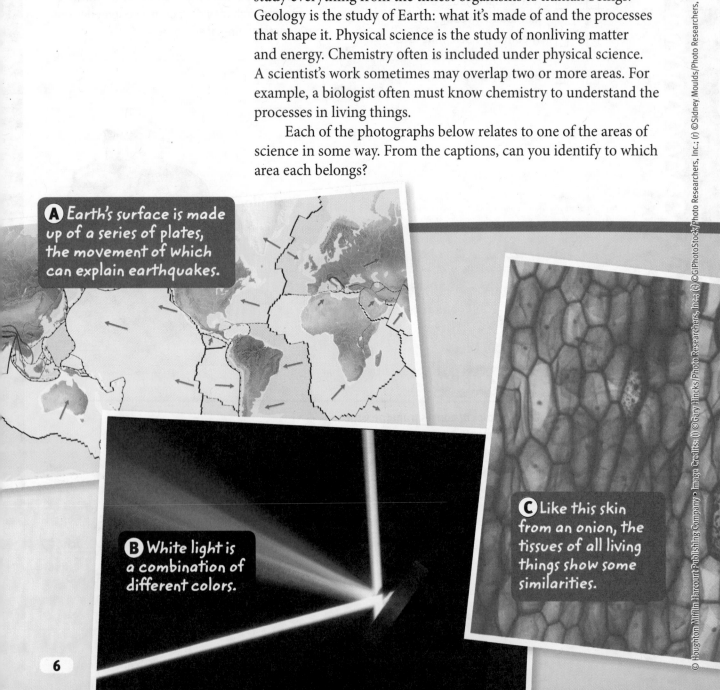

**A** Earth's surface is made up of a series of plates, the movement of which can explain earthquakes.

**B** White light is a combination of different colors.

**C** Like this skin from an onion, the tissues of all living things show some similarities.

# What does science tell us?

**Active Reading** 6 **Identify** Underline what a theory is in science.

You may think that what you read in a science book is accepted by everyone and is unchanging. That is not always the case. The "facts" of science are simply the most widely accepted explanations. Scientific knowledge is and probably always will be changing.

What we learn when we study science are what most scientists agree are the best explanations about how things happen. They are *theories* scientists have about the world. Commonly, we think of a theory as a kind of guess or "hunch." In science, a theory is much more. A scientific theory is an explanation supported by a large amount of evidence. Theories are what most scientists agree to be the best explanations based upon what we now know.

The table below lists three important scientific theories. Each theory relates to one of the areas of science described before. Each also corresponds to a photograph on the previous page. Can you think of what kinds of evidence would support each theory?

## Visualize It!

7 **Identify** For each of the three theories listed in the table below, write the letter of the corresponding photograph at the left. On the lines provided, describe what might be some evidence that would support the theory.

## Scientific Theories

| | What scientists think | What is some evidence? |
|---|---|---|
| Biology | ____ Cell theory: Living things are made up of cells that perform the basic functions of life. | |
| Geology | ____ Plate tectonics: Earth's surface is made up of plates that move. | |
| Physics | ____ Wave theory of light: Each color of visible light has a wave of a specific wavelength. | |

# Not a Theory—

## How do scientific theories differ from laws?

**Active Reading** **8 Identify** As you read, underline a real-world example of Boyle's law.

To understand the nature of scientific knowledge, you must understand how scientists use certain words. Often, the meanings are very specialized. *Law* and *theory* are two familiar words that have very special scientific meanings.

### Laws Describe Principles of Nature

A scientific **law** is a description of a specific relationship under given conditions in the natural world. In short, scientific laws describe the way the world works. They hold anywhere in the universe. You can't escape them.

Boyle's law is one scientific law. According to Boyle's law, at a constant temperature, as the pressure on a gas increases, its volume decreases. To get an appreciation of Boyle's law, think of how it would feel to squeeze a partially deflated beach ball. If you apply pressure by squeezing, the volume, or size, of the ball gets smaller.

You can feel the effects of Boyle's law. A membrane or *eardrum* separates your middle ear from outer ear. Normally, the air spaces on either side are at equal pressure. But sometimes, the pressure on the outer ear can change. For example, the scuba diver in the photo feels an increase in pressure on her eardrum as she descends in the water. By holding her nose and blowing gently, she can force more air into her middle ear. The action momentarily opens the *eustachian tube* connecting the middle ear to the throat. This allows more air from the mouth to rush into the middle ear and equalize the pressure between the two spaces.

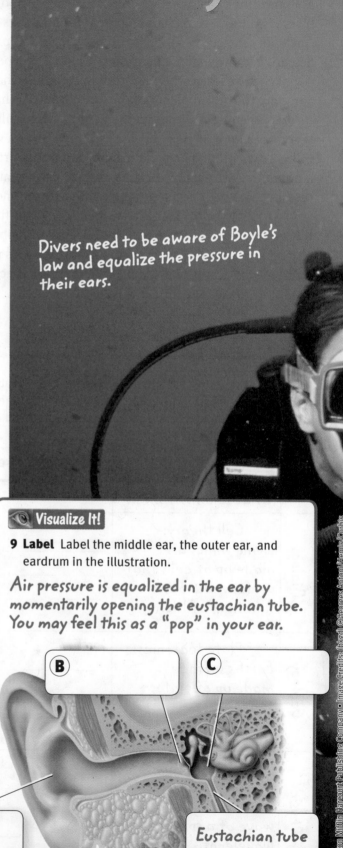

Divers need to be aware of Boyle's law and equalize the pressure in their ears.

**Visualize It!**

**9 Label** Label the middle ear, the outer ear, and eardrum in the illustration.

Air pressure is equalized in the ear by momentarily opening the eustachian tube. You may feel this as a "pop" in your ear.

B

C

A

Eustachian tube

# It's a Law!

## Theories Describe How Things Happen

While laws describe what happens, scientific theories attempt to explain how things happen. A scientific **theory** is a well-supported explanation of nature. Theories help us understand the laws we observe.

For example, the kinetic theory of gases can explain Boyle's law. The kinetic theory describes a gas as being composed of quickly-moving particles. The particles of gas constantly bounce off of the walls of the container they occupy. The pressure of the gas increases the more frequently the particles bounce off the sides of the container.

Two factors increase how frequently the particles of a gas will bounce off the walls of their container: temperature and volume. If the temperature of a gas increases, the particles move more quickly. The particles, therefore, come into contact with the container's walls more often. Decreasing volume also increases the encounters because the particles have less distance to travel before hitting the wall. The container walls can be anything: a metal cylinder, a beach ball, or your eardrum. The illustration below will give you some of idea of how this works.

 **Visualize It!**

**10 Compare** In the table below, circle the signs that show the relationships between the volumes, pressures, and temperatures of the gases in the two cylinders. The first is done for you.

| Cylinder 1 | Relationship | | | Cylinder 2 |
|---|---|---|---|---|
| Volume | < | = | (>) | Volume |
| Pressure | < | = | > | Pressure |
| Temperature | < | = | > | Temperature |

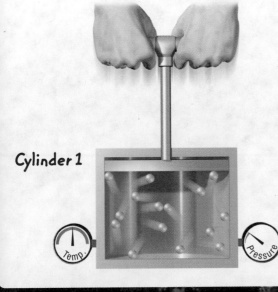

Cylinder 1

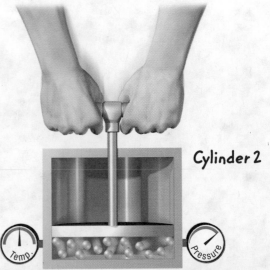

Cylinder 2

9

# What's Your Evidence?

## Where do scientists get their evidence?

Scientists are curious. They look at everything going on around them and ask questions. They collect any information that might help them answer these questions.

Scientific knowledge is based on *empirical evidence*. **Empirical evidence** is all the measurements and data scientists gather in support of a scientific explanation. Scientists get empirical evidence in many different places. Generally, scientific work is categorized as field or laboratory work.

This scientist is a paleontologist. A paleontologist looks for fossilized bones. Here, she is carefully excavating the remains of a 10,000 year-old rhinoceros.

### Visualize It!

**12 Analyze** What empirical evidence might the scientist in the photograph be trying to gather?

_____

_____

_____

## In the Field

Generally, gathering empirical evidence outdoors or where conditions cannot be controlled is known as working in the field or *fieldwork*. Fieldwork gives scientists the opportunity to collect data in an original setting. Biologists and geologists do fieldwork.

A biologist might observe how animals behave in their natural environment. They may look at how the animals gather food or interact with other animals. A geologist may be interested in the minerals in rocks found in a certain area. They may be trying to determine how the rocks formed.

## In the Laboratory

In a laboratory, scientists have the opportunity to collect data in a controlled environment. Unlike in the field, the laboratory allows scientists to control conditions like temperature, lighting, and even what is in the surrounding air. A laboratory is where scientists usually do experiments. In an experiment, scientists try to see what happens under certain conditions. A chemist might be trying to see how two substances react with each other. A physicist might study the energy of a new laser. Even scientists who mainly work in the field, like paleontologists and geologists, may wish to look at a bone or rock in the laboratory.

Laboratories come in many varieties. They can be in the ocean or in the sky. Robotic laboratories even have been sent to Mars!

© Houghton Mifflin Harcourt Publishing Company • Image Credits: (bkgd) ©Annie Griffiths Belt/Corbis; (inset) ©Pierre-Phierre-Phillipe Marcou/AFP/Getty Images

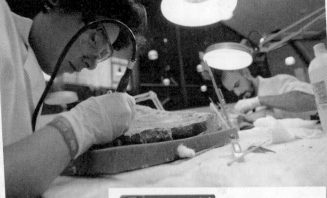

# The **Debate** Continues

## How do scientific ideas change?

Recall that scientific knowledge is agreed-upon knowledge. It is what scientists think are the most-likely explanations for what we see. Over time, these most-likely explanations can change. Sometimes, these changes are very large. More often, they are very small. Why do scientific ideas and explanations change? It's usually because new evidence was found or someone found a better way of explaining the old evidence.

### By New Evidence

The theory of atoms is a good example of how new evidence can modify an established theory. By the mid-1800s, most scientists agreed matter was made of atoms. However, they were not sure what atoms looked like. At first, they thought atoms probably looked like tiny, solid marbles. They assumed atoms of different substances probably differed by their masses.

Later evidence suggested that atoms most likely contained even smaller parts. Scientists observed that these smaller parts carried electric charges and that most of an atom's mass was concentrated at its center. Scientists still saw atoms as extremely small and still often treated them like they were tiny marbles. They came to realize, however, that to best explain how atoms interact, they needed a more complex picture of them.

Today, scientists are still trying to refine the picture of the atom. Much of what they do involves literally smashing atoms into one another. They examine the patterns made by the crashes. It is almost like an atomic game of marbles.

### Active Reading

**15 Identify** Underline an example of a scientific idea that was modified after it was first introduced.

### Visualize It!

**16 Analyze** How does the early model of the atom differ from the current model? What is similar about the two models?

_____

_____

_____

_____

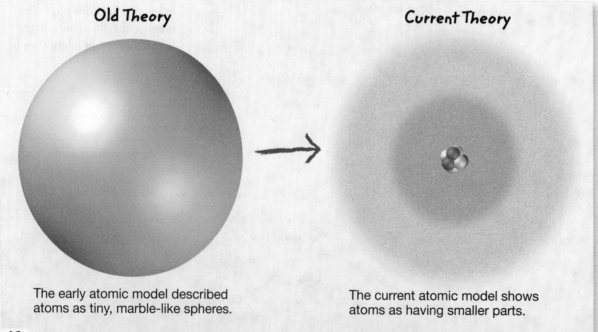

**Old Theory**

**Current Theory**

The early atomic model described atoms as tiny, marble-like spheres.

The current atomic model shows atoms as having smaller parts.

## By Collaboration and Debate

Most scientists do not work in isolation. They collaborate and share ideas. In a way, all scientists are trying to solve a puzzle. Often, many brains are better than one when solving a puzzle.

Scientists regularly gather at meetings to discuss and debate ideas. This helps them to come to an agreement on their ideas. Many ideas are not accepted at first. It is the nature of science to question every idea. Many times, challenges are even welcomed. This rigorous evaluation ensures that scientific knowledge is solidly supported.

### Think Outside the Book — Inquiry

**17 Evaluate** Describe a time when you had to ask for someone's help in solving a problem. Why did you ask for help?

To the left is an example of how scientists study atoms today. The "streaks" show the paths of subatomic particles after two atoms collide. The scientists below study and discuss images like these in a group in hopes to better understand atoms.

# Visual Summary

To complete this summary, fill in the blanks with the correct word or phrase. Then, use the key below to check your answers. You can use this page to review the main concepts of the lesson.

The facts we may think of as science are simply the most widely accepted explanations.

18 A scientific _____ describes what happens, but a scientific _____ describes for what reasons it happens.

**Scientific Knowledge**

Empirical evidence is all the measurements and data scientists gather in support of a scientific explanation.

19 Empirical evidence about rocks might be collected by a _____ doing _____

20 Empirical evidence about how substances combine might be collected by a _____ doing work in the _____

Scientific knowledge often changes with new evidence or new interpretations.

21 Scientists often _____ and _____ to help them interpret complex ideas.

22 **Justify** Could a scientific theory be thought of as a scientific law that doesn't have as much evidence supporting it? Explain your answer.

© Houghton Mifflin Harcourt Publishing Company • Image Credits: (l) ©Pierre-Pierre-Phillippe Marcou/AFP/Getty Images; (r) ©Sidney Moulds/Photo Researchers, Inc.

# Lesson Review

## Vocabulary

Circle the term that best completes each of the following sentences.

**1** A scientific *law / theory* is an explanation for how something occurs. It is supported by a great deal of evidence.

**2** Scientists look for *empirical evidence / laws* either in the field or in the laboratory.

**3** A basic principle that applies everywhere and in all situations is best described as a scientific *law / theory*.

## Key Concepts

**4 List** Into what three areas are the natural sciences commonly divided?

_____

_____

**5 Distinguish** How is the use of the word *theory* in science different from its more common use?

_____

_____

_____

**6 Differentiate** How would you distinguish a scientific theory from a scientific law?

_____

_____

_____

**7 Identify** Name two methods scientists use to obtain empirical evidence.

_____

_____

**8 Apply** What is a difference between research in the field and in the laboratory?

_____

_____

_____

## Critical Thinking

Use this picture to answer the following question.

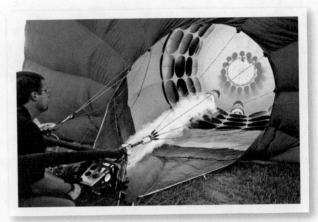

**9 Interpret** As the flames heat the gases in the balloon, the volume of the gases increases. At constant pressure, the volume of all gases increases with increasing temperature. Is this statement a scientific theory or law? Explain.

_____

_____

_____

**10 Defend** Someone tells you that scientific knowledge cannot be changed or modified. How would you answer this statement?

_____

_____

_____

**11 Conclude** Each year, the American Chemical Society holds a national meeting and many regional meetings for chemists. Reports of these meetings are then circulated all over the world. Why do you think this has become standard practice?

_____

_____

_____

_____

# My Notes

# Scientific Investigations

ESSENTIAL QUESTION

## How do scientists work?

By the end of this lesson, you should be able to summarize the processes and characteristics of different kinds of scientific investigations.

Geologists are able to create artificial earthquakes on this model of a portion of Earth's crust. They can investigate the rock types through which seismic waves travel, all from a computer!

TEKS **6.2A** plan and implement comparative and descriptive investigations by making observations, asking well-defined questions, and using appropriate equipment and technology

TEKS **6.2B** design and implement experimental investigations by making observations, asking well-defined questions, formulating testable hypotheses, and using appropriate equipment and technology

Lesson Labs

**Quick Labs**
• Identifying Minerals
• Soil Texture and Water Flow
**Exploration Lab**
• Predicting and Inferring Outcomes

## Engage Your Brain

**1 Predict** Check T or F to show whether you think each statement is true or false.

T  F

☐ ☐ There is only one correct way to carry out a scientific investigation.

☐ ☐ A hypothesis is a conclusion you draw after you carry out a scientific experiment.

☐ ☐ In a controlled experiment, scientists try to control all but one variable.

☐ ☐ Scientists may come up with different interpretations of the same data.

**2 Explain** Observe the hills shown in the picture. Write some questions you would like to investigate about the sedimentary rock layers.

_____

_____

_____

_____

## Active Reading

**3 Synthesize** You can often define an unknown word if you know the meaning of its word parts. Use the word part and sentence below to make an educated guess about the meaning of the term *independent variable*.

| Word part | Meaning |
|-----------|---------|
| *in-* | not |

**Example Sentence**
In an experiment about how light affects plant growth, the <u>independent variable</u> is the number of hours that a plant is exposed to light.

independent variable:

_____

_____

_____

### Vocabulary Terms

• experiment
• observation
• hypothesis
• independent variable
• dependent variable
• data

**4 Identify** This list contains the vocabulary terms you'll learn in this lesson. As you read, underline the definition of each term.

# Detective Story

## What are some types of scientific investigations?

The two basic types of scientific investigations are *experiments* and field *observations*. Most scientists carry out both experiments and observations. Experiments are often based on observations of the world. Experiments also produce observations when they are carried out. But observations do not always lead to experiments.

🔖 **Active Reading**

**5 Identify** As you read these two pages, underline characteristics of the different types of scientific investigations discussed.

### Scientific Investigations

### Experiments

An **experiment** is an organized procedure to study something under controlled conditions. Scientists often conduct experiments to find out the cause of something they have observed.

In 1928, Alexander Fleming found a fungus growing on a nutrient plate that was coated with bacteria. He noticed that there were no bacterial colonies growing close to the fungal colony. He thought that the fungus produced something that killed the bacteria.

Fleming conducted experiments showing that the fungus produced a chemical that kills bacteria. He named the chemical penicillin after the fungus that made it. Based on this work, scientists developed the first antibiotic drugs.

Experiments such as Fleming's are done in a laboratory. Most conditions that might affect the results of an experiment can be controlled in a laboratory. Experiments can also be done in the field, which means outside of a laboratory. Fewer conditions can be controlled in the field. However, field experiments may be needed to show that something found in a laboratory also occurs in nature.

These scientists work in a laboratory called a clean room. A clean room must be free of all possible contaminants.

**6 Infer** Why is it harder to control conditions in the field than in a laboratory?

_____

_____

_____

## Observations and Models

Scientists can also study the natural world without carrying out experiments. **Observation** is the process of gathering information by using the senses. The term can also mean the information gathered by using the senses or special tools.

For example, an archaeologist observes a small bone at a prehistoric site that does not look like a human bone. Based on its size and shape, the scientist questions whether it came from a small animal. Her observation and question can be used to plan a descriptive investigation. She compares the bone to those from various small animals. After making observations, she concludes that people once kept pets at the site.

Another type of investigation is the building of models. Models are representations of an object or system. Models are used to study things that are very small, large, or too complex to study directly. For example, computer models of Earth's atmosphere help scientists forecast the weather.

This scientist is observing flies in their natural habitat.

 **Visualize It!**

**7 Observe** The fruit flies shown here are members of the same species. Carefully observe the flies, paying close attention to detail. You may want to use a hand lens and ruler to better observe details. In the space below, describe differences you observe between the flies. Write one well-defined question about the flies that you could answer during an investigation.

_____
_____
_____
_____
_____
_____
_____
_____
_____
_____
_____
_____

© Houghton Mifflin Harcourt Publishing Company • Image Credits: (t) ©Martin Shields/Photo Researchers, Inc.; (c) ©Francesco Tomasinelli/Photo Researchers, Inc.; (b) ©Martin Shields/Photo Researchers, Inc.

# Parts of a Whole

## What are some parts of scientific investigations?

Scientists study all aspects of the natural world. The work they do varies, but their investigations have some basic elements in common.

### Hypothesis

A **hypothesis** (hy•PAHTH•ih•sis) is a testable idea or explanation that can be used to design and implement an investigation. A scientist may form a hypothesis after making observations or after reading the results of other investigations. The hypothesis can be tested by experiment or observation.

Hypotheses must be carefully constructed so they can be tested in a meaningful way. The hypothesis must be specific and identify the relationship between factors, or variables.

### Prediction

When making a hypothesis, scientists often predict the outcome of an investigation. A prediction is a statement about a cause-and-effect relationship that will occur under specific conditions. Predictions are based on prior knowledge, observations, and reasoning. If you hear thunder, you might predict it will rain.

Predictions and hypotheses are sometimes confused. It may be helpful to remember that a prediction states what may happen next under certain conditions. In contrast, a hypothesis is a testable statement that describes relationships among factors in an investigation.

These plants are being grown in a laboratory and tested under carefully controlled conditions. A scientist could conduct a variety of experiments with these plants.

### 👁 Visualize It!

**8 Develop** Write a hypothesis that could be tested on the plants shown in this photo.

_____

_____

_____

## Independent Variables

Variables are factors that can change in a scientific investigation. An **independent variable** is the factor that is deliberately adjusted in an investigation. The hypothesis identifies the independent variable. For example, Fleming hypothesized that something made by the penicillin fungus stopped the growth of bacteria. The independent variable was the penicillin fungus. The fungus was the factor that caused the change in bacterial growth.

Most experiments have only one independent variable. Other variables are kept constant, or unchanged, so they do not affect the results. Scientists can then conclude that any changes observed are due to the variable that was changed. It is not always possible to control all other variables, however, particularly for investigations in the field.

## Dependent Variables

A **dependent variable** is the factor that changes as a result of adjusting the independent variable. In Fleming's experiments with bacteria, the dependent variable was the survival of the bacteria. The bacteria either lived or died. Both the independent variable and the dependent variable should be identified in the hypothesis for an experiment.

Dependent variables can be measured outside of experiments. Consider the hypothesis that crickets chirp faster at higher temperatures. The independent variable would be the temperature. The dependent variable would be the cricket chirps. If this study is carried out in the field rather than in a lab, it might not be possible to control all variables. Factors such as the presence of females or male competitors must be taken into account.

**9 Apply** Complete the missing parts of the table below, which describes three experiments.

| Investigation | Independent Variable | Dependent Variable |
|---|---|---|
| How is plant height affected by amount of sunlight it receives? | Hours of sunlight per day | |
| | Altitude of water | Boiling temperature |
| How does a person's heart rate change as speed of movement increases? | | Heart rate |

**Active Reading**

**10 Identify** As you read, underline the types of data that scientists record.

## Observations and Data

**Data** are information gathered by observation or experimentation that can be used in calculating or reasoning. Everything a scientist observes must be recorded. The setup and procedures of an experiment also need to be recorded. By carefully recording this data, scientists will not forget important information.

Scientists analyze data to determine the relationship between the independent and dependent variables. Then they conclude whether or not the data support an investigation's hypothesis.

# Many Methods

## What are some scientific methods?

Conducting experiments and other scientific investigations is not like following a cookbook recipe. Scientists do not always use the same steps in every investigation or use steps in the same order. They may even repeat some of the steps. The following graphic shows one path a scientist might follow while conducting an experiment.

**Visualize It!**

**11 Diagram** Using a different color, draw arrows showing another path a scientist might follow if the data from an experiment did not support the hypothesis.

### Asking Well-Defined Questions

After making observations or reading scientific reports, a scientist might be curious about some unexplained aspect of a topic. This may lead the scientist to ask a question that could be answered with an investigation. A scientific question must be well-defined, or precisely stated, so that it can be investigated.

### Planning an Investigation

A scientific investigation must be carefully planned so that it tests a hypothesis in a meaningful way. Scientists need to decide whether an investigation should be done in the field or in a laboratory. They must also determine what equipment and technology are needed and how to get materials for the investigation.

### Forming a Testable Hypothesis and Making Predictions

A hypothesis is a testable explanation that answers a scientific question. A hypothesis must be tested to see if results of the test support the hypothesis. Before testing a hypothesis, scientists make predictions about what might happen. These predictions are based on prior knowledge, reasoning, and observations.

## Identifying Variables

The independent and dependent variables of an experiment are identified in the hypothesis. But scientists need to decide how the independent variable will change. They also must identify other variables that will be controlled and decide how they will measure the results of the experiment. The dependent variable often can be measured in more than one way. For example, if the dependent variable is plant growth, a scientist could measure height, weight, or even flower or fruit production.

## Collecting and Organizing Data

The data collected in an investigation must be recorded and properly organized so that they can be analyzed. Data such as measurements and numbers are often organized into tables, spreadsheets, or graphs. Data from multiple trials are often compared using tables.

A    B

**12 Compare** What are the similarities and differences between these two microscopic organisms?

_____

_____

_____

## Interpreting Data and Analyzing Information

After they finish collecting data, scientists must analyze this information. Their analysis will help them draw conclusions about the results. Scientists may have different interpretations of the same data because they analyze the data using different methods.

## Drawing Conclusions

Scientists conclude whether the results of their investigation support the hypothesis. If the hypothesis is not supported, scientists may think about the problem some more and try to come up with a new hypothesis to test. Or they may repeat an experiment to see if any mistakes were made. When they publish the results of their investigation, scientists must be prepared to defend their conclusions if they are challenged by other scientists.

# Drawing Conclusions

## What are predictions and inferences?

Scientists use both predictions and inferences when they conduct scientific investigations. While a prediction is a statement about a possible outcome, an inference is an explanation. Both predictions and inferences are based on existing knowledge. Developing predictions and making inferences involve critical thinking skills. Both can help support theories or lead to new hypotheses.

### Predictions Show Possible Cause-and-Effect Relationships

A prediction is a statement that shows a cause-and-effect relationship that may occur under specific conditions. A scientific prediction is based on logic and prior knowledge. For example, you likely know from experience that plants need water to live. In an experiment investigating the effect of water on plants, you might predict that a plant will die if not given water for two weeks.

### Inferences are Explanations Based on Known Facts

An inference is an explanation that is based on prior knowledge. For example, you know that plants absorb water, so you may infer that plants absorb water through their roots. Inference also explains events that cannot be directly observed. For example, the orbit of planets around the sun and movement of electrons around the nucleus are based on inferences.

## How do scientists form conclusions?

Scientists interpret the data, or results, from an experiment to form a conclusion. Data must be interpreted in a valid, or correct, way, to arrive at a correct conclusion. The actual data must also be correct and thorough. Incorrect or incomplete data, as well as faulty reasoning, can lead to incorrect conclusions.

For example, imagine that a scientist observed a butterfly in a large field. The butterfly landed only on purple flowers. It would it be incorrect, however, to conclude that all butterflies prefer purple flowers. That conclusion is incorrect because it is based on incomplete data and faulty reasoning. It is not logical to draw conclusions about all butterflies after observing just one. Also, other factors such as flower shape, size, and amount of nectar, were not considered. The scientist could, however, design investigations to find out what factor or factors cause butterflies to visit certain flowers.

Logical reasoning is important in all parts of an investigation, not just to form conclusions. Scientists must decide if data support their predictions and inferences or if the data show they are false.

13 **Reason** Leo's garden is full of spicy pepper plants. He read that birds cannot taste spiciness. He also knows that some birds are attracted to the color red. He predicts that birds will eat the red peppers in his garden but not the green ones. How could Leo see if his prediction is correct?

_____

_____

_____

_____

_____

_____

© Houghton Mifflin Harcourt Publishing Company

# How are inferences and conclusions related?

### Active Reading

**14 Identify** As you read, underline an example of an inference.

An inference is not a fact. Inferences often lead to further investigation or to valid conclusions. For example, you may infer that water moves up the stems of plants. You cannot directly observe this action, but you can carry out an experiment to see if your inference is valid. You could put a stalk of celery in a cup with a small amount of dyed water. After a certain amount of time, you could cut open the celery to see if the dyed water moved up the stalk. If it did, you could make the conclusion that your inference is correct—water does move up the stems of plants.

## Visualize It!

### Excellent Fitness

### Average Fitness

### Poor Fitness

### Recording Heart Rates of Adults of Different Fitness Levels Before and After Activity.

**Prediction:** People with poor fitness levels will have higher heart rates after activity than people with better levels of fitness.

**15 Analyze** Fill in the table with the correct data from the graphs.

| Fitness level | Average heart rate | |
|---------------|-------------------|---|
| | **At rest** | **After 200 m run** |
| **Excellent** | | |
| **Average** | | |
| **Poor** | | |

**16 Analyze** What conclusions can you infer about the heart of an adult with poor fitness compared to an adult with excellent fitness? Write a conclusion based on the data. How does the prediction provided relate to your conclusion?

_____

_____

_____

_____

_____

# Make It Work

**17 Plan** Choose a plant or animal you would like to investigate. How would you learn about what it needs to live, grow, and reproduce? Plan an investigation using scientific methods, including making observations, asking well-defined questions, and listing the equipment and technology that may be needed.

## How are scientific methods used?

Scientific methods are used in physical, life, and Earth sciences. The findings of scientific investigations support previous work and add new knowledge.

### Different Situations Require Different Methods

After forming a hypothesis, scientists decide how they will test it. Some hypotheses can only be tested through observation. Others must be tested in experiments. However, observation and experiments are often used together to build scientific knowledge.

For example, a biologist wants to study the effects of air pollution on a plant species. He makes observations in the field. He gathers data on the plants and the amount of pollutants in the air. Then he conducts experiments under controlled conditions. He exposes plants to different levels of pollution to test how they are affected. He compares his laboratory data with his field data.

If an investigation does not support a hypothesis, it is still useful. The data can help scientists form a better hypothesis. Scientists often go through many cycles of testing and data analysis before they arrive at a hypothesis that is supported.

This photo shows the large jaws of SuperCroc and the smaller jaws of a modern crocodile.

## Different Sciences use Scientific Methods

Active Reading **18 Identify** As you read, underline steps of the scientific method.

Earth science includes the study of fossils, which are the remains of organisms that lived long ago. Scientific methods allow scientists to use fossils to learn about species that lived millions of years ago.

Scientists found a fossilized set of jaws in the Sahara that was 1.8 m (6 ft) long. They could tell from the shape of the jaws and teeth that it was not from a dinosaur. They also knew that rivers once ran through this now dry region. The team hypothesized that the jaws belonged to a giant crocodile that lived in ancient rivers.

However, the scientists needed more data. They were able to find more fossils and assemble half of a crocodile skeleton. The scientists measured the fossils and compared them with the bones of modern crocodiles. Their analysis showed that the giant crocodile grew up to 12 m (40 ft) long and weighed up to 10 tons.

The scientists concluded that the new fossils supported their original hypothesis. They published their findings about the large crocodile called *Sarcosuchus* and nicknamed it "SuperCroc."

**19 Relate** In the space below, write a well-defined question and a testable hypothesis that could have been used in the SuperCroc investigation.

Question:

_____

_____

_____

_____

Hypothesis:

_____

_____

_____

_____

_____

_____

After scientists find fossils, scientific artists draw what they determine the animals looked like. SuperCroc was large enough to snack on T. rex dinosaurs.

# Quality Control

## What makes a good scientific investigation?

The standards for scientific investigations are high. Possible sources of errors, such as poor experimental design or errors in measurements, should be identified and corrected. Experiments should be carried out enough times so that results are reliable. Data and procedures must be carefully recorded. Together, these checks help ensure that good scientific practices are followed.

**Active Reading**

**20 Identify** As you read this page and the next, underline the meanings of *repetition* and *replication*.

**Repetition** occurs when an activity is repeated by the same person. When a person bakes a cake multiple times using the same recipe, it is repetition, and the cake should turn out the same. When a scientist repeats her experiment, she should achieve similar results each time.

© Houghton Mifflin Harcourt Publishing Company

## Repetition and Replication

There are two ways that scientific investigations can be carried out again. First, the scientist who conducted the original investigation can repeat the study. Repetition with similar results provides support for the conclusions. Second, other scientists can replicate the investigation. Replication of the findings by other scientists in other locations also provides support to the results and conclusion.

## Open Communication

Scientists may share their research with each other by publishing reports and papers. Scientific papers must include all parts of the investigation so other scientists may replicate the investigation. Before an investigation can be published in a journal, it is reviewed by scientists who are not involved in the investigation. Open communication between scientists helps decrease the possibility of errors and unethical behavior.

## Where is there reliable scientific information?

The most reliable scientific information is found in peer-reviewed scientific journals. Peer review is the review of investigations by other scientists. But, scientific journals are often difficult to understand for people who are not scientists. Sometimes, reliable summaries of investigations are published in newspapers or on the Internet. Many scientists write books for the public. People who are not scientists but who are knowledgeable about a particular field or topic may also write reliable books and articles.

The most reliable Internet sources are government or academic webpages. Commercial webpages are often unreliable because they are trying to sell something. As a result, the information on these sites may be biased. Information is biased if it has a particular slant that changes how the information is presented.

Replication occurs when an activity is repeated by a different person. When a person bakes a cake using a recipe from someone else, it should be the same as the first person's cake. When a scientist replicates another scientist's experiment, he or she should achieve the same results.

**21 Classify** Read each of the scenarios below. Check one of the boxes next to each statement to classify each scenario as an example of repetition, replication, or both.

**Scenario 1:**
You go to a neighborhood park five times. Each time, you take notes on the birds you see and hear.

☐ Replication
☐ Repetition
☐ Both

**Scenario 2:**
You go to the same neighborhood park with a friend. You give your friend a copy of the notes you took when you went to the park on your own. You and your friend both take notes on the birds you see and hear.

☐ Replication
☐ Repetition
☐ Both

**Scenario 3:**
Your friend goes by himself to the same neighborhood park. Your friend takes notes on the birds he sees and hears.

☐ Replication
☐ Repetition
☐ Both

# Visual Summary

To complete this summary, fill in the blanks with the correct word or phrase. Then use the key below to check your answers. You can use this page to review the main concepts of the lesson.

## Scientific Investigations

Scientific investigations may involve observations, experiments, and models.

Scientific methods include making observations, asking questions, planning experiments, collecting data, and drawing conclusions.

**22** Scientific investigations can be conducted in a(n) _____ or in the field.

**23** The _____ of an experiment must be testable.

**24** In an experiment, the variable that a scientist plans to change is the _____ variable.

**25** The results of an experiment are the _____ collected.

Characteristics of good scientific investigations include using controls, identifying variables, and having reproducible results.

**26** If your classmate repeats an experiment that you have already conducted, that is an example of _____.

**27** One way that the quality of scientific information is evaluated is that it is reviewed by _____.

**28 Identify** Suppose that you soak ten seeds in water and ten seeds in a mixture of water and vinegar to see how acidity affects the sprouting of seeds. You observe them for two weeks. What are the independent and dependent variables of this experiment?

# Lesson Review

## Vocabulary

Circle the term that best completes each of the following sentences.

**1** A(n) *hypothesis/observation* is information gathered by using the senses or other tools.

**2** In an experiment, the *independent/dependent* variable is the one that scientists measure or observe as it changes.

**3** The *data/hypothesis* is/are the result(s) obtained from an experiment.

## Key Concepts

**4 Explain** What is a basic requirement that a scientific hypothesis must have?

_____

_____

**5 Identify** A group of students wants to see how temperature affects the time it takes for spilled water to dry up. In their investigation, what will be the dependent and independent variables?

_____

_____

_____

_____

**6 Assess** What is the difference between repetition and replication of an investigation?

_____

_____

_____

_____

**7 List** Write a list of at least five scientific methods.

_____

_____

_____

_____

_____

## Critical Thinking

Use this photograph to answer the following questions.

**8 Compile** Record your observations about the fossil in the photograph. Be sure to include as much detail as you can observe.

_____

_____

_____

_____

**9 Produce** Write a hypothesis about this fossil that you could test in an investigation.

_____

_____

_____

_____

**10 Formulate** Describe how you would test your hypothesis. You don't need to identify specific tests or instruments. Rather, describe the kinds of information you would want to collect.

_____

_____

_____

_____

_____

# My Notes

TEKS 6.3D

# Dijanna Figueroa

## MARINE BIOLOGIST

Dijanna Figueroa has wanted to be a marine biologist for as long as she can remember. Like many scientists, she now wears a lab coat and safety glasses most days. She spends up to 12 hours a day in the lab. There, she studies the metabolisms of creatures that live in extreme environments. These creatures live more than two kilometers below the ocean's surface, in a habitat that sunlight never reaches. The water pressure is so great that it would crush a human being. Creatures living in these conditions must therefore produce foods in ways that were unknown until only recently. In order to get specimens of these animals for her lab, Dr. Figueroa had to go down to where they live.

Dr. Figueroa's job has taken her onto the big screen, too. She appeared in the IMAX film *Aliens of the Deep*, with other scientists. The film shows footage of expeditions down to the deep-sea ocean vents. These vents may be one of the harshest environments on the planet. The scientists traveled in *Alvin*, a deep-sea submarine.

Dr. Figueroa currently works as a project scientist at the Marine Science Institute in California. She also works to get young people interested in real-life science through fun and exciting hands-on activities.

Dr. Figueroa in *Alvin*—2,400 m deep!

## Language Arts Connection

Think of a science-related job that you would like to know more about. Research the job and write a plan for a documentary film that teaches what you have learned about the job.

Houghton Mifflin Harcourt Publishing Company • Image Credits: (bkgd) ©Science Source/Photo Researchers, Inc.; (bc) Courtesy of Dijanna Figueroa

# JOB BOARD

## Museum Educational Interpreter

**What You'll Do:** Tell students and groups visiting a museum about what they are looking at. You might create educational programs, give tours, and answer questions.

**Where You Might Work:** Likely places are a science museum or a museum of technology.

**Education:** Educational interpreters usually need a bachelor's degree in science, and may need extra training in museums or in teaching.

**Other Job Requirements:** You need to enjoy working with people, be good at public speaking, and be able to answer questions clearly.

## Pyrotechnician

**What You'll Do:** Work with explosives to create explosions and fireworks for special effects. Blow things up in the safest way possible, using a lot of safety measures to keep things from getting out of hand.

**Where You Might Work:** A company that designs special effects or that creates and performs fireworks shows is a possibility. A pyrotechnician spends time in the workshop and on-site, so you may find yourself on a film set blowing up cars, or on a hillside setting off fireworks.

**Education:** You need a high-school diploma with additional training in pyrotechnics and safety.

**Other Job Requirements:** Strong math skills, ability to concentrate, and careful attention to detail are required.

## PEOPLE IN SCIENCE NEWS

# Jon BOHMER

### Cooking with Sunlight

Jon Bohmer isn't the first person to invent an oven that uses sunlight to heat food and water. He's one of many people to use cardboard, foil, and sunlight to build an oven. In some countries, people use firewood for most of their cooking, and must boil all of their water before they drink it. Jon's Kyoto Box oven uses two cardboard boxes painted black on the inside and coated with foil on the outside. It costs only about $5 to make, but it gets hot enough to boil water and cook food.

**Lesson 3**

# Science and Society

**ESSENTIAL QUESTION**

## How does research affect scientific thought and society?

By the end of this lesson, you should be able to describe how science and society impact each other.

Pollinators, such as bees, are important to society because they help us grow plants used for food and for decoration. This structure provides a suitable home for the bee colony, even though it is made of common materials.

**TEKS** 6.3D relate the impact of research on scientific thought and society, including the history of science and contributions of scientists as related to the content

## Lesson Labs

**Quick Labs**
- Contributions of Scientists to Scientific Thought and Society
- Modeling the Atom

**Exploration Lab**
- The Science of Bridges

## Engage Your Brain

**1 List** List three things that our society would not have without scientific research. Draw a picture of one of them in the space below.

_____

_____

_____

**2 Analyze** Write your own caption about the source of electric power for this house in Africa.

_____

_____

_____

_____

## Active Reading

**3 Apply** Use context clues to write your own definition for the word *society*.

**Example sentence**
The people who live within a <u>society</u> live according to certain laws and rules.

society:

_____

_____

_____

## Vocabulary Terms

**4 Identify** As you read, place a question mark next to any words that you don't understand. When you finish reading the lesson, go back and review the text that you marked. If the information is still confusing, consult a classmate or a teacher.

© Houghton Mifflin Harcourt Publishing Company • Image Credits: ©Michael Runkel/Robert Harding World Imagery/Alamy Images

# Seeing Stars

## How has scientific research changed over time?

Many civilizations have contributed to scientific knowledge throughout history. Scientific research and discoveries build on each other to produce a more complete and accurate understanding of the universe and our own world. Scientific research has changed through people making and sharing observations, through the development of scientific methods, and through the use of new technology.

**5 Summarize** How does scientific research change over time?

_____

_____

_____

Ancient Egyptian drawings of constellations, or patterns in the stars, were made by observing the night sky.

## By Observing and Sharing

People throughout the ages have been curious about the world around them. Many people ask questions about the things they observe and try to explain mysteries. Sharing ideas with others expands the base of knowledge.

For example, ancient Egyptians used an early form of written communication called hieroglyphics. Hieroglyphics use pictures to represent symbols or sounds. Scientists today study hieroglyphics to learn about ancient Egyptian culture and their understanding of science. Egyptian hieroglyphics show the stars and the sun as living beings that interact with humans on a personal level. Their observations about nature were shared with future generations through these writings.

**6 Apply** What is some knowledge that was passed down to you?

_____

_____

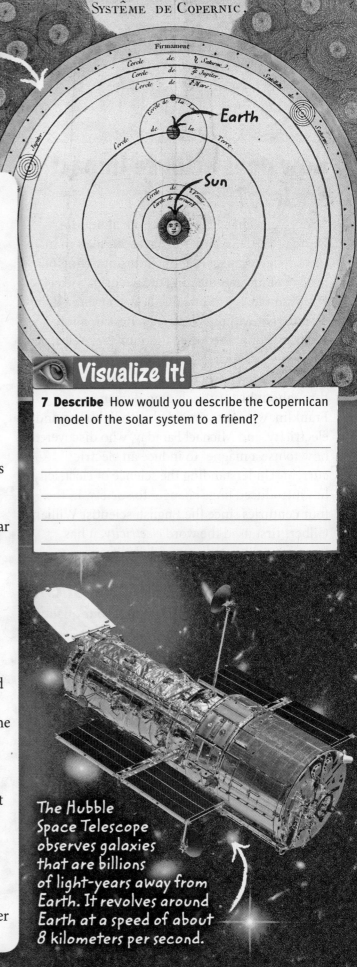

Nicolaus Copernicus used scientific evidence to build this model showing that the planets, including Earth, move around the sun. Before this model, people believed that Earth was at the center of the universe and that all other bodies moved around Earth.

SYSTÈME DE COPERNIC.

Earth

Sun

## By Methodical Investigation

Although ancient societies observed and recorded nature, they did not use science as we know it today. Modern science uses methodical investigation to evaluate an idea. The 16th and 17th centuries were a time called the Scientific Revolution. This is also the time when scientists began using scientific methods. Scientists ask questions, form hypotheses, test hypotheses, analyze data, form conclusions, and report results. Some or all of these steps are part of an investigation using scientific methods.

Nicolaus Copernicus, a 16th-century astronomer and mathematician, studied the motion of planets and stars. By applying concepts of mathematics and motion, he developed a new model of the solar system. This model was built on the idea that the sun is at the center of the solar system and other objects move around it.

## By Using New Technology

New technology has also caused scientific research to change over time. Computers have changed scientific research by allowing scientists to collect, record, and analyze data rapidly. Computers also allow scientists around the world to communicate and work together.

The Hubble Space Telescope, launched by the National Aeronautics and Space Administration in 1990, has expanded our knowledge of the universe. Its advanced telescopes and cameras have recorded galaxies so far away that their light has traveled billions of years to reach Earth.

Scientists have used new technologies, such as computers and telescopes, to build upon and expand the model of the universe. This model differs in many ways from that of Copernicus. Other technologies have led to efficient cars, taller buildings, and more effective medicines.

### Visualize It!

**7 Describe** How would you describe the Copernican model of the solar system to a friend?

_____

_____

_____

_____

The Hubble Space Telescope observes galaxies that are billions of light-years away from Earth. It revolves around Earth at a speed of about 8 kilometers per second.

# Electrifying

## How does science impact society?

Science can change how we think about the world around us, and it impacts our lives in many ways. These impacts can include improving our quality of life and meeting the needs of society. For example, try to imagine how your life might be different without electricity. Research into electricity built the foundation for every electrical device we use today.

Many scientists have studied electricity throughout history, including Benjamin Franklin, who experimented with lightning and electricity, and Michael Faraday, who discovered how to use a magnet to induce an electric current. Understanding the science of electricity has introduced huge changes to society. In the four centuries since the English scientist William Gilbert first used the word *electricity*, it has become an essential part of daily life.

### Science Improves Quality of Life

Many scientific discoveries improve our quality of life. Sometimes one discovery, such as electricity, opens a wide range of new discoveries and practical applications.

Refrigerators and freezers, for example, have increased the types of healthy food available year round. Having healthy foods available improves people's diets. Safe food storage also reduces the risk of illness from food. Other applications of electricity include medical devices and transportation. Computers and electronic communication systems have also had enormous effects on everyday life.

**8 List** When the power goes out, what are some of the things you can't do?

_____

_____

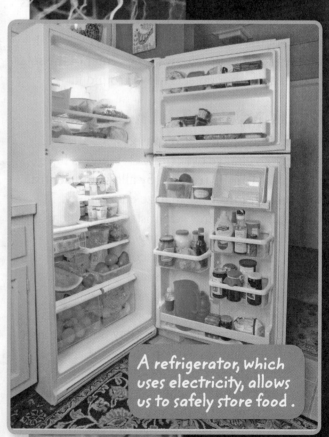

A refrigerator, which uses electricity, allows us to safely store food.

**9 Identify** As you read, underline the products of scientific research that help society.

Many scientific discoveries lead to solutions for a need of society. For example, doctors use medicines to treat diseases and to improve overall health. The development of vaccines and antibiotics has increased the average length of people's lives.

Continuing developments in the ways we grow and distribute food and water improve health in places all over the world. New transportation and communication technologies allow people around the world to interact with one another. Food and manufactured products can be shipped to distant places and traded for products made there.

**10 Apply** Think about a problem in society that science might solve. Then, with a partner, take turns interviewing each other about the problems you have identified. Be sure to ask about how the problem affects society and what type of research might be helpful. Summarize your questions and responses in a few paragraphs.

Electric cars reduce the use of fossil fuel, decrease pollution, and are much quieter than gas-powered cars.

**11 Evaluate** How could transportation technology help the people living in very remote places?

_____

_____

# Waste Not, Want Not

## How can society drive scientific research?

Science can impact scientific thought and society. However, society can also impact science. For example, the needs of society can drive scientific research. Many medicines have been developed to treat particular diseases, which meets a need of society. Society also drives research through decisions about funding and support.

As world populations and demand for resources increase, there is a growing need for finding new resources and reducing waste. Scientists have developed new ways to reuse and recycle many materials as a way to meet this need. Many materials that once ended up as waste in massive landfills have become the starting materials for new products. Scientists continue to work on new ways to recycle waste and turn it into a resource.

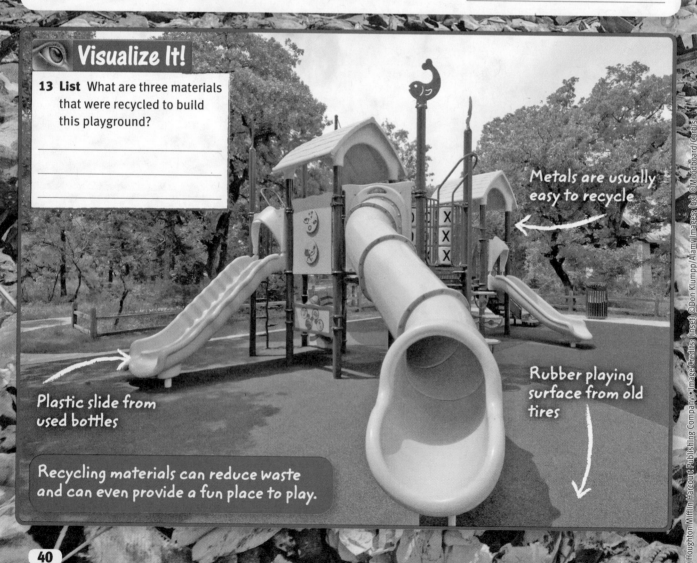

**Visualize It!**

**13 List** What are three materials that were recycled to build this playground?

_____

_____

_____

Metals are usually easy to recycle

Plastic slide from used bottles

Rubber playing surface from old tires

Recycling materials can reduce waste and can even provide a fun place to play.

Plastic-eating fungi have been discovered in the Amazon. These microbes may be used in our landfills to help break down plastic waste.

This plastic bag is 100% degradable* but you can still reuse it!

*From date of manufacture, the plastic will start to degrade in approx. 18 months time. The whole process will take about 3 years. See bottom of bag for date of manufacture.

Manufactured using 100% supplied by ch

epi

We go further so you don't have to

12/05

Waste-to-energy plants convert parts of waste that can be decomposed by bacteria into a type of fuel. Waste such as food, paper, and plastic becomes fuel for electric power generators.

Bioremediation uses microorganisms to break down hazardous waste and pollution in the environment. These vent towers allow harmless gases to escape as bacteria break down buried waste materials.

## Visualize It!

**14 List** In the left column, list two problems in society shown on these pages. In the right column, list the scientific research that has solved, or is solving, each problem.

| Problem in Society | Scientific Research |
|---|---|
|  |  |
|  |  |

# Visual Summary

To complete this summary, fill in the space with the correct word or phrase. Then use the key below to check your answers. You can use this page to review the main concepts of the lesson.

## Science and Society

Different civilizations have made contributions to science throughout history.

**15** The ancient Egyptians used _____ to record and share what they knew about science and the natural world.

Scientific discoveries can change the way we think as well as the way we live.

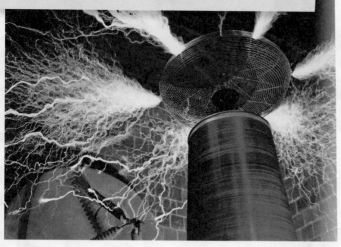

**16** The invention of the _____ was part of the development of modern electrical technologies.

Many scientific discoveries help to satisfy a need of society.

**17** The research that scientists pursue often depends on the research supported by _____ .

Answers: 15 hieroglyphics; 16 tesla coil; 17 society

**18 Analyze** List at least three different products of scientific research you use in your own home. What need do each of these products satisfy?

# Lesson Review

## Vocabulary

Fill in the blank with the term that best completes the following sentence.

**1** Modern scientific research uses scientific _____ to evaluate ideas.

**2** Scientific research is applied to problems in order to meet the _____ of society.

## Key Concepts

**3 Identify** Use an example to show how science builds on earlier discoveries.

_____

_____

_____

_____

**4 Describe** List three ways that our society has been impacted by scientific research.

_____

_____

_____

_____

**5 Analyze** How can society impact science?

_____

_____

_____

**6 Evaluate** Why is methodical investigation an important part of the way new scientific research impacts society?

_____

_____

_____

_____

_____

_____

## Critical Thinking

Use this photo to answer the following question.

**7 Identify** What need of society does the hands-free telephone device in the photo address?

_____

_____

_____

**8 Apply** How was the development of this type of phone based on other scientific and technological discoveries?

_____

_____

_____

**9 Analyze** A scientist wants to research a new house paint that lasts longer than paint products currently on the market. Describe how the needs of society have driven this research and what types of companies may provide funding.

_____

_____

_____

_____

_____

_____

# My Notes

# Unit 1 | Big Idea

Scientists use careful observations and clear reasoning to understand processes and patterns in nature.

## Lesson 1

**ESSENTIAL QUESTION**
**What are the types of scientific knowledge?**

Differentiate the methods that scientists use to gain empirical evidence in a variety of scientific fields, and explain how this leads to scientific change.

## Lesson 2

**ESSENTIAL QUESTION**
**How do scientists work?**

Summarize the processes and characteristics of different kinds of scientific investigations.

## Lesson 3

**ESSENTIAL QUESTION**
**How does research affect scientific thought and society?**

Describe the relationship between science and society throughout history.

## Connect ESSENTIAL QUESTIONS
Lessons 1 and 2

**1 Compare** Explain the difference between scientific investigations and scientific knowledge.

_____

_____

_____

_____

_____

_____

## Think Outside the Book

**2 Synthesize** Choose one of these activities to help synthesize what you have learned in this unit.

☐ Using what you learned in lessons 1 and 3, write a script that includes dialogue between a modern scientist and a scientist from the past. The scientists should discuss how a specific aspect of scientific knowledge has changed over time and how these changes have impacted society.

☐ Using what you learned in lessons 1 and 2, plan an investigation that could be conducted by experimentation or by observation. Write a procedure for both types of investigation, and explain the advantages and disadvantages of each.

# Unit 1 Review

Name _____

## Vocabulary

Fill in the blank with the term that best completes the sentence.

**TEKS 6.2B**

**1** The _____ variable is the factor that is changed in order to test the effect of the change.

**TEKS 6.2B**

**2** A testable idea or explanation that leads to a scientific investigation is called a(n) _____.

**TEKS 6.3A**

**3** A scientific _____ is a well-supported and widely accepted explanation of a natural occurrence.

**TEKS 6.3A**

**4** The cumulative body of observations on which scientific explanations are based is called _____.

**TEKS 6.3A**

**5** A scientific _____ is a description of a specific relationship under given conditions in the natural world.

## Key Concepts

Choose the letter of the best answer.

**TEKS 6.2B**

**6** Which sequence of events is a logical order for a scientific investigation?

**A** experiment → hypothesis → analysis of data → conclusion

**B** hypothesis → experiment → conclusion → analysis of data

**C** analysis of data → conclusion → experiment → hypothesis

**D** hypothesis → experiment → analysis of data → conclusion

**TEKS** 6.2E

**7** The result of an experiment about how the speed of an object changes over time is shown in the following graph.

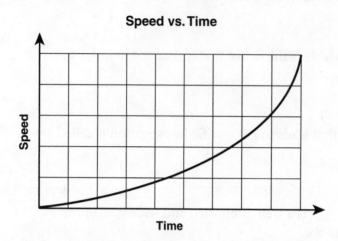

Based on this graph, four different lab groups came to the following conclusions. Which group's conclusion describes the result shown in the graph?

**A** Group 1: The speed of the object increases as time passes.

**B** Group 2: The speed of the object decreases as time passes.

**C** Group 3: The speed of the object does not change as time passes.

**D** Group 4: The speed of the object decreases and then increases as time passes.

**TEKS** 6.3A

**8** Which statement describes how a scientist makes scientific explanations?

**A** A scientist bases scientific explanations on a large body of observations of the natural world.

**B** A scientist bases scientific explanations only on other scientists' opinions.

**C** A scientist bases scientific explanations on personal experience and opinions.

**D** A scientist suggests scientific explanations and makes up evidence to make them true.

**TEKS** 6.3D

**9** Look at the picture.

Which of the following diseases has been significantly reduced by this technology? (Hint: Step 1. Consider which diseases are related to food consumption. Step 2. Identify which of these diseases would be reduced by refrigeration technology.)

**A** cancer

**B** diabetes

**C** heart disease

**D** food poisoning

## Gridded Response

Write your answer in the boxes, then bubble in the corresponding number in the grid below.

**TEKS** 6.2E

**10** In an experiment, heat is added to a liquid at a constant rate of 10 degrees Celsius per minute. If the starting temperature is 25 degrees Celsius, what will the temperature of the liquid be after 5 minutes? Give your answer in degrees Celsius.

## Critical Thinking

Answer the following questions in the space provided.

**11** Why is it important for experimental procedures and results to be reproducible?

_____

_____

_____

TEKS 6.2A

**12** This table shows the average life expectancy for males in the United States.

| Year of birth | Average life expectancy (y) |
|---|---|
| 1900 | 48 |
| 1920 | 56 |
| 1940 | 62 |
| 1960 | 67 |
| 1980 | 70 |
| 2000 | 74 |

What is one inference you can make based on the data in the table? What is one prediction you can make based on the data in the table?

_____

_____

_____

_____

**Connect** ESSENTIAL QUESTIONS
Lessons 1, 2, and 3

Answer the following question in the space provided.

TEKS 6.2A, 6.2B, 6.4A

**13** Explain the characteristics of a good scientific investigation. Discuss how these characteristics affect the validity of a scientific investigation.

_____

_____

_____

_____

_____

**UNIT 2**

# Measurement and Data

**Big Idea**

Scientists use tools to collect, organize, and analyze data while conducting investigations.

## What do you think?

NOAA scientists use the instrument shown here to collect conductivity and temperature data of seawater at different depths. What other data might scientists aboard the Henry B. Bigelow collect while at sea?

# Unit 2
# Measurement and Data

## CITIZEN SCIENCE

# Counting Birds

The National Audubon Society's Great Backyard Bird Count is an annual event that you can participate in. Every year, over a period of four days, citizen scientists all over North America count birds in a specific location. People can count birds in their backyard, a park, a schoolyard, a wildlife refuge, or any spot that birds visit! Whether a person is able to spend 15 minutes or all four days counting, the data collected helps scientists who study birds.

## ① Think About It

**A** Review the history of annual bird counts on the National Audubon Society's website. When was the very first bird count?

_____

_____

**B** What is the collected data used for?

_____

_____

_____

_____

_____

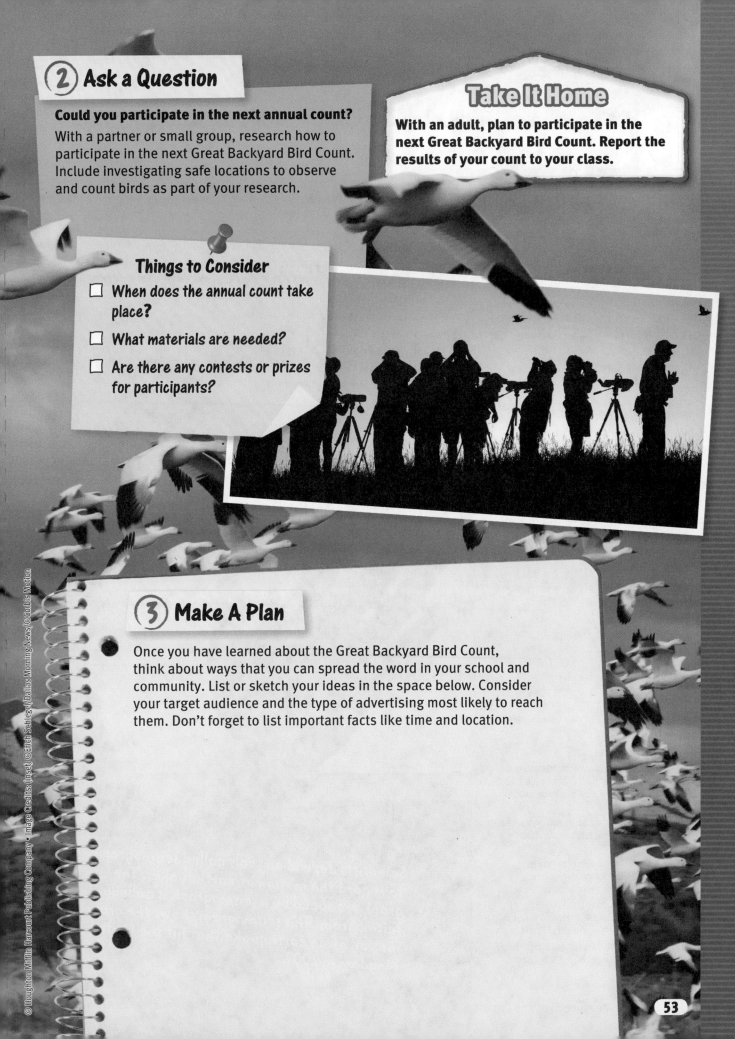

## ② Ask a Question

**Could you participate in the next annual count?**
With a partner or small group, research how to participate in the next Great Backyard Bird Count. Include investigating safe locations to observe and count birds as part of your research.

### Things to Consider

☐ When does the annual count take place?

☐ What materials are needed?

☐ Are there any contests or prizes for participants?

## Take It Home

With an adult, plan to participate in the next Great Backyard Bird Count. Report the results of your count to your class.

## ③ Make A Plan

Once you have learned about the Great Backyard Bird Count, think about ways that you can spread the word in your school and community. List or sketch your ideas in the space below. Consider your target audience and the type of advertising most likely to reach them. Don't forget to list important facts like time and location.

# Representing Data

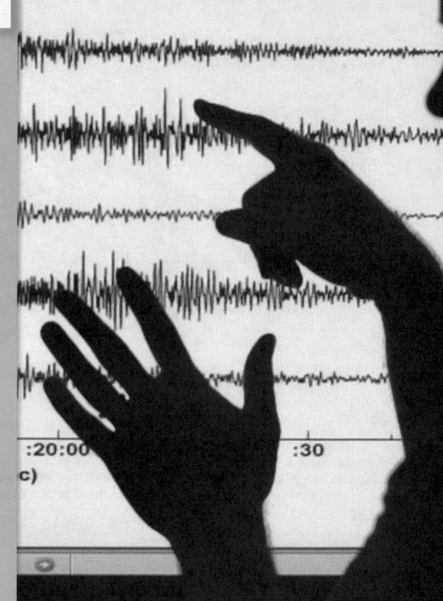

**ESSENTIAL QUESTION**

## In what ways can you make sense of data?

By the end of this lesson, you should be able to use models, simulations, tables, and graphs to display and analyze scientific data.

**TEKS** **6.2C** collect and record data using the International System of Units (SI) and qualitative means such as labeled drawings, writing, and graphic organizers

**TEKS** **6.2D** construct tables and graphs, using repeated trials and means, to organize data and identify patterns

**TEKS** **6.2E** analyze data to formulate reasonable explanations, communicate valid conclusions supported by the data, and predict trends

**TEKS** **6.3B** use models to represent aspects of the natural world such as a model of Earth's layers

**TEKS** **6.3C** identify advantages and limitations of models such as size, scale, properties, and materials

Scientists depend on tools called seismographs to record the motion of earthquakes. The graph produced by a seismograph is called a seismogram. This seismogram shows the ground motion of an earthquake that hit the United Kingdom in 2007.

## Engage Your Brain

**1 Predict** Check T or F to show whether you think each statement is true or false.

T   F

☐  ☐  Scientific models have been used to show results of scientific experiments.

☐  ☐  Certain types of graphs are better than others for displaying specific types of data.

☐  ☐  Most graphs are confusing and unnecessary.

☐  ☐  If something can be shown in a table, then it should not be shown in a graph.

**2 Evaluate** Name two things about the model shown that are similar to the object that the model represents. Then name two things about the model that are different.

_____

_____

_____

_____

_____

_____

_____

_____

_____

## Active Reading

**3 Apply** Many words, such as *model*, have multiple meanings. Use context clues to write your own definition for each meaning of the word *model*.

**Example sentence**
After getting an *A* on another test, Julio's teacher told him he was a <u>model</u> student.

model:

_____

_____

**Example sentence**
For her science project, Samantha created a <u>model</u> of the solar system.

model:

_____

_____

### Vocabulary Terms
- model
- simulation

**4 Identify** As you read this lesson, underline examples of models.

# Crunching Data!

## How do scientists make sense of data?

Before scientists begin an experiment, they often create a data table for recording their data. *Data* are the facts, figures, and other evidence gathered through observations and experimentation. The more data a scientist collects, the greater is the need for the data to be organized in some way. Data tables are one helpful way to organize a lot of scientific data.

## Scientists Organize the Data

A data table provides an organized way for scientists to record the data that they collect. Information types that might be recorded in data tables are times, amounts, and *frequencies*, or the number of times something happens.

When creating a data table, scientists must decide how to organize the table into columns and rows. Any units of measurement, such as seconds or degrees, should be included in the column headings and not in the individual cells. Finally, a title must always be added to describe the data in the table.

The data table below shows the number of movie tickets sold each month at a small theater.

### Movie Tickets Sold Monthly

| Month | Number of tickets |
|-------|-------------------|
| January | 15,487 |
| February | 12,654 |
| March | 15,721 |
| April | 10,597 |
| May | 10,916 |
| June | 11,797 |
| July | 18,687 |
| August | 18,302 |
| September | 16,978 |
| October | 10,460 |
| November | 11,807 |
| December | 17,497 |

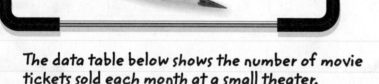

## Do the Math — You Try It

**5 Extend** Circle the row in the table that shows the month when the greatest number of tickets were sold. Then circle the row that shows the month when the least number of tickets were sold. Finally, subtract the least number from the greatest number to find the range of the number of tickets sold.

_____ − _____ = _____

Greatest number of tickets — Least number of tickets — Range

# Scientists Graph and Analyze the Data

In order to analyze their collected data for patterns, it is often helpful for scientists to construct a graph of their data. The type of graph they use depends upon the data they collect and what they want to show.

A *bar graph* is used to display and compare data in a number of separate categories. The length, or height, of each bar represents the number in each category. For example, for the movie theater data, the months are the categories. The lengths of the bars represent the number of tickets sold each month.

Other types of graphs include line graphs and circle graphs. A *line graph* is often used to show continuous change over time. A *circle graph,* or pie chart, is used to show how each group of data relates to all of the data. For example, you could use a circle graph to show the percentages of boys and girls in your class.

**6 Interpret** What kind of data would you display in a bar graph?

_____

_____

_____

## Visualize It!

**7 Analyze** The data in the graph below are the same as the data in the table at the left. During what three months are the most movie theater tickets sold?

_____

_____

_____

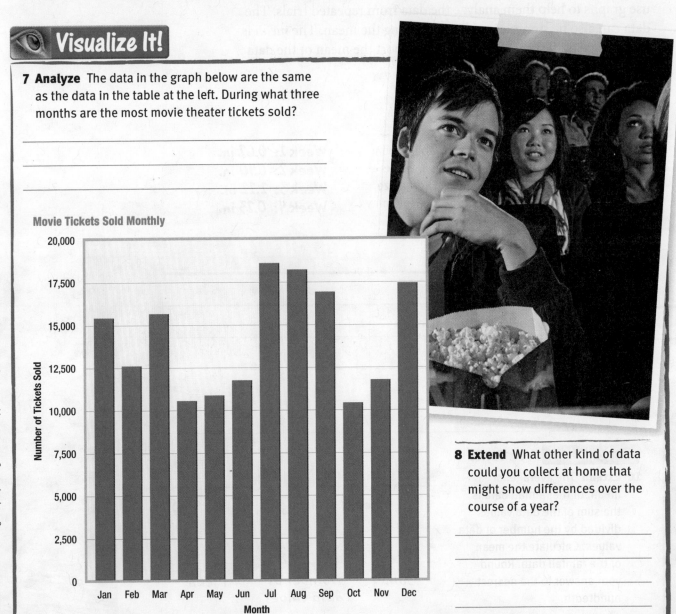

Movie Tickets Sold Monthly

**8 Extend** What other kind of data could you collect at home that might show differences over the course of a year?

_____

_____

_____

_____

# Graph It!

## What do graphs show?

Graphs are visual representations of data. They show information in a way that is often easier to understand than data shown in tables are.

Graphs can help you compare data. They can be used to identify trends and patterns. They can also be used to group data. A bar graph of the total rainfall each month might show increasing and decreasing trends. Months could be easily grouped into low or high rainfall months.

Repeated trials are used in many experiments. The more trials there are, the clearer trends usually become. Scientists often use graphs to help them analyze the data from repeated trials. The data can also be summarized by calculating the mean. The *mean* is the average of the data. Scientists may report the mean of the data from several trials.

### Visualize It!

**9 Complete** The data at the right show the amount of rain, in inches, that fell in each of four weeks at a school. Use the empty table below to organize the data. Include a title for the table, the column headings, and all of the data.

Week 1: 0.62 in.
Week 2: 0.40 in.
Week 3: 1.12 in.
Week 4: 0.23 in.

Title _____

Headings _____

Data _____

### Do the Math — You Try It

**10 Extend** The average, or mean, of the rainfall data is the sum of the data values divided by the number of data values. Calculate the mean of the rainfall data. Round your answer to the nearest hundredth.

_____ + _____ + _____ + _____ = _____

Weeks 1 through 4 · · · · · · · · · · · · Sum

_____ ÷ _____ ≈ _____

Sum · · Number of · · Mean
· · · · · data values

# How are graphs constructed?

To make a bar graph of the rainfall data at the left, first draw a horizontal axis and a vertical axis. Next, write the names of the categories to be graphed along the horizontal axis. Include an overall label for the axis as well. Next, label the vertical axis with the name of the dependent variable. Be sure to include the units of measurement. Then create a scale along the axis by marking off equally spaced numbers that cover the range of the data collected. For each category, draw a solid bar using the scale on the vertical axis to determine the height. Make all the bars the same width. Finally, add a title that describes the graph.

**Active Reading**

**11 Identify** As you read, number the steps used to construct a graph. You may want to rely on signal words that indicate a new step, such as *then* or *next*.

**12 Graph** Construct a bar graph of the rainfall data at the left. On the lines provided, include a title for the graph and axis labels. Use a scale of 0.20 in. for the horizontal axis, and label the bars on the vertical axis.

Title: _____

Amount of Rainfall (in.)

0.0

Week 1 _____ _____ _____ _____

_____

**Visualize It!**

**13 Analyze** During which week was the rainfall amount approximately twice what it was during week 4? Use your graph to explain.

_____
_____
_____
_____
_____

This rain gauge is used to gather and measure liquid precipitation.

# Model It!

## What types of models can be used to represent data?

### Active Reading

**14 Apply** As you read, underline different ways that scientists use models.

A crash-test dummy, a mathematical equation, and a road map are all models that represent real things. A **model** is a representation of an object or a process that allows scientists to study something in greater detail. A model uses something familiar to help you understand something that is not familiar.

Models can represent things that are too small to see, such as atoms. They can also represent things that are too large to see fully, such as Earth. Models can be used to explain the past and the present. They can even be used to predict future events. Kinds of scientific models include physical models, conceptual models, mathematical models, and simulations.

## Physical and Conceptual Models

*Physical models* are models that you can touch. Toy cars, models of buildings, maps, and globes are all physical models. *Conceptual models* are representations of how parts are related or organized. A diagram is an example of a conceptual model. For example, this model of Earth shows that Earth is divided into three layers—the crust, the mantle, and the core. The table shows the estimated densities of each of Earth's layers.

### Density of Earth's Layers

| Layer | Density (g/cm³) |
|-------|-----------------|
| crust | 2.6–2.9 |
| mantle | 3.4–5.6 |
| core | 9.9–13.1 |

### Visualize It!

**15 Apply** Explain how a peach could be used as a physical model of the Earth's layers.

_____

_____

_____

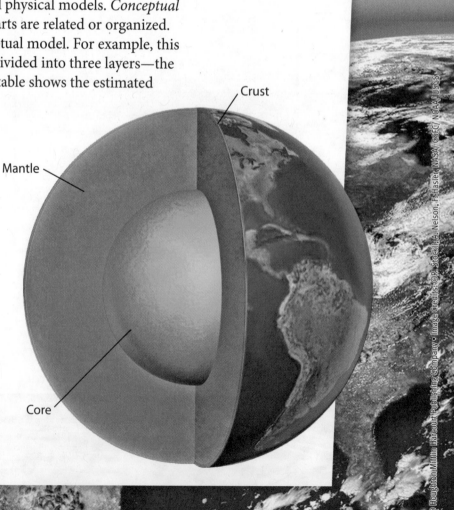

Crust

Mantle

Core

## Mathematical Models

Every day, people try to predict the weather. One way to predict the weather is to use *mathematical models*. A mathematical model is made up of mathematical equations and data. Some mathematical models are simple. These models allow you to calculate things such as how far a car will travel in an hour or how much you would weigh on the moon. A chemical equation is another example of a mathematical model.

Other mathematical models are very complex. Computers are often used to process them. Some of these very complex models, such as population growth models, have many variables. Sometimes, certain variables that no one thought of exist in the model. A change in any variable could cause the model to fail.

# What are some benefits and limitations of models?

Models are used to represent things that are too small or too large to see. Models also benefit scientists in other ways. They allow scientists to do experiments without affecting or harming the subject of the study. For example, crash-test dummies simulate how car accidents affect people.

All models are limited because they are simpler versions of the systems that they try to explain. The simpler model is easier to understand and use. However, information is left out when a model is made.

The size and scale of a model can differ from the real thing. Models have different properties. They are often made of different materials than the real thing. These factors influence how models behave. This means that models do not function exactly like the object or system they represent.

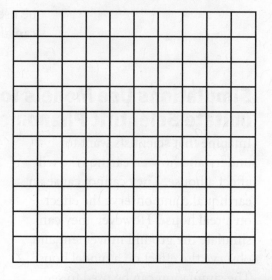

**Do the Math** You Try It

**16 Calculate** The air we breathe is made up of 78% nitrogen, 21% oxygen, and 1% other gases. Use three different colored pencils to color the appropriate number of squares in the grid for each of these percentages.

**Think Outside the Book** Inquiry

**17 Apply** With a classmate, discuss the benefits and limitations of globes and maps as physical models.

# How do simulations represent data?

A **simulation** uses a model to copy the function, behavior, or process of the thing it represents. The model used in a simulation can be a physical model. Computer simulations are also common. Simulations are often used to study systems that are large or complex, such as weather systems. They can also imitate processes that are difficult to study directly. For example, they could be used to study earthquakes or the melting of the polar ice caps.

Scientists observe and collect data from the simulation. It can be used to explain events in the past and the present. Simulations can also be used to make predictions.

**Active Reading**

**18 Identify** As you read, underline three different reasons that scientists use simulations.

## Simulations Use Models to Imitate Scientific Phenomena

Imagine that scientists want to understand how an earthquake will affect a house. They cannot cause an earthquake and observe the effect on a real house. However, they can simulate the ground movement and observe the effect on a model house. The simulation can be used to see how the house moves, what damage occurs, or how the materials react. The simulation is not exactly the same as the real thing; there are always some variables that differ. However, it is a practical way to learn more about real events.

## Simulations Help Explain Scientific Phenomena

An earthquake simulation may show that a house has been damaged. This information is not useful on its own. Scientists also need to understand why the damage occurred.

A simulation can be used to analyze events in detail. Scientists can then understand the causes of events. The information gained from earthquake simulations can be used in design. Houses can be designed with features that help reduce damage. More simulations could be used to test the features to see if they work. If they do not work, scientists would again ask why.

Scientists can simulate how the movement of an earthquake affects different types of structures.

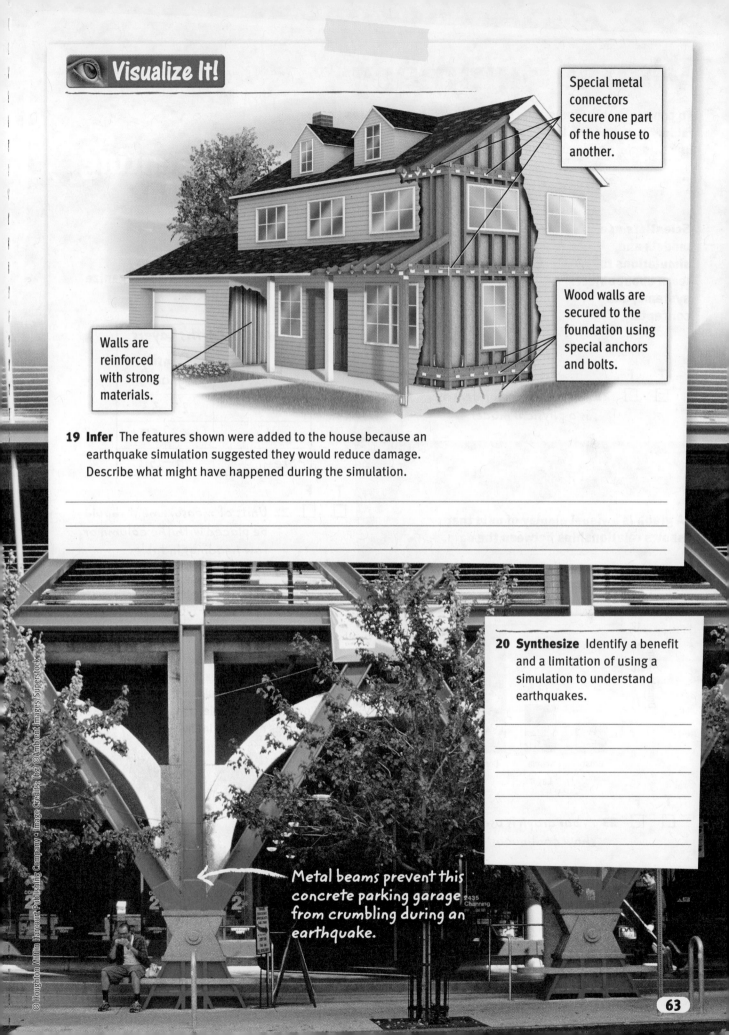

**Visualize It!**

Special metal connectors secure one part of the house to another.

Wood walls are secured to the foundation using special anchors and bolts.

Walls are reinforced with strong materials.

**19 Infer** The features shown were added to the house because an earthquake simulation suggested they would reduce damage. Describe what might have happened during the simulation.

_____

_____

_____

**20 Synthesize** Identify a benefit and a limitation of using a simulation to understand earthquakes.

_____

_____

_____

_____

_____

_____

Metal beams prevent this concrete parking garage from crumbling during an earthquake.

# Visual Summary

To complete this summary, check the box that indicates true or false. Then, use the key below to check your answers. You can use this page to review the main concepts of the lesson.

**Representing Data**

Scientists use models and simulations to learn about objects, systems, and concepts.

**T   F**
☐   ☐   **21** The equation for density is a physical model.

A table can be used to record and organize data as it is being collected.

| Density of Earth's Layers | |
|---|---|
| Layer | Density (g/cm³) |
| crust | 2.7–3.3 |
| mantle | 3.3–5.7 |
| core | 9.9–13.1 |

**T   F**
☐   ☐   **22** Units of measurement should be placed with the column or row headings in tables.

Answers: 21 False; 22 True; 23 False

A graph is a visual display of data that shows relationships between the data.

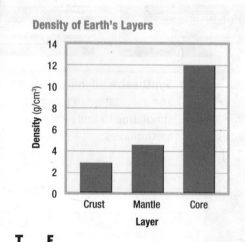

Density of Earth's Layers

**T   F**
☐   ☐   **23** A bar graph is used to show continuous data.

**24 Synthesize** Provide an example of something in the natural world that could be depicted in each of the following ways: a table, a graph, and a model. (Use examples not given in this lesson.)

# Lesson Review

## Vocabulary

Fill in the blank with the term that best completes the following sentences.

**1** A(n) _____ can be a visual or mathematical representation of an object, system, or concept.

**2** A(n) _____ imitates the function, behavior, or process of the thing it represents.

**3** Data can be arranged in visual displays called _____ to make identifying trends easier.

## Key Concepts

**4 Differentiate** How is a diagram different from a simulation?

_____

_____

_____

_____

**5 Predict** A data table shows the height of a person on his birthday each year from age 2 to 12. What trend would you expect to see in a line graph of the data?

_____

_____

_____

_____

_____

**6 Judge** Which kind of graph would be best for depicting data collected on the weight of a baby every month for six months?

_____

_____

_____

_____

**7 Apply** What kind of model would you use to represent the human heart?

_____

_____

## Critical Thinking

Use this graph to answer the following questions.

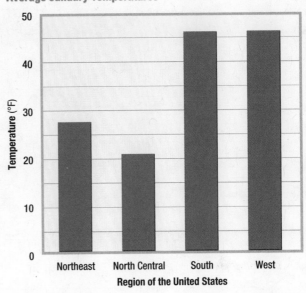

Average January Temperatures

**8 Identify** Which region of the country has the coldest January temperatures?

_____

**9 Estimate** What was the average temperature of the South in January? How did you arrive upon your answer?

_____

_____

_____

_____

_____

**10 Apply** Give an example of a physical model, and explain one limitation of the model. Then give an example of a mathematical model, and explain one limitation.

_____

_____

_____

_____

_____

# My Notes

# Making Conclusions from Evidence

TEKS 6.2E analyze data to formulate reasonable explanations, communicate valid conclusions supported by the data, and predict trends

TEKS 6.3A in all fields of science, analyze, evaluate, and critique scientific explanations by using empirical evidence, logical reasoning, and experimental and observational testing, including examining all sides of scientific evidence of those scientific explanations, so as to encourage critical thinking by the student

In scientific investigations, you will be asked to collect data and summarize your findings. Sometimes, a set of data can be interpreted in more than one way and lead to more than one conclusion. A reliable investigation will allow you to make conclusions that are supported by the data you have collected, and that reflect the findings of other scientists.

## Tutorial

**Take these steps as you analyze findings and evaluate a conclusion made from the findings.**

### Flu Prevention Breakthrough

A medical study has shown that a new drug, Compound Z, protected children from the flu. The results of the study that was conducted last year showed that only 5% of students who were taking Compound Z were affected by the flu. During the same period of time, 20% of the general population was affected by the flu.

Researchers do not know exactly how Compound Z protects children from the flu.

**1 What conclusion is made by the study?** Identify the conclusion or interpretation of the data that is being made in the study.

**2 What evidence or data is given and does the data support the conclusion?** Identify all the observations and findings that are presented to support the conclusion. Decide whether the findings support the conclusion. Look for information and data in other studies that replicate the experiments and verify the conclusion.

Other data should be considered before the conclusion above can be supported. For example, data should be gathered to determine the percentage of children who were not taking Compound Z and got the flu. And, within the 20% of the general population who got the flu, what percentage were children?

**3 Should other data be considered before accepting the conclusion as true?** There may be more than one way to interpret findings of scientific work, and important questions left unanswered. When this happens, plan to make observations, look for more information, or do further experiments that could eliminate one explanation as a possibility.

# You Try It!

**Climate change is one of the most debated issues in modern science.**

In the past 100 years, Earth's average global temperature has risen more than 0.74° C. In 2008, the cold La Niña current in the Pacific caused the average global temperature to drop, but the global average was still warmer than any year from 1880 to 1996. The concentration of the greenhouse gas carbon dioxide ($CO_2$), rose by about 76 parts per million from 1958 to 2008. Many scientists interpret this to mean that human activity is causing global climate change. At the same time, evidence from the geologic record shows that Earth's climate has experienced even larger climate changes in the past.

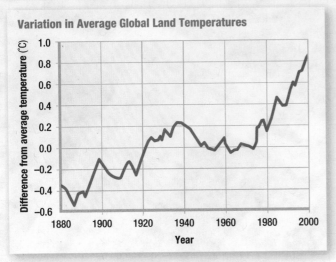

Variation in Average Global Land Temperatures

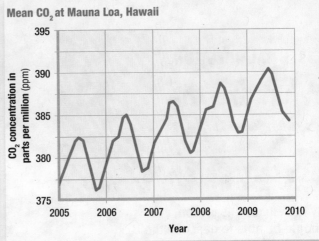

Mean $CO_2$ at Mauna Loa, Hawaii

**1 Evaluating Data** The graphs shown above are taken from a study on climate change. Identify trends or patterns that you can observe in the data on the graphs.

_____

_____

_____

_____

**2 Drawing Conclusions** Draw a conclusion that is supported by these trends. Summarize your conclusion in a single paragraph.

_____

_____

_____

_____

_____

_____

**3 Justifying Conclusions** Which conclusions in the reading are supported by the data in the graphs? Which are not supported by the data?

_____

_____

_____

_____

**4 Identifying Relationships** What other data do you need to further support your conclusion?

_____

_____

_____

## Take It Home

**Find an article that makes a conclusion based on a scientific study. Evaluate the conclusion and determine whether the evidence given supports the conclusion. Bring the article to class and be prepared to discuss it.**

# Scientific Tools and Measurement

## ESSENTIAL QUESTION

### What are the tools and units used in science?

By the end of this lesson, you should be able to describe the different tools and units of measurement used in scientific investigations.

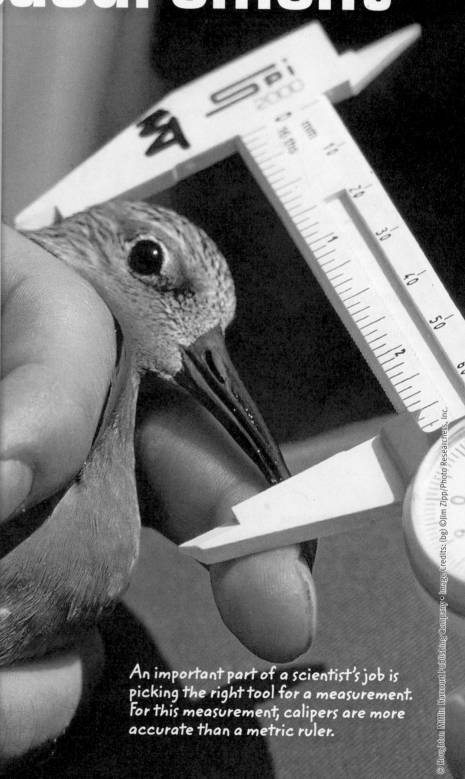

An important part of a scientist's job is picking the right tool for a measurement. For this measurement, calipers are more accurate than a metric ruler.

**TEKS** **6.2C** collect and record data using the International System of Units (SI) and qualitative means such as labeled drawings, writing, and graphic organizers;

**TEKS** **6.4A** use appropriate tools to collect, record, and analyze information, including journals/notebooks, beakers, Petri dishes, meter sticks, graduated cylinders, hot plates, test tubes, triple beam balances, microscopes, thermometers, calculators, computers, timing devices, and other equipment as needed to teach the curriculum

## Lesson Labs

**Quick Labs**
- Investigate Making Measurements
- Investigating Density

**Field Lab**
- Use a Sextant to Make a Map

 **Engage Your Brain**

**1 Predict** Check T or F to show whether you think each statement is true or false.

| T | F | |
|---|---|---|
| ☐ | ☐ | A lab journal or notebook is considered a scientific tool. |
| ☐ | ☐ | Scientists worldwide use the same units of measurement. |
| ☐ | ☐ | It is sometimes appropriate for scientists to estimate measurements. |
| ☐ | ☐ | Precision describes how close a measured value comes to the true value of the measurement. |

**2 Infer** Describe how the scientist might use this electron microscope for a scientific investigation.

 **Active Reading**

**3 Apply** Use context clues to write your own definition for the term *standard*.

**Example sentence**
A scientist uses a <u>standard</u> unit of measurement to compare the lengths of different bacteria.

standard:

_____
_____
_____
_____

### Vocabulary Terms
- measurement
- scientific notation
- accuracy
- precision

**4 Apply** As you learn the definition of each vocabulary term in this lesson, create your own definition or sketch to help you remember the meaning of the term.

# For Good Measure

## What is measurement?

In science, the ability to describe an observation is an important skill. A description is a statement that reports what has been observed. Often, a scientist uses a measurement to describe an observation. A **measurement** is a description that includes a number and a unit. Measurement can also refer to the process of obtaining a quantitative description of something.

## Why do we use standard units of measurement?

Measurements were once based on parts of the body, such as arms or feet, but this method caused problems with accuracy. Body parts vary in size from one person to another, which made it difficult for two people to get the same measurement for an object.

Over time, societies realized that they needed to make units of measurement standard. Using standard units makes it possible for people working in different places to work with the same quantities. Standard units also allow scientists to repeat one another's experiments. Experiments must be repeatable to determine if the results are valid.

*Whether you are in the kitchen or the laboratory, it is difficult to work with nonstandard units of measurement.*

99s
dash of vanilla
pinch of salt
3 cups all-purpo
1 teaspoon bak

1 tsp.

## Visualize It!

**6 List** Which units of measurement in this recipe are not standard?

_____

_____

_____

### Active Reading

**5 Compare** What is the difference between a description and a measurement?

_____

_____

_____

_____

# What is the International System of Units?

In the late 1700s, the French government requested that the French Academy of Sciences improve their own existing official measurement system. The academy responded by creating the original metric system. The system has undergone several changes over the years. The modern metric system is called the International System of Units (SI). Scientists around the world use the SI to collect measurements and record data. The table shows the SI units that apply to the quantities of length, mass, time, temperature, volume, weight, and density. Each SI unit is represented by a symbol. A number and a unit, or representative symbol, are required to correctly record a measurement.

A thermometer is used to measure temperature.

| Measurement | SI unit | Symbol |
|---|---|---|
| length | meter | m |
| mass | kilogram | kg |
| time | second | s |
| temperature | kelvin | K |
| volume | cubic meter | m³ |
| weight | newton | N |
| density | grams per cubic centimeter (milliliter) | g/cm³ or g/mL |

## What are the advantages of using the SI?

There are many advantages of using the SI rather than other systems of measurement. One advantage is that SI measurements provide a common international language for scientists. Scientists worldwide can share and compare their observations and results. A second advantage is that changing from one unit to another is easier in SI than in other systems. Almost all SI units are based on the number 10. Within one type of measurement, you can convert from one unit to another by multiplying or dividing by a power of 10. Conversions in non-SI systems are more complicated, as when converting between inches, feet, and yards.

**Think Outside the Book**

**7 Apply** Do one of the following:
• Write a blog entry as a member of the 1790 French National Assembly explaining the need for a standard measurement system.
• Research the history of a common measurement, such as the yard, and write a report explaining how it came into use.

A meterstick is used to measure length.

# Made to Measure

## What are some tools used to measure SI units?

Scientists use specific tools for each type of measurement. These tools are designed to measure quantities in SI units. Each type of quantity is labeled using an SI base unit. For example, the SI unit for length is the *meter* (m). Length can be measured using a meterstick, ruler, or measuring tape. The *kilogram* (kg) is the SI unit for mass. Mass is measured with a balance. There are different types of balances, including electronic balances and triple beam balances. The SI unit for time is the *second* (s). Time can be measured using a stopwatch. The *kelvin* (K) is the SI unit used for temperature. You usually measure temperature with a thermometer.

Some measurements combine basic SI units to create a new unit. For example, volume is the amount of space that something occupies. The SI unit for volume is the cubic meter (m³). Liquid volume is often expressed in liters (L) or milliliters (mL), which are smaller units than a cubic meter. The volume of liquids can be measured by placing the substance in a graduated cylinder.

 **Visualize It!**

**8 Label** Identify the measurement associated with each tool in the image below.

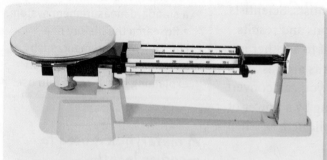

a. The triple beam balance is used to measure _____.

b. The graduated cylinder is used to measure _____.

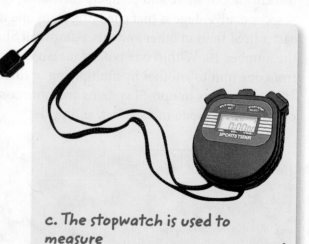

c. The stopwatch is used to measure _____.

© Houghton Mifflin Harcourt Publishing Company • Image Credits: (all) ©HMH

# Mixed-up Measurements

NEW FRONTIERS

When scientists make a mistake in measurement, it usually doesn't cost $125 million. But that's exactly what a metric mess-up cost the National Aeronautics and Space Administration (NASA) in 1999.

## Next Stop: Mars

NASA planned a space mission to Mars to study the planet's atmosphere and climate. After a journey of 286 days, the Mars Climate Orbiter finally reached its destination. The engine of the spacecraft fired to send the craft into orbit around Mars. That is when problems arose—the spacecraft came much too close to the planet. It could not maintain an orbit. The mission failed.

## Small Details, Big Problems

Scientists soon figured out the problem. The team at NASA had been using SI units to calculate the spacecraft's orbit. The team at the private company that built the spacecraft, however, programmed the craft using English units, such as miles.

## Extend

Inquiry

9 **Infer** What can you infer about the relationship between SI units and English units from this article?

10 **Research** Find out how NASA responded to this problem. What did NASA do to ensure that costly mistakes such as this one do not happen again?

11 **Justify** People in the United States still use English units such as inches and pounds for many types of measurements, while most other countries use the SI. Do you think the United States should switch exclusively to the SI? Why or why not?

# How can we make very large or small measurements easy to work with?

**Active Reading**

**12 Identify** As you read, underline examples of SI prefixes.

Some scientific numbers are much smaller or much larger than those we use in everyday life. Measurements that are very big or very small can be confusing to work with. There are two ways that scientists can make working with very large or very small numbers easier: using prefixes and scientific notation.

## We Can Use Prefixes

A prefix is one or more letters or syllables added to the beginning of a word to change its meaning. In the SI, a prefix is used to express an SI unit that is larger or smaller than a base unit. For example, *kilo-* means 1,000 times, so a kilometer is 1,000 meters. The prefix *milli-* indicates 1/1,000 times, so a millimeter is 1/1,000 of a meter. The prefix used depends on the size of the object being measured. The table below shows common SI prefixes.

| SI Prefixes | | |
|---|---|---|
| **Prefix** | **Symbol** | **Factor** |
| *kilo–* | k | 1,000 |
| *hecto–* | h | 100 |
| *deca–* | da | 10 |
| | | 1 |
| *deci–* | d | 0.1 |
| *centi–* | c | 0.01 |
| *milli–* | m | 0.001 |
| *micro–* | μ | 0.000001 |

**13 Apply** The table below shows how prefixes can be used with the unit for length. Complete the table by filling in the blanks.

| Prefix with the base unit meter | Symbol | Number of meters |
|---|---|---|
| kilometer | km | |
| | hm | 100 |
| decameter | dam | |
| millimeter | | 0.001 |

# We Can Use Scientific Notation

**Scientific notation** is a short way of representing very large numbers or very small numbers. Numbers in scientific notation are written in the form $a \times 10^b$. For example, the speed of light in standard notation is 300,000,000 m/s. It is $3 \times 10^8$ m/s in scientific notation.

To find $a$, move the decimal point to make a number greater than or equal to 1 and less than 10. To find $b$, count how many places the decimal point moved. When the decimal moves to the left, $b$ is a positive number. When the decimal moves to the right, $b$ is a negative number. For 300,000,000 m/s, the decimal point is at the right of the last 0. Move the decimal 8 places to the left, until it is to the right of the number 3, to get the value $3 \times 10^8$ m/s.

To convert from scientific notation to standard notation, look at the exponent. If the exponent is positive, move the decimal point $b$ places to the right. If the exponent is negative, move the decimal point $b$ places to the left. For the speed of light, $3 \times 10^8$ m/s, the exponent is 8, which is positive, so move the decimal eight places to the right to write it as 300,000,000 m/s again.

## Do the Math

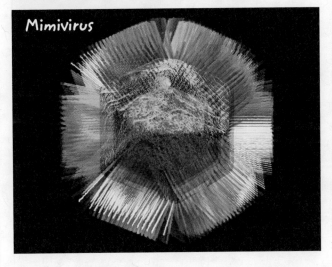

Mimivirus

Red blood cells

### Sample Problem

The diameter of this Mimivirus is 0.000000750 m. Write this number in scientific notation.

Use the form $a \times 10^b$. The decimal number that begins with the first nonzero digit is $a$. The number of decimal places to move is $b$.

To get $a$, move the decimal 7 places to the right.

$$a = 7.5, \ b = -7$$

$$0.000000750 \ m = 7.50 \times 10^{-7} \ m$$

### You Try It

**14 Calculate** The diameter of a human red blood cell is 0.000006 m. Write the diameter in scientific notation.

# Why are accuracy and precision important?

A scientist wants to use tools that can provide a measurement very close to the actual value. **Accuracy** is a description of how close a measurement is to the true value of the quantity measured. The smaller the difference between the measurement and the true value, the more accurate the measurement is. **Precision** is the exactness of a measurement. A precise measurement is repeatable and reliable. If a high-precision measurement is repeated, the number obtained will be the same or very nearly the same.

In a game of horseshoes, the most accurate and precise player wins. Accurate throws are close to the stake. Precise throws are close together.

👁 **Visualize It!**

**15 Illustrate** Draw a fourth set of horseshoes that represents low accuracy and low precision.

Low accuracy, high precision

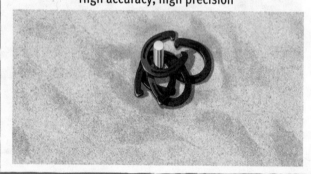

High accuracy, low precision

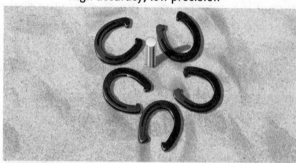

High accuracy, high precision

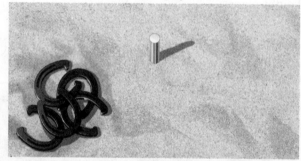

Low accuracy, low precision

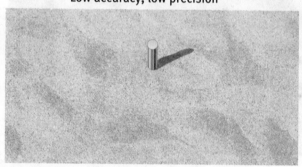

# Why do scientists sometimes estimate measurements?

People estimate measurements doing everyday tasks such as making salsa or rearranging furniture. Scientists also make estimates of measurements. Scientists may use estimates to see if the data they collected are reasonable. Scientists may also use estimates to determine which tool is best suited for making the measurements they need. For example, if you needed to measure a paperclip and a table, you could estimate their lengths and then choose which object to measure with a metric ruler and which object to measure with a measuring tape.

**Think Outside the Book** Inquiry

**16 Apply** Choose an everyday object, and design a method to measure that object that is both accurate and precise. What tool or tools would you use? Explain your answer.

# How do scientists collect and record qualitative data?

The data discussed so far use numbers, measurements, and SI units. These types of data are called quantitative data because they refer to a quantity, or number, of something.

However, some data are not expressed using numbers or measurements. These are called qualitative data because they refer to a quality something has. Observations that describe the color, texture, smell, taste, behavior, or appearance of something are examples of qualitative data. Suppose a scientist is studying a troop, or group, of gorillas. Qualitative observations of a gorilla might include its body color, how it sounds, or a description of the way it moves.

Like quantitative data, qualitative data can be recorded in a lab notebook, in a journal, or on a computer. Scientists also use labeled drawings and graphic organizers, such as an idea web, to collect, record, and analyze qualitative data.

**Active Reading**

**17 Identify** As you read, underline examples of qualitative data.

**Visualize It!**

**18 Observe** On the lines below, list three qualitative observations about the gorillas in the photograph and sketch.

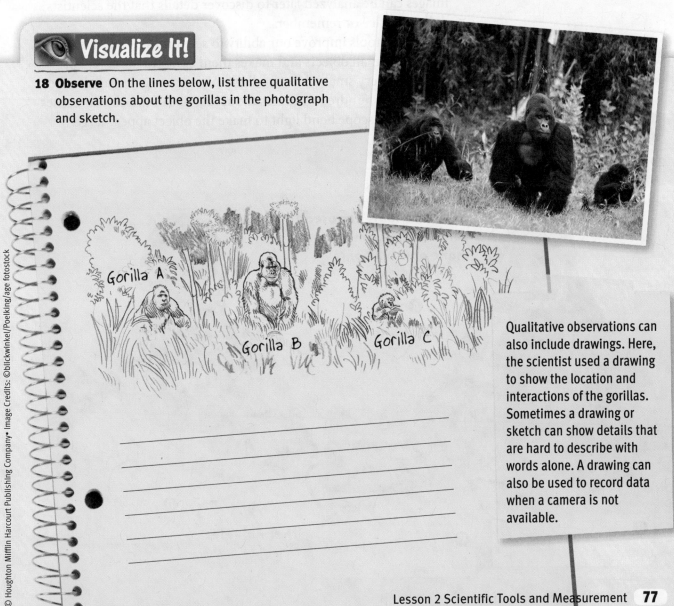

Gorilla A

Gorilla B     Gorilla C

_____

_____

_____

_____

_____

Qualitative observations can also include drawings. Here, the scientist used a drawing to show the location and interactions of the gorillas. Sometimes a drawing or sketch can show details that are hard to describe with words alone. A drawing can also be used to record data when a camera is not available.

# Tools of the Trade

## How are tools used in a science laboratory?

**Active Reading**

**19 Identify** As you read, underline the names of scientific tools.

Scientists use tools for tasks other than measuring. Scientists also needs tools to perform experiments and analyze data. For example, test tubes can hold samples of materials. To increase the temperature of a substance, you can pour the substance into a beaker and warm it on a hot plate. If you need to store samples or grow cell cultures or bacteria, you can use a petri dish. A petri dish is a shallow, circular dish with a lid.

Lab journals or lab notebooks and pencils are tools that can be used to record and analyze data and observations. Scientists use digital cameras to record images of objects or environments. These images can be analyzed later to discover details that the scientists did not notice or remember.

Some tools improve our ability to see things. A hand lens magnifies small objects and makes them easier to observe. For observing very small objects, a light microscope can magnify the image up to hundreds of times the actual size of the object. Lenses in the microscope bend light to make the object appear larger.

**Visualize It!**

**20 Identify** On each line, write the name of the tool that the student is using.

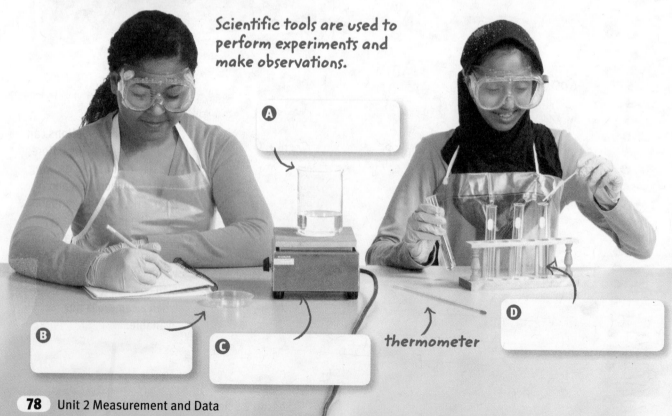

Scientific tools are used to perform experiments and make observations.

**Ⓐ**

**Ⓑ**

**Ⓒ**

**Ⓓ**

thermometer

# How are computers and technology used by scientists?

The use of science for practical purposes is called *technology*. Calculators and computers are two examples of technological devices. They allow scientists to calculate quickly and accurately. They can also analyze data by creating graphs and solving complex equations. With computers, scientists can build spreadsheets, design models, or run simulations. Computers also help scientists share data and ideas and publish reports about their research.

Another type of technology is *probeware*. Probeware is a measuring tool linked to a computer. Probeware allows scientists to collect, record, and analyze data, all with the same tool. Probeware can be used to measure factors such as temperature, acidity, or oxygen levels.

New technology can expand scientists' ability to collect data. The light microscope allowed scientists to discover and observe living cells. Today, electron microscopes have extended those observations to individual atoms. Electron microscopes use beams of electrons to collect data that are translated into an image by a computer. With an electron microscope, scientists can magnify an object by factors of thousands or millions.

Just as technology leads to new scientific discoveries, new scientific discoveries lead to the development of new technologies. Thanks to the discovery of semiconductors, you can put an entire computer in your lap. The first computers filled up large rooms!

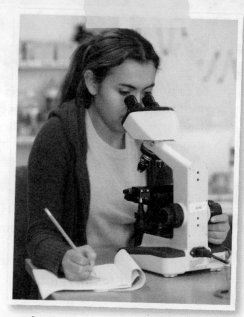

Light microscopes show very small features.

![Active Reading]

**21 Distinguish** What is the difference between a light microscope and an electron microscope?

_____

_____

_____

## Electron Microscope

**22 Hypothesize** Electron microscopes use beams of electrons to make images of objects as small as atoms. Why might an electron microscope be used in manufacturing computer chips?

_____

_____

_____

_____

_____

_____

_____

_____

An electron microscope magnifies an object and creates a digital file of the data. The images can be observed using a computer screen.

# Visual Summary

To complete this summary, circle the correct word or phrase. Then, use the key below to check your answers. You can use this page to review the main concepts of the lesson.

## Scientific Tools and Measurement

**The International System of Units (SI) is the standard system of measurement used in science.**

23 The SI unit for mass is the kilogram / newton.

24 The SI unit for time is the hour / second.

**Scientific tools are used to make observations, collect and analyze data, and share results.**

25 Scientists were only able to observe individual living cells after the invention of the light / electron microscope.

26 A common container in the laboratory used for holding small samples of liquid is a hot plate / test tube.

Gorilla A

Gorilla B

Gorilla C

**Scientists use tools to record and analyze qualitative and quantitative data.**

27 Computers may be used at every stage / only to calculate results of a scientific investigation.

28 An example of a qualitative / quantitative statement would be stating that there are three gorillas in this sketch.

29 **Summarize** Why are tools and technology important for scientific investigations?

# Lesson Review

## Vocabulary

Draw a line to connect the following terms to their definitions.

**1** precision       **A** closeness to the true value

**2** accuracy      **B** description with a number and a unit

**3** measurement      **C** way to write very large or small numbers

**4** scientific notation      **D** the repeatability of a measurement

## Key Concepts

**5 Summarize** Which of the following is not an advantage of using SI units?

**A** allows scientists to compare observations and results

**B** can compare measurements made years apart

**C** based on the number 5, which is easy to use in calculations

**D** uses prefixes to express measurements that are small or large

**6 Calculate** What is 0.003 in scientific notation?

**A** $10 \times 10^3$

**B** $3 \times 10^{-3}$

**C** $3 \times 10^3$

**D** $10 \times 3^{-10}$

**7 Identify** What is the SI unit for temperature?

**A** the kelvin

**B** degrees Celsius

**C** degrees Fahrenheit

**D** the newton

## Critical Thinking

Use this photo to answer the following questions.

**8 Conclude** Name the type of measurement the student in the photo is making.

_____

**9 Apply** The prefix for the measurement the student is making is *milli-*. What does *milli-* mean?

_____

**10 Evaluate** The student measured the volume of water as 80.0 mL. She discovered that the actual volume was 80.1 mL. Is her measurement accurate? Explain.

_____
_____
_____

**11 Compare** How might the student's recorded data differ if she were recording qualitative data instead of quantitative data?

_____
_____
_____

# My Notes

# Engineering Design Process

| Skills |
| --- |
| Identify a need |
| Conduct research |
| ✓ Brainstorm solutions |
| ✓ Select a solution |
| ✓ Design a prototype |
| ✓ Build a prototype |
| ✓ Test and evaluate |
| Redesign to improve |
| ✓ Communicate results |

## Objectives

- List and rank insulation materials according to effectiveness.
- Design a technological solution to keep an ice cube frozen.
- Test a prototype insulated ice cooler and communicate whether it achieved the desired results.

## Building an Insulated Cooler

What do freezers, ovens, and polar bears have in common? They are all insulated! *Insulation* is a type of material that slows the transfer of energy such as heat. Refrigerators and freezers use insulation to keep the food inside cold. Insulation around ovens keeps energy inside the oven. And some animals have hair, fur, and fat layers that provide them with insulation, too.

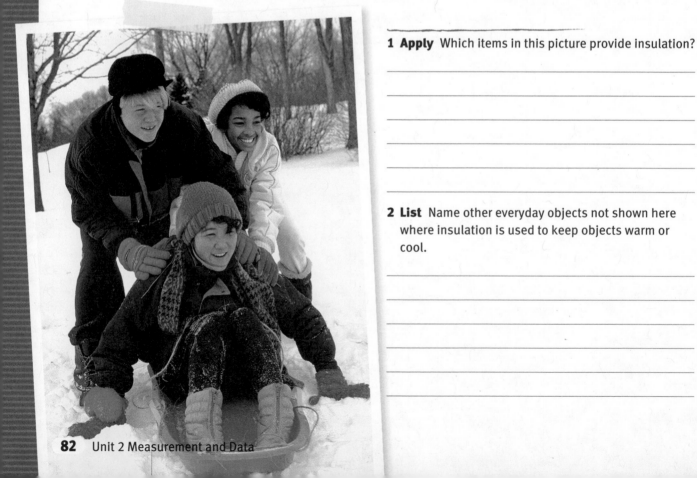

**1 Apply** Which items in this picture provide insulation?

_____

_____

_____

_____

_____

**2 List** Name other everyday objects not shown here where insulation is used to keep objects warm or cool.

_____

_____

_____

_____

_____

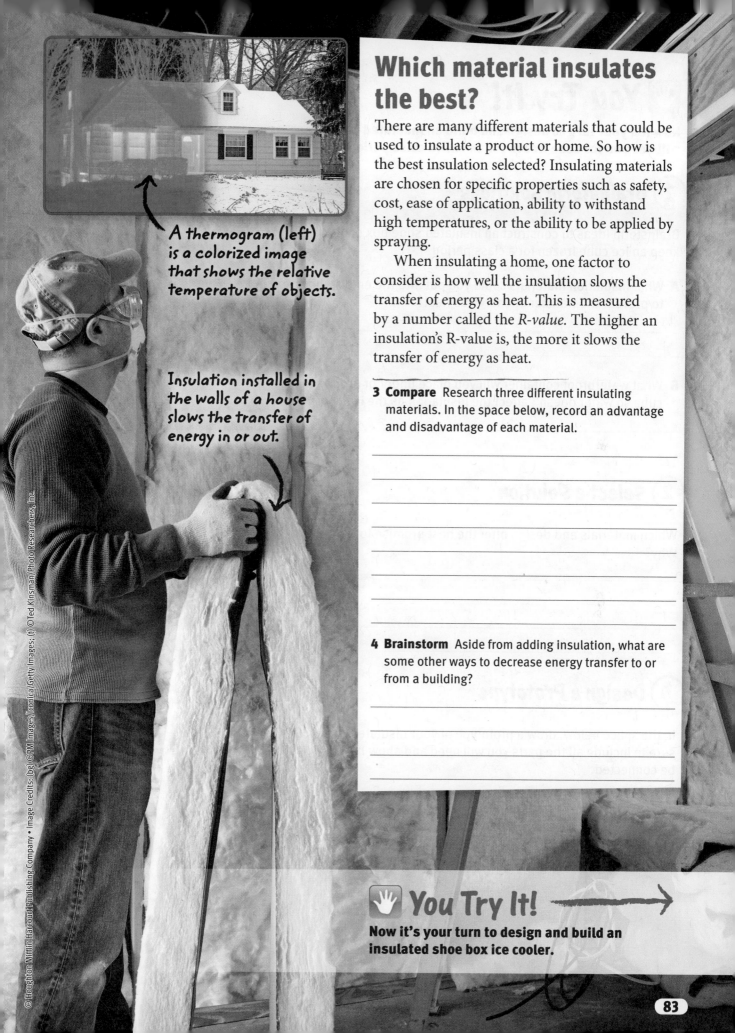

A thermogram (left) is a colorized image that shows the relative temperature of objects.

Insulation installed in the walls of a house slows the transfer of energy in or out.

# Which material insulates the best?

There are many different materials that could be used to insulate a product or home. So how is the best insulation selected? Insulating materials are chosen for specific properties such as safety, cost, ease of application, ability to withstand high temperatures, or the ability to be applied by spraying.

When insulating a home, one factor to consider is how well the insulation slows the transfer of energy as heat. This is measured by a number called the *R-value*. The higher an insulation's R-value is, the more it slows the transfer of energy as heat.

3 **Compare** Research three different insulating materials. In the space below, record an advantage and disadvantage of each material.

_____
_____
_____
_____
_____
_____
_____

4 **Brainstorm** Aside from adding insulation, what are some other ways to decrease energy transfer to or from a building?

_____
_____
_____
_____

🖐 You Try It! ⟶

Now it's your turn to design and build an insulated shoe box ice cooler.

 You Try It!

Now it's your turn to design and build an insulated cooler that will keep an ice cube frozen for an entire class period.

## 1 Brainstorm Solutions

Brainstorm ideas to construct an insulated shoe box cooler that will keep an ice cube frozen for a class period.

**A** What insulation materials could you put into the empty shoe box to prevent the transfer of energy as heat?

_____

_____

**B** What waterproof container will you place under or around the ice cube so water doesn't affect the insulation as the ice cube melts?

_____

_____

## 2 Select a Solution

Which materials and design offer the best promise for success? Why?

_____

_____

_____

_____

## 3 Design a Prototype

In the space below, draw a prototype of your insulated cooler. Be sure to include all the parts you will need and show how they will be connected.

### You Will Need

✔ balance

✔ duct tape or packing tape

✔ ice cube

✔ insulation material

✔ plastic bag or waterproof container

✔ shoe box, empty

## (4) Build a Prototype

Now build your insulated cooler. What parts, if any, did you have to revise as you were building the prototype?

_____

_____

_____

_____

## (5) Test and Evaluate

**A** At the beginning of a class period, find the mass of an ice cube. Record your result below.

_____

**B** Place the ice cube in your cooler and close it. At the end of the class period, open the cooler and observe the ice cube. Find the ice cube's mass and record your result below.

_____

**C** Was part of the ice still frozen? Calculate the fraction of the ice cube that remained frozen.

_____

## (6) Communicate Results

**A** Did your cooler provide effective insulation? Explain.

_____

_____

_____

_____

**B** Is there anything you could have done to increase the amount of ice remaining?

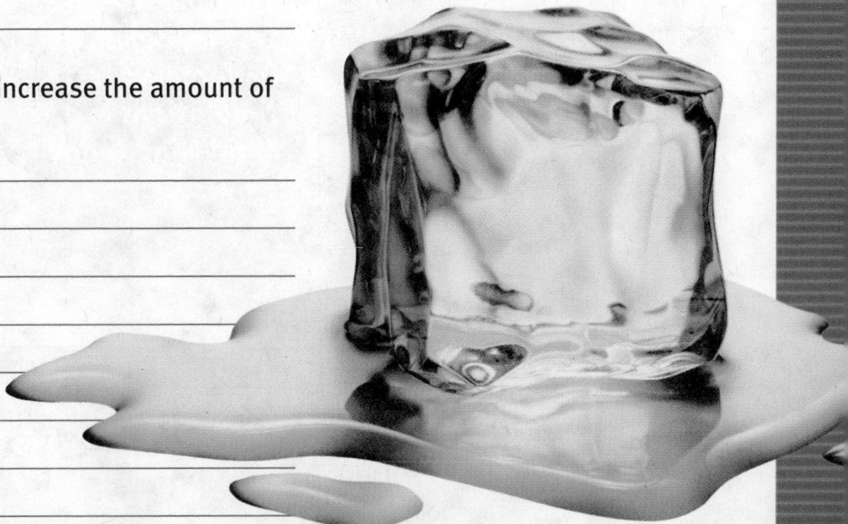

_____

_____

_____

_____

_____

_____

_____

# Models and Simulations

## ESSENTIAL QUESTION

## How do scientists use models and simulations?

By the end of this lesson, you should be able to explain how scientists use models and simulations to represent systems, explain phenomena, and make predictions.

This full-size test model is undergoing test simulations in a giant wind tunnel.

**TEKS** **6.3B** use models to represent aspects of the natural world such as a model of Earth's layers

**TEKS** **6.3C** identify advantages and limitations of models such as size, scale, properties, and materials

**Lesson Labs**

**Quick Labs**
- Modeling Eye Images
- Interpreting Models

**S.T.E.M. Lab**
- Exploring Convection

## Engage Your Brain

**1 Predict** Check T or F to show whether you think each statement is true or false.

T F

☐ ☐ Models can have the same general appearance as real-life objects.

☐ ☐ Models of airplanes have all of the same operating parts as real airplanes do.

☐ ☐ Models can represent systems and processes.

**2 Describe** Write your own caption to this photo.

_____

_____

_____

_____

## Active Reading

**3 Synthesize** Many English words have their roots in other languages. Use the Latin word below to make an educated guess about the meaning of the word *simulation*.

| Latin word | Meaning |
|------------|-------------|
| *simulatio* | make-believe |

**Example sentence:**
A flight <u>simulation</u> lets pilots practice flying an airplane in dangerous conditions.

simulation:

_____

_____

_____

### Vocabulary Terms

- model
- simulation
- physical model
- mathematical model
- conceptual model

**4 Identify** As you read, create a reference card for each vocabulary term. On one side of the card, write the term and its meaning. On the other side, draw an image that illustrates or makes a connection to the term. These cards can be used as bookmarks in the text so that you can refer to them while studying.

# To Be a Model Scientist...

## Why do scientists use models and simulations?

Models and simulations help us to understand the world around us. A scientific **model** shows the structure of an object, system, or concept. **Simulations** use models to imitate the function, behavior, or process of whatever the models represent.

### To Answer Difficult Questions

What is the structure of an atom? How much fuel do we need to reach the moon? How many fish can we catch each year without drastically reducing the fish population? These questions are all difficult to answer. A difficult question is a question that cannot be answered quickly by direct observation. Models and simulations are tools that can help answer these questions. Models let us test many possible ideas to find the solutions to difficult questions.

### To Represent Complex Systems

In the real world, systems are complex and made up of many interacting parts. Scientists can use models to represent these systems. For example, a building is a complex system that has many parts that interact. Scientists can study the way a model building will behave during an earthquake. Data from simulations on a model building can help to produce an earthquake-resistant building design.

**Active Reading** **5 Identify** What is one example of a complex system that can be represented by a model?

_____

_____

Model buildings can be tested for earthquake resistance before real buildings are constructed.

**Inquiry**

**6 Infer** How can using model buildings in earthquake simulations produce more earthquake-resistant building designs?

_____

_____

_____

_____

# ...Use Models!

## To Test New Ideas

People have new ideas all the time. Some ideas are good and lead to useful technologies. Other ideas are never developed. Modeling can separate good ideas from ideas that will never be developed.

Testing is needed before time and money are spent developing new ideas. For example, someone might propose using wind turbines and solar cells as an environmentally friendly way to generate electrical energy in a community. However, before building these expensive systems, computer modeling can be used to determine if these technologies will actually be energy efficient.

## To Make Predictions

Models are used to make predictions that affect our everyday lives. For example, meteorologists make weather predictions by entering data for different weather elements into complex computer programs. Models are also used to make predictions about phenomena that occur far from Earth. For example, the sun has periods of intense magnetic activity. These periods are identified by the number of sunspots that appear on the sun's surface. Solar activity can damage satellites and affect communications. Models of sunspot activity can be built using past sunspot activity. With these models, researchers can predict future sunspot activity and minimize satellite damage and communications interruptions.

Computer models can test designs, such as this turbine, before they are built.

## Visualize It!

**7 Analyze** Use the graph to predict sunspot activity in 2020.

_____

_____

_____

_____

_____

_____

_____

Mathematical models are used to make predictions.

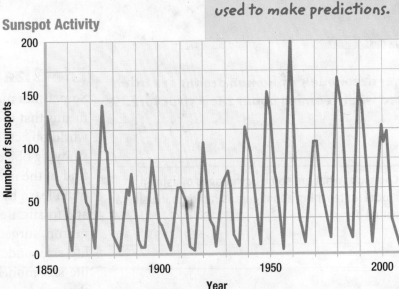

**Sunspot Activity**

Year

# It's a Matter of Scale

## What are some types of physical models?

Toy cars are physical models that represent real cars. A **physical model** represents the physical structure of an object or system. Physical models often look and act like the object or system they represent. Toy cars look like real cars and roll like real cars. However, toy cars usually don't have working engines.

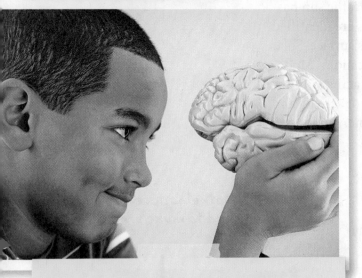

Molecular models help us to imagine the structure of tiny molecules.

Life-size models of human organs are often used when learning about their structure.

### Scale Models

Scale models are used to estimate distance, volume, or quantity. Scale models are also used to study objects or systems that are too small to see or are too big to see completely. *Scale* is the relationship between a model's measurements and the real object's measurements. A one-eighth scale model of a boat is one-eighth the size of the real boat. Scientists use scale models to estimate the properties of actual objects or systems. For example, the internal structure of atoms is simply too small to see, so we study atoms using models.

> **Inquiry**
>
> **8** What are three examples of objects that are too large to easily study without using models?
>
> _____
>
> _____

### Life-Size Models

Sometimes models are made to be life-size. This means that the model is the same size as a real-world object. Life-size models are useful for studying objects that are rare or are difficult to find in the natural world. For example, students often learn by using models of human organs and fossils. Before performing surgery on a living person, surgeons practice their technique on life-size models of human organs. Museums use life-size models of dinosaurs to show how large these creatures were when they were alive.

**9 Compare** What are some advantages of using a model for teaching about organs rather than using an actual organ?

_____

_____

# What are some advantages and disadvantages of physical models?

Physical models allow scientists to study objects or systems that are too small to see or too big to see completely. They are also used when objects are too far away, too dangerous, or too expensive to study, or when they no longer exist. Like other models, physical models do not always behave like the real thing.

## Physical Models Are Easier and Safer to Work With

Physical models are often easier and less dangerous to work with than the objects that they represent. For example, scale models of ships are used for training shiphandlers and for testing the hydraulic systems that control the ships. For accuracy, the models must consider different variables such as wind, currents, and water depth. Flight simulators on the ground are used to train pilots to fly. The same instruments that are found in a real airplane are used in a flight simulator. Using a simulator is easier, cheaper, and much safer than training pilots in a real plane.

## Physical Models Are Not Always Like the Real Thing

Ideally, physical models should work exactly like the objects that they represent. In reality, physical models have limitations. They may not behave in the exact same way as the object or system that they have been made to represent. This may occur if a model is being studied outside of its natural environment. For instance, a model may not function the same way in a laboratory as it would in the real world. Also, a physical model may not be the best way to represent a complex system. It may be impossible to account for every variable in a complex model.

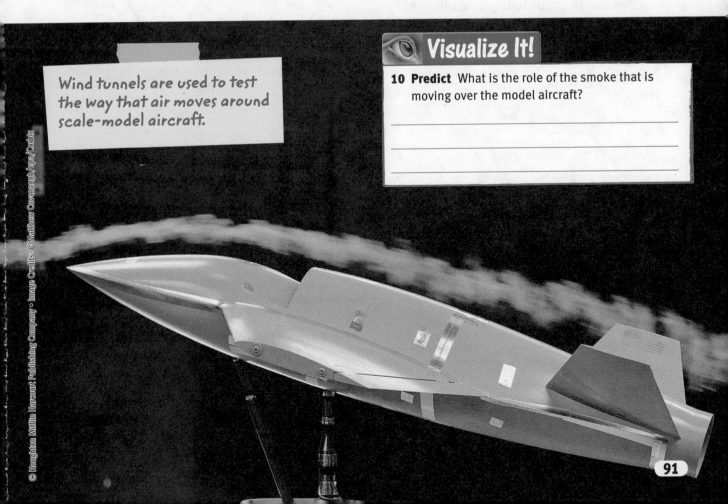

Wind tunnels are used to test the way that air moves around scale-model aircraft.

### Visualize It!

**10 Predict** What is the role of the smoke that is moving over the model aircraft?

_____

_____

_____

# It's All in the Numbers

## What are some types of mathematical models?

Models that represent processes are more abstract than models that represent objects. Some of the most useful process models are mathematical models. A **mathematical model** uses different forms of data to represent the way a system or process works.

### Equations and Graphs

Mathematical models are made up of numbers and equations. These models can often be shown as graphs and are used to predict future trends. For example, in order to plan for future services, a city needs to predict future populations. Based on past data, it is known that populations tend to grow at an increasingly faster rate. Such growth is called *exponential* (ek•spuh•NEN•shuhl). When population data are illustrated on a graph, future populations can be predicted by extending the curve. As with all models, assumptions have been made. In this case, the model assumes that the rate of growth remains the same.

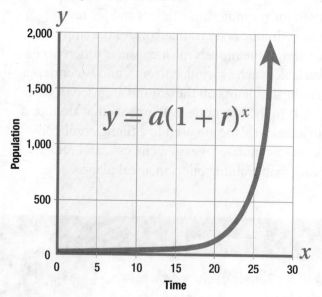

**Model of Exponential Growth**

$$y = a(1 + r)^x$$

(y-axis: Population, 0 to 2,000; x-axis: Time, 0 to 30)

---

The process of photosynthesis can be shown as a mathematical model.

$$6CO_2 + 6H_2O \xrightarrow{\text{sunlight}} C_6H_{12}O_6 + 6O_2$$

**11 Interpret** What do the large and small numbers represent in a chemical equation?

_____

_____

_____

_____

### Chemical Formulas and Equations

Drawing the chemical structure of each molecule when writing chemical reactions would take too long and use a lot of space. Using words would also be difficult. Instead, chemical symbols from the periodic table are used to represent atoms, just as $x$ and $y$ represent variables in an equation. A number to the right of and below the atom's symbol shows how many of each atom are in a molecule. This number is called the *subscript*. A number before the molecule shows how many of each molecule are in the reaction. This number is called the *coefficient*.

© Houghton Mifflin Harcourt Publishing Company

# What are some advantages and disadvantages of mathematical models?

Mathematical models are useful for showing patterns and making predictions. They are easy to change and adjust. But some systems that have many variables are too complex to model easily. If key variables are not considered, the model could contain errors.

## Mathematical Models are Powerful Predictors

One advantage of mathematical models is that they are useful in making predictions. For obtaining the detailed predictions of a mathematical model, computers are often essential. Computers can process many variables quickly using complex mathematical equations. And they can do so without making the calculation errors that humans often make. Computer modeling is useful for determining how a large number of objects interact or change. For example, weather predictions are made using computer models. Economic forecasts are also made using computer models. Computer models can even be used to predict the sizes and shapes of spots on giraffes.

## Mathematical Models Can Be Oversimplified

Mathematical models also have limitations. They are based on current data, which might not be of use in the future. Also, they may exclude variables that did not seem to be important. Sometimes systems are too large or too complex for mathematical modeling, even using computers. To save computer processing time, some variables might need to be left out of a model. Or, to simplify a calculation, only a small portion of the system might be studied. Taking these steps could result in a model that gives misleading results.

**Active Reading** **12 Explain** What are two ways in which a computer model might be oversimplified?

_____

_____

Mathematical models can be used to predict the size of spots on animals.

# It's Kind of Abstract

## What are some characteristics of conceptual models?

Another type of model used in science is the conceptual model. A **conceptual model** is a representation of how parts of a system are related or organized. Conceptual models can be used to simplify complex relationships.

### Conceptual Models Have Different Uses

**Active Reading** **13 List** As you read, underline the uses of conceptual models.

Conceptual models are useful in identifying patterns and similarities for classifications. The periodic table is a type of conceptual model. The elements in each horizontal row of the periodic table have the same number of electron shells. The elements in each vertical row have similar chemical properties.

Conceptual models are often used to represent processes that cannot be directly observed. The rock cycle, which is shown below, is an example. Because conceptual models represent how parts of a system are related, they can help predict the effect that changing one part of a system will have on the whole system.

### Conceptual Models May Have Limitations

Like all models, conceptual models may have limitations. Models may not be able to take certain data or ideas into account. Therefore, one limitation of conceptual models is that they may be oversimplified. In this case, a model may not be a true representation of the complex relationships that exist in a system. This leads us to a second limitation of conceptual models. If a model is not a true representation of the relationships that exist in a system, then the model can lead to misconceptions. A model that is oversimplified and that can lead to misconceptions can produce incomplete predictions.

### Think Outside the Book

**14 Diagram** Create a conceptual model that shows the relationships among groups of people you spend time with, such as friends, family, classmates, or teammates. Use arrows with captions to help explain the relationships.

This is a conceptual model of the rock cycle.

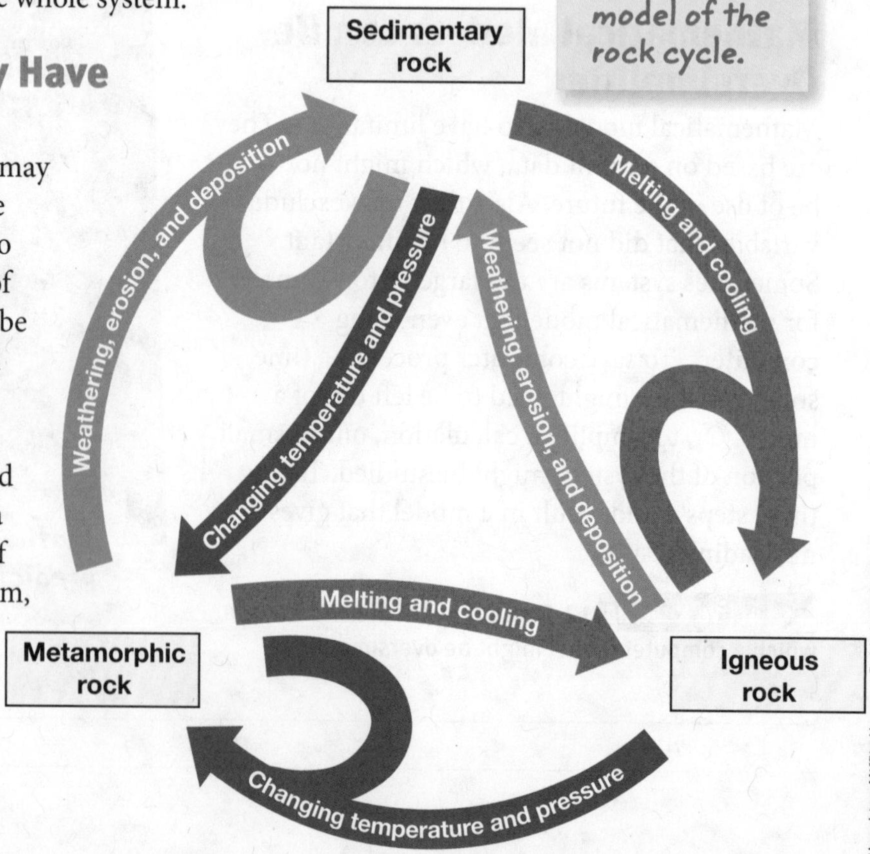

Sedimentary rock

Weathering, erosion, and deposition

Melting and cooling

Changing temperature and pressure

Weathering, erosion, and deposition

Melting and cooling

Metamorphic rock

Changing temperature and pressure

Igneous rock

# How are simulations used?

Simulations use models to show how an object or system works. Simulations can be used to improve the performance of a piece of technology. Quality control, safety, training, and education are other reasons for using simulations. In research, simulations allow scientists to control variables when conducting tests and to determine what happens when variables are changed.

## To Test Designs in a Controlled Environment

Simulations may show how an event would occur under specific circumstances to test a hypothesis. Simulations can test hypotheses by changing certain conditions. Complex technologies can be tested in a variety of environments before they are put in use. For example, the *Mars Exploration Rovers* were designed based on the experiences of previous space expeditions. So, before sending the rovers to Mars, extensive tests were conducted using models on Earth. In this way, researchers could change variables to determine an outcome. During testing, design flaws may be found that can be corrected. This can prevent damage to an expensive piece of equipment or people being injured because of faulty design.

## To Test Designs in a Safer, Less Expensive Way

Simulations can prevent costly and dangerous errors in design. Imagine building an expensive rocket, then launching it without knowing if it would work. That's how early rocket designs were tested. Today, new rocket designs are first tested in simulations.

Simulations can also be used to predict future events. Astronauts train in an underwater environment that simulates the weightlessness of space. The astronauts "spacewalk" inside a tank that is 12 m deep and holds 23.5 million liters of water. They put on their spacesuits and practice working on a model of the *Hubble Space Telescope* to prepare for future missions in space.

To improve vehicle safety, crashes are simulated in controlled environments.

Procedures planned for space are always simulated first on Earth.

**15 Explain** Why is an actual car with realistic passengers needed to simulate the effects of a crash in safety tests?

_____

_____

**16 Infer** Why do astronauts train using underwater simulations?

_____

_____

# Visual Summary

To complete this summary, answer the following True or False questions. Then, use the key below to check your answers. You can use this page to review the main concepts of the lesson.

## Models and Simulations

**A physical model represents an object or system.**

T  F
17 ☐  ☐  Models always behave exactly like the thing they represent.

**Mathematical models use numbers and equations to represent the way a system or process works.**

T  F
18 ☐  ☐  Computer modeling is useful for determining how objects interact with one another or change.

**A simulation uses a model to imitate the function, behavior, or process of the thing it represents.**

T  F
19 ☐  ☐  Complex objects or processes are easier to simulate.

**A conceptual model shows how parts of a system are related or organized.**

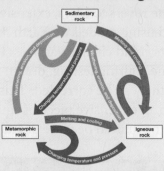

T  F
20 ☐  ☐  Conceptual models can represent a process that cannot be observed directly.

Answers: 17 F; 18 T; 19 F; 20 T

---

21 **Synthesize** How can models and simulations be used to build safer cars?

# Lesson Review

## Vocabulary

Draw a line to connect each type of model to its matching examples.

**1** physical model

**2** conceptual model

**3** mathematical model

**A** water cycle, rock cycle, family tree

**B** chemical reaction, population growth, sunspot activity

**C** architectural model, atomic structure, an artificial organ

## Key Concepts

**4 Identify** What are three advantages of using conceptual models?

_____

_____

_____

_____

**5 Explain** Models are often used to represent very small objects or very large objects. Why is it also useful to create life-size models of some objects?

_____

_____

_____

_____

_____

**6 List** What are two advantages and two limitations of physical models?

_____

_____

_____

## Critical Thinking

Use this graph to answer the following questions.

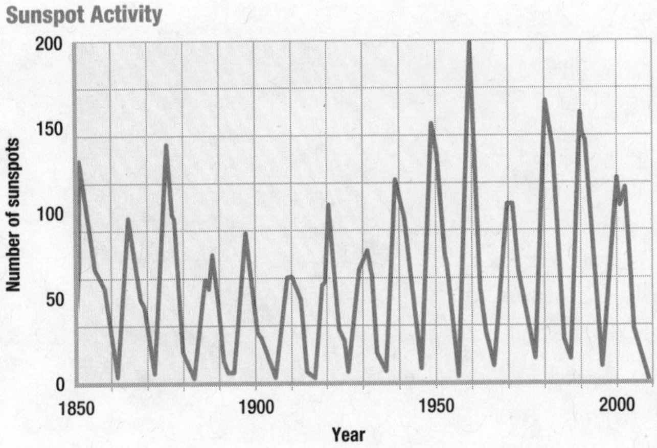

**Sunspot Activity**

**7 Analyze** What is the length of time between peaks in sunspot activity?

_____

_____

**8 Evaluate** Evaluate the following statement. *By using the sunspot graph above, you can predict the exact number of sunspots for any year in the future.*

_____

_____

_____

_____

_____

**9 Infer** Computers are fast and do not make errors when doing calculations. Does this mean that computer models are always correct? Explain your answer.

_____

_____

_____

_____

_____

_____

_____

# My Notes

# Unit 2 〈Big Idea〉 Scientists use tools to collect, organize, and analyze data while conducting investigations.

### Lesson 1
**ESSENTIAL QUESTION**
*In what ways can you make sense of data?*

Use models, simulations, tables, and graphs to display and analyze scientific data.

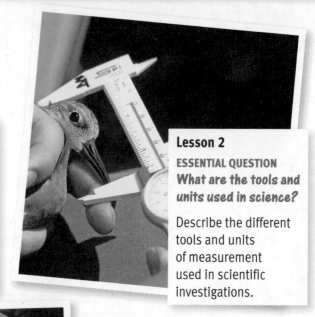

### Lesson 2
**ESSENTIAL QUESTION**
*What are the tools and units used in science?*

Describe the different tools and units of measurement used in scientific investigations.

### Lesson 3
**ESSENTIAL QUESTION**
*How do scientists use models and simulations?*

Explain how scientists use models and simulations to represent systems, explain phenomena, and make predictions.

---

**Connect** **ESSENTIAL QUESTIONS**
Lessons 1 and 3

**1 Synthesize** Compare the ways in which a scientist would use a graph and a model in investigations.

_____

_____

_____

_____

_____

## Think Outside the Book

**2 Synthesize** Choose one of these activities to help synthesize what you have learned in this unit.

☐ Using what you learned in lessons 1 and 2, measure and graph air temperature changes during the day. Include data points for every hour between 6:00 a.m. and 6:00 p.m.

☐ Using what you learned in lessons 2 and 3, describe the measurements and the type of model that a meteorologist would use to predict the weather created by a developing storm.

# Unit 2 Review

Name _____

## Vocabulary

Fill in the blank with the term that best completes the sentence.

**1** _____ is a short way of representing very large numbers or very small numbers without writing all of the place-holding zeros.

**TEKS** 6.3B

**2** A(n) _____ uses a model to test the function, behavior, or process of the thing the model represents.

**TEKS** 6.3C

**3** A toy car is an example of a _____ that represents a real car.

**TEKS** 6.2C

**4** The International System of Units, or SI, was developed to make it possible to compare _____ made by people in different locations using different tools.

**5** _____ is the exactness and consistency of measurements.

## Key Concepts

Choose the letter of the best answer.

**TEKS** 6.3C

**6** The picture shows a model of the solar system.

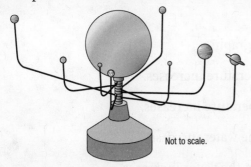

Not to scale.

Which is a limitation of the model?

**A** It cannot show the relative sizes of each planet.

**B** It cannot show how the planets orbit the sun.

**C** It does not show the gravitational force exerted by each planet.

**D** It does not show the correct order of the planets, starting from the sun.

# Unit 2 Review continued

TEKS 6.2D, 6.2E

7 The maximum amount of a substance that can be dissolved in a solvent is called solubility. The solubility of a substance often changes with the temperature of the water, a common solvent. The graph shows the solubility of $NaNO_3$ (sodium nitrate) and HCl (hydrochloric acid) at different temperatures.

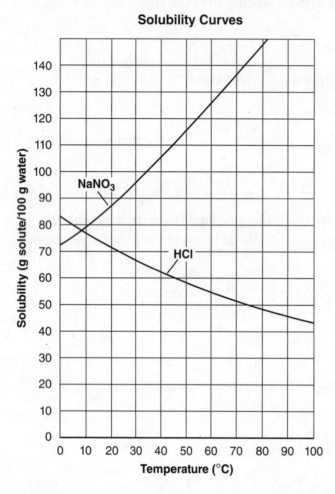

Which statement best summarizes the data shown in the graph?

**A** The solubility of both substances increases as the temperature increases.

**B** The solubility of both substances decreases as the temperature increases.

**C** The solubility of HCl increases as the temperature of the water increases.

**D** The solubility of $NaNO_3$ increases as the temperature of the water increases.

Name _____

Unit 2 Review

## Gridded Response

Write your answer in the boxes, then bubble in the corresponding number in the
grid below.

**TEKS 6.2C**

**8** A student is exploring a salt water solution in science lab.
She measures the mass of the salt water solution, then
boils off the water, and then measures the mass of the salt
remaining in the flask.

By how many grams did the mass of the contents of the flask change during
this lab?

© Houghton Mifflin Harcourt Publishing Company

Unit 2 Review **103**

## Critical Thinking

Answer the following question in the space provided.

TEKS 6.4A

**9** For each of the following measurements, list one tool that could be used to make the measurement:

| | |
|---|---|
| 2.9 g : | |
| 35.20 s : | |
| 17 cm : | |
| 37 °C : | |

**Connect** ESSENTIAL QUESTIONS
Lessons 1 and 3

Answer the following question in the space provided.

TEKS 6.3B

**10** Define *mathematical model* and *conceptual model*. Give at least one example of each. What kind of data would each represent?

_____

_____

_____

_____

_____

_____

_____

_____

_____

_____

_____

_____

_____

_____

# UNIT 3
# Matter

**Big Idea**

Matter is described by its properties and may undergo changes.

## What do you think?

A large iceberg floats in water, but an anchor sinks. What is different about these two objects that causes them to behave differently in water?

# Unit 3
# Matter

# Deep Freeze

When outdoor temperatures reach 0 °C (32 °F), liquid water can freeze to form a solid. Snow, ice, sleet, and hail are examples of the solid form of water. Understanding the properties of water in its different states helps people to stay safe during icy weather.

## ① Think About It

How is liquid water different from solid ice?

_____

_____

_____

This truck is applying salt to an icy road. Do you know what effect this will have on the ice?

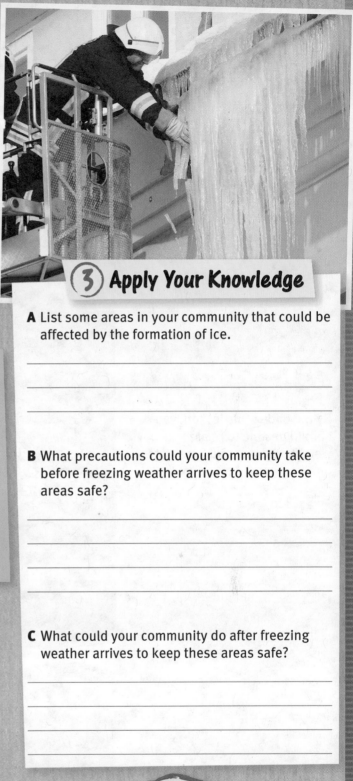

## ② Ask A Question

### What precautions should be taken during freezing weather?

Would you believe that the ice on these fruit trees is actually protecting them? The trees are being sprayed with water, which turns to ice in freezing weather. The formation of ice helps to keep the plants warmer. With a partner, research some of the ways in which people protect other areas and living things during icy weather.

### Think about the impact that ice could have on

✔ plants

✔ people

✔ bodies of water

✔ pets and other animals

## ③ Apply Your Knowledge

**A** List some areas in your community that could be affected by the formation of ice.

_____

_____

_____

**B** What precautions could your community take before freezing weather arrives to keep these areas safe?

_____

_____

_____

_____

**C** What could your community do after freezing weather arrives to keep these areas safe?

_____

_____

_____

_____

### Take It Home

How do you prepare your home for icy weather? Draw a map of your home and the surrounding area. Identify areas on your map that could become hazardous in freezing conditions. Then, create a plan for protecting these areas.

# Introduction to Matter

**ESSENTIAL QUESTION**

## What properties define matter?

By the end of this lesson, you should be able to relate mass, weight, volume, and density to one another.

*Hot air takes balloons aloft because hot air is less dense than the cooler air around it.*

© Houghton Mifflin Harcourt Publishing Company • Image Credits: (bkgd) ©Christian Kober/John Warburton-Lee Photography/Photolibrary

**TEKS** **6.6B** calculate density to identify an unknown substance

**Quick Labs**
- Mass and Weight
- Finding Volume by Displacement
- How Much Mass?

**Exploration Lab**
- Comparing Buoyancy

 **Engage Your Brain**

**1 Describe** Fill in the blank with the word or phrase that you think correctly completes the following sentences.

A(n) _____ can hold a greater volume of water than a mug.

A hamster weighs less than a(n) _____ .

A bowling ball is harder to lift than a basketball because _____
_____ .

**2 Explain** List some similarities and differences between the golf ball on the left and the table-tennis ball on the right in the photo below.

_____
_____
_____
_____
_____

**Active Reading**

**3 Apply** Many scientific words, such as *matter*, also have everyday meanings. Use context clues to write your own definition for each meaning of the word *matter*.

**Example sentence**
What is this gooey <u>matter</u> on the table?

Matter:

_____
_____
_____

**Example sentence**
Please vote! Your opinions <u>matter</u>.

Matter:

_____
_____
_____

**Vocabulary Terms**
- matter
- mass
- weight
- volume
- density

**4 Identify** This list contains the vocabulary terms you'll learn in this lesson. As you read, circle the definition of each term.

# What's the MATTER?

## What is matter?

Suppose your class takes a field trip to a museum. During the course of the day you see mammoth bones, sparkling crystals, hot-air balloons, and an astronaut's space suit. All of these things are matter.

As you will see, **matter** is anything that has mass and takes up space. Your body is matter. The air that you breathe and the water that you drink are also matter. Matter makes up the materials around you.

However, not everything is matter. Light and sound, for example, are not matter. Light does not take up space or have mass in the same way that a table does. Although air is matter, a sound traveling through air is not.

**Active Reading** **5 Explain** How can you tell if something is matter?

_____

_____

_____

**Visualize It!**

**6 Identify** Name three examples of matter found in this photo.

_____

_____

_____

# What is mass?

You cannot always tell how much matter is in an object simply by observing the object's size. But you *can* measure the object's mass. **Mass** describes the amount of matter in an object.

Compare the two balloons at the right. The digital scales show that the balloon filled with compressed air has a greater mass than the other balloon. This is because the compressed air adds mass to the balloon. Air may seem to be made of nothing, but it has mass. The readings on the scale are in grams (g). A gram is the unit of mass you will use most often in science class.

Objects that are the same size can be made up of different amounts of matter. For example, a large sponge is about the same size as a brick. But the brick contains more matter. Therefore, the brick has a greater mass than the sponge.

The readings on these digital scales show that all matter, even air, has mass.

0.010 g

0.005 g

# How does mass differ from weight?

The words *weight* and *mass* are often used as though they mean the same thing, but they do not. **Weight** is a measure of the gravitational force (grav•ih•TAY•shuhn•uhl FAWRS) on an object. Gravitational force keeps objects on Earth from floating into space. The gravitational force between an object and Earth depends partly on the object's mass. The greater that the mass of an object is, the greater the gravitational force on the object will be and the greater the object's weight will be.

An object's weight can change depending on the object's location. For example, you would weigh less on the moon than you do on Earth because the moon has less mass—and therefore exerts less gravitational force—than Earth does. However, you would have the same mass in both places. An object's mass does not change unless the amount of matter in an object changes.

The weight of this dachshund on the moon is about one-sixth of its weight on Earth.

**Active Reading** 7 **Explain** Why do astronauts weigh less on the moon than they do on Earth?

_____

_____

The balance below works by moving the masses on the right along the beams until they "balance" the pan on the left. Moving the masses changes the amount of force the levers exert on the pan. The more massive the object on the pan, the more force will be needed on the levers to balance the two sides.

**8 Infer** Would this balance give the same value for mass if used on the moon? Explain.

_____

_____

_____

_____

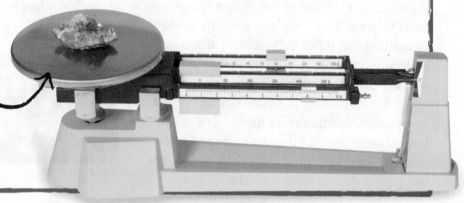

A triple-beam balance can be used to measure the mass of small objects such as this geode fragment.

The spring scale gives weight in pounds (lb).

## How are mass and weight measured?

Mass is often measured by using a triple-beam balance such as the one shown above. The balance compares an object's mass to known standards of mass called *countermasses*. The countermasses slide across each of three beams. When the countermasses balance the mass of the object in the balance pan, the pointer will rest at 0. Then, the mass can be read from the position of the countermasses on the beams.

Weight is measured with devices such as the spring scale shown at the left. The spring measures the force between the mass in the pan and Earth. The more massive the object placed in the pan, the more forceful is the attraction between it and Earth, and the more the spring will stretch. Greater stretch means greater weight.

Because weight is a measure of gravitational force, it is given in units of force. You probably are most familiar with weight given in pounds (lb), like the units shown on the scale. The standard scientific unit for weight, however, is the newton (N). A 100-g mass weighs approximately 1 N on Earth. One newton is about one-fourth of a pound.

# Measuring Space

## How is the amount of space occupied by matter measured?

All matter takes up space. The amount of space that an object takes up, or occupies, is known as the object's **volume.**

Objects with the similar volumes do not always have the same mass. In the photos, the bowling ball and the balloon have about the same volume, but the bowling ball contains a lot more mass than the balloon. You know this because the bowling ball weighs much more than the balloon. The different masses take up about the same amount of space, so both objects have about the same volume.

**Active Reading** **9 Define** What does volume measure?

_____

_____

The bowling ball has a lot more mass than the balloon.

The balloon is similar in volume but has much less mass than the bowling ball.

### Think Outside the Book (Inquiry)

**10 Infer** Big things can look very small when seen from far away. Describe how you know big things far away aren't really small.

**113**

# How can volume be determined?

There are different ways to find the volume of an object. For objects that have well-defined shapes, you can take a few measurements and calculate the volume using a formula. For objects that are irregularly shaped, such as a rock, you can use water displacement to measure volume. For liquids, you can use a graduated cylinder.

## Using a Formula

Some objects have well-defined shapes. For these objects, the easiest way to find their volume is to measure the dimensions of the object and use a formula. Different shapes use different volume formulas. For example, to find the volume of a rectangular box, you would use a different formula than if you were to find the volume of a spherical ball.

The volume of a solid is measured in units of length cubed. For example, if you measure the length, width, and height of a box in centimeters (cm), the volume of the box has units of centimeters multiplied by centimeters multiplied by centimeters, or cubic centimeters ($cm^3$). In order to calculate volume, make sure that all the measurements are in the same units.

> To find the volume of a rectangular box, use the following formula:
>
> $$Volume = (length)(width)(height)$$
> $$V = lwh$$

 **Do the Math**  **Sample Problem**

Find the volume of the lunch box.

### Identify

**A.** What do you know?

length = 25 cm, width = 18 cm, height = 10 cm

**B.** What do you want to find?  Volume

### Plan

**C.** Draw and label a sketch:

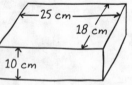

**D.** Write the formula:  $V = lwh$

**E.** Substitute into the formula:  $V = (25\ cm)(18\ cm)(10\ cm)$

### Solve

**F.** Multiply:  $(25\ cm)(18\ cm)(10\ cm) = 4{,}500\ cm^3$

**G.** Check that your units agree:  The given units are centimeters, and the measure found is volume. Therefore, the units should be $cm^3$. The units agree.

**Answer:** $4{,}500\ cm^3$

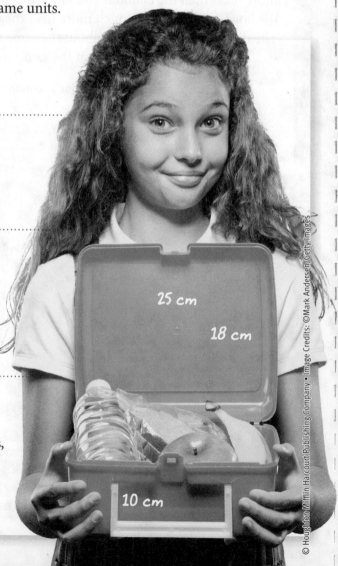

> The volume of your locker will tell you how much stuff will fit inside.

30 cm

200 cm

40 cm

### Do the Math   You Try It

**11 Calculate** Find the volume of a locker that is 30 cm long, 40 cm wide, and 200 cm high.

#### Identify

**A.** What do you know?

**B.** What do you want to find?

#### Plan

**C.** Draw and label a sketch:

**D.** Write the formula:

**E.** Substitute the given values into the formula:

#### Solve

**F.** Multiply:

**G.** Check that your units agree:

**Answer:**

## Using Water Displacement

In the lab, you can use a beaker or graduated cylinder to measure the volume of liquids. Graduated cylinders are used to measure liquid volume when accuracy is important. The volume of liquids is often expressed in liters (L) or milliliters (mL). Milliliters and cubic centimeters are equivalent; in other words, $1 \text{ mL} = 1 \text{ cm}^3$. The volume of any amount of liquid, from one raindrop to an entire ocean, can be expressed in these units.

Two objects cannot occupy the same space at the same time. For example, as a builder stacks bricks to build a wall, she adds each brick on top of the other. No brick can occupy the same place that another brick occupies. Similarly, when an object is placed in water, the object pushes some of the water out of the way. This process, called *displacement*, can be used to measure the volume of an irregularly shaped solid object.

In the photos at the right, you can see that the level of the water in the graduated cylinder has risen after the chess piece is placed inside. The volume of water displaced is found by subtracting the original volume in the graduated cylinder from the new volume. This is equal to the volume of the chess piece.

When deciding the units of the volume found using water displacement, it is helpful to remember that 1 mL of water is equal to $1 \text{ cm}^3$. Therefore, you can report the volume of the object in cubic centimeters.

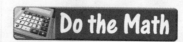

# Do the Math

### You Try It

**12 Calculate** The two images below show a graduated cylinder filled with water before and after a chess piece is placed inside. Use the images to calculate the volume of the chess piece.

Volume without chess piece = _____

Volume with chess piece = _____

Volume of chess piece = _____

Don't forget to check the units of volume of the chess piece!

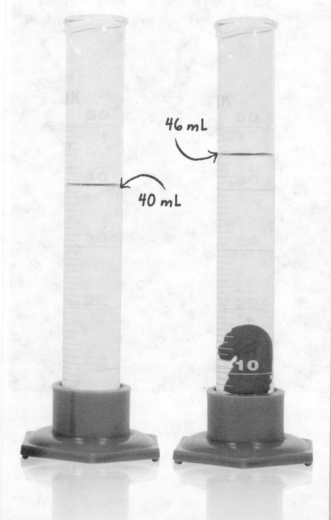

46 mL

40 mL

# Packing It In!

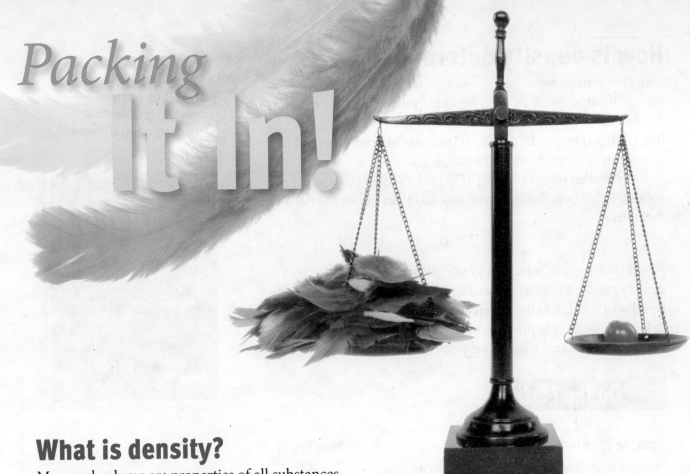

## What is density?

Mass and volume are properties of all substances. These two properties are related to another property called density (DEN•sih•tee). **Density** is a measure of the amount of mass in a given volume. Objects containing the same amount of mass can take up different amounts of space. For example, the pile of feathers above takes up more space than the tomato. But they have the same mass. This is because the tomato is more dense. The tomato has more mass in a smaller space.

The density of a given substance remains the same no matter how much of the substance you have. For example, if you divide a piece of clay in half, both halves will have the same density as the original piece.

The tomato and the pile of feathers have similar masses, but the tomato has less volume. This means that the tomato is more dense.

**13 Explain** What is density?

_____

_____

_____

**14 Predict** Circle the item in each pair that is more dense.

| | | |
|---|---|---|
| Golf ball | Empty milk carton | Foam ball |
| Table-tennis ball | Milk carton full of milk | Baseball |

# How is density determined?

Units for density consist of a mass unit divided by a volume unit. Units that are often used for density are grams per cubic centimeter (g/cm³) for solids, and grams per milliliter (g/mL) for liquids. In other words, density is the mass in grams divided by the volume in cubic centimeters or milliliters.

To find an object's density (*D*), find its mass (*m*) and its volume (*V*). Then, use the given formula to calculate the density of the object.

$$D = \frac{m}{V}$$

The density of water is 1 g/mL (g/cm³). Any object with a density greater than 1 g/mL will sink in water and with a density less than 1 g/mL will float. Density, therefore, can be a useful thing to know. The sample problem below shows how to calculate the density of a volcanic rock called pumice.

Pumice and obsidian are two igneous volcanic rocks with very different densities.

## Do the Math

### Sample Problem

Pumice is an igneous volcanic rock, formed by the rapid cooling of lava. What is the density of a 49.8 g piece of pumice that has a volume of 83 cm³?

**Identify**

**A.** What do you know?

mass = 49.8 g, volume = 83 cm³

**B.** What do you want to find?  Density

**Plan**

**C.** Write the formula:  $D = \dfrac{m}{V}$

**D.** Substitute the given values into the formula:

$D = \dfrac{49.8 \text{ g}}{83 \text{ cm}^3}$

**Solve**

**E.** Divide:  $\dfrac{49.8 \text{ g}}{83 \text{ cm}^3} = 0.6 \text{ g/cm}^3$

**F.** Check that your units agree:  The given units are grams and cubic centimeters, and the measure found is density. Therefore, the units should be g/cm³. The units agree.

**Answer:** 0.6 g/cm³

### You Try It

**15 Calculate**  Obsidian is another type of igneous rock. What is the density of a piece of obsidian that has a mass of 239.2 g and a volume of 92 cm³?

**Identify**

**A.** What do you know?

**B.** What do you want to find?

**Plan**

**C.** Write the formula:

**D.** Substitute the given values into the formula:

**Solve**

**E.** Divide:

**F.** Check that your units agree:

**Answer:**

### Sample Problem

A basalt rock displaces 16 mL of water. The density of the rock is 3.0 g/cm³. What is the mass of the rock?

### Identify

**A.** What do you know?

volume = 16 mL, density = 3.0 g/cm³

**B.** What do you want to find?  Mass

### Plan

**C.** Rearrange the formula $D = \dfrac{m}{V}$ to solve for mass. You can do this by multiplying each side by $V$.

$$D = \frac{m}{V}$$
$$m = D \cdot V$$

**D.** Substitute the given values into the formula. Recall that 1 mL = 1 cm³, so 16 mL = 16 cm³.

$$m = \frac{3.0 \text{ g}}{\text{cm}^3} \cdot 16 \text{ cm}^3$$

### Solve

**E.** Multiply: $\dfrac{3.0 \text{ g}}{\text{cm}^3} \cdot 16 \text{ cm}^3 = 48 \text{ g}$

**F.** Check that your units agree:  The given units are g/cm³ and mL, and the measure found is mass. Therefore, the units should be g. The units agree.

**Answer:** 48 g

### You Try It

**16 Calculate**  A rhyolite rock has a volume of 9.5 mL. The density of the rock is 2.6 g/cm³. What is the mass of the rock?

### Identify

**A.** What do you know?

**B.** What do you want to find?

### Plan

**C.** Write the formula:

**D.** Substitute the given values into the formula:

### Solve

**E.** Multiply:

**F.** Check that your units agree:

**Answer:**

Kilauea is the youngest volcano on the Big Island of Hawaii. "Kilauea" means "spewing" or "much spreading," apparently in reference to the lava flows that it erupts.

# Visual Summary

To complete this summary, check the box that indicates true or false. Then, use the key below to check your answers. You can use this page to review the main concepts of the lesson.

## Relating Mass, Weight, Volume, and Density

Mass is the amount of matter in an object. Weight is a measure of the gravitational force on an object.

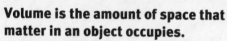

Mass  Weight

   T F

**17** ☐ ☐ An object's weight is the amount of space it occupies.

**18** ☐ ☐ The mass of an object is equal to its weight.

---

Volume is the amount of space that matter in an object occupies.

To find the volume of a rectangular box, use the formula:

$$V = lwh$$

  T F

**19** ☐ ☐ The volume of a solid can be expressed in units of cm³.

Answers: 17 F; 18 F; 19 T; 20 T

---

Density describes the mass of a substance in a given volume.

To find the density of a substance, use the formula:

$$D = \frac{m}{V}$$

  T F

**20** ☐ ☐ An object that floats in water is less dense than water.

---

**21 Describe** Write a set of instructions that describe how to find the density of an object. Write the instructions so that they work for a regularly shaped object and for an irregularly shaped object.

# Lesson Review

## Vocabulary

Fill in the blank with the term that best completes the following sentence.

**1** _____ is the amount of space that matter in an object occupies.

**2** _____ is anything that has mass and takes up space.

**3** _____ is the amount of matter in an object.

**4** _____ is a measure of the amount of matter in a given amount of space.

**5** _____ is a measure of the gravitational force on an object.

## Key Concepts

**6 Classify** Is air matter? How can you tell?

_____

_____

_____

**7 Describe** Is it possible for an object's weight to change while its mass remains constant? Explain.

_____

_____

_____

**8 Compare** Explain why a golf ball is heavier than a table-tennis ball, even though the balls are the same size.

_____

_____

_____

**9 Calculate** A block of wood has a mass of 120 g and a volume of 200 cm³. What is the density of the wood?

## Critical Thinking

Use this table to answer the following questions.

| Substance | Density (g/cm³) |
|-----------|-----------------|
| Zinc (solid) | 7.13 |
| Silver (solid) | 10.50 |
| Lead (solid) | 11.35 |

**10 Identify** Suppose that 273 g of one of the substances listed above displaces 26 mL of water. What is the substance?

_____

_____

_____

**11 Evaluate** How many mL of water would be displaced by 408 g of lead?

_____

_____

_____

**12 Predict** How can you determine that a coin is not pure silver if you know the mass and volume of the coin?

_____

_____

_____

_____

_____

**13 Calculate** A truck whose bed is 2.5 m long, 1.5 m wide, and 1.0 m high is delivering sand for a sand-sculpture competition. About how many trips must the truck make to deliver 7 m³ of sand?

# My Notes

# Evaluating Scientific Evidence

TEKS 6.3A in all fields of science, analyze, evaluate, and critique scientific explanations by using empirical evidence, logical reasoning, and experimental and observational testing, including examining all sides of scientific evidence of those scientific explanations, so as to encourage critical thinking by the student

TEKS 6.3D relate the impact of research on scientific thought and society, including the history of science and contributions of scientists as related to the content

Many people and companies claim to use scientific evidence to support their ideas, arguments, or products. Some of this evidence may be strong and well-supported by scientific investigation. But some evidence may be biased, or may not be supported by valid scientific investigation. How can you recognize the difference?

## Tutorial

**The advertisement below highlights some things that you should consider as you try to evaluate scientific evidence.**

Grow your best Indian blanket wildflowers using new Fertilizer Formulation!

**Fertilizer Formulation**

We tested 20 patches of Indian blanket wildflowers in the Valdosta, Georgia, area. Plants that received the recommended amount of fertilizer grew an average of 30% taller. This fertilizer is made of all-natural ingredients and provides the best mixture of nutrients for any garden.

Everyone should use this fertilizer!

**Weakness** This sample is biased. The advertisement says that everyone should use the fertilizer, but the sample plants were all from the Valdosta, Georgia, area. An unbiased test would include samples from other parts of the country.

**Weakness** "All-natural ingredients" is a vague statement that advertisers use because people tend to believe that "natural" is better. However, in many cases that statement doesn't really mean anything. The minerals found in all fertilizers are "natural".

**Weakness** This generalization is not supported by the evidence. The fertilizer was only tested on Indian blanket wildflowers. It is impossible to say, based on that evidence, whether the fertilizer would be good for gardens with other types of plants.

# You Try It!

**Read the following advertisement, and answer the questions below to evaluate whether the evidence supports the claims being made.**

## GroBig
### Soil Additive

**GroBig will work on all types of wildflowers!**

**Buy GroBig today, and watch your flowers grow!**
**$19.95 per liter**

*"I've found the secret to the best wildflower garden—using GroBig Soil Additive. Now, you can have your best garden, too."*
— A. Gardener

Botanists at a private nursery near Tampa, Florida, selected two tall samples of a common wildflower, the narrow-leaved sunflower. One plant received the recommended amount of GroBig Soil Additive. The other did not. After 2 weeks, the plant given GroBig Soil Additive had grown 4 cm. The other plant had grown just 2 cm. What a difference!

**1 Identifying Conclusions** Identify the claim that the advertisers are making.

_____

_____

_____

**2 Evaluating Evidence** Identify two weaknesses in the evidence presented in this advertisement.

_____

_____

_____

_____

_____

**3 Applying Concepts** List three questions you would need to answer in order to support the claims being made about GroBig.

_____

_____

_____

_____

_____

_____

_____

### Take It Home

**Find an article or advertisement in a newspaper or magazine that contains a scientific claim and supporting information. Identify the evidence that is being used to support the claims in the article or advertisement. Write a paragraph that summarizes the article or advertisement and its scientific evidence.**

Lesson **2**

# Properties of Matter

**ESSENTIAL QUESTION**

## What are physical and chemical properties of matter?

By the end of this lesson, you should be able to classify and compare substances based on their physical and chemical properties.

To harvest cranberries, the dry beds are flooded with water. Next, water reels loosen the berries from the vines. Since cranberries are less dense than water, they float. Harvesters take advantage of this property to gather and easily float them toward collection sites.

**TEKS** **6.6A** compare metals, nonmetals, and metalloids using physical properties such as luster, conductivity, or malleability

**TEKS** **6.6B** calculate density to identify an unknown substance

## Lesson Labs

**Quick Labs**
• Comparing Two Elements
• Observe Physical Properties

**Exploration Lab**
• Identifying an Unknown Substance

## Engage Your Brain

**1 Predict** Check T or F to show whether you think each statement is true or false.

T    F

☐    ☐    Liquid water freezes at the same temperature at which ice melts: 0 °C.

☐    ☐    A bowling ball weighs less than a foam ball of the same size.

☐    ☐    An object with a density greater than the density of water will float in water.

☐    ☐    Solubility is the ability of one substance to dissolve in another.

**2 Describe** If you were asked to describe an orange to someone who had never seen an orange, what would you tell the person?

_____

_____

_____

_____

_____

_____

## Active Reading

**3 Synthesize** Many English words have their roots in other languages. The root of the word *solubility* is the Latin word *solvere,* which means "to loosen." Make an educated guess about the meaning of the word *solubility*.

_____

_____

_____

_____

### Vocabulary Terms

• physical property
• chemical property

**4 Apply** As you learn the definition of each vocabulary term in this lesson, create your own definition or sketch to help you remember the meaning of the term.

# Physical Education

## What are physical properties of matter?

What words would you use to describe a table? You would probably say something about the shape, color, and size of the table. Next, you might consider whether the table is hard or soft, smooth or rough. Normally, when describing an object like a table, you list its easily observable properties.

### They Are Used to Describe a Substance

A characteristic of a substance that can be observed or measured without changing the identity of the substance is called a **physical property**. Gold is one metal prized for its physical properties. Gold can be bent and shaped easily and has a lasting shine. Both properties make it an excellent metal for making coins and jewelry.

All of your senses can be used to observe physical properties. Color, shape, size, odor, and texture are a few of the physical properties you encounter. Think of how you would describe an object to a friend. Most likely, your description would be a list of the object's physical properties.

Active Reading **5 Apply** List six physical properties.

_____
_____
_____
_____
_____
_____

Gold is a highly sought-after metal for making jewelry. Gold is dense, soft, and shiny. Gold is often mixed with other metals to make it stronger.

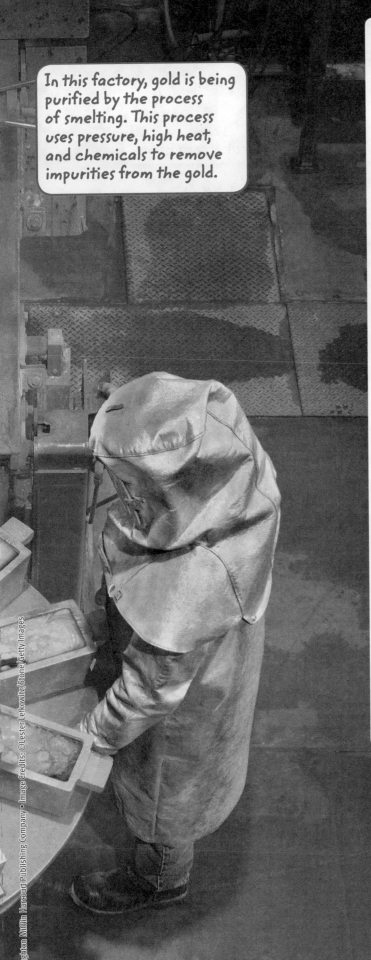

In this factory, gold is being purified by the process of smelting. This process uses pressure, high heat, and chemicals to remove impurities from the gold.

## They Can Be Observed or Measured without Changing the Identity of a Substance

The physical properties of an object can be observed with the senses. Some properties can be measured, too. For example, you can look at a table to observe its relative size. Or, you can measure its length, width, and height by using a tool like a measuring tape. When you observe a physical property, you do not change the substance's identity. The material that makes up the table stays the same.

Imagine that you conducted an experiment to measure the temperature at which water boils. This temperature, called the boiling point, is a physical property. You placed a beaker of water over a heating source and measured the increase in water temperature using a thermometer. Once the water reached its boiling point, some of the water had become a gas. In this experiment, the water had to change to a gas before you could record the boiling point of water. However, the water did not change its identity. The substance is water whether it is a solid, liquid, or gas.

### Visualize It!

6 **Apply** Describe how you could measure a physical property of the gold bars shown in this image.

_____

_____

_____

_____

### Think Outside the Book

7 **Apply** Describe a common object by naming its properties. Trade your mystery-object description with a classmate's and try to guess what object he or she has described.

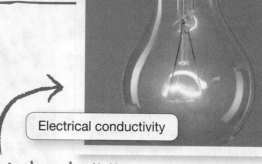

# Visualize It!

# Common Physical Properties

On these two pages, you can read about some common physical properties. The physical properties of a substance often describe how the substance can be useful.

Electrical conductivity

Electrical conductivity is a measure of how well electric charges can move through a substance.

Density

Density is a measure of the amount of mass in a given amount of volume.

**8 Explain** The photo above shows oil and vinegar in a pitcher. The top layer is the oil. Describe the density of the vinegar compared to the density of the oil.

_____

_____

_____

Thermal conductivity

Thermal conductivity is the rate at which a substance transfers heat.

Solubility

Solubility is the ability of a substance to dissolve in another substance. This powdered drink mix is dissolving in water. When fully dissolved, the particles of the drink mix will be spread throughout the water.

**9 Predict** If you let all of the liquid evaporate out of the pitcher, would you be able to see the solid particles of the drink mix? Explain.

_____

_____

_____

_____

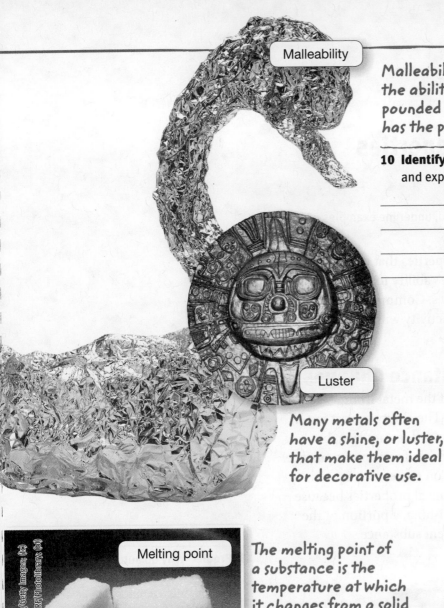

Malleability

Malleability (MAL·ee·uh·bil·i·tee) is the ability of a substance to be rolled or pounded into various shapes. Aluminum has the property of malleability.

**10 Identify** Name something made of aluminum and explain why malleability is a useful property.

_____

_____

_____

Some metals are magnetic. Magnets can act at a distance.

Luster

Many metals often have a shine, or luster, that make them ideal for decorative use.

Magnetism

Melting point

The melting point of a substance is the temperature at which it changes from a solid to a liquid.

Minerals are often described by relative hardness. Quartz can scratch calcite because it is harder than calcite.

Hardness

Calcite

Quartz

**11 Summarize** Identify three physical properties you could use to organize a set of cookware.

_____

_____

_____

_____

_____

# Identity Theft

## What are chemical properties of matter?

Active Reading **12 Identify** As you read, underline examples of chemical properties.

Physical properties are not the only properties that describe matter. A **chemical property** describes a substance's ability to change into a new substance with different properties. Common chemical properties include flammability and reactivity with substances such as oxygen, water, and acids.

### They Describe How a Substance Changes

Can you think of a chemical property of the metal iron? When left outdoors in wet weather, iron rusts. The ability to rust is a chemical property of iron. The metal silver does not rust, but eventually a darker substance, called tarnish, forms on its surface. You may have noticed a layer of tarnish on some silver spoons or jewelry. Rusting and tarnishing are chemical properties because the metal changes. After rusting or tarnishing, a portion of the metal is no longer the metal but a different substance.

**13 Predict** Why do automobiles rust more easily in wet climates than in drier climates?

_____

_____

_____

_____

Iron can form rust, turning a once shiny car into a crumbling relic.

## They Can Be Observed by Attempting to Change the Identity of a Substance

One way to identify a chemical property is to observe the changes that a substance undergoes. Wood for a campfire has the chemical property of flammability—the ability to burn. When wood burns, new substances are formed: water, carbon dioxide, and ash. These new substances have different properties than the wood had. Reactivity is another chemical property that can be identified by observing changes. Reactivity is the ability of a substance to interact with another substance and form one or more new substances.

You can also observe a chemical property of a substance by attempting to change the substance, even if no change occurs. For example, you can observe that gold is nonflammable by attempting to burn it. A chemical property of gold is that it is nonflammable.

Reactivity is a chemical property. Vinegar and baking soda react to make water, a salt, and carbon dioxide gas.

Flammability, or the ability of a substance to burn, is a chemical property. For example, the wood building in the photo is flammable, and the suits that help keep the firefighters safe are flame resistant.

# Property [Boundaries]

## What is the difference between physical and chemical properties?

A physical property can always be observed without changing the identity of a substance. The mass of a log can be observed without changing the log. A chemical property, however, is observed by attempting to change the identity of a substance. To witness a log's flammability, you must try to set the log on fire.

A substance always has physical and chemical properties. For example, a log is flammable even when it's not burning.

**Active Reading** **14 Compare** Describe the difference between a physical property and a chemical property.

_____

_____

_____

_____

### Visualize It!

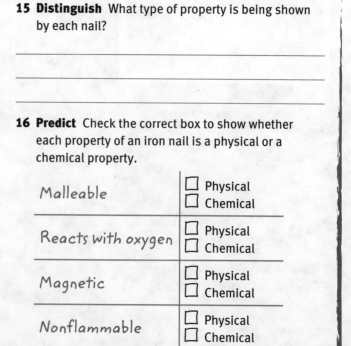

Bending an iron nail will change its shape but not its identity.

An iron nail can react with oxygen in the air to form iron oxide, or rust.

**15 Distinguish** What type of property is being shown by each nail?

_____

_____

**16 Predict** Check the correct box to show whether each property of an iron nail is a physical or a chemical property.

| Malleable | ☐ Physical ☐ Chemical |
|---|---|
| Reacts with oxygen | ☐ Physical ☐ Chemical |
| Magnetic | ☐ Physical ☐ Chemical |
| Nonflammable | ☐ Physical ☐ Chemical |

# At the Scene

**FORENSIC SCIENCE**

The collection and study of physical evidence in a criminal investigation is known as *forensic science.* **Forensic scientists are experts in observing the physical and chemical properties of evidence at crime scenes.**

### Arson Investigation
A forensic scientist can gently heat ashes from an arson scene to help determine what chemicals were used to start the fire. If detectives know how the fire began, then they might be able to determine who is responsible for the crime.

### Studying Paint
Flecks of paint left on a tree where a car hit it can be examined with a special microscope. How the paint absorbs light can reveal what chemicals were used in the paint. This information could help authorities determine what kind of vehicle a criminal suspect drove.

### Fiber Analysis
Magnified fibers, like those shown above, can provide clues, too. An acrylic fiber might be material from a boat cover or a rug. Polyester could also have come from a suspect's shirt.

## Extend

**Inquiry**

**17 Identify** List physical and chemical properties used to identify evidence at a crime scene.

**18 Predict** When examining evidence, why might investigators want to be more careful examining chemical properties than physical properties?

**19 Evaluate** By examining the physical and chemical properties of evidence at a crime scene, investigators can often be more certain about what a substance is not than about what it is. Why do you think this is?

# Identify Yourself

## How can physical and chemical properties identify a substance?

Properties unique to a substance are its *characteristic properties*. Characteristic properties can be physical properties, such as density, or chemical properties, such as flammability. Characteristic properties stay the same regardless of the amount of a sample. They can help identify a substance.

Iron pyrite is one of several minerals having a color similar to that of gold. Miners can find iron pyrite, or "fool's gold," near deposits of gold and sometimes mistake it for gold. Color and location, however, are about the only properties iron pyrite shares with gold. The two substances have quite different characteristic properties. For example, gold flattens when hit with a hammer, but iron pyrite shatters. When rubbed on a ceramic plate, gold leaves a yellow streak, but iron pyrite leaves a greenish black one. Gold keeps its shine even if beneath the sea for years, but iron pyrite turns green if exposed to water.

An easy way for miners to tell iron pyrite and gold apart is by density. Miners collect gold by sifting through dirt in pans. Because of its high density, gold stays in the pan while dirt and most other substances wash over the side as the miner swirls the contents in the pan. Gold has a density almost four times that of iron pyrite, so distinguishing gold from iron pyrite should be an easy task for the experienced miner. Density is a characteristic property of matter.

> **To find the density of a substance, use the following formula, where *D* is density, *m* is mass, and *V* is volume:**
>
> $$D = \frac{m}{V}$$

---

**20 Infer** Check the box to show which would tell you for sure that you had a sample of real gold and not of iron pyrite.

|  | Yes | No |
|---|---|---|
| Color of your sample | ☐ | ☐ |
| What happens when you strike your sample with a hammer | ☐ | ☐ |
| The location where your sample was found | ☐ | ☐ |

In pan mining, as the contents in the pan are swirled, less dense substances are washed away.

© Houghton Mifflin Harcourt Publishing Company • Image Credits: ©Neil Overy//Getty Images

 **Do the Math**

## Sample Problem

A sample of gold has a mass of 579 g. The volume of the sample is 30 cm³. What is the density of the gold sample?

## Identify

**A.** What do you know?

mass = 579 g, volume = 30 cm³

**B.** What do you want to find?  Density

## Plan

**C.** Write the formula:  $D = \dfrac{m}{V}$

**D.** Substitute the given values into the formula:

$D = \dfrac{579 \text{ g}}{30 \text{ cm}^3}$

## Solve

**E.** Divide:  $\dfrac{579 \text{ g}}{30 \text{ cm}^3} = 19.3 \text{ g/cm}^3$

**F.** Check that your units agree:

The given units are grams and cubic centimeters, and the measure found is density. Therefore, the units should be g/cm³. The units agree.

**Answer:** 19.3 g/cm³

Gold

Iron pyrite

## You Try It

**21 Calculate**  A student finds an object with a mass of 64.54 g and a volume of 14 cm³. Find the density of the object. Could the object be gold?

## Identify

**A.** What do you know?

**B.** What do you want to find?

## Plan

**C.** Write the formula:

**D.** Substitute the given values into the formula:

## Solve

**E.** Divide:

**F.** Check that your units agree:

**Answer:**

|  | Yes | No |
|---|---|---|
| Could the object be gold? | ☐ | ☐ |

# Visual Summary

To complete this summary, circle the correct words. Then use the
key below to check your answers. You can use this page to review
the main concepts of the lesson.

## Physical and Chemical Properties

A chemical property is a property that describes
a substance's ability to form new substances.

**24** Reactivity with water / Magnetism is a
chemical property.

**25** Flammability is the ability of a substance to
transfer heat / burn.

A physical property is a property that can be
observed or measured without changing the
identity of the substance.

**22** Solubility / Flammability is a physical
property.

**23** The melting point of a substance is the
temperature at which the substance
changes from a solid to a gas / liquid.

The properties that are most useful in
identifying a substance are its characteristic
properties. Characteristic properties can be
physical properties or chemical properties.

**26** The characteristic properties of a substance
do / do not depend on the size of the sample.

Answers: 22 Solubility; 23 liquid; 24 Reactivity with
water; 25 burn; 26 do not.

**27 Synthesize** You have two solid substances that look the same. What
measurements would you take and which tests would you perform to
determine whether they actually are the same?

# Lesson Review

## Vocabulary

Fill in the blanks with the term that best completes the following sentences.

**1** Flammability is an example of a _____ property.

**2** Electrical conductivity is an example of a _____ property.

## Key Concepts

**3 Identify** What are three physical properties of aluminum foil?

_____

_____

_____

_____

**4 Identify** Give an example of a physical property that is also a characteristic property.

_____

_____

_____

**5 Explain** Describe how a physical property, such as mass or texture, can change without causing a change in the substance.

_____

_____

_____

_____

**6 Justify** Must new substances be formed when you observe a chemical property? Explain.

_____

_____

_____

_____

## Critical Thinking

Use this table to answer the following question.

| Element | Melting Point (°C) | Boiling Point (°C) |
|---------|--------------------|--------------------|
| Bromine | −7.2 | 59 |
| Chlorine | −100 | −35 |
| Iodine | 110 | 180 |

**7 Infer** You are given samples of the substances shown in the table. The samples are labeled A, B, and C. At room temperature, sample A is a solid, sample B is a liquid, and sample C is a gas. What are the identities of samples A, B, and C? (Hint: Room temperature is about 20 °C.)

_____

_____

_____

**8 Analyze** A scientist observes a 5-mL sample of an unknown substance. It is a blue liquid with a density of $1.2 \text{ g/cm}^3$. The substance reacts with carbon dioxide. List each of the properties of matter the scientist observed and whether it is a characteristic property of matter.

_____

_____

_____

_____

_____

**9 Predict** Suppose you need to build a raft to cross a fast-moving river. Describe the physical and chemical properties of the raft that would be important to ensure your safety.

_____

_____

_____

_____

_____

# My Notes

# Physical and Chemical Changes

**ESSENTIAL QUESTION**

## What are physical and chemical changes of matter?

By the end of this lesson, you should be able to distinguish between physical and chemical changes of matter.

Rusty beams are all that remain of these large boats. The rust is the result of an interaction of the iron beams with water and air.

**TEKS** 6.5D identify the formation of a new substance by using the evidence of a possible chemical change such as production of a gas, change in temperature, production of a precipitate, or color change

---

## Engage Your Brain

**1 Predict** Check T or F to show whether you think each statement is true or false.

| T | F | |
|---|---|---|
| ☐ | ☐ | When an ice cube melts, it is still water. |
| ☐ | ☐ | Matter is lost when a candle is burned. |
| ☐ | ☐ | When your body digests food, the food is changed into new substances. |

**2 Describe** Write a word or phrase beginning with each letter of the word CHANGE that describes changes you have observed in everyday objects.

C _____

H _____

A _____

N _____

G _____

E _____

## Active Reading

**3 Preview** Before you begin reading this lesson, look through the pages and read the headings and subheadings. The headings show how information is organized in the lesson. After you read the headings and subheadings, write a short description of what the lesson will cover.

_____

_____

_____

_____

_____

_____

_____

### Vocabulary Terms

- physical change
- chemical change
- law of conservation of mass
- law of conservation of energy

**4 Apply** As you learn the definition of each vocabulary term in this lesson, create your own definition or sketch to help you remember the meaning of the term.

# Change of Appearance

## What are physical changes of matter?

A physical property of matter is any property that can be observed or measured without changing the chemical identity of the substance. A **physical change** is a change that affects one or more physical properties of a substance. Physical changes occur when a substance changes from one form to another. However, the chemical identity of the substance remains the same.

### Changes in Observable Properties

The appearance, shape, or size of a substance may be altered during a physical change. For example, the process of turning wool into a sweater requires that the wool undergo physical changes. Wool is sheared from the sheep. The wool is then cleaned, and the wool fibers are separated from one another. Shearing and separating the fibers are physical changes that change the shape, volume, and texture of the wool.

### Physical Changes Turn Wool into a Sweater

**Ⓐ** Wool is sheared from the sheep. The raw wool is then cleaned and placed into a machine that separates the wool fibers from one another.

**Ⓑ** The wool fibers are spun into yarn. Again, the shape and volume of the wool change. The fibers are twisted so that they are packed more closely together and are intertwined with one another.

**Ⓒ** The yarn is dyed. The dye changes the color of the wool, but it does not change the wool into another substance. This type of color change is a physical change.

## Changes That Do Not Alter the Chemical Identity of the Substance

During the process of turning wool into a sweater, many physical changes occur in the wool. However, the wool does not change into some other substance as a result of these changes. Therefore, physical changes do not change the chemical identity of a substance.

Another example of a physical change happens when you fill an ice-cube tray with water and place it inside a freezer. If the water gets cold enough, it will freeze to form ice cubes. Freezing water does not change its chemical makeup. In fact, you could melt the ice cube and have liquid water again! Changes of state, like all physical changes, do not change the chemical makeup of the substance.

**6 Identify** The list below gives several examples of physical changes. Write your own examples of physical changes on the blank lines.

Examples of Physical Changes
Stretching a rubber band
Dissolving sugar in water
Cutting your hair
Melting butter
Bending a paper clip
Crushing an aluminum can

_____
_____
_____

**D** Knitting the yarn into a sweater also does not change the wool into another substance. A wool sweater is still wool, even though it no longer resembles the wool on the sheep.

### Visualize It!

**7 Analyze** How does the yarn in the sweater differ from the wool on the sheep?

_____
_____
_____

# Change from

## What are chemical changes of matter?

Think about what happens to the burning logs in a campfire. They start out dry, rough, and dense. After flames surround them, the logs emerge as black and powdery ashes. The campfire releases a lot of heat and smoke in the process. Something has obviously happened, something more than simply a change of appearance. The wood has stopped being wood. It has undergone a chemical change.

### Changes in Substance Identity

A **chemical change** occurs when one or more substances change into entirely new substances with different properties. For example, in the campfire, the dry, dense wood became the powdery ashes—new substances with different properties. When a cake is baked, the liquid cake batter becomes the solid, spongy treat. Whenever a new substance is formed, a chemical change has occurred.

Be aware that chemical *changes* are not exactly the same as chemical *properties*. Burning is a chemical change; flammability is a chemical property. The chemical properties of a substance describe which chemical changes can or cannot happen to that substance. Chemical changes are the *processes* by which substances actually change into new substances. You can learn about a substance's chemical properties by watching the chemical changes that substance undergoes.

### Visualize It!

**8 Identify** Use the boxes provided to identify the wood, ashes, and flames involved in the chemical change shown in the photo. Then write a caption on the lines below that describes the chemical changes you see.

_____

_____

_____

# the Inside

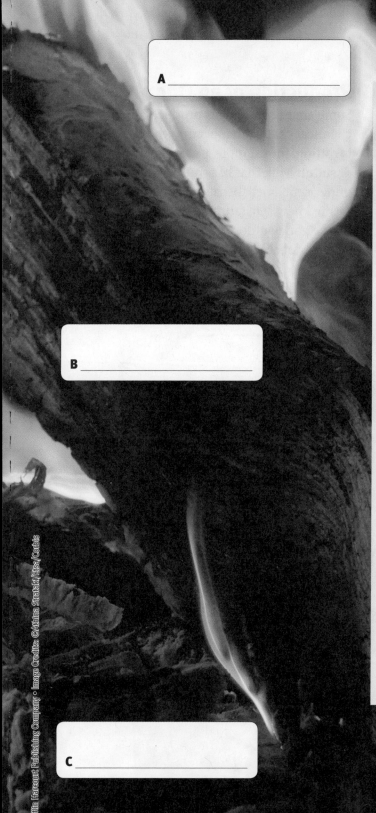

A _____

B _____

C _____

## Changes to the Chemical Makeup of a Substance

In a chemical change, a substance's identity changes because its chemical makeup changes. This happens as the particles and chemical bonds that make up the substance get rearranged. For example, when iron rusts, molecules of oxygen from the air combine with iron atoms to form a new compound. Rust is not iron or oxygen. It is a new substance made up of oxygen and iron joined together.

Because chemical changes involve changes in the arrangements of particles, they are often influenced by temperature. At higher temperatures, the particles in a substance have more average kinetic energy. They move around a lot more freely and so rearrange more easily. Therefore, at higher temperatures, chemical reactions often happen more quickly. Think of baking a cake. The higher the temperature of the oven, the less time the cake will need to bake because the faster the chemical reactions occur.

**Active Reading** **9 Explain** How do higher temperatures influence a chemical change?

_____
_____
_____
_____

## Think Outside the Book Inquiry

**10 Infer** Think of ways you control temperature to influence chemical changes during a typical day. (Hint: cooking, art class)

# Look for the Signs

## How can you tell a chemical change has happened?

Physical changes and chemical changes are different. Chemical changes result in new substances, while physical changes do not. However, it may not be obvious that any new substances have formed during a chemical change. On this page and the next, you will read about some signs that a chemical change may have occurred. If you observe two or more of these signs during a change, you likely are observing a chemical change.

**Active Reading** **11 Compare** How are physical and chemical changes different?

_____

_____

_____

_____

## Production of an Odor

Some chemical changes produce odors. The chemical change that occurs when an egg is rotting, for example, produces the smell of sulfur. Milk that has soured also has an unpleasant smell, because bacteria have formed new substances in the milk. And if you've gone outdoors after a thunderstorm, you've probably noticed a distinct smell. This odor is an indication that lightning has caused a chemical change in the air.

## Production of a Gas

Chemical changes often cause fizzing or foaming. For example, a chemical change is involved when an antacid tablet is dropped into a glass of water. As the tablet makes contact with the water and begins to react with it, bubbles of gas appear. One of the new substances that is formed is carbon dioxide gas, which forms the bubbles that you see.

It is important to note that some physical changes, such as boiling, can also produce gas bubbles. Therefore, the only way to know for sure whether a chemical change has taken place is to identify the new substances.

*Bubbles form when an antacid tablet reacts with water. The bubbles contain a new, gaseous substance, which signals that a chemical change has happened.*

© Houghton Mifflin Harcourt Publishing Company • Image Credits: ©PhotoSpin, Inc/Alamy

## Formation of a Precipitate

Chemical changes may result in products in different physical states. Liquids sometimes combine to form a solid called a *precipitate*. For example, colorless potassium iodide and lead nitrate combine to form the bright yellow precipitate lead iodide, as shown below.

Bright yellow lead iodide precipitates from the clear solution.

## Change in Color

A color change is often an indication of a chemical change. For example, when gray iron rusts, the product that forms is brown.

## Change in Energy

Chemical changes can cause energy to change from one form into another. For example, in a burning candle, the chemical energy stored in the candle converts to heat and light energy.

A change in temperature is often a sign of a chemical change. The change need not always be as dramatic as the one in the photo, however.

The reaction of powdered aluminum with a metal oxide releases so much heat that it is often used to weld metals together. Here it is being used to test the heat-resistant properties of steel.

**12 Infer** List the observations you might make as you witness each of the changes below. Then classify each change as a physical change or a chemical change.

| Change | Signs/observations | Type of change |
|---|---|---|
| Boiling water | | |
| Baking a cake | | |
| Burning wood | | |
| Painting a door | | |

# Conservation is the Law

## What happens to energy and mass during physical and chemical changes?

### Active Reading

**13 Identify** As you read, underline examples of physical and chemical changes.

If you freeze 10 g of water and then let the ice melt, you have 10 g of water again. You can freeze and melt the water many times, and mass of the water will not change. Mass is a measure of the amount of matter in a substance. Freezing water and melting ice are physical changes. Most physical changes can be reversed.

Now consider a chemical change, such as burning logs in a campfire. The ashes remaining after a fire contain much less mass than the logs that produced them. Matter seems to vanish. In other chemical changes, such as those that cause the growth of plants, matter seems to appear out of nowhere. This puzzled scientists for years. Where did the matter go? Where did it come from?

*The water may freeze or the ice may melt, but the amount of matter in this glass will stay the same.*

### Overall, Mass Is Conserved

In the 1770s, the French chemist Antoine Lavoisier (an•TWAHN luh•VWAH•zee•ay) studied chemical changes in which substances seemed to lose or gain mass. He showed that mass was most often lost to or gained from gases in the air. Lavoisier demonstrated these transformations of mass by observing chemical changes in sealed glass bulbs. He carefully measured the substances involved before and after a chemical reaction. The masses were the same. This was the first demonstration of the law of conservation of mass. The **law of conservation of mass** states that in ordinary chemical and physical changes, mass is not created or destroyed. Mass is only transformed into different substances. This law is sometimes called the law of conservation of matter. Physical and chemical changes both follow the law of conservation of mass or matter.

**14 Infer** How could a chemist find out how much mass is given off as gas during a chemical reaction?

_____

_____

_____

## Overall, Energy Is Conserved

Ordinary physical and chemical changes also follow the law of conservation of energy. The **law of conservation of energy** states that energy cannot be created or destroyed. Energy can only change from one form to another. Energy can be released or absorbed during physical and chemical changes. Changes that absorb energy are called *endothermic*. Changes that release energy are called *exothermic*. During a physical or chemical change, the total amount of energy in the substances and their surroundings remains constant.

**15 Apply** When an egg is boiled, a chemical reaction takes place that turns the egg from a clear liquid into an opaque solid. What happens to the energy used to boil an egg?

Visualize It!

## Conservation of Mass and Energy

When vinegar and baking soda are combined, they undergo an exothermic chemical change that releases energy and carbon dioxide gas. Without the balloon to catch it, the gas would seem to disappear. But when the gas is captured, you can see that the mass of the starting materials is the same as the mass of the products. Energy that was stored in the chemical bonds is released as heat. The total amount of energy also stayed the same.

Before
vinegar
baking soda
equals
After

When vinegar and baking soda combine, carbon dioxide gas is produced.

**16 Infer** What would you observe about the mass in the flask if you did not put the balloon on top? Why?

© Houghton Mifflin Harcourt Publishing Company • Image Credits: ©Victoria Smith/HMH Photo

# Visual Summary

To complete this summary, circle the correct word or phrase. Then use the key below to check your answers. You can use this page to review the main concepts of the lesson.

**How Matter Changes**

A physical change is a change of matter from one form to another without a change in the identity of the substance.

**17** Burning / Dyeing wool is an example of a physical change.

A chemical change is a change of matter that occurs when one or more substances change into entirely new substances with different properties.

**18** The formation of a precipitate signals a physical / chemical change.

Chemical changes often cause the production of an odor, fizzing or foaming, the formation of a precipitate, or changes in color or temperature.

**19** This physical / chemical change results in the formation of new substances.

The laws of conservation of mass and energy state that mass and energy cannot be created or destroyed in ordinary physical and chemical changes.

**20** In the chemical reaction between baking soda and vinegar, mass / energy / both mass and energy is / are conserved.

Answers: 17 Dyeing; 18 chemical; 19 chemical; 20 both mass and energy

---

**21 Explain** Do changes that cannot be easily reversed, such as burning, observe the law of conservation of mass? Explain.

# Lesson Review

## Vocabulary

In your own words, define the following terms.

**1** physical change

_____

_____

_____

**2** chemical change

_____

_____

_____

**3** law of conservation of mass

_____

_____

_____

## Key Concepts

**4 Identify** Give an example of a physical change and an example of a chemical change.

_____

_____

_____

_____

**5 Compare** How is a chemical change different from a physical change?

_____

_____

_____

_____

_____

**6 Apply** Suppose a log's mass is 5 kg. After burning, the mass of the ash is 1 kg. Explain what may have happened to the other 4 kg.

_____

_____

_____

_____

_____

## Critical Thinking

Use this photo to answer the following questions.

**7 Analyze** As the bright sun shines upon the water, the water slowly disappears. The sunlight also gives energy to the surrounding plants to convert water and carbon dioxide into sugar and oxygen gas. Which change is physical, and which is chemical?

_____

_____

_____

**8 Infer** How does the law of conservation of energy relate to the processes going on in the water and in the plants?

_____

_____

_____

_____

_____

_____

**9 Compare** Relate the statement "You can't get something for nothing" to the law of conservation of mass.

_____

_____

_____

_____

_____

# My Notes

TEKS 6.2B design and implement experimental investigations by making observations, asking well-defined questions, formulating testable hypotheses, and using appropriate equipment and technology

TEKS 6.2E analyze data to formulate reasonable explanations, communicate valid conclusions supported by the data, and predict trends

# Forming Hypotheses

Before beginning an investigation, a scientist should collect as much evidence and background knowledge as possible. This allows the scientist to create a clear, informed hypothesis. A scientist must be open to the fact that the results of an investigation may not completely support the hypothesis. They may even contradict it! However, revising or forming a new hypothesis may lead a scientist to make a breakthrough that could be the basis of a new discovery.

## Tutorial

**The following procedure explains the steps that you will use to develop and evaluate a hypothesis.**

**Make Observations**

**1 Making Observations** Scientific investigations commonly begin with observations. Your observations may lead to a question. For example, you may wonder how, why, or when something happens.

**Form a Hypothesis**

**2 Forming a Hypothesis** To answer your question, you can start by forming a hypothesis. A hypothesis is a clear idea or explanation that can be investigated. Start to form a hypothesis by stating the probable answer to your question based on your observations.

**Test a Hypothesis**

**3 Testing a Hypothesis** A useful hypothesis must be testable. To determine whether your hypothesis is testable, identify experiments that you can perform or observations that you can make to find out whether the hypothesis is supported or not.

**Evaluate a Hypothesis**

**4 Evaluating a Hypothesis** After analyzing your data, you can determine if your results support your hypothesis. If your data support your hypothesis, you may want to repeat your observations or experiments to verify your results. If your data do not support your hypothesis, you may have to check your procedure for errors. Or, you may have to reject your hypothesis and form a new one.

**Report Your Results**

# You Try It!

Alloys are solutions that are formed by dissolving substances into a molten metal and then allowing the solution to cool and harden. Alloys can be made up of different ratios of substances such as lead, nickel, and carbon. Different alloys have different engineering applications. Use the data below to form a hypothesis about lead-antimony alloys.

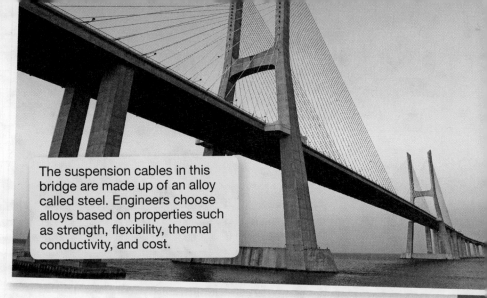

The suspension cables in this bridge are made up of an alloy called steel. Engineers choose alloys based on properties such as strength, flexibility, thermal conductivity, and cost.

**1 Making Observations** Examine these data about alloys. Then, circle the higher value of the two given in each box.

An alloy's *tensile strength* is tested by pulling a given sample until it breaks or changes shape. Tensile strength is recorded in units of force per area.

**Lead = 16.5 MPa      Antimony = 11.2 MPa**

*Brinell hardness* describes the force required to create a measured indentation in an alloy. It is also recorded in units of force per area.

**Lead = 38.3 MPa      Antimony = 294 MPa**

An alloy's *thermal conductivity* measures how quickly energy as heat is transferred through it. Thermal conductivity is measured in watts per meter-kelvin (W/m·K).

**Lead = 35 W/m·K      Antimony = 24 W/m·K**

**2 Forming a Hypothesis** Use the data above to form a testable hypothesis about how the amount of antimony in a lead-antimony alloy will affect the alloy's properties. Your hypothesis should be supported by all of your data.

_____

_____

_____

_____

_____

_____

## Properties of Lead-Antimony Alloys

| Alloy composition | | Tensile strength (MPa) | Brinell hardness (MPa) | Thermal conductivity (W/m·K) |
|---|---|---|---|---|
| Lead | Antimony | | | |
| 92% | 8% | 32.2 | 93.2 | 27 |
| 94% | 6% | 28.4 | 82.4 | 29 |
| 96% | 4% | 28.1 | 78.5 | 31 |

**3 Testing a Hypothesis** Scientists tested three lead-antimony alloys and recorded their results in the table above. Do these new observations support your hypothesis?

_____

**4 Evaluating a Hypothesis** How would you revise your original hypothesis based on these data?

_____

_____

_____

_____

_____

### Take It Home

Use the Internet to find videos that demonstrate tensile strength testing. Research tensile strength, and write a scientific paper containing your findings. Be sure to include an introduction and a list of works cited.

# Pure Substances
## and Mixtures

**ESSENTIAL QUESTION**

## How do pure substances and mixtures compare?

By the end of this lesson, you should be able to distinguish between pure substances and mixtures.

Seawater is a unique mixture that contains many dissolved substances. One such substance, called calcium carbonate, is used by these stony coral to build their hard skeletons.

**TEKS 6.5A** know that an element is a pure substance represented by chemical symbols

**TEKS 6.5C** differentiate between elements and compounds on the most basic level

## Lesson Labs

**Quick Labs**
- Observing Mixtures
- Identifying Elements and Compounds

**Exploration Lab**
- Investigate Separating Mixtures

## Engage Your Brain

**1 Predict** Check T or F to show whether you think each statement is true or false.

**T   F**

☐   ☐   Atoms combine in different ways to make up all of the substances you encounter every day.

☐   ☐   Saltwater can be separated into salt and water.

☐   ☐   A mixture of soil has the same chemical composition throughout.

**2 Apply** Think of a substance that does not dissolve in water. Draw a sketch below that shows what happens when this substance is added to water.

## Active Reading

**3 Synthesize** Many English words have their roots in other languages. Use the Greek words below to make an educated guess about the meanings of the words *homogeneous* and *heterogeneous*.

| Greek word | Meaning |
|------------|---------|
| *genus* | type |
| *homos* | same |
| *heteros* | different |

**Example sentence**
Saltwater is <u>homogeneous</u> throughout.

**homogeneous:**

_____

_____

**Example sentence**
A <u>heterogeneous</u> mixture of rocks varies from handful to handful.

**heterogeneous:**

_____

_____

### Vocabulary Terms

- atom
- element
- compound
- mixture
- pure substance
- heterogeneous
- homogeneous

**4 Identify** This list contains the key terms you'll learn in this lesson. As you read, circle the definition of each term.

© Houghton Mifflin Harcourt Publishing Company • Image Credits: © Jeff Rotman/Rise/Getty Images

# A Great Combination

## How can matter be classified?

What kinds of food could you make with the ingredients shown below? You could eat slices of tomato as a snack. Or, you could combine tomato slices with lettuce to make a salad. Combine more ingredients, such as bread and cheese, and you have a sandwich. Just as these meals are made up of simpler foods, matter is made up of basic "ingredients" known as *atoms*. **Atoms** are the smallest unit of an element that maintains the properties of that element. Atoms, like the foods shown here, can be combined in different ways to produce different substances.

The substances you encounter every day can be classified into one of the three major classes of matter: *elements, compounds,* and *mixtures*. Atoms are the basic building blocks for all three types of matter. Elements, compounds, and mixtures differ in the way that atoms are combined.

Active Reading **5 Compare** What do elements, compounds, and mixtures have in common?

_____

_____

**Think Outside the Book** Inquiry

**6 Predict** If you have ever baked a cake or bread, you know that the ingredients that combine to make it taste different from the baked food. Why do you think that is?

Just as these ingredients combine to make a tasty sandwich, atoms are the basic "ingredients" that make up matter.

# Matter Can Be Classified into Elements, Compounds, and Mixtures

You can think of atoms as the building blocks of matter. Like these toy blocks, atoms can be connected in different ways. The models below show how atoms make up elements and compounds. Elements and compounds, in turn, make up mixtures.

 An atom is like a building block of matter.

 An **element** is made up of one or more of the same kind of atom chemically combined.

Oxygen

 A **compound** is made up of different kinds of atoms chemically combined. Compounds have different properties from the elements that make them up.

Water

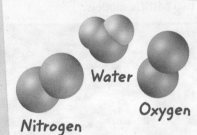 A **mixture** contains a variety of elements and compounds that are not chemically combined with each other.

Water

Oxygen

Nitrogen

## Visualize It!

**7 Analyze** Why are the spheres representing nitrogen and oxygen different colors?

_____

_____

_____

_____

# Pure Genius

## What are pure substances?

Elements and compounds are **pure substances**. A pure substance is a substance that has definite physical and chemical properties such as appearance, melting point, and reactivity. No matter the amount of a pure substance you have, it will always have the same properties. This is because pure substances are made up of one type of particle.

### Pure Substances Are Made Up of One Type of Particle

Copper, like all elements, is a pure substance. Take a look at the element copper, shown below. The atoms that make up copper are all the same. No matter where in the world you find pure copper, it will always have the same properties.

Compounds are also pure substances. Consider water, shown on the next page. Two different kinds of atoms make up each chemically combined particle, or *molecule*. Every water molecule is identical. Each molecule is made up of exactly two hydrogen atoms and one oxygen atom. Because water is a pure substance, we can define certain properties of water. For example, at standard pressure, water always freezes at 0 °C and boils at 100 °C.

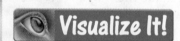 Visualize It!

**8 Identify** Fill in the blanks to label the two particle models.

A Copper _____

**9 Explain** Copper is an element. How do these images of copper illustrate this?

_____
_____
_____
_____

# Pure Substances Cannot Be Formed or Broken Down by Physical Changes

Physical changes such as melting, freezing, cutting, or smashing do not change the identity of pure substances. For example, if you cut copper pipe into short pieces, the material is still copper. And if you freeze liquid water, the particles that make up the ice remain the same: two hydrogen atoms combined with one oxygen atom.

The chemical bonds that hold atoms together cannot be broken easily. To break or form chemical bonds, a chemical change is required. For example, when an electric current is passed through water, a chemical change takes place. The atoms that make up the compound break apart into two elements: hydrogen and oxygen. When a pure substance undergoes a chemical change, it is no longer that same substance. A chemical change changes the identity of the substance. Individual atoms cannot be broken down into smaller parts by normal physical or chemical changes.

**Active Reading** **11 Identify** What happens when a pure substance undergoes a chemical change?

_____

_____

_____

_____

**B** Water _____

**10 Explain** Water is a compound. How do these images of water illustrate this?

_____

_____

_____

_____

© Houghton Mifflin Harcourt Publishing Company • Image Credits: (bkgd) ©Imagewerks//Getty Images; (b) ©Yamada Taro/Riser/Getty Images

Lesson 4 Pure Substances and Mixtures  **157**

# Classified Information

## How can elements be classified?

**Active Reading**

**12 Identify** As you read, underline the ways in which elements are organized on the periodic table.

Differences in physical and chemical properties allow us to classify elements. By knowing the category to which an element belongs, you can predict some of its properties. Elements are broadly classified as metals, nonmetals, or metalloids. Most metals are shiny, conduct heat and electricity well, and can be shaped into thin sheets and wires. Nonmetals are not shiny and do not conduct heat or electricity well. Metalloids have some properties of both metals and nonmetals.

Over 100 elements are known to exist. Each element has a place in an arrangement called the periodic table of the elements. The periodic table is a useful tool that can help you to identify elements that have similar properties. Metals, nonmetals, and metalloids occupy different regions in the periodic table. Metals start at the left and make up most of the elements in the periodic table. Nonmetals are at the right and are often shaded with a color different from that of the metals. Not surprisingly, the metalloids lie between the metals and nonmetals. In many instances, you can even predict which elements combine with others to form compounds based on their positions in the periodic table.

*Aluminum, like many metals, can be formed into a thin foil.*

*Charcoal, made mostly of carbon atoms, is brittle and dull like many other nonmetals.*

# How can compounds be classified?

You are surrounded by compounds. Compounds make up the food you eat, the school supplies you use, and the clothes you wear—even you! There are so many compounds that it would be very difficult to list or describe them all. Fortunately, these compounds can be grouped into a few basic categories by their properties.

## By Their pH

Compounds can be classified as acidic, basic, or neutral by measuring a special value known as *pH.* Acids have a pH value below 7. Vinegar contains acetic acid, which gives a sharp, sour taste to salad dressings. Bases, on the other hand, have pH values greater than 7. Baking soda is an example of a basic compound. Bases have a slippery feel and a bitter taste. Neutral compounds, such as pure water and table salt, have a pH value of 7. Water and salt are formed when an acid and a base react. A type of paper called litmus paper can be used to test whether a compound is an acid or a base. Blue litmus paper turns red in the presence of an acid. Red litmus paper turns blue in the presence of a base. Although some foods are acidic or basic, you should NEVER taste, smell, or touch a non-food chemical to classify it. Many acids and bases can damage your body or clothing.

**13 Classify** Read about some of the ways in which compounds can be classified. Then fill in the blanks to complete the photo captions.

Baking soda is an example of a(n) _____

## As Organic or Inorganic

You may have heard of organically-grown foods. But in chemistry, the word *organic* refers to compounds that contain carbon and hydrogen. Organic compounds are found in most foods. They can also be found in synthetic goods. For example, gasoline contains a number of organic compounds, such as octane and heptane.

The compounds that make up plastic are _____ because they contain carbon.

## By Their Role in the Body

Organic compounds that are made by living things are called biochemicals. Biochemicals are divided into four categories: carbohydrates, lipids, proteins, and nucleic acids. *Carbohydrates* are used as a source of energy and include sugars, starches, and fiber. *Lipids* are biochemicals that store excess energy in the body and make up cell membranes. Lipids include fats, oils, and waxes. *Proteins* are one of the most abundant types of compounds in your body. They regulate chemical activities of the body and build and repair body structures. *Nucleic acids* such as DNA and RNA contain genetic information and help the body build proteins.

Your body gets _____ such as sugars, starches, and fiber, from many of the foods you eat.

© Houghton Mifflin Harcourt Publishing Company • Image Credits: (c) ©Terry Vine/Blend Images/Corbis; (b) ©MIB Pictures/UpperCut Images/Getty Images

# Mix and Match

## What are mixtures?

Imagine that you roll out some dough, add tomato sauce, and sprinkle some cheese on top. Then you add green peppers, mushrooms, and pepperoni. What have you just made? A pizza, of course! But that's not all. You have also created a mixture.

A mixture is a combination of two or more substances that are combined physically but not chemically. When two or more materials are put together, they form a mixture if they do not change chemically to form a new substance. For example, cheese and tomato sauce do not react when they are combined to make a pizza. They keep their original identities and properties. So, a pizza is a mixture.

## Mixtures Are Made Up of More Than One Type of Particle

Unlike elements and compounds, mixtures are not pure substances. Mixtures contain more than one type of substance. Each substance in a mixture has the same chemical makeup it had before the mixture formed.

Unlike pure substances, mixtures do not have definite properties. Granite from different parts of the world could contain different minerals in different ratios. Pizzas made by different people could have different toppings. Mixtures do not have defined properties because they do not have a defined chemical makeup.

 **Visualize It!**

**14 Describe** This student is going to make and separate a mixture of sand and salt. Complete these captions to describe what is taking place in each photo.

A Sand and salt are poured into a single beaker. The result is a mixture because

_____

_____

_____

_____

## Mixtures Can Be Separated by Physical Changes

You don't like mushrooms on your pizza? Just pick them off. This change is a physical change of the mixture because the identities of the substances do not change. But not all mixtures are as easy to separate as a pizza. You cannot just pick salt out of a salt water mixture. One way to separate the salt from the water is to heat the mixture until the water evaporates. The salt is left behind. Other ways to separate mixtures are shown at the right and below.

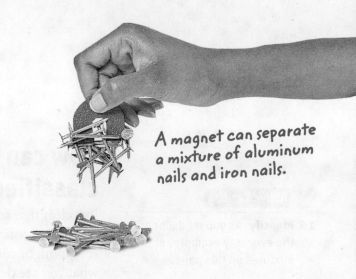

A magnet can separate a mixture of aluminum nails and iron nails.

Active Reading **15 Devise** How could you separate a mixture of rocks and sand?

_____

_____

_____

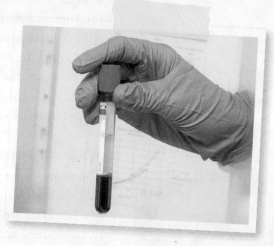

A machine called a centrifuge separates mixtures by the densities of the components. It can be used to separate the different parts of blood.

**B** When water is added to the sand-salt mixture,

_____

_____

_____

_____

**C** When the liquid is poured through a filter,

_____

_____

_____

_____

**D** The remaining salt water is heated until

_____

_____

_____

_____

# A Simple Solution

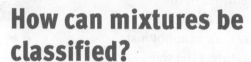

A snow globe contains a suspension.

## How can mixtures be classified?

**16 Identify** As you read, underline the everyday examples of mixtures on this page.

It is clear that something is a mixture when you can see the different substances in it. For example, if you scoop up a handful of soil, it might contain dirt, rocks, leaves, and even insects. Exactly what you see depends on what part of the soil is scooped. Such a mixture is called a heterogeneous (het•uhr•uh•JEE•nee•uhs) mixture. A **heterogeneous** mixture is one that does not have a uniform composition. In other types of mixtures, the substances are evenly spread throughout. If you add sugar to a cup of water, the sugar dissolves. Each part of the sugar-water mixture has the same sweet taste. This is called a **homogeneous** (hoh•muh•JEE•nee•uhs) mixture.

### As Suspensions

The snow globe (above) contains a type of heterogeneous mixture called a *suspension*. Suspensions are mixtures in which the particles of a material are spread throughout a liquid or gas but are too large to stay mixed without being stirred or shaken. If a suspension is allowed to sit, the particles will settle out.

### As Solutions

Tea is an example of a type of homogeneous mixture known as a *solution*. In a solution, one substance is dissolved in another substance. When you make tea, some of the compounds inside the tea leaves dissolve in the hot water. These compounds give your tea its unique color and taste. Many familiar solutions are liquids. However, solutions may also be gases or solids. Air is an example of a gaseous solution. Alloys, such as brass and steel, are solid solutions in which substances are dissolved in metals.

Tea is a solution.

### As Colloids

*Colloids* are a third type of mixture that falls somewhere between suspensions and solutions. As in a suspension, the particles in a colloid are spread throughout a liquid or gas. Unlike the particles in a suspension, colloid particles are small and do not settle out quickly. Milk and gelatin are colloids. Colloids look homogeneous, but we consider them to be heterogeneous.

Gelatin is a colloid.

**17 Summarize** Complete the graphic organizer below by filling in the blanks with terms from this lesson. Then add definitions or sketches of each term inside the appropriate box.

## Classifying Matter

**Matter**
Definition:

Matter is anything that has mass and takes up space. Matter is made up of building blocks called atoms.

**Pure Substances**
Definition:

_____
_____
_____
_____

Sketch:

**Elements**
Sketch:

Definition:

_____
_____
_____
_____

Sketch:

**Homogeneous**
Definition:

_____
_____
_____
_____

**Suspensions**
Sketch:

**Colloids**
Definition:

_____
_____
_____

Definition:

_____
_____
_____
_____

# Visual Summary

To complete this summary, circle the correct word or phrase. Then use the key below to check your answers. You can use this page to review the main concepts of the lesson.

Pure substances are made up of a single type of particle and cannot be formed or broken down by physical changes.

18 Water is a pure substance / mixture.

19 Water is a(n) element / compound.

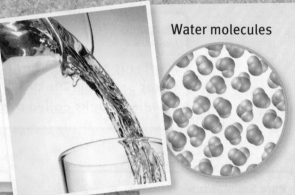

Water molecules

## Pure Substances and Mixtures

Mixtures are made up of more than one type of particle and can be separated into their component parts by physical changes.

20 Saltwater and sand can be separated with a magnet / filter.

21 Saltwater is a homogeneous / heterogeneous mixture.

Answers: 18 pure substance; 19 compound; 20 filter; 21 homogeneous

22 **Predict** Why do you think that the particles of a suspension settle out but the particles of a colloid do not?

# Lesson Review

## Vocabulary

Fill in the blanks with the term that best completes the following sentences.

**1** The basic building blocks of matter are called

_____

**2** A(n) _____ is a substance that is made up of a single kind of atom.

**3** Elements and compounds are two types of

_____

**4** A(n) _____ is a combination of substances that are combined physically but not chemically.

## Key Concepts

**5 Identify** What kind of mixture is a solution? A suspension? A colloid?

_____

_____

_____

**6 Apply** Fish give off the compound ammonia, which has a pH above 7. To which class of compounds does ammonia belong?

**7 Compare** Fill in the following table with properties of elements and compounds.

| How are elements and compounds similar? | How are elements and compounds different? |
|---|---|
|  |  |

Use this drawing to answer the following question.

**8 Identify** What type of mixture is this salad dressing?

_____

## Critical Thinking

**9 Explain** Could a mixture be made up of only elements and no compounds? Explain.

_____

_____

_____

_____

_____

**10 Synthesize** Describe a procedure to separate a mixture of sugar, black pepper, and pebbles.

_____

_____

_____

_____

_____

_____

_____

_____

_____

# My Notes

# Atoms and Elements

**ESSENTIAL QUESTION**

## How are atoms and elements related?

By the end of this lesson, you should be able to describe the properties of atoms and elements.

**TEKS** **6.5A** know that an element is a pure substance represented by chemical symbols

**TEKS** **6.5B** recognize that a limited number of the many known elements comprise the largest portion of solid Earth, living matter, oceans, and the atmosphere

**TEKS** **6.6A** compare metals, nonmetals, and metalloids using physical properties such as luster, conductivity, or malleability

Earth is made of many elements. The fantastic formations in this cave contain atoms of calcium, carbon, and oxygen.

## 🧠 Engage Your Brain

**1 Predict** Check T or F to show whether you think each statement is true or false.

| T | F | |
|---|---|---|
| ☐ | ☐ | Atoms are smaller than electrons. |
| ☐ | ☐ | Single atoms can be seen with a powerful light microscope. |
| ☐ | ☐ | There are more than 100 elements on the periodic table of elements. |

**2 Infer** Why do the two elements silver and iron have different properties?

_____
_____
_____
_____
_____
_____
_____

## ✏️ Active Reading

**3 Synthesize** Many English words have their roots in other languages. Use the Greek word below to make an educated guess about the meaning of the word *atom*.

| Greek word | Meaning |
|---|---|
| *atomos* | indivisible |

**Example sentence**
All matter is made up of particles called <u>atoms</u>.

*atom:*

_____
_____
_____
_____

### Vocabulary Terms

- atom
- proton
- neutron
- electron
- element
- atomic number
- chemical symbol
- physical property

**4 Identify** As you read, create a reference card for each vocabulary term. On one side of the card, write the term and its meaning. On the other side, draw an image that illustrates or makes a connection to the term. These cards can be used as bookmarks in the text so that you can refer to them while studying.

# A Small World

These dots of ink, like all matter, are made up of much smaller particles called atoms.

## What are atoms?

When you magnify printed letters in a book, you can see that they are made up of small dots of ink. A fixed ratio of magenta and cyan ink dots make a light purple color. In the same way, all matter is made up of very small particles called atoms. **Atoms** are the basic building blocks of matter, because they are the smallest particles that can have the same properties as the stuff they make up. Different atoms can be combined in different ratios to form all of the substances we encounter every day. Unlike dots of ink, atoms are so small that they cannot be seen using a light microscope.

## What are the parts of an atom?

These tiny atoms contain even smaller particles called *subatomic* particles. **Protons** are subatomic particles that have a positive electric charge. Protons are found at the center, or *nucleus,* of the atom. The nucleus also contains another type of subatomic particle called **neutrons.** Neutrons have no charge. The protons and neutrons in the nucleus make up most of the mass of an atom.

A third type of subatomic particles are called **electrons.** Electrons are negatively charged and are much smaller than protons and neutrons. Electrons are found outside the nucleus in a region called the *electron cloud.* Atoms are electrically neutral overall because they have the same number of protons as electrons. The positive charges of the protons balance out the negative charges of the electrons.

## Visualize It!

**6 Apply** This model represents an atom and its parts. Label the parts of the atom.

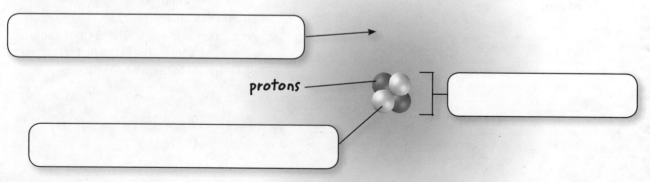
protons

**Why It Matters**

# Nanotechnology

Nanotechnology is the use of materials and processes designed on the atomic scale. Incredibly small electric circuits, machines, and medicine delivery systems are just a few nanotechnology applications that scientists are working to develop.

## How It Works

In traditional manufacturing, materials are cut away or shaped to make a product. In nanotechnological manufacturing, materials are built by putting atoms together. The electric wires in this robotic "skin" are built from carbon atoms.

## What Can You Make?

Scientists don't yet know all the possible uses of nanotechnology. Someday, tiny robots may be able to deliver medicine exactly where it is needed to treat disease. This drawing shows a model of a robot on a red blood cell.

## Extend

Inquiry

**7 Explain** How does nanotechnology differ from other ways to make objects and materials?

**8 Explain** What could be the potential benefits of atomic-scale medicine delivery systems?

**9 Research** Use the library or the Internet to research a possible new device or material in the field of nanotechnology. Make a poster to present what you learn to your class.

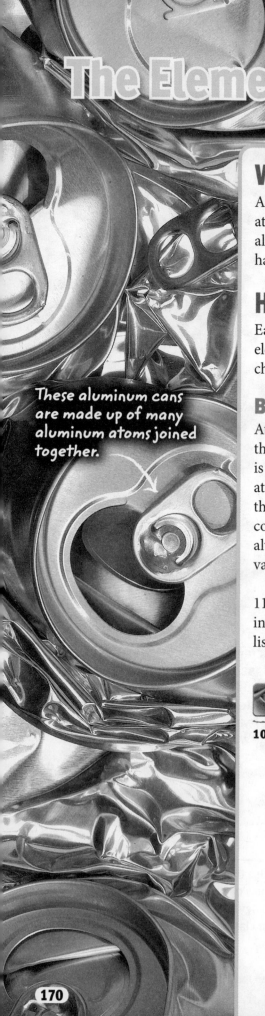

These aluminum cans are made up of many aluminum atoms joined together.

# The Element of Surprise

## What is an element?

An **element** is a pure substance that is made up of only one type of atom. For example, the metal aluminum is an element made up of aluminum atoms. An atom is the smallest unit of an element that has the properties of that element.

## How are elements described?

Each element has its own properties that differ from those of other elements. Elements can be identified by their atomic numbers and chemical symbols.

### By Their Atomic Numbers

Atoms of one element differ from atoms of another element by the number of protons they have. The **atomic number** of an element is the number of protons in the nucleus of one of its atoms. Every atom of a given element has the same atomic number. For example, the atomic number of aluminum is 13. Each atom of aluminum contains 13 protons. While the number of protons in the nucleus is always the same for a given element, the number of neutrons can vary. All aluminum atoms found in nature have 14 neutrons.

The periodic table of elements is used to organize over 110 known elements. The periodic table is organized in rows by increasing atomic number. The atomic number of each element is listed at the top of that element's square in the periodic table.

### Visualize It!

**10 Apply** In the space below, draw a model of an atom of the element aluminum. Use information from this lesson to determine how many protons, neutrons, and electrons to include in your model.

# By Their Chemical Symbols

**Active Reading** **11 Identify** As you read, underline the chemical symbols of elements.

Elements can also be described by their chemical symbols. A **chemical symbol** is an abbreviation that represents an element. Most elements have a one- or two-letter chemical symbol. The first letter is always capitalized, and the other letters are always lowercase. These symbols are like nicknames that allow chemists to write chemical names in a shorter form. A few elements at the end of the periodic table have three-letter chemical symbols, such as Uut. These symbols are placeholders for elements that have not yet been discovered or that do not have official names. The discovery of a new element has to be approved by an international committee of scientists. Then the element is given a permanent name and a one- or two-letter chemical symbol.

A chemical symbol often contains letters from the element's name. For example, hydrogen is represented by H, and zinc is represented by Zn. Some chemical symbols come from the names of the elements in other languages. The chemical symbol of gold is Au, from the Latin word for gold—*aurum*. The symbol for tungsten, W, comes from its German name—*wolfram*.

## Visualize It!

**12 Describe** Helium appears in the top-right corner of the periodic table. What are the atomic number and chemical symbol for helium?

_____

_____

---

### 13
### Al
### Aluminum
### 26.98

Different periodic tables may show different information about each element. The square above shows the atomic number, the chemical symbol, the full name, and the average atomic mass of aluminum. The table below shows less information about each element. Each square shows only the atomic number and the chemical symbol for each element.

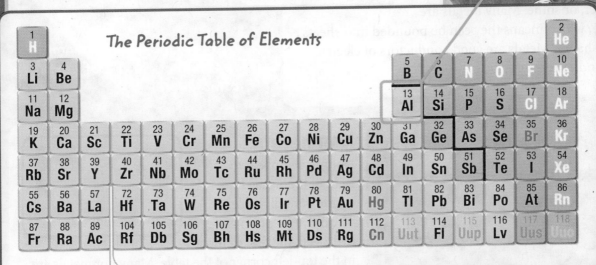

The Periodic Table of Elements

© Houghton Mifflin Harcourt Publishing Company • Image Credits: (bg) ©Don Farrall/Getty Images

# The Head of the Class

## What are the three main classes of elements?

The periodic table is arranged into columns and rows. Elements in each column have similar properties. Also, the properties of the elements in each row change in a predictable way.

The periodic table contains three main classes of elements: metals, nonmetals, and metalloids. Each class of elements can be found in a specific area of the periodic table. A zigzag line on some periodic tables marks the locations of the metals, nonmetals, and metalloids. Each class of elements also has unique properties. A **physical property** is a characteristic of a substance that can be observed and measured without changing the identity of the substance. Color, density, and conductivity are all physical properties. Thermal conductivity is a measure of how well a substance transfers energy as heat. Conductivity also describes how well an electric current flows through a substance.

### Metals

Most elements are classified as metals. Metals appear to the left of the zigzag line on the periodic table. Most metals are solid and can be recognized by their luster, or shine. Many metals are malleable, which means they can be pounded into sheets or other shapes. Metals are good conductors of electric current and of energy as heat.

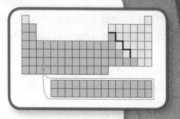

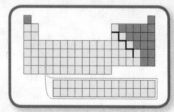

Nitrogen gas, N$_2$, is a nonmetal that makes up 78% of Earth's atmosphere.

This fence is made of wrought iron. Iron is a metal that is used in many building materials.

### Nonmetals

Nonmetals appear to the right of the zigzag line on the periodic table. The only exception is hydrogen, the first element in the top-left corner of the table. Many nonmetals are gases at room temperature. Nonmetals are typically dull; in other words, they lack luster. Solid nonmetals are brittle, or not malleable. Nonmetals are poor conductors of electric current and of energy as heat.

# Metalloids

Metalloids appear between metals and nonmetals along the zigzag line on the periodic table. Metalloids are elements that have some properties of metals and some properties of nonmetals. Metalloids are typically solids and have a somewhat metallic luster. Metalloids are less malleable than metals but not as brittle as nonmetals. Metalloids are known as semiconductors. They conduct electric current better than nonmetals but not as well as metals.

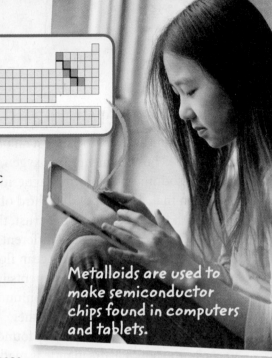

Metalloids are used to make semiconductor chips found in computers and tablets.

**Active Reading** 13 **Describe** Where are metalloids found on the periodic table?

_____

## Visualize It!

14 **Compare** Use the physical properties in the table to label each of these elements as a metal, nonmetal, or metalloid.

| Substance | Appearance | Malleability | Thermal conductivity (mW/cm*K) |
|---|---|---|---|
| A | shiny solid | malleable | 804 |
| B | shiny solid | brittle | 602 |
| C | shiny solid | malleable | 4,010 |
| D | yellowish-green gas | not malleable | 0.089 |

Ⓐ _____

Ⓑ _____

Ⓒ _____

Ⓓ _____

15 **Extend** What additional physical properties could help you compare these elements?

_____

_____

_____

# Elements in Our World

## What elements make up Earth?

Nine elements account for almost all of the matter that makes up our planet. These elements are oxygen, silicon, aluminum, calcium, sodium, potassium, magnesium, nickel, and iron. Iron makes up about one-third of Earth's mass.

Earth has three layers: the crust, the mantle, and the core. Each layer has a different mix of elements. The continents and ocean floor are parts of the crust. The main elements in the crust are oxygen, silicon, and aluminum. Along with smaller amounts of other elements, they form the minerals found in rocks and soil. Earth's mantle is made of rock that is so hot that it flows slowly. Most of this rock is made of silicon, oxygen, iron, and magnesium. The main elements in Earth's core are the metals iron and nickel.

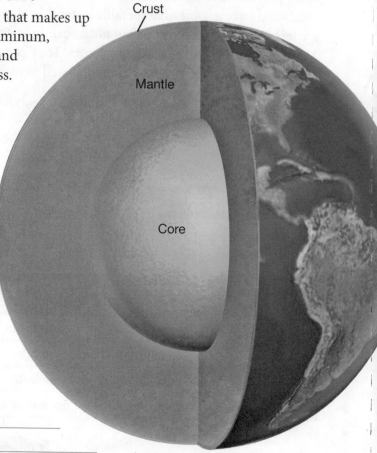

Crust

Mantle

Core

**Active Reading** **16 Identify** What are the main elements in Earth's core? Which class do these elements belong to?

_____

_____

**17 Infer** Despite the many different colors on the canyon walls, all the sandstone is mostly made of the same elements. What do you think the most common elements are? Check your answer with library or Internet resources.

_____

_____

_____

_____

_____

# What elements make up the atmosphere and ocean?

The atmosphere and ocean are above Earth's crust. The atmosphere is a layer of gases surrounding Earth. It is composed of about 78% nitrogen and 21% oxygen. The remaining 1% of the atmosphere is made up of gases such as argon, helium, neon, and carbon dioxide.

The ocean is mainly water. Water molecules are made of hydrogen and oxygen atoms joined together. These two elements are the most abundant in Earth's oceans. If you have ever tasted ocean water, you know that it is salty. Salt compounds make up a small percentage of the ocean. In all, ocean water contains about 30 elements. The salts in the ocean contain the elements sodium, chlorine, sulfur, magnesium, calcium, and potassium.

# What elements make up living things?

All living things–and things that were once alive–contain the element carbon. This includes fossil fuels, such as coal and petroleum. These fuels come from the remains of organisms that lived millions of years ago. Other elements that are abundant in living things include hydrogen, oxygen, nitrogen, phosphorus, and calcium. Living things need a variety of other elements, such as iron, in small amounts. You can get some of these elements from the food you eat. Eating a variety of healthy foods will help you to get all the elements your body needs.

This sea lion, as well as the water and air that it needs to survive, is composed of just a few elements joined in different ways.

**18 Compare** In the table below, write the names and chemical symbols of elements found in Earth, the atmosphere, the oceans, and living things. Use the periodic table in the Look It Up! section to look up unfamiliar chemical symbols.

| Earth | Earth's Atmosphere | Earth's Oceans | Living Things |
|-------|--------------------|--------------------|---------------|
|       |                    |                    |               |
|       |                    |                    |               |
|       |                    |                    |               |
|       |                    |                    |               |
|       |                    |                    |               |

# Visual Summary

To complete this summary, fill in the blanks with the correct word or phrase. Then use the key below to check your answers. You can use this page to review the main concepts of the lesson.

## Atoms and Elements

**Atoms are the basic building blocks of matter.**

19 Atoms are made up of protons, electrons, and _____

**An element is a pure substance that can be described by its atomic number and chemical symbol.**

13
**Al**
Aluminum
26.98

20 The atomic number of an element is the number of _____ in an atom's nucleus.

**A small number of elements make up Earth, the atmosphere, the oceans, and living things.**

21 The most common elements in the atmosphere are _____ and _____

22 The most common elements in the ocean are _____ and _____, which make up water.

Answers: 19 neutrons; 20 protons; 21 nitrogen, oxygen; 22 hydrogen, oxygen

23 **Synthesize** An unknown mineral sample contains the element calcium. What information could you learn about calcium and its properties from the periodic table?

# Lesson Review

## Vocabulary

Draw a line to connect the following terms to their definitions.

**1** nucleus

**2** element

**3** chemical symbol

**A** a pure substance made up of one type of atom

**B** letters that represent an element

**C** the central region of an atom

## Key Concepts

**4 Relate** Explain how the terms *atom* and *element* are related.

_____

_____

_____

**5 Summarize** What are the three main classes of elements? Provide two physical properties for each class of elements.

_____

_____

_____

_____

_____

_____

_____

_____

**6 Infer** The atomic number of barium is 56. What do you know about the subatomic particles in an atom of this element?

_____

_____

_____

**7 Explain** Atoms contain positively charged protons and negatively charged electrons. Why does an ordinary atom have no charge?

_____

_____

_____

## Critical Thinking

Use this diagram to answer the questions below.

**Elements in Amazonite**

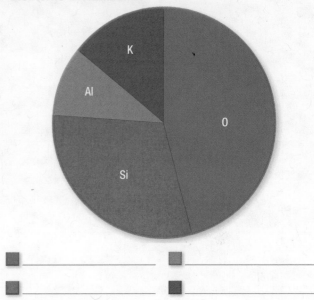

**8 Classify** Each color and chemical symbol on the chart represents an element. Write the name of each element next to the matching color box.

**9 Analyze** According to the chart, which element is most abundant in amazonite?

_____

_____

**10 Infer** Based on its chemical makeup, where do you think amazonite is found? Explain.

_____

_____

_____

**11 Synthesize** Thermal energy is generated in Earth's core and mantle. Do you think this heat stays within those layers, or can it be transferred to Earth's surface? Explain.

_____

_____

_____

# My Notes

# Unit 3 | Big Idea

Matter is described by its properties and may undergo changes.

### Lesson 1
**ESSENTIAL QUESTION**
**What properties define matter?**

Relate mass, weight, volume, and density to one another.

### Lesson 4
**ESSENTIAL QUESTION**
**How do pure substances and mixtures compare?**

Distinguish between pure substances and mixtures.

### Lesson 2
**ESSENTIAL QUESTION**
**What are physical and chemical properties of matter?**

Classify and compare substances based on their physical and chemical properties.

### Lesson 5
**ESSENTIAL QUESTION**
**What particles make up matter?**

Describe atoms and how the atoms of an element are alike.

### Lesson 3
**ESSENTIAL QUESTION**
**What are physical and chemical changes of matter?**

Distinguish between physical and chemical changes of matter.

## Connect ESSENTIAL QUESTIONS
Lessons 1 and 5

**1 Synthesize** There are countless different types of matter on Earth, yet this matter is made of the same handful of elements. How is this possible?

_____

_____

_____

_____

_____

_____

## Think Outside the Book

**2 Synthesize** Choose one of these activities to help synthesize what you have learned in this unit.

☐ Using what you learned in lessons 1, 2, 3, and 4, create an informative brochure to explain how matter can be classified by its physical and chemical properties. Include examples of both pure substances and mixtures.

☐ Using what you learned in lessons 1 and 4, create a demonstration that shows how the properties of matter can be used to separate substances in a mixture.

## Vocabulary

Check the box to show whether each statement is true or false.

| T | F | |
|---|---|---|
| ☐ | ☐ | **TEKS 6.6B** <br> 1 <u>Density</u> is anything that has mass and takes up space. |
| ☐ | ☐ | **TEKS 6.6A** <br> 2 A <u>physical property</u> can be measured without changing the identity of the substance. |
| ☐ | ☐ | 3 <u>Matter</u> is anything that has mass and takes up space. |
| ☐ | ☐ | 4 A <u>proton</u> is a negatively charged subatomic particle. |
| ☐ | ☐ | **TEKS 6.5A** <br> 5 Each element is a pure substance that cannot be broken down into simpler materials by ordinary means and is represented by a unique chemical symbol. |

## Key Concepts

Choose the letter of the best answer.

**TEKS 6.5D**

6 Trini adds 10 g of baking soda to 100 g of vinegar. The mixture begins to bubble. When the bubbling stops, Trini finds the mass of the resulting mixture. She determines its mass is 105 g.

| Before mixing | | After mixing |
|---|---|---|
| Mass, baking soda | Mass, vinegar | Mass, mixture |
| 10 g | 100 g | 105 g |

Why has the mass changed? (Hint: Step 1. Find the sum of the masses of the baking soda and the vinegar. Step 2. Compare that sum to the mass of the mixture. Step 3. Determine the cause of the difference.)

**A** A gas has formed and left the mixture.

**B** Vinegar evaporated during the experiment.

**C** Mixtures always are less massive than their parts.

**D** Mass was destroyed when vinegar reacted with baking soda.

TEKS 6.4A

**7** The instrument below is used to measure an object.

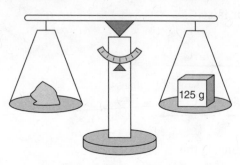

What is the instrument measuring?

**A** gravity

**B** weight

**C** density

**D** mass

TEKS 6.6A

**8** Luster, conductivity, and malleability are physical properties of metals. What makes these properties different from chemical properties?

**A** Physical properties relate to elements rather than compounds.

**B** Physical properties appear only after a chemical change occurs.

**C** Physical properties can be observed without attempting to change the identity of the substance.

**D** Physical properties describe elements in the solid state rather than in the liquid or gas state.

TEKS 6.3B

**9** Every atom has a nucleus and an electron cloud. The diagram below is a model of an atom.

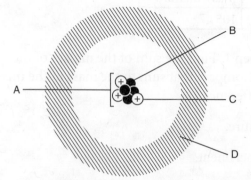

Which label points to a neutron?

**A** A

**B** B

**C** C

**D** D

Name _____

TEKS 6.5C

**10** Which of the following is a way in which elements and compounds are different?

    **A** Elements are pure substances, but compounds are not.

    **B** Compounds can be broken down by physical changes, but elements cannot.

    **C** Elements are made of identical atoms, whereas compounds are made of identical molecules.

    **D** A compound contains many different kinds of elements, whereas an element contains many different kinds of atoms.

## Gridded Response

Write your answer in the boxes, then bubble in the corresponding number in the grid below.

TEKS 6.4A

**11** A rock is dropped into a graduated cylinder filled with 35 mL of water.

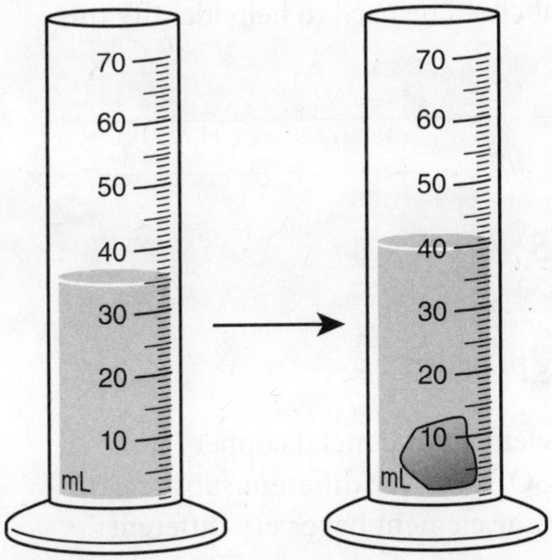

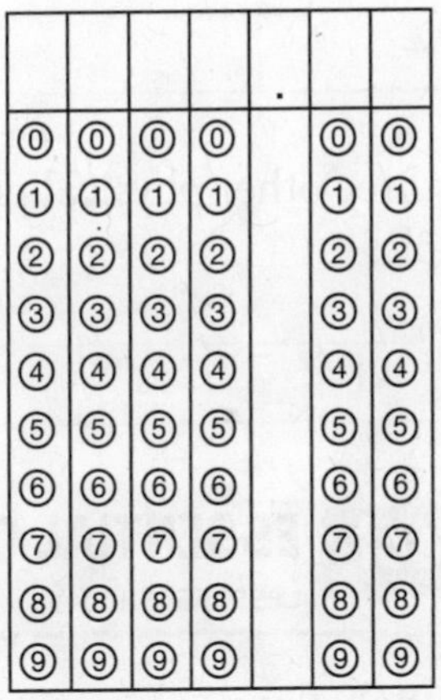

What is the volume of the rock? (Hint: 1 mL water = 1 $cm^3$ )

## Critical Thinking

Answer the following question in the space provided.

**TEKS** 6.6B

**12** An unknown substance has a volume of 2 cm³ and a mass of 38.6 grams.

| Material | Density (g/cm³) |
|----------|-----------------|
| water | 1.0 |
| aluminum | 2.7 |
| iron | 7.9 |
| silver | 10.5 |
| gold | 19.3 |

Find the density of the unknown sample. Then use the chart above to determine its identity.

_____

_____

_____

List three other physical properties that could be used to help identify this sample.

_____

_____

## Connect ESSENTIAL QUESTIONS
Lessons 2 and 5

Answer the following question in the space provided.

**13** Although they both contain the same element, the metal copper (Cu) and the compound copper sulfate ($CuSO_4$) are very different substances. Why can substances that contain the same element have very different properties?

_____

_____

_____

_____

_____

_____

# Energy, Motion, and Forces

## Big Idea

Energy is always conserved but can change from one form to another and can be transferred from one object to another or within a substance.

Machines are found everywhere—even in the skate park.

## What do you think?

Machines make work and play easier. Skateboards are complex machines made of simple machines. Can you identify two basic parts of this skateboard?

Simple machines make up complex machines.

## Unit 4
# Energy, Motion, and Forces

# CITIZEN SCIENCE

# A Day at the Races

Both simple and complex machines can make work easier and play more exciting. Creating a small-scale downhill racing machine is a fun way to learn about simple machines.

## 1 Think about It

**A** Investigate some ways to create a small-scale downhill racer with everyday objects. Make notes about your research.

_____

**B** Most downhill racers will have two axles and four wheels. Define *axle* and *wheel* below and explain what function each would serve in a racer.

_____

**C** Check out the recycling bin in your school, classroom, or home. Can you use any recyclable materials to make a downhill racer? (Safety note: Some materials are toxic or dangerous. Before you touch anything, ask your teacher.)

_____

## ② Ask a Question

What are some ways that you could make a downhill racer go faster? Do some research and write notes below.

_____

_____

_____

_____

_____

## ③ Make a Plan

Draw a sketch of a small-scale downhill racer that you would make. Label it, and note if any of the parts are reused or recyclable.

The downhill racer is traveling over 20 mph! Do you think the driver is frightened or exhilarated?

### Take It Home

With an adult, make the small-scale downhill racer you designed. Challenge the adult to design and help you make a different downhill racer. Conduct a race to find out which racer was faster. Think about how the design may affect speed.

# Lesson 1

# Introduction to Energy

**ESSENTIAL QUESTION**

## What is energy?

By the end of this lesson, you should be able to describe how energy is conserved through transformation between different forms.

The chemical energy contained in fireworks is transformed into sound, light, and heat when the fireworks shells explode.

**TEKS** **6.8A** compare and contrast potential and kinetic energy

**TEKS** **6.9C** demonstrate energy transformations such as energy in a flashlight battery changes from chemical energy to electrical energy to light energy

188

© Houghton Mifflin Harcourt Publishing Company • Image Credits: (bg) ©Thinkstock/Getty Images

## ✋ Lesson Labs

**Quick Labs**
• Setting Objects in Motion
• Conservation of Energy
• Bungee Jumping

**S.T.E.M. Lab**
• Designing a Simple Device

## Engage Your Brain

**1 Predict** Check T or F to show whether you think each statement is true or false.

**T   F**

☐   ☐   Energy can change from one form to another.

☐   ☐   An object can have only one type of energy at a time.

☐   ☐   If an object has energy, it must be moving.

☐   ☐   All energy travels in waves.

**2 Describe** Write a caption for this picture that includes the concept of sound energy.

_____

_____

_____

## ✏️ Active Reading

**3 Apply** The phrase *conservation of energy* has an everyday meaning. We speak of trying to conserve, or save, energy for environmental reasons. It also refers to a law of nature. Use context clues to write your own definition for the meaning of the *law of conservation of energy*.

**Example sentence**
According to the <u>law of conservation of energy</u>, when a rolling ball slows, the energy of the ball does not disappear. Instead, it changes to energy as heat generated from moving across the ground.

*law of conservation of energy:*

_____

_____

_____

_____

### Vocabulary Terms

• **energy**
• **kinetic energy**
• **potential energy**
• **mechanical energy**
• **energy transformation**
• **law of conservation of energy**

**4 Apply** As you learn the definition of each vocabulary term in this lesson, create your own definition or sketch to help you remember the meaning of the term.

# Get Energized!

© Houghton Mifflin Harcourt Publishing Company • Image Credits: ©Paul A. Souders/Corbis

## What are two types of energy?

In science, **energy** is the ability to cause change. Energy takes many different forms and has many different effects. There are two general types of energy: kinetic energy and potential energy.

### Kinetic Energy

**Kinetic energy** (kih•NET•ik EN•er•jee) is the energy of an object that is due to motion. All moving objects have kinetic energy. The amount of kinetic energy an object has depends on its mass and its speed. Kinetic energy increases as mass increases. Imagine that a bowling ball and a soccer ball roll across the floor at the same speed. The bowling ball has more kinetic energy than the soccer ball has because the bowling ball has a greater mass.

Kinetic energy also increases as speed increases. If two bowling balls with the same mass roll across the floor at different speeds, the faster ball will have the greater kinetic energy.

**Active Reading**

**5 Identify** As you read this page and the next, underline the factors that affect an object's kinetic and potential energy.

As the skater moves up the ramp, he gains height but loses speed. Some of his kinetic energy is converted back to potential energy. The rest of it is transferred as heat due to friction.

**D**

At the bottom of the ramp, the skater's kinetic energy is at its peak because he is going the fastest. His potential energy is at its lowest because he is closer to the ground than at any other point on the ramp.

**C**

## Potential Energy

**Potential energy** (puh•TEN•shuhl EN•er•jee) is the energy that an object has due to its position, condition, or chemical composition. A ball held above the ground has potential energy because the force of gravity can pull it to the ground. Potential energy that is the result of an object's position is called gravitational potential energy. Gravitational potential energy increases as the object's height or mass increases.

A change in condition can also affect potential energy. For example, stretching a rubber band increases its potential energy.

Chemical potential energy depends on chemical composition. As bonds break and new bonds form between atoms during a chemical change, energy can be released.

## Can objects have potential and kinetic energy at the same time?

An object can have both kinetic and potential energy. For example, the skater in the picture below has kinetic energy as he moves down the ramp. He has potential energy due to his position on the ramp. A flying bird has kinetic energy because of its speed and mass, and potential energy due to its height from the ground.

**6 Summarize** Compare and contrast potential energy and kinetic energy.

_____

_____

_____

_____

_____

_____

_____

At the top of the ramp, the skater has potential energy because gravity can pull him downward. He has no speed, so he has no kinetic energy.

**A**

As the skater moves closer to the ground, the decrease in potential energy is equal to the increase in his kinetic energy. As he rolls down the ramp, his potential energy decreases because his distance from the ground decreases. His kinetic energy increases because his speed increases.

**B**

**7 Analyze** Do you think that the skater has any gravitational potential energy at point C? Why?

_____

_____

_____

_____

_____

_____

_____

_____

Lesson 1 Introduction to Energy **191**

© Houghton Mifflin Harcourt Publishing Company • Image Credits: ©Paul A. Souders/Corbis

# In Perfect Form

## What forms can energy take?

Kinetic energy and potential energy are two types of energy that can come in many different forms. Some common forms of energy include mechanical, sound, electromagnetic, electrical, chemical, thermal, and nuclear energy. Energy is expressed in joules (J) (JOOLZ).

### Mechanical Energy

**Mechanical energy** is the sum of an object's kinetic energy and potential energy. Remember that kinetic energy is the energy of motion, and potential energy is the energy of position. So mechanical energy is the energy of position and motion. A moving car has mechanical energy. An object's mechanical energy can be all potential energy, all kinetic energy, or a combination of potential and kinetic energy.

### Sound Energy

Sound energy is kinetic energy caused by the vibration of particles in a medium such as steel, water, or air. As the particles vibrate, they transfer the sound energy to other particles. The sound a guitar makes is caused by the vibrations of its strings transferring energy to the air around it. You hear the sound because special structures in your ears detect the vibrations of the particles in the air.

A _____

 **Visualize It!**

**8 Identify** Label the three forms of energy represented in this image.

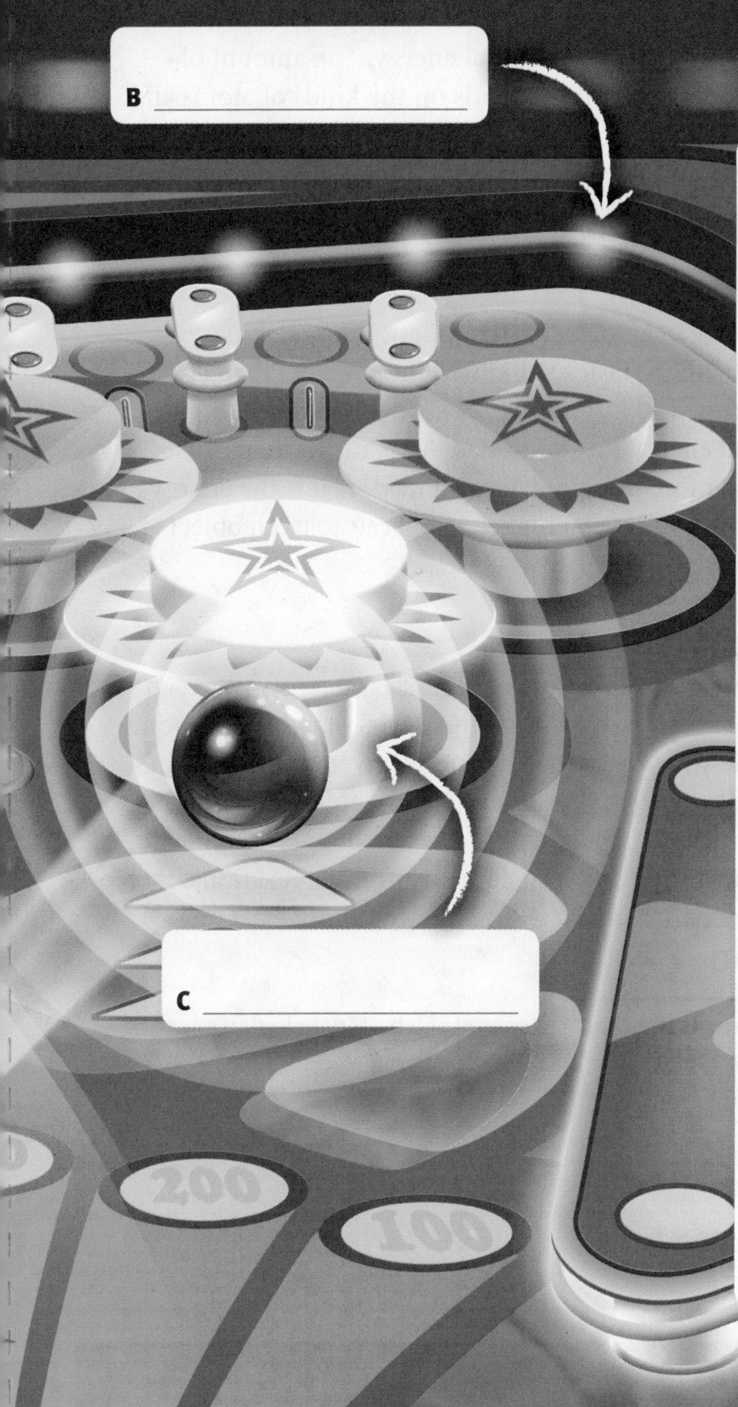

**B** _____

## Electromagnetic Energy

Electromagnetic energy is transmitted through space in the form of electromagnetic waves. These waves are caused by the vibration of electrically charged particles. Electromagnetic waves include visible light, x-rays, and microwaves. X-rays are high-energy waves used by doctors and dentists to look at your bones. Microwaves can be used to cook food or to transmit cellular telephone calls. The sun releases a large amount of electromagnetic energy, some of which reaches Earth as radiant energy.

## Electrical Energy

Electrical energy is the energy that results from the position or motion of charged particles. The electrical energy that powers the lights overhead is associated with negatively charged particles moving in a wire. The wire also has positively charged particles that do not move. The negatively charged particles move within the wire and create an electric current.

**C** _____

**9 Compare** How does electrical energy differ from electromagnetic energy?

_____
_____
_____

**10 Infer** Would you expect to detect electrical energy if you played the pinball game shown in the picture? Explain your answer.

_____
_____
_____
_____
_____

## Chemical Energy

Chemical energy is a form of potential energy. The amount of chemical energy in a molecule depends on the kinds of atoms and their arrangement. During a chemical change, bonds between these atoms break, and new bonds form. The foods you eat, batteries, and matches are sources of chemical energy.

## Thermal Energy

The thermal energy of an object is the kinetic energy of its particles. Particles move faster at higher temperatures than at lower temperatures. The faster the molecules in an object move, the more thermal energy the object has. Also, the more particles an object has, the more thermal energy it has. Heat is the energy transferred from an object at a higher temperature to an object at a lower temperature.

## Nuclear Energy

The nucleus of an atom is the source of nuclear energy. When an atom's nucleus breaks apart, or when the nuclei of two small atoms join together, energy is released. The energy given off by the sun comes from nuclear energy. In the sun, hydrogen nuclei join to make a helium nucleus. This reaction gives off a huge amount of energy. The sun's light and heat come from these reactions. Without nuclear energy from the sun, life would not exist on Earth.

**Active Reading**

**11 Identify** As you read, underline the source of energy in a chemical reaction.

**12 Synthesize** Why is the chemical energy of a battery potential energy and not kinetic energy?

_____

_____

_____

_____

Solar flares are explosions of hot gases on the sun. They can release electromagnetic energy that reaches all the way to Earth.

# Space Weather and Technology

Every time you turn on a TV or use a cell phone, you may be affected by the "weather" in space. Space weather includes any activity happening in space that might affect Earth's environment, such as solar flares. A solar flare can release a million times more energy than the largest earthquake. It is an intense release of electromagnetic energy as a burst of radiation.

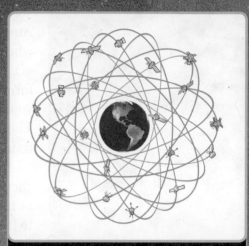

### Space Weather Can Damage Satellites
Many of the satellites orbiting Earth provide telephone service. Damage from space weather can interrupt phone communications.

### Space Weather Can Affect Navigation
Space weather can also cause navigation errors by interrupting satellite signals to Global Positioning System (GPS) receivers.

### Space Weather Can Ground Planes
Auroras like the one shown here are caused by electrically charged particles of the solar winds hitting Earth's magnetic field. This activity can interrupt airplane communications, forcing the planes to land.

## Extend

Inquiry

**13 Identify** What type of energy is monitored by scientists forecasting future space weather?

**14 Infer** Why is space weather a bigger concern now than it was in the past?

**15 Research** How do scientists forecast space weather? Why?

# Transformers

## What is an energy transformation?

An **energy transformation** (EN•er•jee trans•fohr•MAY•shuhn) occurs when energy changes from one form into another form. Any form of energy can change into any other form of energy. Often, one form of energy changes into more than one form. When you rub your hands together, you hear a sound, and your hands get warm. This demonstrates the mechanical energy of your moving hands transforming into both sound energy and energy as heat.

Another example of an energy transformation is when chemical energy is converted in the body. Why is eating breakfast so important? Eating breakfast gives your body the energy needed to help you start your day. Chemical potential energy is stored in the food you eat. Your body breaks down the components of the food to access the energy stored in them. Some of this energy is then changed to the kinetic energy that allows you to move and play. Some of the chemical energy is converted into heat energy that keeps your body warm.

© Houghton Mifflin Harcourt Publishing Company • Image Credits: (bg) ©SuperStock Rf/SuperStock

### Visualize It!

Some examples of energy transformation are illustrated in this flashlight. Follow the captions to learn how energy is transformed into the light energy that you rely on when you turn on a flashlight.

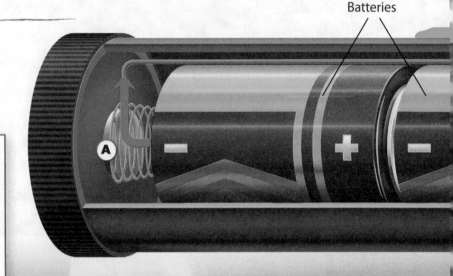

Batteries

(A) *The chemical energy from the batteries is transformed into electrical energy.*

**16 Describe** Give two examples of other devices in which the chemical energy in a battery is transformed into electrical energy.

_____

_____

_____

# Is energy conserved?

A closed system is a group of objects that transfers energy only to one another. For example, a roller coaster can be considered a closed system if it includes everything involved, such as the track, the cars, and the air around them. Energy is conserved in all closed systems. The **law of conservation of energy** states that energy cannot be created or destroyed. It can only change forms. All of the different forms of energy in a closed system always add up to the same total amount of energy. It does not matter how many energy transformations take place.

For example, on a roller coaster some mechanical energy gets transformed into sound and heat energy as the roller coaster goes down a hill. The total of the coaster's mechanical energy at the bottom of the hill, the extra heat energy, and the sound energy is the same as the original amount of mechanical energy. In other words, total energy is conserved.

**Active Reading** **17 Relate** How are energy transformations related to the law of conservation of energy?

_____

_____

_____

_____

© Houghton Mifflin Harcourt Publishing Company • Image Credits: (bg) ©SuperStock RF/SuperStock

**18 Apply** Have you ever thought about how an MP3 player works? What form of energy is used to power an MP3 player? What form of energy do you use from an MP3 player? Can you think of any other forms of energy that may be used inside of an MP3 player?

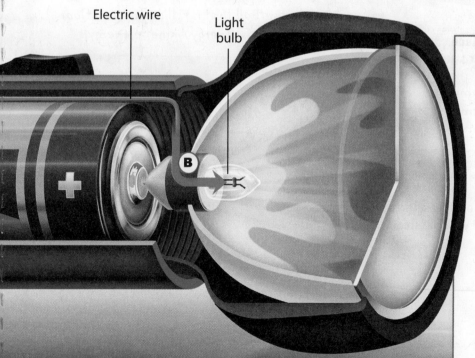

Electric wire

Light bulb

B

**B** The electrical energy in the wire is transformed into light in the light bulb. Some of the electrical energy is also transformed into energy as heat.

**19 Describe** Give another example of electrical energy being transformed into light.

_____

_____

_____

_____

_____

# Visual Summary

To complete this summary, circle the correct word. Then use the key below to check your answers. You can use this page to review the main concepts of the lesson.

## Introduction to Energy

Energy is the ability to cause change. Energy cannot be created or destroyed.

**20** The total energy in a closed system remains the same / changes as energy changes forms.

Potential energy results from an object's position, composition, or condition, and kinetic energy results from an object's motion.

**21** A basketball that is balanced on the rim of a basketball hoop has potential energy / kinetic energy.

**22** A basketball that is rolling across a floor has potential energy / kinetic energy.

Energy transformation takes place when energy changes from one form to another.

**23** When a candle is burned, some chemical energy is transformed into nuclear / heat energy.

**24 Apply** Identify and give examples of at least three types of energy you see being used as you look around your classroom.

# Lesson Review

## Vocabulary

Draw a line to connect the following terms to their definitions.

1  kinetic energy

**A**  energy of position

2  mechanical energy

**B**  sum of energy of motion and energy of position

3  potential energy

**C**  energy of motion

## Key Concepts

4  **Describe**  What happens to the kinetic energy of a snowball as it rolls across the lawn and gains mass?

_____

_____

5  **Relate**  How is the sun related to nuclear, electromagnetic, and heat energy?

_____

_____

_____

_____

_____

_____

6  **Apply**  When a person uses an iron to remove the wrinkles from a shirt, why does heat travel from the iron to the shirt?

_____

_____

_____

7  **Explain**  What determines the amount of chemical energy a substance has?

_____

_____

_____

## Critical Thinking

Use the picture below to answer the following questions.

8  **Identify**  Name at least three types of energy associated with the microwave.

_____

_____

9  **Hypothesize**  How is electromagnetic energy from the microwave transformed into heat energy?

_____

_____

_____

_____

10  **Infer**  Explain the law of conservation of energy.

_____

_____

_____

_____

_____

# My Notes

Lesson **2**

# Temperature

**ESSENTIAL QUESTION**

## How is temperature related to kinetic energy?

By the end of this lesson, you should be able to relate the temperature of a substance to the kinetic energy of its particles.

**TEKS** **6.9A** investigate methods of thermal energy transfer, including conduction, convection, and radiation

**TEKS** **6.9B** verify through investigations that thermal energy moves in a predictable pattern from warmer to cooler until all the substances attain the same temperature such as an ice cube melting

What does it mean to be hot or cold? You can tell that this environment is cold because there is ice and because the person is in a hat and coat.

© Houghton Mifflin Harcourt Publishing Company • Image Credits: ©Steve Allen/Photo Researchers, Inc.

**200** Unit 4 Energy, Motion, and Forces

## Lesson Labs

**Quick Labs**
- Exploring Temperature
- Understanding Temperature Scales

## Engage Your Brain

**1 Predict** Check T or F to show whether you think each statement is true or false.

| T | F | |
|---|---|---|
| ☐ | ☐ | Solids and liquids are made of particles, but gases are made of air, which is not made of particles. |
| ☐ | ☐ | Kinetic energy is the energy of motion. |
| ☐ | ☐ | Kinetic energy depends on mass and speed. |

**2 Illustrate** Think about a time when you were very cold. Then draw a picture of a time when you were very hot. Write a caption about the differences between the two situations.

## Active Reading

**3 Synthesize** Many English words have their roots in other languages. Use the Greek words below to make an educated guess about the meaning of the word *thermometer*. A context sentence is provided for help. Then, write a sentence using the word correctly.

| Greek word | Meaning |
|---|---|
| *thermos* | warm |
| *metron* | to measure |

**Example sentence**
This thermometer indicates that it is 72 °F in this room.

**Define thermometer:**

**Sentence with thermometer:**

### Vocabulary Terms

- **kinetic theory of matter**
- **temperature**
- **degree**
- **thermometer**

**4 Identify** This list contains the key terms you'll learn in this lesson. As you read, circle the definition of each term.

# Particle Party

## What is the kinetic theory of matter?

All matter is made of atoms. These particles are always moving, even if it doesn't look like they are. The **kinetic theory of matter** states that all of the particles that make up matter are constantly in motion. Because the particles are in motion, they have kinetic energy. The faster the particles are moving, the more kinetic energy they have.

While the particles of matter are constantly moving, the particles move in different directions and at different speeds. This motion is random. Therefore, the individual particles of matter have different amounts of kinetic energy. The average kinetic energy of all these particles takes into account their different random movements. As seen in this picture, solids, liquids, and gases have different average kinetic energies.

This bridge is a solid, so its particles are close together and vibrate.

In this hot pool, the liquid particles are moving around.

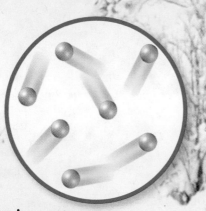

The particles in the gas in the air are far apart and moving quickly.

The particles in this cold river water are moving freely.

# How do particles move in solids, liquids, and gases?

The kinetic theory of matter explains the motion of particles in solids, liquids, and gases.

- The particles in a solid, such as concrete, are not free to move around very much. They vibrate back and forth in the same position and are held tightly together by forces of attraction.
- The particles in a liquid, such as water in a pool, move much more freely than particles in a solid. They are constantly sliding around and tumbling over each other as they move.
- In a gas, such as the air around you, particles are far apart and move around at high speeds. Particles collide with one another, but otherwise they do not interact much.

**Active Reading** **5 Describe** In your own words, describe the difference between the movement of particles in liquids and the movement of particles in gases.

_____

_____

_____

_____

## Visualize It!

**6 Illustrate** Locate another solid, liquid, or gas in this photo. Sketch a representation of the particles that make up the solid, liquid, or gas. Make sure to indicate how fast you think the particles might be moving based on temperature. Then, write a caption describing the particle movement.

_____

_____

_____

_____

# Mercury Rising

## How does temperature relate to kinetic energy?

**Temperature** (TEM•per•uh•chur) is a measure of the average kinetic energy of all the particles in an object. In the picture on the previous page, the particle diagrams for two different liquids are shown. For the colder liquid, the particles are moving slower. For the warmer liquid, the particles are moving faster. If an iron is hot, the particles in the solid are vibrating very fast and have a high average kinetic energy. If the iron has a low temperature, the particles in the solid are vibrating more slowly and have a lower average kinetic energy.

*Absolute zero* is the temperature at which the motion of particles stops. It is not possible to actually reach absolute zero, though temperatures very close to absolute zero have been reached in laboratories.

## How is temperature measured?

Suppose you hear on the radio that the temperature outside is 30 degrees. Do you need to wear a warm coat to spend the day outside? The answer depends on the temperature scale being used. There are three common temperature scales, all of which measure the average kinetic energy of particles. These scales are called Celsius, Fahrenheit, and Kelvin. However, 30 degrees on one scale is quite different from 30 degrees on the other scales.

To establish a temperature scale, two known values and the number of units between the values are needed. The freezing and boiling points of pure water are often used as the standard values. These points are always the same under the same conditions, and they are easy to reproduce. In the Celsius and Fahrenheit scales, temperature is measured in units called degrees. **Degrees** (°) are equally spaced units between two points. The space between degrees can vary from scale to scale. In the Kelvin scale, no degree sign is used. Instead, the unit is just called a kelvin. Temperature is measured using an instrument called a **thermometer**.

**Active Reading** **7 Explain** How does a substance's temperature change when the average kinetic energy of its particles increases? When it decreases?

_____

_____

_____

**8 Produce** Write a story about someone who travels from one extreme temperature to another. Make sure to talk about how your character adjusts to the change in temperature. How are the character's daily activities or decisions affected?

## Celsius Scale

The temperature scale most commonly used around the world, and often used by scientists, is the Celsius (SEL•see•uhs) scale (°C). This scale was developed in the 1740s by Anders Celsius. On the Celsius scale, pure water freezes at 0 °C and boils at 100 °C, so there are 100 degrees—100 equal units—between these two temperatures.

## Fahrenheit Scale

The scale used most commonly in the United States for measuring temperature is the Fahrenheit scale (°F). It was developed in the early 1700s by Gabriel Fahrenheit. On the Fahrenheit scale, pure water freezes at 32 °F and boils at 212 °F. Thus, there are 180 degrees—180 equal units—between the freezing point and the boiling point of water.

## Kelvin Scale

A temperature scale used commonly by physicists is the Kelvin scale. This scale was not developed until the 20th century. The equal units in the Kelvin scale are called kelvins, not degrees. On the kelvin scale, pure water freezes at 273 K and boils at 373 K. There are 100 kelvins—100 equal units—between these two temperatures. The lowest temperature on the Kelvin scale is absolute zero, or 0 K.

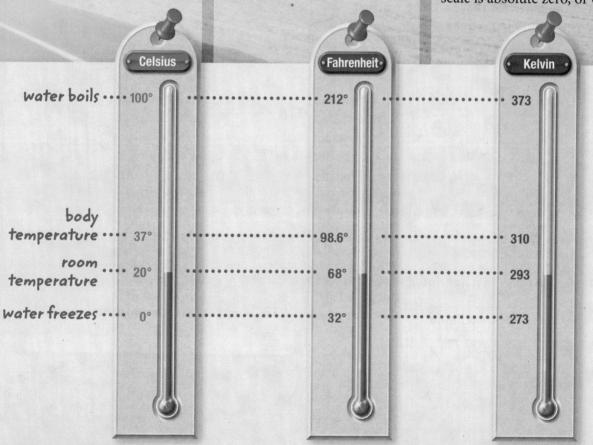

| | Celsius | Fahrenheit | Kelvin |
|---|---|---|---|
| water boils | 100° | 212° | 373 |
| body temperature | 37° | 98.6° | 310 |
| room temperature | 20° | 68° | 293 |
| water freezes | 0° | 32° | 273 |

**9 Identify** What is body temperature in the Celsius scale? In the Fahrenheit scale? In the Kelvin scale?

_____

_____

**10 Apply** The water in swimming pools is typically about 80 °F. Mark this temperature on the Fahrenheit thermometer above. Estimate what temperature this is in the Celsius and Kelvin scales.

_____

_____

# Visual Summary

To complete this summary, fill in the blanks with the correct word. Then use the key below to check your answers. You can use this page to review the main concepts of the lesson.

## Temperature

Temperature is a measure of the average kinetic energy of all the particles in an object. Temperature is measured using one of three scales: Celsius, Fahrenheit, or Kelvin.

Fahrenheit

212°

98.6°

68°

32°

All of the particles that make up matter are constantly in motion.

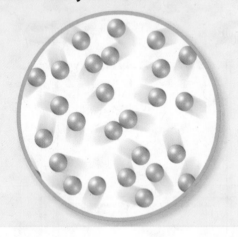

11 The particles in a hot liquid move _____ than the particles in a cold liquid.

12 Temperature is measured using a _____.

13 **Infer** If a puddle of water is frozen, do particles in the ice have kinetic energy? Explain.

# Lesson Review

## Vocabulary

For each pair of terms, write a sentence using both words that demonstrates the definition of each word.

**1** Kinetic theory of matter and temperature

_____

_____

_____

_____

_____

**2** Thermometer and degree

_____

_____

_____

_____

_____

## Key Concepts

**3 Relate** Describe the relationship between temperature and kinetic energy.

_____

_____

_____

_____

**4 Apply** Particles in a warmer substance have a _____ average kinetic energy than particles in the substance when it is cooler.

**5 Identify** What are the three scales used to measure temperature? What are the units of each scale?

_____

_____

_____

## Critical Thinking

Use the art below to answer the following questions.

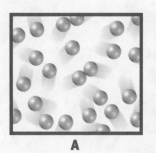 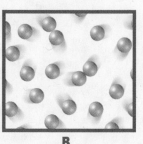

A                         B

**6 Observe** Which illustration represents the substance at a higher temperature? Explain.

_____

_____

_____

**7 Predict** What would happen to the particles in illustration A if the substance were chilled? What would happen if the particles in illustration B were warmed?

_____

_____

_____

_____

_____

**8 Apply** Using your knowledge of the difference between the three different temperature scales, what do you think would happen if a human's body temperature was 98.6 °C? Why do doctors worry more about a fever of a couple of degrees Celsius than a fever of a couple of degrees Fahrenheit?

_____

_____

_____

_____

# My Notes

# Thermal Energy and Heat

**ESSENTIAL QUESTION**

## What is the relationship between heat and temperature?

By the end of this lesson, you should be able to analyze the relationship between heat, temperature, and thermal energy.

The Afar Depression, in Eastern Africa, is one of the hottest places on Earth. In the summer, temperatures average over 100 °F!

**TEKS** **6.9A** investigate methods of thermal energy transfer, including conduction, convection, and radiation

**TEKS** **6.9B** verify through investigations that thermal energy moves in a predictable pattern from warmer to cooler until all the substances attain the same temperature such as an ice cube melting

## Lesson Labs

**Quick Labs**
- Simple Heat Engine
- Observing the Transfer of Energy
- Exploring Thermal Conductivity

**Field Lab**
- Building a Solar Cooker

## Engage Your Brain

**1 Describe** Fill in the blanks with the words that you think correctly complete the following sentences.

When you put your hands on a cold object, like a glass of ice water, your hands become

_____ The glass of water

becomes _____ if you

leave your hands on it for a long time. If you

leave the glass of ice water out in the sun, the

ice will start to _____

**2 Describe** Write your own caption for this photo.

_____

_____

_____

_____

## Active Reading

**3 Apply** Many scientific words, such as *conductor*, also have everyday meanings. Use context clues to write your own definition for each meaning of the word *conductor*.

**Example sentence**
That school's band is very good because its <u>conductor</u> is a great teacher.

conductor:

_____

_____

**Example sentence**
That metal spoon is a good <u>conductor</u>, so it will get hot if you put it into boiling soup.

conductor:

_____

_____

### Vocabulary Terms

- **thermal energy**
- **heat**
- **calorie**
- **conduction**
- **conductor**
- **insulator**
- **convection**
- **radiation**

**4 Apply** As you learn the definition of each vocabulary term in this lesson, create your own definition or sketch to help you remember the meaning of the term.

There are more water molecules in this lake than in the glass of water on the right.

# Thermal,

## What is thermal energy?

**Thermal energy** is the total kinetic energy of all particles in a substance. In the SI system, thermal energy is measured in joules (J). Remember that temperature is not energy, but it does give a measure of the average kinetic energy of all the particles in a substance. If you have two identical glasses of water and one is at a higher temperature than the other, the particles in the hotter water have a higher average kinetic energy. The water at a higher temperature will have a higher amount of thermal energy.

## What is the difference between thermal energy and temperature?

Temperature and thermal energy are different from each other. Temperature is related to the average kinetic energy of particles, while thermal energy is the total kinetic energy of all the particles. A glass of water can have the same temperature as a lake, but the lake has much more thermal energy because the lake contains many more water molecules.

After you put ice cubes into a pitcher of lemonade, energy is transferred from the warmer lemonade to the colder ice. The lemonade's thermal energy decreases and the ice's thermal energy increases. Because the particles in the lemonade have transferred some of their energy to the particles in the ice, the average kinetic energy of the particles in the lemonade decreases. Thus, the temperature of the lemonade decreases.

**Active Reading** **5 Explain** What are two factors that determine the thermal energy of a substance?

_____

_____

# Under Where?

There are fewer water molecules in this glass than in the lake.

**6 Apply** For each object pair in the table below, circle the object that has more thermal energy. Assume that both objects are at the same temperature.

| bowl of soup | small balloon | tiger |
|---|---|---|
| pot of soup | large balloon | house cat |

# Heat It Up!

## What is heat?

You might think of the word *heat* as having to do with things that feel hot. But heat also has to do with things that feel cold. Heat causes objects to feel hot or cold or to get hot or cold under the right conditions. You probably use the word *heat* every day to mean different things. However, in science, **heat** is the energy transferred from an object at a higher temperature to an object at a lower temperature.

When two objects at different temperatures come into contact, energy is always transferred from the object that has the higher temperature to the object that has the lower temperature. Energy in the form of heat always flows from hot to cold. For example, if you put an ice cube into a glass of water, energy is transferred from the warmer water to the colder ice cube.

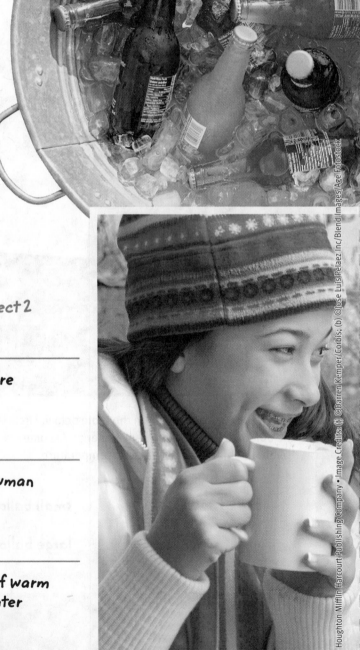

Energy in the form of heat flows from the warm drinks to the cold ice. The ice melts.

---

**7 Apply** For each object pair in the table below, draw an arrow in the direction in which energy in the form of heat would flow.

| Object 1 | Direction of heat flow | Object 2 |
|---|---|---|
| metal rod | | fire |
| hat | | snowman |
| ice cube | | glass of warm water |

© Houghton Mifflin Harcourt Publishing Company • Image Credits: (t) ©Darren Kemper/Corbis; (b) ©Jose Luis Pelaez Inc/Blend Images/Age Fotostock

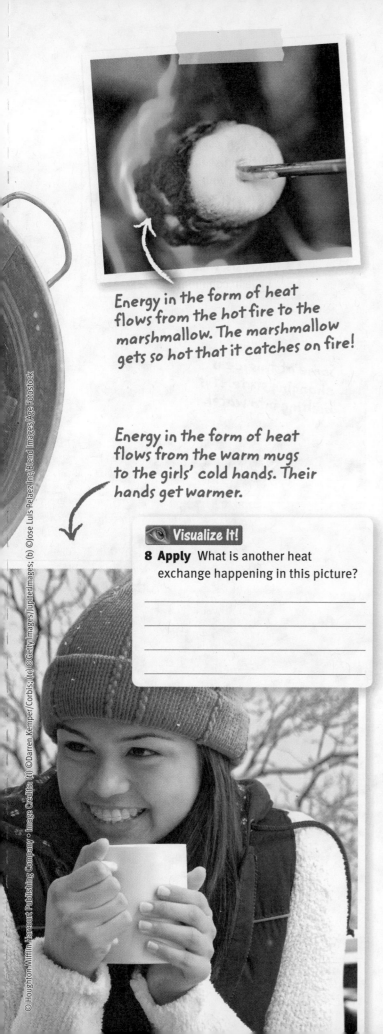

Energy in the form of heat flows from the hot fire to the marshmallow. The marshmallow gets so hot that it catches on fire!

Energy in the form of heat flows from the warm mugs to the girls' cold hands. Their hands get warmer.

**Visualize It!**

**8 Apply** What is another heat exchange happening in this picture?

_____

_____

_____

# How is heat measured?

Heat is measured in two ways. One way is the calorie (cal). One **calorie** is equal to the amount of energy needed to raise the temperature of 1 g of water by 1 °C. Heat can also be measured in joules (J) because heat is a form of energy. One calorie is equal to 4.18 J.

You probably think of calories in terms of food. However, in nutrition, one Calorie—written with a capital C—is actually one kilocalorie, or 1,000 calories. This means that one Calorie (Cal) contains enough energy to raise the temperature of 1 kg of water by 1 °C. Each Calorie in food contains 1,000 cal of energy.

To find out how many Calories are in an apple, the apple is burned inside an instrument called a calorimeter. A thermometer measures the increase in temperature, which is used to calculate how much energy is released. This amount is the number of Calories.

# How is heat related to thermal energy?

Adding or removing heat from a substance will affect its temperature and thermal energy. Heat, however, is not the same as thermal energy and temperature. These are properties of a substance. Heat is the energy involved when these properties change.

Think of what happens when two objects at different temperatures come into contact. Energy as heat flows from the object at the higher temperature to the object at the lower temperature. When both objects come to the same temperature, no more energy as heat flows. Just because the temperature of the two objects is the same does not mean they have the same thermal energy. One object may be larger than the other and thus have more particles in motion.

**Active Reading** **9 Relate** What will happen if two objects at different temperatures come into contact?

_____

_____

_____

# How can heat affect the state of an object?

The matter that makes up a frozen juice bar is the same whether the juice bar is frozen or has melted. The matter is just in a different form, or state. Remember that the kinetic theory of matter states that the particles that make up matter move around at different speeds. The state of a substance depends on the speed of its particles. Adding energy in the form of heat to a substance may result in a change of state. The added energy may cause the bonds between particles to break. This is what allows the state to change. Adding energy in the form of heat to a chunk of glacier may cause the ice to melt into water. Removing energy in the form of heat from a substance may also result in a change of state.

**Active Reading** **11 Predict** What are two ways to change the state of a substance?

_____

_____

**Think Outside the Book** Inquiry

**10 Compare** Have you ever needed to touch a very hot object? What did you use to touch it without burning yourself? Make a list. Have you ever needed to protect yourself from being cold? What sorts of things did you use? Make a list. Now, looking at the two lists, what do the things have in common?

Some of this ice is changing state. It is melting into water.

How do polar bears stay warm?

© Houghton Mifflin Harcourt Publishing Company • Image Credits: ©Arcticphoto /Alamy

# Keep Your Cool

## What is conduction?

There are three main ways to transfer energy as heat: conduction, convection, and radiation. **Conduction** is the transfer of energy as heat from one substance to another through direct contact. It occurs any time that objects at different temperatures come into contact with each other. The average kinetic energy of particles in the warmer object is greater than the average kinetic energy of the particles in the cooler object. As the particles collide, some of the kinetic energy of the particles in the warmer object is transferred to the cooler object. As long as the objects are in contact, conduction continues until the temperatures of the objects are equal.

Conduction can also occur within a single object. In this case, energy in the form of heat is transferred from the warmer part of the object to the cooler part of the object. Imagine you put a metal spoon into a cup of hot cocoa. Energy will be conducted from the warm end of the spoon to the cool end until the temperature of the entire spoon is the same.

## Conductors

Some materials transfer the kinetic energy of particles better than others. A **conductor** is a material that transfers heat very well. Metals are typically good conductors. You know that when one end of a metal object gets hot, the other end quickly becomes hot as well. Consider pots or pans that have metal handles. A metal handle becomes too hot to touch soon after the pan is placed on a hot stove.

## Insulators

An **insulator** (IN•suh•lay•ter) is a material that is a poor conductor of heat. Some examples of insulators are wood, paper, and plastic foam. Plastic foam is a good insulator because it contains many small spaces that are filled with air. A plastic foam cup will not easily transfer energy in the form of heat by conduction. That is why plastic foam is often used to keep hot drinks hot. Think about the metal pan handle mentioned above. It can be dangerous to have handles get hot so quickly. Instead, pot handles are often made of an insulator, such as wood or plastic. Although a plastic handle will also get hot when the pot is on the stove, it takes a much longer time for it to get hot than it would for a metal handle.

---

**12 Classify** Decide whether each object below is a conductor or an insulator. Then check the correct box.

| Flannel shirt | ☐ Conductor |
| | ☐ Insulator |
| Iron skillet | ☐ Conductor |
| | ☐ Insulator |
| Copper pipe | ☐ Conductor |
| | ☐ Insulator |
| Oven mitt | ☐ Conductor |
| | ☐ Insulator |

This is a photo of polar bear hair magnified about 350 times! Notice that it is hollow inside. The air inside is a good insulator.

## What is convection?

Energy in the form of heat can also be transferred through the movement of gases or liquids. **Convection** (kuhn•VEK•shuhn) is the transfer of energy as heat by the movement of a liquid or gas. In most substances, as temperature increases, the density of the liquid or gas decreases. Convection occurs when a cooler, denser mass of a gas or liquid replaces a warmer, less dense mass of a gas or liquid by pushing it upward.

When you boil water in a pot, the water moves in roughly circular patterns because of convection. The water at the bottom of the pot gets hot because there is a source of heat at the bottom. As the water heats, it becomes less dense. The warmer water rises through the denser, cooler water above it. At the surface, the warm water begins to cool. The particles move closer together, making the water denser. The cooler water then sinks back to the bottom, is heated again, and the cycle repeats. This cycle causes a circular motion of liquids or gases. The motion is due to density differences that result from temperature differences. The motion is called a *convection current*.

## What is radiation?

Radiation is another way in which heat can be transferred. **Radiation** is the transfer of energy by electromagnetic waves. Some examples of electromagnetic waves include visible light, microwaves, and infrared light. The sun is the most significant source of radiation that you experience on a daily basis. However, all objects—even you—emit radiation and release energy.

When radiation is emitted from one object and then absorbed by another, the result is often a transfer of heat. Like conduction and convection, radiation can transfer heat from warmer to cooler objects. However, radiation differs from conduction and convection in a very significant way. Radiation can travel through empty space, as it does when it moves from the sun to Earth.

**Active Reading**

**13 Identify** As you read, underline examples of heat transfer.

This pot of boiling water shows how convection currents move.

**14 Classify** Fill in the blanks in the chart below.

| Example | Conduction, Convection, or Radiation |
|---|---|
| When you put some food in the microwave, it gets hot. | |
| | Conduction |
| A heater on the first floor of the school makes the air on the second floor warm. | |

# Practical Uses of Radiation

Do you think that you could cook your food using the energy from the sun? Using a device called a solar cooker, you could! A solar cooker works by concentrating the radiation from the sun into a small area using mirrors. Solar cookers aren't just fun to use—they also help some people eat clean food!

### As a hobby
This woman demonstrates how her solar cooker works. Many people like to use solar cookers because they do not require any fuel. They also do not release any emissions that are harmful to the planet.

### In a refugee camp
This woman, who lives in a refugee camp in Sudan, is making tea with water that she boiled in a solar cooker. For many people living far from electricity or a source of clean water, a solar cooker provides a cheap and portable way to sterilize their water. This helps to prevent disease.

## Extend

Inquiry

**15 Identify** Two examples of radiation are shown in the photos above. What is the source of the radiation in the examples?

**16 Relate** Research other places throughout the world where solar cookers are being used.

**17 Produce** Explain how solar cookers are useful to society by doing one of the following:
- Make a solar cooker and demonstrate how it works.
- Write a story about a family who uses a solar cooker to stay healthy and safe.

# Visual Summary

To complete this summary, circle the correct word or phrase. Then use the key below to check your answers. You can use this page to review the main concepts of the lesson.

**Thermal energy is the total kinetic energy of all particles in a substance.**

18 If two objects are at the same temperature, the one with more / fewer / the same amount of particles will have a higher thermal energy.

**Heat is the energy transferred from an object at a higher temperature to an object at a lower temperature.**

19 Heat always flows from cold to hot / hot to cold / left to right.

**Heat**

**Heat can change the state of a substance.**

20 Adding heat to an object causes bonds between particles to form / break / combine. This is what allows the state change.

**There are three main ways to transfer energy as heat: conduction, convection, and radiation.**

conduction

convection

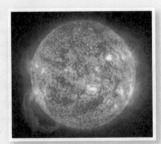

radiation

21 Conduction is the transfer of energy from a warmer object to a cooler object through a gas / empty space / direct contact.

22 Energy from the sun travels to Earth through conduction / convection / radiation.

Answers: 18 more; 19 hot to cold; 20 break; 21 direct contact; 22 radiation

23 **Conclude** Suppose you are outside on a hot day and you move into the shade of a tree. Which form of energy transfer are you avoiding? Explain.

# Lesson Review

## Vocabulary

In your own words, define the following terms.

**1** heat

_____

_____

_____

**2** thermal energy

_____

_____

_____

**3** conduction

_____

_____

_____

**4** convection

_____

_____

_____

**5** radiation

_____

_____

_____

## Key Concepts

**6 Compare** What is the difference between heat and temperature?

_____

_____

_____

_____

**7 Predict** If two objects at different temperatures are in contact with each other, what happens to their temperatures?

_____

_____

_____

_____

Use this photo to answer the following questions.

**8 Classify** Which type of energy transfer is occurring at each lettered area?

A _____

B _____

C _____

## Critical Thinking

**9 Synthesize** Describe the relationships among temperature, heat, and thermal energy.

_____

_____

_____

_____

**10 Synthesize** Do you think that solids can undergo convection? Explain.

_____

_____

_____

_____

_____

# My Notes

# Motion and Speed

**ESSENTIAL QUESTION**

## How are distance, time, and speed related?

By the end of this lesson, you should be able to analyze how distance, time, and speed are related.

The personal watercraft in this photo is going fast. How can we measure how fast it is going?

**TEKS** **6.8B** identify and describe the changes in position, direction, and speed of an object when acted upon by unbalanced forces

**TEKS** **6.8C** calculate average speed using distance and time measurements

**TEKS** **6.8D** measure and graph changes in motion

## Lesson Labs

**Quick Labs**
- Investigate Changing Positions
- Create a Distance-Time Graph

**S.T.E.M. Lab**
- Investigate Average Speed

## Engage Your Brain

**1 Predict** Circle the correct words in the paragraph below to make true statements.

A dog usually moves faster than a bug. That means that if I watch them move for one minute, then the dog would have traveled a *greater/smaller* distance than the bug. However, a car usually goes *faster/slower* than a dog. If the car and the dog both traveled to the end of the road, then the *car/dog* would get there first.

**2 Explain** Draw or sketch something that you might see move. Write a caption that answers the following questions: How would you describe its motion? Is it moving at a constant speed, or does it speed up and slow down?

## Active Reading

**3 Define** Fill in the blank with the word that best completes the following sentences.

If an object changes its position, then it is

_____

The speed of a car describes

_____

_____

### Vocabulary Terms
- position
- reference point
- motion
- speed
- vector
- velocity

**4 Apply** As you learn the definition of each vocabulary term in this lesson, make your own definition or sketch to help you remember the meaning of the term.

# Location, location,

## How can you describe the location of an object?

Have you ever gotten lost while looking for a specific place? If so, you probably know that the description of the location can be very important. Imagine that you are trying to describe your location to a friend. How would you explain where you are? You need two pieces of information: a position and a reference point.

### With a Position

**Position** describes the location of an object. Often, you describe where something is by comparing its position with where you currently are. For example, you might say that a classmate sitting next to you is two desks to your right, or that a mailbox is two blocks south of where you live. Each time you identify the position of an object, you are comparing the location of the object with the location of another object or place.

### With a Reference Point

When you describe a position by comparing it to the location of another object or place, you are using a reference point. A **reference point** is a location to which you compare other locations. In the example above of a mailbox that is two blocks south of where you live, the reference point is "where you live."

Imagine that you are at a zoo with some friends. If you are using the map to the right, you could describe your destination using different reference points. Using yourself as the reference point, you might say that the red panda house is one block east and three blocks north of your current location. Or you might say the red panda house is one block north and one block east of the fountain. In this example, the fountain is your reference point.

**Active Reading** **5 Apply** How would you describe where this question is located on the page? Give two different answers using two different reference points.

_____

_____

_____

_____

# location

## ZOO MAP

| | A | B | C | D | E | F | G | H |
|---|---|---|---|---|---|---|---|---|
| 1 | | Elephants | | | | | | |
| 2 | | | | | Cafe | | Gorillas | |
| 3 | Zebras | | Rhino | | | | | |
| 4 | | | | | Tigers | | | Reptiles |
| 5 | | Monkey Island | | | Red Panda | | | |
| 6 | | | | | | Birds | N | |
| 7 | Petting Zoo | Carousel | | Fountain | | | | |
| 8 | Gift Shop | | YOU ARE HERE | | | | | |
| 9 | | Zoo Entrance | | | Cafe | | | |

**Guest Services**

- 👫 Restrooms
- 🍴 Food
- ➕ First Aid
- ℹ️ Information

## Visualize It!

**6 Apply** One of your friends is at the southeast corner of Monkey Island. He would like to meet you. How would you describe your location to him?

_____

_____

_____

**7 Apply** You need to go visit the first aid station. How would you describe how to get there?

_____

_____

_____

223

# MOVE It!

## What is motion?

An object moves, or is in motion, when it changes its position relative to a reference point. **Motion** is a change in position over time. If you were to watch the biker pictured to the right, you would see him move. If you were not able to watch him, you might still know something about his motion. If you saw that he was in one place at one time and a different place later, you would know that he had moved. A change in position is evidence that motion has happened.

If the biker returned to his starting point, you might not know that he had moved. The starting and ending positions cannot tell you everything about motion.

## How is distance measured?

Suppose you walk from one building to another building that is several blocks away. If you could walk in a straight line, you might end up 500 meters from where you started. The actual distance you travel, however, would depend on the exact path you take. If you take a route that has many turns, the distance you travel might be 900 meters or more.

The way you measure distance depends on the information you want. Sometimes you want to know the straight-line distance between two positions, or the displacement. Sometimes, however, you might need to know the total length of a certain path between those positions.

When measuring any distances, scientists use a standard unit of measurement. The standard unit of length is the meter (m), which is about 3.3 feet. Longer distances can be measured in kilometers (km), and shorter distances in centimeters (cm). In the United States, distance is often measured in miles (mi), feet (ft), or inches (in).

The distance from point A to point B depends on the path you take.

### Visualize It!

**8 Illustrate** Draw a sample path on the maze that is a different distance than the one in red but still goes from the start point, "A," to the finish point, "B."

*This biker is in motion.*

# What is speed?

A change in an object's position tells you that motion took place, but it does not tell you how quickly the object changed position. The **speed** of an object is a measure of how far something moves in a given amount of time. In other words, speed measures how quickly or slowly the object changes position. In the same amount of time, a faster object would move farther than a slower moving object would.

# What is average speed?

The speed of an object is rarely constant. For example, the biker in the photo above may travel quickly when he begins a race but may slow down as he gets tired at the end of the race. *Average speed* is a way to calculate the speed of an object that may not always be moving at a constant speed. Instead of describing the speed of an object at an exact moment in time, average speed describes the speed over a stretch of time.

**Active Reading** **9 Compare** What is the difference between speed and average speed?

_____

_____

_____

**Think Outside the Book** Inquiry

**10 Analyze** Research the top speeds of a cheetah, a race car, and a speed boat. How do they rank in order of speed? Make a poster showing which is fastest and which is slowest. How do the speeds of the fastest human runners compare to the speeds you found?

# Speed It Up!

## How is average speed calculated?

Speed can be calculated by dividing the distance an object travels by the time it takes to cover the distance. Speed is shown in the formula as the letter $s$, distance as the letter $d$, and time as the letter $t$. The formula shows how distance, time, and speed are related. If two objects travel the same distance, the object that took a shorter amount of time will have the greater speed. An object with a greater speed will travel a longer distance in the same amount of time than an object with a lower speed will.

© Houghton Mifflin Harcourt Publishing Company • Image Credits: ©Specialist Stock/Corbis

> The following equation can be used to find average speed:
>
> $$\text{average speed} = \frac{distance}{time}$$
>
> $$s = \frac{d}{t}$$

The standard unit for speed is meters per second (m/s). Speed can also be given in kilometers per hour (km/h). In the United States, speeds are often given in miles per hour (mi/h or mph). One mile per hour is equal to 0.45 m/s.

**Active Reading**

**11 Identify** As you read, underline sentences that relate distance and time.

---

###  Do the Math   Sample Problem

A penguin swimming underwater goes 20 meters in 8 seconds. What is its average speed?

................................................................

**Identify**

**A.** What do you know? $d = 20$ m, $t = 8$ s

**B.** What do you want to find out?  average speed

................................................................

**Plan**

**C.** Draw and label a sketch:   |———— 20 m ————|
                                       8 sec

**D.** Write the formula: $s = d/t$

**E.** Substitute into the formula: $s = \frac{20 \text{ m}}{8 \text{ s}}$

................................................................

**Solve**

**F.** Calculate and simplify: $s = \frac{20 \text{ m}}{8 \text{ s}} = 2.5$ m/s

**G.** Check that your units agree:  Unit is m/s. Unit of speed is distance/time. Units agree.

**Answer:** 2.5 m/s

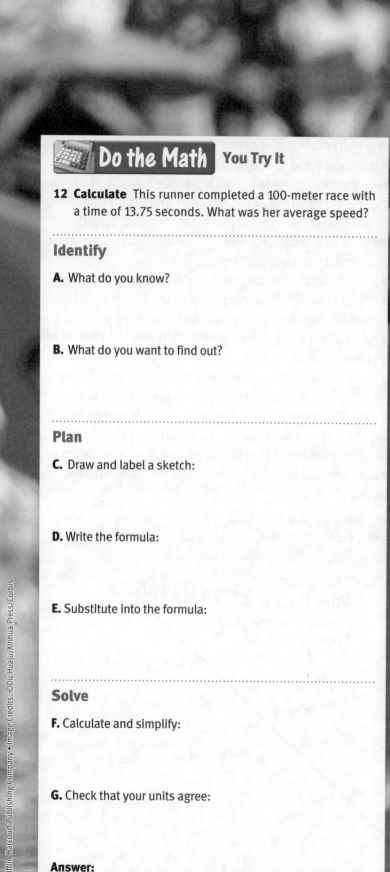

## Do the Math    You Try It

**12 Calculate** This runner completed a 100-meter race with a time of 13.75 seconds. What was her average speed?

### Identify

**A.** What do you know?

**B.** What do you want to find out?

### Plan

**C.** Draw and label a sketch:

**D.** Write the formula:

**E.** Substitute into the formula:

### Solve

**F.** Calculate and simplify:

**G.** Check that your units agree:

**Answer:**

# Fast Graphs

## How is constant speed graphed?

A convenient way to show the motion of an object is by using a graph that plots the distance the object has traveled against time. This type of graph is called a distance-time graph. You can use it to see how both distance and speed change with time.

How far away the object is from a reference point is plotted on the y-axis. So the y-axis expresses distance in units such as meters, centimeters, or kilometers. Time is plotted on the x-axis, and can display units such as seconds, minutes, or hours. If an object moves at a constant speed, the graph is a straight line.

You can use a distance-time graph to determine the average speed of an object. The slope, or steepness, of the line is equal to the average speed of the object. You calculate the average speed for a time interval by dividing the change in distance by the change in time for that time interval.

Suppose that an ostrich is running at a constant speed. The distance-time graph of its motion is shown below. To calculate the speed of the ostrich, choose two data points from the graph below and calculate the slope of the line. The calculation of the slope is shown below. Since we know that the slope of a line on a distance-time graph is its average speed, then we know that the ostrich's speed is 14 m/s.

How can you calculate slope?

$$\text{slope} = \frac{\text{change in } y}{\text{change in } x}$$

$$= \frac{140 \text{ m} - 70 \text{ m}}{10 \text{ s} - 5 \text{ s}}$$

$$= \frac{70 \text{ m}}{5 \text{ s}}$$

$$= 14 \text{ m/s}$$

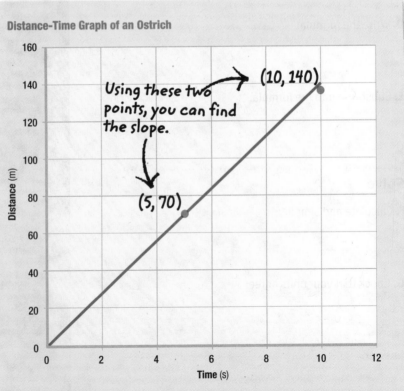

**Distance-Time Graph of an Ostrich**

Using these two points, you can find the slope.

(10, 140)

(5, 70)

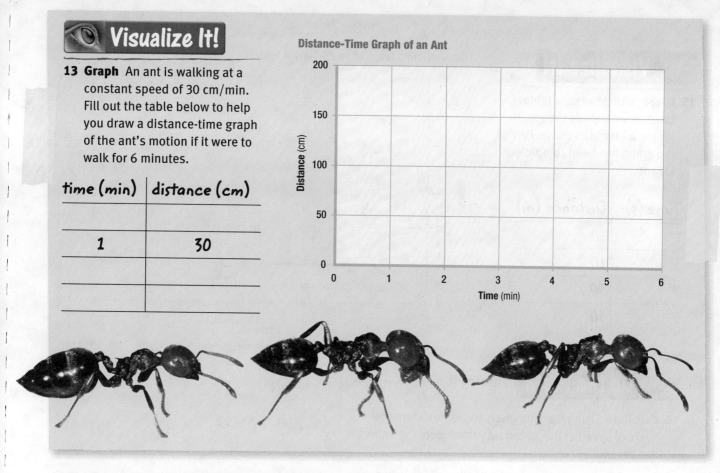

## Visualize It!

**13 Graph** An ant is walking at a constant speed of 30 cm/min. Fill out the table below to help you draw a distance-time graph of the ant's motion if it were to walk for 6 minutes.

| time (min) | distance (cm) |
|---|---|
|  |  |
| 1 | 30 |
|  |  |
|  |  |

**Distance-Time Graph of an Ant**

# How are changing speeds graphed?

Some distance-time graphs show the motion of an object with a changing speed. In these distance-time graphs, the change in the slope of a line indicates that the object has either sped up, slowed down, or stopped.

As an object moves, the distance it travels increases with time. The motion can be seen as a climbing line on the graph. The slope of the line indicates speed. Steeper lines show intervals where the speed is greater than intervals with less steep lines. If the line gets steeper, the object is speeding up. If the line gets less steep, the object is slowing. If the line becomes flat, or horizontal, the object is not moving. In this interval, the speed is zero meters per second.

For objects that change speed, you can calculate speed for a specific interval of time. You would choose two points close together on the graph. Or, you can calculate the average speed over a long interval of time. You would choose two points far apart on the graph to calculate an average over a long interval of time.

**Active Reading** **14 Analyze** If a line on a distance-time graph becomes steeper, what has happened to the speed of the object? What if it becomes a flat horizontal line?

_____

_____

_____

 **Visualize It!**

**15 Graph** Using the data table provided, complete the graph for the all-terrain vehicle. Part of the graph has been completed for you.

| Time (s) | Distance (m) |
|----------|--------------|
| 1 | 10 |
| 3 | 10 |
| 4 | 30 |
| 5 | 50 |

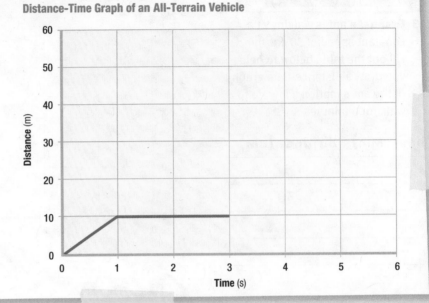

**Distance-Time Graph of an All-Terrain Vehicle**

 **Do the Math** You Try It

**16 Calculate** Using the data given above, calculate the average speed of the all-terrain vehicle over the entire five seconds.

**Identify**

**A.** What do you know?

**B.** What do you want to find out?

**Plan**

**C.** Draw and label a sketch:

**D.** Write the formula:

**E.** Substitute into the formula:

**Solve**

**F.** Calculate and simplify:

**G.** Check that your units agree:

**Answer:**

What would the distance-time graph of this ATV's motion look like?

# Follow Directions

## What is velocity?

Suppose that two birds start from the same place and fly at 10 km/h for 5 minutes. Why might they not end up at the same place? Because the birds were flying in different directions! There are times when the direction of motion must be included in a measurement. A **vector** is a quantity that has both size and direction.

In the example above, the birds' speeds were the same, but their velocities were different. **Velocity** [vuh•LAHS•ih•tee] is speed in a specific direction. If a police officer gives a speeding ticket for a car traveling 100 km/h, the ticket does not list a velocity. But it would list a velocity if it described the car traveling south at 100 km/h.

Because velocity includes direction, it is possible for two objects to have the same speed but different velocities. In the picture to the right, the chair lifts are going the same speed but in opposite directions: some people are going up the mountain while others are going down the mountain.

Average velocity is calculated in a different way than average speed. Average speed depends on the total distance traveled along a path. Average velocity depends on the straight-line distance from the starting point to the final point, or the displacement. A chair lift might carry you up the mountain at an average speed of 5 km/h, giving you an average velocity of 5 km/h north. After a round-trip ride, your average traveling speed would still be 5 km/h. Your average velocity, however, would be 0 km/h because you ended up exactly where you started.

These chair lifts have opposite velocities because they are going at the same speed but in opposite directions.

---

**17 Compare** Fill in the Venn diagram to compare and contrast speed and velocity.

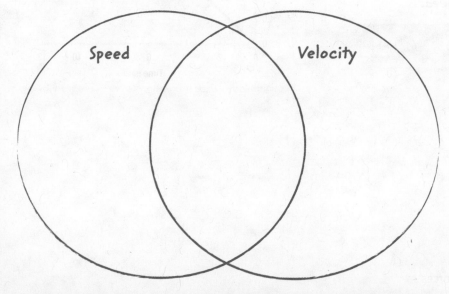

Speed          Velocity

# Visual Summary

To complete this summary, check the box that indicates true or false. Then use the key below to check your answers. You can use this page to review the main concepts of the lesson.

YOU ARE HERE

Motion is a change in position over time.

|  | T | F |  |
|---|---|---|---|
| **18** | ☐ | ☐ | A reference point is a location to which you compare other locations. |
| **19** | ☐ | ☐ | Distance traveled does not depend on the path you take. |

Speed measures how far something moves in a given amount of time.

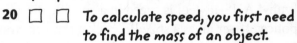

$$s = \frac{d}{t}$$

|  | T | F |  |
|---|---|---|---|
| **20** | ☐ | ☐ | To calculate speed, you first need to find the mass of an object. |
| **21** | ☐ | ☐ | Average speed is a way to describe the speed of an object that may not always be moving at a constant speed. |

## Motion and Speed

A distance-time graph plots the distance traveled by an object and the time it takes to travel that distance.

|  | T | F |  |
|---|---|---|---|
| **22** | ☐ | ☐ | In the graph at the right, the object is moving at a constant speed. |

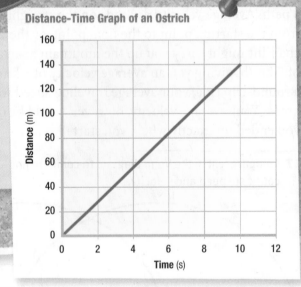

Distance-Time Graph of an Ostrich

**23 Predict** Amy and Ellie left school at the same time. Amy lives farther away than Ellie, but she and Ellie arrived at their homes at the same time. Compare the girls' speeds.

# Lesson Review

## Vocabulary

Draw a line to connect the following terms to their definitions.

**1** velocity

**2** reference point

**3** speed

**4** position

**A** describes the location of an object

**B** speed in a specific direction

**C** a location to which you compare other locations

**D** a measure of how far something moves in a given amount of time

## Key Concepts

**5 Describe** What information do you need to describe an object's location?

_____

_____

**6 Predict** How would decreasing the time it takes you to run a certain distance affect your speed?

_____

_____

_____

**7 Calculate** Juan lives 100 m away from Bill. What is Juan's average speed if he reaches Bill's home in 50 s?

_____

_____

_____

_____

**8 Describe** What do you need to know to describe the velocity of an object?

_____

_____

_____

Use this graph to answer the following questions.

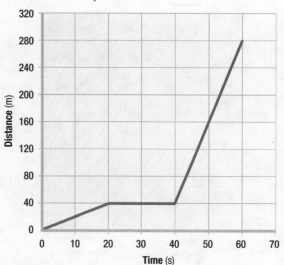

Distance-Time Graph of a Zebra

**9 Analyze** When is the zebra in motion? When is it not moving?

In motion: _____

Not moving: _____

**10 Calculate** What is the average speed of the zebra during the time between 0 s and 40 s?

_____

_____

_____

_____

## Critical Thinking

**11 Apply** Look around you to find an object in motion. Describe the object's motion by discussing its position and direction of motion in relation to a reference point. Then explain how you could determine the object's speed.

_____

_____

_____

_____

_____

_____

# My Notes

TEKS MATH **6.1D** communicate mathematical ideas, reasoning, and their implications using multiple representations, including symbols, diagrams, graphs, and language as appropriate

TEKS MATH **6.1F** analyze mathematical relationships to connect and communicate mathematical ideas

# Interpreting Graphs

A visual display, such as a graph or table, is a useful way to show data that you have collected in an experiment. The ability to interpret graphs is a necessary skill in science, and it is also important in everyday life. You will come across various types of graphs in newspaper articles, medical reports, and, of course, textbooks. Understanding a report or article's message often depends heavily on your ability to read and interpret different types of graphs.

## Tutorial

**Ask yourself the following questions when studying a graph.**

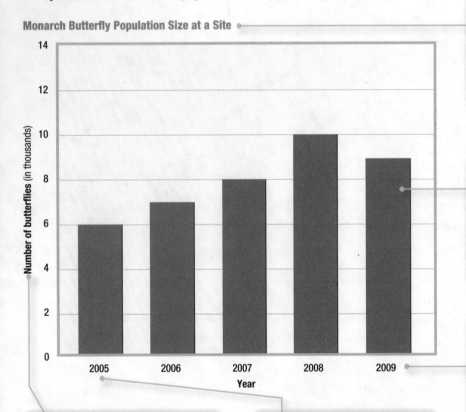

Monarch Butterfly Population Size at a Site

**What is the title of the graph?** Reading the title can tell you the subject or main idea of the graph. The subject here is monarch butterfly population size.

**What type of graph is it?** Bar graphs, like the one here, are useful for comparing categories or total values. The lengths of the bars are proportional to the value they represent.

**Do you notice any trends in the graph?** After you understand what the graph is about, look for patterns. For example, here the monarch butterfly population increased each year from 2005 to 2008. But in 2009, the monarch butterfly population decreased.

**What are the labels and headings in the graph? What is on each axis of the graph?** Here, the vertical axis shows the population in thousands. Each bar represents a different year from 2005 to 2009. So from 2005 to 2009, the monarch butterfly population ranged from 6,000 to 10,000.

**Can you describe the data in the graph?** Data can be numbers or text. Analyze the information you read at specific data points. For example, the graph here tells us that there were 6,000 monarch butterflies in 2005.

# You Try It!

A member of your research group has made the graph shown below about an object in motion. Study the graph, then answer the questions that follow.

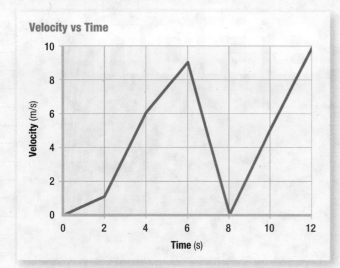

Velocity vs Time

**1 Interpreting Graphs** Study the graph shown above. Identify the title of this graph, the *x*-axis, the *y*-axis, and the type of graph.

**A** title of graph _____

**B** *x*-axis _____

**C** *y*-axis _____

**D** type of graph _____

**2 Identify** Study the graph shown above and record the velocity at the indicated times.

| Time (s) | Velocity (m/s) |
|----------|----------------|
| 2        |                |
| 4        |                |
| 6        |                |
| 8        |                |
| 10       |                |

**3 Using Graphs** Use the graph to answer the following questions.

**A** What is the approximate velocity of the object at 5 seconds?

_____

**B** During what time interval is the object slowing down? Explain how you can tell.

_____

_____

_____

_____

**C** At what time or times was the velocity of the object about 4 m/s?

_____

**4 Communicating Results** In a short paragraph, describe the motion of the object.

_____

_____

_____

_____

_____

_____

## Take It Home

Find a newspaper or magazine article that has a graph. What type of graph is it? Study the graph and determine its main message. Bring the graph to class and be prepared to discuss your interpretation of the graph.

Lesson **5**

# Acceleration

**ESSENTIAL QUESTION**

## How does motion change?

By the end of this lesson, you should be able to analyze how acceleration is related to time and velocity.

The riders on this roller coaster are constantly changing direction and speed.

**TEKS** **6.8D** measure and graph changes in motion

**236**

© Houghton Mifflin Harcourt Publishing Company • Image Credits: © Chad Slattery/Stone/Getty Images

## Lesson Labs

**Quick Labs**
- Acceleration and Slope
- Mass and Acceleration

**S.T.E.M. Lab**
- Investigate Acceleration

## Engage Your Brain

**1 Predict** Check T or F to show whether you think each statement is true or false.

T    F

☐    ☐    A car taking a turn at a constant speed is accelerating.

☐    ☐    If an object has low acceleration, it isn't moving very fast.

☐    ☐    An accelerating car is always gaining speed.

**2 Identify** The names of the two things that can change when something accelerates are scrambled together below. Unscramble them!

P E D S E

_____

C D E I I N O R T

_____

## Active Reading

**3 Synthesize** You can often define an unknown word if you know the meaning of its word parts. Use the word parts and sentence below to make an educated guess about the meaning of the word *centripetal*.

| Word part | Meaning |
|-----------|---------|
| *centri-* | center |
| *pet-* | tend toward |

**Example Sentence:**
Josephina felt the <u>centripetal</u> force as she spun around on the carnival ride.

*centripetal:*

_____

_____

_____

### Vocabulary Terms

- acceleration
- centripetal acceleration

**4 Distinguish** As you read, draw pictures or make a chart to help remember the relationship between distance, velocity, and acceleration.

© Houghton Mifflin Harcourt Publishing Company • Image Credits: ©Chad Slattery/Stone/Getty Images

# Getting up to

## How do we measure changing velocity?

Imagine riding a bike as in the images below. You start off not moving at all, then move slowly, and then faster and faster each second. Your velocity is changing. You are accelerating.

**Active Reading** **5 Identify** Underline the two components of a vector.

### Acceleration Measures a Change in Velocity

Just as velocity measures a rate of change in position, acceleration measures a rate of change in velocity. **Acceleration** (ack•SELL•uh•ray•shuhn) is the rate at which velocity changes. Velocity is a vector, having both a magnitude and direction, and if either of these change, then the velocity changes. So, an object accelerates if its speed, its direction of motion, or both change.

Keep in mind that acceleration depends not only on how much velocity changes, but also on how much time that change takes. A small change in velocity can still be a large acceleration if the change happens quickly, and a large change in velocity can be a small acceleration if it happens slowly. Increasing your speed by 5 m/s in 5 s is a smaller acceleration than to do the same in 1 s.

Each second, the cyclist's southward velocity increases by 1 m/s south.

| 1 m/s | 2 m/s | 3 m/s | 4 m/s | 5 m/s |

# Speed

## How is average acceleration calculated?

Acceleration is a change in velocity as compared with the time it takes to make the change. You can find the average acceleration experienced by an accelerating object using the following equation.

$$\text{average acceleration} = \frac{(\text{final velocity} - \text{starting velocity})}{\text{time}}$$

Velocity is expressed in meters per second (m/s) and time is measured in seconds (s). So acceleration is measured in meters per second per second, or meters per second squared (m/s²).

As an example, consider an object that starts off moving at 8 m/s west, and then 16 s later is moving at 48 m/s west. The average acceleration of this object can be calculated as shown below.

$$a = \frac{(48\ m/s - 8\ m/s)}{16\ s}$$
$$a = 2.5\ m/s^2\ west$$

**Active Reading**

**6 Identify** Underline the units of acceleration.

This formula is often abbreviated as

$$a = \frac{(v_2 - v_1)}{t}$$

## Visualize It!

**7 Analyze** What is the change in velocity of the biker below as he travels from point B to point C? What is his acceleration from point B to point C?

_____

_____

**8 Calculate** Find the average acceleration of the cyclist moving from point A to point B, and over the whole trip (from point A to point D).

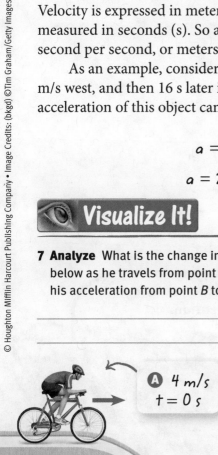

**A** 4 m/s
t = 0 s

**B** 8 m/s
t = 1 s

**C** 8 m/s
t = 2 s

**D** 7 m/s
t = 3 s

The cyclist is riding at 4 m/s. One second later, at the bottom of the hill, he is riding at 8 m/s. After going up a small incline, he has slowed to 7 m/s.

# What a Drag!

## How can accelerating objects change velocity?

Like velocity, acceleration is a vector, with a magnitude and a direction.

### Accelerating Objects Change Speed

Although the word *acceleration* is commonly used to mean an increasing speed, in scientific use, the word applies to both increases and decreases in speed.

When you slide down a hill, you go from a small velocity to a large one. An increase in velocity like this is called *positive acceleration*. When a race car slows down, it goes from a high velocity to a low velocity. A decrease in velocity like this is called *negative acceleration*.

What is the acceleration when an object decreases speed? Because the initial velocity is larger than the final velocity, the term $(v_2 - v_1)$ will be negative. So the acceleration $a = \dfrac{(v_2 - v_1)}{t}$ will be a negative.

When acceleration and velocity (rate of motion) are in the same direction, the speed will increase. When acceleration and velocity are in opposing directions, the acceleration works against the initial motion in that direction, and the speed will decrease.

**Active Reading**

**9 Identify** Underline the term for an increase in velocity and the term for a decrease in velocity.

The parachute dragging on the air slows the car down, causing a negative acceleration.

Sliding down a hill causes a positive acceleration.

© Houghton Mifflin Harcourt Publishing Company • Image Credits: (l) ©Mel Yates/Photodisc/Getty Images; (r) ©Leo Mason/Corbis

# Accelerating Objects Change Direction

An object changing direction of motion experiences acceleration even when it does not speed up or slow down. Think about a car that makes a sharp left turn. The direction of velocity changes from "forward" to "left." This change in velocity is an acceleration, even if the speed does not change. As the car finishes the turn, the acceleration drops to zero.

What happens, however, when an object is *always* turning? An object traveling in a circular motion is always changing its direction, so it always experiences acceleration. Acceleration in circular motion is known as **centripetal acceleration**. (sehn•TRIP•ih•tahl ack•SELL•uh•ray•shuhn)

A skater rounding a curve experiences centripetal acceleration.

 Inquiry

**10 Conclude** An acceleration in the direction of motion increases speed, and an acceleration opposite to the direction of motion decreases speed. What direction is the acceleration in centripetal acceleration, where speed does not change but direction does?

_____

_____

_____

 Do the Math

**11 Calculate** The horse is galloping at 13 m/s. Five seconds later, after climbing the hill, the horse is moving at 5.5 m/s. Find the acceleration that describes this change in velocity.

$$a = \frac{(v_2 - v_1)}{t}$$

5.5 m/s
5 seconds

Running uphill is tough to do without slowing down!

13 m/s
0 seconds

# Visual Summary

To complete this summary, complete the statements below by filling in the blanks. You can use this page to review the main concepts of the lesson.

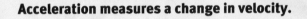

## Acceleration

**Acceleration measures a change in velocity.**

1 m/s          5 m/s

12 The formula for calculating average acceleration is

_____

**Acceleration can be a change in speed or a change in direction of motion.**

13 When acceleration and velocity are in the same direction, the speed will
_____

14 When acceleration and velocity are in opposing directions, the speed will
_____

15 Objects traveling in _____ motion experience centripetal acceleration.

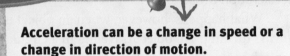

Answers: 12 $a = \dfrac{(v_2 - v_1)}{t}$ ;
13 increase; 14 decrease; 15 circular

16 **Synthesize** Explain why a moving object cannot come to a stop instantaneously (in zero seconds). Hint: Think about the acceleration that would be required.

# Lesson Review

## Vocabulary

Fill in the blank with the term that best completes the following sentences.

**1** Acceleration is a change in _____

**2** _____ occurs when an object travels in a curved path.

**3** A decrease in the magnitude of velocity is called _____

**4** An increase in the magnitude of velocity is called _____

## Key Concepts

**5 State** The units for acceleration are

_____

**6 Label** In the equation $a = \dfrac{(v_2 - v_1)}{t}$, what do $v_1$ and $v_2$ represent?

_____

_____

**7 Calculate** What is the acceleration experienced by a car that takes 10 s to reach 27 m/s from rest?

**8 Identify** Acceleration can be a change in speed or _____

**9 Identify** A helicopter flying west begins experiencing an acceleration of 3 m/s² east. Will the magnitude of its velocity increase or decrease?

_____

## Critical Thinking

**10 Model** Describe a situation when you might travel at a high velocity, but with low acceleration.

_____

_____

_____

Use this graph to answer the following questions. Assume Jenny's direction did not change.

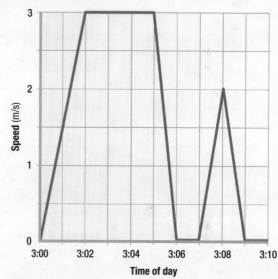

**11 Analyze** During what intervals was Jenny negatively accelerating?

_____

_____

**12 Analyze** During what intervals was Jenny positively accelerating?

_____

_____

**13 Analyze** During what intervals was Jenny not accelerating at all?

_____

_____

_____

# My Notes

# Forces

**ESSENTIAL QUESTION**

## How do forces affect motion?

By the end of this lesson, you should be able to describe different types of forces and explain the effect force has on motion.

Even though this skydiver is not touching the ground, a force is still being exerted on him by Earth.

**TEKS** **6.8B** identify and describe the changes in position, direction, and speed of an object when acted upon by unbalanced forces

244

✋ **Lesson Labs**

**Quick Labs**
• Net Force
• First Law of Skateboarding

**S.T.E.M. Lab**
• Newton's Laws of Motion

## 🧠 Engage Your Brain

**1 Illustrate** Draw a diagram showing how forces act on a ball tossed into the air.

**2 Describe** Write a caption for this photo.

## ✏️ Active Reading

**3 Apply** Many scientific words, such as *net*, also have everyday meanings. Use context clues to write your own definition for each meaning of the word *net*.

**Example sentence**
The fisherman scooped his catch out of the water with a <u>net</u>.

net:

_____

_____

**Example sentence**
Subtract the mass of the container from the total mass of the substance and the container to determine the <u>net</u> mass of the substance.

net:

_____

_____

_____

### Vocabulary Terms

• force        • inertia
• net force

**4 Apply** As you learn the definition of each vocabulary term in this lesson, create your own definition or sketch to help you remember the meaning of the term.

# A Tour de Forces

## What is a force, and how does it act on an object?

You have probably heard the word *force* used in conversation. People say, "Don't force the issue," or "Our team is a force to be reckoned with." Scientists also use the word *force*. What exactly is a force, as it is used in science?

### A Force Is a Push or a Pull

🖍️ **Active Reading** **5 Identify** As you read, underline the unit that is used to express force.

In science, a **force** is simply a push or a pull. All forces have both a size and a direction. A force can cause an object to change its speed or direction. When you see a change in an object's motion, one or more forces caused the change. The unit used to express force is the newton (N). You will learn how to calculate force a little later in this lesson.

Forces exist only when there is an object for them to act on. However, forces do not always cause an object to move. When you sit in a chair, the chair does not move. Your downward force on the chair is balanced by the upward force from the floor.

 **Visualize It!**

**6 Identify** Draw arrows to represent the pushing forces in the image at left and the pulling forces in the image at right.

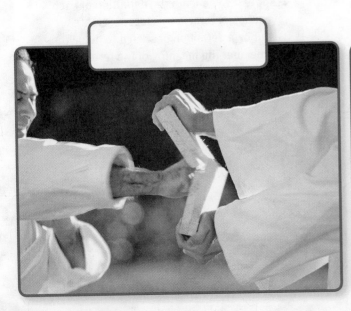

## A Force Can Act Directly on an Object

It is not always easy to tell what is exerting a force or what is being acted on by a force. When one object touches or bumps into another object, we say that the objects are in contact with each other. A force exerted during contact between objects is a contact force. Friction is an example of a contact force between two surfaces. Suppose you slide a book across your desk. The amount of friction between the surface of the desk and the book cover determines how easily the book moves. Car tires rely on friction to keep a moving car from sliding off a road. Cars may slide on icy roads because ice lowers the force of friction on the tires.

## A Force Can Act on an Object from a Distance

Forces can also act at a distance. One force that acts at a distance is called gravity. When you jump, gravity pulls you back to the ground even though you are not touching Earth. Magnetic force is another example of a force that can act at a distance. Magnetic force can be a push or a pull. A magnet can hold paper to a metal refrigerator door. The magnet touches the paper, not the metal, so the magnetic force is acting on the refrigerator door at a distance. Magnetic force also acts at a distance when the like poles of two magnets push each other apart. A magnetic levitation train floats because magnetic forces push the train away from its track.

### Visualize It!

**7 Identify.** The arrows in the picture below represent contact and distance forces. Label each arrow with a "C" if it is a contact force or "D" if it is a distance force.

# In the Balance

## What happens when multiple forces act on an object?

Usually, more than one force is acting on an object. The combination of all the forces acting on an object is called the **net force**. How do you determine net force? The answer depends on the directions of the forces involved.

When forces act in the same direction, you simply add them together to determine the net force. For example, when forces of 1 N and 2 N act in the same direction on an object, the net force is 1 N + 2 N = 3 N. When forces act in opposite directions, you subtract the smaller force from the larger force to determine the net force: 2 N − 1 N = 1 N.

**Active Reading**

**8 Identify** As you read, underline how one determines net force.

**Visualize It!**

**9 Calculate** Calculate the net force acting on the appliance box and use it to determine if the box will move.

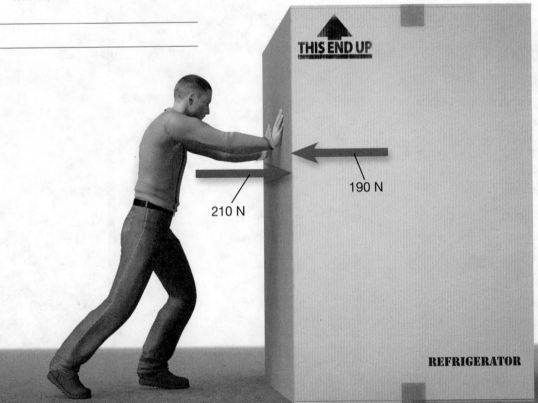

THIS END UP

190 N

210 N

REFRIGERATOR

## The Forces Can Be Balanced

When the forces on an object produce a net force of 0 N, the forces are balanced. Balanced forces will not cause a change in the motion of a moving object or cause a nonmoving object to start moving. Many objects around you have only balanced forces acting on them. A light hanging from the ceiling does not move, because the force of gravity pulling downward on the light is balanced by the force of the chain pulling the light upward.

## The Forces Can Be Unbalanced

When the net force on an object is not 0 N, the forces are unbalanced. Unbalanced forces produce a change in the object's motion. It could be a change in its speed or direction or both. This change in motion is called acceleration. The acceleration is always in the direction of the net force. For example, when a big dog and a small dog play with a tug toy, the bigger dog pulls with greater force, so the acceleration is in the direction of the bigger dog.

**10 Apply** The arrows in the first image show that the forces on the rope are balanced. Draw arrows on the second image to show how the forces on the rope are unbalanced.

These two tug-of-war teams are pulling on the rope with equal force to produce a net force of 0 N. The rope does not move.

One of these teams is pulling on the rope with more force. The rope moves in the direction of the stronger team.

# It's the Law

## What is Newton's First Law of Motion?

Force and motion are related. In the 1680s, British scientist Sir Isaac Newton explained this relationship between force and motion with three laws of motion.

Newton's first law describes the motion of an object that has a net force of 0 N acting on it. The law states: *An object at rest stays at rest, and an object in motion stays in motion at the same speed and direction, unless it experiences an unbalanced force.* Let's look at the two parts of this law more closely.

### An Object at Rest Stays at Rest

**Active Reading** **11 Identify** As you read, underline examples of objects affected by inertia.

Newton's first law is also called the law of inertia. **Inertia** (ih•NER•shuh) is the tendency of all objects to resist a change in motion. An object will not move until a force makes it move. So a chair will not slide across the floor unless a force pushes the chair, and a golf ball will not leave the tee until a force pushes it off.

**Visualize It!**

**12 Explain** In your own words, explain why the dishes remain in place when the magician pulls the cloth out from under them.

_____

_____

_____

# An Object in Motion Stays in Motion

Now let's look at the second part of Newton's first law of motion. It states that an object in motion stays in motion at the same speed and direction, or velocity, unless it experiences an unbalanced force. Think about coming to a sudden stop while riding in a car. The car stops because the brakes apply friction to the wheel, making the forces acting on the car unbalanced. You keep moving forward until your seat belt applies an unbalanced force on you. This force stops your forward motion.

Both parts of the law are really stating the same thing. After all, an object at rest has a velocity—its velocity is zero!

When this car was in motion, the test dummy was moving forward at the same velocity as the car. When the car hit the barrier and stopped, the dummy kept moving until it, too, was acted on by a net backward force.

FO4305OZ02

0001768

## Visualize It!

**14 Infer** What forces acted on the test dummy to stop its forward motion?

_____

_____

_____

_____

_____

# What is Newton's Second Law of Motion?

**15 Identify** As you read, underline Newton's second law of motion.

When an unbalanced force acts on an object, the object accelerates. Newton's second law describes this motion. The law states: *The acceleration of an object depends on the mass of the object and the amount of force applied.*

In other words, objects that have different masses will have different accelerations if the same amount of force is used. Imagine pushing a shopping cart. When the cart is empty, you need only a small force to accelerate it. But if the cart is full of groceries, the same amount of force causes a much smaller acceleration.

## Force Equals Mass Times Acceleration

Newton's second law links force, mass, and acceleration. We can express this relationship using the equation $F = ma$, where $F$ stands for applied force, $m$ stands for mass, and $a$ stands for acceleration. This equation tells us that a given force applied to a large mass will result in a small acceleration. When the same force is applied to a smaller mass, the acceleration will be larger.

## Do the Math   Sample Problem

These players train by pushing a massive object. If the players push with a force of 150 N, and the object has a mass of 75 kg, what is the object's acceleration? One newton is equal to 1 kg•m/s².

**Use Newton's law:**

$$F = ma$$
$$150 \text{ kg·m/s}^2 = (75 \text{ kg})(a)$$
$$a = \frac{150}{75} \text{ m/s}^2$$
$$a = 2.0 \text{ m/s}^2$$

### You Try It

**16 Calculate** For a more difficult training session, the mass to be pushed is increased to 160 kg. If the players still push with a force of 150 N, what is the acceleration of the object?

**Use Newton's law:**

$$F = ma$$
$$150 \text{ N} =$$

# Newton's Second Law and You

Think about the last time you rode on a roller coaster or in a car on a hilly road. Did you feel like you were going to float out of your seat when you went over a big hill? Newton's second law can explain that feeling.

## Going Up

When the roller coaster is going up a hill, you have two important forces acting on you—the force of gravity and the upward force exerted by the roller coaster seat.

## Coming Down

Once the roller coaster starts down the other side, it accelerates downward, and your seat does not support your full weight.

flight path

## Practicing for Space

Astronauts take special flights to train for space missions. The airplane's path looks like a roller coaster hill. As the plane accelerates downward, the astronauts lose contact with the plane and fall toward Earth. This condition is called free fall.

## Extend

Inquiry

**17 Infer** Suppose you were standing on a scale in an elevator in free fall. What would the scale read?

**18 Synthesize** Explain why the feeling of weightlessness in free fall is not the same as truly being weightless.

**19 Compare** In what ways are roller coaster rides similar to and different from training simulations in a NASA plane?

# What is Newton's Third Law of Motion?

Newton also devised a third law of motion. The law states: *Whenever one object exerts a force on a second object, the second object exerts an equal and opposite force on the first.*

So when you push against a wall, Newton's law tells you that the wall is actually pushing back against you.

## Objects Exert Force on Each Other

Newton's third law also can be stated as: All forces act in pairs. Whenever one object exerts a force on a second object, the second object exerts an equal and opposite force on the first. There are action forces and reaction forces. Action and reaction forces are present even when there is no motion. For example, you exert a force on a chair when you sit on it. Your weight pushing down on the chair is the action force. The reaction force is the force exerted by the chair that pushes up on your body.

## Forces in Pairs Have Equal Size but Opposite Directions

When an object pushes against another object, that object pushes back equally hard. But the second object pushes back in the opposite direction. In the pool below, the swimmer's feet push against the wall as he moves forward. This push is the action force. The wall also exerts a force on the swimmer. This is the reaction force, and it moves the swimmer forward. The forces do not act on the same object. Read on to find out why the swimmer moves but the wall does not!

**Visualize It!**

**20 Apply** The arrow below represents the action force exerted by the swimmer. Draw an arrow that represents the reaction force.

When a swimmer pushes off against a wall, the wall pushes back against the swimmer.

## Forces Acting in Pairs Can Have Unequal Effects

Even though action and reaction forces are equal in size, their effects are often different. Gravitation is a force pair between two objects. If you drop a ball, gravity in an action force pulls the ball toward Earth. But the reaction force pulls Earth toward the ball! It's easy to see the effect of the action force. Why don't you see the effect of the reaction force—Earth being pulled upward? Newton's second law answers this question. The force on the ball is the same size as the force on Earth. However, Earth has much more mass than the ball. So Earth's acceleration is much smaller than that of the ball!

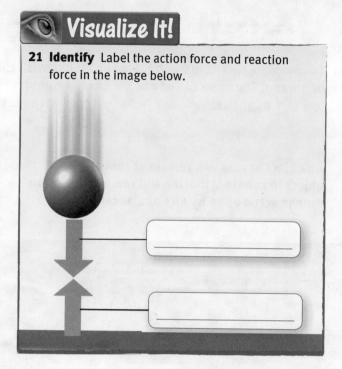

**Visualize It!**

**21 Identify** Label the action force and reaction force in the image below.

## Forces Can Act in Multiple Pairs

An object can have multiple forces acting on it at once. When this happens, each force is part of a force pair. For example, when a baseball bat hits a baseball, the bat does not fly backward. A force is exerted on the ball by the bat. The bat does not fly backward, because the player's hands are exerting another force on the bat. What then keeps the player's hands from flying backward when the bat hits the ball? The bones and muscles in the player's arms exert a force on the hands. As you can see, a simple activity such as playing baseball involves the action of many forces at the same time.

**22 Describe** In your own words, explain Newton's third law of motion.

_____

_____

# Visual Summary

To complete this summary, fill in the blanks with the correct word or phrase. Then use the key below to check your answers. You can use this page to review the main concepts of the lesson.

## Forces

An object at rest will remain at rest and an object in constant motion will remain in motion unless acted upon by an unbalanced force.

**23** Newton's first law is also called the law of _____

When an unbalanced force acts on an object, the object moves with accelerated motion.

**24** In the formula F = ma, m stands for _____

Whenever one object exerts a force on a second object, the second object exerts an equal and opposite force on the first.

**25** Forces in the same pair have equal size but opposite_____

**26 Synthesize** A car designer is designing a new model of a popular car. He wants to use the same engine as in the old model, but improve the new car's acceleration. Use Newton's second law to explain how to improve the car's acceleration without redesigning the engine.

© Houghton Mifflin Harcourt Publishing Company • Image Credits: (l) ©Fstop/Photodisc/Getty Images; (r) ©HMH

# Lesson Review

## Vocabulary

Draw a line to connect the following terms to their definitions.

**1** force

**2** inertia

**3** newton

**A** resistance of an object to a change in motion

**B** the unit that expresses force

**C** a push or a pull

## Key Concepts

**4 Describe** What is the action force and the reaction force when you sit down on a chair?

_____

_____

_____

_____

_____

**5 Summarize** How do you determine net force?

_____

_____

_____

_____

_____

_____

**6 Explain** How do tests with crash dummies, seat belts, and air bags illustrate Newton's first law of motion?

_____

_____

_____

_____

_____

## Critical Thinking

Use this photo to answer the following questions.

**7 Identify** This rock, known as Balanced Rock, sits on a thin spike of rock in a canyon in Idaho. Explain the forces that keep the rock balanced on its tiny pedestal.

_____

_____

_____

_____

**8 Calculate** Balanced Rock has a mass of about 36,000 kg. If the acceleration due to gravity is 9.8 m/s², what is the force that the rock is exerting on its pedestal?

_____

_____

_____

_____

_____

**9 Infer** What would happen to the moon if Earth stopped exerting the force of gravity on it?

_____

_____

_____

_____

# My Notes

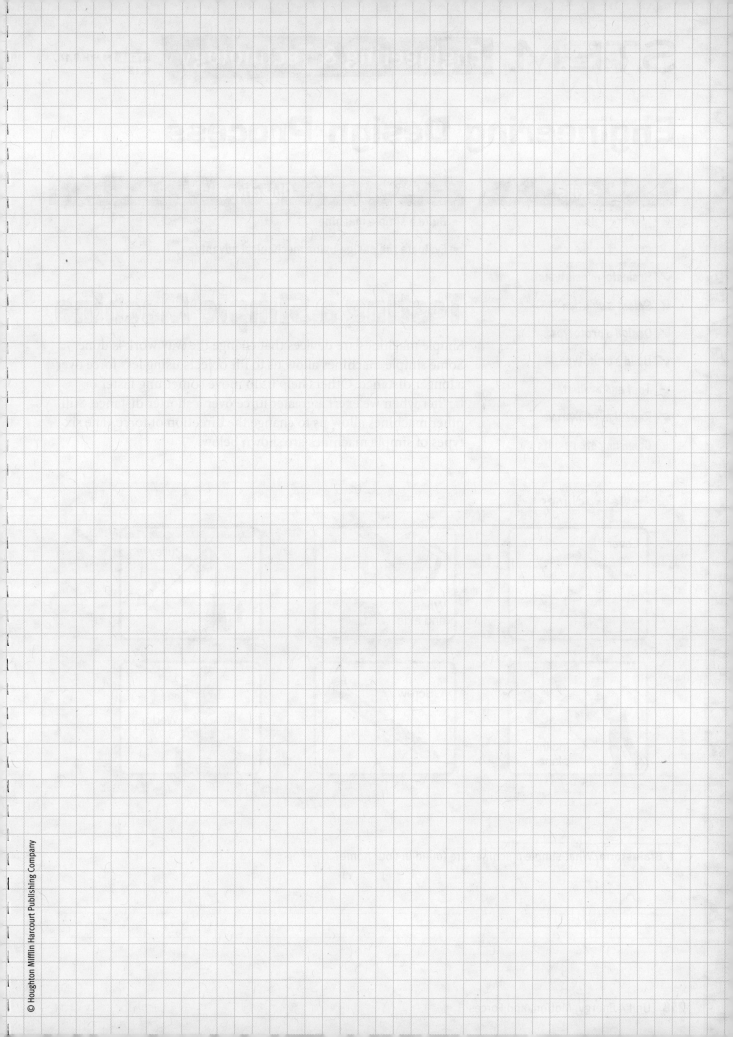

# Engineering Design Process

| Skills | Objectives |
|---|---|
| Identify a need | • Build a simple machine. |
| Conduct research | • Evaluate the design using mechanical advantage. |
| ✓ Brainstorm solutions | |
| ✓ Select a solution | |
| ✓ Design a prototype | |
| ✓ Build a prototype | |
| ✓ Test and evaluate | |
| ✓ Redesign to improve | |
| ✓ Communicate results | |

## Testing a Simple Machine

Simple machines are devices that change the way work is done. Some simple machines allow us to lift objects using less force over a longer distance. Others help us to move something faster or farther when we exert a greater force over a shorter distance. Still other machines allow us to change the direction of force. The six types of simple machines are shown below.

Six simple machines

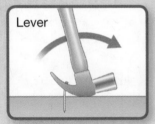

Lever

Wheel and axle

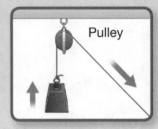

Pulley

Inclined plane

Screw

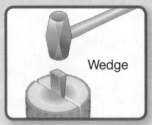

Wedge

**1 Brainstorm** What simple machines are found in your home?

_____

_____

_____

_____

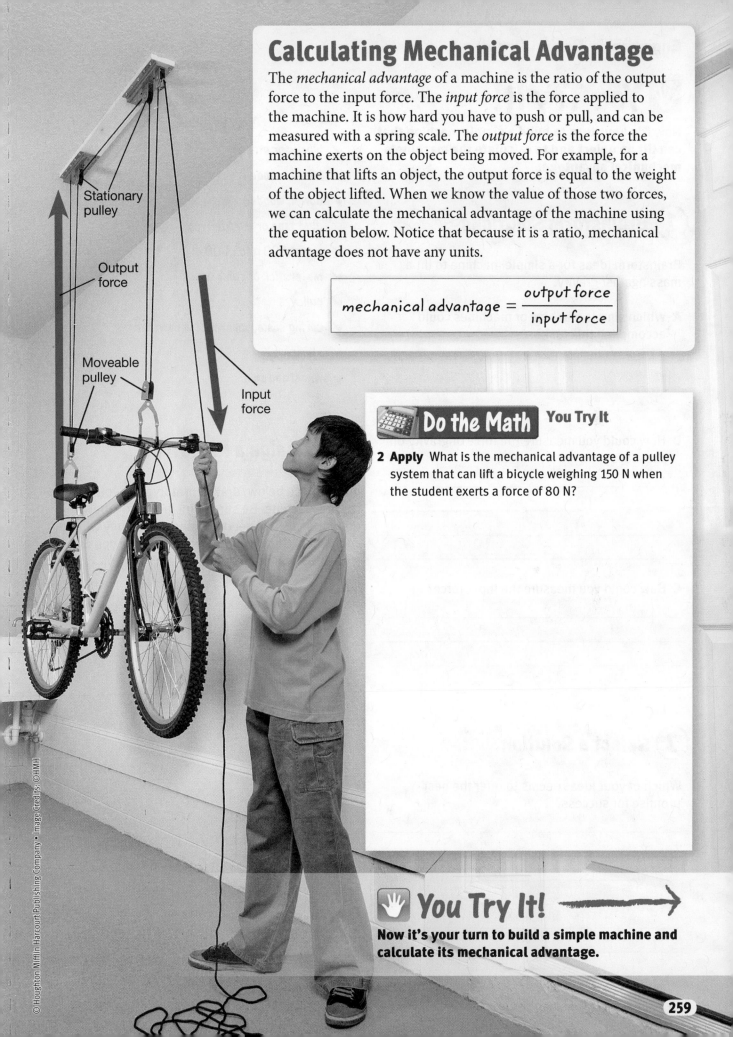

# Calculating Mechanical Advantage

The *mechanical advantage* of a machine is the ratio of the output force to the input force. The *input force* is the force applied to the machine. It is how hard you have to push or pull, and can be measured with a spring scale. The *output force* is the force the machine exerts on the object being moved. For example, for a machine that lifts an object, the output force is equal to the weight of the object lifted. When we know the value of those two forces, we can calculate the mechanical advantage of the machine using the equation below. Notice that because it is a ratio, mechanical advantage does not have any units.

$$\text{mechanical advantage} = \frac{\text{output force}}{\text{input force}}$$

Stationary pulley

Output force

Moveable pulley

Input force

**Do the Math** You Try It

**2 Apply** What is the mechanical advantage of a pulley system that can lift a bicycle weighing 150 N when the student exerts a force of 80 N?

✋ **You Try It!** ⟶

**Now it's your turn to build a simple machine and calculate its mechanical advantage.**

# You Try It!

**Now it's your turn to build a simple machine that can lift an object and to calculate the machine's mechanical advantage.**

## ① Brainstorm Solutions

Brainstorm ideas for a simple machine to lift a mass against gravity.

**A** Which simple machine or machines could accomplish this task?

_____

_____

_____

**B** How could you measure the force of gravity on the mass?

_____

_____

_____

_____

**C** How could you measure the input force?

_____

_____

_____

_____

_____

## ② Select a Solution

Which of your ideas seems to offer the best promise for success?

_____

_____

_____

_____

_____

## You Will Need

✔ blocks or stands

✔ board, wooden

✔ dowel, wooden

✔ duct tape or masking tape

✔ mass, 200 g to 1,000 g

✔ meterstick or ruler

✔ pulley

✔ spring scale, calibrated in newtons

✔ string

✔ wheel and axle

## ③ Design a Prototype

In the space below, draw a prototype of your simple machine. Be sure to include and label all the parts you will need and show how they will be connected. Show where on the machine you will measure the input force.

## (4) Build a Prototype

Now build your lifting device. Were there any parts you had to revise as you were building the prototype?

_____

_____

_____

## (5) Test and Evaluate

What is the output force (the weight in newtons that was lifted)? What is the input force needed to raise the mass? Calculate the mechanical advantage of your machine.

Output force: _____

Input force: _____

Mechanical advantage = _____

## (6) Redesign to Improve

**A** How could you redesign your machine to increase its mechanical advantage?

_____

_____

**B** Make a change and take measurements to see if the mechanical advantage has increased. How many revisions did you have to make to see an increase in mechanical advantage?

_____

_____

## (7) Communicate Results

What is the largest mechanical advantage that you measured? As the mechanical advantage increased, did you notice any change in function of the machine? Why do you think that was the case?

_____

_____

_____

_____

# Machines

**ESSENTIAL QUESTION**

## How do simple machines work?

By the end of this lesson, you should be able to describe different types of simple machines and to calculate the mechanical advantages and efficiencies of various simple machines.

Machines come in all shapes and sizes. This huge Ferris wheel contains a type of simple machine known as a wheel and axle.

**TEKS** **6.8E** investigate how inclined planes and pulleys can be used to change the amount of force to move an object

## Lesson Labs

**Quick Labs**
• Mechanical Efficiency
• Investigate Pulleys

**S.T.E.M. Lab**
• Compound Machines

---

## Engage Your Brain

**1 Identify** Unscramble the letters below to find the names of some simple machines. Write your words on the blank lines.

VEERL _____

EGDWE _____

YPLLUE _____

HELWE DAN EXAL _____

**2 Compare** How is using the stairs similar to and different from using a ramp to get into a building?

_____

_____

_____

_____

_____

_____

_____

---

## Active Reading

**3 Apply** Use context clues to write your own definition for the phrases *input force* and *output force*.

**Example sentence**
An <u>input force</u> was applied to the pedal to make it move.

*input force:*

_____

_____

**Example sentence**
The <u>output force</u> of the pedal made the gear of the bike turn.

*output force:*

_____

_____

### Vocabulary Terms

• machine
• mechanical advantage
• mechanical efficiency
• lever
• fulcrum
• wheel and axle
• pulley
• inclined plane

**4 Identify** As you read, create a reference card for each vocabulary term. On one side of the card, write the term and its meaning. On the other side, draw an image that illustrates or makes a connection to the term. These cards can be used as bookmarks in the text so that you can refer to them while studying.

# Simply Easier

## What do simple machines do?

What do you think of as a machine—maybe a car or a computer? A **machine** is any device that helps people do work by changing the way work is done. The machines that make up other machines are called *simple machines*. The six types of simple machines are *levers, wheels and axles, pulleys, inclined planes, wedges,* and *screws.*

### Change the Way Work Is Done

The wheelbarrow and rake shown below contain simple machines. They change the way you do work. Work is the use of force to move an object some distance. The force you apply to a machine through a distance is called the *input force*. The work that you do on a machine is called *work input.* You do work on a wheelbarrow when you lift the handles. You pull up on the handles to make them move. The wheelbarrow does work on the leaves. The work done by the machine on an object is called *work output*. The *output force* is the force a machine exerts on an object. The wheelbarrow exerts an output force on the leaves to lift them up.

**Visualize It!**

**6 Identify** The person raking leaves applies an input force to the handle of the rake. The output force is applied to the leaves. Label the input force and the output force on the rake.

Machines, such as a wheelbarrow and rake, make yard work easier.

Output force

Input force

A _____

B _____

## Change the Size of a Force and the Distance

Machines make tasks easier without decreasing the amount of work done. Work is equal to force times distance. If you apply less force with a machine, you apply that force through a longer distance. So the amount of work done remains the same. A ramp is an example of a machine that can change the magnitude, or size, of the force needed to move an object. You apply less force when you push a box up a ramp than when you lift the box. However, you apply the force through a longer distance. The amount of work you do is the same as when you lift the box to the same height, if friction is ignored. Other machines increase the amount of force needed, but you apply the force over a shorter distance.

The work done on the box is equal to the input force needed to lift the box times the height to which the box is lifted.

Less force is applied through a longer distance when the box is pushed up a ramp. But the work done on the box is the same.

**7 Summarize** Complete the table below by filling in the word *larger*, *smaller*, or *same* to compare lifting the box with pushing it up the ramp.

|  | Lifting box | Using ramp |
|---|---|---|
| Force applied | larger | smaller |
| Distance through which force is applied |  |  |
| Work done |  |  |

## Change the Direction of a Force

Some machines change the way you do work by changing the direction of a force. For example, you apply a downward force when you pull on the rope to raise a flag. The rope runs over a pulley at the top of the flagpole. The rope exerts an upward force on the flag, and the flag goes up. The direction of the force you applied has changed. But the magnitude of force and distance through which you apply the force are the same.

The pulley on the flagpole changed only the direction of the force. However, other machines can change the direction of a force, the magnitude of the force, and the distance through which the force is applied.

Pulling down on the rope pulls up the flag.

Input force

# Input and Output

## What is mechanical advantage?

Machines change force by different amounts. A machine's **mechanical advantage** is the number of times the machine multiplies the input force. It is a way of comparing the input force with the output force. Ignoring friction, you can calculate mechanical advantage, MA, of any machine by dividing the output force by the input force.

$$\text{mechanical advantage} = \frac{\text{output force}}{\text{input force}}$$

The bottle opener, pulley, and hammer shown below have different mechanical advantages. A machine that has a mechanical advantage greater than one multiplies the input force, producing greater output force. A machine that has a mechanical advantage equal to one changes only the direction of the force. A machine that has a mechanical advantage less than one requires greater input force, but the output force is applied through a longer distance.

**Active Reading**

**8 Identify** As you read, underline what happens when the mechanical advantage of a machine is equal to one.

### Do the Math

**Sample Problem**

The bottle opener changes the input force of 1 N to an output force of 2 N. Calculate the mechanical advantage of the bottle opener.

Output Force · Input Force

$$MA = \frac{\text{output force}}{\text{input force}}$$
$$= 2\,N / 1\,N$$
$$= 2$$

**You Try It**

**9 Calculate** The pulley changes the direction of a 5 N input force. The output force is equal to the input force. Calculate the mechanical advantage.

Input Force · Output Force

MA = _____

= _____

= _____

**You Try It**

**10 Calculate** The input force applied on the hammer is 6 N. The output force applied to the nail is 2 N. Calculate the mechanical advantage.

Output Force · Input Force

MA = _____

= _____

= _____

# What is mechanical efficiency?

Ideally, the work a machine does on an object is the same as the work that you put into it. But even when the mechanical advantage is greater than one, the work input is greater than the work output because some work is done to overcome friction. **Mechanical efficiency** is a comparison of a machine's work output with the work input. Mechanical efficiency, ME, is equal to the work output divided by the work input, expressed as a percentage.

$$\text{mechanical efficiency} = \frac{\text{work output}}{\text{work input}} \times 100\%$$

## Do the Math

### Sample Problem

Suppose 5,000 J of work is put into a go-cart engine. The work output of the engine is 1,250 J. What is the mechanical efficiency of the engine?

$$ME = \frac{\text{work output}}{\text{work input}} \times 100\%$$

$$= \frac{1,250 \text{ J}}{5,000 \text{ J}} \times 100\%$$

$$= 25\%$$

### What Happens to Input Work

Work output 25%

Unusable work 75%

Only 25% of work that goes into the engine is used to move the go-cart.

## You Try It!

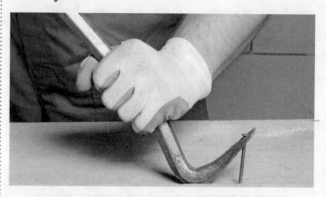

**11 Calculate** A person does 500 J of work on a crowbar. The crowbar does 475 J of work on a nail. What is the mechanical efficiency of the crowbar?

**12 Graph** Draw and label a pie graph that shows the percentages of work output and unusable work.

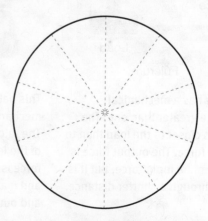

# Gaining Leverage

## What are the classes of levers?

What do hammers, seesaws, and baseball bats have in common? They are all levers. A **lever** is a simple machine that has a bar that pivots at a fixed point. This fixed point is called a **fulcrum**. Levers are used to apply a force to move an object. The force of the object is called the load.

*Ideal mechanical advantage* is the mechanical advantage of a simple machine that does not take friction into account. In other words, ideal mechanical advantage is the mechanical advantage of a machine that is 100% efficient. The ideal mechanical advantage of a lever is equal to the distance from input force to fulcrum ($d_{input}$) divided by the distance from output force to fulcrum ($d_{output}$).

$$\text{ideal mechanical advantage} = \frac{d_{input}}{d_{output}}$$

### 👁 Visualize It!

**14 Illustrate** In box C, draw and label a first-class lever that has an ideal mechanical advantage less than one.

### First-Class Levers

There are three classes of levers that differ based on the positions of the fulcrum, the load, and the input force. A seesaw is an example of a *first-class lever*. In a first-class lever, the fulcrum is between the input force and the load. First-class levers always change the direction of the input force. They may also increase the force or the distance through which the force is applied. The ideal mechanical advantage of first-class levers can be greater than one, equal to one, or less than one, depending on the location of the fulcrum.

**Active Reading** **13 Describe** Where is the fulcrum located in a first-class lever?

_____

_____

_____

**A**

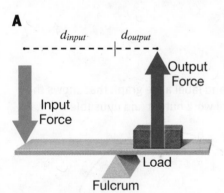

This lever has a mechanical advantage greater than one. The fulcrum is closer to the load than to the input force. The output force is larger than the input force, but it is applied through a shorter distance.

**B**

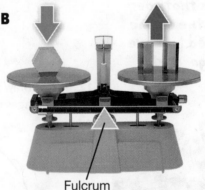

This balance is a lever that has a mechanical advantage equal to one. The fulcrum is exactly in the middle of the lever. The direction of the force is changed, but the distance and magnitude of the input force and output force are the same.

**C**

This lever has a mechanical advantage of less than one. The fulcrum is closer to the input force than to the load. The output force is less than the input force, but it is applied through a longer distance.

## Second-Class Levers

In a *second-class lever,* the load is between the fulcrum and the input force. Second-class levers do not change the direction of the input force. They allow you to apply less force than the load. But you must exert the input force through a greater distance. The ideal mechanical advantage for a second-class lever is always greater than one. Wheelbarrows, bottle-cap openers, and staplers are second-class levers. A stapler pivots at one end when you push on the other end. The output force of the stapler drives the staple into the paper. The output force is applied between where you push and where the stapler pivots.

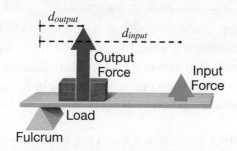

The load is between the fulcrum and input force in a stapler.

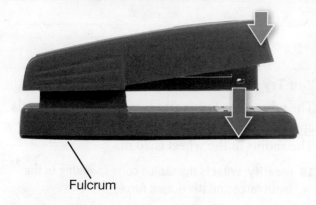

Fulcrum

## Third-Class Levers

In a *third-class lever,* the input force is between the fulcrum and the load. Like second-class levers, third-class levers do not change the direction of the input force. The mechanical advantage for a third-class lever is always less than one. The output force is less than the input force. But the output force is applied through a longer distance. Hammers and baseball bats are examples of third-class levers. When you swing a baseball bat, the fulcrum is at the base of the handle. The output force is at the end of the bat where it hits the ball. A bat applies a force to the ball in the same direction as you swing the bat. Your hands move a much shorter distance than the end of the bat moves when you swing.

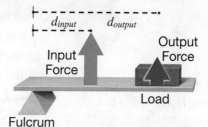

The input force is between the fulcrum and the load in a baseball bat.

---

### Do the Math   You Try It!

**15 Calculate** The input force of a third-class lever is 5 cm away from the fulcrum. The output force is 20 cm away from the fulcrum. What is the ideal mechanical advantage of the lever?

**16 Model** Draw and label a diagram of the lever described in question 15. Make sure to show the correct relative distances of the input and output forces from the fulcrum.

# Turn, Turn, Turn

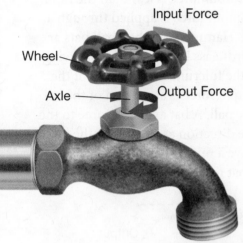

**Input Force**

Wheel

Axle

**Output Force**

The axle of this faucet turns when an input force is applied to the wheel. The axle rotates through a shorter distance than the wheel does. So the output force is larger than the input force.

## What is a wheel and axle?

A **wheel and axle** is a simple machine that is made of a wheel connected to a smaller cylindrical object, the axle. Doorknobs, tires, and screwdrivers are machines that contain wheels and axles.

The ideal mechanical advantage of a wheel and axle equals the radius corresponding to the input force divided by the radius corresponding to the output force.

$$\text{ideal mechanical advantage} = \frac{radius_{input}}{radius_{output}}$$

The radius of the wheel is always larger than the radius of the axle. The mechanical advantage is greater than one when the input force is applied to the wheel, such as when you turn on a faucet. The mechanical advantage is less than one when the input force is applied to the axle, such as when a Ferris wheel is turned.

**Active Reading** **17 Describe** When does a wheel and axle have a mechanical advantage greater than one?

_____

_____

### Do the Math

#### Sample Problem

The faucet has a wheel radius of 5 cm and an axle radius of 1 cm. What is its ideal mechanical advantage?

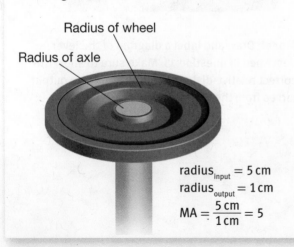

Radius of wheel

Radius of axle

$radius_{input} = 5\,cm$
$radius_{output} = 1\,cm$
$MA = \dfrac{5\,cm}{1\,cm} = 5$

#### You Try It!

The wheel of a Ferris wheel turns when a force is applied to the axle. The radius of its axle is 1 m. The radius of the wheel is 20 m.

**18 Identify** What is the radius corresponding to the input force and the output force?

$radius_{input}$: _____

$radius_{output}$: _____

**19 Calculate** What is the ideal mechanical advantage of the Ferris wheel?

# What are the types of pulleys?

When you open window blinds by pulling on a cord, you're using a pulley. A **pulley** is a simple machine that has a grooved wheel that holds a rope or a cable. A load is attached to one end of the rope, and an input force is applied to the other end. There are three different types of pulleys.

## Fixed Pulleys

The pulley at the top of a flagpole is a *fixed pulley*. A fixed pulley is attached to something that does not move. It allows you to pull down on the rope to lift the load up. The wheel of the pulley turns and changes the direction of the force. Fixed pulleys do not change the size of the force. The size of the output force is the same as the size of the input force. Therefore, a fixed pulley has an ideal mechanical advantage of one.

Input Force

Output Force

## Movable Pulleys

Unlike a fixed pulley, the wheel of a *movable pulley* is attached to the object being moved. One end of the rope is fixed. You can pull on the other end of the rope to make the wheel and load move along the rope. A movable pulley moves up with the load as the load is lifted. A movable pulley does not change the direction of a force, but does increase the force. The ideal mechanical advantage of all movable pulleys is two. They also increase the distance through which the input force must be applied. The rope must be pulled twice the distance that the load is moved.

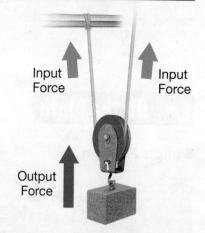

Input Force

Input Force

Output Force

## Block and Tackle Pulleys

A *block and tackle pulley* is a pulley system made by combining a fixed pulley and a movable pulley. Cranes at construction sites use block and tackle pulleys to lift heavy objects. Block and tackle pulleys change the direction of the force and increase the force. The ideal mechanical advantage of a block and tackle pulley depends on the number of rope segments. The ideal mechanical advantage of a block and tackle with four rope segments is four. It multiplies your input force by four. But you have to pull the rope four times as far.

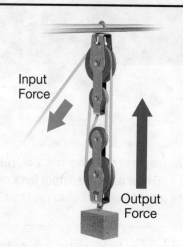

Input Force

Output Force

**20 Identify** Which type(s) of pulley could you use to increase your output force?

_____

_____

# So Inclined

## What are inclined planes?

Why is pushing furniture up a ramp easier than lifting the furniture? When you push something up a ramp, you are using a machine called an *inclined plane*. An **inclined plane** is a simple machine that is a straight, slanted surface. A smaller input force is needed to move an object using an inclined plane than is needed to lift the object. However, the force must be applied through a longer distance. So, the amount of work done on the object is the same. The ideal mechanical advantage of an inclined plane can be calculated by dividing the length of the incline by the height that the load is lifted.

**Active Reading**

**21 Identify** As you read, underline how an inclined plane changes the force and the distance through which the force is applied.

$$\text{ideal mechanical advantage} = \frac{length}{height}$$

## Do the Math

### Sample Problem

Length

Height

The length of the ramp is 4.2 m. The height of the ramp is 1.2 m. How does the output force on the chair compare to the input force applied to the chair?

$$\text{ideal mechanical advantage} =$$
$$\frac{length}{height} = \frac{4.2 \text{ m}}{1.2 \text{ m}} = 3.5$$

The output force on the chair is 3.5 times the input force.

### You Try It!

**22 Illustrate** Use the grid below to draw and label a diagram of an inclined plane that has a length of 6 meters and an ideal mechanical advantage of 3. Use the squares to approximate the length. (Hint: In the space below, use the mechanical advantage to calculate the height.)

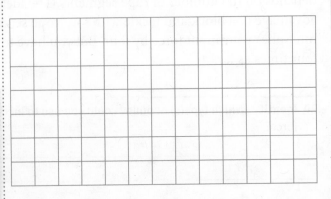

# What are wedges?

Sculptors use chisels to break rock and wood. Chisels, ax heads, and knife blades are wedges. A *wedge* is a pair of inclined planes that move. They have one thick end and one thin end. Wedges are used to cut and split objects. For example, a sculptor applies an input force to the thick end of a chisel. The thin end of the chisel exerts an outward force that splits open the object. The output force of the wedge is greater than the input force, but the output force is applied through a shorter distance. The longer and thinner the wedge is, the greater its ideal mechanical advantage. So a longer chisel has a greater mechanical advantage than a shorter chisel that is the same width at the thick end.

Wedges have two sloped sides and help split objects.

# What are screws?

Screws are often used to hold wood together. A *screw* is an inclined plane that is wrapped in a spiral around a cylinder. Think of wrapping a long triangular piece of paper around a pencil, as shown below. The ridges formed by the paper are like the threads of a screw. When a screw is turned, a small force is applied through the distance along the inclined plane of the screw. The screw applies a large force through the short distance it is pushed.

Imagine unwinding the inclined plane of a screw. You would see that the plane is very long and has a gentle slope. The longer an inclined plane is compared with its height, the greater its ideal mechanical advantage. Similarly, the longer the spiral on a screw is and the closer together the threads are, the greater the screw's mechanical advantage.

The threads of a screw are made by wrapping an inclined plane around a cylinder.

## Think Outside the Book (Inquiry)

**23 Apply** Make a list of simple machines you use every day. In a small group, try to classify all the machines identified by the group members.

# Visual Summary

To complete this summary, check the box that indicates true or false. Then, use the key below to check your answers. You can use this page to review the main concepts of the lesson.

## Machines

Mechanical efficiency is a way to compare a machine's work output with work input.

The six types of simple machines:

- levers
- wheel and axles
- pulleys
- inclined planes
- wedges
- screws

|  | T | F |  |
|---|---|---|---|
| 24 | ☐ | ☐ | Mechanical advantage is calculated by dividing the output force by the input force and multiplying by 100. |
| 25 | ☐ | ☐ | Friction causes the real mechanical advantage of a ramp to be less than the ideal mechanical advantage. |

|  | T | F |  |
|---|---|---|---|
| 26 | ☐ | ☐ | The location of the fulcrum differs for first-class levers, second-class levers, and third-class levers. |
| 27 | ☐ | ☐ | Types of pulleys include fixed pulleys, movable pulleys, and wheel and axles. |
| 28 | ☐ | ☐ | Using ramps, wedges, and screws reduces the amount of work that is done. |

Answers: 24 False; 25 True; 26 True; 27 False; 28 False

**29 Apply** A third-class lever has an ideal mechanical advantage of less than one. Explain why it is useful for some tasks, and identify two examples of third-class levers.

© Houghton Mifflin Harcourt Publishing Company • Image Credits: (tl) ©HMH; (tr) ©Tetra Images/Getty Images

# Lesson Review

## Vocabulary

Draw a line to connect the following terms to their definitions.

**1** machine

**2** lever

**3** wheel and axle

**4** pulley

**5** inclined plane

**A** a simple machine that has a grooved wheel that holds a rope

**B** a simple machine consisting of two circular objects of different sizes

**C** a simple machine that is a straight, slanted surface

**D** a device that helps people do work by changing the way work is done

**E** a simple machine that has a bar that pivots at a fixed point

## Key Concepts

**6 Explain** In what two ways can machines change the way work is done?

_____

_____

_____

_____

**7 Identify** What equation would you use to calculate the ideal mechanical advantage of a wheel and axle if the input force is applied to the axle?

_____

_____

_____

**8 Solve** A stone block is pushed up a ramp that is 120 m long and 20 m high. What is the ideal mechanical advantage of the ramp?

_____

_____

## Critical Thinking

**9 Apply** A person does 50 J of work to lift a crate using a pulley. The pulley's work output is 42 J. What is the pulley's mechanical efficiency?

_____

_____

Use this drawing to answer the following questions.

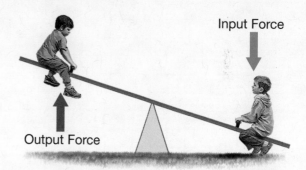

Input Force

Output Force

**10 Classify** What type of lever is the seesaw? Explain.

_____

_____

**11 Calculate** The input force is 245 N, and the output force is 245 N. Calculate the ideal mechanical advantage of the seesaw.

_____

_____

**12 Predict** The boy applying the input force moves so that he is 1.5 m from the fulcrum. The seesaw applies an output force to the other boy, who is 2 m from the fulcrum. What is the new ideal mechanical advantage?

_____

_____

_____

_____

# My Notes

# Unit 4

**Big Idea** Energy is always conserved but can change from one form to another and can be transferred from one object to another or within a substance.

### Lesson 1
**ESSENTIAL QUESTION**
**What is energy?**

Describe how energy is conserved through transformation between different forms.

### Lesson 2
**ESSENTIAL QUESTION**
**How is temperature related to kinetic energy?**

Relate the temperature of a substance to the kinetic energy of its particles.

### Lesson 3
**ESSENTIAL QUESTION**
**What is the relationship between heat and temperature?**

Analyze the relationship between heat, temperature, and thermal energy.

### Lesson 4
**ESSENTIAL QUESTION**
**How are distance, time, and speed related?**

Analyze how distance, time, and speed are related.

### Lesson 5
**ESSENTIAL QUESTION**
**How does motion change?**

Analyze how acceleration is related to time and velocity.

### Lesson 6
**ESSENTIAL QUESTION**
**How do forces affect motion?**

Describe different types of forces, and explain the effect force has on motion.

### Lesson 7
**ESSENTIAL QUESTION**
**How do simple machines work?**

Describe different types of simple machines, and calculate the mechanical advantages and efficiencies of various simple machines.

---

**Connect** **ESSENTIAL QUESTIONS**
Lessons 1 and 3

**1 Apply** Give an example of an energy transformation that results in a temperature change.

_____

_____

_____

## Think Outside the Book

**2 Synthesize** Choose one of these activities to help synthesize what you have learned in this unit.

☐ Using what you learned in lessons 1, 2, and 3, make a poster that explains the movement of particles in a cold glass of water as energy is transferred to the glass from warm hands.

☐ Using what you learned in lessons 5 and 6, use everyday examples to explain the relationship among force, acceleration, and gravity to a group of younger students.

# Unit 4 Review

Name _____

## Vocabulary

Fill in the blank with the term that best completes the sentence.

**1** The _____ of an object describes the speed and the direction in which it is going.

**2** _____ is the energy transferred from an object at a higher temperature to an object at a lower temperature.

**TEKS** 6.8A

**3** The _____ theory of matter states that all of the particles that make up matter are constantly in motion.

**4** _____ is the sum of an object's kinetic and potential energy.

## Key Concepts

Choose the letter of the best answer.

**TEKS** 6.8C, 6.8D

**5** Joanna's family drove 360 km on a trip. The graph below represents their motion.

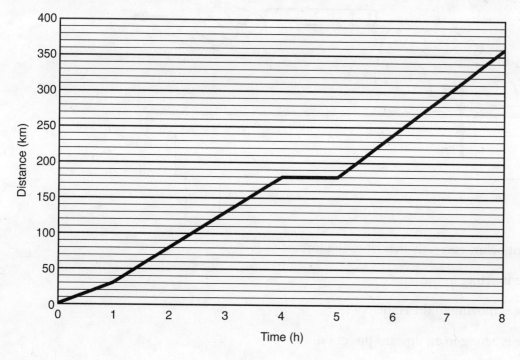

What was the average speed during the last 3 h of the trip?

**A** 45 km/h          **C** 120 km/h

**B** 60 km/h          **D** 180 km/h

TEKS 6.8C

**6** An airplane leaves New York to fly to Los Angeles. It travels 3850 km in 5.5 hours. What is the average speed of the airplane?

**A** 700 km

**C** 700 km/hour

**B** 700 hours

**D** 7000 hours/km

**7** Julia is in a car with her father. The car is undergoing centripetal acceleration. What is happening to the car?

**A** The car is slowing down.

**B** The car is stopping suddenly.

**C** The car is changing direction and speeding up.

**D** The car is changing direction at a constant speed.

TEKS 6.8B

**8** The diagram below shows the forces acting on a sneaker. As the force $F$ is applied, the sneaker does not move.

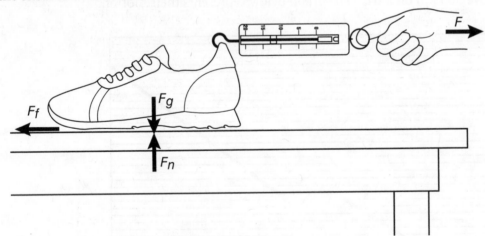

Which statement below correctly describes the forces?

**A** The net force is acting to the left.

**B** The net force is moving to the right.

**C** The net force is acting in an upward direction.

**D** The net force is zero, and all the forces are balanced.

© Houghton Mifflin Harcourt Publishing Company

TEKS 6.9B, 6.2E

**9** Addison warms a pure, solid substance. He records the changes in temperature over time in the left-hand column of the following data table. In the right-hand column, he records the state of the substance.

| Temperature (°C) | State |
|---|---|
| 0 | solid |
| X | liquid |
| Y | boiling liquid |
| Z | gas |

Which of the following could represent the missing values in Addison's data table? (Hint: Step 1. Think about the relative temperatures at which a solid becomes a liquid, boils, and becomes gaseous. Step 2. Determine if the temperature will increase or decrease as the substance changes phases.)

**A** $X = 50$; $Y = 100$; $Z = 50$   **C** $X = -50$; $Y = -100$; $Z = -50$

**B** $X = 50$; $Y = 100$; $Z = 150$   **D** $X = -50$; $Y = -100$; $Z = -150$

TEKS 6.9A

**10** Which of the following is the transfer of energy as heat by the movement of a liquid or gas?

**A** radiation

**B** emission

**C** convection

**D** conduction

TEKS 6.4A

**11** A student collects and records the following data throughout the day.

| Time | Temperature (°C) |
|---|---|
| 9 a.m. | 12 |
| 11 a.m. | 14 |
| 3 p.m. | 16 |
| 5 p.m. | 13 |

Which instrument did the student use to collect the temperature data?

**A** scale

**B** balance

**C** barometer

**D** thermometer

TEKS 6.8A

12 A mass hanging from a spring moves up and down. The mass stops moving temporarily each time the spring is extended to its fullest at position 2 and each time it returns to its tight coil at position 4.

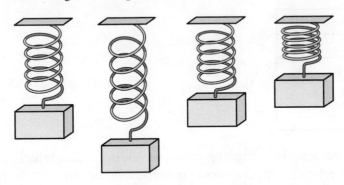

Position 1    Position 2    Position 3    Position 4

Which answer choice best describes the type of energy the spring has at Position 1?

**A** kinetic energy

**C** both potential energy and kinetic energy

**B** potential energy

**D** neither potential energy or kinetic energy

TEKS 6.9C

13 A person flips a switch to turn on a lamp. Instantly, light is produced. What is one other form of energy that the person should expect to observe from the lamp?

**A** sound

**C** thermal

**B** nuclear

**D** chemical

TEKS 6.8E

14 Movers roll a piano up a ramp and into a building. If the ramp has a mechanical advantage of 6, which of the following could be true about the length of the ramp and the height of its incline? (Hint: Step 1. Think about how mechanical advantage is calculated. Step 2. Calculate the mechanical advantage of each of the answer choices. Step 3. Compare the mechanical advantage of each answer choice to the required mechanical advantage of 6.)

**A** The ramp is 3 meters long, and the incline is 2 meters high.

**B** The ramp is 6 meters long, and the incline is 3 meters high.

**C** The ramp is 12 meters long, and the incline is 2 meters high.

**D** The ramp is 18 meters long, and the incline is 6 meters high.

## Gridded Response

Write your answer in the boxes, then bubble in the corresponding number in the grid below.

**TEKS** 6.8E

**15** A worker moves a heavy load into a house with the aid of an inclined plane. If the plane has a length of 8.5 meters and an ideal mechanical advantage of 3.5, what is the height, in meters, of the inclined plane?

## Critical Thinking

Answer the following questions in the space provided.

**TEKS** 6.8B

**16** Marek is trying to push a box of sports equipment across the floor. The arrow on the box is a vector representing the force that Marek exerts.

Besides the force that Marek exerts, which other forces are acting upon the box? Describe each one.

_____

_____

_____

_____

TEKS **6.8B**

**17** What does the formula $F = ma$ mean, and which of Newton's three laws does it describe?

_____

_____

_____

_____

TEKS **6.8A, 6.9C**

**18** Describe the law of conservation of energy. Then, give two examples of energy being transformed from one type to another.

_____

_____

_____

_____

## Connect ESSENTIAL QUESTIONS
Lessons 1, 6, and 7

Answer the following question in the space provided.

TEKS **6.8A, 6.8E**

**19** Explain how an inclined plane makes loading a piano into a truck easier. Refer to the changing potential energy and kinetic energy of the piano as it (a) sits on the ground, (b) is being moved into the truck, and (c) sits in the truck.

_____

_____

_____

_____

_____

_____

_____

_____

# Energy Resources

## Big Idea

Humans depend on natural resources for materials and for energy.

Common building materials such as lumber, bricks, and glass are all made from natural resources.

## What do you think?

Texas has the resources that humans need to live. These resources are found on Earth or come from the sun. What would happen if one or more of these resources were used up?

285

# Unit 5
# Energy Resources

# Texas Energy Sources

Texas is known for its energy resources. Vast amounts of oil, natural gas, coal, and uranium have been produced from Texas resources. For economic and environmental reasons, oil production in Texas has fallen drastically and is not expected to fully recover. How we use, reuse, or use up Texas resources is important to your generation and the future.

## ① Think About It

Every time you walk into school on a normal school day, the lights are on, the rooms are comfortable, and there are material resources available for teacher and student use. Where does your school get its energy? Is it from a renewable or nonrenewable resource? Could the energy be used more efficiently?

_____

_____

_____

Solar panels increase this school's efficiency.

## ② Ask a Question

### What is the energy source for your school's heating and cooling system?

With a partner or as a class, learn more about the source of energy for your school's heating and cooling system and the energy efficiency of your school building. Some Texas schools have installed solar panels or other systems for harnessing renewable energy. As you talk about it, consider the items below.

### Things to Consider

☐ Does your school have more than one energy source?

☐ Is your school building energy efficient?

## ③ Make a Plan

Once you have learned about your school building's energy efficiency, develop a proposal for your principal. Propose an alternative energy source for the heating and cooling system and ways to improve the building's energy efficiency.

**A** Describe the current energy source for your school's heating and cooling system.

_____

_____

**B** Describe one alternative energy source your school could use.

_____

_____

**C** List any noted energy inefficiencies and suggestions for improvements.

_____

_____

_____

Ideas for saving resources can help schools save money.

Oil pump jacks such as this one are a familiar sight across Texas. They bring fossil fuels to the surface. As interest in renewable energy sources increases, wind turbines are becoming a common sight in oil fields across the country.

### Take It Home

What energy sources supply your home? With an adult, talk about possible ways to improve energy efficiency where you live.

## Lesson 1

# Natural Resources

**ESSENTIAL QUESTION**

## What are Earth's natural resources?

By the end of this lesson, you should be able to understand the types and uses of Earth's natural resources.

*Light produced from electrical energy helps people see at night. Natural resources are needed to produce electrical energy.*

**TEKS** **6.7B** design a logical plan to manage energy resources in the home, school, or community

## Lesson Labs

**Quick Labs**
- Renewable or Not?
- Production Impacts
- Managing Energy Resources

**Field Labs**
- Natural Resources Used at Lunch

## Engage Your Brain

**1 Predict** Check T or F to show whether you think each statement is true or false.

T   F

☐   ☐   Energy from the sun can be used to make electrical energy.

☐   ☐   All of Earth's resources will last forever.

☐   ☐   Food, cloth, rope, lumber, paper, and rubber come from plants.

☐   ☐   Human activity can negatively affect Earth's resources.

**2 Describe** Name one item that you use every day. Describe the natural resources that you think are used to make this item.

_____

_____

_____

_____

_____

_____

_____

## Active Reading

**3 Preview** Before you begin reading this lesson, look through the pages and read the headings and subheadings. The headings show how information is organized in the lesson. After you read the headings and subheadings, write a short description of what the lesson will cover.

_____

_____

_____

_____

_____

_____

_____

_____

_____

_____

_____

_____

_____

### Vocabulary Terms

- natural resource
- renewable resource
- nonrenewable resource
- fossil fuel
- material resource
- energy resource

**4 Identify** This list contains the key terms you'll learn in this lesson. As you read, circle the definition of each term.

# It's Only Natural

## What are natural resources?

What do the water you drink, the paper you write on, the gasoline used in cars, and the air you breathe all have in common? They all come from Earth's natural resources. A **natural resource** is any natural material that is used by humans. Natural resources include air, soil, minerals, water, oil, plants, and animals.

Earth's natural resources provide everything needed for life. The atmosphere contains the air we breathe. Rainfall from the atmosphere renews the water in oceans, rivers, lakes, and underground. In turn, these water sources provide water for drinking, industry, and other uses. Earth's soil provides nutrients necessary for plants to grow. Plants provide food for some animals and humans. Animals provide food as well. Many of Earth's resources, such as oil and wind, provide energy for human use. The energy in these resources comes from the sun's energy. Earth's resources are also used to make products that make people's lives more convenient.

**Active Reading**

**5 Identify** List four examples of natural resources.

_____

_____

_____

## How can we manage resources?

As human populations continue to grow, we will need more and more resources in order to survive. People can make sure that resources continue to be available by practicing stewardship and conservation. *Stewardship* is the careful and responsible management of resources. *Conservation* is the protection and wise use of natural resources.

**Visualize It!**

**6 Illustrate** Draw or label the missing natural resources.

(A)

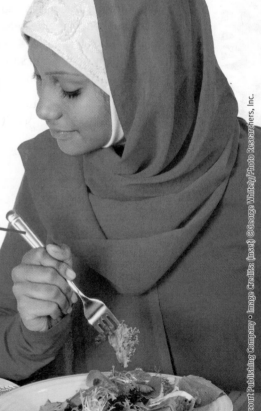

Bauxite is a rock that is used to make aluminum.

# How can we categorize natural resources?

There are many different types of natural resources. Some can be replaced more quickly than others. A natural resource may be categorized as a renewable resource or a nonrenewable resource.

**Think Outside the Book** Inquiry

**7 Debate** Research why water or soil can be a renewable or nonrenewable resource. Discuss your points with a classmate.

## Renewable Resources

Some natural resources can be replaced in a relatively short time. A natural resource that can be replaced at the same rate at which it is consumed is a **renewable resource**. Solar energy, water, and air are all renewable resources. Some renewable resources are considered to be *inexhaustible resources* [in•ig•ZAW•stuh•buhl REE•sohrs•iz] because the resources can never be used up. Solar energy and wind energy, which is powered by the sun, are examples of inexhaustible resources. Other renewable resources are not inexhaustible. Trees and crops that are used for food must be replanted and regrown. Water must be managed so that it does not become scarce.

## Nonrenewable Resources

A resource that forms much more slowly than it is consumed is a **nonrenewable resource**. Some natural resources, such as minerals, form very slowly. Iron ore and copper are important minerals. A **fossil fuel** is a nonrenewable resource formed from the buried remains of plants and animals that lived long ago. Coal, oil, and natural gas are examples of fossil fuels. Coal and oil take millions of years to form. Once these resources are used up, humans will have to find other resources to use instead. Some renewable resources, such as water and wood, may become nonrenewable if they are not used wisely.

**8 Compare** List some examples of renewable and nonrenewable resources.

| Renewable resources | Nonrenewable resources |
|---|---|
|  |  |
|  |  |
|  |  |
|  |  |

Natural fibers from cotton plants are processed to make fabric.

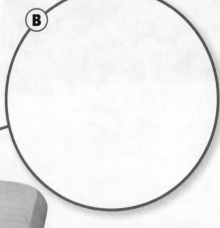

B

© Houghton Mifflin Harcourt Publishing Company • Image Credits: (Inset) ©Inga Spence/Visuals Unlimited/Getty Images

# A Material World

## How do we use material resources?

Look around your classroom. The walls, windows, desks, pencils, books, and even the clothing you see are made of material resources. Natural resources that are used to make objects, food, or drink are called **material resources**. Material resources can be either renewable or nonrenewable. The cotton used in T-shirts is an example of a renewable resource. The metal used in your desk is an example of a nonrenewable resource.

## To Make Food or Drink

Material resources come from Earth's atmosphere, crust, and waters. They also come from organisms that live on Earth. Think about what you eat and drink every day. All foods and beverages are made from material resources. Some foods come from plants, such as the wheat in bread or the corn in tortillas. These resources are renewable, since farmers can grow more. Other foods, such as milk, cheese, eggs, and meat, come from animals. Juices, sodas, and sport drinks contain water, which is a renewable resource.

**Active Reading**

**9 Identify** As you read, underline examples of material resources.

**Visualize It!**

**10 List** List two types of food or drink that are made from the material resources in each picture.

A

B

C

# To Make Objects

Any object you see is made from material resources. For example, cars are made of steel, plastic, rubber, glass, and leather. Steel comes from iron, which is mined from rock. Plastic is made from oil, which must be drilled from areas underground. Natural rubber comes from tropical trees. Glass is made from minerals found in sand. Leather comes from the hides of animals.

Iron, oil, and sand are nonrenewable. If these materials are used too quickly, they can run out. Rubber, leather, and wood are renewable resources. The plants and animals that produce these resources can be managed so that these resources do not run out.

## Visualize It!

**11 Label** Write the name of each material resource that is used to make objects in this house.

*A house is made from many material resources.*

A

B

C

D

limestone

# Change It Up!

**Active Reading**

**12 Identify** As you read, underline the different forms of energy.

## How do we use energy resources?

Many objects need energy in order to be useful. For example, a bus needs energy so that it can move people around. Natural resources used to generate energy are called **energy resources**.

Energy is often stored in objects or substances. Stored energy is called *potential energy*. Food and products made from oil have potential energy that is stored in their chemical bonds. For this energy to be useful, it must be converted to *kinetic energy*, which is the energy of movement. Body cells perform chemical reactions that convert the potential energy in food to the kinetic energy that moves your body. Gasoline engines break the bonds in gasoline to convert potential energy to the kinetic energy that moves a car.

An object can have potential energy because of its position. An object that is high above the ground has more potential energy than an object that is close to the ground. Potential energy is converted to kinetic energy when the object falls, such as when water falls over a dam to produce electricity in a power plant.

The gasoline being pumped into this car has potential energy in its chemical bonds.

This car's engine burns gasoline, converting the potential energy in the fuel into the kinetic energy of the moving car.

**13 List** Look at the examples in the table. Write down three more situations in which potential energy changes to kinetic energy.

| When Does Potential Energy Change to Kinetic Energy? |
|---|
| when coal burns to produce electrical energy in a power plant |
| when your body digests food to give you energy to move |
| |
| |
| |

# How do everyday objects convert energy?

Energy cannot be created or destroyed, and energy must be converted to be useful. Energy conversions happen around us every day. Think about the appliances in your home. An electric oven warms food by converting electrical energy to energy as heat. A television converts electrical energy to light energy and sound energy, which is a type of kinetic energy. A fan moves by converting electrical energy to kinetic energy. Your body converts the chemical energy in food to kinetic energy as well as thermal energy. When you talk on the phone, the sound energy from your voice is converted to electrical energy. The phone on the other end of the conversation changes the electrical energy back to sound.

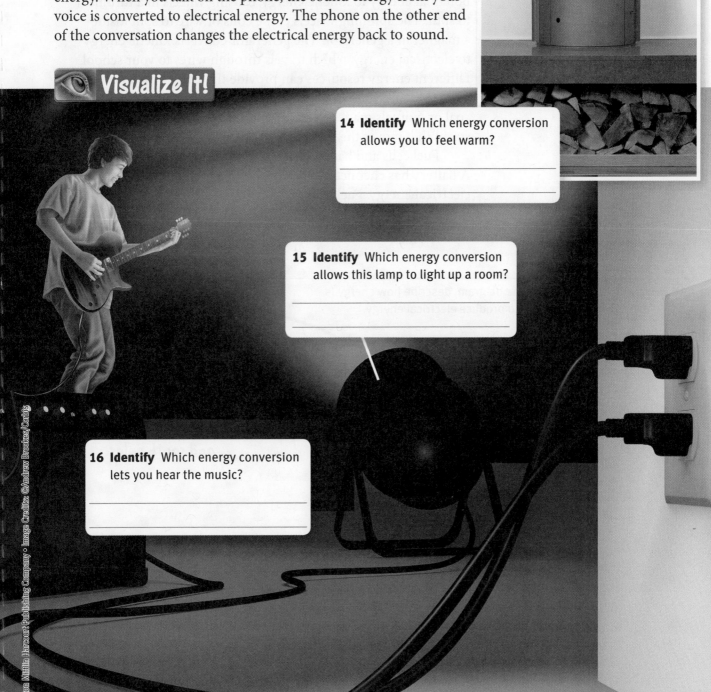

**Visualize It!**

**14 Identify** Which energy conversion allows you to feel warm?

_____

_____

**15 Identify** Which energy conversion allows this lamp to light up a room?

_____

_____

**16 Identify** Which energy conversion lets you hear the music?

_____

_____

# Power Trip

**17 Identify** As you read, underline the resources that can provide energy for a power plant.

## How is electrical energy produced?

Computers and appliances need electrical energy to work. Electrical energy is available from outlets, but how does this energy get to the outlets?

In most electrical power plants, an energy source converts potential energy to kinetic energy, causing wheels in a turbine to spin. The spinning wheels cause coils of wire to spin inside a magnet in a generator. The generator converts kinetic energy to electrical energy, which travels through wires to your school. Different energy resources can provide the energy for a power plant. Moving wind or water can turn wheels in a turbine. Burning coal or biofuels made from crop plants can warm water, producing steam that moves the turbine.

Fuel cells and batteries are other sources of electrical energy. A battery has chemicals inside that convert chemical energy to electrical energy. Fuel cells convert chemical energy from hydrogen to produce electrical energy.

### Visualize It!

**18 Describe** After looking at the diagram, describe how energy is converted in a power plant to produce electrical energy.

Energy source

Turbine

Generator

Powerlines

N

S

Steam

Electrical energy is generated when coils of wire are turned inside a large magnet. This magnet might look different from bar magnets you have seen, but it still has north and south poles.

_____

_____

_____

_____

_____

_____

## Why It Matters

# Clean Machines

Many car companies are introducing vehicles with hydrogen fuel cells. Hydrogen fuel cells use chemical reactions to produce electrical energy. These reactions produce no pollutants. If hydrogen fuel is made using renewable energy sources, these cars could truly be clean machines.

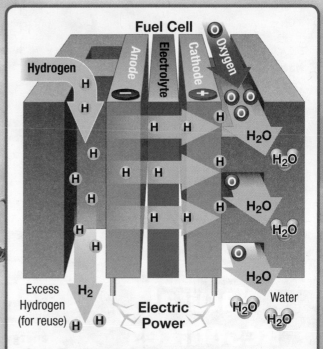

Fuel Cell

Hydrogen · Anode · Electrolyte · Cathode · Oxygen

$H_2O$

Excess Hydrogen (for reuse) · $H_2$ · Electric Power · Water · $H_2O$

### Small Packages

The hydrogen fuel cell in a car is about the size of a microwave oven.

HYDROGEN FUEL CELL ELECTRIC

### Cell Technology

The fuel cell removes electrons from hydrogen atoms. Electron movement generates electrical energy. Hydrogen then combines with oxygen to form water. Water and excess hydrogen are the products of this reaction. No carbon dioxide or other pollutants are produced.

driving the future

---

## Extend

Inquiry

**19 Explain** What kind of energy conversion happens in a hydrogen fuel cell?

**20 Compare** How is the process of energy conversion different between a fuel-cell vehicle and a gasoline vehicle?

**21 Infer** Hydrogen fuel must be produced by splitting water into hydrogen and oxygen. This process requires energy. Does it matter if nonrenewable energy is used to produce hydrogen fuel? Support your answer.

# Visual Summary

To complete this summary, answer the questions using the lines provided. Then, use the key below to check your answers. You can use this page to review the main concepts of the lesson.

Natural resources can be renewable or nonrenewable.

**22** What makes a resource renewable?

_____

_____

Material resources are used to make objects, food, and drink.

**23** What are two material resources in this picture?

_____

_____

## Natural Resources

Energy can be converted from one form to another. Potential energy in energy resources can be converted to kinetic energy.

**24** What are all the energy conversions that happen when wood burns?

_____

_____

**25 Illustrate** Think of a natural resource that can be used as both a material resource and as an energy resource. Draw two pictures to illustrate each use of the resource.

# Lesson Review

## Vocabulary

Draw a line to connect the following terms to their definitions.

**1** fossil fuel

**2** material resource

**3** natural resource

**A** resource used to make objects, food, or drink

**B** any natural material used by people

**C** a nonrenewable resource formed by buried remains of plants and animals

## Key Concepts

**4 List** Name two material resources and give an example of how each is used.

_____

_____

_____

**5 Describe** What makes a resource nonrenewable?

_____

_____

_____

_____

**6 Explain** How can the conversion from potential energy to kinetic energy provide energy that is useful to people?

_____

_____

_____

_____

_____

## Critical Thinking

**7 Apply** What could people do in order to make nonrenewable resources last longer?

_____

_____

_____

_____

Use the drawing to answer the following questions.

**8 Analyze** What energy conversions are occurring in the illustration?

_____

_____

_____

_____

**9 Infer** What form of energy that is not useful is being released from the flashlight when it is on?

_____

_____

**10 Relate** Assume that the batteries in the flashlight are rechargeable. What energy conversion would have to take place in order to recharge the batteries?

_____

_____

_____

# My Notes

# Lesson 2

# Nonrenewable Energy Resources

## ESSENTIAL QUESTION

## How do we use nonrenewable energy resources?

By the end of this lesson, you should be able to describe how humans use energy resources and the role of nonrenewable energy resources in society.

The energy that lights up this city and powers the vehicles comes from energy resources. Most of our energy resources are being used up faster than natural processes can replace them.

**TEKS** 6.7A research and debate the advantages and disadvantages of using coal, oil, natural gas, nuclear power, biomass, wind, hydropower, geothermal, and solar resources

## Engage Your Brain

**1 Identify** Unscramble the letters below to find substances that are nonrenewable resources.

ALCO _____

AUNTRLA SGA _____

NUUIMAR _____

MLPEOUTRE _____

**2 Describe** Write your own caption for this photo.

_____

_____

_____

_____

 Active Reading

**3 Synthesize** Many English words have their roots in other languages. Use the Latin word below to make an educated guess about the meaning of the word *fission*.

| Latin word | Meaning |
|------------|---------|
| *fissus* | to split |

**Example sentence**
An atomic nucleus can undergo <u>fission</u>.

*fission:*

_____

_____

_____

### Vocabulary Terms

• energy resource       • nuclear energy
• fossil fuel             • fission

**4 Identify** This list contains the vocabulary terms you'll learn in this lesson. As you read, circle the definition of each term.

# Be Resourceful!

## What are the two main types of nonrenewable energy resources?

An **energy resource** is a natural resource that humans use to generate energy and can be renewable or nonrenewable. *Renewable resources* are replaced by natural processes at least as quickly as they are used. *Nonrenewable resources* are used up faster than they can be replaced. Most of the energy used in the United States comes from nonrenewable resources.

### Fossil Fuels

A **fossil fuel** is a nonrenewable energy resource that forms from the remains of organisms that lived long ago. Fossil fuels release energy when they are burned. This energy can be converted to electricity or used to power engines. Fossil fuels are the most commonly used energy resource because they are relatively inexpensive to locate and process.

### Nuclear Fuel

The energy released when the nuclei of atoms are split or combined is called **nuclear energy**. This energy can be obtained by two kinds of nuclear reactions—fusion and fission. Today's nuclear power plants use fission, because the technology for fusion power plants does not currently exist. The most common nuclear fuel is uranium. Uranium is obtained by mining and processing uranium ore, which is a nonrenewable resource.

**6 Compare** Fill in the Venn diagram to compare and contrast fossil fuels and nuclear fuel.

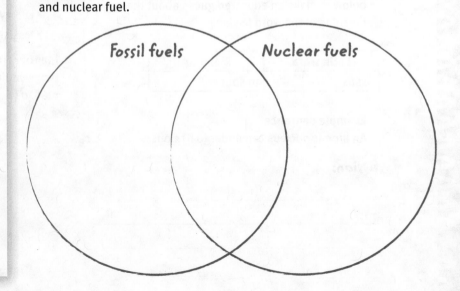

Fossil fuels        Nuclear fuels

# What are the three main types of fossil fuels?

All living things contain the element carbon. Fossil fuels form from the remains of living things, so they also contain carbon. Most of this carbon is in the form of hydrocarbons, which are compounds made of hydrogen and carbon. Fossil fuels can be liquids, gases, or solids. Fossil fuels include petroleum, natural gas, and coal.

**Active Reading** **7 Identify** As you read, underline the state of matter for each fossil fuel.

## Petroleum

Petroleum, or *crude oil,* is a liquid mixture of complex hydrocarbon compounds. Crude oil is extracted from the ground by drilling then processed for use. This process, called *refining,* separates the crude oil into different products such as gasoline, kerosene, and diesel fuel. More than 35 percent of the world's energy comes from crude oil products. Crude oil is also used to make products such as ink, bubble gum, and plastics.

This crude oil will be refined into gasoline, diesel fuel, heating oil, kerosene, and other products.

## Natural Gas

Natural gas is a mixture of gaseous hydrocarbons. Most natural gas is used for heating and cooking, but some is used to generate electricity. Also, some vehicles use natural gas as fuel.

Methane is the main component of natural gas. Butane and propane can also be separated from natural gas. Butane and propane are used as fuel for camp stoves and outdoor grills. Some rural homes also use propane as a heating fuel.

Natural gas is a popular fuel for cooking because it is inexpensive.

## Coal

The fossil fuel most widely used for generating electrical power is a solid called coal. Coal was once used to heat homes and for transportation. In fact, many trains in the 1800s and early 1900s were pulled by coal-burning steam locomotives. Now, most people use gasoline for transportation fuel. But more than half of our nation's electricity comes from coal-burning power plants.

Coal is a fossil fuel often used to generate electricity.

© Houghton Mifflin Harcourt Publishing Company • Image Credits: (t) ©Pablo Paul/Alamy; (c) ©IFMC/Alamy; (b) ©Dmitriy Sechin/Alamy Images

# How do fossil fuels form?

How might a sunny day 200 million years ago relate to your life today? If you traveled to school by bus or car, you likely used energy from sunlight that warmed Earth that long ago.

Fossil fuels form over millions of years from the buried remains of ancient organisms. Fossil fuels differ in the kinds of organisms from which they form and in how they form. This process is continuing, too. The fossil fuels forming today will be available for use in a few million years!

## Petroleum and Natural Gas Form from Marine Organisms

Petroleum and natural gas form mainly from the remains of microscopic sea organisms. When these organisms die, their remains sink and settle on the ocean floor. There, the dead organisms are gradually buried by sediment. The sediment is compacted by more layers of dead organisms and sediment. Over time the sediment layers become layers of rock.

Over millions of years, heat and pressure turn the remains of the organisms into petroleum and natural gas. The petroleum and natural gas, along with groundwater, flow into pores in the rock. A rock with pores is a *permeable rock*. Permeable rocks become reservoirs where the petroleum and natural gas are trapped and concentrated over time. Humans can extract the fuels from these reservoirs.

**Think Outside the Book** Inquiry

**8 Research** Write a summary on the advantages and disadvantages of using coal, oil, natural gas, and nuclear energy.

### Petroleum and Natural Gas Formation

**1** Microscopic marine organisms die and settle to the bottom of the sea.

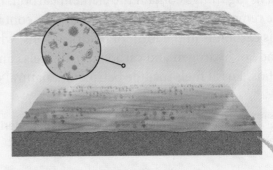

**2** Layers of sediment slowly bury the dead marine organisms.

**3** Heat and pressure on these layers slowly turn the remains of these organisms into petroleum and natural gas.

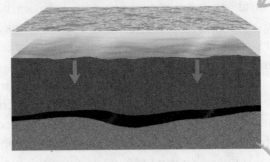

**4** Petroleum and natural gas flow through permeable rocks, where they are trapped and become concentrated into reservoirs.

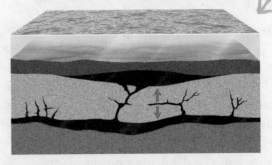

## Coal Formation

**1 Peat** Partially decayed swamp plants sink and change into peat.

**2 Lignite** As sediment buries the peat, increases in temperature and pressure change peat to lignite.

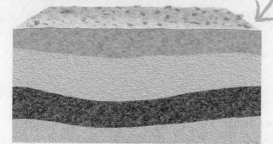

**3 Bituminous Coal** As sediment builds, increased temperature and pressure change lignite to bituminous coal.

**4 Anthracite** As sediments accumulate and temperature and pressure rise, bituminous coal changes to anthracite.

# Coal Forms from Plant Remains

Active Reading **9 Identify** As you read, underline the factors that convert the buried plants into coal.

Coal is formed over millions of years from the remains of swamp plants. When the plants die, they sink to the swamp floor. Low oxygen levels in the water keep many plants from decaying and allow the process of coal formation to begin. Today's swamp plants may eventually turn into coal millions of years from now.

The first step of coal formation is plant matter changing into peat. Peat is made mostly of plant material and water. Peat is not coal. In some parts of the world, peat is dried and burned for warmth or used as fuel. Peat that is buried by layers of sediment can turn into coal after millions of years.

Over time, pressure and high temperature force water and gases out of the peat. The peat gradually becomes harder, and its carbon content increases. The amount of heat and pressure determines the type of coal that forms. Lignite forms first, followed by bituminous coal and, finally, anthracite. Anthracite is highly valued because it has the highest carbon content and gives off the most energy as heat when burned.

Today, all three types of coal are mined around the world. When burned, coal releases energy as heat and pollutes the air. The greater the carbon content of the coal, the fewer pollutants are released and the cleaner the coal burns.

Visualize It!

**10 Compare** What is similar about the way petroleum and coal form? What is different?

_____

_____

_____

_____

_____

_____

# Power Trip

## How are fossil fuels used as energy sources?

In the United States, petroleum fuels are mainly used for transportation and heating. Airplanes, trains, boats, and cars all use petroleum for energy. Some people also use petroleum as a heating fuel. There are some oil-fired power plants in the United States, but most are found in other parts of the world.

Natural gas can be used as transportation fuel but is mainly used for heating and cooking. The use of natural gas as a source of electrical power is increasing. The U.S. Department of Energy projects that most power plants in the near future will use natural gas. Today, coal is mainly used in the U.S. to generate electricity, which we use for lighting and to power appliances and technology.

**Active Reading**

**11 Identify** As you read, underline the uses of fossil fuels.

*Burning coal heats water to produce steam. The steam turns the turbines to generate electricity. Scrubbers and filters in the smokestack help reduce air pollution.*

**Coal-Fired Power Plant**

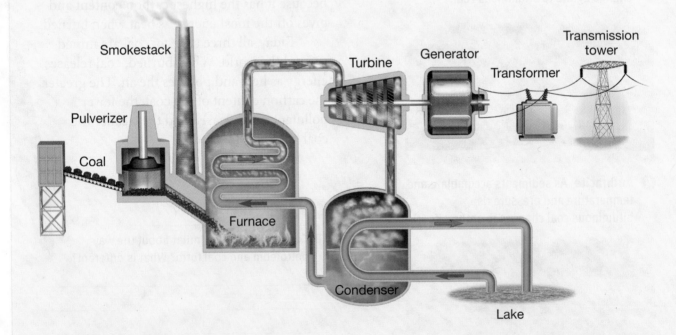

Smokestack

Pulverizer

Coal

Furnace

Turbine

Generator

Transformer

Transmission tower

Condenser

Lake

# How is energy produced from nuclear fuels?

During **fission**, the nuclei of radioactive atoms are split into two or more fragments. A small particle called a neutron hits and splits an atom. This process releases large amounts of energy as heat and radiation. Fission also releases more neutrons that bombard other atoms. The process repeats as a chain reaction. Fission takes place inside a reactor core. Fuel rods containing uranium, shown in green below, provide the material for the chain reaction. Control rods that absorb neutrons are used to regulate the chain reaction. The energy is released, which is used to generate electrical power. A closed reactor system contains the radioactivity. Nuclear wastes are contained separately for disposal.

During nuclear reactions, energy in the form of heat is released, which turns water into steam. Steam turns the turbines to generate electricity.

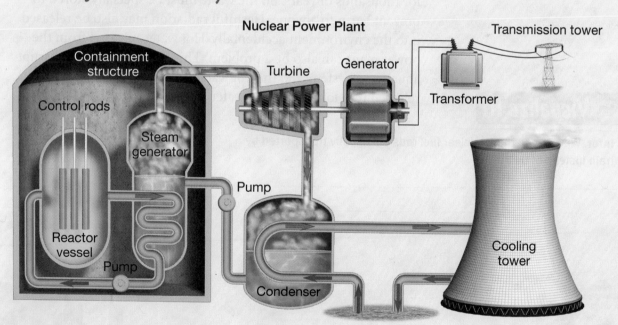

Nuclear Power Plant

12 **Compare** How are the two types of power plants similar? How are they different?

**Similar**

_____

_____

_____

_____

**Different**

_____

_____

_____

_____

# The Pros and Cons

## How can we evaluate nonrenewable energy resources?

There are advantages and disadvantages to using nonrenewable energy resources. Nonrenewable resources provide much of the energy that humans need to power transportation, warm homes, and produce electricity relatively cheaply. But the methods of obtaining and using these resources can have negative effects on the environment.

### The Pros and Cons of Nuclear Fuel

Nuclear fission produces a large amount of energy and does not cause air pollution because no fuel is burned. Mining uranium also does not usually result in massive strip mines or a large loss of habitat.

However, nuclear power does have drawbacks. Nuclear power plants produce dangerous wastes that remain radioactive for thousands of years. So the waste must be specially stored to prevent harm to anyone. Harmful radiation may also be released into the environment accidentally. Hot water released from the power plant can also be a problem. This heated water can disrupt aquatic ecosystems. So the hot water must be cooled before it is released into local bodies of water.

**Active Reading**

**13 Identify** As you read, underline the effects that nuclear power plants have on their surroundings.

**Visualize It!**

**14 Infer** Why do you think nuclear fuel rods are usually transported by train instead of by trucks?

_____

_____

Used nuclear fuel rods must be transported in specially built steel containers.

# The Pros and Cons of Fossil Fuels

Fossil fuels are relatively inexpensive to obtain and use. However, there are problems associated with their use. Burning coal can release sulfur dioxide, which combines with moisture in the air to form acid rain. Acid rain causes damage to structures and the environment. Coal mining also disturbs habitats, lowers water tables, and pollutes water.

Environmental problems are also associated with using oil. In 2010, a blown oil well spilled an estimated 200 million gallons of crude oil in the Gulf of Mexico for 86 days. The environmental costs may continue for years.

Burning fossil fuels can cause smog, especially in cities with millions of vehicles. Smog is a brownish haze that can cause respiratory problems and contribute to acid rain. Burning fossil fuels also releases carbon dioxide into the atmosphere. Increases in atmospheric carbon dioxide can lead to global warming.

Some coal is mined by removing the tops of mountains to expose the coal. This damages habitats and can cause water pollution as well.

**15 Debate** In the chart below, list the advantages and disadvantages of both nuclear energy and fossil fuels to have a classroom debate.

| Type of energy | Pros | Cons |
|---|---|---|
| nuclear energy | | |
| fossil fuels (coal, oil, and natural gas) | | |

# Visual Summary

**To complete this summary, check the box that indicates true or false. Then use the key below to check your answers. You can use this page to review the main concepts of the lesson.**

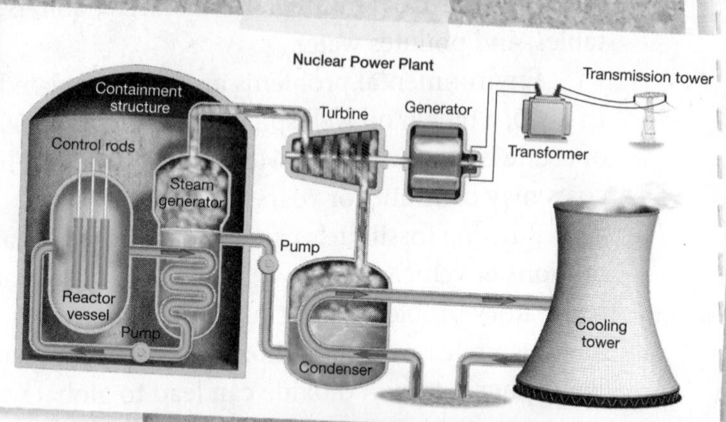


**Nuclear fuel is an energy resource that undergoes the process of fission to release energy for human use.**

| | T | F | |
|---|---|---|---|
| 16 | ☐ | ☐ | Uranium is often used as fuel in nuclear fission. |
| 17 | ☐ | ☐ | One disadvantage of nuclear fission is that it produces only a small amount of energy. |

## Nonrenewable Energy Resources

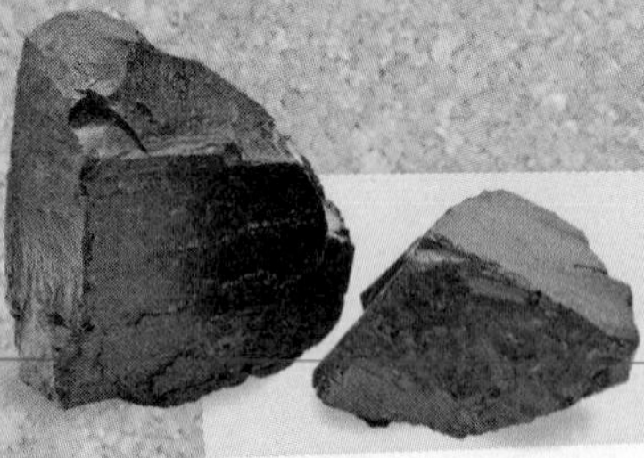

**Most of the energy used today comes from fossil fuels, which include petroleum, natural gas, and coal.**

| | T | F | |
|---|---|---|---|
| 18 | ☐ | ☐ | Natural gas forms from microscopic marine organisms. |
| 19 | ☐ | ☐ | Most transportation fuels are products of coal. |
| 20 | ☐ | ☐ | Burning fossil fuels decreases the amount of carbon dioxide in the atmosphere. |

Answers: 16 True; 17 False; 18 True; 19 False; 20 False

**21 Summarize** Identify the advantages and disadvantages for both fossil fuels and nuclear fuels.

# Lesson Review

## Vocabulary

Fill in the blank with the term that best completes the following sentences.

**1** _____ is energy in an atom's nucleus.

**2** Crude oil is a liquid kind of _____

**3** _____ can be renewable or nonrenewable.

**4** During the process of _____, the nuclei of radioactive atoms are split into two or more smaller nuclei.

## Key Concepts

**5 Describe** Describe how fossil fuels are converted into usable energy.

_____

_____

_____

_____

**6 Sequence** Which of the following sequences of processes best describes how electricity is generated in a nuclear power plant?

**A** fission reaction, produce steam, turn turbine, generate electricity, cool water

**B** produce steam, fission reaction, turn turbine, generate electricity, cool water

**C** cool water, fission reaction, produce steam, turn turbine, generate electricity

**D** produce steam, turn turbine, cool water, fission reaction, generate electricity

**7 Identify** Which is an example of how people use nonrenewable energy resources?

**A** eating a banana

**B** sailing a boat

**C** walking to school

**D** driving a car

## Critical Thinking

**8 Hypothesize** Why do some places in the United States have deposits of coal but others have deposits of petroleum and natural gas?

_____

_____

_____

_____

Use the graph to answer the following questions.

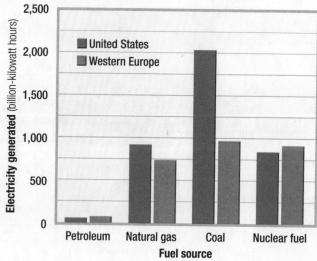

**Electricity Produced from Nonrenewable Energy Resources in 2007**

**9 Calculate** About how much more coal than petroleum is used to generate electricity in the United States and Western Europe?

_____

_____

_____

**10 Analyze** What patterns of energy resource use do you see in the graph?

_____

_____

_____

# My Notes

# Think Science

# Scientific Debate

Not all scientific knowledge is gained through experimentation. It is also a result of a great deal of research, debate, and risk analysis.

**TEKS 6.3A** in all fields of science, analyze, evaluate, and critique scientific explanations by using empirical evidence, logical reasoning, and experimental and observational testing, including examining all sides of scientific evidence of those scientific explanations, so as to encourage critical thinking by the student

**6.7A** research and debate the advantages and disadvantages of using coal, oil, natural gas, nuclear power, biomass, wind, hydropower, geothermal, and solar resources

## Tutorial

**As you research a topic about which there is much debate, look for the following from your sources.**

**Reliability** Reliable research can strengthen your argument. Scientific studies published in major journals are reviewed by other scientists and are more reliable than non-reviewed studies.

**Lack of bias** Bias is the tendency to favor a particular point of view or outcome. Determine whether your source favors a particular side of the topic. Science journals and university and government publications are less likely to be affected by bias than articles in magazines, newspapers, blogs, and commercial webpages.

**Fact-based conclusions** Scientific studies in journals are called primary sources. Secondary sources are reports that explain the findings of scientific studies. A tertiary source is a news item or magazine report about a scientific study. If using a secondary or tertiary source, does it provide references to its source information? Does it contain information for which you cannot find a source? Or does it have phrases such as "Experts say . . ." or "Most people know . . . " without providing reliable references?

**Read the passage, and answer the questions.**

Extracting natural gas and oil from places that were once too difficult to mine is now possible. One process involves injecting large amounts of fluids under high pressure deep into layers of shale, a type of sedimentary rock. This process is called *hydraulic fracturing,* or *fracking*. The fluid "pushes out" gas or oil trapped in the shale. The extracted gas or oil rises up the well and is collected at the surface. A well may be deeper than 2.5 km (about 1.5 miles) below the surface. Fracking fluid is approximately 90% water, 9% sand, and 1% additives. The additives include chemicals that reduce bacterial growth and reduce friction for the drilling equipment.

There is debate about the safety and environmental impact of fracking. Opponents of fracking are concerned about the potential health effects the additives have on people and animals, the high noise levels and high traffic volumes caused by fracking operations, and where the fracking fluids can leak to once underground. Supporters of fracking say that the drilling methods are safe, the fluids used do not pose a health risk, natural gas is a cleaner fuel than coal or oil, and fracking creates many jobs.

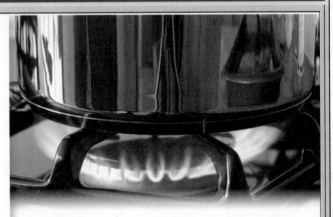

**1 Identify the argument in favor of fracking.**

_____
_____
_____
_____

**2 What is fracking fluid made of?**

_____
_____
_____
_____

Sources: *American Petroleum Institute; Chesapeake Energy; U.S. Environmental Protection Agency; U.S. Dept. of Energy.*

# You Try It!

Imagine a fracking well is to be built near your community. You want to learn more about the fracking process. Review this diagram and answer the questions that follow to help you develop an understanding of the debate.

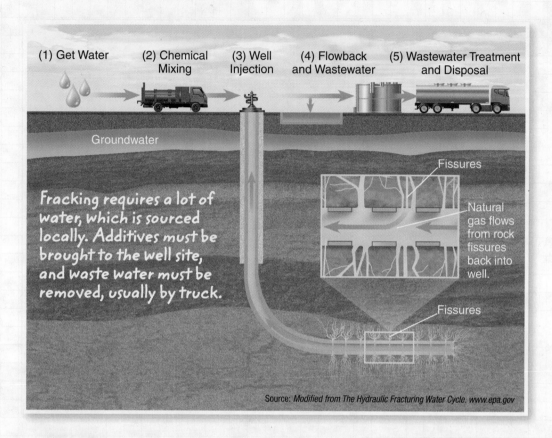

(1) Get Water    (2) Chemical Mixing    (3) Well Injection    (4) Flowback and Wastewater    (5) Wastewater Treatment and Disposal

Groundwater

*Fracking requires a lot of water, which is sourced locally. Additives must be brought to the well site, and waste water must be removed, usually by truck.*

Fissures

Natural gas flows from rock fissures back into well.

Fissures

Source: *Modified from The Hydraulic Fracturing Water Cycle. www.epa.gov*

**1 Interpreting Graphics** Using the image above, explain the fracking process in your own words.

_____

_____

_____

_____

_____

**2 Investigating Sources** What additional information do you want to know about fracking that is not shown in the graphic? Is this information in the reading passage at left?

_____

_____

_____

_____

_____

**3 Communicating Ideas** Do you think the benefits of fracking outweigh the risks? Discuss and debate your position with a classmate. Complete the table below to show the points on which you agree and disagree.

| Agree | Disagree |
|---|---|
| | |
| | |
| | |

# Lesson 3

# Renewable Energy Resources

## ESSENTIAL QUESTION

### How do humans use renewable energy resources?

By the end of this lesson, you should be able to describe how humans use energy resources and the role of renewable energy resources in society.

**TEKS 6.7A** research and debate the advantages and disadvantages of using coal, oil, natural gas, nuclear power, biomass, wind, hydropower, geothermal, and solar resources

Panels such as these can turn an unused city roof into a miniature solar energy plant.

## Lesson Labs

**Quick Labs**
- Design a Turbine
- Understanding Solar Panels

**S.T.E.M. Labs**
- Advantages and Disadvantages of Renewable Energy Resources
- Modeling Geothermal Power

## Engage Your Brain

**1 Predict** Check T or F to show whether you think each statement is true or false.

| T | F | |
|---|---|---|
| ☐ | ☐ | Renewable energy resources can never run out. |
| ☐ | ☐ | Renewable energy resources do not cause any type of pollution. |
| ☐ | ☐ | Solar energy is the most widely used renewable energy resource in the United States. |
| ☐ | ☐ | Renewable energy resources include solar energy, wind energy, and geothermal energy. |

**2 Describe** Write a caption to explain how the sun's energy is being used in this photo. Share and discuss your caption with a partner.

_____

_____

_____

_____

## Active Reading

**3 Synthesize** You can often define an unknown word if you know the meaning of its word parts. Use the word parts and sentence below to make an educated guess about the meaning of the word *geothermal*.

| Word part | Meaning |
|---|---|
| *geo-* | Earth |
| *therm-* | heat |

**Example sentence**
A <u>geothermal</u> power plant uses steam produced deep in the ground to generate electricity.

*geothermal:*

_____

_____

_____

### Vocabulary Terms
- energy resource
- wind energy
- hydroelectric energy
- solar energy
- biomass
- geothermal energy

**4 Apply** As you learn the definition of each vocabulary term in this lesson, create your own definition or sketch to help you remember the meaning of the term.

# Energy *Déjà Vu*

## What are the two main sources of renewable energy?

An **energy resource** is a natural resource used to generate electricity and other forms of energy. Most of the energy used by humans comes from *nonrenewable resources*. These resources are used more quickly than they can be replaced. But *renewable resources* can be replaced almost as quickly as they are used. Most renewable energy resources come from the sun and some from Earth itself.

### The Sun

The sun's energy is a result of nuclear fusion. Fusion is the process by which two or more nuclei fuse together to form a larger nucleus. Fusion produces a large amount of energy, which is released into space as light and heat.

Solar energy warms Earth, causing the movement of air masses. Moving air masses form winds and some ocean currents. Solar energy also fuels plant growth. Animals get energy by eating plants. Humans can harness energy from wind, moving water, plant and animal materials, and directly from the light and heat that comes from the sun.

### Earth

Energy from within Earth comes from two sources. One source is the decay of radioactive elements in Earth's mantle and crust, caused by nuclear fission. Fission is the splitting of the nuclei of radioactive atoms. The second source of energy within Earth is energy stored during Earth's formation. The heat produced from these sources radiates outward toward Earth's surface. Humans can harness this heat to use as an energy source.

**5 Contrast** Explain how energy production in the sun differs from energy production in Earth's interior.

_____

_____

_____

_____

_____

_____

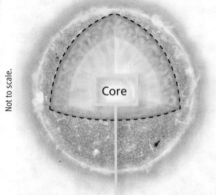

Not to scale.

Core

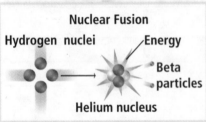

**Nuclear Fusion**

Hydrogen nuclei

Energy

Beta particles

Helium nucleus

When atomic nuclei fuse, energy is released.

Not to scale.

Core

Earth's internal energy comes from the process of nuclear fission and the events that formed Earth.

# How might a renewable energy resource become nonrenewable?

All of the energy resources you will learn about in this lesson are renewable. That doesn't mean that they can't become nonrenewable resources. Trees, for example, are a renewable resource. Some people burn wood from trees to heat their homes and cook food. However, some forests are being cut down but are not being replanted in a timely manner. Others are being cut down and replaced with buildings. If this process continues, eventually these forests will no longer be considered renewable resources.

**6 Apply** Read the caption below, then describe what might happen if the community uses too much of the water in the reservoir.

_____

_____

_____

_____

**7 Distinguish** What is the difference between nonrenewable and renewable energy resources?

_____

_____

_____

_____

### Think Outside the Book

**8 Apply** Write an interview with a renewable resource that is afraid it might become nonrenewable. Be sure to include questions and answers.

A community uses this reservoir for water. The dam at the end of the reservoir uses moving water to produce electricity for the community.

# Turn, Turn, Turn

## How do humans use wind energy?

Wind is created by the sun's uneven heating of air masses in Earth's atmosphere. **Wind energy** uses the force of moving air to drive an electric generator or do other work. Wind energy is renewable because the wind will blow as long as the sun warms Earth. Wind energy is harnessed by machines called wind turbines. Electricity is generated when moving air turns turbine blades that drive an electric generator. Clusters of wind turbines, called wind farms, generate large amounts of electricity.

Although wind energy is a renewable energy resource, it has several disadvantages. Wind farms can be placed only in areas that receive large amounts of wind. The equipment required to collect and convert wind energy is also expensive to produce and maintain. And the production and maintenance of this equipment produces a small amount of pollution. The turbine blades can also be hazardous to birds.

Windmills such as these have been used for centuries to grind grain and pump surface water for irrigation.

A wind-powered water pump can pull water from deep underground when electricity is not available.

**9 Infer** What is the main benefit of placing these turbines in open water?

_____

_____

_____

_____

Wind farms are a form of clean energy, because they do not generate air pollution as they generate electricity.

# How do humans get energy from moving water?

## Active Reading

**10 Identify** Underline the kind of energy that is found in moving water.

Like wind, moving water has kinetic energy. People have harnessed the energy of falling or flowing water to power machines since ancient times. Some grain and saw mills still use water to power their equipment. Electrical energy produced by moving water is called **hydroelectric energy**. Hydroelectric energy is renewable because the water cycle is driven by the sun. Water that evaporates from oceans and lakes falls on higher elevations and flows downhill in streams, rivers, and waterfalls. The energy in flowing water is converted to electrical energy when it spins turbines connected to electric generators inside the dam.

Hydroelectric energy is a good source of energy only in locations where there are large, reliable amounts of flowing water. Another disadvantage of hydroelectric energy is that hydroelectric dams and their technology are expensive to build. The dams also can block the movement of fish between the sea and their spawning grounds. Special fish ladders must be built to allow fish to swim around the dam.

## Visualize It!

**11 Explain** What is the purpose of the lake that is located behind the dam of a hydroelectric plant?

_____

_____

_____

_____

_____

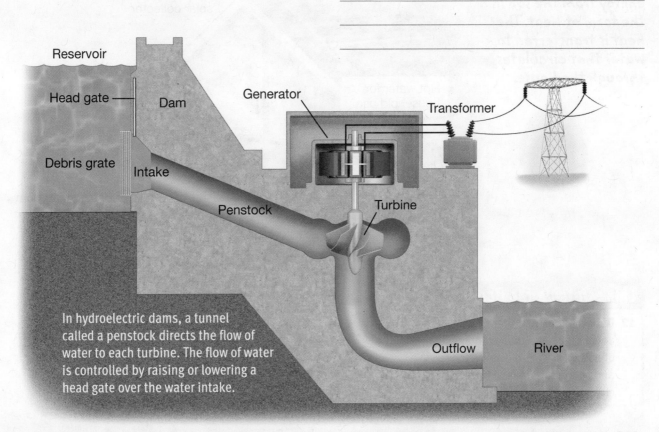

In hydroelectric dams, a tunnel called a penstock directs the flow of water to each turbine. The flow of water is controlled by raising or lowering a head gate over the water intake.

# Let the Sunshine In

## How do humans use solar energy?

Most forms of energy come from the sun—even fossil fuels begin with the sun as an energy resource. **Solar energy** is the energy received by Earth from the sun in the form of radiation. Solar energy can be used to warm buildings directly. Solar energy can also be converted into electricity by solar cells.

## To Provide Energy as Heat

We can use liquids warmed by the sun to warm water and buildings. Some liquids, such as water, have a high capacity for absorbing and holding heat. When the heat is absorbed by the liquid in a solar collector, it can be transferred to water that circulates through a building. The hot water can be used for bathing or other household uses, or to warm the building. The only pollution generated by solar heating systems comes from the manufacture and maintenance of their equipment. Solar heating systems work best in areas with large amounts of sunlight.

*Solar collectors absorb energy from the sun in the form of heat. The heat is transferred to water that circulates through the house.*

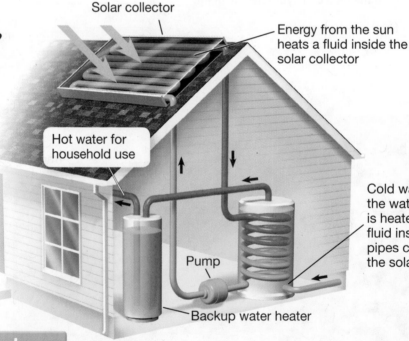

Solar collector

Energy from the sun heats a fluid inside the solar collector

Hot water for household use

Cold water from the water supply is heated by hot fluid inside the pipes coming from the solar collector

Pump

Backup water heater

### Think Outside the Book

**12 Debate** Research the advantages and disadvantages of using wind, hydropower, and solar resources to have a classroom debate.

Active Reading **13 Identify** As you read, underline the characteristics of a photovoltaic cell.

## To Produce Electricity

Solar collectors can also be used to generate electricity. First, heated fluid is used to produce steam. Then, the steam turns a turbine connected to an electric generator.

Electricity can also be generated when sunlight is absorbed by a photovoltaic cell. A single photovoltaic cell produces a small amount of electricity. The electricity from joined photovoltaic cells can power anything from calculators to entire communities. Many cells must be joined together to form each solar panel, as shown in the solar power plant below. Solar power plants must be built in places with adequate space and abundant sunshine year-round. These requirements increase the costs of solar power.

*This calculator is powered by solar cells instead of a battery.*

## Visualize It! (Inquiry)

**14 Infer** Based on this image and your reading, what might be a disadvantage to using solar energy to supply electricity to a large community?

_____

_____

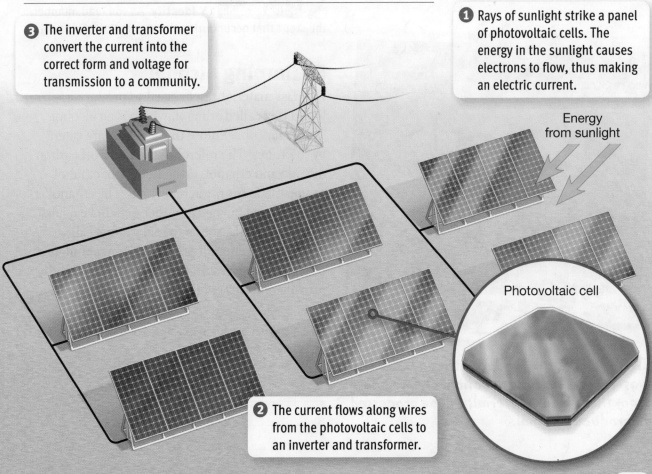

**3** The inverter and transformer convert the current into the correct form and voltage for transmission to a community.

**1** Rays of sunlight strike a panel of photovoltaic cells. The energy in the sunlight causes electrons to flow, thus making an electric current.

Energy from sunlight

Photovoltaic cell

**2** The current flows along wires from the photovoltaic cells to an inverter and transformer.

# How do humans get energy from living things?

Plants absorb light energy from the sun and convert it to chemical energy through *photosynthesis*. This energy is stored in leaves, stems, and roots. Chemical energy is also present in the dung of animals. These sources of energy make up biomass.

## By Burning Biomass

**Biomass** is organic matter from plants and from animal waste that contains chemical energy. Biomass can be burned to release energy. This energy can be used to cook food, provide warmth, or power an engine. Biomass sources include trees, crops, animal waste, and peat.

Biomass is inexpensive and can usually be replaced relatively quickly, so it is considered to be a renewable resource. Some types of biomass renew more slowly than others. Peat renews so slowly in areas where it is used heavily that it is treated as a nonrenewable resource. Like fossil fuels, biomass produces pollutants when it burns.

*These peat pellets will be used to generate steam in the power plant in the background. The steam will generate electricity by turning turbines.*

**Active Reading** **15 Identify** As you read, number the steps that occur during the production of ethanol.

## By Burning Alcohol

Biomass material can be used to produce a liquid fuel called ethanol, which is an alcohol. The sugars or cellulose in the plants are eaten by microbes. The microbes then give off carbon dioxide and ethanol. Over 1,000 L of ethanol can be made from 1 acre of corn. The ethanol is collected and burned as a fuel. Ethanol can also be mixed with gasoline to make a fuel called gasohol. The ethanol produced from about 40% of one corn harvest in the United States would provide only 10% of the fuel used in our cars!

**16 List** What are three examples of how biomass can be used for energy?

_____

_____

_____

_____

*These wagons are loaded with sugar cane wastes from sugar production. The cellulose from these plant materials will be processed to produce ethanol.*

© Houghton Mifflin Harcourt Publishing Company • Image Credits: (t) ©Hank Morgan/Photo Researchers, Inc.; (b) ©Christian Tragni/Aurora Photos/Alamy Images

# How do humans use geothermal energy?

The water in the geyser above is heated by geothermal energy. **Geothermal energy** is energy produced by heat from Earth's interior. Geothermal energy heats rock formations deep within the ground. Groundwater absorbs this heat and forms hot springs and geysers where the water reaches Earth's surface. Geothermal energy is used to produce energy as heat and electricity.

## To Provide Energy as Heat

Geothermal energy can be used to warm and cool buildings. A closed loop system of pipes runs from underground into the heating system of a home or building. Water pumped through these pipes absorbs heat from the ground and is used to warm the building. Hot groundwater can also be pumped in and used in a similar way. In warmer months, the ground is cooler than the air, so this system can also be used for cooling.

## To Produce Electricity

Geothermal energy is also used to produce electricity. Wells are drilled into areas of superheated groundwater, allowing steam and hot water to escape. Geothermal power plants pump the steam or hot water from underground to spin turbines that generate electricity, as shown at right. A disadvantage of geothermal energy is pollution that occurs during production of the technology needed to capture it. The technology is also expensive to make and maintain.

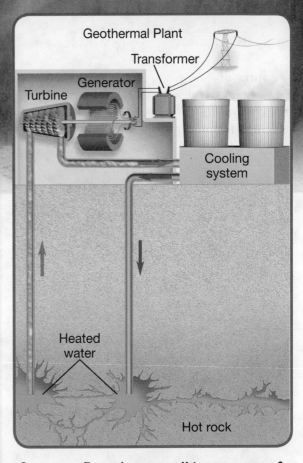

Because Earth's core will be very hot for billions of years, geothermal energy will be available for a long time.

### Think Outside the Book

**17 Debate** Research the advantages and disadvantages of using biomass and geothermal energy to have a classroom debate.

# Visual Summary

To complete this summary, fill in the blanks with the correct word or phrase. Then, use the key below to check your answers. You can use this page to review the main concepts of the lesson.

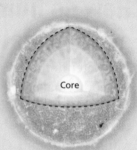

## Renewable Energy Resources

The source of geothermal energy is energy from within Earth.

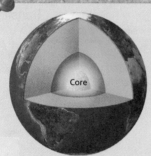

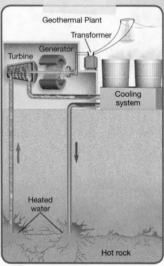

Most of the renewable energy resources that people use come from the sun.

**18** In geothermal power plants, hot water or _____ is pumped from within Earth's crust to produce electricity.

**19** Renewable resources that come from the sun include _____ _____ _____

Answers: 18 steam; 19 biomass, solar energy, wind energy, and hydroelectric energy

**20 Synthesize** Which type of renewable energy resource would be best to use to provide electricity for your town? Explain your answer.

# Lesson Review

## Vocabulary

Fill in the blanks with the term that best completes the following sentences.

**1** Organic matter that contains stored energy is called _____

**2** A resource that humans can use to produce energy is a(n) _____

**3** _____ is an energy resource harnessed from flowing water.

## Key Concepts

**4 Describe** Identify a major advantage and a major disadvantage of using renewable energy resources to produce electricity.

_____

_____

_____

_____

_____

_____

**5 Explain** If renewable energy resources can be replaced, why do we need to conserve them? Use an example to support your answer.

_____

_____

_____

_____

_____

_____

**6 Describe** What is the source of energy that powers wind and flowing water?

_____

_____

_____

_____

_____

## Critical Thinking

Use this graph to answer the following questions.

**Total Renewable Energy Resources Consumed in 2009 in the United States**

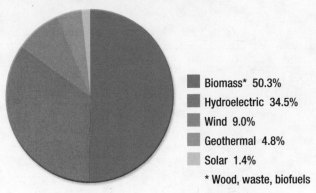

- Biomass* 50.3%
- Hydroelectric 34.5%
- Wind 9.0%
- Geothermal 4.8%
- Solar 1.4%

\* Wood, waste, biofuels

*Source:* Annual Energy Review 2009, U.S. Energy Information Administration

**7 Evaluate** Which is the most used renewable energy resource in the United States? Why do you think this is the case?

_____

_____

_____

_____

**8 Evaluate** Which is the least used renewable energy resource in the United States? Why do you think this is the case?

_____

_____

_____

_____

_____

_____

**9 Relate** How are biomass and alcohol production related to energy from the sun?

_____

_____

_____

_____

# My Notes

# Unit 5 〔Big Idea〕 Humans depend on natural resources for materials and for energy.

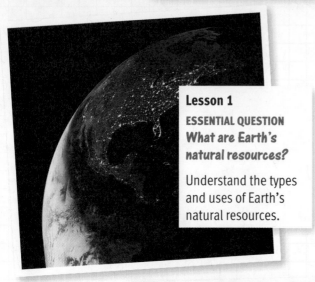

### Lesson 1

**ESSENTIAL QUESTION**
**What are Earth's natural resources?**

Understand the types and uses of Earth's natural resources.

### Lesson 2

**ESSENTIAL QUESTION**
**How do we use nonrenewable energy resources?**

Describe how humans use energy resources and the role of nonrenewable energy resources in society.

### Lesson 3

**ESSENTIAL QUESTION**
**How do humans use renewable energy resources?**

Describe how humans use energy resources and the role of renewable energy resources in society.

## 〔Connect〕 ESSENTIAL QUESTIONS
Lessons 2 and 3

**1 Apply** What kind of energy resources are best suited for use in your area? Explain your choices.

_____

_____

_____

_____

_____

_____

_____

_____

### Think Outside the Book

**2 Synthesize** Choose one of these activities to help synthesize what you have learned in this unit.

☐ Using what you learned in lessons 1, 2, and 3, create a poster presentation that compares and contrasts one renewable resource and one nonrenewable resource. Include a discussion of at least one drawback for each resource type.

☐ Using what you learned in lessons 1 and 2, write a short story about a fossil fuel that follows the fuel from its formation to its use by humans.

# Unit 5 Review

Name _____

## Vocabulary

Check the box to show whether each statement is true or false.

| T | F | |
|---|---|---|
| ☐ | ☐ | **TEKS** 6.7A<br>**1** Petroleum is a fossil fuel that can be used to make plastics. |
| ☐ | ☐ | **2** An energy resource is a resource that humans can use to make food or beverages. |
| ☐ | ☐ | **TEKS** 6.7A<br>**3** Biomass energy comes from organic matter such as plant material and manure. |
| ☐ | ☐ | **TEKS** 6.7A<br>**4** A material resource is a renewable resource that is used to make objects. |
| ☐ | ☐ | **TEKS** 6.7A<br>**5** Rocks, water, air, minerals, forests, wildlife, and soil are all examples of natural resources. |

## Key Concepts

Choose the letter of the best answer.

**TEKS** 6.7A

**6** What is the original source of the energy stored in coal? (Hint: Step 1. Recall the process by which coal is formed. Step 2. Identify the original source of energy in the process. Step 3. Choose the statement below that correctly identifies the original source of the energy stored in coal.)

**A** wind  **C** plants

**B** the sun  **D** soil

**TEKS** 6.7A

**7** The chemicals released by burning petroleum in car engines contribute to which local and worldwide effects?

**A** smog and global warming

**B** fog and radioactivity

**C** acid rain and UV radiation

**D** cloudy weather and ozone buildup

# Unit 5 Review continued

TEKS 6.7A, 6.2E, 6.3B

**8** The diagram below shows changes to the nucleus of an atom.

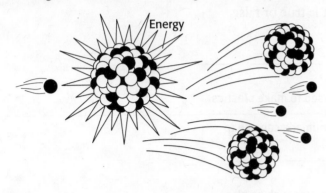

Which process is occurring in the diagram?

**A** Energy is released as a result of atomic fission.

**B** Energy is absorbed as a result of atomic fission.

**C** Energy is released during the combustion of a fossil fuel.

**D** Energy is being stored during the formation of a fossil fuel.

TEKS 6.7A

**9** Sometimes a renewable resource can be considered nonrenewable because it is used up faster than it can be replenished. What is one example of this?

**A** coal supply dwindling because it takes millions of years to form

**B** forests being cut down at a quicker rate than they can grow

**C** solar energy being used to provide electricity to a home

**D** water in streams replaced by rainfall from the atmosphere

TEKS 6.7B

**10** As part of a natural resources management plan, the owner of an apartment building wants to reduce overall water usage. Which recommendation should she give that would help her renters conserve water?

**A** Buy drinking water from the store.

**B** Don't let water run while brushing your teeth.

**C** Bathe only in the afternoon while others are out.

**D** Shower before entering the swimming pool.

Name _____

**11** The picture shows a scene from a campground.

Which energy conversion is taking place in the picture? (Hint: Step 1. Identify the type of energy stored in wood. Step 2. Identify the type of energy represented by fire. Step 3. Choose the statement below that correctly summarizes the type of energy conversion taking place.)

**A** chemical energy to thermal energy

**B** nuclear energy to chemical energy

**C** electrical energy to mechanical energy

**D** electromagnetic energy to chemical energy

## Gridded Response

Write your answer in the boxes, then bubble in the corresponding number in the grid below.

**12** All of the electricity in the United States is produced using several natural resources. Some are nonrenewable, and some are renewable. Nuclear energy accounts for 19.9 percent of all the electricity produced in the United States, and 9.3 percent is produced using natural gas. Hydroelectric energy produces another 9.2 percent, and petroleum and other sources produce 2.3 percent. Coal is the source of energy for producing all of the rest of the electricity used in the United States. What percentage of electricity is produced by coal energy in the United States?

## Critical Thinking

Answer the following question in the space provided.

**TEKS** 6.7B, 6.2E

**13** Below is a graph of the production and use of petroleum in the United States in the past and present and likely usage in the future.

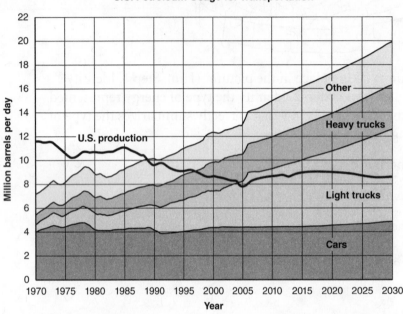

U.S. Petroleum Usage for Transportation

Based on current production and current usage, what could you predict about petroleum resources? Design a logical plan that could help to conserve petroleum resources.

_____

_____

_____

**Connect** **ESSENTIAL QUESTIONS**
Lessons 1 and 3

Answer the following question in the space provided.

**TEKS** 6.7A, 6.2E, 6.3A

**14** The picture shows technology used for alternative energy.
Name one benefit and one disadvantage of using this type of energy.

_____

_____

# Minerals and Rocks

The rock in this abandoned Australian copper mine has been colored by different compounds of copper.

## Big Idea

Minerals and rocks are basic building blocks of Earth and can change over time from one type of mineral or rock to another.

## What do you think?

Minerals and rocks have a variety of uses in products that people use every day. What minerals or rocks are mined in your community?

Copper was one of the first metals used by humans, because it can be found in a nearly pure form, like this native copper.

## Unit 6
# Minerals and Rocks

# Mineral Resources

Minerals and rocks are mined in large open-pit mines or quarries, or within deep underground tunnels. These natural resources are used to build homes, to pave roads, and to manufacture many everyday consumer items. Some common mineral resources are granite, limestone, and marble; sand and gravel; gypsum; coal; and iron and copper ore.

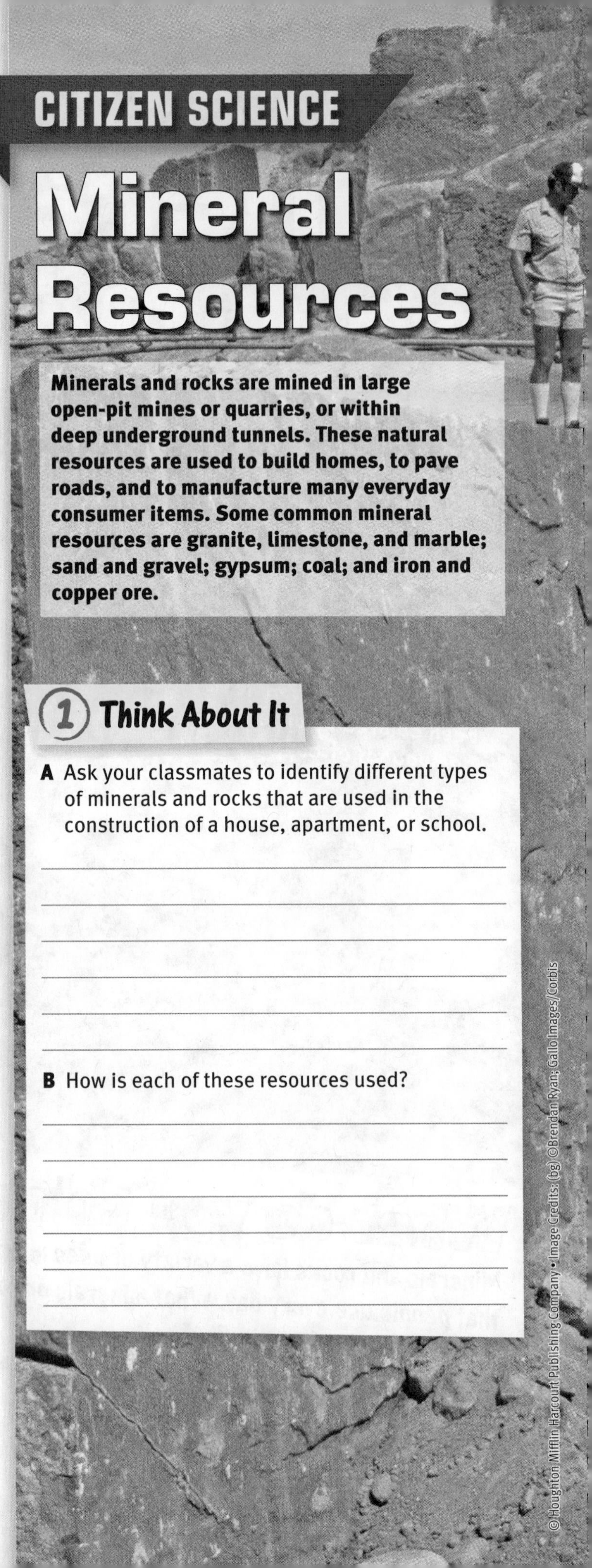

## (1) Think About It

**A** Ask your classmates to identify different types of minerals and rocks that are used in the construction of a house, apartment, or school.

_____

_____

_____

_____

_____

**B** How is each of these resources used?

_____

_____

_____

_____

_____

_____

## ② Ask a Question

**What is the environmental impact of mining minerals and rocks?**
Opening a mine requires clearing the land and moving soil and rock. Do some research on how mining affects the environment. What are some ways in which mining can harm the environment?

_____

_____

_____

_____

_____

Workers must carefully plan how to remove large blocks or sheets of granite from a quarry.

## ③ Make a Plan

Imagine that a mining operation is coming to a place near you. Make a plan for two regulations you would like to see the mining company have to follow in order to protect the environment.

_____

_____

_____

_____

_____

_____

_____

_____

Marble, also mined from quarries, can become beautiful works of art.

### Take It Home

**Search your local newspaper or the Internet for news stories that involve the environmental impact of mining.**

**Lesson 1**

# Minerals

## ESSENTIAL QUESTION

## What are minerals, how do they form, and how can they be identified?

By the end of this lesson, you should be able to describe the basic structure of minerals and identify different minerals by using their physical properties.

This cave was once full of water. Over millions of years, dissolved minerals in the water slowly formed these gypsum crystals, which are now considered to be the largest mineral crystals in the world!

**TEKS** **6.6C** test the physical properties of minerals, including hardness, color, luster, and streak

**Lesson Labs**

**Quick Labs**
• Cooling Rate and Crystal Size
• Scratch Test

**Exploration Lab**
• Intrinsic Identification of Minerals

 **Engage Your Brain**

**1 Identify** Which of the materials listed below is a mineral?

| Yes | No | |
|-----|-----|------|
| ☐ | ☐ | ice |
| ☐ | ☐ | gold |
| ☐ | ☐ | wood |
| ☐ | ☐ | diamond |
| ☐ | ☐ | table salt |

**2 Explain** Describe how you think the minerals in the picture below may have formed.

_____

_____

_____

 **Active Reading**

**3 Synthesize** Many of this lesson's vocabulary terms are related to each other. Locate the terms in the Glossary and see if you can find connections between them. When you find two terms that are related to each other, write a sentence using both terms in a way that shows the relationship. An example is done for you.

**Example Sentence**
Each element is made of only one kind of atom.

_____

_____

_____

_____

**Vocabulary Terms**
• mineral          • crystal
• element          • streak
• atom             • luster
• compound         • cleavage
• matter

**4 Apply** As you learn the definition of each vocabulary term in this lesson, create your own definition or sketch to help you remember the meaning of the term.

# Animal, Vegetable,

## What do minerals have in common?

When you hear the word *mineral,* you may think of sparkling gems. But, in fact, most minerals are found in groups that make up rocks. So what is a mineral? A **mineral** is a naturally occurring, usually inorganic solid that has a definite crystalline structure and chemical composition.

## Definite Chemical Composition

To understand what a definite chemical composition is, you need to know a little about elements. **Elements** are pure substances that cannot be broken down into simpler substances by ordinary chemical means. Each element is made of only one kind of atom. All substances are made up of atoms, so **atoms** can be thought of as the building blocks of matter. Stable particles that are made up of strongly bonded atoms are called *molecules.* And, if a substance is made up of molecules of two or more elements, the substance is called a **compound.**

The chemical composition of a mineral is determined by the element or compound that makes up the mineral. For example, minerals such as gold and silver are composed of only one element. Such a mineral is called a *native element.* The mineral quartz is a compound in which silicon atoms can each bond with up to four oxygen atoms in a repeating pattern.

### Inquiry

**5 Synthesize** What is the relationship between elements, atoms, and compounds?

_____

_____

_____

_____

## Solid

**Matter** is anything that has volume and mass. *Volume* refers to the amount of space an object takes up. For example, a golf ball has a smaller volume than a baseball does. Matter is generally found in one of three states: solid, liquid, or gas. A mineral is a solid—that is, it has a definite volume and shape. A substance that is a liquid or a gas is not a mineral. However, in some cases its solid form is a mineral. For instance, liquid water is not a mineral, but ice is because it is solid and has all of the other mineral characteristics also.

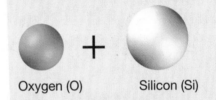

**Atoms** The mineral quartz is made up of atoms of oxygen and silicon.

Oxygen (O)      +      Silicon (Si)

**Compound** An atom of silicon can typically bond with up to four oxygen atoms to form a molecule. One or more of these molecules form a compound.

# or Mineral?

## Usually Inorganic

Most substances made by living things are categorized as organic substances, such as kidney stones and wood. However, a few substances made by animals, such as clam shells, are categorized as inorganic. An inorganic substance is usually one that is not made up of living things or the remains of living things. And, although a few organic substances such as kidney stones are categorized as minerals, most minerals are inorganic. And, unlike clam shells, most of the processes that form minerals usually take place in the non-living environment.

## Crystalline Structure

Minerals have a crystalline structure because they are composed of crystals. A **crystal** is a solid, geometric form that results from a repeating pattern of atoms or molecules. A crystal's shape is produced by the arrangement of the atoms or molecules within the crystal. This arrangement is determined by the kinds of atoms or molecules that make up the mineral and the conditions under which it forms. All minerals can be placed into crystal classes according to their specific crystal shape. This diagram shows how silica compounds can be arranged in quartz crystals.

**Crystal Structure** In crystals, molecules are arranged in a regular pattern.

## Naturally Occurring

Minerals are formed by many different natural processes that occur on Earth and throughout the universe. On Earth, the mineral halite, which is used for table salt, forms as water evaporates and leaves behind the salt it contained. Some minerals form as molten rock cools. Talc, a mineral that can be used to make baby powder, forms deep in Earth as high temperature and pressure change the rock. Some of the other ways in which minerals form are on the next page.

**6 Classify** Circle *Y* for "yes" or *N* for "no" to determine whether the two materials below are minerals.

|  | Cardboard | Topaz |
|---|---|---|
| Definite chemical composition? | Y (N) | (Y) N |
| Solid? | Y N | (Y) N |
| Inorganic? | Y N | Y N |
| Naturally occurring? | Y N | Y N |
| Crystalline structure? | Y (N) | Y N |
| Mineral? | Y N | Y N |

**Mineral Crystal** Billions of molecules arranged in a crystalline structure form these quartz crystals.

# Crystal Clear!

## How are minerals formed?

Minerals form within Earth or on Earth's surface by natural processes. Recall that each type of mineral has its own chemical makeup. Therefore, which types of minerals form in an area depends in part on which elements are present there. Temperature and pressure also affect which minerals form.

### As Magma and Lava Cool

Many minerals grow from magma. Magma—molten rock inside Earth—contains most of the types of atoms that are found in minerals. As magma cools, the atoms join together to form different minerals. Minerals also form as lava cools. Lava is molten rock that has reached Earth's surface. Quartz is one of the many minerals that crystallize from magma and lava.

### By Metamorphism

Temperature and pressure within Earth cause new minerals to form as bonds between atoms break and reform with different atoms. The mineral garnet can form and replace the minerals chlorite and quartz in this way. At high temperatures and pressures, the element carbon in rocks forms the mineral diamond or the mineral graphite, which is used in pencils.

**Visualize It!**

**7 Compare** How are the ways in which pluton and pegmatite minerals form similar?

_____

_____

**Cooling Magma Forms Plutons**
As magma rises, it can stop moving and cool slowly. This forms rocks like this granite, which contains minerals like quartz, mica, and feldspar.

**Cooling Magma Forms Pegmatites**
Magma that cools very slowly can form pegmatites. Some crystals in pegmatites, such as this topaz, can grow quite large.

**Metamorphism** Minerals like these garnets form when temperature and pressure causes the chemical and crystalline makeup of minerals to change.

# From Solutions

Water usually has many substances dissolved in it. As water evaporates, these substances form into solids and come out of solution, or *precipitate*. For example, the mineral gypsum often forms as water evaporates. Minerals can also form from hot water solutions. Hot water can dissolve more materials than cold water. As a body of hot water cools, dissolved substances can form into minerals such as dolomite, as they precipitate out of solution.

**8 Summarize** Describe three ways minerals form.

A _____

_____

B _____

_____

C _____

_____

**Precipitating from an Evaporating Solution** When a body of salt water evaporates, minerals such as this halite precipitate and are left behind on the shoreline.

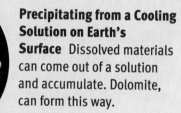

**Precipitating from a Cooling Solution on Earth's Surface** Dissolved materials can come out of a solution and accumulate. Dolomite, can form this way.

**Precipitating from a Cooling Solution Beneath Earth's Surface** Water works its way downward and is heated by magma. It then reacts with minerals to form a solution. Dissolved elements, such as gold, precipitate once the fluid cools to form new mineral deposits.

## Think Outside the Book

**9 Apply** Find out what your state mineral is and how it forms.

# Sort It Out

## How are minerals classified?

The most common classification of minerals is based on chemical composition. Minerals are divided into two groups based on their composition. These groups are the silicate (SIL'ih•kayt) minerals and the nonsilicate (nawn•SIL'ih•kayt) minerals.

## Silicate Minerals

Silicon and oxygen are the two most common elements in Earth's crust. Minerals that contain a combination of these two elements are called *silicate minerals*. Silicate minerals make up most of Earth's crust. The most common silicate minerals in Earth's crust are feldspar and quartz. Most silicate minerals are formed from basic building blocks called *silicate tetrahedrons*. Silicate tetrahedrons are made of one silicon atom bonded to four oxygen atoms. Most silicate minerals, including mica and olivine, are composed of silicate tetrahedrons combined with other elements, such as aluminum or iron.

Active Reading **10 Explain** Why is Earth's crust made up mostly of silicate minerals?

_____

_____

*The mineral zircon is a silicate mineral. It is composed of the element zirconium and silicate tetrahedrons.*

## Nonsilicate Minerals

Minerals that do not contain the silicate tetrahedron building block form a group called the *nonsilicate minerals*. Some of these minerals are made up of elements such as carbon, oxygen, fluorine, iron, and sulfur. The table on the next page shows the most important classes of nonsilicate minerals. A nonsilicate mineral's chemical composition determines its class.

**Do the Math** You Try It

**11 Calculate** Calculate the percent of non-silicates in Earth's crust to complete the graph's key.

Minerals in Earth's Crust

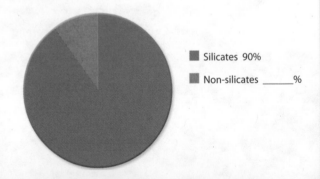

- Silicates  90%
- Non-silicates _____%

# Classes of Nonsilicate Minerals

**Native elements** are minerals that are composed of only one element. Copper (Cu) and silver (Ag) are two examples. Native elements are often used to make electronics.

Silver, Ag

**Carbonates** are minerals that contain carbon (C) and oxygen (O) in the form of the carbonate ion $CO_3^{2-}$. We use carbonate minerals in cement, building stones, and fireworks.

Calcite, $CaCO_3$

**Halides** are compounds that form when elements such as fluorine (F) and chlorine (Cl), combine with elements such as calcium (Ca). Halides are used in the chemical industry and in detergents.

Fluorite, $CaF_2$

**Oxides** are compounds that form when an element, such as aluminum (Al) or iron (Fe), combines with oxygen. Oxide minerals are used to make abrasives, aircraft parts, and paint.

Corundum, $Al_2O_3$

**Sulfates** are minerals that contain sulfur (S) and oxygen (O) in the form of the sulfate ion $SO_4^{2-}$. Sulfates are used in cosmetics, toothpaste, cement, and paint.

Barite, $BaSO_4$

**Sulfides** are minerals that contain one or more elements, such as lead (Pb), or iron (Fe), combined with sulfur (S). Sulfide minerals are used to make batteries and medicines.

Pyrite, $FeS_2$

## Visualize It!

**12 Classify** Examine the chemical formulas for the two minerals at right. Classify the minerals as a silicate or nonsilicate. If it is a nonsilicate, also write its class.

Gypsum, $CaSO_4 \cdot 2H_2O$

Kyanite, $Al_2SiO_5$

_____     _____

_____     _____

# Name That Mineral!

## What properties can be used to identify minerals?

If you closed your eyes and tasted different foods, you could probably determine what the foods are by noting properties such as saltiness or sweetness. You can also determine the identity of a mineral by noting different properties. In this section, you will learn about the properties that will help you identify minerals.

### Color

The same mineral can come in different colors. For example, pure quartz is colorless. However, impurities can make quartz pink, orange, or many other colors. Other factors can also change a mineral's color. Pyrite is normally golden, but turns black or brown if exposed to air and water. The same mineral can be different colors, and different minerals can be the same color. So, color is helpful but usually not the best way to identify a mineral.

### Streak

The color of the powdered form of a mineral is its **streak**. A mineral's streak is found by rubbing the mineral against a white tile called a *streak plate*. The mark left is the streak. A mineral's streak is not always the same as the color of the mineral, but all samples of the same mineral have the same streak color. Unlike the surface of a mineral, the streak is not affected by air or water. For this reason, streak is more reliable than color in identifying a mineral.

**Active Reading**

**13 Identify** Underline the name of the property on this page that is most reliable for identifying a mineral.

**Visualize It!**

**14 Evaluate** Look at these two mineral samples. What property indicates that they may be the same mineral?

_____

_____

_____

## Mineral Lusters

**Metallic**

**Silky**

**Vitreous**

**Waxy**

**Submetallic**

**Pearly**

**Resinous**

**Earthy**

## Luster

The way a surface reflects light is called **luster**. When you say an object is shiny or dull, you are describing its luster. The two major types of luster are metallic and nonmetallic. Pyrite has a metallic luster. It looks as if it is made of metal. A mineral with a nonmetallic luster can be shiny, but it does not appear to be made of metal. Different types of lusters are shown above.

## Cleavage and Fracture

The tendency of a mineral to split along specific planes of weakness to form smooth, flat surfaces is called **cleavage**. When a mineral has cleavage, it breaks along flat surfaces that generally run parallel to planes of weakness in the crystal structure. For example, mica tends to split into parallel sheets. Many minerals, however, do not break along cleavage planes. Instead, they fracture, or break unevenly, into pieces that have curved or irregular surfaces. Scientists describe a fracture according to the appearance of the broken surface. For example, a rough surface has an irregular fracture, and a curved surfaces has a conchoidal (kahn•KOY•duhl) fracture.

👁 **Visualize It!**

**15 Identify** Write the correct description, either *cleavage* or *fracture*, under the two broken mineral crystals shown here.

## Mohs Scale

**1** Talc

**2** Gypsum

Your fingernail has a hardness of about 2.5, so it can scratch talc and gypsum.

**3** Calcite

**4** Fluorite

**5** Apatite

**6** Feldspar

A steel file has a hardness of about 6.5. You can scratch feldspar with it.

**7** Quartz

**8** Topaz

**9** Corundum

**10** Diamond

Diamond is the hardest mineral. Only a diamond can scratch another diamond.

### Visualize It!

**16 Determine** A mineral can be scratched by calcite but not by a fingernail. What is its approximate hardness?

_____

## Density

If you pick up a golf ball and a table-tennis ball, which will feel heavier? Although the balls are of similar size, the golf ball will feel heavier because it is denser. *Density* is the measure of how much matter is in a given amount of space. Density is usually measured in grams per cubic centimeter. Gold has a density of 19 g/cm³. The mineral pyrite looks very similar to gold, but its density is only 5 g/cm³. Because of this, density can be used to tell gold from pyrite. Density can also be used to tell many other similar-looking minerals apart.

## Hardness

A mineral's resistance to being scratched is called its *hardness*. To determine the hardness of minerals, scientists use the Mohs hardness scale, shown at left. Notice that talc has a rating of 1 and diamond has a rating of 10. The greater a mineral's resistance to being scratched, the higher its hardness rating. To identify a mineral by using the Mohs scale, try to scratch the surface of a mineral with the edge of one of the 10 reference minerals. If the reference mineral scratches your mineral, the reference mineral is as hard as or harder than your mineral.

## Special Properties

All minerals exhibit the properties that were described earlier in this section. However, a few minerals have some additional, special properties that can help identify those minerals. For example, the mineral magnetite is a natural magnet. The mineral calcite is usually white in ordinary light, but in ultraviolet light, it often appears red. Another special property of calcite is shown below.

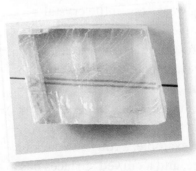

A clear piece of calcite placed over an image will cause a double image.

# Made from Minerals

Many minerals contain useful substances. Rutile and several other minerals contain the metal titanium. Titanium can resist corrosion and is about as strong as steel, but it is 47% lighter than steel. These properties make titanium very valuable.

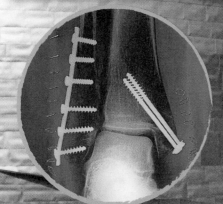

## Devices for Doctors

Surgical procedures like joint replacements require metal implantations. Titanium is used because it can resist body fluid corrosion and its low density and elasticity is similar to human bone.

## Marvels for Mechanics

Motorcycle exhaust pipes are often made out of titanium, which dissipates heat better than stainless steel.

## An Aid to Architects

Titanium doesn't just serve practical purposes. Architect Frank Gehry used titanium panels to cover the outside of the Guggenheim Museum in Bilbao, Spain. He chose titanium because of its luster.

## Extend

Inquiry

**17 Infer** How do you think the density of titanium-containing minerals would compare to the density of minerals used to make steel? Explain.

**18 List** Research some other products made from minerals. Make a list summarizing your research.

**19 Determine** Choose one of the products you researched. How do the properties of the minerals used to make the product contribute to the product's characteristics or usefulness?

# Visual Summary

To complete this summary, fill in the blanks with the correct words or phrase. Then use the key below to check your answers. You can use this page to review the main concepts of the lesson.

## Minerals make up Earth's crust.

**20** A mineral:

- has a definite chemical composition
- is a solid
- is usually inorganic
- is formed in nature
- _____

## Minerals are classified by composition.

**21** Minerals are classified in two groups as:

Quartz, $SiO_2$        Calcite, $CaCO_3$

_____        _____

## Minerals

## Minerals form by natural processes.

**22** Minerals form by:

- metamorphism
- the cooling of magma and lava
- _____

## Minerals are identified by their properties.

**23** Properties used to identify minerals include:

- color and luster
- _____
- cleavage or fracture
- density and hardness
- special properties

Answers: 20 has a crystalline structure. 21 silicates (left), nonsilicates (right); 22 precipitating from solutions; 23 streak

**24 Apply** Ice ($H_2O$) is a mineral. Classify it as silicate or nonsilicate. List two of its properties.

# Lesson Review

## Vocabulary

Fill in the blank with the term that best completes the following sentence.

**1** The way light bounces off a mineral's surface is described by the mineral's _____

**2** The color of a mineral in powdered form is the mineral's _____

**3** Each element is made up of only one kind of _____

## Key Concepts

**4 Explain** How could you determine whether an unknown substance is a mineral?

_____
_____
_____
_____
_____

**5 Determine** If a substance is a mineral, how could you identify what type of mineral it is?

_____
_____
_____

**6 Organize** In the space below, draw a graphic organizer showing how minerals can be classified. Be sure to include the six main classes of nonsilicate minerals.

## Critical Thinking

Use the diagram below to answer question 7.

**Carbon Bonds in Graphite**

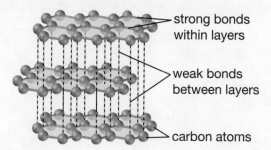

strong bonds within layers

weak bonds between layers

carbon atoms

**7 Evaluate** The diagram above shows the crystal structure of graphite, a mineral made up of carbon atoms that are bonded together in a regular pattern. Do you think graphite would most likely display cleavage or fracture? Explain your answer.

_____
_____
_____
_____
_____

**8 Infer** How do you think the hardness and density of a mineral that formed through metamorphism would compare to a mineral that formed through evaporation? Explain.

_____
_____
_____
_____
_____
_____
_____
_____
_____
_____

# My Notes

**Lesson 2**

# Three Classes of Rock

**ESSENTIAL QUESTION**

## How do rocks form?

By the end of this lesson, you should be able to describe the formation and classification of sedimentary, igneous, and metamorphic rocks.

Wind and water have eroded the softer rock surrounding Ship Rock, an igneous landform in New Mexico.

**TEKS 6.10B** classify rocks as metamorphic, igneous, or sedimentary by the processes of their formation

© Houghton Mifflin Harcourt Publishing Company • Image Credits: (bg) ©Danny Lehman/Corbis

**Lesson Labs**

**Quick Labs**
- Stretching Out
- Observing Rocks

**S.T.E.M. Lab**
- Modeling Rock Formation

## Engage Your Brain

**1 Predict** Check T or F to show whether you think each statement is true or false.

**T    F**

☐    ☐    All rocks form deep beneath Earth's surface.

☐    ☐    Some rocks are made up of materials from living things.

☐    ☐    Some rocks take millions of years to form.

☐    ☐    All rocks are made up of the same kinds of minerals.

☐    ☐    Some rocks form from particles of other rocks.

**2 Identify** How do you think rocks might form as a result of the volcanic activity shown here?

_____

_____

_____

_____

## Active Reading

**3 Apply** Use context clues to write your own definition for the words *composition* and *texture*.

**Example sentence:**
The <u>composition</u> of the trail mix was 50% nuts, 30% dried fruit, and 20% granola.

composition:

_____

_____

**Example sentence:**
Because glass is smooth, flat, and shiny, it has a much different <u>texture</u> than wood does.

texture:

_____

_____

**Vocabulary Terms**
- rock
- texture
- composition

**4 Apply** As you learn the definition of each vocabulary term in this lesson, create your own definition or sketch to help you remember the meaning of the term.

# A Rocky World

## How are rocks classified?

A combination of one or more minerals or organic matter is called **rock**. Scientists divide rock into three classes based on how each class of rock forms. The three classes of rock are igneous, sedimentary, and metamorphic. Each class of rock can be further divided into more specific types of rock. For example, igneous rocks can be divided based on where they form. All igneous rock forms when molten rock cools and solidifies. However, some igneous rocks form on Earth's surface and others form within Earth's crust. Sedimentary and metamorphic rocks are also divided into more specific types of rock. How do scientists understand how to classify rocks? They observe their composition and texture.

### By Mineral Composition

The minerals and organic matter a rock contains determine the **composition**, or makeup, of that rock, as shown below. Many rocks are made up mostly of the minerals quartz and feldspar, which contain a large amount of the compound silica. Other rocks have different compositions. The limestone rock shown below is made up mostly of the mineral calcite.

**Active Reading**

**5 Identify** As you read, underline two properties that are used to classify rock.

**Do the Math**

**6 Graph** Fill in the percentage grid on the right to show the amounts of calcite and aragonite in limestone.

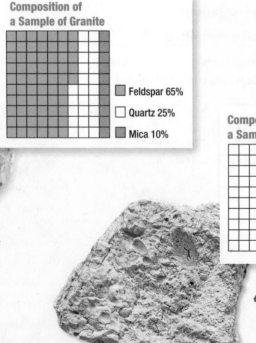

**Composition of a Sample of Granite**

- Feldspar 65%
- Quartz 25%
- Mica 10%

**Composition of a Sample of Limestone**

- Calcite 95%
- Aragonite 5%

Granite is made of silica minerals.

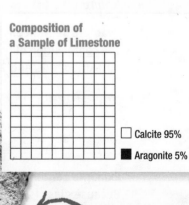

Limestone is made of carbonate minerals.

## By Texture

The size, shape, and positions of the grains that make up a rock determine a rock's **texture**. Coarse-grained rock has large grains that are easy to see with your eyes. Fine-grained rock has small grains that can only be seen by using a hand lens or microscope. The texture of a rock may give clues as to how and where it formed. Igneous rock can be fine-grained or coarse-grained depending on the time magma takes to cool. The texture of metamorphic rock depends on the rock's original composition and the temperature and pressure at which the rock formed. The rocks shown below look different because they formed in different ways.

### Visualize It!

**7 Describe** Observe the sedimentary rocks on this page and describe their texture as coarse-grained, medium-grained, or fine-grained.

This sandstone formed from sand grains that once made up a sand dune.

A _____

_____

This mudstone is made up of microscopic particles of clay.

B _____

_____

This breccia is composed of broken fragments of rock cemented together.

C _____

_____

# The Furnace Below

## What are two kinds of igneous rock?

Igneous rock forms when hot, liquid magma cools into solid rock. Magma forms when solid rock melts below Earth's surface. Magma flows through passageways up toward Earth's surface. Magma can cool and harden below Earth's surface, or it can make its way above Earth's surface and become lava.

### Intrusive Igneous Rock

When magma does not reach Earth's surface, it cools in large chambers, in cracks, or between layers in the surrounding rock. When magma pushes into, or intrudes, surrounding rock below Earth's surface and cools, the rock that forms is called *intrusive igneous rock*. Magma that is well insulated by surrounding rock cools very slowly. The minerals form large, visible crystals. Therefore, intrusive igneous rock generally has a coarse-grained texture. Examples of intrusive igneous rock are granite and diorite. A sample of diorite is shown at the left.

Diorite is an example of intrusive igneous rock.

**8 Infer** How can you tell that diorite is an intrusive igneous rock?

_____

_____

**Deep Inside Earth** The amount of time magma takes to cool determines the texture of an igneous rock.

**Crystals** Slow-cooling magma has time to form large mineral crystals. The resulting rock is coarse-grained.

**Magma chamber** Magma chambers deep inside Earth contain pools of molten rock. Magma cools slowly in large chambers such as this.

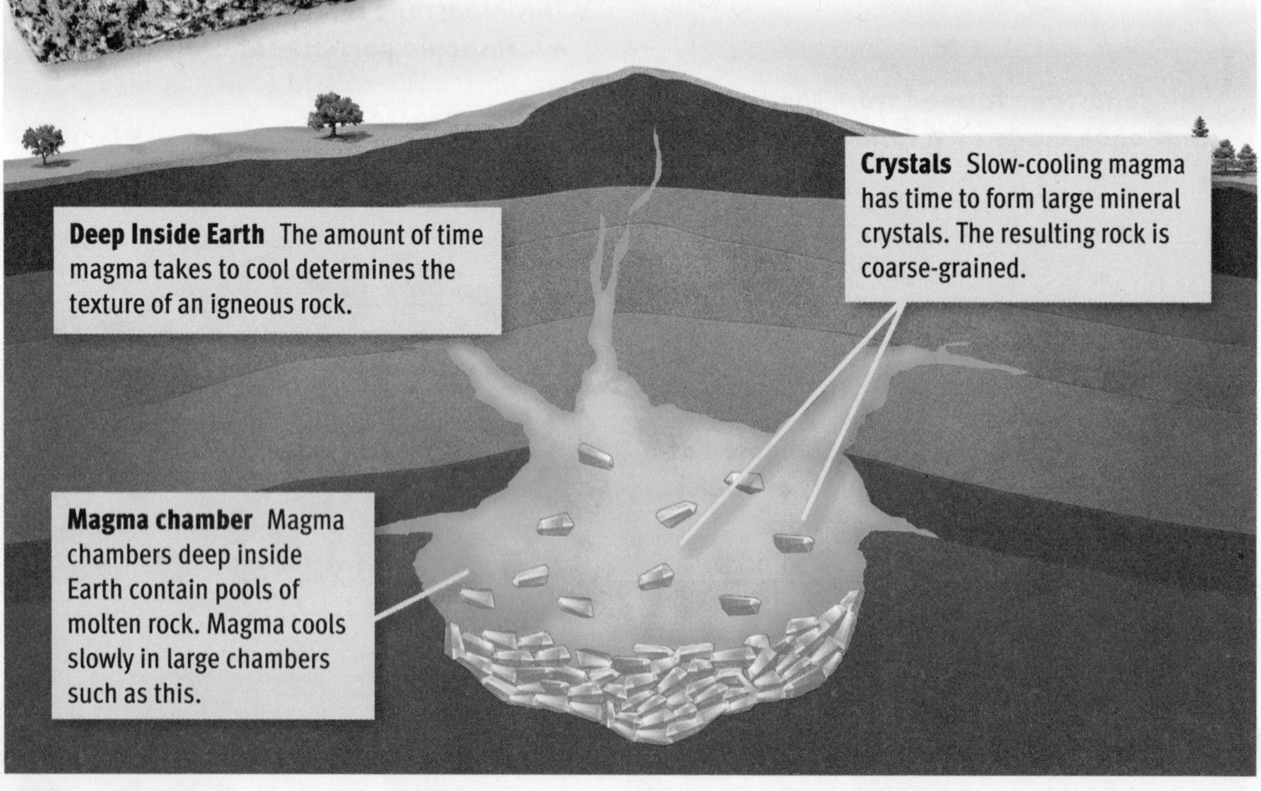

© Houghton Mifflin Harcourt Publishing Company • Image Credits: ©Dirk Wiersma/Photo Researchers, Inc.

© Houghton Mifflin Harcourt Publishing Company • Image Credits: (t) ©Images & Volcans/Photo Researchers, Inc.; (b) ©Harry Taylor/Dorling Kindersley/Getty Images

**Near or at Earth's Surface**
Fine-grained igneous rock forms as lava cools quickly at Earth's surface.

## Extrusive Igneous Rock

Igneous rock that forms when lava erupts, or extrudes, onto Earth's surface is called *extrusive igneous rock*. Extrusive igneous rock is common around the sides and bases of volcanoes. Lava cools very quickly at Earth's surface. So, there is very little time for crystal formation. Because there is little time for crystals to form, extrusive rocks are made up of very small crystals and have a fine-grained texture. Obsidian (ahb•SID•ee•uhn) is an extrusive rock that cools so rapidly that no crystals form. Obsidian looks glassy, so it is often called *volcanic glass*. Other common extrusive igneous rocks are basalt and andesite.

Lava flows form when lava erupts from a volcano. The photo above shows an active lava flow. Sometimes lava erupts and flows from long cracks in Earth's crust called *fissures*. It also flows on the ocean floor at places where tension is causing Earth's crust to pull apart.

**Active Reading** **9 Explain** How does the rate at which magma cools affect the texture of igneous rock?

_____

_____

*Basalt is an example of extrusive igneous rock.*

**10 Compare** Use the Venn diagram to compare and contrast intrusive igneous rock and extrusive igneous rock.

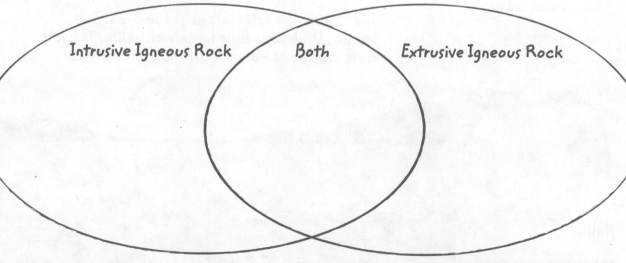

Intrusive Igneous Rock          Both          Extrusive Igneous Rock

# Lay It On!

## What are three types of sedimentary rock?

All the processes that form sedimentary rock occur mainly at or near the surface of Earth. Some of these processes include weathering, erosion, deposition, burial, and cementation. Based on the way that they form, scientists classify sedimentary rocks as clastic, chemical, and organic sedimentary rock.

### Clastic Sedimentary Rock

Clastic sedimentary rock forms when sediments are buried, compacted, and cemented together by calcite or quartz. The size of the sediment, or clasts, that makes up the rock is used to classify clastic sedimentary rocks. Fine-grained sedimentary rocks, in which grains are too small to be seen, include mudstone, siltstone, and shale. Sandstone, which is shown at the left, is a medium-grained clastic sedimentary rock with visible grains. Breccia and conglomerate are coarse-grained clastic sedimentary rocks made of large particles, such as pebbles, cobbles, and boulders.

### Chemical Sedimentary Rock

Chemical sedimentary rocks form when water, usually seawater, evaporates. Most water contains dissolved minerals. As water evaporates, the minerals in water become concentrated to the point that they precipitate out of solution and crystallize. Halite, or rock salt, is an example of chemical sedimentary rock. It is made of sodium chloride, $NaCl$. Halite forms when sodium ions and chlorine ions in shallow bodies of water become so concentrated that halite crystallizes from solution.

Horizontal layers of clastic sedimentary rocks and volcanic ash are exposed at Badlands National Park in South Dakota.

Sandstone

 Visualize It!

**11 Identify** How would you describe the texture of the halite shown below?

_____

_____

The Bonneville Salt Flats near the Great Salt Lake in Utah are made largely of halite. The salt flats are the remains of an ancient lake bed.

Halite

The White Cliffs of Dover on the English sea coast are made up of the skeletons of the marine alga that is shown below.

Skeleton of a marine alga

## Organic Sedimentary Rock

Organic sedimentary rock forms from the remains or fossils, of once-living plants and animals. Most limestone forms from the fossils of organisms that once lived in the ocean. Over time, the skeletons of these marine organisms, which are made of calcium carbonate, collect on the ocean floor. These animal remains, together with sediment, are eventually buried, compacted, and cemented together to form *fossiliferous* [fahs•uh•LIF•er•uhs] limestone.

Coquina is a fossiliferous limestone that consists of the shells of marine mollusks that have been cemented together by calcite. Chalk is a soft, white limestone that is made up of the skeletons of microorganisms that collect in huge numbers on the floor of the deep ocean.

Coal is another type of organic sedimentary rock. It forms when plant material is buried and changes into coal as a result of increasing heat and pressure. This process occurs over millions of years.

**Active Reading** **12 Identify** What are two types of organic sedimentary rock?

_____

_____

**13 Compare** Use the table to compare and contrast clastic, chemical, and organic sedimentary rock.

### Three Types of Sedimentary Rock

| Clastic | Chemical | Organic |
|---------|----------|---------|
|         |          |         |

# The Heat Is On!

Sedimentary shale

Slate

Phyllite

When shale is exposed to increasing temperature and pressure, different foliated metamorphic rocks form.

## What are two types of metamorphic rock?

As a rock is exposed to high temperature and pressure, the crystal structures of the minerals in the rock change to form new minerals. This process results in the formation of metamorphic rock, which has either a foliated texture or a nonfoliated texture.

### Foliated Metamorphic Rock

The metamorphic process in which mineral grains are arranged in planes or bands is called *foliation* (foh•lee•AY•shuhn). Foliation occurs when pressure causes the mineral grains in a rock to realign to form parallel bands.

Metamorphic rocks with a foliated texture include slate, phyllite, schist (SHIST), and gneiss (NYS). Slate and phyllite are commonly produced when shale, a fine-grained sedimentary rock, is exposed to an increase in temperature and pressure. The minerals in slate and phyllite are squeezed into flat, sheet-like layers. With increasing temperature and pressure, phyllite may become schist, a coarse-grained foliated rock. With further increases in temperature and pressure, the minerals in schist separate into alternating bands of light and dark minerals. Gneiss is a coarse-grained, foliated rock that forms from schist. Slate, phyllite, schist, and gneiss can all begin as shale, but they are very different rocks. Each rock forms under a certain range of temperatures and pressures, and contains different minerals.

Schist

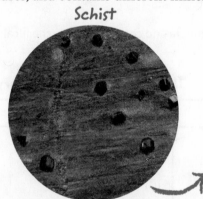

Gneiss

**14 Describe** What happens to the minerals as gneiss forms from schist?

_____

_____

# Nonfoliated Metamorphic Rock

Metamorphic rocks that do not have mineral grains that are aligned in planes or bands are called *nonfoliated*. Nonfoliated metamorphic rocks are commonly made of one or only a few minerals. During metamorphism, mineral grains or crystals may change size or shape, and some may change into another mineral.

Two common nonfoliated metamorphic rocks are quartzite and marble. Quartzite forms when quartz sandstone is exposed to high temperature and pressure. This causes the sand grains to grow larger and the spaces between the sand grains disappear. For that reason, quartzite is very hard and not easily broken down.

When limestone undergoes metamorphism, the limestone becomes marble. During the process of metamorphism, the calcite crystals in the marble grow larger than the calcite grains in the original limestone.

The mineral grains in quartzite (top) and crystals in marble (bottom) do not form bands.

**Active Reading** **15 Apply** What are two characteristics of nonfoliated metamorphic rocks?

_____

_____

Marble is a nonfoliated metamorphic rock that forms when limestone is metamorphosed. Marble is used to build monuments and statues.

**Think Outside the Book** Inquiry

**16 Apply** With a classmate, discuss how different types of rocks can be used as building or construction materials.

© Houghton Mifflin Harcourt Publishing Company • Image Credits: (t) ©Colin Keates/Natural History Museum London/Dorling Kindersley/Getty Images; (c) ©HMH; (b) ©Grant Faint/The Image Bank/Getty Images

# Visual Summary

To complete this summary, fill in the blanks. Then, use the key below to check your answers. You can use this page to review the main concepts of the lesson.

Sedimentary rock may form from layers of sediment that are cemented together.

**17** Sedimentary rocks can be classified into three groups:

_____,

_____, and

_____

## Three Classes of Rock

**Igneous rock forms from magma or lava that has cooled and hardened.**

**18** Igneous rocks can be classified into two groups:

_____

and _____

**Metamorphic rock forms under high temperature or pressure deep within Earth's crust.**

**19** Metamorphic rocks can be classified into two groups:

_____

and _____

Answers: 17 clastic, chemical, organic; 18 intrusive, extrusive; 19 foliated, nonfoliated

**20 Synthesize** While hiking in the mountains, you see a large outcrop of marble. Describe one process by which the metamorphic rock marble forms from the sedimentary rock limestone.

# Lesson Review

## Vocabulary

Fill in the blank with the term that best completes the following sentence.

**1** Sedimentary rocks that are made up of large pebbles and stones have a coarse-grained

_____

**2** Most granite has a _____ of quartz, mica, and feldspar.

**3** _____ can be considered to be mixtures of minerals.

## Key Concepts

**4 Summarize** How does the cooling rate of magma or lava affect the texture of the igneous rock that forms?

_____
_____
_____
_____
_____
_____

**5 Describe** How does clastic sedimentary rock form?

_____
_____
_____
_____

**6 Explain** What is the difference between foliated and nonfoliated metamorphic rock?

_____
_____
_____
_____
_____
_____

## Critical Thinking

Use this photo to answer the following questions.

**7 Identify** What type of rock is shown here? How do you know?

_____
_____
_____

**8 Describe** How did this rock form?

_____
_____
_____

**9 Infer** Suppose this rock was exposed to high temperatures and pressure. What would most likely happen to it?

_____
_____

**10 Infer** What information can a foliated metamorphic rock provide you about the conditions under which it formed?

_____
_____
_____
_____
_____

# My Notes

# Analyzing Technology

| Skills |
| --- |
| *Identify risks* |
| *Identify benefits* |
| ✓ Evaluate cost of technology |
| ✓ Evaluate environmental impact |
| ✓ Propose improvements |
| *Propose risk reduction* |
| ✓ Compare technology |
| ✓ Communicate results |

| Objectives |
| --- |
| • Analyze the life cycle of an aluminum can. |
| • Analyze the life cycle of a glass bottle. |
| • Evaluate the cost of recycling versus disposal of technology. |
| • Analyze the environmental impact of technology. |

## Analyzing the Life Cycles of Aluminum and Glass

A life cycle analysis is a way to evaluate the real cost of a product. The analysis considers how much money an item costs to make. It also examines how making the product affects the economy and the environment through the life of the product. Engineers, scientists, and technologists use this information to improve processes and to compare products.

## Costs of Production

Have you ever wondered where an aluminum soda can comes from? Have you wondered where the can goes when you are done with it? If so, you have started a life cycle analysis by asking the right questions. Aluminum is a metal found in a type of rock called *bauxite*. To get aluminum, first bauxite must be mined. The mined ore is then shipped to a processing plant. There, the bauxite is melted to get aluminum in a process called *smelting*. After smelting, the aluminum is processed. It may be shaped into bicycle parts or rolled into sheets to make cans. Every step in the production involves both financial costs and environmental costs that must be considered in a life cycle analysis.

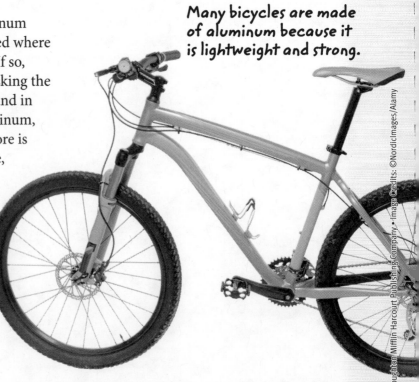

*Many bicycles are made of aluminum because it is lightweight and strong.*

# Costs of Disposal

After an aluminum can is used it can travel either to a landfill or to a recycling plant. The process of recycling an aluminum can does require the use of some energy. However, the financial and environmental costs of disposing of a can and mining ore are much greater than the cost of recycling a can. Additionally, smelting bauxite produces harmful wastes. A life cycle analysis of an aluminum can must include the cost and environmental effects of mining, smelting, and disposing of the aluminum can.

**1 Analyze** After a can is recycled, which steps are no longer part of the life cycle?

_____

_____

_____

_____

_____

**Bauxite mining**

Most bauxite mining occurs far away from where aluminum is used. Large ships or trains transport the ore before it is made into aluminum products.

Aluminum is one of the easiest materials to recycle. Producing a ton of aluminum by shredding and remelting uses about 5% of the energy needed to process enough bauxite to make a ton of aluminum.

**Remelting**

**Shredding**

**Smelting**

**Fabrication**

# Life Cycle of an Aluminum Can

**Recycling**

**Manufacturing**

**Consumer use**

**2 Evaluate** In the life cycle shown here, which two steps could include an arrow to indicate disposal?

_____

_____

_____

✋ **You Try It!** ⟶

**Now it's your turn to analyze the life cycle of a product.**

# ✋ You Try It!

Now, apply what you have learned about the life cycle of aluminum to analyze the life cycle of a glass bottle. Glass is made by melting silica from sand or from mineral deposits mined from the Earth. A kiln heats the silica until it melts to form a red-hot glob. Then, the glass is shaped and cooled to form useful items.

## ① Evaluate Cost of Technology

As a group, discuss the steps that would be involved in making a glass bottle. List the steps in the space below. Start with mining and end at a landfill. Include as many steps in the process as you can think of. Beside each step, tell whether there would be financial costs, environmental costs, or both.

*Life Cycle of a Glass Bottle*

## ② Evaluate Environmental Impact

Use the table below to indicate which of the steps listed above would have environmental costs, and what type of cost would be involved. A step can appear in more than one column.

| Cause pollution | Consume energy | Damage habitat |
|---|---|---|
| | | |

# (3) Propose Improvements

In your group, discuss how you might improve the life cycle of a glass bottle and reduce the impact on the environment. Draw a life cycle that includes your suggestions for improvement.

# (4) Compare Technology

How does your improved process decrease the environmental effects of making and using glass bottles?

_____

_____

_____

_____

# (5) Communicate Results

Imagine that you are an accountant for a company that produces glass bottles. In the space below, write an argument for using recycled glass that is based on financial savings for your company.

_____

_____

_____

_____

# The Rock Cycle

**ESSENTIAL QUESTION**

## What is the rock cycle?

By the end of this lesson, you should be able to describe the series of processes and classes of rocks that make up the rock cycle.

It may be hard to believe, but these mountains actually move. Wyoming's Teton Mountains rise by millimeters each year. An active fault is uplifting the mountains. In this lesson, you will learn about uplift and other processes that change rock.

**TEKS 6.10B** classify rocks as metamorphic, igneous, or sedimentary by the processes of their formation

## Engage Your Brain

**1 Describe** Fill in the blank with the word or phrase that you think correctly completes the following sentences.

Most of Earth is made of _____

Rock is _____ changing.

The three main classes of rock are igneous, metamorphic, and _____

**2 Describe** Write your own caption for this photo.

_____

_____

_____

## Active Reading

**3 Synthesize** Many English words have their roots in other languages. Use the Latin words below to make an educated guess about the meaning of the words *erosion* and *deposition*.

| Latin Word | Meaning |
|------------|---------|
| *erosus* | eaten away |
| *depositus* | laid down |

### Vocabulary Terms

- weathering
- erosion
- deposition
- igneous rock
- sedimentary rock
- metamorphic rock
- rock cycle
- uplift
- subsidence
- rift zone

**4 Apply** As you learn the definition of each vocabulary term in this lesson, create your own definition or sketch to help you remember the meaning of the term.

Erosion:

_____

_____

Deposition:

_____

_____

# Let's Rock!

## What is rock?

The solid parts of Earth are made almost entirely of rock. Scientists define rock as a naturally occurring solid mixture of one or more minerals that may also include organic matter. Most rock is made of minerals, but some rock is made of nonmineral material that is not organic, such as glass. Rock has been an important natural resource as long as humans have existed. Early humans used rocks as hammers to make other tools. For centuries, people have used different types of rock, including granite, marble, sandstone, and slate, to make buildings, such as the pyramids shown below.

It may be hard to believe, but rocks are always changing. People study rocks to learn how areas have changed through time.

**5 List** How is rock used today?

_____
_____
_____
_____

The ancient Egyptians used a rock called limestone to construct the Great Sphinx and the pyramids at Giza.

These rock formations in Goreme, Turkey, are known as fairy chimneys. They were shaped by erosion.

**Think Outside the Book**

**6 Design** Create a travel brochure for Goreme, Turkey.

# What processes change rock?

Natural processes make and destroy rock. They change each type of rock into other types of rock and shape the features of our planet. These processes also influence the type of rock that is found in each area of Earth's surface.

**Active Reading** **7 Identify** As you read, underline the processes and factors that can change rock.

## Weathering, Erosion, and Deposition

The process by which water, wind, ice, and changes in temperature break down rock is called **weathering**. Weathering breaks down rock into fragments called *sediment*. The process by which sediment is moved from one place to another is called **erosion.** Water, wind, ice, and gravity can erode sediments. These sediments are eventually deposited, or laid down, in bodies of water and other low-lying areas. The process by which sediment comes to rest is called **deposition.**

## Temperature and Pressure

Rock that is buried can be squeezed by the weight of the rock or the layers of sediment on top of it. As pressure increases with depth beneath Earth's surface, so does temperature. If the temperature and pressure are high enough, the buried rock can change into metamorphic rock. In some cases, the rock gets hot enough to melt and forms *magma*, or molten rock. If magma reaches Earth's surface, it is called *lava*. The magma or lava eventually cool and solidify to form new rock.

# Classified Information!

## What are the classes of rocks?

Rocks fall into three major classes based on how they form. **Igneous rock** forms when magma or lava cools and hardens to become solid. It forms beneath or on Earth's surface. **Sedimentary rock** forms when minerals that form from solutions or sediment from older rocks get pressed and cemented together. **Metamorphic rock** forms when pressure, temperature, or chemical processes change existing rock. Each class can be divided further, based on differences in the way rocks form. For example, some igneous rocks form when lava cools on Earth's surface, and others form when magma cools deep beneath the surface. Therefore, igneous rock can be classified based on how and where it forms.

**Active Reading**

**8 Identify** As you read the paragraph, underline the three main classes of rocks.

**Think Outside the Book** **Inquiry**

**9 Apply** With a classmate, discuss the processes that might have shaped the rock formations in the Valley of Fire State Park.

These formations in Valley of Fire State Park in Nevada are made of sandstone, a sedimentary rock.

sandstone

### Sedimentary

Sedimentary rock is composed of minerals formed from solutions or sediments from older rock. Sedimentary rock forms when the weight from above presses down on the layers of minerals or sediment, or when minerals dissolved in water solidify between sediment pieces and cement them together.

Sedimentary rocks are named according to the size and type of the fragments they contain. For example, the rock shown here is made of sand and is called sandstone. Rock made primarily of the mineral calcite (calcium carbonate) is called limestone.

Enchanted Rock in Texas is a large dome made of granite, an intrusive igneous rock.

## Igneous Rock

Igneous rock forms from cooling lava and magma. As molten rock cools and becomes solid, the minerals crystallize and grow. The longer the cooling takes, the more time the crystals have to grow. The granite shown here cooled slowly and is made of large crystals. Rock that forms when magma cools beneath Earth's surface is called intrusive igneous rock. Rock that forms when lava cools on Earth's surface is called extrusive igneous rock.

granite

## Metamorphic Rock

Metamorphic rock forms when high temperature and pressure change the texture and mineral content of rock. For example, a rock can be buried in Earth's crust, where the temperature and pressure are high. Over millions of years, the solid rock changes, and new crystals are formed. Metamorphic rocks may be changed in four ways: by temperature, by pressure, by temperature and pressure combined, or by fluids or other chemicals. Gneiss, shown here, is a metamorphic rock. It forms at high temperatures deep within Earth's crust.

gneiss

Gneiss is a metamorphic rock that is made up of bands of light and dark minerals.

**10 Compare** Fill in the chart to compare and contrast sedimentary, igneous, and metamorphic rock.

### Classes of Rocks

| Sedimentary rock | Igneous rock | Metamorphic rock |
|------------------|--------------|------------------|
|                  |              |                  |

# What is the rock cycle?

**Active Reading** 11 **Apply** As you read, underline the rock types that metamorphic rock can change into.

Rocks may seem very permanent, solid, and unchanging. But over millions of years, any of the three rock types can be changed into another of the three types. For example, igneous rock can change into sedimentary or metamorphic rock, or back into another kind of igneous rock. This series of processes in which rock changes from one type to another is called the **rock cycle**. Rocks may follow different pathways in the cycle. Examples of these pathways are shown here. Factors, including temperature, pressure, weathering, and erosion, may change a rock's identity. Where rock is located on a tectonic plate and whether the rock is at Earth's surface also influence how it forms and changes.

When igneous rock is exposed at Earth's surface, it may break down into sediment. Igneous rock may also change directly into metamorphic rock while still beneath Earth's surface. It may also melt to form magma that becomes another type of igneous rock.

When sediment is pressed together and cemented, the sediment becomes sedimentary rock. With temperature and pressure changes, sedimentary rocks may become metamorphic rocks, or they may melt and become igneous rock. Sedimentary rock may also be broken down at Earth's surface and become sediment that forms another sedimentary rock.

Under certain temperature and pressure conditions, metamorphic rock will melt and form magma. Metamorphic rock can also be altered by heat and pressure to form a different type of metamorphic rock. Metamorphic rock can also be broken down by weathering and erosion to form sediment that forms sedimentary rock.

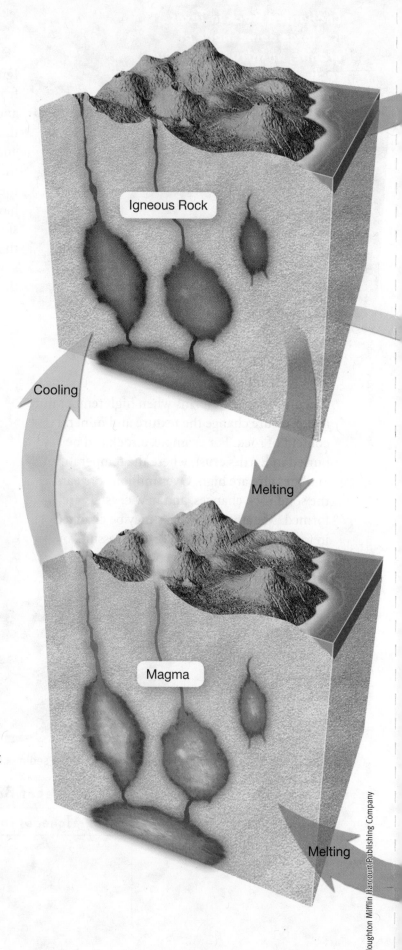

Igneous Rock

Cooling

Melting

Magma

Melting

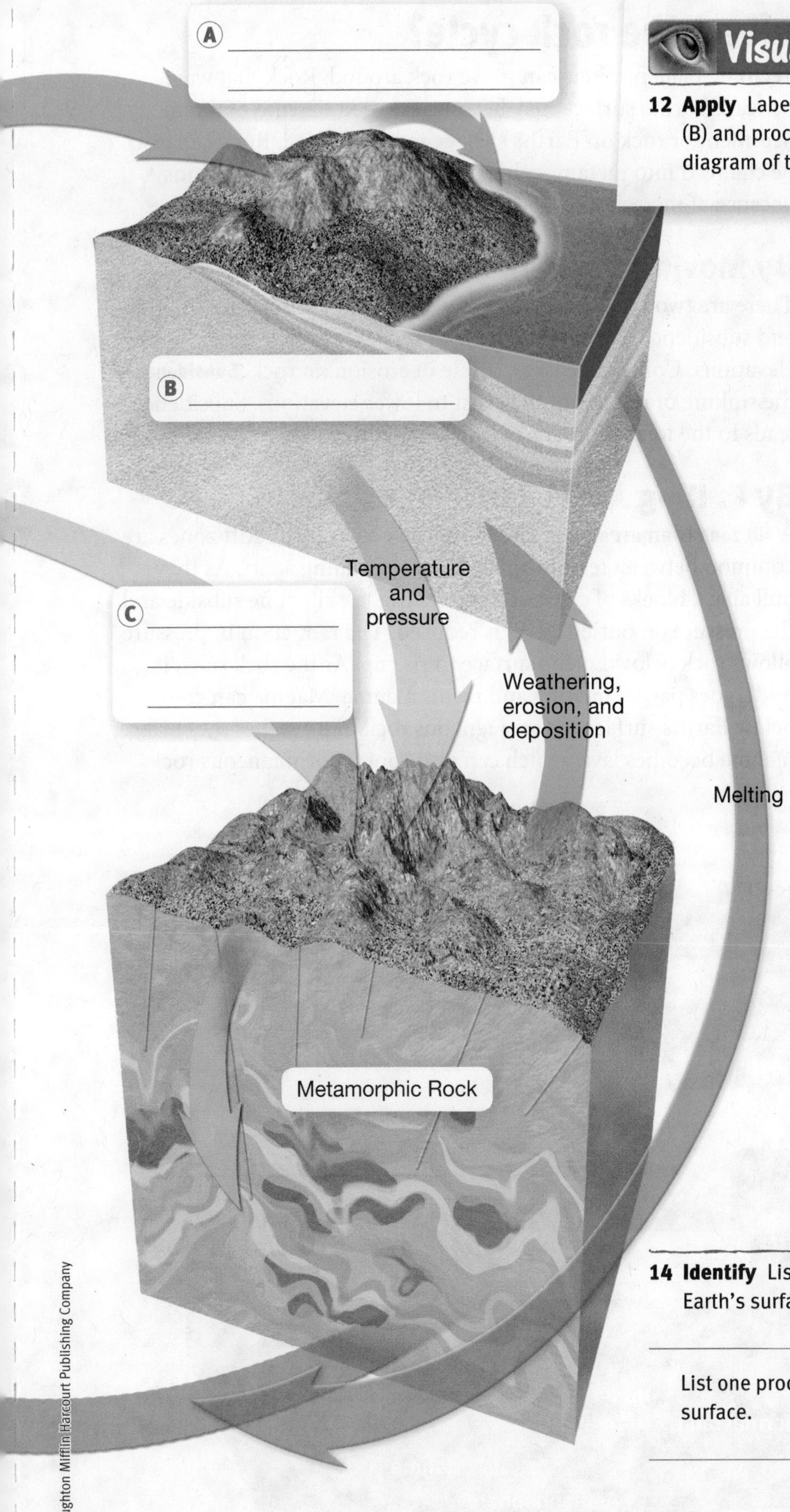

(A) _____

_____

**Visualize It!**

**12 Apply** Label the missing rock type (B) and processes (A and C) on the diagram of the rock cycle.

(B) _____

Temperature
and
pressure

(C) _____

_____

_____

Weathering,
erosion, and
deposition

Melting

**Think Outside the Book**

**13 Apply** Write a series of blog entries from the viewpoint of igneous rock that is changing into sedimentary rock.

Metamorphic Rock

**14 Identify** List one process that happens above Earth's surface.

_____

List one process that happens below Earth's surface.

_____

# How do tectonic plate motions affect the rock cycle?

Tectonic plate motions can move rock around. Rock that was beneath Earth's surface may become exposed to wind and rain. Sediment or rock on Earth's surface may be buried. Rock can also be changed into metamorphic rock by tectonic plate collisions because of increased temperature and pressure.

## By Moving Rock Up or Down

There are two types of vertical movements in Earth's crust: uplift and subsidence. **Uplift** is the rising of regions of the crust to higher elevations. Uplift increases the rate of erosion on rock. **Subsidence** is the sinking of regions of the crust to lower elevations. Subsidence leads to the formation of basins where sediment can be deposited.

## By Pulling Apart Earth's Surface

A **rift zone** is an area where a set of deep cracks form. Rift zones are common between tectonic plates that are pulling apart. As they pull apart, blocks of crust in the center of the rift zone subside and the pressure on buried rocks is reduced. The reduction in pressure allows rock below Earth's surface to rise up. As the rock rises, it undergoes partial melting and forms magma. Magma can cool below Earth's surface to form igneous rock. If it reaches the surface, magma becomes lava, which can also cool to form igneous rock.

**15 Compare** How does uplift differ from subsidence?

_____

_____

_____

**Visualize It! Inquiry**

**16 Predict** Label uplift and subsidence on this diagram. What pathway in the rock cycle might rock take next if it is subjected to uplift? Explain.

_____

_____

_____

Before

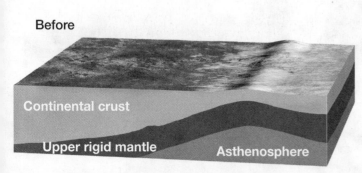

Continental crust

Upper rigid mantle          Asthenosphere

After

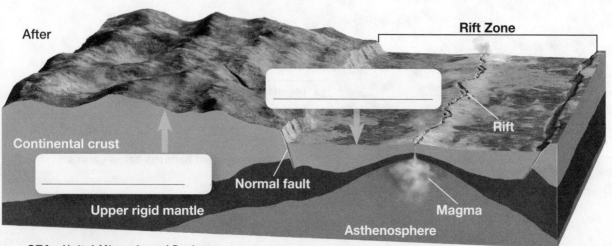

Rift Zone

Rift

Continental crust

Normal fault

Magma

Upper rigid mantle

Asthenosphere

## Why It Matters
# Cliff Dwellings

Can you imagine living on the side of a cliff? Some ancient peoples could! They created dwellings from cliff rock. They also decorated rock with art, as you can see in the pictographs shown below.

### Cliff Palace
This dwelling in Colorado is called the Cliff Palace. It was home to the Ancient Puebloans from about 550 to 1300 CE.

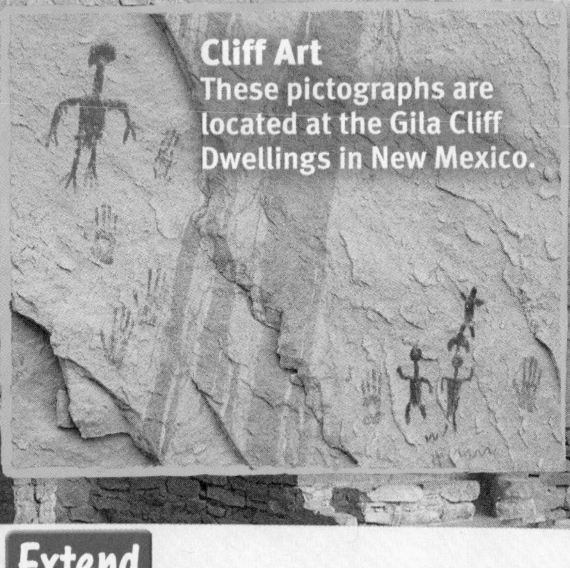

### Cliff Art
These pictographs are located at the Gila Cliff Dwellings in New Mexico.

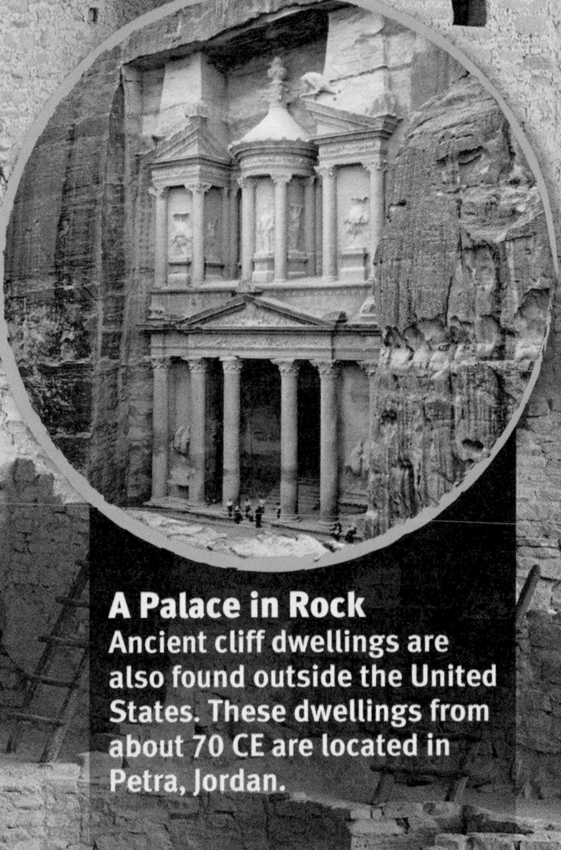

### A Palace in Rock
Ancient cliff dwellings are also found outside the United States. These dwellings from about 70 CE are located in Petra, Jordan.

## Extend

Inquiry

**17 Identify** Describe how ancient people used rock to create shelter.

**18 Research** Find out how people lived in one of the cliff dwelling locations. How did living in a rock environment affect their daily lives?

**19 Produce** Illustrate how the people lived by doing one of the following: write a play, write a song, or create a graphic novel.

# Visual Summary

To complete this summary, use what you know about the rock cycle to fill in the blanks below. Then use the key below to check your answers. You can use this page to review the main concepts of the lesson.

Each rock type can change into another of the three types.

**20** When sediment is pressed together and cemented, the sediment becomes

_____

**21** When lava cools and solidifies,

_____ forms.

**22** Metamorphic rock can be altered by temperature and pressure to form a different type of

_____

## Rock Cycle

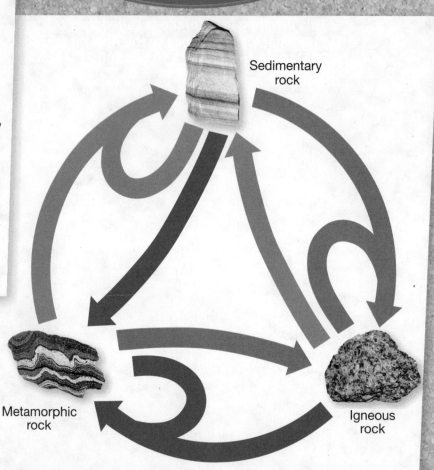

Sedimentary rock

Metamorphic rock

Igneous rock

Answers: 20 sedimentary rock; 21 igneous rock; 22 metamorphic rock

**23 Explain** What factors and processes can affect the pathway that igneous rock takes in the rock cycle?

© Houghton Mifflin Harcourt Publishing Company • Image Credits: (sedimentary) ©Joyce Photographics/Photo Researchers, Inc.; (morphic) ©Dirk Wiersma/Photo Researchers, Inc.; (igneous) ©Joyce Photographics/Photo Researchers, Inc.

# Lesson Review

## Vocabulary

In your own words, define the following terms.

**1** Rock cycle

_____

_____

**2** Weathering

_____

_____

**3** Rift zone

_____

_____

## Key Concepts

Use these photos to classify the rock as sedimentary, igneous, or metamorphic.

| Example | Type of rock |
|---|---|
| **4 Classify** This rock is made up of the mineral calcite, and it formed from the remains of organisms that lived in water. |  |
| **5 Classify** Through high temperature and pressure, this rock formed from a sedimentary rock. | |
| **6 Classify** This rock is made of tiny crystals that formed quickly when molten rock cooled at Earth's surface. |  |

**7 Describe** How can sedimentary rock become metamorphic rock?

_____

_____

_____

**8 Explain** How can subsidence lead to the formation of sedimentary rock?

_____

_____

_____

**9 Explain** Why are rift zones common places for igneous rock to form?

_____

_____

_____

## Critical Thinking

**10 Hypothesize** What would happen to the rock cycle if erosion did not occur?

_____

_____

**11 Criticize** A classmate states that igneous rock must always become sedimentary rock next, according to the rock cycle. Explain why this statement is not correct.

_____

_____

_____

**12 Predict** Granite is an igneous rock that forms from magma cooled below Earth's surface. Why would granite have larger crystals than igneous rocks formed from lava cooled above Earth's surface?

_____

_____

_____

# My Notes

# Unit 6 > Big Idea

Minerals and rocks are basic building blocks of Earth and can change over time from one type of mineral or rock to another.

### Lesson 1

**ESSENTIAL QUESTION**
**What are minerals, how do they form, and how can they be identified?**

Describe the basic structures of minerals, and identify different minerals by using their physical properties.

### Lesson 2

**ESSENTIAL QUESTION**
**How do rocks form?**

Describe the formation and classification of sedimentary, igneous, and metamorphic rocks.

### Lesson 3

**ESSENTIAL QUESTION**
**What is the rock cycle?**

Describe the series of processes and classes of rocks that make up the rock cycle.

## Connect ESSENTIAL QUESTIONS
Lessons 1 and 2

**1 Synthesize** Describe a process by which one mineral can change into another mineral.

_____

_____

_____

_____

_____

## Think Outside the Book

**2 Synthesize** Choose one of these activities to help synthesize what you have learned in this unit.

☐ Using what you learned in lessons 1, 2, and 3, explain in a short essay how a chemical sedimentary rock formed, beginning with a lake full of dissolved gypsum minerals.

☐ Using what you learned in lessons 1, 2, and 3, create a poster presentation to describe the type and texture of a rock formed by an explosive volcanic event.

# Unit 6 Review

Name _____

## Vocabulary

Fill in the blank with the term that best completes the sentence.

**1** The _____ is a series of geologic processes in which rock can form, change from one type to another, be destroyed, and form again.

**2** The rising of regions of Earth's crust to higher elevations is called _____.

**3** A(n) _____ is a naturally occurring, solid combination of one or more minerals or organic matter.

**4** _____ is a physical property used to describe how the surface of a mineral reflects light.

## Key Concepts

Choose the letter of the best answer.

**TEKS** 6.6C, 6.2E

**5** The table below lists the masses and volumes of four mineral samples.

| Mineral | Mass (g) | Volume (mL) |
|---------|----------|-------------|
| feldspar | 16 | 6.2 |
| galena | 9 | 1.2 |
| garnet | 12 | 3.0 |
| quartz | 10 | 3.7 |

Which mineral has the greatest density? (Hint: Step 1. Use the density equation to find the density of each mineral in the table. Step 2. Compare the densities you calculate to find the greatest value.)

**A** feldspar

**B** galena

**C** garnet

**D** quartz

TEKS **6.10B**

**6** Declan observed a rock that he found at the beach. He concluded that the rock was sedimentary. Which observation best supports this conclusion? (Hint: Step 1. Recall how sedimentary rock is formed. Step 2. Decide which property sedimentary rock will have because of the way it forms.)

**A** the yellow color          **C** the layers within the rock

**B** the hardness of the rock          **D** the location where the rock was found

TEKS **6.10B**

**7** Which of the following best describes how sedimentary rock forms?

**A** Molten rock beneath the surface of the Earth cools and becomes solid.

**B** Layers of material become compressed to form rock.

**C** Chemical processes or changes in pressure or temperature change the texture and composition of a rock.

**D** Molten rock reaches the surface and cools to become solid rock.

TEKS **6.10B, 6.3B**

**8** The diagram shows portions of the rock cycle.

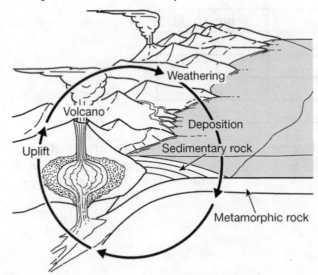

Suppose you were to add an arrow to show subsidence in the diagram. How would you draw the arrow?

**A** It would extend horizontally across the diagram.

**B** It would point upward toward the metamorphic rock.

**C** It would point downward from the metamorphic rock.

**D** It would point in the same direction as the uplift arrow.

TEKS 6.6C, 6.2B

**9** A student is shining a light on several different mineral samples. For which type of mineral should the student expect the greatest luster?

**A** a dull, chalky mineral

**B** a rough, grey mineral

**C** a shiny, metallic mineral

**D** a clear, translucent mineral

## Gridded Response

Write the answer in the boxes, then bubble in the corresponding number in the grid below.

TEKS 6.6C

**10** The table below shows the Mohs hardness scale.

| Hardness | Mineral |
|---|---|
| 1 | talc |
| 2 | gypsum |
| 3 | calcite |
| 4 | fluorite |
| 5 | apatite |
| 6 | feldspar |
| 7 | quartz |
| 8 | topaz |
| 9 | corundum |
| 10 | diamond |

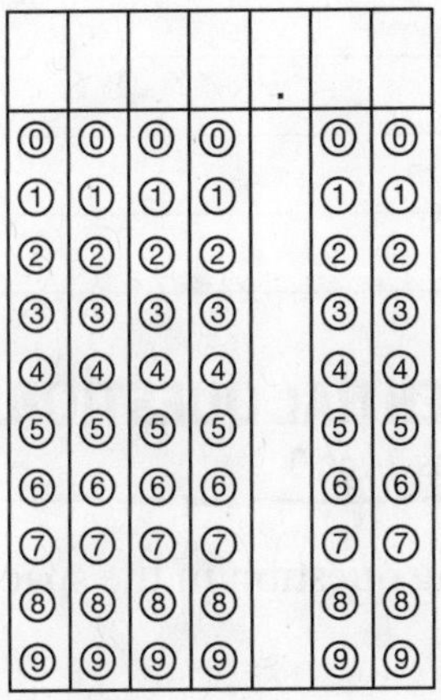

A student determines that the hardness of a penny is exactly between the hardnesses of calcite and fluorite. What is the hardness of the penny?

# Unit 6 Review continued

## Critical Thinking

Answer the following questions in the space provided.

**11** Explain how both the texture and the composition of a rock can provide scientists with information on the rock's history. Give an example of each.

_____

_____

_____

_____

_____

**TEKS** 6.10B

**12** Explain a way that a sedimentary rock could form, then over time break down into smaller pieces, and become sedimentary rock again in another location.

_____

_____

_____

_____

_____

**Connect** ESSENTIAL QUESTIONS
Lessons 2 and 3

Answer the following question in the space provided.

**TEKS** 6.10B, 6.3B

**13** A student is developing a model to show how one type of rock can undergo several changes and eventually form the same type of rock again. Describe two pathways the student can use to show how a metamorphic rock could become another type of rock and then become metamorphic once again.

_____

_____

_____

_____

_____

_____

_____

# The Dynamic Earth

© Houghton Mifflin Harcourt Publishing Company • Image Credits: (bkgd) ©NASA; (br)

## Big Idea

The movement of tectonic plates accounts for important features of Earth's surface and for major geologic events.

The Cleveland volcano in Alaska erupts.

## What do you think?

Earth is continuously changing. Volcanoes and earthquakes are powerful forces of change. Volcanoes form new rock and reshape the land. Earthquakes move rocks. How did the landscape around you form?

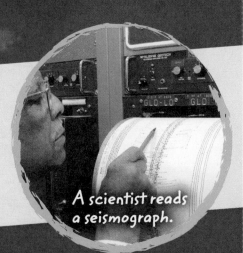

A scientist reads a seismograph.

# CITIZEN SCIENCE

# Texas Volcanoes

Volcanoes in Texas? Yes! In fact, many of the mountains and rock formations in Big Bend National Park are the result of ancient volcanic activity. Around 30 million years ago, a series of volcanic eruptions occurred in the area near the Chisos Mountains. These eruptions happened periodically over millions of years and helped to shape the landscape we see today.

## (1) Think About It

**A** Where would you expect to find evidence of volcanic activity?

_____

_____

**B** What mountain-building materials do you think are produced by volcanoes?

_____

_____

**C** Use the Internet to research the history of volcanic activity in Big Bend National Park. Take notes on your findings on a separate sheet of paper.

*The South Rim of the Chisos Mountains in Big Bend National Park*

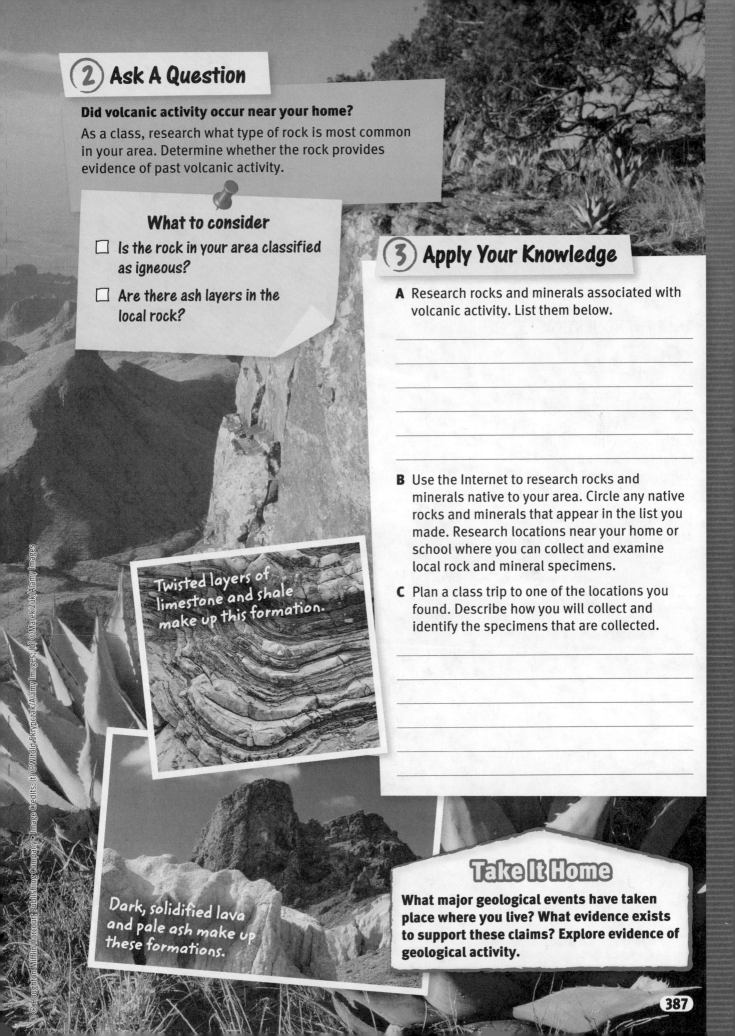

## ② Ask A Question

**Did volcanic activity occur near your home?**

As a class, research what type of rock is most common in your area. Determine whether the rock provides evidence of past volcanic activity.

### What to consider

☐ Is the rock in your area classified as igneous?

☐ Are there ash layers in the local rock?

## ③ Apply Your Knowledge

**A** Research rocks and minerals associated with volcanic activity. List them below.

_____

_____

_____

_____

_____

_____

**B** Use the Internet to research rocks and minerals native to your area. Circle any native rocks and minerals that appear in the list you made. Research locations near your home or school where you can collect and examine local rock and mineral specimens.

**C** Plan a class trip to one of the locations you found. Describe how you will collect and identify the specimens that are collected.

_____

_____

_____

_____

_____

Twisted layers of limestone and shale make up this formation.

Dark, solidified lava and pale ash make up these formations.

### Take It Home

**What major geological events have taken place where you live? What evidence exists to support these claims? Explore evidence of geological activity.**

# Lesson 1
# Earth's Layers

**ESSENTIAL QUESTION**

## What are Earth's layers?

By the end of this lesson, you should be able to identify Earth's compositional and physical layers and describe their properties.

If you could dig below this canyon, you would discover that Earth is made up of different layers below its surface.

**TEKS** **6.10A** build a model to illustrate the structural layers of Earth, including the inner core, mantle, crust, asthenosphere, and lithosphere

© Houghton Mifflin Harcourt Publishing Company • Image Credits: ©Phil Schermeister/Corbis

## Lesson Labs

**Quick Labs**
- Layers of Earth
- Ordering Earth's Layers

**S.T.E.M. Lab**
- Models of Earth

## Engage Your Brain

**1 Predict** Check T or F to show whether you think each statement is true or false.

| T | F | |
|---|---|---|
| ☐ | ☐ | The outermost layer of solid Earth is sometimes called the crust. |
| ☐ | ☐ | The crust is the densest layer. |
| ☐ | ☐ | The mantle is the layer between the crust and the core. |
| ☐ | ☐ | Earth's core is divided into five parts. |

**2 Describe** If you were asked to describe this apple, how many layers would you say it has? How would you describe the layers?

_____

_____

_____

_____

_____

## Active Reading

**3 Synthesize** You can often define an unknown word if you know the meaning of its word parts. Use the word parts and sentence below to make an educated guess about the meaning of the word *mesosphere*.

| Word part | Meaning |
|-----------|---------|
| *meso-* | middle |
| *-sphere* | ball |

**Example sentence**
The <u>mesosphere</u> is more than 2,000 km thick.

**Vocabulary Terms**
- crust
- mantle
- convection
- core
- lithosphere
- asthenosphere
- mesosphere

**4 Apply** As you learn the definition of each vocabulary term in this lesson, create your own definition or sketch to help you remember the meaning of the term.

Mesosphere:

_____

_____

_____

# Peeling the Layers

## What is inside Earth?

If you tried to dig to the center of Earth, what do you think you would find? Would Earth be solid or hollow? Would it be made of the same material throughout? Actually, Earth is made of several layers. The materials that make up each layer have characteristic properties that vary from layer to layer. Scientists think about Earth's layers in two ways—in terms of their chemical composition and in terms of their physical properties.

**Think Outside the Book** **Inquiry**

**5 Apply** With a classmate, discuss why scientists might have two ways for thinking about Earth's layers.

## What are Earth's compositional layers?

Earth can be divided into three layers based on chemical composition. These layers are called the *crust*, the *mantle*, and the *core*. Each compositional layer is made up of a different mixture of chemicals.

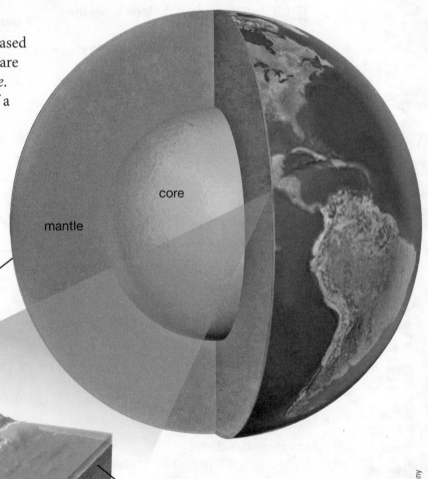

Earth is divided into three layers based on the chemical composition of each layer.

crust

mantle

core

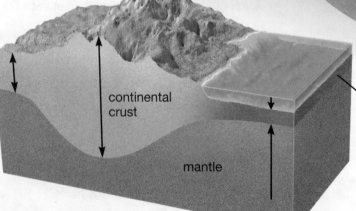

continental crust

oceanic crust

mantle

Continental crust is thicker than oceanic crust.

## Crust

The outermost solid layer of Earth is the **crust.** There are two types of crust—continental and oceanic. Both types are made mainly of the elements oxygen, silicon, and aluminum. However, the denser oceanic crust has almost twice as much iron, calcium, and magnesium. These elements form minerals that are denser than those in the continental crust.

### Active Reading

**6 Identify** List the compositional layers in order of most dense to least dense.

_____

_____

_____

## Mantle

The **mantle** is located between the core and the crust. It is a region of hot, slow-flowing, solid rock. When convection takes place in the mantle, cooler rock sinks and warmer rock rises. **Convection** is the movement of matter that results from differences in density caused by variations in temperature. Scientists can learn about the mantle by observing mantle rock that has risen to Earth's surface. The mantle is denser than the crust. It contains more magnesium and less aluminum and silicon than the crust does.

## Core

The **core** extends from below the mantle to the center of Earth. Scientists think that the core is made mostly of iron and some nickel. Scientists also think that it contains much less oxygen, silicon, aluminum, and magnesium than the mantle does. The core is the densest layer. It makes up about one-third of Earth's mass.

### Active Reading **7 Identify** What element makes up most of Earth's core? _____

# What are Earth's physical layers?

Earth can also be divided into layers based on physical properties. The properties considered include whether the layer is solid or liquid, and how the layer moves or transmits waves. The five physical layers are the *lithosphere*, *asthenosphere*, *mesosphere*, *outer core*, and *inner core*.

**Active Reading** **8 Label** Write the names of the compositional layers shown below in the spaces provided.

**Visualize It!**

**9 Analyze** Which of Earth's compositional layers make up the lithosphere?

_____

## Lithosphere

The outermost, rigid layer of Earth is the **lithosphere.** The lithosphere is made of two parts—the crust and the rigid, upper part of the mantle. The lithosphere is divided into pieces called *tectonic plates*.

## Asthenosphere

The **asthenosphere** is a layer of weak or soft mantle that is made of rock that flows slowly. Tectonic plates move on top of this layer.

## Mesosphere

The strong, lower part of the mantle is called the **mesosphere.** Rock in the mesosphere flows more slowly than rock in the asthenosphere does.

## Outer Core

The outer core is the liquid layer of Earth's core. It lies beneath the mantle and surrounds the inner core.

## Inner Core

The inner core is the solid, dense center of our planet that extends from the bottom of the outer core to the center of Earth, which is about 6,380 km beneath the surface.

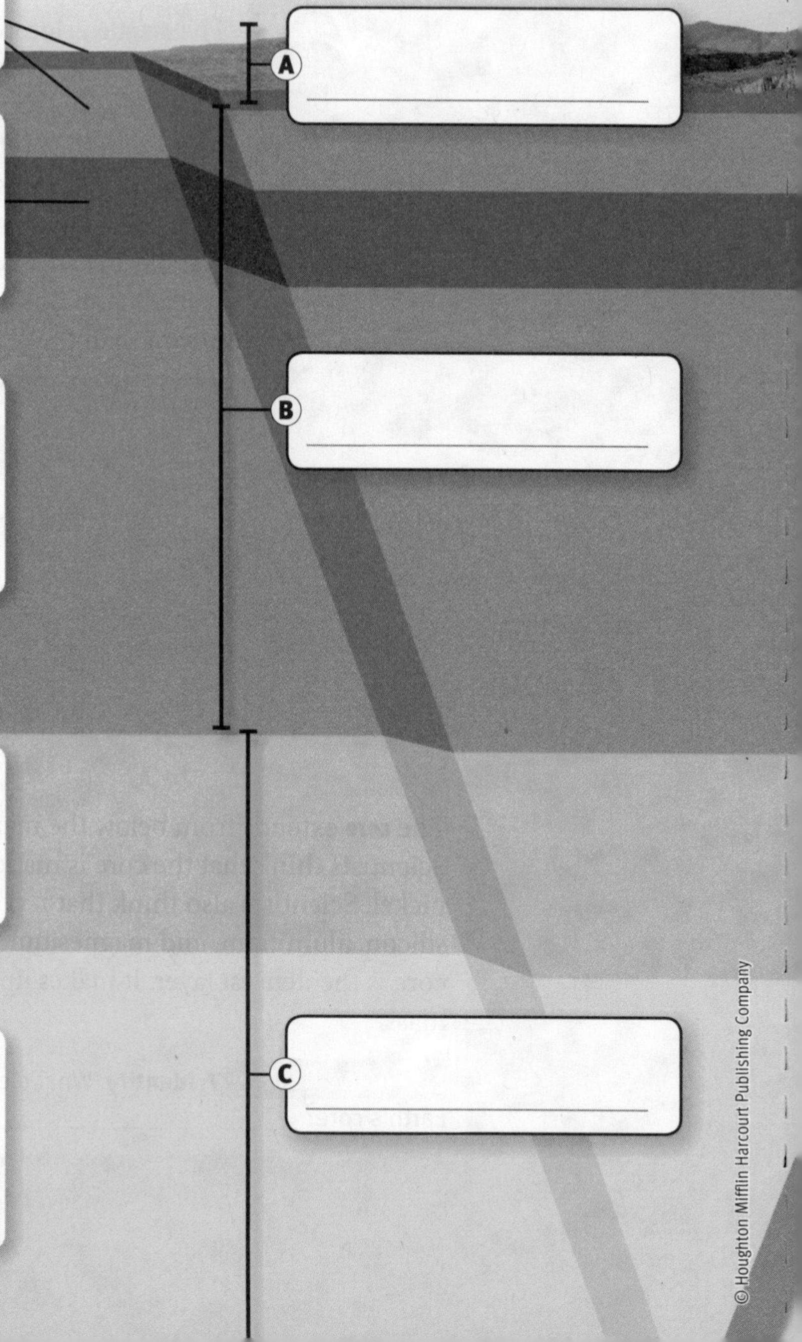

**A**

**B**

**C**

 **Do the Math** Sample Problem

Here's an example of how to find the percentage thickness of the core that is the outer core.

| Physical | Compositional |
|---|---|
| Continental lithosphere (150 km) | Continental crust (30 km) |
| Asthenosphere (250 km) | Mantle (2,900 km) |
| Mesosphere (2,550 km) | |
| Outer core (2,200 km) | Core (3,430 km) |
| Inner core (1,230 km) | |

### Identify

**A.** What do you know?
core = 3,430 km    outer core = 2,200 km

**B.** What do you want to find out?
Percentage of core that is outer core

### Plan

**C.** Write the formula:

Percentage (%) of core that is outer core =

$\left( \dfrac{\text{thickness of outer core}}{\text{thickness of core}} \right) \times 100\%$

**D.** Substitute into the formula:

$\% = \dfrac{(2,200)}{(3,430)} \times 100\%$

### Solve

**E.** Calculate and simplify:

$\% = 0.6414 \times 100\% = 64.14\%$

**Answer:** 64.14%

---

**Do the Math** You Try It

**10 Calculate** What percentage thickness of the continental lithosphere is continental crust?

### Identify

**A.** What do you know?

**B.** What do you want to find out?

### Plan

**C.** Write the formula:

**D.** Substitute into the formula:

### Solve

**E.** Calculate and simplify:

**Answer:**

# Visual Summary

To complete this summary, fill in the blanks with the correct word or phrase. Then, use the key below to check your answers. You can use this page to review the main concepts of the lesson.

**Earth is divided into three compositional layers.**

11  The outermost compositional layer of the Earth is the _____ .

12  The _____ is denser than the crust and contains more magnesium.

**Earth is divided into five physical layers.**

13  The _____ is divided into pieces called tectonic plates.

14  The _____ core is the liquid layer of Earth's core.

## Earth's Layers

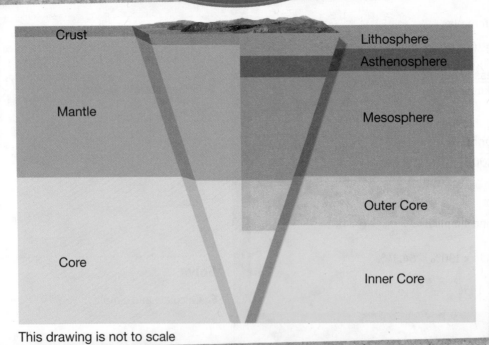

Crust

Mantle

Core

Lithosphere

Asthenosphere

Mesosphere

Outer Core

Inner Core

This drawing is not to scale

15  **Synthesize** Which physical layers correspond to which compositional layers?

# Lesson Review

## Vocabulary

Fill in the blank with the term that best completes the following sentence.

**1** The _____ is a region of hot, slow-flowing, solid rock between the core and the crust.

**2** The _____ is the densest compositional layer and makes up one-third of Earth's mass.

**3** The _____ is the outermost, rigid physical layer of Earth.

## Key Concepts

Use this diagram to answer the following questions.

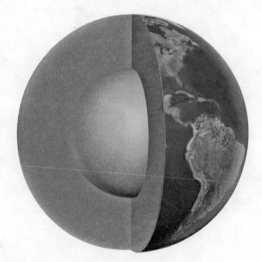

**4 Identify** Which model of Earth's interior does this image show?

_____

**5 Identify** Which of these layers is made mostly of iron and nickel?

_____

**6 Compare** Explain the differences between the inner core and the outer core.

_____

_____

_____

## Critical Thinking

**7 Compare** Explain the difference between the lithosphere and the crust.

_____

_____

_____

_____

**8 Hypothesizing** Scientists find dense rock on Earth's surface that is made of magnesium and smaller amounts of aluminum and silicon. What layer of Earth might this rock help scientists study? Explain your answer.

_____

_____

_____

_____

_____

_____

**9 Apply** In a model of Earth's layers that is determined by physical properties, how might the atmosphere be classified? Would it be part of the lithosphere, or a separate layer? Explain your answer.

_____

_____

_____

_____

_____

_____

_____

_____

_____

_____

# My Notes

# Plate Tectonics

## ESSENTIAL QUESTION

## What is plate tectonics?

By the end of this lesson, you should be able to explain the theory of plate tectonics, to describe how tectonic plates move, and to identify geologic events that occur because of tectonic plate movement.

The San Andreas Fault is located where two tectonic plates slide past each other.

The course of this river has been shifted as a result of tectonic plate motion.

**TEKS** 6.10C identify the major tectonic plates, including Eurasian, African, Indo-Australian, Pacific, North American, and South American

**Lesson Labs**

**Quick Labs**
• Tectonic Ice Cubes
• Mantle Convection
• Reconstructing Land Masses

**Exploration Lab**
• Sea-floor Spreading

## Engage Your Brain

**1 Predict** Check T or F to show whether you think each statement is true or false.

T   F

☐  ☐  Earth's surface is all one piece.

☐  ☐  Scientists think the continents once formed a single landmass.

☐  ☐  The sea floor is smooth and level.

☐  ☐  All tectonic plates are the same.

**2 Illustrate** Imagine that you could slice planet Earth in half. Draw a picture of what you might see inside Earth.

## Active Reading

**3 Apply** Many scientific words, such as *divergent*, also have everyday meanings or are related to words with everyday meanings. Use context clues to write your own definition for each underlined word.

**Example sentence**
They argued about the issue because their opinions about it were <u>divergent</u>.

divergent:

_____

_____

**Example sentence**

The two rivers <u>converged</u> near the town.

convergent:

_____

_____

### Vocabulary Terms

• Pangaea
• plate tectonics
• tectonic plate
• sea-floor spreading
• convergent boundary
• divergent boundary
• transform boundary
• convection

**4 Identify** This list contains key terms you'll learn in this lesson. As you read, underline the definition of each term.

# Puzzling Evidence

## What evidence suggests that continents move?

Have you ever looked at a map and noticed that continents look like they could fit together like a puzzle? In 1912, Alfred Wegener (AL•frid VAY•guh•ner) proposed his hypothesis of *continental drift*. It said that the continents were once joined together. Over time, they broke up and then drifted apart. This was supported by many types of evidence. For example, the same fossil species are found on continents now separated by an ocean. These species could not have crossed the ocean. Separated continents also have matching coastlines, similar land features, similar rock layers, and evidence of similar past climates.

This map shows some of the geologic evidence that supports the hypothesis of continental drift.

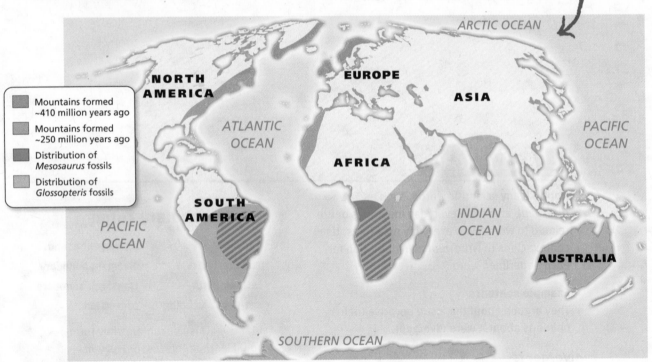

Legend:
- Mountains formed ~410 million years ago
- Mountains formed ~250 million years ago
- Distribution of *Mesosaurus* fossils
- Distribution of *Glossopteris* fossils

**Visualize It!** **5 Summarize** Using the map and legend, complete the table to describe evidence that supports that each continent was once joined.

|  | Fossil evidence | Mountain evidence |
|---|---|---|
| South America and Africa |  |  |
| North America and Europe |  |  |

# What is Pangaea?

**Active Reading** **6 Identify** As you read, underline what happened during the formation of Pangaea.

Using evidence from many scientific fields, scientists formed a model of continental change. About 200–300 million years ago, the continents were joined in a single large landmass called **Pangaea** (pan•JEE•uh). When the continents collided to form Pangaea, huge forces slowly crumpled Earth's rocky outer layer, called the crust, forming mountains. A single, large ocean called Panthalassa surrounded Pangaea.

About 200 million years ago, a large rift formed, and Pangaea began to break into two continents: *Laurasia* (law•RAY•zhuh) and *Gondwana* (gahnd•WAH•nuh). Slowly, Laurasia began to drift northward and rotate. A new rift formed, separating Laurasia into the continents of North America and Eurasia. Gondwana broke apart, too. It formed five separate continents. The continents continue their slow movements today.

# What is plate tectonics?

After Wegener introduced his hypothesis, scientists continued to search for evidence to explain their observations. Based on evidence gathered over many decades, scientists concluded that the entire surface of Earth was moving, not just the continents. Finally, in the 1960s, a theory was formed to explain these movements. **Plate tectonics** is a theory that states that Earth's outer layer is broken into large, slowly moving pieces. Earth's outer layer is called the lithosphere (LITH•uh•sfir). Each piece of the lithosphere is called a **tectonic plate**.

Tectonic plates may be made up of whole continents, parts of continents, and parts of the sea floor. The plates move as they ride atop the soft, but solid rock of the mantle. Mantle rock moves in cycles called *convection currents*: denser rock sinks down and less dense rock is pushed up. The motion of tectonic plates depends partly on how the mantle is moving below. Plate motion shapes the land as plates push together, pull apart, and slide past each other. This motion also causes events, such as earthquakes.

**The Breakup of Pangaea**

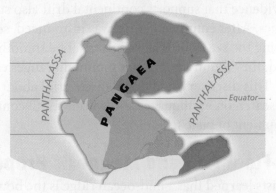

200–300 million years ago

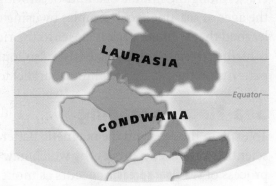

200 million years ago

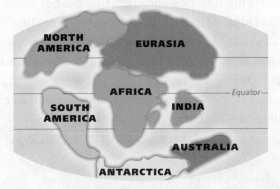

65 million years ago

3 million years ago

# What evidence led to the theory of plate tectonics?

The evidence that supports continental drift also supports plate tectonics. After continental drift was introduced, scientists began exploring the sea floor. They expected it be smooth and flat. Instead, they found underwater mountain ranges called *mid-ocean ridges*. This discovery, additional discoveries about the sea floor, and research on earthquakes and volcanoes all contributed to the development of plate tectonics.

## Sea-Floor Age and Magnetic Properties

Scientists learned that a mid-ocean ridge is the boundary between two plates moving away from each other. This motion forms deep cracks along the middle of a mid-ocean ridge. Scientists also found the ages of sea-floor rock samples by using dating techniques. They learned that younger rock is closer to the ridge and older rock is further from the ridge. Scientists also found striped magnetic patterns on the sea floor, running parallel to the mid-ocean ridges.

## Sea-Floor Spreading

To explain the ages and the magnetic patterns of sea-floor rock, scientists proposed a process by which new sea floor forms. This process of **sea-floor spreading** occurs as molten rock within Earth rises through cracks along a mid-ocean ridge. The molten rock cools, forming new oceanic crust that pushes older crust away from the ridge. This process is repeated over time and the sea floor slowly spreads. As the sea floor moves, so do any continents that are on the same tectonic plate. Scientists also found that Earth's magnetic poles have flipped back and forth over Earth's history. The magnetic patterns on the sea floor formed as minerals in new rock aligned with Earth's magnetic field.

**7 Infer** Before scientists were able to view and study the ocean floor directly, why might they have expected the ocean floor to be smooth and flat?

_____

_____

_____

_____

_____

_____

_____

The red lines on this map show the locations of mid-ocean ridges.

## Ocean Trenches

If the sea floor is spreading, why is Earth not getting larger? Scientists discovered the answer when they found huge *trenches*, like deep underwater canyons, on the sea floor. At trenches, denser oceanic plates sink into the asthenosphere, as shown in the diagram below. Older sea floor is drug down with the plate. Plates are destroyed in trenches at about the same rate they form at mid-ocean ridges. Thus, Earth remains the same size.

With new evidence, such as sea-floor spreading, magnetic patterns, and subduction, scientists could begin to understand why plates, and therefore continents, were moving.

## Distribution of Earthquakes and Volcanoes

As scientists and explorers mapped the world, they noticed that earthquakes and volcanoes were found in some locations but not in others. They found that these events most often occur in certain areas—along and near tectonic plate boundaries. The movement of plates relative to one another results in the earthquakes and volcanoes that occur along these boundaries.

**Active Reading**

**8 Identify** Why is Earth not getting larger if sea-floor spreading is adding new crust to the surface?

_____

_____

_____

 **Visualize It!**

**9 Interpret** Label the youngest rock and the oldest rock on this diagram of sea-floor spreading.

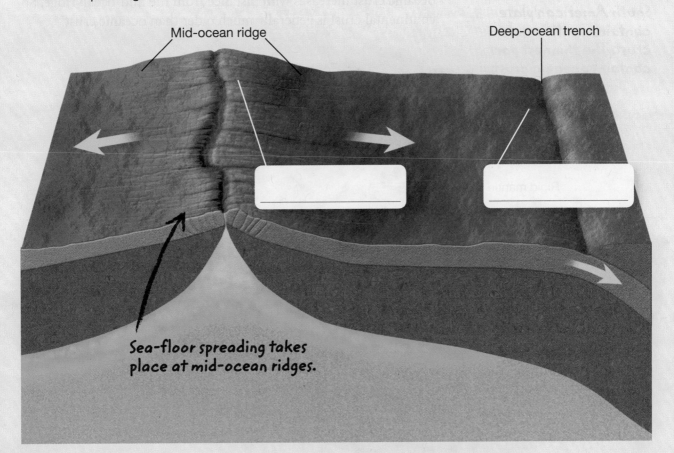

Mid-ocean ridge

Deep-ocean trench

*Sea-floor spreading takes place at mid-ocean ridges.*

# Plate Traits

**Active Reading**

**10 Identify** As you read, underline the names of the major tectonic plates.

## What are the properties of tectonic plates?

Tectonic plates all move in different directions and at different speeds. Continents and the sea floor are located on the tops of the tectonic plates, so they move along with the plates. Each plate fits together with the plates that surround it.

The major tectonic plates include the Pacific, North American, Nazca, South American, African, Indo-Australian, Eurasian, and Antarctic plates. Not all tectonic plates are the same. The South American plate has an entire continent on it and has oceanic crust. The Nazca plate has only oceanic crust. The Indo-Australian plate has a developing boundary, shown with a dotted line on the map on the next page. Because of this developing boundary, the Indo-Australian plate is sometimes considered to be two plates: the Indian plate and the Australian plate.

Tectonic plates of different shapes and sizes make up the lithosphere. Where continental crust is found, plates are thicker. Where oceanic crust is found, plates are thinner. The age of the oceanic crust increases with distance from the mid-ocean ridge. So continental crust is generally much older than oceanic crust.

*The thickest part of the South American plate contains continental crust. The thinnest part contains oceanic crust.*

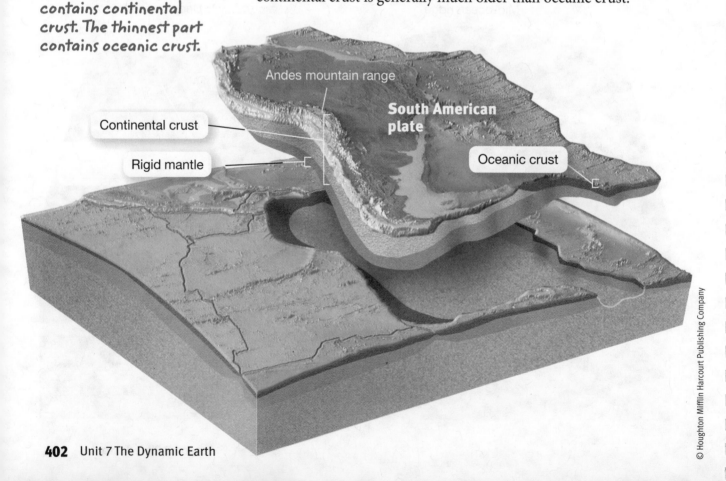

Andes mountain range

Continental crust

Rigid mantle

**South American plate**

Oceanic crust

**11 Identify** Most tectonic plates include one or more continents. Plates are often named after the continents they contain. Using the list and hints below, write the tectonic plate names on the map.

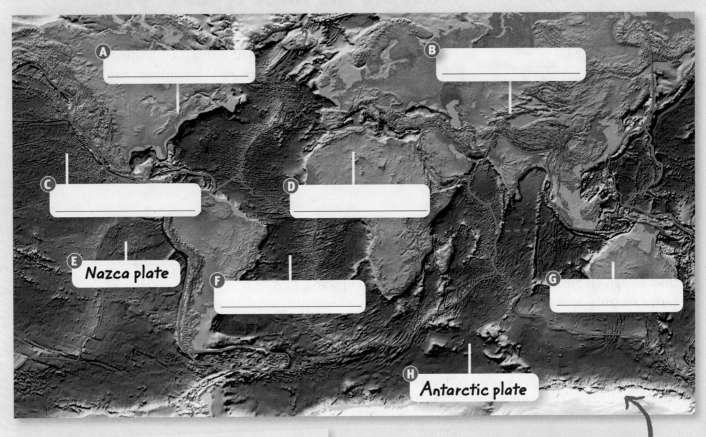

A _____

B _____

C _____

D _____

E Nazca plate

F _____

G _____

H Antarctic plate

The tectonic plates fit together like the pieces of a jigsaw puzzle.

**Tectonic Plate Names**

Pacific plate

Eurasian plate

~~Nazca plate~~

Indo-Australian plate

North American plate

South American plate

~~Antarctic plate~~

African plate

Hint: The word *Eurasian* is a combination of the words *Europe* and *Asia*.

Hint: The word *Indo-Australian* is a combination of the words *India* and *Australia*.

**Think Outside the Book**

**12 Apply** Choose a tectonic plate to research. Design a magazine article with text, images, and captions to describe the plate, its location, and its properties.

# Boundaries

## What are the three types of plate boundaries?

**Active Reading**

**13 Identify** As you read, underline the locations where plate boundaries may be found.

The most dramatic changes and land features on Earth often occur along plate boundaries. Some plate boundaries run along the ocean floor. Others are found along the edges of continents or within continents. There are three types of plate boundaries: divergent, convergent, and transform. Each type of plate boundary is associated with different types of land features.

## Convergent Boundaries

**Convergent boundaries** form where two plates collide. Three types of collisions can happen at convergent boundaries. When two tectonic plates of continental lithosphere collide, they buckle and thicken, which pushes some of the continental crust upward. This forms mountains and can cause earthquakes. When an oceanic plate collides with a continental plate, the denser oceanic plate sinks into the mantle. When two oceanic plates collide, one is always denser. The denser plate sinks under the other plate. Boundaries where one plate sinks beneath another plate are called *subduction zones*. Plates are subducted, or pulled down, beneath another plate. Subduction forms deep-ocean trenches. This process also causes volcanism and large earthquakes.

**Inquiry**

**14 Infer** Why do you think the denser plate subducts in a collision?

_____

_____

_____

_____

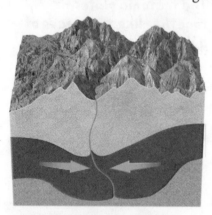

**Continent-Continent Collisions**
When two plates of continental lithosphere collide, they buckle and thicken. This causes rock to fold and break, forming mountains.

**Continent-Ocean Collisions**
When a plate of oceanic lithosphere collides with a plate of continental lithosphere, the denser oceanic lithosphere is subducted This causes volcanic mountain chains to form.

**Ocean-Ocean Collisions**
When two plates of oceanic lithosphere collide, the older, denser plate is subducted. This causes volcanic island chains to form.

# Divergent Boundaries

At a **divergent boundary,** two plates move away from each other. This separation allows hot rock below to melt. The melted rock below ground is called *magma*. Magma rises and erupts out of volcanoes on Earth's surface, where it becomes lava. Lava cools to form new rock.

As the crust and the upper part of the mantle cool and become rigid, they form new lithosphere. This lithosphere is thin, warm, and light. This warm, light rock sits higher than the surrounding sea floor because it is less dense. It forms mid-ocean ridges. Most divergent boundaries are located on the ocean floor. However, rift valleys may also form where continents are separated by plate movement.

At divergent boundaries, plates separate.

# Transform Boundaries

A boundary at which two plates move past each other horizontally is called a **transform boundary**. The plate edges do not slide along smoothly. Instead, they may get stuck or locked against each other until they suddenly slip. When they slip, huge amounts of energy are released, causing earthquakes. Unlike other types of boundaries, transform boundaries generally do not produce magma. The San Andreas Fault in California is a major transform boundary. It is a boundary between the North American plate and the Pacific plate. Transform motion also occurs at divergent boundaries. Short segments of mid-ocean ridges are connected by transform faults called fracture zones.

At transform boundaries, plates slide past each other horizontally.

**Active Reading**

**15 Contrast** How are transform boundaries different from convergent and divergent boundaries?

_____

_____

_____

_____

# What causes tectonic plates to move?

**Active Reading** **16 Identify** As you read, underline the names of the three mechanisms scientists have proposed to explain plate motion.

Scientists have proposed three mechanisms to explain how tectonic plates move. Mantle convection drags plates along as mantle material moves beneath tectonic plates. Ridge push moves plates away from mid-ocean ridges as rock cools and becomes more dense. Slab pull tugs plates along as the edge of a denser plate sinks beneath a less dense plate at a subduction zone.

## Mantle Convection

As atoms in Earth's core and mantle undergo radioactive decay, energy is released as heat. Some parts of the mantle become hotter than other parts. The cooler parts are more dense and sink. The sinking, denser material pushes up the hotter parts that are less dense. As the hotter parts rise, they begin to cool. As these parts cool, they become denser again. This cycling of material due to differences in density is called **convection**. Convection causes the overlying tectonic plates to move, but scientists do not know the exact nature of this force. Convection does not fully explain the huge amount of force that would be needed to move tectonic plates.

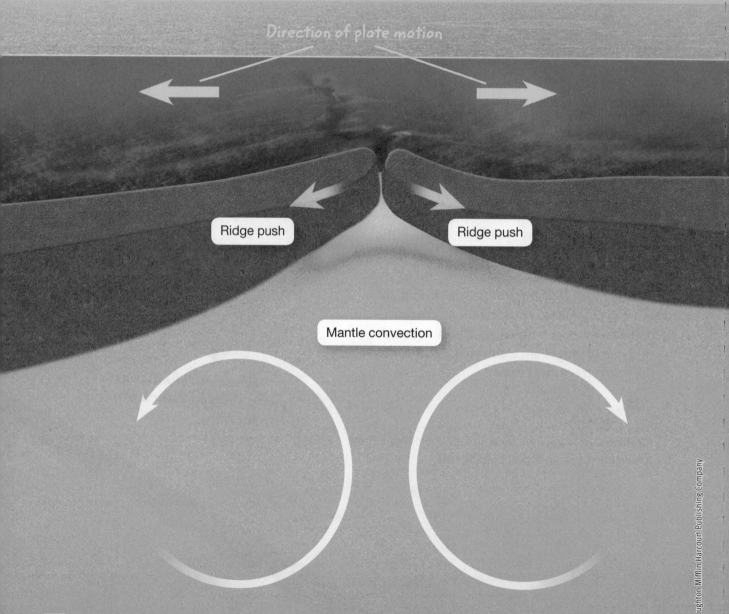

Direction of plate motion

Ridge push

Ridge push

Mantle convection

## Ridge Push

Newly formed rock at a mid-ocean ridge is warmer and less dense than the surrounding older rock. Because of its lower density, the new rock rests at a higher elevation than the older rock. The cooler, older rock slopes downward away from the ridge. As the new rock cools, it also becomes more dense and moves down the slope, away from the ridge. When this happens, the older rock is pushed away from the ridge as well. This force, called *ridge push*, pushes tectonic plates away from mid-ocean ridges.

## Slab Pull

At subduction zones, one tectonic plate sinks beneath another plate. The denser plate always subducts beneath the less dense plate. The leading edge of the subducting plate is colder and denser than the mantle. As it sinks, the leading edge of the plate pulls the rest of the plate with it. This process is called *slab pull*. In general, subducting plates move faster than other plates do. This evidence leads many scientists to think that slab pull may be the most important mechanism driving tectonic plate motion.

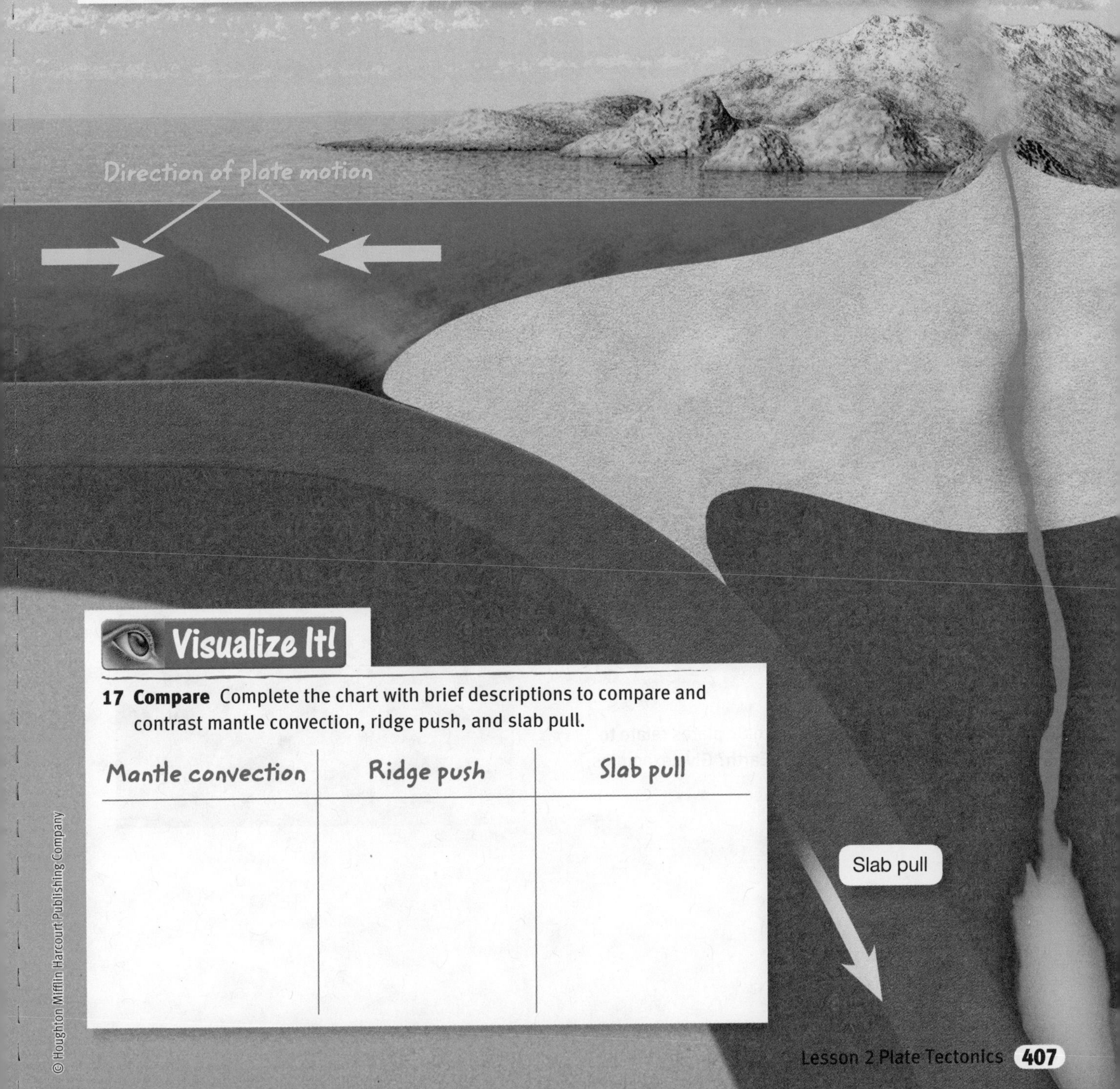

*Direction of plate motion*

Slab pull

## Visualize It!

**17 Compare** Complete the chart with brief descriptions to compare and contrast mantle convection, ridge push, and slab pull.

| Mantle convection | Ridge push | Slab pull |
|---|---|---|
| | | |

# Visual Summary

To complete this summary, fill in the blanks to complete the label or caption. Then, use the key below to check your answers. You can use this page to review the main concepts of the lesson.

**Plate Tectonics**

**The continents were once joined in a single landmass.**

18 Scientists call this landmass _____

**Tectonic plates differ in size and composition.**

19 The United States is part of the _____ plate.

**There are three types of plate boundaries: convergent, divergent, and transform.**

20 This image shows a _____ boundary.

**Three mechanisms drive plate motion: mantle convection, slab pull, and ridge push.**

21 The mechanism that scientists think is most important is _____

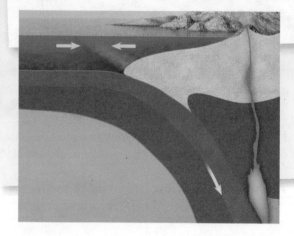

Answers:18 Pangaea; 19 North American; 20 transform; 21 slab pull

22 **Synthesize** How do moving tectonic plates relate to land features and processes on Earth? Give examples.

# Lesson Review

## Vocabulary

Fill in the blanks with the term that best completes the following sentences.

**1** The lithosphere is divided into pieces called

_____

**2** The theory that describes large-scale movements of Earth's lithosphere is called

_____

**3** The movement of material due to differences in density is called _____

## Key Concepts

**4 Describe** How is continental lithosphere different from oceanic lithosphere?

_____
_____
_____

**5 Name** Identify eight major tectonic plates by writing their names on the lines below.

_____
_____
_____
_____
_____
_____

**6 List** What key evidence supports the hypothesis of continental drift?

_____
_____
_____
_____
_____

**7 List** What additional evidence supports the theory of plate tectonics?

_____
_____
_____
_____
_____
_____

## Critical Thinking

Use this diagram to answer the following questions.

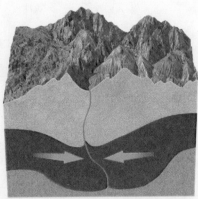

**8 Identify** What type of plate boundary is shown?

_____

**9 Identify** What landform might form here?

_____

**10 Explain** Why is subduction not occurring at this plate boundary?

_____
_____
_____
_____

**11 Synthesize** Describe ridge push and slab pull. Then describe the type of plate boundary at which each process occurs .

_____
_____
_____
_____
_____
_____
_____
_____
_____
_____
_____

# My Notes

# Estella Atekwana

## GEOPHYSICIST

Dr. Estella Atekwana studies changes on Earth's surface. Some of the changes may tell us how life on Earth developed. Others may help us to detect whether life exists somewhere else in the universe.

Some of Dr. Atekwana's work takes her to Botswana and Zambia in Africa. There she is studying the formation of a new rift valley. Rift valleys are places where continents break apart. (For example, long ago a rift valley formed, and Africa broke apart from South America.) Studying this rift valley, Dr. Atekwana hopes to learn more about how new landmasses form. Further, the ground reveals the remains of plants and animals that once lived there. These remains can tell us more about the climate that existed there millions of years ago.

Currently, Dr. Atekwana is doing brand new research in a new field of geology known as biogeophysics. She is looking at the effects that microorganisms have on rocks. She is using new technologies to study how rock changes after microorganisms have mixed with it. This research may one day help scientists detect evidence of life on other planets. Looking for the same geophysical changes in the rocks on Mars might be a way of detecting whether life ever existed on that planet. If the rocks show the same changes as the rocks on Earth, it could be because microorganisms once lived in them.

Dr. Atekwana's research included this visit to Victoria Falls on the Zambezi River in Africa.

## Social Studies Connection

Dr. Atekwana studies rift valleys—areas where the tectonic plates are pulling apart. Research to find out where else in the world scientists have located rift valleys.

# JOB BOARD

## Surveying and Mapping Technicians

**What You'll Do:** Help surveyors take measurements of outdoor areas. Technicians hold measuring tapes and adjust instruments, take notes, and make sketches.

**Where You Might Work:** Outdoors and indoors entering measurements into a computer.

**Education:** Some post-secondary education to obtain a license.

**Other Job Requirements:** Technicians must be able to visualize objects, distances, sizes, and shapes. They must be able to work with great care, precision, and accuracy because mistakes can be expensive. They must also be in good physical condition.

## Petroleum Technician

**What You'll Do:** Measure and record the conditions in oil or gas wells to find out whether samples contain oil and other minerals.

**Where You Might Work:** Outdoors, sometimes in remote locations and sometimes in your own town or city.

**Education:** An associate's degree or a certificate in applied science or science-related technology.

**Other Job Requirements:** You need to be able to take accurate measurements and keep track of many details.

## Geologist

**What You'll Do:** Study the history of Earth's crust. Geologists work in many different businesses. You may explore for minerals, oil, or gas. You may find and test ground water supplies. You may work with engineers to make sure ground is safe to build on.

**Where You Might Work:** In the field, where you collect samples, and in the office, where you analyze them. Geologists work in mines, on oil rigs, on the slopes of volcanoes, in quarries, and in paleontological digs.

**Education:** A four-year bachelor's degree in science.

**Other Job Requirements:** Geologists who work in the field must be in good physical condition. Most geologists do field training. Geologists need strong math skills, analytical skills, and computer skills. They also need to be able to work well with other members of a team.

# Mountain Building

**ESSENTIAL QUESTION**

## How do mountains form?

By the end of this lesson, you should be able to describe how the movement of Earth's tectonic plates causes mountain building.

**TEKS** **6.10D** describe how plate tectonics causes major geological events such as ocean basins, earthquakes, volcanic eruptions, and mountain building

The highest peak in the Alps mountain range is Mont Blanc at just over 4,800 m tall.

## Engage Your Brain

**1 Predict** Check T or F to show whether you think each statement is true or false.

| T | F | |
|---|---|---|
| ☐ | ☐ | Mountains can originate from a level surface that is folded upward. |
| ☐ | ☐ | Rocks can be pulled apart by the movement of tectonic plates. |
| ☐ | ☐ | All mountains are created by volcanoes. |
| ☐ | ☐ | A mountain range can form only at the edge of a tectonic plate. |

**2 Hypothesize** The Appalachian Mountains were once taller than the Rocky Mountains. What do you think happened to the mountains? Explain.

_____

_____

_____

Rocky Mountains

Appalachian Mountains

## Active Reading

**3 Compare** The terms *compression* and *tension* have opposite meanings. Compare the two sentences below, then write your own definition for *compression* and *tension*.

| Vocabulary | Sentence |
|---|---|
| compression | The stack of books on Jon's desk caused the bottom book to be flattened by <u>compression</u>. |
| tension | Keisha pulled the piece of string so hard, the <u>tension</u> caused the string to break. |

### Vocabulary Terms

- deformation
- folding
- fault
- shear stress
- tension
- compression

**4 Apply** As you learn the definition of each vocabulary term in this lesson, create your own definition or sketch to help you remember the meaning of the term.

compression:

_____

_____

tension:

_____

_____

# Stressed Out

## How can tectonic plate motion cause deformation?

The movement of tectonic plates places stress on rocks. A *tectonic plate* is a block of lithosphere that consists of crust and the rigid outermost part of the mantle. *Stress* is the amount of force per unit area that is placed on an object. Rocks can bend or break under stress. In addition, low temperatures make materials more brittle, or easily broken. High temperatures can allow rock to bend.

When a rock is placed under stress, it deforms, or changes shape. **Deformation** (dee•fohr•MAY•shuhn) is the process by which rocks change shape when under stress. Rock can bend if it is under high temperature and pressure for long periods of time. If the stress becomes too great, or is applied quickly, rock can break. When rocks bend, folds form. When rocks break, faults form.

**Active Reading**

**5 Identify** List some objects near you that can bend or break from deformation.

_____

_____

_____

_____

By applying stress, the boy is causing the spaghetti to deform. Similarly, stress over a long period of time can cause rock to bend.

Like the spaghetti, stress over a short period of time or great amounts of stress can cause rock to break.

**Visualize It!**

**6 Correlate** How can the same material bend in one situation but break in another?

_____

_____

_____

_____

# What are two kinds of folds?

Folded rock layers appear bent or buckled. **Folding** occurs when rock layers bend under stress. The bends are called *folds*. Scientists assume that all rock layers start out as horizontal layers deposited on top of each other over time. Sometimes, different layers of rocks can still be seen even after the rocks have been folded. When scientists see a fold, they know that deformation has happened. Two common types of folds are synclines and anticlines.

### Think Outside the Book

**7 Model** Stack several sheets of paper together. Apply stress to the sides of the paper to create a model of a syncline and an anticline. Share your model with your teacher.

## Synclines and Anticlines

Folds are classified based on the age of the rock layers. In a *syncline* (SIN•klyn), the youngest layers of rock are found at the core of a fold. The oldest layers are found on the outside of the fold. Synclines usually look like rock layers that are arched upward, like a bowl. In an *anticline* (AN•tih•klyn), the oldest layers of rock are found at the core of the fold. The youngest layers are found on the outside of the fold. Anticlines often look like rock layers that are arched downwards and high in the middle. Often, both types of folds will be visible in the same rock layers, as shown below.

*The hinge is the middle point of the bend in a syncline or anticline.*

 **Visualize It!**

**8 Identify** Rock layers are labeled on the image below. Which rock layers are the youngest and oldest?

_____

_____

How do you know? _____

_____

_____

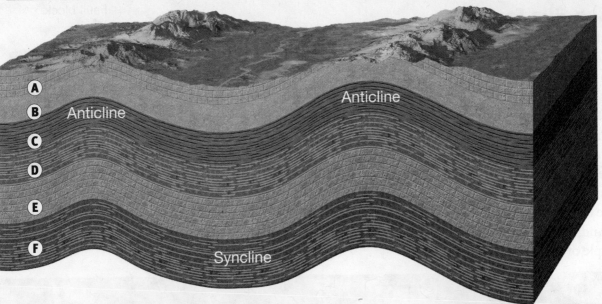

# Faulted

## What are the three kinds of faults?

Tectonic plate movement places stress on rock and can cause it to break. Imagine a rock unit that breaks into two blocks. The crack that forms between the two blocks is called a **fault**. The blocks of rock on either side of a fault, called *fault blocks,* are able to move. Sometimes, a fault block suddenly slips and causes the ground to shake. This event is called an *earthquake*.

Rocks tend to move in predictable directions along faults. There are three main kinds of faults: strike-slip faults, normal faults, and reverse faults. Scientists classify faults based on the way fault blocks move relative to each other. The location where two fault blocks meet is called the *fault plane*. A fault plane can be oriented horizontally, vertically, or at an angle. For any fault, except a perfectly vertical fault, the block above the fault plane is called the *hanging wall*. The block below the fault plane is the *footwall*.

The movement of faults can create mountains and other types of landforms. At any tectonic plate boundary, the amount of stress on rock is complex. Therefore, any of the three types of faults can occur at almost all plate boundaries.

**Active Reading**

**9 Identify** As you read, underline the direction of movement of the fault blocks in each type of fault.

## Strike-Slip Faults

In a strike-slip fault, the fault blocks move past each other horizontally. Strike-slip faults form when rock is under shear stress. **Shear stress** is stress that pushes rocks in parallel but opposite directions as seen in the image. As rocks are deformed deep in Earth's crust, energy builds. The release of this energy can cause earthquakes as the rocks slide past each other. Strike-slip faults are common along transform boundaries, where tectonic plates move past each other. The San Andreas fault system in California is an example of a strike-slip fault.

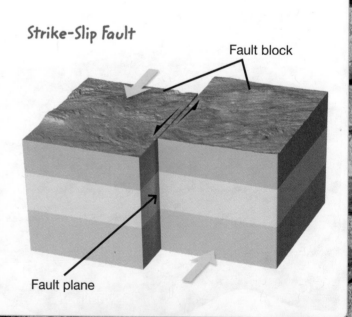

Strike-Slip Fault

Fault block

Fault plane

## Normal Faults

In the normal fault shown on the right, the hanging wall moves down relative to the footwall. The faults are called normal because the blocks move in a way that you would *normally* expect as a result of gravity. Normal faults form when the rock is under tension. **Tension** (TEN•shun) is stress that stretches or pulls rock apart. Therefore, normal faults are common along divergent boundaries. Earth's crust can also stretch in the middle of a tectonic plate. The Basin and Range area of the southwestern United States is an example of a location with many normal fault structures.

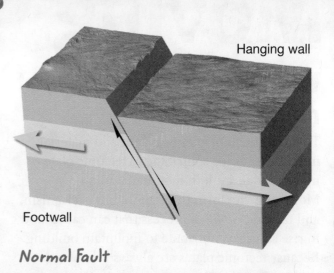

Hanging wall

Footwall

*Normal Fault*

## Reverse Faults

In the reverse fault shown on the right, the hanging wall moves up relative to the footwall. The faults are called reverse because the hanging blocks move up, which is the reverse of what you would expect as a result of gravity. Reverse faults form when rocks undergo compression. **Compression** (kuhm•PRESH•uhn) is stress that squeezes or pushes rock together. Reverse faults are common along convergent boundaries, where two plates collide. The San Gabriel Mountains in the United States were formed by reverse faults.

*Reverse Fault*

👁 **Visualize It!**

**10 Identify** Label the fault plane, hanging wall, and footwall on the reverse fault to the right.

© Houghton Mifflin Harcourt Publishing Company • Image Credits: (bkgd) ©William D. Bachman/Photo Researchers, Inc.

**Think Outside the Book** Inquiry

**11 Compile** Create a memory matching game of the types of faults. Create as many cards as you can with different photos, drawings, or written details about the types of faults. Use the cards to quiz yourself and your classmates.

# Moving On Up

## What are the three kinds of mountains?

The movement of energy as heat and material in Earth's interior contribute to tectonic plate motions that result in mountain building. Mountains can form through folding, volcanism, and faulting. *Uplift,* a process that can cause land to rise can also contribute to mountain building. Because tectonic plates are always in motion, some mountains are constantly being uplifted.

**Active Reading** **12 Identify** As you read, underline examples of folded, volcanic, and fault-block mountains.

### Folded Mountains

Folded mountains form when rock layers are squeezed together and pushed upward. They usually form at convergent boundaries, where plates collide. For example, the Appalachian Mountains (ap•uh•LAY•chun) formed from folding and faulting when the North American plate collided with the Eurasian and African plates millions of years ago.

In Europe, the Pyrenees (PIR•uh•neez) are another range of folded mountains, as shown below. They are folded over an older, pre-existing mountain range. Today, the highest peaks are over 3,000 m tall.

The Pyrenees Mountains are folded mountains that separate France from Spain.

### Visualize It!

**13 Identify** What evidence do you see that the Pyrenees Mountains are folded mountains?

_____

_____

_____

## Volcanic Mountains

Volcanic mountains form when melted rock erupts onto Earth's surface. Many major volcanic mountains are located at convergent boundaries. Volcanic mountains can form on land or on the ocean floor. Volcanoes on the ocean floor can grow so tall that they rise above the surface of the ocean, forming islands. Most of Earth's active volcanoes are concentrated around the edge of the Pacific Ocean. This area is known as the Ring of Fire. Many volcanoes, including Mt. Griggs in the image to the right, are located on the Northern rim of the Pacific plate in Alaska.

Mt. Griggs volcano on the Alaskan Peninsula is 2,317 m high.

The Teton Mountains in Wyoming are fault-block mountains.

## Fault-Block Mountains

Fault-block mountains form when tension makes the lithosphere break into many normal faults. Along the faults, pieces of the lithosphere drop down compared with other pieces. The pieces left standing form fault-block mountains. The Teton Mountains (TEE•tuhn) and the Sierra Nevadas are fault-block mountains.

---

**14 Identify** Draw a simple version of each type of mountain below.

| Folded | Volcanic | Faulted |
|--------|----------|---------|
|        |          |         |

# Visual Summary

To complete this summary, fill in the blanks with the correct word or phrase. Then use the key below to check your answers. You can use this page to review the main concepts of the lesson.

## Mountain Building

**Rocks can bend or break under stress.**

15 The process by which rocks change shape under stress is called _____

**Folds occur when rock layers bend.**

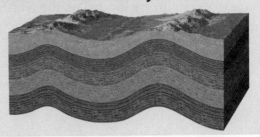

16 A rock structure with the oldest rocks at the core of the fold is called a/an _____

**Faults occur when rock layers break.**

Footwall

Hanging wall

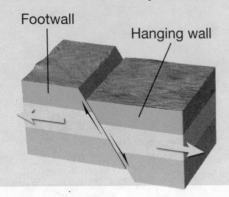

17 The type of fault pictured is a _____ fault.

**Mountains form through folding, volcanism, and faulting.**

18 The type of mountains pictured are _____ mountains.

Answers: 15 deformation; 16 anticline; 17 normal; 18 fault-block

19 **Synthesize** The middle of tectonic plates tend to have fewer mountains than locations near tectonic plate boundaries. What might be one possible explanation for this?

# Lesson Review

## Vocabulary

Fill in the blank with the term that best completes the following sentences.

**1** A normal fault is a result of a type of stress known as _____

**2** A strike-slip fault is a result of _____ stress.

**3** A reverse fault is caused by a type of stress known as _____

## Key Concepts

Fill in the table below by identifying the type of mountain described in the example question.

| Example | Type of Mountain |
|---|---|
| **4 Identify** The Basin and Range province is characterized by many normal faults. | |
| **5 Identify** The Cascade Range in the U.S. was built up by eruptions | |
| **6 Identify** The Pyrenees Mountains have many synclines and anticlines. | |

**7 Describe** How does the movement of tectonic plates cause events such as earthquakes?

_____

_____

_____

**8 Compare** How do folded, volcanic, and fault-block mountains differ?

_____

_____

_____

_____

_____

## Critical Thinking

Use the diagram below to answer the following questions.

**9 Apply** What kind of fault is shown? What kind of stress formed this fault?

_____

_____

**10 Identify** Which fault block is the hanging wall and which is the footwall?

_____

_____

_____

**11 Analyze** Can rock undergo compression, tension, and shear stress all at once? Explain.

_____

_____

_____

**12 Conclude** Imagine you are walking along a roadway and see a syncline. What can you conclude about the formation of that fold?

_____

_____

_____

_____

# My Notes

## Lesson 4

# Volcanoes

**ESSENTIAL QUESTION**

## How do volcanoes change Earth's surface?

By the end of this lesson, you should be able to describe what the various kinds of volcanoes and eruptions are, where they occur, how they form, and how they change Earth's surface.

**TEKS** 6.10D describe how plate tectonics causes major geological events such as ocean basins, earthquakes, volcanic eruptions, and mountain building

The Arenal volcano in Costa Rica has been active since 1968. The volcano has erupted on and off for over 7,000 years.

## Lesson Labs

**Quick Labs**
• Modeling an Explosive Eruption
• Volcano Mapping

**Exploration Lab**
• Modeling Lava Viscosity

## Engage Your Brain

**1 Predict** Check T or F to show whether you think each statement is true or false.

| T | F | |
|---|---|---|
| ☐ | ☐ | Volcanoes create new landforms such as mountains. |
| ☐ | ☐ | Tectonic plate boundaries are the only locations where volcanoes form. |
| ☐ | ☐ | Volcanic eruptions are often accompanied by earthquakes. |
| ☐ | ☐ | Volcanoes form new rocks and minerals. |

**2 Hypothesize** You are a news reporter assigned to cover a story about the roadway in the image below. Describe what you think happened in this photo.

_____

_____

_____

_____

## Active Reading

**3 Synthesize** You can often define an unknown word if you know the meaning of its word parts. Use the word parts and sentence below to make an educated guess about the meaning of the word *pyroclastic*.

| Word part | Meaning |
|---|---|
| *pyro-* | heat or fire |
| *-clastic* | pieces |

**Example sentence**
Pyroclastic material was ejected into the atmosphere with explosive force during the eruption of the volcano.

pyroclastic:

_____

_____

### Vocabulary Terms

• volcano
• magma
• lava
• vent
• tectonic plate
• hot spot

**4 Apply** As you learn the definition of each vocabulary term in this lesson, create your own definition or sketch to help you remember the meaning of the term.

# Magma MAGIC

## What is a volcano?

What do volcanoes look like? Most people think of a steep mountain with smoke coming out of the top. In fact, a **volcano** is any place where gas, ash, or melted rock come out of the ground. A volcano can be a tall mountain, as shown below, or a small crack in the ground. Volcanoes occur on land and underwater. There are even volcanoes on other planets. Not all volcanoes actively erupt. Many are *dormant,* meaning an eruption has not occurred in a long period of time.

Volcanoes form as rock below the surface of Earth melts. The melted rock, or **magma**, is less dense than solid rock, so it rises toward the surface. **Lava** is magma that has reached Earth's surface. Lava and clouds of ash can erupt from a **vent**, or opening of a volcano.

### Visualize It!

**5 Identify** Label the parts of the volcano. Include the following terms: *magma, lava, vent, ash cloud.*

Lava can reach temperatures of more than 1,200 °C.

# What are the kinds of volcanic landforms?

The location of a volcano and the composition of magma determine the type of volcanic landforms created. Shield volcanoes, cinder cones, composite volcanoes, lava plateaus, craters, and calderas are all types of volcanic landforms.

## Volcanic Mountains

Materials ejected from a volcano may build up around a vent to create volcanic mountains. *Viscosity* (vyz•SKAHZ•ih•tee) is the resistance of a liquid material, such as lava, to flow. The viscosity of lava determines the explosiveness of an eruption and the shape of the resulting volcanic mountain. Low-viscosity lava flows easily, forms low slopes, and erupts without large explosions. High-viscosity lava does not flow easily, forms steep slopes, and can erupt explosively. *Pyroclastic materials* (py•roh•KLAHZ•tyk), or hot ash and bits of rock, may also be ejected into the atmosphere.

**Active Reading**

**7 Identify** As you read, underline the main features of each type of volcanic mountain.

- **Shield Volcanoes** Volcanoes with a broad base and gently sloping sides are *shield volcanoes*. Shield volcanoes cover a wide area and generally form from mild eruptions. Layers of lava flow out from the vent, harden, and slowly build up to form the cone. The Hawaiian Islands are shield volcanoes.

- **Cinder Cones** Sometimes, ash and pieces of lava harden in the air and can fall to the ground around a small vent. The hardened pieces of lava are called cinders. The cinders and ash build up around the vent and form a steep volcano called a *cinder cone*. A cinder cone can also form at a side vent on other volcanic mountains, such as on shield or composite volcanoes.

- **Composite Volcanoes** Alternating layers of hardened lava flows and pyroclastic material create *composite volcanoes* (kuhm•PAHZ•iht). During a mild eruption, lava flows cover the sides of the cone. During an explosive eruption, pyroclastic material is deposited around the vent. Composite volcanoes commonly develop into large and steep volcanic mountains.

Layers of lava

Magma

Pyroclastic material

Ash and cinders

Conduit

Pyroclastic material

Lava and ash layers

**Think Outside the Book** **Inquiry**

**6 Apply** Small fragments of rock material that are ejected from a volcano are known as *volcanic ash*. Volcanic ash is a form of pyroclastic material. The material does not dissolve in water and is very abrasive, meaning it can scratch surfaces. Ash can build up to great depths in locations around a volcano. Write a cleanup plan for a town that explains how you might safely remove and dispose of volcanic ash.

## Fissures and Lava Plateaus

Fissure eruptions (FIH•shohr ee•RUHP•shuhnz) happen when lava flows from giant cracks, or *fissures*, in Earth's surface. The fissures are found on land and on the ocean floor. A fissure eruption has no central opening. Lava flows out of the entire length of the fissure, which can be many kilometers long. As a result, a thick and mostly flattened layer of cooled lava, called a *lava plateau* (plah•TOH), can form. One example of a lava plateau is the Columbia Plateau Province in Washington, Oregon, and Idaho, as shown to the right.

The Palouse Falls in Washington plunge deep into exposed layers of the Columbia lava plateau.

## Craters and Calderas

A *volcanic crater* is an opening or depression at the top of a volcano caused by eruptions. Inside the volcano, molten rock can form an expanded area of magma called a *magma chamber*, as shown to the right. When the magma chamber below a volcano empties, the roof of the magma chamber may collapse and leave an even larger, basin-shaped depression called a *caldera* (kahl•DAHR•uh). Calderas can form from the sudden drain of a magma chamber during an explosive eruption or from a slowly emptied magma chamber. More than 7,000 years ago, the cone of Mount Mazama in Oregon collapsed to form a caldera. The caldera later filled with water and is now called Crater Lake.

A caldera can be more than 100 km in diameter.

**Visualize It!**

**8 Describe** How does the appearance of land surfaces change before and after a caldera forms?

_____

_____

_____

Before

Expanded magma chamber

After

Collapsed magma chamber

# ERUPTION!

## Where do volcanoes form?

Volcanoes can form at plate boundaries or within the middle of a plate. Recall that **tectonic plates** are giant sections of lithosphere on Earth's surface. Volcanoes can form at *divergent plate boundaries* where two plates are moving away from each other. Most fissure eruptions occur at divergent boundaries. Shield volcanoes, fissure eruptions, and cinder cones can also occur away from plate boundaries within a plate at *hot spots*. The type of lava normally associated with these volcanoes has a relatively low viscosity, few trapped gases, and is usually not explosive.

Composite volcanoes are most common along *convergent plate boundaries* where oceanic plates subduct. In order for the rock to melt, it must be hot and the pressure on it must drop, or water and other fluids must be added to it. Extra fluids from ocean water form magma of higher viscosity with more trapped gases. Thus, composite volcanoes produce the most violent eruptions. The *Ring of Fire* is a name used to describe the numerous explosive volcanoes that form on convergent plate boundaries surrounding the Pacific Ocean.

**Active Reading**

**9 Identify** As you read, underline three locations where volcanoes can form.

## Plate Tectonic Boundaries and Volcano Locations Worldwide

**Visualize It!**

**10 Describe** How do the locations of volcanoes relate to tectonic plate boundaries?

_____

_____

_____

## At Divergent Boundaries

At divergent boundaries, plates move away from each other. The lithosphere stretches and gets thinner, so the pressure on the mantle rock below decreases. As a result, the asthenosphere bulges upward and magma forms. This magma rises through fissures in the lithosphere, out onto the land or the ocean floor.

Most divergent boundaries are on the ocean floor. When eruptions occur in these areas, undersea volcanoes develop. These volcanoes and other processes lead to the formation of a long, underwater mountain range known as a *mid-ocean ridge*. Two examples of mid-ocean ridges are the East Pacific Rise in the Pacific Ocean and the Mid-Atlantic Ridge in the Atlantic Ocean. The youngest rocks in the ocean are located at mid-ocean ridges.

Shield volcanoes and cinder cones are common in Iceland, where the Mid-Atlantic Ridge runs through the country. As the plates move away from each other, new crust forms. When a divergent boundary is located in the middle of a continent, the crust stretches until a rift valley is formed, as shown below.

**Active Reading** 11 **Identify** What types of volcanic landforms occur at divergent plate boundaries?

_____

_____

_____

Divergent plate boundaries create fissure eruptions and shield volcanoes.

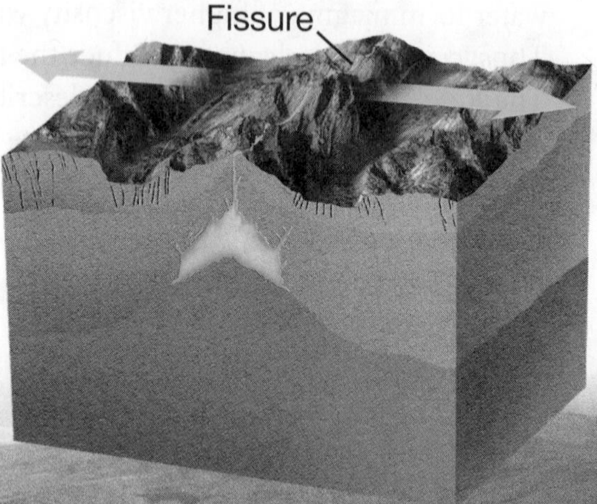

Fissure

The Great Rift Valley in Africa is a location where the crust is stretching and separating.

Tectonic plates move away from each other at divergent boundaries.

## At Convergent Boundaries

At convergent boundaries, two plates move toward each other. In most cases, one plate sinks beneath the other plate. As the sinking plate dives into the mantle, fluids in the sinking plate become super heated and escape. These escaping fluids cause the rock above the sinking plate to melt and form magma. This magma rises to the surface and erupts to form volcanoes.

The magma that forms at convergent boundaries has a high concentration of fluids. As the magma rises, decreasing pressure causes the fluid trapped in the magma to form gas bubbles. But, because the magma has a high viscosity, these bubbles cannot escape easily. As the bubbles expand, the magma rises faster. Eventually, the magma can erupt explosively, forming calderas or composite volcanoes. Gas, ash, and large chunks of rock can be blown out of the volcanoes. The Cascade Range is a chain of active composite volcanoes in the northwestern United States, as shown to the right. In 1980, Mt. St. Helens erupted so violently that the entire top of the mountain was blown away.

**12 Identify** Draw two arrows in the white boxes to indicate the direction of motion of the plates that formed the Cascade volcanoes.

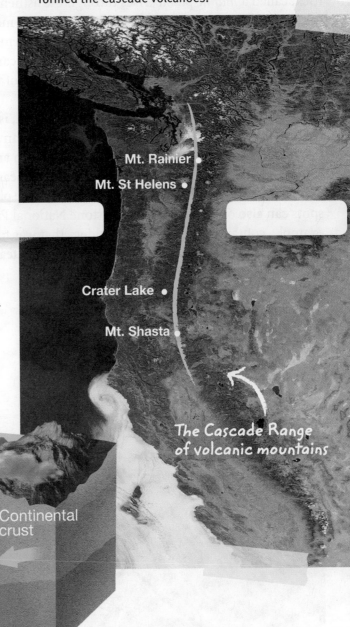

Mt. Rainier
Mt. St Helens
Crater Lake
Mt. Shasta

The Cascade Range of volcanic mountains

Tectonic plates move toward each other at convergent boundaries.

Oceanic crust

Continental crust

**13 Summarize** List the characteristics of divergent-boundary volcanoes and convergent-boundary volcanoes below.

| Volcanoes at divergent boundaries | Volcanoes at convergent boundaries |
|---|---|
| | |
| | |
| | |

# At Hot Spots

Volcanoes can form within a plate, away from the plate boundaries. A **hot spot** is a location where a column of extremely hot mantle rock, called a *mantle plume*, rises through the asthenosphere. As the hot rock reaches the base of the lithosphere, it melts partially to form magma that can rise to the surface and form a volcano. Eruptions at a hot spot commonly form shield volcanoes. As tectonic plates move over a mantle plume, chains of volcanic mountains can form, as shown below.

The youngest Hawaiian island, the Big Island, is home to Kilauea (kih•loh•AY•uh). The Kilauea volcano is an active shield volcano located over a mantle plume. To the north and west of Kilauea is a chain of progressively-older shield volcanoes. These volcanoes were once located over the same mantle plume. Hot spots can also occur on land. Yellowstone National Park, for example, contains a huge volcanic caldera that was formed by the same mantle plume that created the Columbia Plateau.

## Visualize It!

**14 Analyze** Which location, *A*, *B*, or *C*, do you think is the oldest volcano? How do you know?

_____

_____

_____

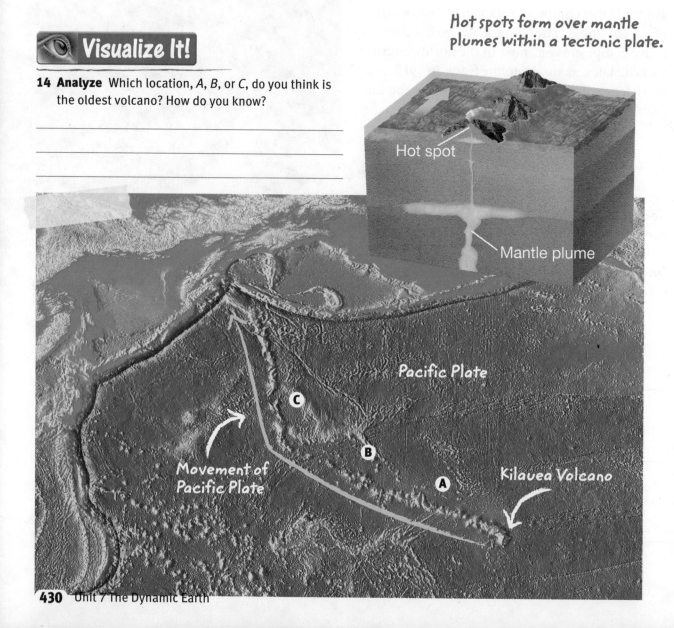

Hot spots form over mantle plumes within a tectonic plate.

Hot spot

Mantle plume

Pacific Plate

C

B

A

Kilauea Volcano

Movement of Pacific Plate

# Living Near a Volcano

Volcanoes occur around the world. Many people live near volcanoes because the soils around a volcano can be very rich with essential minerals. These minerals make the soils fertile for growing a variety of crops. Living near a volcano also has its hazards. Sudden and unexpected eruptions can cause people to lose their homes and their lives.

## Not All Bad
Volcanic rocks are used in jewelry, in making concrete, and in water filtration systems. Even cat litter and facial scrubs can contain volcanic rock.

## Destruction
Earthquakes, fires, ash, and lava flows during an eruption can destroy entire cities.

## Ash in the Air
Volcanic ash can cause breathing problems, bury crops, and damage engines. The weight of falling ash can cause buildings to collapse.

## Extend

Inquiry

**15 Identify** Are all characteristics of volcanoes dangerous?

**16 Apply** Research the eruption of a specific volcano of your choice. Describe how the volcano affected the environment and the people near the volcano.

**17 Design** Create a poster that outlines a school safety plan for events that can occur before, during, and after a volcanic eruption.

# Visual Summary

To complete this summary, check the box that indicates true or false. Then, use the key below to check your answers. You can use this page to review the main concepts of the lesson.

**Lava and magma are different.**

T F
18 ☐ ☐ Lava is inside Earth's crust and may contain trapped gases.

**The three types of volcanic mountains are shield volcanoes, cinder cones, and composite volcanoes.**

T F
19 ☐ ☐ The type of volcano shown is a shield volcano.

## Volcanoes

**Volcanoes can form at tectonic plate boundaries.**

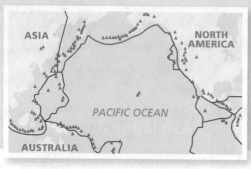

ASIA

NORTH AMERICA

PACIFIC OCEAN

AUSTRALIA

T F
20 ☐ ☐ At divergent plate boundaries, plates move toward each other.

**Volcanoes can form at hot spots.**

Hot spot

Mantle plume

T F
21 ☐ ☐ Hot spots are restricted to tectonic plate boundaries.

Answers: 18 False; 19 True; 20 False; 21 False

22 **Explain** How do volcanoes contribute to the formation of new landforms?

# Lesson Review

## Vocabulary

Write 1 or 2 sentences that describe the differences between the two terms.

**1** magma      lava

_____

_____

_____

**2** volcano      vent

_____

_____

_____

**3** tectonic plate      hot spot

_____

_____

_____

## Key Concepts

Use the image to answer the following question.

**4 Identify** How did the composite volcano in the image get its layered interior?

_____

_____

_____

**5 Analyze** Is pyroclastic material likely to form from low-viscosity lava or high-viscosity lava? Explain.

_____

_____

_____

Describe the location and characteristics of the types of volcanic landforms in the table below.

| Volcanic landform | Description |
|---|---|
| **6 Hot-spot volcanoes** | |
| **7 Cinder cones** | |
| **8 Calderas** | |

## Critical Thinking

**9 Hypothesize** In Iceland, the Mid-Atlantic Ridge runs through the center of the country. What can you conclude about the appearance of Iceland many thousands of years from now?

_____

_____

_____

_____

**10 Analyze** Why do you think the location surrounding the Pacific Ocean is known as the Ring of Fire?

_____

_____

_____

_____

# My Notes

# Comparing Earthquake Magnitudes

**TEKS** MATH **6.1D** communicate mathematical ideas, reasoning, and their implications using multiple representations, including symbols, diagrams, graphs, and language as appropriate

**TEKS** MATH **6.1E** create and use representations to organize, record, and communicate mathematical ideas

**TEKS** MATH **6.7A** generate equivalent numerical expressions using order of operations, including whole number exponents and prime factorization

Scales are used to describe and compare things. For example, you could rate something on a scale from 1 to 10. In science, different types of scales are used to describe the natural world.

A linear scale is a scale you might be familiar with. Each step along a linear scale is the same size. For example, on a ruler, 2 cm is twice as long as 1 cm, and 3 cm is three times as long as 1 cm. Another type of scale is called a logarithmic scale. See the steps below to learn more about logarithmic scales.

## Sample Problem

**1 Reading a Scale** Logarithmic scales are used to describe things with a large range of values in a meaningful way. The scale below is a *base-ten logarithmic scale*.

**2 Identifying Relationships** On the logarithmic scale below, each step shows an increase by a factor of ten.

**3 Calculating Logarithms** The colored boxes below show how each value along the scale can be calculated. The smaller number after the 10 is the exponent. $10^2$ means ten to the power of

two, and the exponent is 2. This means ten is used as a factor two times: 10 x 10 = 100. Any number to the power of zero is equal to 1.

**4 Applying Concepts** Look at the cubes above the number line. For each step, the number of cubes increases by a factor of ten.

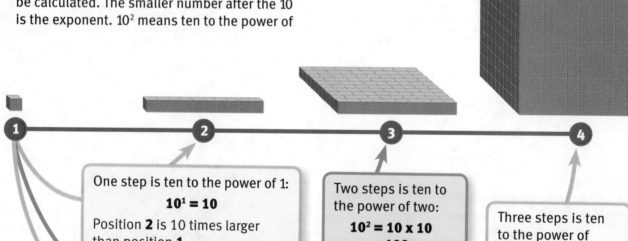

One step is ten to the power of 1:
$$10^1 = 10$$
Position **2** is 10 times larger than position **1**.

Two steps is ten to the power of two:
$$10^2 = 10 \times 10$$
$$= 100$$
Position **3** is 100 times larger than position **1**.

Three steps is ten to the power of three:
$$10^3 = 10 \times 10 \times 10$$
$$= 1,000$$
Position **4** is 1,000 times larger than position **1**.

# You Try It!

Earthquakes happen when a section of rock moves along a fault, or a break in Earth's surface. This motion releases energy and causes the ground to shake. The magnitude, or size, of an earthquake can be expressed using the moment magnitude scale. Just like the scale on the previous page, this is a base-ten logarithmic scale. Each step represents a ten-fold increase in earthquake magnitude. This scale is used because there is a very large range in earthquake magnitudes.

*This is a base-ten logarithmic scale used to represent earthquake magnitude.*

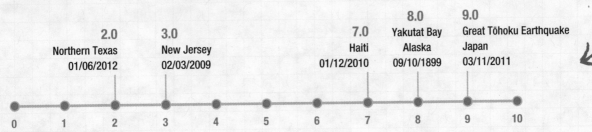

1 **Reading a Scale** What type of scale is shown above? What does this scale represent?

2 **Identifying Relationships** How much does the strength of an earthquake increase with 1 step on this scale? With 2 steps?

3 **Calculating Logarithms**

A Draw an arrow under the number line from the Northern Texas earthquake to the New Jersey earthquake.

B Below the arrow, write the number of steps between the two earthquakes.

C The number of steps is equal to the exponent. Remember that this is a base-ten logarithmic scale. How much larger is the magnitude 3.0 New Jersey earthquake than the magnitude 2.0 Northern Texas earthquake? Show your calculations and answer below the arrow.

4 Repeat steps 3A to 3C to compare the Northern Texas earthquake to the Haiti earthquake. Then, repeat the steps again to compare two more earthquakes of your choice.

5 **Applying Concepts** Explain why a logarithmic scale is appropriate to display earthquake magnitudes.

## Take It Home

Do research to find something else that can be described using a base-ten logarithmic scale. Make a poster showing the scale, and describe the meaning of the scale's values. Include images and other information that will help explain how to read the scale.

# Earthquakes

**ESSENTIAL QUESTION**

## Why do earthquakes happen?

By the end of this lesson, you should be able to describe the causes of earthquakes and to identify where earthquakes happen.

The 1995 Kobe earthquake in Japan destroyed more than 200,000 buildings and structures including this railroad track.

**TEKS** **6.10D** describe how plate tectonics causes major geological events such as ocean basins, earthquakes, volcanic eruptions, and mountain building

## Engage Your Brain

**1 Predict** Fill in any words or numbers that you think best complete each of the statements below.

Each year there are approximately _____ earthquakes detected around the world.

In the United States, the state with the most earthquakes on average is _____

Every year, earthquakes cause _____ of dollars in damages in the United States.

Most earthquakes only last for several _____ of time.

**2 Analyze** Using the image, list in column 1 some of the hazards that can occur after an earthquake. In column 2, explain why you think these items or situations would be hazardous.

| Hazards | Why? |
|---------|------|
|         |      |
|         |      |
|         |      |
|         |      |

## Active Reading

**3 Synthesize** You can often define an unknown word if you know the meaning of its word parts. Use the word parts and sentence below to make an educated guess about the meaning of the word *epicenter*.

| Word part | Meaning |
|-----------|---------|
| *epi-*    | on, upon, or over |
| *-center* | the middle |

**Example sentence**
The <u>epicenter</u> of the earthquake was only 3 km from our school.

epicenter:

_____

_____

### Vocabulary Terms

- earthquake
- focus
- epicenter
- tectonic plate boundary
- fault
- deformation
- elastic rebound

**4 Apply** As you learn the definition of each vocabulary term in this lesson, create your own definition or sketch to help you remember the meaning of the term.

# Let's Focus

## Active Reading

**5 Identify** As you read, underline the definitions of *focus* and *epicenter*.

## What is an earthquake?

Earthquakes can cause extreme damage and loss of life. **Earthquakes** are ground movements that occur when blocks of rock in Earth move suddenly and release energy. The energy is released as seismic waves which cause the ground to shake and tremble.

Earthquake waves can be tracked to a point below Earth's surface known as the focus. The **focus** is a place within Earth along a fault at which the first motion of an earthquake occurs. Motion along a fault causes stress. When the stress on the rock is too great, the rock will rupture and cause an earthquake. The earthquake releases the stress. Directly above the focus on Earth's surface is the **epicenter** (EP•i•sen•ter). Seismic waves flow outward from the focus in all directions.

## Visualize It!

**6 Identify** Label the epicenter, focus, and fault on the diagram.

Seismic waves

# What causes earthquakes?

Most earthquakes occur near the boundaries of tectonic plates. A **tectonic plate boundary** is where two or more tectonic plates meet. As tectonic plates move, pressure builds up near the edges of the plates. These movements break Earth's crust into a series of faults. A **fault** is a break in Earth's crust along which blocks of rock move. The release of energy that accompanies the movement of the rock along a fault causes an earthquake.

## Elastic Rebound

When rock is put under tremendous pressure, stress may deform, or change the shape of, the rock. **Deformation** (dee•for•MAY•shun) is the process by which rock becomes deformed and changes shape due to stress. As stress increases, the amount of energy that is stored in the rock increases, as seen in image B to the right.

Stress can change the shape of rock along a fault. Once the stress is released, rock may return to its original shape. When rock returns to nearly the same shape after the stress is removed, the process is known as *elastic deformation*. Imagine an elastic band that is pulled tight under stress. Once stress on the elastic band is removed, there is a *snap!* The elastic band returns to its original shape. A similar process occurs during earthquakes.

Similar to an elastic band, rock along tectonic plate boundaries can suddenly return to nearly its original shape when the stress is removed. The sudden *snap* is an earthquake. The return of rock to its original shape after elastic deformation is called **elastic rebound**. Earthquakes accompany the release of energy during elastic rebound. When the rock breaks and rebounds, it releases energy as seismic waves. The seismic wave energy radiates from the focus of the earthquake in all directions. This energy causes the ground to shake for a short time. Most earthquakes last for just a few seconds.

## Visualize It!

**7 Compare** Did an earthquake occur between images A and B or between images B and C? How do you know?

_____

_____

_____

Along a fault, rocks are pushed or pulled in different directions and at different speeds.

As stress increases and energy builds within the rock, the rock deforms but remains locked in place.

Too much stress causes the rock to break and rebound to its original shape, releasing energy.

# Unstable Ground

## Where do earthquakes happen?

### Active Reading

**8 Identify** As you read, underline the locations where earthquakes occur.

Each year, approximately 500,000 earthquakes are detected worldwide. The map below shows some of these earthquakes. Movement of material and energy in the form of heat in Earth's interior contribute to plate motions that result in earthquakes.

Most earthquakes happen at or near tectonic plate boundaries. Tectonic plate boundaries are areas where Earth's crust experiences a lot of stress. This stress occurs because the tectonic plates are colliding, separating, or grinding past each other horizontally. There are three main types of tectonic plate boundaries: divergent, convergent, and transform. The movement and interactions of the plates causes the crust to break into different types of faults. Earthquakes happen along these faults.

## Plate Tectonic Boundaries and Earthquake Locations Worldwide

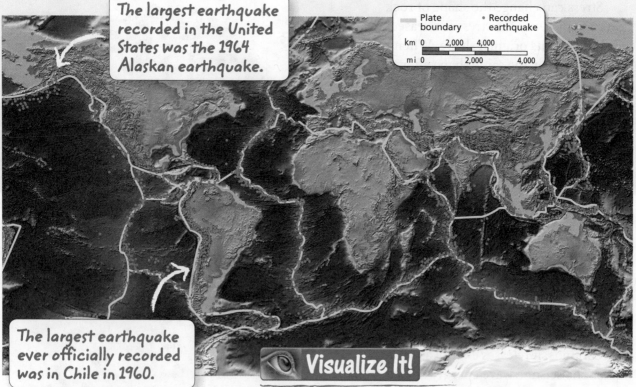

The largest earthquake recorded in the United States was the 1964 Alaskan earthquake.

The largest earthquake ever officially recorded was in Chile in 1960.

Plate boundary — Recorded earthquake

km 0    2,000    4,000
mi 0         2,000         4,000

### Visualize It!

**9 Identify** Where are most of Earth's earthquakes located? How do you know?

_____

_____

_____

**10 Correlate** In the caption for each diagram, write in the type of fault that is common at each of the types of tectonic plate boundaries.

## At Divergent Boundaries

At a divergent boundary, plates pull apart, causing the crust to stretch. Stress that stretches rock and makes rock thinner is called *tension*. Normal faults commonly result when tension pulls rock apart.

Most of the crust at divergent boundaries is thin, so the earthquakes tend to be shallow. Most earthquakes at divergent boundaries are no more than 20 km deep. A mid-ocean ridge is an example of a divergent boundary where earthquakes occur.

At divergent boundaries, earthquakes are common along _____ faults.

## At Convergent Boundaries

Convergent plate boundaries occur when plates collide, causing rock to be squeezed. Stress that shortens or squeezes an object is known as *compression*. Compression causes the formation of reverse faults. Rocks are thrust over one another at reverse faults.

When two plates come together, both plates may crumple up to form mountains. Or one plate can subduct, or sink, underneath the other plate and into the mantle. The earthquakes that happen at convergent boundaries can be very strong. Subduction zone earthquakes occur at depths of up to 700 km.

At convergent boundaries, earthquakes are common along _____ faults.

## At Transform Boundaries

A transform boundary is a place where two tectonic plates slide past each other horizontally. Stress that distorts a body by pushing different parts of the body in opposite directions is called *shear stress*. As the plates move, rocks on both sides of the fault are sheared, or broken, as they grind past one another in opposite directions.

Strike–slip faults are common at transform boundaries. Most earthquakes along the faults at transform boundaries are relatively shallow. The earthquakes are generally within the upper 50 km of the crust.

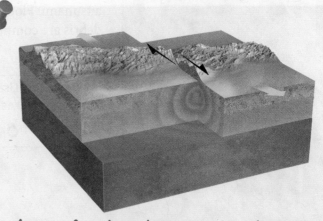

At transform boundaries, earthquakes are common along _____ faults.

# What are some effects of earthquakes?

Many earthquakes do not cause major damage. However, some strong earthquakes can cause billions of dollars in property damage. Earthquakes may even cause human injuries and loss of life. In general, areas closest to the epicenter of an earthquake experience the greatest damage.

## Danger to People and Structures

The shaking of an earthquake can cause structures to move vertically and horizontally. When structures cannot withstand the shaking, major destruction can occur. Following the release of seismic waves, buildings can shake so violently that a total or partial collapse can happen, as shown below.

Much of the injury and loss of life that happen during and after earthquakes is caused by structures that collapse. In addition, fires, gas leaks, floods, and polluted water supplies can cause secondary damages following an earthquake. The debris left after an earthquake can take weeks or months to clean up. Bridges, roadways, homes, and entire cities can become disaster zones.

## Tsunamis

An earthquake under the ocean can cause a vertical movement of the sea floor that displaces an enormous amount of water. This displacement may cause a tsunami to form. A *tsunami* (sue•NAH•mee) is a series of extremely long waves that can travel across the ocean at speeds of up to 800 km/h. Tsunami waves travel outward in all directions from the point where the earthquake occurred. As the waves approach a shoreline, the size of the waves increases. The waves can be taller than 30 m. Tsunami waves can cause major destruction and take many lives as they smash and wash away anything in their path. Many people may drown during a tsunami. Floods, polluted water supplies, and large amount of debris are common in the aftermath.

11 **Design** You are an emergency management professional. You have been assigned to create an earthquake safety brochure for your town. Create a brochure that demonstrates ways people can protect themselves during an earthquake.

**Think Outside the Book** Inquiry

Although most of this building is left standing, the entire area is a hazard to citizens in the town.

12 **Identify** List some of the hazards associated with earthquakes on land and underwater.

| On Land | Underwater |
|---------|------------|
|         |            |

© Houghton Mifflin Harcourt Publishing Company • Image Credits: ©PBNJ Productions/Corbis

# Killer Quake

Imagine losing half the people in your city. On December 26, 2004, a massive tsunami destroyed approximately one-third of the buildings in Banda Aceh, Indonesia, and wiped out half the population.

**Before**

**Epicenter**

**Affected coastal areas**

INDIA
MYANMAR
BANGLADESH
THAILAND
Andaman Is.
SRI LANKA
Nicobar Is.
MALDIVES
Banda Aceh
MALAYSIA
INDONESIA
INDIAN OCEAN

## How Tsunamis Form

In the ocean, tsunami waves are fast but not very tall. As the waves approach a coast, they slow down and get much taller.

## Before the Earthquake

The Banda Aceh tsunami resulted from a very strong earthquake in the ocean. Banda Aceh was very close to the epicenter.

## Major Damages

The destruction to parts of Asia were so massive that geographers had to redraw the maps of some of the countries.

**After**

## Extend

Inquiry

**13 Identify** In what ocean did the earthquake occur?

**14 Research** Investigate one other destructive tsunami and find out where the earthquake that caused it originated.

**15 Debate** Many of the people affected by the tsunami were poor. Why might earthquakes be more damaging in poor areas of the world?

# Visual Summary

To complete this summary, fill in the correct word. Then use the key below to check your answers. You can use this page to review the main concepts of the lesson.

## Earthquakes

**Earthquakes occur along faults.**

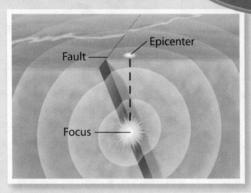

Epicenter

Fault

Focus

**16** The epicenter of an earthquake is directly above the _____

**Rocks break and snap back to their original shape in an earthquake.**

**17** Earthquakes happen when rocks bend and snap back in a process called _____

**Earthquakes usually happen along plate boundaries.**

**18** The three types of plate boundaries are

_____

_____

_____

**Earthquakes can cause a lot of damage.**

**19** An example of the dangers of earthquakes is _____

**20 Hypothesize** Can earthquakes be prevented?

# Lesson Review

## Vocabulary

In your own words, define the following terms.

**1** Elastic rebound

_____

_____

_____

**2** Focus

_____

_____

_____

**3** Fault

_____

_____

_____

## Key Concepts

| Example | Type of Boundary |
|---|---|
| **4 Identify** Most of the earthquakes in Japan are a result of one plate sinking under another. | |
| **5 Identify** The African Rift Valley is a location where plates are moving apart. | |
| **6 Identify** The San Andreas fault is a location where tectonic plates move horizontally past each other. | |

**7 Explain** What causes an earthquake?

_____

_____

_____

_____

## Critical Thinking

Use the image to answer the following questions.

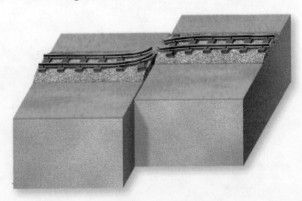

**8 Analyze** How does the image demonstrate that deformation has taken place?

_____

_____

_____

_____

_____

**9 Apply** How does Earth's surface and the structures on the surface change as a result of an earthquake?

_____

_____

_____

_____

_____

_____

**10 Hypothesize** Why do you think there is often only a short amount of time to evacuate an area before an earthquake?

_____

_____

_____

_____

_____

_____

# My Notes

# Unit 7 〔Big Idea〕 The movement of tectonic plates accounts for important features of Earth's surface and for major geologic events.

### Lesson 1
**ESSENTIAL QUESTION**
**What are Earth's layers?**

Identify Earth's compositional and physical layers, and describe their properties.

### Lesson 4
**ESSENTIAL QUESTION**
*How do volcanoes change Earth's surface?*

Describe what the various kinds of volcanoes and eruptions are, where they occur, how they form, and how they change Earth's surface.

### Lesson 2
**ESSENTIAL QUESTION**
*What is plate tectonics?*

Explain the theory of plate tectonics, describe how tectonic plates move, and identify geologic events that occur because of tectonic plate movement.

### Lesson 5
**ESSENTIAL QUESTION**
*Why do earthquakes happen?*

Describe the causes of earthquakes, and identify where earthquakes happen.

### Lesson 3
**ESSENTIAL QUESTION**
*How do mountains form?*

Describe how the movement of Earth's tectonic plates causes mountain building.

## 〔Connect〕 ESSENTIAL QUESTIONS
Lessons 2 and 5

**1 Synthesize** Explain why tectonic plate boundaries are usually areas of intense geological activity.

_____

_____

_____

_____

## Think Outside the Book

**2 Synthesize** Choose one of these activities to help synthesize what you have learned in this unit.

☐ Using what you learned in lessons 2, 3, 4, and 5, prepare a poster presentation that summarizes plate tectonic activity at convergent boundaries.

☐ Using what you learned in lessons 2, 3, and 5, prepare a poster presentation that summarizes plate tectonic activity at divergent boundaries.

## Vocabulary

Fill in the blank with the term that best completes the sentence.

**TEKS 6.10A**

1  The _____ is the layer of rock between Earth's crust and core.

2  _____ is the theory that explains how large pieces of Earth's outermost layer move and change shape.

**TEKS 6.10D**

3  _____ is the bending of rock layers due to stress.

4  A(n) _____ is a vent or fissure in Earth's surface through which magma and gases are expelled.

5  A(n) _____ is a movement or trembling of the ground that is caused by a sudden release of energy when rocks move along a fault.

## Key Concepts

Choose the letter of the best answer.

**TEKS 6.10A**

6  Evelyn is making a model of Earth to show how the physical layers correspond to the compositional layers. Which of the following should Evelyn show in her model? (Hint: Step 1. List the physical layers of Earth. Step 2. List the compositional layers of Earth. Step 3. Identify the statement that correctly relates the physical and compositional layers.)

**A** The physical layers exactly match the compositional layers.

**B** The crust is the only compositional layer not included in the physical layers.

**C** The physical layer of the asthenosphere includes the compositional layer of the crust.

**D** The physical layers of the inner core and outer core form a single compositional layer.

TEKS 6.10A

**7** Which of the following is a major difference between Earth's inner core and outer core?

**A** The inner core is liquid, and the outer core is solid.

**B** The inner core is solid, and the outer core is liquid.

**C** The inner core is gas, and the outer core is solid.

**D** The inner core is solid, and the outer core is gas.

TEKS 6.10A

**8** Earth can be divided into five layers: the lithosphere, the asthenosphere, the mesosphere, the outer core, and the inner core. Which properties are used to make these divisions?

**A** compositional properties      **C** chemical properties

**B** physical properties      **D** elemental properties

TEKS 6.10C, 6.10D

**9** The illustration below shows some of Earth's tectonic plates. The arrows indicate the direction in which some of these plates are moving.

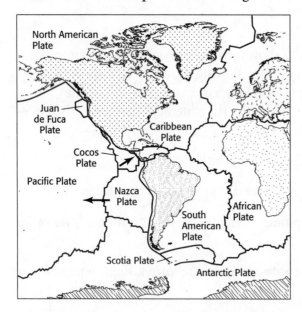

Based on the direction of the Cocos Plate, what type of plate boundary likely exists between the Cocos Plate and the Caribbean Plate? (Hint: Step 1. Analyze the likely relative motions of the Caribbean Plate and the Cocos Plate. Step 2. Relate the relative motions of plates to the type of plate boundary.)

**A** transform boundary      **C** convection boundary

**B** divergent boundary      **D** convergent boundary

## Gridded Response

Write your answer in the boxes, then bubble in the corresponding number in the grid below.

**TEKS** 6.2E

**10** The table below identifies the relationship between the strength of earthquakes and how often earthquakes happen.

| Worldwide Frequency of Earthquakes of Different Magnitudes | | |
|---|---|---|
| **Descriptor** | **Magnitude** | **Average number annually** |
| great | 8.0 and higher | 1 |
| major | 7.0–7.9 | 17 |
| strong | 6.0–6.9 | 134 |
| moderate | 5.0–5.9 | 1,319 |
| light | 4.0–4.9 | about 13,000 |
| minor | 3.0–3.9 | about 130,000 |
| very minor | 2.0–2.9 | about 1,300,000 |

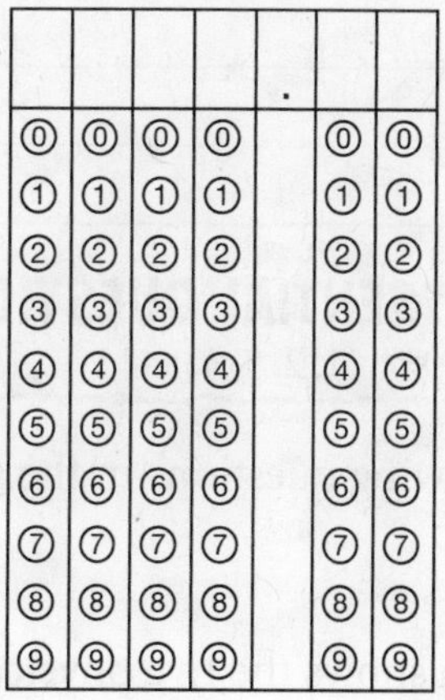

Approximately how many earthquakes classified as moderate to great happen each year?

## Critical Thinking

Answer the following questions in the space provided.

**TEKS** 6.10D

**11** Explain how a convergent boundary is different from a transform boundary. Then, name one thing that commonly occurs along both convergent boundaries and transform boundaries.

_____

_____

_____

_____

_____

_____

_____

_____

**TEKS** 6.10D

**12** Explain how forces from tectonic plate movement can build these three types of mountains: folded mountains, fault block mountains, and volcanic mountains.

_____

_____

_____

_____

_____

_____

**Connect** **ESSENTIAL QUESTIONS**
Lessons 1, 2, 3, 4, and 5

Answer the following questions in the space provided.

**TEKS** 6.10A, 6.3B

**13** The diagram shows the five physical layers of Earth.

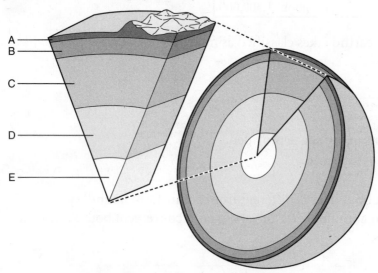

Identify the physical layers A, B, and C. Describe the relationship between these layers and how this relationship is important to understanding the function of the different layers of Earth's interior.

_____

_____

_____

_____

_____

_____

# UNIT 8
# The Solar System

A brass orrery shows the rotation of planets around the sun.

## Big Idea

Planets and a variety of other bodies form a system of objects orbiting the sun.

## What do you think?

For thousands of years, scientists have created models to help us understand the solar system. What are some different ways in which scientists have modeled the solar system?

The Human Orrery models the solar system.

453

# Unit 8
# The Solar System

## CITIZEN SCIENCE

# Solar System Discoveries

Today's knowledge of the solar system is the result of discoveries that have been made over the centuries. Discoveries will continue to change our view of the solar system.

**Moons of Jupiter, 1610**
On January 7, 1610, Galileo used a telescope he had improved and discovered the four largest moons of Jupiter. The moons are some of the largest objects in our solar system!

*Ganymede is the largest of Jupiter's moons.*

William Herschel

Comet Hyakutake

**Comet Hyakutake, 1996**
Amateur astronomer Yuji Hyakutake discovered Comet Hyakutake on January 31, 1996, using a pair of powerful binoculars. This comet will approach Earth only once every 100,000 years.

**Uranus, 1781**
British astronomer Sir William Herschel discovered Uranus on March 13, 1781. It was the first planet discovered with a telescope. Our knowledge of the solar system expanded in ways people had not expected.

**Neptune, 1846**
Mathematics helped scientists discover the planet Neptune. Astronomers predicted Neptune's existence based on irregularities in Uranus's orbit. On September 23, 1846, Neptune was discovered by telescope almost exactly where it was mathematically predicted to be.

Neptune

## Take It Home   Future Explorations

### ① Think About It

What are some recent discoveries that have been made about the solar system?

_____

_____

_____

_____

**B** Will crewed missions to distant places in the solar system ever be possible? Justify your answer.

_____

_____

_____

_____

_____

### ② Ask Some Questions

Research efforts such as NASA's Stardust spacecraft to learn more about how space is being explored now.

**A** How is information being transmitted back to Earth?

_____

_____

### ③ Make A Plan

Design a poster to explain why humans are exploring the solar system. Be sure to include the following information:

• How we are using technology for exploration

• Why it benefits all of us to learn about the solar system

# Historical Models
## of the Solar System

**ESSENTIAL QUESTION**

## How have people modeled the solar system?

By the end of this lesson, you should be able to compare various historical models of the solar system.

TEKS **6.3D** relate the impact of research on scientific thought and society, including the history of science and contributions of scientists as related to the content

TEKS **6.11A** describe the physical properties, locations, and movements of the Sun, planets, Galilean moons, meteors, asteroids, and comets

The Earth-centered model of the solar system was accepted for almost 1,400 years. It was replaced by the sun-centered model of the solar system, which is shown in this 17th-century illustration.

## Lesson Labs

**Quick Labs**
- The Geocentric Model of the Solar System
- The Heliocentric Model of the Solar System
- Orbital Ellipses

**Field Lab**
- Investigating Parallax

## Engage Your Brain

**1 Predict** Check T or F to show whether you think each statement is true or false.

| T | F | |
|---|---|---|
| ☐ | ☐ | The sun and planets circle Earth. |
| ☐ | ☐ | Most early astronomers placed the sun at the center of the solar system. |
| ☐ | ☐ | The planets orbit the sun in ellipses. |
| ☐ | ☐ | The telescope helped to improve our understanding of the solar system. |

**2 Evaluate** What, if anything, is wrong with the model of the solar system shown below?

_____

_____

_____

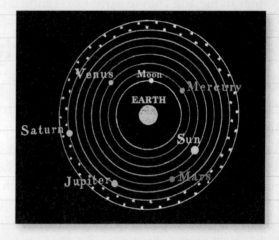

## Active Reading

**3 Synthesis** You can often define an unknown word if you know the meaning of its word parts. Use the word parts and sentence below to make an educated guess about the meaning of the word *heliocentric*.

| Word part | Meaning |
|-----------|---------|
| helio- | sun |
| -centric | centered |

**Example sentence**
The <u>heliocentric</u> model of the solar system was first proposed by Aristarchus.

**heliocentric:**

_____

_____

_____

### Vocabulary Terms

- solar system
- heliocentric
- geocentric
- parallax

**4 Apply** As you learn the definition of each vocabulary term in this lesson, create your own definition or sketch to help you remember the meaning of the term.

# What is the Center

## What is the solar system?

The **solar system** is the sun and all of the bodies that orbit the sun. Our current model of the solar system is the *sun-centered* or *heliocentric* (hee•lee•oh•SEN•trik) model. In the **heliocentric** model, Earth and the other planets orbit the sun. The earliest models for the solar system assumed that the Earth was at the center of the solar system, with the sun, moon, and planets circling it. These models, which used Earth as the center, are called *Earth-centered* or **geocentric** (jee•oh•SEN•trik) models. The heliocentric model was not generally accepted until the work of Copernicus and Kepler in the late 16th to early 17th centuries.

**Active Reading**

**5 Identify** As you read the text, underline the definitions of geocentric and heliocentric.

## Who proposed some early models of the solar system?

Until Galileo improved on the telescope in 1609, people observed the heavens with the naked eye. To observers, it appeared that the sun, the moon, the planets, and the stars moved around Earth each day. This caused them to conclude that Earth was not moving. If Earth was not moving, then Earth must be the center of the solar system and all other bodies revolved around it.

This geocentric model of the solar system became part of ancient Greek thought beginning in the 6th century BCE. Aristotle was among the first thinkers to propose this model.

**Think Outside the Book**

**6 Research** Use different sources to research a geocentric model of the solar system from either ancient Greece, ancient China, or Babylon. Write a short description of the model you choose.

Aristotle (384–322 BCE)

### Aristotle

Aristotle (AIR•ih•staht'l) was a Greek philosopher. Aristotle thought Earth was the center of all things. His model placed the moon, sun, planets, and stars on a series of circles that surrounded Earth. He thought that if Earth went around the sun, then the relative positions of the stars would change as Earth moves. This apparent shift in the position of an object when viewed from different locations is known as **parallax** (PAIR•uh•laks). In fact, the stars are so far away that parallax cannot be seen with the naked eye.

© Houghton Mifflin Harcourt Publishing Company • Image Credits: (bkgd) ©Ian McKinnell/Photographer's Choice/Getty Images; (b) ©After Lysippos/The Bridgeman Art Library/Getty Images

# of the Solar System?

## Aristarchus

Aristarchus (air•i•STAHR•kuhs) was a Greek astronomer and mathematician. Aristarchus is reported to have proposed a heliocentric model of the solar system. His model, however, was not widely accepted at the time. Aristarchus attempted to measure the relative distances to the moon and sun. This was a major contribution to science. Aristarchus's ratio of distances was much too small but was important in the use of observation and geometry to solve a scientific problem.

Aristarchus (about 310–230 BCE)

Aristotle thought that if Earth were moving, the positions of the stars should change as Earth moved. In fact, stars are so far away that shifts in their positions can only be observed by telescope.

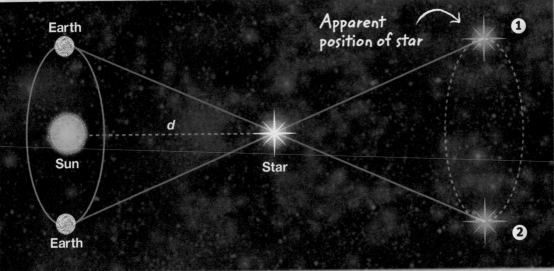

Diagram showing the shift in apparent position of a star at two different times of year seen from a telescope on Earth. A star first seen at point 1 will be seen at point 2 six months later.

### Visualize It!

**7 Predict** If a star appears at position 1 during the summer, during which season will it appear at position 2?

_____

_____

_____

Ptolemy (about 100–170 CE)

# Ptolemy

Ptolemy (TOHL•uh•mee) was an astronomer, geographer, and mathematician who lived in Alexandria, Egypt, which was part of ancient Rome. His book, the *Almagest*, is one of the few books that we have from these early times. It was based on observations of the planets going back as much as 800 years. Ptolemy developed a detailed geocentric model that was used by astronomers for the next 14 centuries. He believed that a celestial body traveled at a constant speed in a perfect circle. In Ptolemy's model, the planets moved on small circles that in turn moved on larger circles. This "wheels-on-wheels" system fit observations better than any model that had come before. It allowed prediction of the motion of planets years into the future.

## Visualize It!

**8 Describe** Use the diagram at the right to describe Ptolemy's geocentric model of the solar system.

_____

_____

_____

_____

_____

## Ptolemaic Model

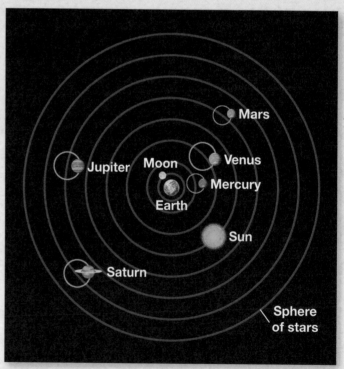

**Think Outside the Book** Inquiry

**9 Defend** As a class activity, defend Ptolemy's geocentric model of the solar system. Remember that during Ptolemy's time people were limited to what they could see with the naked eye.

## Copernicus

The Polish astronomer Nicolaus Copernicus (nik•uh•LAY•uhs koh•PER•nuh•kuhs) felt that Ptolemy's model of the solar system was too complicated. He was aware of the heliocentric idea of Aristarchus when he developed the first detailed heliocentric model of the solar system. In Copernicus's time, data was still based on observations with the naked eye. Because data had changed little since the time of Ptolemy, Copernicus adopted Ptolemy's idea that planetary paths should be perfect circles. Like Ptolemy, he used a "wheels-on-wheels" system. Copernicus's model fit observations a little better than the geocentric model of Ptolemy. The heliocentric model of Copernicus is generally seen as the first step in the development of modern models of the solar system.

Nicolaus Copernicus (1473–1543)

### Copernican Model

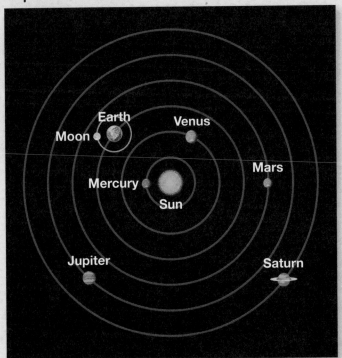

**10 Compare** How does Copernicus's model of the solar system differ from Ptolemy's model of the solar system?

| Ptolemaic model | Copernican model |
| --- | --- |
|  |  |

**11 Identify** Underline text that summarizes Kepler's three laws.

## Kepler

Johannes Kepler (yoh•HAH•nuhs KEP•luhr) was a German mathematician and astronomer. After carefully analyzing observations of the planets, he realized that requiring planetary motions to be exactly circular did not fit the observations perfectly. Kepler then tried other types of paths and found that ellipses fit best.

Kepler formulated three principles, which today are known as Kepler's laws. The first law states that planetary orbits are ellipses with the sun at one focus. The second law states that planets move faster in their orbits when closer to the sun. The third law relates the distance of a planet from the sun to the time it takes to go once around its orbit.

**12 Analyze** How did Kepler's first law support the idea of a heliocentric solar system?

_____

_____

_____

_____

Johannes Kepler (1571–1630)

**Kepler's First Law**

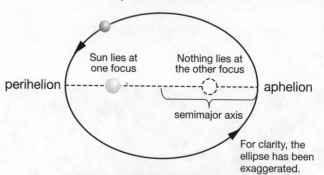

Sun lies at one focus

Nothing lies at the other focus

perihelion - - - - - - - - - - - - - - - - aphelion

semimajor axis

For clarity, the ellipse has been exaggerated.

## Galileo

Galileo Galilei (gahl•uh•LAY•oh gahl•uh•LAY) was a scientist who approached questions in the fashion that today we call *scientific methods*. Galileo made significant improvements to the newly invented telescope. He then used his more powerful telescope to view celestial objects. Galileo observed the moons Io, Europa, Callisto, and Ganymede orbiting Jupiter. Today, these moons are known as the Galilean satellites. His observations showed that Earth was not the only object that could be orbited. This gave support to the heliocentric model. He also observed that Venus went through phases similar to the phases of Earth's moon. These phases result from changes in the direction that sunlight strikes Venus as Venus orbits the sun.

Galileo Galilei (1564–1642)

# Galileo

Galileo Galilei was an Italian mathematician, physicist, and astronomer who lived during the 16th and 17th centuries. Galileo demonstrated that all bodies, regardless of their mass, fall at the same rate. He also argued that moving objects retain their velocity unless an unbalanced force acts upon them. Galileo made improvements to telescope technology. He used his telescopes to observe sunspots, the phases of Venus, Earth's moon, the four Galilean moons of Jupiter, and a supernova.

## Galileo's Telescopes

This reconstruction of one of Galileo's telescopes is on exhibit in Florence, Italy. Galileo's first telescopes magnified objects at 3 and then 20 times.

## The *Galileo* Spacecraft

The *Galileo* spacecraft was launched from the space shuttle *Atlantis* in 1989. *Galileo* was the first spacecraft to orbit Jupiter. It studied the planet and its moons.

Inquiry

## Extend

**13 Identify** What were Galileo's most important contributions to astronomy?

**14 Research** Galileo invented or improved upon many instruments and technologies, such as the compound microscope, the thermometer, and the geometric compass. Research one of Galileo's technological contributions.

**15 Create** Describe one of Galileo's experiments concerning the motion of bodies by doing one of the following:

- make a poster

- recreate the experiment

- draw a graphic novel of Galileo conducting an experiment

# Visual Summary

To complete this summary, fill in the blanks with the correct word or phrase. Then use the key below to check your answers. You can use this page to review the main concepts of the lesson.

## Models of the Solar System

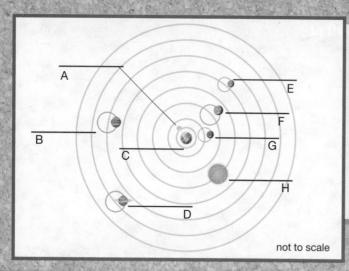

not to scale

**Early astronomers proposed a geocentric solar system.**

16 Label the solar system bodies as they appear in the geocentric model.

17 Which astronomers are associated with this model of the solar system?

_____

_____

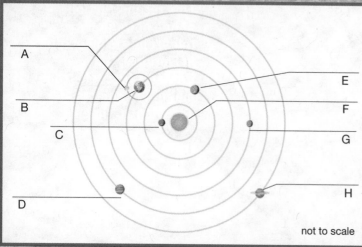

not to scale

**The heliocentric solar system is the current model.**

18 Label the solar system bodies as they appear in the heliocentric model.

19 Which astronomers are associated with this model of the solar system?

_____

_____

_____

20 **Compare** How does the geocentric model of the solar system differ from the heliocentric model of the solar system?

# Lesson Review

## Vocabulary

Fill in the blank with the term that best completes the following sentences.

**1** The _____ is the sun and all of the planets and other bodies that travel around it.

**2** Until the time of Copernicus, most scientists thought the _____ model of the solar system was correct.

**3** An apparent shift in the position of an object when viewed from different locations is called _____.

## Key Concepts

In the following table, write the name of the correct astronomer next to that astronomer's contribution.

| Contribution | Astronomer |
|---|---|
| **4 Identify** Who first observed the phases of Venus? | |
| **5 Identify** Who attempted to measure the relative distances to the moon and the sun? | |
| **6 Identify** Who replaced circles with ellipses in a heliocentric model of the universe? | |
| **7 Identify** Whose geocentric model of the solar system was accepted for 1,400 years? | |
| **8 Identify** Whose heliocentric model is seen as the first step in the development of modern models of the solar system? | |

## Critical Thinking

Use the illustration to answer the following question.

**9 Appraise** How did data gathered using Galileo's early telescope support the heliocentric model?

_____

_____

_____

_____

**10 Explain** How did Aristotle's inability to detect parallax lead him to propose a geocentric model of the solar system?

_____

_____

_____

_____

_____

# My Notes

TEKS MATH **6.3D** add, subtract, multiply, and divide integers fluently

TEKS MATH **6.3E** multiply and divide positive rational numbers fluently

# Mean, Median, Mode, and Range

You can analyze both the measures of central tendency and the variability of data using mean, median, mode, and range.

## Tutorial

**Orbit eccentricity measures how oval-shaped the elliptical orbit is. The closer a value is to 0, the closer the orbit is to a circle. Examine the eccentricity values below.**

| Orbit Eccentricities of Planets in the Solar System | | | |
|---|---|---|---|
| Mercury | 0.205 | Jupiter | 0.049 |
| Venus | 0.007 | Saturn | 0.057 |
| Earth | 0.017 | Uranus | 0.046 |
| Mars | 0.094 | Neptune | 0.011 |

| | |
|---|---|
| **Mean**<br>The mean is the sum of all of the values in a data set divided by the total number of values in the data set. The mean is also called the *average*. | $$\frac{0.007 + 0.011 + 0.017 + 0.046 + 0.049 + 0.057 + 0.094 + 0.205}{8}$$<br>**1** Add up all of the values.<br>**2** Divide the sum by the number of values.<br>**mean** = 0.061 |
| **Median**<br>The median is the value of the middle item when data are arranged in numerical order. If there is an odd number of values, the median is the middle value. If there is an even number of values, the median is the mean of the two middle values. | 0.007  0.011  0.017  0.046  0.049  0.057  0.094  0.205<br>————————→ ←————————<br>**1** Order the values.<br>**2** The median is the middle value if there is an odd number of values. If there is an even number of values, calculate the mean of the two middle values.<br>**median** = 0.0475 |
| **Mode**<br>The mode is the value or values that occur most frequently in a data set. Order the values to find the mode. If all values occur with the same frequency, the data set is said to have no mode. | 0.007  0.011  0.017  0.046  0.049  0.057  0.094  0.205<br>**1** Order the values.<br>**2** Find the value or values that occur most frequently.<br>**mode** = none |
| **Range**<br>The range is the difference between the greatest value and the least value of a data set. | 0.205 − 0.007<br>**1** Subtract the least value from the greatest value.<br>**range** = 0.198 |

# You Try It!

The data table below shows the masses and densities of the planets.

| Mass and Density of the Planets | | |
|---|---|---|
| | Mass (× 10²⁴ kg) | Density (g/cm³) |
| Mercury | 0.33 | 5.43 |
| Venus | 4.87 | 5.24 |
| Earth | 5.97 | 5.52 |
| Mars | 0.64 | 3.34 |
| Jupiter | 1,899 | 1.33 |
| Saturn | 568 | 0.69 |
| Uranus | 87 | 1.27 |
| Neptune | 102 | 1.64 |

**②**

**Using Formulas** Find the mean, median, mode, and range for the density of the planets.

**①**

**Using Formulas** Find the mean, median, mode, and range for the mass of the planets.

**③**

**Analyzing Data** Find the mean density of the inner planets (Mercury through Mars). Find the mean density of the outer planets (Jupiter through Neptune). Compare these values.

**Mean density of the inner planets:** _____

**Mean density of the outer planets:** _____

**Comparison:**

_____

**④**

**Evaluating Data** The mean mass of the outer planets (Jupiter, Saturn, Uranus, and Neptune) is 225 times greater than the mean mass of the inner planets. How does this comparison and the comparison of mean densities support the use of the term *gas giants* to describe the outer planets? Explain your reasoning.

_____

_____

# Gravity and the Solar System

**ESSENTIAL QUESTION**

## Why is gravity important in the solar system?

By the end of this lesson, you should be able to explain the role that gravity played in the formation of the solar system and in determining the motion of the planets.

Gravity keeps objects, such as these satellites, in orbit around Earth. Gravity also affects the way in which planets move and how they are formed.

**TEKS** **6.11B** understand that gravity is the force that governs the motion of our solar system

## Lesson Labs

**Quick Labs**
- Gravity's Effect
- Gravity and the Orbit of a Planet

**Exploration Lab**
- Weights on Different Celestial Bodies

##  Engage Your Brain

**1 Predict** Check T or F to show whether you think each statement is true or false.

| T | F | |
|---|---|---|
| ☐ | ☐ | Gravity keeps the planets in orbit around the sun. |
| ☐ | ☐ | The planets follow circular paths around the sun. |
| ☐ | ☐ | Sir Isaac Newton was the first scientist to describe how the force of gravity behaved. |
| ☐ | ☐ | The sun formed in the center of the solar system. |
| ☐ | ☐ | The terrestrial planets and the gas giant planets formed from the same material. |

**2 Draw** In the space below, draw what you think the solar system looked like before the planets formed.

##  Active Reading

**3 Synthesize** You can often define an unknown word if you know the meaning of its word parts. Use the word parts and sentence below to make an educated guess about the meaning of the word *protostellar*.

| Word part | Meaning |
|---|---|
| *proto-* | first |
| *-stellar* | of or having to do with a star or stars |

**Example sentence**
The protostellar disk formed after the collapse of the solar nebula.

protostellar:

_____

_____

### Vocabulary Terms

- gravity
- orbit
- aphelion
- perihelion
- centripetal force
- solar nebula
- planetesimal

**4 Apply** This list contains the key terms you'll learn in this section. As you read, circle the definition of each term.

# Gravity

## What is gravity?

**Active Reading** **5 Identify** Underline the definition of and the effects of gravity.

**Gravity** is a force of attraction between objects that is due to their masses and the distances between them. Every object in the universe pulls on every other object. Objects with greater masses have a greater force of attraction than objects with lesser masses have. Objects that are close together have a greater force of attraction than objects that are far apart have.

Gravity is the weakest force in nature. A toy magnet can overcome the gravitational force acting on a paperclip by the entire mass of Earth. Yet, gravity is one of the most important forces in the universe. It accounts for the formation of planets, stars, and galaxies. It also keeps smaller bodies in orbit around larger bodies. An **orbit** is the path that a body follows as it travels around another body in space. For example, the moon orbits Earth, and Earth orbits the sun.

When astronauts are in orbit, Earth's gravity still pulls them downward toward the planet. However, they appear to be weightless and floating. They "float" because everything around them is falling at the same speed.

# What are Kepler's laws?

The 16th-century Polish astronomer Nicolaus Copernicus (nik•uh•LAY•uhs koh•PER•nuh•kuhs) (1473–1543) changed our view of the solar system. He discovered that the motions of the planets could be best explained if the planets orbited the sun. But, like astronomers who came before him, Copernicus thought the planets followed circular paths around the sun.

Danish astronomer Tycho Brahe (TY•koh BRAH) (1546–1601) built what was at the time the world's largest observatory. Tycho used special instruments to measure the motions of the planets. His measurements were made over a period of 20 years and were very accurate. Using Tycho's data, Johannes Kepler (yoh•HAH•nuhs KEP•luhr) (1571–1630) made discoveries about the motions of the planets. We call these *Kepler's laws of planetary motion.*

Kepler found that objects that orbit the sun follow elliptical orbits. When an object follows an elliptical orbit around the sun, there is one point, called **aphelion** (uh•FEE•lee•uhn), where the object is farthest from the sun. There is also a point, called **perihelion** (perh•uh•HEE•lee•uhn), where the object is closest to the sun. Today, we know that the orbits of the planets are only slightly elliptical. However, the orbits of objects such as Pluto and comets are highly elliptical.

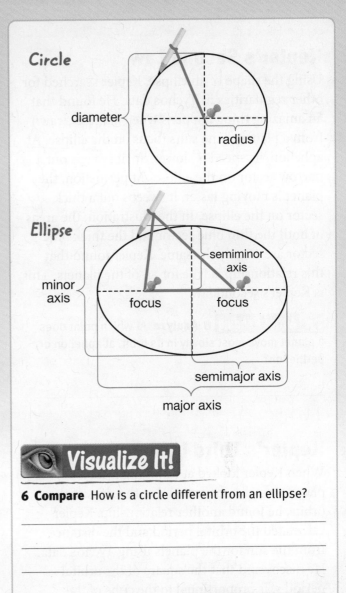

**Visualize It!**

**6 Compare** How is a circle different from an ellipse?

_____

_____

_____

_____

## Kepler's First Law

Kepler's careful plotting of the orbit of Mars kept showing Mars's orbit to be a deformed circle. It took Kepler eight years to realize that this shape was an ellipse. This clue led Kepler to propose elliptical orbits for the planets. Kepler placed the sun at one of the foci of the ellipse. This is Kepler's first law.

**Active Reading** **7 Contrast** What is the difference between Copernicus's and Kepler's description of planetary orbits?

_____

_____

**Kepler's First Law**

Sun lies at one focus

Nothing lies at the other focus

perihelion

aphelion

semimajor axis

Each planet orbits the sun in an ellipse with the sun at one focus. (For clarity, the ellipse is exaggerated here.)

## Kepler's Second Law

Using the shape of an ellipse, Kepler searched for other regularities in Tycho's data. He found that an amazing thing happens when a line is drawn from a planet to the sun's focus on the ellipse. At aphelion, its speed is slower. So, it sweeps out a narrow sector on the ellipse. At perihelion, the planet is moving faster. It sweeps out a thick sector on the ellipse. In the illustration, the areas of both the thin blue sector and the thick blue sector are exactly the same. Kepler found that this relationship is true for all of the planets. This is Kepler's second law.

**Active Reading** **8 Analyze** At which point does a planet move most slowly in its orbit, at aphelion or perihelion?

As a planet moves around its orbit, it sweeps out equal areas in equal times.

**Kepler's Second Law**

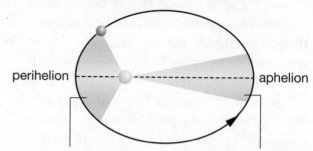

Near perihelion, a planet sweeps out an area that is short but wide.

Near aphelion, in an equal amount of time, a planet sweeps out an area that is long but narrow.

## Kepler's Third Law

When Kepler looked at how long it took for the planets to orbit the sun and at the sizes of their orbits, he found another relationship. Kepler calculated the orbital period and the distance from the sun for the planets using Tycho's data. He discovered that the square of the orbital period was proportional to the cube of the planet's average distance from the sun. This law is true for each planet. This principle is Kepler's third law. When the units are years for the period and AU for the distance, the law can be written:

(orbital period in years)² = (average distance from the sun in astronomical units [AU])³

The square of the orbital period is proportional to the cube of the planet's average distance from the sun.

**Kepler's Third Law**

$p^2$ yrs = $a^3$ AU

perihelion ————— a ————— aphelion

**9 Summarize** In the table below, summarize each of Kepler's three laws in your own words.

| First law | Second law | Third law |
|---|---|---|
| | | |

# What is the law of universal gravitation?

Using Kepler's laws, Sir Isaac Newton (EYE•zuhk NOOT'n) became the first scientist to mathematically describe how the force of gravity behaved. How could Newton do this in the 1600s before the force could be measured in a laboratory? He reasoned that gravity was the same force that accounted for both the fall of an apple from a tree and the movement of the moon around Earth.

In 1687, Newton formulated the *law of universal gravitation*. The law of universal gravitation states that all objects in the universe attract each other through gravitational force. The strength of this force depends on the product of the masses of the objects. Therefore, the gravity between objects increases as the masses of the objects increase. Gravitational force is also inversely proportional to the square of the distance between the objects. Stated another way this means that as the distance between two objects increases, the force of gravity decreases.

**Sir Isaac Newton**
**(1642–1727)**

 **Do the Math**

Newton's law of universal gravitation says that the force of gravity:
- increases as the masses of the objects increase and
- decreases as the distance between the objects increases

In these examples, $M$ = mass, $d$ = distance, and $F$ = the force of gravity exerted by two bodies.

---

## Sample Problems

**A.** In the example below, when two balls have masses of $M$ and the distance between them is $d$, then the force of gravity is $F$. If the mass of each ball is increased to 2M (to the right) and the distance stays the same, then the force of gravity increases to 4F.

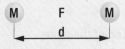

**B.** In this example, we start out again with a distance of $d$ and masses of $M$, and the force of gravity is $F$. If the distance is decreased to ½ d, then the force of gravity increases to 4F.

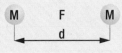

## You Try It

Recall that $M$ = mass, $d$ = distance, and $F$ = the force of gravity exerted by two bodies.

**10 Calculate** Compare the example below to the sample problems. What would the force of gravity be in the example below? Explain your answer.

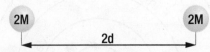

_____
_____
_____
_____
_____

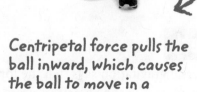 

# How does gravity affect planetary motion?

The illustrations on this page will help you understand planetary motion. In the illustration at the right, a girl is swinging a ball around her head. The ball is attached to a string. The girl is exerting a force on the string that causes the ball to move in a circular path. The inward force that causes an object to move in a circular path is called **centripetal** (sehn•TRIP•ih•tuhl) **force**.

In the illustration at center, we see that if the string breaks, the ball will move off in a straight line. This fact indicates that when the string is intact, a force is pulling the ball inward. This force keeps the ball from flying off and moving in a straight line. This force is centripetal force.

In the illustration below, you see that the planets orbit the sun. A force must be preventing the planets from moving out of their orbits and into a straight line. The sun's gravity is the force that keeps the planets moving in orbit around the sun.

As the girl swings the ball, she is exerting a force on the string that causes the ball to move in a circular path.

Centripetal force pulls the ball inward, which causes the ball to move in a curved path.

direction ball would move if string broke —

direction centripetal force pulls the ball

— Center of rotation

String

path ball takes when — moving around the center of rotation

Just as the string is pulling the ball inward, gravity is keeping the planets in orbit around the sun.

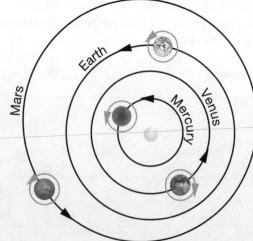

**11 Explain** In the illustration at the top of the page, what does the hand represent, the ball represent, and the string represent? (Hint: Think of the sun, a planet, and the force of gravity.)

_____

_____

_____

_____

# Collapse

## How did the solar system form?

The formation of the solar system is thought to have begun 4.6 billion years ago when a cloud of dust and gas collapsed. This cloud, from which the solar system formed, is called the **solar nebula** (SOH•ler NEB•yuh•luh). In a nebula, the inward pull of gravity is balanced by the outward push of gas pressure in the cloud. Scientists think that an outside force, perhaps the explosion of a nearby star, caused the solar nebula to compress and then to contract under its own gravity. It was in a single region of the nebula, which was perhaps several light-years across, that the solar system formed. The sun probably formed from a region that had a mass that was slightly greater than today's mass of the sun and planets.

**Active Reading** **12 Define** What is the solar nebula?

_____

_____

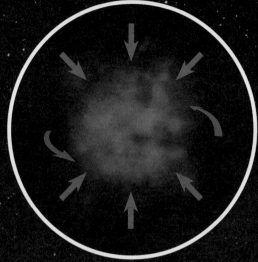

A cloud of dust and gas collapsed 4.6 billion years ago, then began to spin. It may have spun around its axis of rotation once every million years.

## A Protostellar Disk Formed from the Collapsed Solar Nebula

As a region of the solar nebula collapsed, gravity pulled most of the mass toward the center of the nebula. As the nebula contracted, it began to rotate. As the rotation grew faster, the nebula flattened out into a disk. This disk, which is called a *protostellar disk* (PROH•toh•stehl•er DISK), is where the central star, our sun, formed.

As a region of the solar nebula collapsed, it formed a slowly rotating protostellar disk.

## The Sun Formed at the Center of the Protostellar Disk

As the protostellar disk continued to contract, most of the matter ended up in the center of the disk. Friction from matter that fell into the disk heated up its center to millions of degrees, eventually reaching its current temperature of 15,000,000 °C. This intense heat in a densely packed space caused the fusion of hydrogen atoms into helium atoms. The process of fusion released large amounts of energy. This release of energy caused outward pressure that again balanced the inward pull of gravity. As the gas and dust stopped collapsing, a star was born. In the case of the solar system, this star was the sun.

**Active Reading** **13 Identify** How did the sun form?

_____
_____
_____
_____
_____

This is an artist's conception of what the protoplanetary disk in which the planets formed might have looked like.

 **Visualize It!**

**14 Describe** Use the terms *planetesimal* and *protoplanetary disk* to describe the illustration above.

_____
_____
_____
_____
_____

## Planetesimals Formed in the Protoplanetary Disk

As the sun was forming, dust grains collided and stuck together. The resulting *dust granules* grew in size and increased in number. Over time, dust granules increased in size until they became roughly meter-sized bodies. Trillions of these bodies occurred in the protostellar disk. Collisions between these bodies formed larger bodies that were kilometers across. These larger bodies, from which planets formed, are called **planetesimals** (plan•ih•TES•ih•muhls). The protostellar disk had become the *protoplanetary disk*. The protoplanetary disk was the disk in which the planets formed.

Dust grains collided and stuck together.

Over time, dust granules grew to become meter-sized bodies.

Planetesimals formed from the collisions of meter-sized bodies.

## Visualize It! Inquiry

**15 Explain** How can objects as small as dust grains become the building blocks of planets?

_____

_____

_____

_____

© Houghton Mifflin Harcourt Publishing Company• Image Credits: (bkgd) ©NASA/JPL-Caltech; (inset) ©Detlev van Ravenswaay/Photo Researchers, Inc.

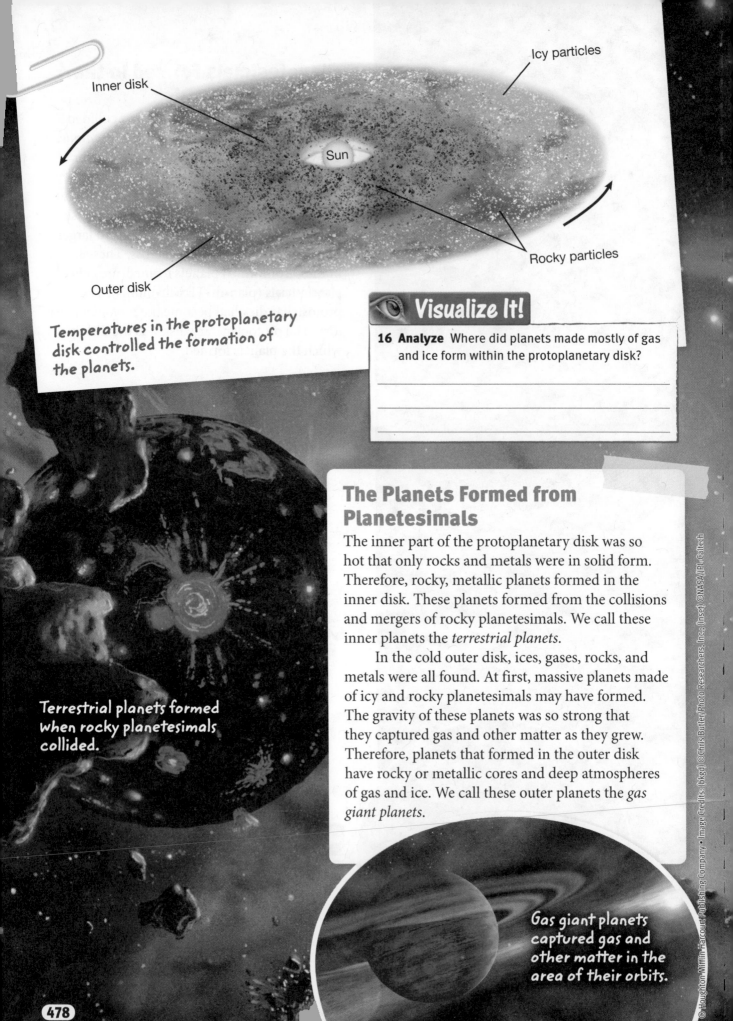

Icy particles

Inner disk

Sun

Rocky particles

Outer disk

Temperatures in the protoplanetary disk controlled the formation of the planets.

## Visualize It!

**16 Analyze** Where did planets made mostly of gas and ice form within the protoplanetary disk?

_____

_____

_____

Terrestrial planets formed when rocky planetesimals collided.

## The Planets Formed from Planetesimals

The inner part of the protoplanetary disk was so hot that only rocks and metals were in solid form. Therefore, rocky, metallic planets formed in the inner disk. These planets formed from the collisions and mergers of rocky planetesimals. We call these inner planets the *terrestrial planets*.

In the cold outer disk, ices, gases, rocks, and metals were all found. At first, massive planets made of icy and rocky planetesimals may have formed. The gravity of these planets was so strong that they captured gas and other matter as they grew. Therefore, planets that formed in the outer disk have rocky or metallic cores and deep atmospheres of gas and ice. We call these outer planets the *gas giant planets*.

Gas giant planets captured gas and other matter in the area of their orbits.

**Visualize It!**

**17 Describe** In the spaces on the left, describe Steps 2 and 4 in the formation of the solar system. In the spaces on the right, draw the last two steps in the formation of the solar system.

# Steps in the Formation of the Solar System

## Step 1 The Solar Nebula Collapses

A cloud of dust and gas collapses. The balance between the inward pull of gravity and the outward push of pressure in the cloud is upset. The collapsing cloud forms a rotating protostellar disk.

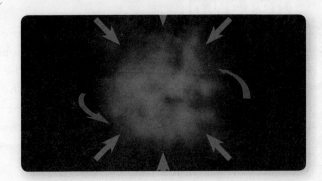

## Step 2 The Sun Forms

_____

_____

_____

_____

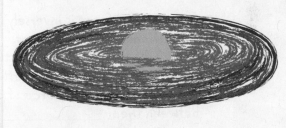

## Step 3 Planetesimals Form

Dust grains stick together and form dust granules. Dust granules slowly increase in size until they become meter-sized objects. These meter-sized objects collide to form kilometer-sized objects called _planetesimals_.

## Step 4 Planets Form

_____

_____

_____

_____

_____

# Visual Summary

To complete this summary, fill in the blank with the correct word or phrase. Then, use the key below to check your answers. You can use this page to review the main concepts of the lesson.

## The Law of Universal Gravitation

### Mass affects the force of gravity.

**18** The strength of the force of gravity depends on the product of the _____ of two objects. Therefore, as the masses of two objects increase, the force that the objects exert on one another _____.

### Distance affects the force of gravity.

**19** Gravitational force is inversely proportional to the square of the _____ between two objects. Therefore, as the distance between two objects increases, the force of gravity between them _____.

### Gravity affects planetary motion.

**20** The sun exerts a _____, indicated by line B, on a planet so that at point C it is moving around the sun in orbit instead of moving off in a _____ as shown at line A.

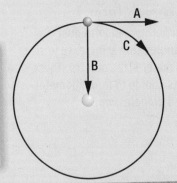

Answers: 18 masses, increases; 19 distance, decreases; 20 gravitational force or centripetal force, straight line

---

**21 Explain** In your own words, explain Newton's law of universal gravitation.

_____

# Lesson Review

## Vocabulary

Fill in the blank with the term that best completes the following sentences.

**1** Small bodies from which the planets formed are called _____

**2** The path that a body follows as it travels around another body in space is its _____

**3** The _____ is the cloud of gas and dust from which our solar system formed.

## Key Concepts

**4 Define** In your own words, define the word *gravity*.

_____

_____

_____

**5 Describe** How did the sun form?

_____

_____

_____

_____

_____

_____

_____

**6 Describe** How did planetesimals form?

_____

_____

_____

_____

_____

_____

_____

## Critical Thinking

Use the illustration below to answer the following question.

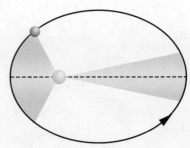

**7 Identify** What law is illustrated in this diagram?

_____

_____

**8 Analyze** How does gravity keep the planets in orbit around the sun?

_____

_____

_____

_____

_____

_____

_____

**9 Explain** How do temperature differences in the protoplanetary disk explain the arrangement of the planets in the solar system?

_____

_____

_____

_____

_____

_____

_____

_____

# My Notes

# The Sun

**ESSENTIAL QUESTION**

## What are the properties of the sun?

By the end of this lesson, you should be able to describe the location of the sun, the structure and rotation of the sun, energy production and energy transport in the sun, and solar activity on the sun.

*Prominence*

*Different types of activity occur on the sun's surface. This loop of gas that extends outward from the sun's surface is a prominence.*

**TEKS 6.11A** describe the physical properties, locations, and movements of the Sun, planets, Galilean moons, meteors, asteroids, and comets

**Lesson Labs**

**Quick Labs**
- Model Solar Composition
- Model Solar Rotation

**S.T.E.M. Lab**
- Create a Model of the Sun

## Engage Your Brain

**1 Predict** Check T or F to show whether you think each statement is true or false.

| T | F | |
|---|---|---|
| ☐ | ☐ | The sun is composed mostly of hydrogen and helium. |
| ☐ | ☐ | Energy is produced in the sun's core. |
| ☐ | ☐ | The process by which energy is produced in the sun is known as nuclear fission. |
| ☐ | ☐ | Energy is transferred to the surface of the sun by the processes of radiation and conduction. |
| ☐ | ☐ | A dark area of the sun's surface that is cooler than the surrounding areas is called a *sunspot*. |

**2 Explain** In your own words, explain the meaning of the word *sunlight*.

_____
_____
_____
_____
_____
_____
_____

## Active Reading

**3 Synthesize** You can often define an unknown word if you know the meaning of its word parts. Use the word parts and sentence below to make an educated guess about the meaning of the word *photosphere*.

| Word Part | Meaning |
|---|---|
| *photo-* | light |
| *-sphere* | ball |

**Example sentence**
Energy is transferred to the sun's <u>photosphere</u> by convection cells.

*photosphere:*

_____
_____
_____

### Vocabulary Terms
- nuclear fusion
- sunspot
- solar flare
- prominence

**4 Apply** This list contains the key terms you'll learn in this section. As you read, circle the definition of each term.

# The Sun:
# The Center of Attention

## Where is the sun located?

The sun rises every day in the east. It appears to travel across the sky in a predictable way before it sets in the west. The apparent motion of the sun led many early astronomers to believe that the sun moved around Earth. In the early 1500s, astronomer Nicolaus Copernicus (koh•PER•nuh•kuhs) developed a different model. He proposed that Earth revolved around the sun.

## The Sun Is the Center of the Solar System

We now know that Copernicus was correct. The sun is located at the center of the solar system. The solar system includes the sun and all of the objects that travel around it. Planets, dwarf planets, asteroids, and comets revolve around the sun in paths called *orbits*. Earth is one of eight planets that orbit the sun and is the third planet from the sun. The sun is by far the largest and most massive object in the solar system. Its gravitational attraction keeps the other objects in the solar system in orbit around it.

**Active Reading**

**5 Explain** Why does every object in the solar system revolve around the sun?

_____

_____

_____

_____

**Visualize It!**

**6 Analyze** What do the thin, curved lines that go through each planet represent?

_____

_____

_____

_____

Sizes and distances are not to scale

## The Sun Is Located in the Milky Way Galaxy

The sun looks small from Earth because it is located so far away. In the 1700s, Edmund Halley found a way to calculate the distance between Earth and the sun. The distance is almost 150 million km. This discovery gave scientists a model with which to determine distances between objects in the solar system.

All of the stars you can see are much farther away than the sun. Like the sun, they are part of the Milky Way galaxy. Hundreds of billions of stars make up the Milky Way. Our solar system is located in a partial spiral arm of the Milky Way about 25,000 light years from the galaxy center.

## The Sun Is Located in the Local Group

The Milky Way galaxy is one of possibly 100 billion or more galaxies in the universe. As scientists gather data from great distances in the universe, they discover that galaxies are not spaced out evenly. They are found in groups, or clusters. The Milky Way is located in the Local Group. The Local Group is a cluster of about 30 galaxies that is approximately ten million light-years across. The Andromeda (an•DRAHM•ih•duh) galaxy is part of the Local Group. It is the closest large galaxy to the Milky Way. The Local Group is in the part of the universe that astronomers know the most about.

### Visualize It!

**7 Describe** Use the graphic organizer below to indicate the location of the sun in the universe.

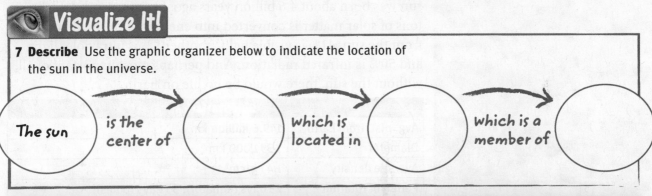

The sun → is the center of → (  ) which is located in → (  ) which is a member of → (  )

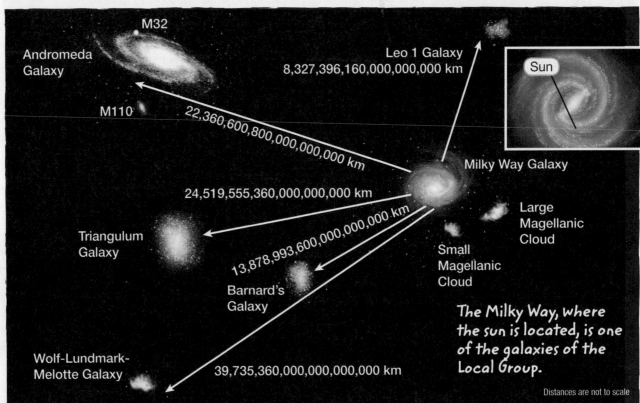

M32

Andromeda Galaxy

Leo 1 Galaxy
8,327,396,160,000,000,000,000 km

M110

22,360,600,800,000,000,000,000 km

Milky Way Galaxy

Sun

24,519,555,360,000,000,000,000 km

Triangulum Galaxy

Large Magellanic Cloud

13,878,993,600,000,000,000,000 km

Small Magellanic Cloud

Barnard's Galaxy

Wolf-Lundmark-Melotte Galaxy

39,735,360,000,000,000,000,000 km

*The Milky Way, where the sun is located, is one of the galaxies of the Local Group.*

Distances are not to scale

# Here Comes the Sun

**8 Identify** As you read the text, underline different discoveries that scientists have made about the sun.

## What are the physical properties of the sun?

Since early in human history, people have marveled at the sun. Civilizations have referred to the sun by different names. Gods and goddesses who represented the sun were worshipped in different cultures. In addition, early astronomical observatories were established to track the sun's apparent motion across the sky.

By the mid-19th century, astronomers had discovered that the sun was actually a hot ball of gas that is composed mostly of the elements hydrogen and helium. Scientists now know that the sun was born about 4.6 billion years ago. Every second, 4 million tons of solar matter is converted into energy. Of the light emitted from the sun, 41% is visible light, another 9% is ultraviolet light, and 50% is infrared radiation. And perhaps most important of all, without the sun, there would be no life on Earth.

| Sun Statistics | |
|---|---|
| Avg. dist. from Earth | 149.6 million km |
| Diameter | 1,391,000 km |
| Average density | 1.41 g/cm³ |
| Period of rotation | 25 days (equator); 35 days (poles) |
| Avg. surface temp. | 5,500 °C |
| Core temp. | 15,000,000 °C |
| Composition | 74% hydrogen, 25% helium, 1% other elements |

**Do the Math** You Try It

**9 Calculate** The diameter of Earth is 12,742 km. How many times greater is the sun's diameter than the diameter of Earth?

_____

_____

_____

A solar flare, which is shown in this image, is a sudden explosive release of energy in the sun's atmosphere.

# What is the structure of the sun?

The composition of the sun and Earth are different. However, the two bodies are similar in structure. Both are spheres. And both have a layered atmosphere and an interior composed of layers.

In the middle of the sun is the core. This is where energy is produced. From the core, energy is transported to the sun's surface through the radiative zone and the convective zone.

The sun's atmosphere has three layers—the photosphere, the chromosphere, and the corona. The sun's surface is the photosphere. Energy escapes the sun from this layer. The chromosphere is the middle layer of the sun's atmosphere. The temperature of the chromosphere rises with distance from the photosphere. The sun's outer atmosphere is the corona. The corona extends millions of kilometers into space.

**10 Analyze** How does the structure of the sun relate to energy production and transfer in the sun?

_____
_____
_____
_____
_____
_____

**Corona** The corona is the outer atmosphere of the sun. Temperatures in the corona may reach 2,000,000 °C.

**Chromosphere** The chromosphere is the middle layer of the sun's atmosphere. Temperatures in the chromosphere increase outward and reach a maximum of about 20,000 °C.

**Photosphere** The photosphere is the visible surface of the sun. It is the layer from which energy escapes into space. The photosphere has an average temperature of 5,500 °C.

**Convective Zone** The convective zone is the layer of the sun through which energy travels by convection from the radiative zone to the photosphere.

**Radiative Zone** The radiative zone is the layer of the sun through which energy is transferred away from the core by radiation.

**Core** The core is the very dense center of the sun. The core has a temperature of 15,000,000 °C, which is hot enough to cause the nuclear reactions that produce energy in the sun.

# Let's Get Together

## How does the sun produce energy?

Early in the 20th century, physicist Albert Einstein proposed that matter and energy are interchangeable. Matter can change into energy according to his famous equation $E = mc^2$. $E$ is energy, $m$ is mass, and $c$ is the speed of light. Because $c$ is such a large number, tiny amounts of matter can produce huge amounts of energy. Using Einstein's formula, scientists were able to explain the huge quantities of energy produced by the sun.

Scientists know that the sun generates energy through the process of *nuclear fusion*. **Nuclear fusion** is the process by which two or more low-mass atomic nuclei fuse to form a heavier nucleus. Nuclear fusion takes place in the core of stars. In stars that have core temperatures similar to the sun's, the fusion process that fuels the star starts with the fusion of two hydrogen nuclei. In older stars in which core temperatures are hotter than the sun's, the fusion process involves the fusion of helium into carbon.

### Think Outside the Book — Inquiry

11 **Debate** Einstein's equation $E = mc^2$ is probably the most famous equation in the world. With your classmates, debate the benefits and risks of technologies that rely on the conversion of matter to energy.

### Visualize It!

12 **Identify** Fill in the circles to label the particles in the diagrams.

P Proton
N Neutron

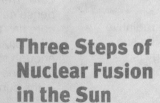

## Three Steps of Nuclear Fusion in the Sun

**Step 1: Deuterium** Two hydrogen nuclei (protons) collide. One proton emits particles and energy and then becomes a neutron. The proton and neutron combine to produce a heavy form of hydrogen called *deuterium*.

# By the Fusion of Hydrogen into Helium

The most common elements in the sun are hydrogen and helium. Under the crushing force of gravity, these gases are compressed and heated in the sun's core, where temperatures reach 15,000,000 °C. In the sun's core, hydrogen nuclei sometimes fuse to form a helium nucleus. This process takes three steps to complete. This three-step process is illustrated below.

Most of the time, when protons are on a collision course with other protons, their positive charges instantly repel them. The protons do not collide. But sometimes one proton will encounter another proton and, at that exact moment, turn into a neutron and eject an electron. This collision forms a nucleus that contains one proton and one neutron. This nucleus is an isotope of hydrogen called *deuterium*. The deuterium nucleus collides with another proton and forms a variety of helium called *helium-3*. Then, two helium-3 nuclei collide and form a helium-4 nucleus that has two protons and two neutrons. The remaining two protons are released back into the sun's core.

The entire chain of fusion reactions requires six hydrogen nuclei and results in one helium nucleus and two hydrogen nuclei. There are approximately $10^{38}$ collisions between hydrogen nuclei taking place in the sun's core every second, which keeps the sun shining.

**13 Identify** As you read the text, underline the steps in the nuclear fusion process in the sun.

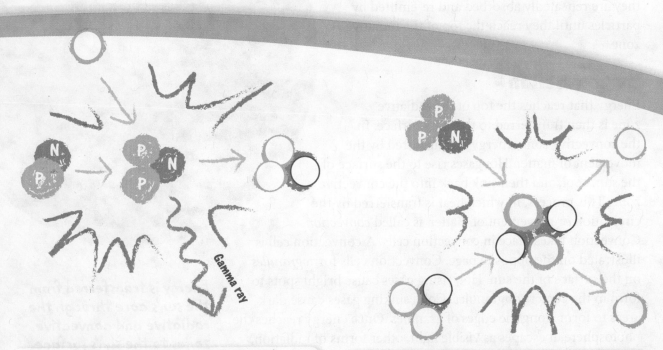

**Step 2: Helium-3** Deuterium combines with another hydrogen nucleus to form a variety of helium called *helium-3*. More energy, including gamma rays, is released.

**Step 3: Helium-4** Two helium-3 nuclei combine to form helium-4, which releases more energy and a pair of hydrogen nuclei (protons).

© Houghton Mifflin Harcourt Publishing Company

# Mixing It Up

## How is energy transferred to the sun's surface?

Energy is transferred to the surface of the sun by two different processes. Energy that is transferred from the sun's core through the radiative zone is transferred by the process of radiation. Energy that is transferred from the top of the radiative zone through the convective zone to the photosphere is transferred by the process of convection. Energy flow from the sun's core outward to the sun's surface by radiation and convection happens continuously.

### By Radiation

When energy leaves the sun's core, it moves into the radiative zone. Energy travels through the radiative zone in the form of electromagnetic waves. The process by which energy is transferred as electromagnetic waves is called *radiation*. The radiative zone is densely packed with particles such as hydrogen, helium, and free electrons. Therefore, electromagnetic waves cannot travel directly through the radiative zone. Instead, they are repeatedly absorbed and re-emitted by particles until they reach the top of the radiative zone.

### By Convection

Energy that reaches the top of the radiative zone is then transferred to the sun's surface. In the convective zone, energy is transferred by the movement of matter. Hot gases rise to the surface of the sun, cool, and then sink back into the convective zone. This process, in which heat is transferred by the circulation or movement of matter, is called *convection*. Convection takes place in convection cells. A convection cell is illustrated on the opposite page. Convection cells form *granules* on the surface of the sun. Hot, rising gases cause bright spots to form in the centers of granules. Cold, sinking gases cause dark areas to form along the edges of granules. Once energy reaches the photosphere, it escapes as visible light, other forms of radiation, heat, and wind.

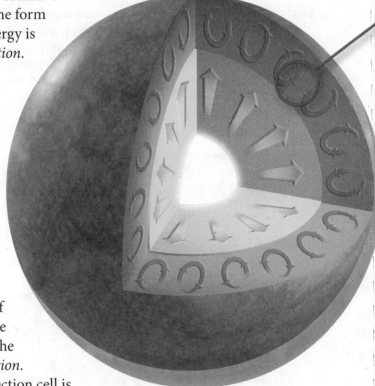

*Energy is transferred from the sun's core through the radiative and convective zones to the sun's surface.*

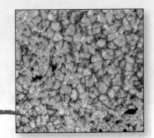

The tops of convection cells form granules on the sun's surface.

Hot, rising gases and colder, sinking gases form convection cells in the convective zone.

**14 Compare** How is energy transferred from the sun's core to the sun's surface in the radiative zone and in the convective zone?

| Radiative zone | Convective zone |
|---|---|
|  |  |
|  |  |
|  |  |
|  |  |
|  |  |

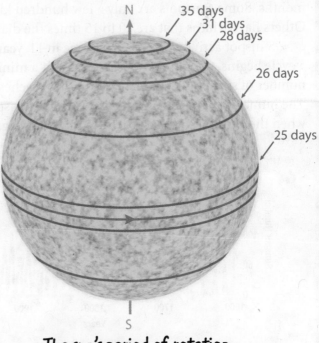

N

35 days
31 days
28 days

26 days

25 days

S

The sun's period of rotation varies with latitude.

# How does the sun rotate?

The sun rotates on its axis like other large bodies in the solar system. However, because the sun is a giant ball of gas, it does not rotate in the same way as a solid body like Earth does. Instead, the sun rotates faster at its equator than it does at higher latitudes. This kind of rotation is known as differential rotation. *Differential rotation* is the rotation of a body in which different parts of a body have different periods of rotation. Near the equator, the sun rotates once in about 25 days. However, at the poles, the sun rotates once in about 35 days.

Even stranger is the fact that the sun's interior does not rotate in the same way as the sun's surface does. Scientists think that the sun's core and radiative zone rotate together, at the same speed. Therefore, the sun's radiative zone and core rotate like Earth.

**15 Define** In your own words, define the term *differential rotation*.

_____

_____

_____

_____

# The Ring of Fire

## What is solar activity?

Solar activity refers to variations in the appearance or energy output of the sun. Solar activity includes dark areas that occur on the sun's surface known as *sunspots*. Solar activity also includes sudden explosive events on the sun's surface, which are called *solar flares*. Prominences are another form of solar activity. *Prominences* are vast loops of gases that extend into the sun's outer atmosphere.

## Sunspots

Dark areas that form on the surface of the sun are called **sunspots**. They are about 1,500 °C cooler than the areas that surround them. Sunspots are places where hot, convecting gases are prevented from reaching the sun's surface.

Sunspots can appear for periods of a few hours or a few months. Some sunspots are only a few hundred kilometers across. Others have widths that are 10 to 15 times the diameter of Earth.

Sunspot activity occurs on average in 11-year cycles. When a cycle begins, the number of sunspots is at a minimum. The number of sunspots then increases until it reaches a maximum. The number then begins to decrease. A new sunspot cycle begins when the sunspot number reaches a minimum again.

Sunspots, solar flares, and prominences are three kinds of solar activity that occur on the sun's surface.

Sunspot

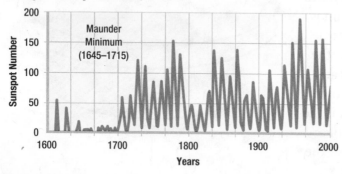

Sunspot Activity from 1600 to 2000

Maunder Minimum (1645–1715)

Sunspot Number

Years

### Do the Math  You Try It

**16 Analyze** The sunspot range is the difference between the maximum number of sunspots and the minimum number of sunspots for a certain period of time. To find this range, subtract the minimum number of sunspots from the maximum number of sunspots. What is the range of sunspot activity between 1700 and 1800?

_____

_____

_____

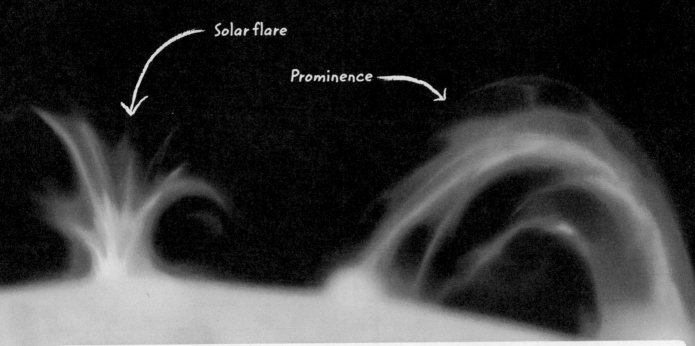

Solar flare

Prominence

## Solar Flares

Solar flares appear as very bright spots on the sun's photosphere. A **solar flare** is an explosive release of energy that can extend outward as far as the sun's outer atmosphere. During a solar flare, enormous numbers of high-energy particles are ejected at near the speed of light. Radiation is released across the entire electromagnetic spectrum, from radio waves to x-rays and gamma rays. Temperatures within solar flares reach millions of degrees Celsius.

## Prominences

Huge loops of relatively cool gas that extend outward from the photosphere thousands of kilometers into the outer atmosphere are called **prominences**. Several objects the size of Earth could fit inside a loop of a prominence. The gases in prominences are cooler than the surrounding atmosphere.

Prominences generally last from several hours to a day. However, some prominences can last for as long as several months.

**17 Compare** Use the Venn diagram below to compare solar flares and prominences.

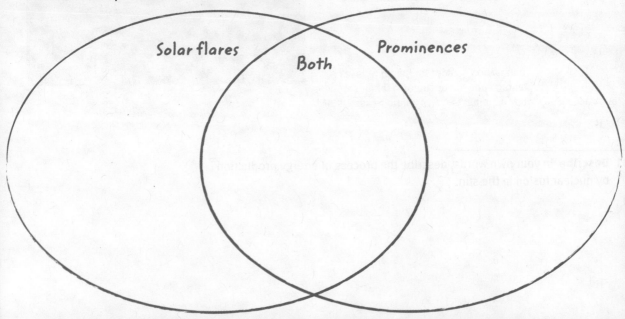

Solar flares    Both    Prominences

# Visual Summary

To complete this summary, fill in the blanks with the correct word or phrase. Then use the key below to check your answers. You can use this page to review the main concepts of the lesson.

**The Sun**

**The sun is located at the center of the solar system.**

**18** What are the paths of objects around the sun called?

_____

**The sun is composed of layers.**

**19** Identify the six layers of the sun, beginning with the innermost layer.

_____

_____

_____

_____

**Energy is transferred from the sun's core to the photosphere.**

**20** By what process is the sun's energy transported in layer A?

_____

By what process is the sun's energy transported in layer B?

_____

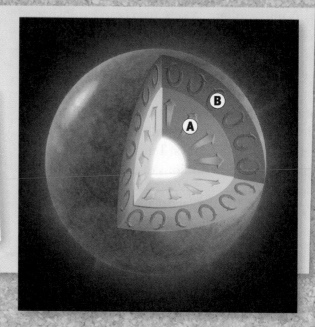

**21 Describe** In your own words, describe the process of energy production by nuclear fusion in the sun.

# Lesson Review

## Vocabulary

Fill in the blank with the term that best completes the following sentences.

**1** The process by which two or more low-mass atomic nuclei fuse to form a heavier nucleus is called _____.

**2** A _____ is a dark area on the surface of the sun that is cooler than the surrounding areas.

**3** A _____ is a loop of relatively cool gas that extends above the photosphere.

## Key Concepts

In the following table, write the name of the correct layer next to the definition.

| Definition | Layer |
|---|---|
| **4 Identify** What is the layer of the sun from which energy escapes into space? | |
| **5 Identify** What is the layer of the sun in which energy is produced? | |
| **6 Identify** What is the layer of the sun through which energy is transferred away from the core by radiation? | |

**7 Describe** What is the composition of the sun?

_____

_____

**8 Describe** Where in the universe is the sun located?

_____

_____

_____

## Critical Thinking

Use the illustration to answer the following questions.

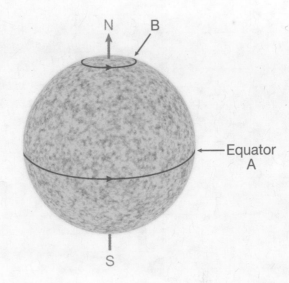

**9 Determine** How many days does it take for the sun to spin once on its axis at location A? How many days does it take for the sun to spin once on its axis at location B?

_____

_____

**10 Compare** How is the rotation of the sun different from the rotation of Earth?

_____

_____

_____

_____

**11 Explain** In your own words, explain how energy is transported from the core to the surface of the sun by radiation and by convection.

_____

_____

_____

_____

# My Notes

# The Terrestrial Planets

**ESSENTIAL QUESTION**

## What is known about the terrestrial planets?

By the end of this lesson, you should be able to describe some of the properties of the terrestrial planets and how the properties of Mercury, Venus, and Mars differ from the properties of Earth.

Mars

Earth

Venus

Mercury

The terrestrial planets are the four planets that are closest to the sun. Distances between the planets shown here are not to scale.

sun

**TEKS** **6.11A** describe the physical properties, locations, and movements of the Sun, planets, Galilean moons, meteors, asteroids, and comets

**Engage Your Brain**

**1 Define** Circle the term that best completes the following sentences.

*Venus/Earth/Mars* is the largest terrestrial planet.

*Mercury/Venus/Mars* has clouds that rain sulfuric acid on the planet.

Huge dust storms sweep across the surface of *Mercury/Venus/Mars*.

*Venus/Earth/Mars* is the most geologically active of the terrestrial planets.

*Mercury/Venus/Earth* has the thinnest atmosphere of the terrestrial planets.

**2 Identify** What are properties of Earth that make it a special place in the solar system? Share and discuss your answer with a partner.

_____
_____
_____
_____

**Active Reading**

**3 Synthesize** Many English words have their roots in other languages. Use the Latin words below to make an educated guess about the meaning of the word *astronomy*.

| Latin word | Meaning |
|---|---|
| astrón | star |
| nomos | law |

**Example sentence**
Some students who are interested in the night sky enter college to study <u>astronomy</u>.

astronomy:

_____
_____

**Vocabulary Terms**

• terrestrial planet
• astronomical unit

**4 Apply** As you learn the definition of each vocabulary term in this lesson, create your own definition or sketch to help you remember the meaning of the term.

# Extreme to the Core

**5 Identify** As you read the text, underline important characteristics of the planet Mercury.

## Statistics Table for Mercury

| | |
|---|---|
| Distance from the sun | 0.39 AU |
| Period of rotation (length of Mercury day) | 58 days 15.5 h |
| Period of revolution (length of Mercury year) | 88 days |
| Tilt of axis | 0° |
| Diameter | 4,879 km |
| Density | 5.44 g/cm³ |
| Surface temperature | -184 °C to 427 °C |
| Surface gravity | 38% of Earth's gravity |
| Number of satellites | 0 |

## What are the terrestrial planets?

The **terrestrial planets** are the four small, dense, rocky planets that orbit closest to the sun. In order by distance from the sun, these planets are Mercury, Venus, Earth, and Mars. The terrestrial planets have similar compositions and consist of an outer crust, a central core, and a mantle that lies between the crust and core.

## What is known about Mercury?

Mercury (MUR•kyuh•ree) is the planet about which we know the least. Until NASA's *Mariner 10* spacecraft flew by Mercury in 1974, the planet was seen as a blotchy, dark ball of rock. Today, scientists know that the planet's heavily cratered, moon-like surface is composed largely of volcanic rock and hides a massive iron core.

Mercury orbits only 0.39 AU from the sun. The letters *AU* stand for *astronomical unit*, which is the term astronomers use to measure distances in the solar system. One **astronomical unit** equals the average distance between the sun and Earth, or approximately 150 million km. Therefore, Mercury lies nearly halfway between the sun and Earth.

Although this may look like the moon, it is actually the heavily cratered surface of the planet Mercury.

# Mercury Has the Most Extreme Temperature Range in the Solar System

On Earth, a day lasts 24 h. On Mercury, a day lasts almost 59 Earth days. What does this fact have to do with temperatures on Mercury? It means that temperatures on that part of Mercury's surface that is receiving sunlight can build for more than 29 days. When it is day on Mercury, temperatures can rise to 427 °C, a temperature that is hot enough to melt certain metals. It also means that temperatures on the part of Mercury's surface that is in darkness can fall for more than 29 days. When it is night on Mercury, temperatures can drop to –184 °C. This means that surface temperatures on Mercury can change by as much as 600 °C between day and night. This is the greatest difference between high and low temperatures in the solar system.

## Mercury Has a Large Iron Core

Mercury is the smallest planet in the solar system. It has a diameter of only 4,879 km at its equator. Amazingly, Mercury's central core is thought to be around 3,600 km in diameter, which accounts for most of the planet's interior. Scientists originally thought that Mercury had a core of solid iron. However, by observing changes in Mercury's spin as it orbits the sun, astronomers now think that the core is at least partially molten. Why is the core so large? Some scientists think that Mercury may have been struck by another object in the distant past and lost most of the rock that surrounded the core. Other scientists think that long ago the sun vaporized the planet's surface and blasted it away into space.

### Think Outside the Book

**6 Plan** You are an astronaut who will be exploring Mercury. What equipment would you take to Mercury to help you survive?

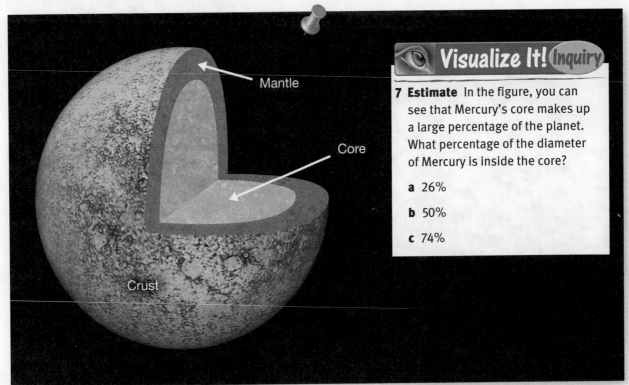

Mantle

Core

Crust

### Visualize It! Inquiry

**7 Estimate** In the figure, you can see that Mercury's core makes up a large percentage of the planet. What percentage of the diameter of Mercury is inside the core?

a 26%

b 50%

c 74%

# Harsh Planet

## What is known about Venus?

Science-fiction writers once imagined Venus (VEE•nuhs) to be a humid planet with lush, tropical forests. Nothing could be further from the truth. On Venus, sulfuric acid rain falls on a surface that is not much different from the inside of an active volcano.

## Venus Is Similar to Earth in Size and Mass

Venus has often been called "Earth's twin." At 12,104 km, the diameter of Venus is 95% the diameter of Earth. Venus's mass is around 80% of Earth's. And the gravity that you would experience on Venus is 89% of the gravity on Earth.

The rotation of Venus is different from the rotation of Earth. Earth has prograde rotation. *Prograde rotation* is the counterclockwise spin of a planet about its axis as seen from above the planet's north pole. Venus, however, has retrograde rotation. *Retrograde rotation* is the clockwise spin of a planet about its axis as seen from above its north pole.

Venus differs from Earth not only in the direction in which it spins on its axis. It takes more time for Venus to rotate once about its axis than it takes for the planet to revolve once around the sun. Venus has the slowest period of rotation in the solar system.

Venus has landforms such as highlands and plains, volcanoes, and impact craters.

### Statistics Table for Venus

| | |
|---|---|
| Distance from the sun | 0.72 AU |
| Period of rotation | 243 days (retrograde rotation) |
| Period of revolution | 225 days |
| Tilt of axis | 177.4° |
| Diameter | 12,104 km |
| Density | 5.20 g/cm³ |
| Average surface temperature | 465 °C |
| Surface gravity | 89% of Earth's gravity |
| Number of satellites | 0 |

Gula Mons volcano is approximately 300 km wide and 3 km high.

Impact crater Cunitz, which is 48.5 km wide, was named after Maria Cunitz, a 17th-century European astronomer and mathematician.

## Venus Has Craters and Volcanoes

In 1990, the powerful radar beams of NASA's *Magellan* spacecraft pierced the dense atmosphere of Venus. This gave us our most detailed look ever at the planet's surface. There are 168 volcanoes on Venus that are larger than 100 km in diameter. Thousands of volcanoes have smaller diameters. Venus's surface is also cratered. These craters are as much as 280 km in diameter. The sizes and locations of the craters on Venus suggest that around 500 million years ago something happened to erase all of the planet's older craters. Scientists are still puzzled about how this occurred. But volcanic activity could have covered the surface of the planet in one huge outpouring of magma.

## The Atmosphere of Venus Is Toxic

Venus may have started out like Earth, with oceans and water running across its surface. However, after billions of years of solar heating, Venus has become a harsh world. Surface temperatures on Venus are hotter than those on Mercury. Temperatures average around 465 °C. Over time, carbon dioxide gas has built up in the atmosphere. Sunlight that strikes Venus's surface warms the ground. However, carbon dioxide in the atmosphere traps this energy, which causes temperatures near the surface to remain high.

Sulfuric acid rains down onto Venus's surface, and the pressure of the atmosphere is at least 90 times that of Earth's atmosphere. No human—or machine—could survive for long under these conditions. Venus is a world that is off limits to human explorers and perhaps all but the hardiest robotic probes.

**9 Contrast** How is the landscape of Venus different from the landscape of Earth?

_____

_____

_____

_____

_____

 Active Reading

**10 Identify** As you read the text, underline those factors that make Venus an unlikely place for life to exist.

# No Place Like Home

## What is special about Earth?

As far as scientists know, Earth is the only planet in the solar system that has the combination of factors needed to support life. Life as we know it requires liquid water and an energy source. Earth has both. Earth's atmosphere contains the oxygen that animals need to breathe. Matter is continuously cycled between the environment and living things. And a number of ecosystems exist on Earth that different organisms can inhabit.

## Earth Has Abundant Water and Life

Earth's vast liquid-water oceans and moderate temperatures provided the ideal conditions for life to emerge and flourish. Around 3.5 billion years ago, organisms that produced food by photosynthesis appeared in Earth's oceans. During the process of making food, these organisms produced oxygen. By 560 million years ago, more complex life forms arose that could use oxygen to release energy from food. Today, the total number of species of organisms that inhabit Earth is thought to be anywhere between 5 million and 30 million.

**Active Reading**

**11 Identify** As you read the text, underline characteristics that make Earth special.

| Statistics Table for Earth | |
|---|---|
| Distance from the sun | 1.0 AU |
| Period of rotation | 23 h 56 min |
| Period of revolution | 365.3 days |
| Tilt of axis | 23.45° |
| Diameter | 12,756 km |
| Density | 5.52 g/cm³ |
| Temperature | -89 °C to 58 °C |
| Surface gravity | 100% of Earth's gravity |
| Number of satellites | 1 |

From space, Earth presents an entirely different scene from that of the other terrestrial planets. Clouds in the atmosphere, blue bodies of water, and green landmasses are all clues to the fact that Earth is a special place.

© Houghton Mifflin Harcourt Publishing Company • Image Credits: ©Astromujoff/The Image Bank/Getty Images

## Earth Is Geologically Active

Earth is the only terrestrial planet whose surface is divided into tectonic plates. These plates move around Earth's surface, which causes the continents to change positions over long periods of time. Tectonic plate motion, together with weathering and erosion, has erased most surface features older than 500 million years.

## Humans Have Set Foot on the Moon

Between 1969 and 1972, 12 astronauts landed on the moon. They are the only humans to have set foot on another body in the solar system. They encountered a surface gravity that is only about one-sixth that of Earth. Because of the moon's lower gravity, astronauts could not walk normally. If they did, they would fly up in the air and fall over.

Like Mercury, the moon's surface is heavily cratered. It is estimated that about 500,000 craters larger than 1 km dot the moon. There are large dark areas on the moon's surface. These are plains of solidified lava. There are also light-colored areas. These are the lunar highlands.

The moon rotates about its axis in the same time it orbits Earth. Therefore, it keeps the same side facing Earth. During a lunar day, which is a little more than 27 Earth days, the daytime surface temperature can reach 127 °C. The nighttime surface temperature can fall to −173 °C.

The moon is the only other body in the solar system where humans have been.

| Statistics Table for the Moon | |
|---|---|
| Distance from Earth | 384,400 km (0.0026 AU) |
| Period of rotation | 27.3 days |
| Period of revolution | 27.3 days |
| Axial tilt | 1.5° |
| Diameter | 3,476 km |
| Density | 3.34 g/cm³ |
| Temperature | −173° C to 127° C |
| Surface gravity | 16.5% of Earth's gravity |

 **Visualize It!**

**12 Identify** In the image, circle any signs of life that you see.

# Is It Alive?

### Think Outside the Book

**13 Debate** Research the surface features of the northern and southern hemispheres of Mars. Decide which hemisphere you would rather explore. With your class, debate the merits of exploring one hemisphere versus the other.

## What is known about Mars?

A fleet of spacecraft is now in orbit around Mars (MARZ) studying the planet. Space rovers have also investigated the surface of Mars. These remote explorers have discovered a planet with an atmosphere that is 100 times thinner than Earth's and temperatures that are little different from the inside of a freezer. They have seen landforms on Mars that are larger than any found on Earth. And these unmanned voyagers have photographed surface features on Mars that are characteristic of erosion and deposition by water.

### Mars Is a Rocky, Red Planet

The surface of Mars is better known than that of any other planet in the solar system except Earth. It is composed largely of dark volcanic rock. Rocks and boulders litter the surface of Mars. Some boulders can be as large as a house. A powdery dust covers Martian rocks and boulders. This dust is the product of the chemical breakdown of rocks rich in iron minerals. This is what gives the Martian soil its orange-red color.

### Statistics Table for Mars

| | |
|---|---|
| Distance from the sun | 1.52 AU |
| Period of rotation | 24 h 37 min |
| Period of revolution | 1.88 y |
| Tilt of axis | 25.3° |
| Diameter | 6,792 km |
| Density | 3.93 g/cm³ |
| Temperature | -140°C to 20°C |
| Surface gravity | 37% of Earth's gravity |
| Number of satellites | 2 |

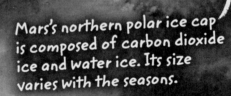

Mars's northern polar ice cap is composed of carbon dioxide ice and water ice. Its size varies with the seasons.

## Mars Has Interesting Surface Features

The surface of Mars varies from hemisphere to hemisphere. The northern hemisphere appears to have been covered by lava flows. The southern hemisphere is heavily cratered.

Large volcanoes are found on Mars. At 27 km high and 600 km across, Olympus Mons (uh•LIM•puhs MAHNZ) is the largest volcano and mountain in the solar system. Mars also has very deep valleys and canyons. The canyon system Valles Marineris (VAL•less mar•uh•NAIR•iss) runs from west to east along the Martian equator. It is about 4,000 km long, 500 km wide, and up to 10 km deep. It is the largest canyon in the solar system.

Olympus Mons is the largest volcano in the solar system.

## Mars Has a Thin Atmosphere

Mars has a very thin atmosphere that is thought to have been thicker in the past. Mars may have gradually lost its atmosphere to the solar wind. Or a body or bodies that collided with Mars may have caused much of the atmosphere to have been blown away.

Unlike Earth, Mars's atmosphere is composed mostly of carbon dioxide. During the Martian winter, temperatures at the planet's poles grow cold enough for carbon dioxide to freeze into a thin coating. During the summer, when temperatures grow warmer, this coating vanishes.

Winds on Mars can blow with enough force to pick up dust particles from the planet's surface. When this happens, giant dust storms can form. At times, these storms cover the entire planet.

**Active Reading** 14 **Explain** What are two possible reasons why the atmosphere on Mars is so thin?

_____

_____

_____

Hebes Chasma is a 6,000 m–deep depression that is located in the Valles Marineris region.

15 **Compare** Compare and contrast the physical properties of Mars to the physical properties of Earth.

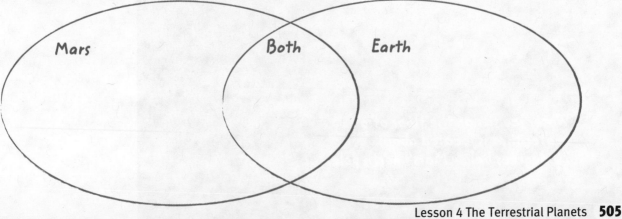

Mars        Both        Earth

# Liquid Water Once Flowed on Mars

A number of features on Mars provide evidence that liquid water once flowed on the planet's surface. Many of these features have been struck by asteroids. These asteroid impacts have left behind craters that scientists can use to find the approximate dates of these features. Scientists estimate that many of these features, such as empty river basins, existed on Mars more than 3 billion years ago. Since then, little erosion has taken place that would cause these features to disappear.

In 2000, the *Mars Global Surveyor* took before-and-after images of a valley wall on Mars. Scientists observed the unmistakable trace of a liquid substance that had flowed out of the valley wall and into the valley. Since 2000, many similar features have been seen. The best explanation of these observations is that water is found beneath Mars's surface. At times, this water leaks out onto the Martian surface like spring water on Earth.

This image shows gullies on the wall of a Martian crater. Water that may be stored close to the Martian surface has run downhill into the crater.

 **Visualize It!**

**16 Describe** How do the features in the image at the right indicate that liquid water once flowed on Mars?

_____

_____

_____

_____

Water ice sits on the floor of a crater that is located about 20 degrees below Mars's north pole.

# Roving Mars

The Mars Exploration Rovers *Spirit* and *Opportunity* landed safely on Mars in January 2004. The 185-kg rovers were designed to explore Mars for 90 days. However, in 2009, both rovers were still exploring Mars. They are searching for rocks and soils that indicate that water once flowed on the Martian surface. The rovers are also looking for environments in which life may have existed.

## The Martian Surface

Mars's surface is made up mostly of the volcanic rock *basalt*, which is also found on Earth. Boulders of basalt cover the Martian landscape.

## Testing the Rovers on Earth

Before leaving Earth, the rovers were tested under conditions that were similar to those that they would encounter on the Martian surface.

## Collecting Data on Mars

The Mars rover *Spirit* took this picture of itself collecting data from the Martian surface.

## Extend

Inquiry

**17 Infer** What advantages would a robotic explorer, such as *Spirit* or *Opportunity*, have over a manned mission to Mars?

**18 Hypothesize** What kind of evidence would the Mars Exploration Rovers be looking for that indicated that water once flowed on Mars?

# Visual Summary

To complete this summary, write the answers to the questions on the lines. Then, use the key below to check your answers. You can use this page to review the main concepts of the lesson.

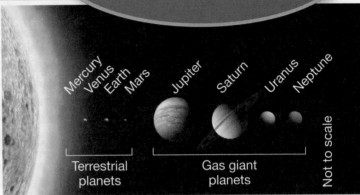

Mercury  Venus  Earth  Mars      Jupiter      Saturn      Uranus  Neptune

Terrestrial planets        Gas giant planets        Not to scale

**Mercury orbits near the sun.**

**19** Why do temperatures on Mercury vary so much?

_____

_____

_____

**Venus is covered with clouds.**

**20** Why is Venus's surface temperature so high?

_____

_____

_____

**Earth has abundant life.**

**21** What factors support life on Earth?

_____

_____

_____

**Mars is a rocky planet.**

**22** What makes up the surface of Mars?

_____

_____

_____

Answers: 19 Long periods of sunlight and darkness cause temperatures to rise and fall dramatically; 20 Carbon dioxide in Venus's atmosphere traps energy, which causes temperatures near the surface to remain high; 21 liquid water, breathable air, and a source of energy; 22 dark volcanic rock (basalt), red-orange dust

**23 Compare** How are important properties of Mercury, Venus, and Mars different from important properties of Earth?

_____

# Lesson Review

## Vocabulary

Fill in the blanks with the terms that best complete the following sentences.

**1** The _____ are the dense planets nearest the sun.

**2** An _____ is equal to the distance between the sun and Earth.

## Key Concepts

In the following table, write the name of the correct planet next to the property of that planet.

| Properties | Planet |
|---|---|
| **3 Identify** Which planet has the highest surface temperature in the solar system? | |
| **4 Identify** Which planet has very large dust storms? | |
| **5 Identify** Which planet is the most heavily cratered of the terrestrial planets? | |
| **6 Identify** Which planet has the highest surface gravity of the terrestrial planets? | |

**7 Explain** What is the difference between prograde rotation and retrograde rotation?

_____

_____

_____

_____

**8 Describe** What characteristics of Venus's atmosphere make the planet so harsh?

_____

_____

_____

## Critical Thinking

Use this table to answer the following questions.

| Planet | Period of rotation | Period of revolution |
|---|---|---|
| Mercury | 58 days 15.5 h | 88 days |
| Venus | 243 days (retrograde rotation) | 225 days |
| Earth | 23 h 56 min | 365.3 days |
| Mars | 24 h 37 min | 1.88 y |

**9 Analyze** Which planet rotates most slowly about its axis?

_____

**10 Analyze** Which planet revolves around the sun in less time than it rotates around its axis?

_____

**11 Analyze** Which planet revolves around the sun in the shortest amount of time?

_____

**12 Explain** Why are the temperatures on each of the other terrestrial planets more extreme than the temperatures on Earth?

_____

_____

_____

_____

_____

_____

_____

_____

_____

_____

_____

_____

# My Notes

# A. Wesley Ward

## GEOLOGIST

Geologist Dr. Wesley Ward lives in a desert region of the western United States. The living conditions are sometimes harsh, but the region offers some fascinating places to study. For a geologist like Dr. Ward, who tries to understand the geologic processes on another planet, the desert may be the only place to be.

Dr. Ward was a leading scientist on the Mars Pathfinder mission. The surface of Mars is a lot like the western desert. Dr. Ward helped scientists map the surface of Mars and plan for the Pathfinder's landing. Using data from the Pathfinder, Dr. Ward studied how Martian winds have shaped the planet's landscape. This information will help scientists better understand what conditions are like on the surface of Mars. More importantly, the information will guide scientists in choosing future landings sites. Dr. Ward's work may determine whether human beings can safely land on Mars.

You could say that Dr. Ward's scientific career has hit the big-time. He helped in the making of the Discovery Channel's documentary *Planet Storm*. The program features scientists describing weather conditions on other planets. Dr. Ward and the scientists worked with special effects artists to simulate what these conditions might feel like to astronauts.

The Mars Pathfinder rover *Sojourner* was designed to withstand the fierce Martian dust storms, such as the one shown.

## Social Studies Connection

The Pathfinder is not the first attempt scientists have made to explore the surface of Mars. In fact, scientists in different countries have been exploring Mars for over 50 years. Research other missions to Mars and attempts to send rovers to Mars, and present your research in a timeline. Remember to identify where the mission started, what its goals were, and whether it achieved them.

# JOB BOARD

## Science Writer

**What You'll Do:** Research and write articles, press releases, reports, and sometimes books about scientific discoveries and issues for a wide range of readers. Science writers who write for a broad audience must work to find the stories behind the science in order to keep readers interested.

**Where You Might Work:** For a magazine, a newspaper, or a museum, or independently as a freelance writer specializing in science. Some science writers may work for universities, research foundations, government agencies, or non-profit science and health organizations.

**Education:** A bachelor's degree in a scientific field, with courses in English or writing.

**Other Job Requirements:** Strong communications skills. Science writers must not only understand science, but must also be able to interview scientists and to write clear, interesting stories.

## Telescope Mechanic

**What You'll Do:** Keep telescopes at large observatories working, climbing heights of up to 30 meters to make sure the telescope's supports are in good shape, which includes welding new components, cleaning, and sweeping.

**Where You Might Work:** A large observatory or research institution with large telescopes, possibly in the desert.

**Education:** A high-school diploma with some experience performing maintenance on delicate equipment.

**Other Job Requirements.** Strong communications skills to consult with other mechanics and the scientists who use the telescopes. Mechanics must be able to weld and to use tools. Mechanics must also have good vision (or wear glasses to correct their vision), and be able to climb up high and carry heavy equipment.

## PEOPLE IN SCIENCE NEWS

# Anthony Wesley

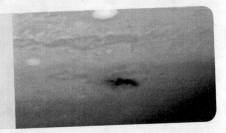

### Witnessing Impact

Anthony Wesley was sitting in his backyard in Australia on July 19, 2009, gazing at Jupiter through his custom-built telescope, when he saw a dark spot or "scar" on the planet (shown). Wesley sent his tip to the National Aeronautics and Space Administration (NASA).

NASA has much more powerful telescopes than a citizen scientist usually does. Scientists at NASA confirmed that a comet had crashed into the planet, leaving a scar. Coincidentally, this crash happened almost exactly 15 years after another comet crashed into Jupiter.

# The Gas Giant Planets

**ESSENTIAL QUESTION**

## What is known about the gas giant planets?

By the end of this lesson, you should be able to describe some of the properties of the gas giant planets and how these properties differ from the physical properties of Earth.

The gas giant planets are the four planets that orbit farthest from the sun. Distances between the planets shown here are not to scale.

Neptune

Uranus

Saturn

Jupiter

**TEKS** **6.11A** describe the physical properties, locations, and movements of the Sun, planets, Galilean moons, meteors, asteroids, and comets

## Engage Your Brain

**1 Predict** Circle the term that best completes the following sentences.

*Jupiter/Saturn/Uranus* is the largest planet in the solar system.

*Jupiter/Uranus/Neptune* has the strongest winds in the solar system.

*Saturn/Uranus/Neptune* has the largest ring system of the gas giant planets.

*Jupiter/Saturn/Neptune* has more moons than any other planet in the solar system.

*Jupiter/Uranus/Neptune* is tilted on its side as it orbits the sun.

**2 Identify** What are the objects that circle Saturn? What do you think they are made of?

_____

_____

_____

## Active Reading

**3 Apply** Many scientific words, such as *gas*, also have everyday meanings. Use context clues to write your own definition for each meaning of the word *gas*.

**Example sentence**
Vehicles, such as cars, trucks, and buses, use gas as a fuel.

**gas:**

_____

_____

**Example sentence**
Gas is the most common state of matter in Earth's atmosphere.

**gas:**

_____

_____

_____

### Vocabulary Terms

- gas giant
- Galilean moons
- planetary ring

**4 Apply** With a classmate, identify the paragraphs in this lesson that contain the highlighted vocabulary terms. Take turns reading these paragraphs to each other. When it is your turn to listen, take notes. After each of you has taken notes, compare the main points of each paragraph.

# A Giant Among

Jupiter's high winds circle the planet and cause cloud bands to form. Storms, such as the Great Red Spot shown here, form between the cloud bands.

## Statistics Table for Jupiter

| | |
|---|---|
| Distance from the sun | 5.20 AU |
| Period of rotation | 9 h 55 min |
| Period of revolution | 11.86 y |
| Tilt of axis | 3.13° |
| Diameter | 142,984 km |
| Density | 1.33 g/cm³ |
| Mean surface temperature | −150 °C |
| Surface gravity | 253% of Earth's gravity |
| Number of satellites | 66 |

### Active Reading

**5 Identify** As you read the text, underline important physical properties of the planet Jupiter.

## What is a gas giant planet?

Jupiter, Saturn, Uranus, and Neptune are the gas giant planets. They orbit far from the sun. **Gas giants** have deep, massive gas atmospheres, which are made up mostly of hydrogen and helium. These gases become denser the deeper you travel inside. All of the gas giants are large. Neptune, the smallest gas giant planet, is big enough to hold 58 Earths within its volume. The gas giant planets are cold. Mean surface temperatures range from about −150 °C on Jupiter to −210 °C on Neptune.

## What is known about Jupiter?

Jupiter (JOO•pih•ter) is the largest planet in the solar system. Its volume can contain more than 1,300 Earths. Jupiter is also the most massive planet. Its mass is twice that of the other seven planets combined. Jupiter has the highest surface gravity in the solar system at 253% that of Earth. And although all of the gas giant planets rotate rapidly, Jupiter rotates the fastest of all. Its period of rotation is just under 10 h. A day on Jupiter is less than half of a day on Earth. Wind speeds on Jupiter are high. They can reach 540 km/h. By contrast, Earth's wind-speed record is 372 km/h.

# Giants!

## Jupiter Has the Deepest Atmosphere of Any Planet

Jupiter may have a small, rocky core at its center. However, its atmosphere accounts for most of the planet's huge volume and mass. Earth's atmosphere is much thinner and composed of mostly nitrogen and oxygen. In addition to hydrogen and helium, Jupiter's atmosphere contains traces of ammonia, methane, water, and other substances. As the depth of the atmosphere increases, the pressure becomes much greater than the atmospheric pressure on Earth. The pressure is so great that hydrogen gas turns into liquid hydrogen.

Fast-moving winds in Jupiter's atmosphere cause clouds to form bands that circle the planet. The higher, light-colored clouds are made mostly of frozen ammonia. The clouds in the darker-colored bands are located lower in the atmosphere. Scientists do not yet know what causes their reddish color.

The banded appearance of Jupiter's atmosphere is caused by strong winds that blow clouds in opposite directions.

**6 Contrast** Compare Jupiter's atmosphere to the atmosphere of Earth.

_____

_____

_____

## Huge Storms Travel Across Jupiter's Surface

Jupiter has some of the strangest weather conditions in the solar system. The winds on Jupiter circle the planet. Clouds are stretched into bands that run from east to west. Storms appear as white or red spots between cloud bands. The best known of these storms is the Great Red Spot. The east–west width of this storm is three times the diameter of Earth. Incredibly, astronomers on Earth have observed this storm for nearly 350 years. Recently, scientists observed three storms combine to form the Little Red Spot.

Wind speeds in the storms on Jupiter are faster than the winds that travel around the planet. In the Little Red Spot, wind speeds have reached about 620 km/hr.

### Think Outside the Book

**7 Model** Select one of the following topics about weather on Jupiter to research: belts and zones; jet streams; storms. Present your findings to the rest of the class in the form of a model. Your model may be handcrafted, may be an art piece, or may be a computer presentation.

Sizes and distances are not to scale.

# What are the Galilean moons?

Jupiter has the most moons of any planet in the solar system. Scientists have discovered more than 60 satellites orbiting Jupiter. The **Galilean moons** (gal·uh·LAY·uhn MOONZ) are the four largest moons of Jupiter. In order of closest to farthest from Jupiter, these moons are Io, Europa, Ganymede, and Callisto. They were first observed by the Italian astronomer Galileo Galilei in 1610 using a weak telescope.

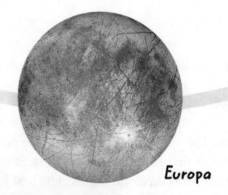

Jupiter

## Io

Io is the third largest of Jupiter's moons. The internal structure of Io is not completely known. However, it does have an iron core.

Io is stretched and squeezed by the gravitational attraction of Jupiter and the three other Galilean moons. These forces generate huge amounts of heat and pressure within Io. In fact, Io is more volcanically active than any other object in the solar system. Its surface is covered with volcanoes, some of which are erupting.

**Active Reading** **8 Identify** What physical feature on Io is also found on the surface of Earth?

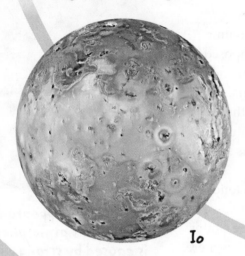

Io

## Europa

Europa is the second-closest Galilean moon to Jupiter. It is the fourth-largest moon of Jupiter. It has a layered, rocky structure and may have a small, metallic core. The surface of Europa is mostly flat with few craters, indicating that the moon is geologically active. Dark streaks cover the moon's surface. These streaks may be caused by volcanic eruptions or by geysers.

Images from spacecraft indicate that the surface of Europa is covered by ice. Data have led scientists to conclude that an ocean of liquid water may be located beneath the moon's surface. If so, Europa may be the only body in the solar system, other than Earth, with the conditions necessary to support life as we know it.

Europa

**Visualize It!**

**9 Explain** What may be the origin of the dark streaks on Europa?

_____

_____

## Ganymede

Ganymede (GAN•uh•meed) is the largest of Jupiter's moons. In fact, it is the largest satellite in the solar system. It is even bigger than the planet Mercury. Io and Europa are closer to Jupiter than Ganymede is. Ganymede has a layered internal structure with an icy crust, rocky mantle, and molten iron core. Because of its core, Ganymede is the only moon in the solar system that produces its own magnetic field. The surface of Ganymede is heavily cratered and likely has been altered by tectonic activity. Scientists think that the planet's icy crust flows slowly over time.

Ganymede

## Callisto

Callisto is the farthest Galilean moon from Jupiter. It is second largest of Jupiter's moons and is about the size of Mercury. Unlike Ganymede, Callisto does not appear to have a layered internal structure. Its composition is about 60 percent rock and 40 percent ice. Callisto is the most heavily cratered object in the solar system. Valhalla, the largest crater on Callisto, is about 3,000 km in diameter. Callisto does not show much current geologic activity. Its craters are about 4 billion years old. So Callisto has the oldest surface features in the solar system.

Callisto

# What is the motion of the Galilean moons?

Three of the Galilean moons—Io, Europa, and Ganymede—affect each other's orbits. Because of forces between the moons and Jupiter, the ratio of the number of orbits the moons complete in the same amount of time is exactly 1:2:4. In other words, in the time it takes Ganymede to orbit Jupiter once, Europa has orbited Jupiter twice, and Io has orbited Jupiter four times.

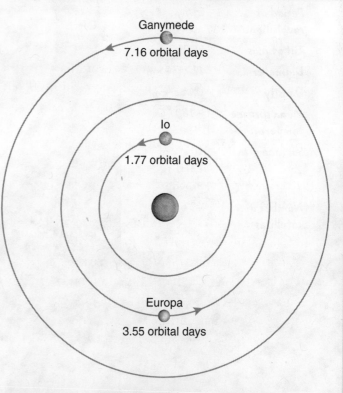

Ganymede
7.16 orbital days

Io
1.77 orbital days

Europa
3.55 orbital days

 **Do the Math**

**10 Calculate** How many orbits will Ganymede have made after Europa orbits Jupiter once and Io orbits Jupiter twice?

_____

_____

© Houghton Mifflin Harcourt Publishing Company • Image Credits: (t) ©Science Source/Photo Researchers, Inc. (c) ©Science Source/Photo Researchers, Inc.

# King of the Rings!

## What is known about Saturn?

Saturn (SAT•ern) is a near-twin to Jupiter. It is the second-largest gas giant planet and is made mostly of hydrogen and helium. About 760 Earths could fit inside the volume of Saturn. Amazingly, the planet's density is less than that of water.

## Saturn Has a Large Ring System

The planetary ring system that circles Saturn's equator is the planet's most spectacular feature. A **planetary ring** is a disk of material that circles a planet and consists of orbiting particles. Saturn's ring system has many individual rings that form complex bands. Between bands are gaps that may be occupied by moons.

The edge of the outermost ring is nearly 500,000 km from the center of Saturn. The rings range in thickness from tens of meters to thousands of kilometers. They consist of trillions of small, icy bodies that are a few millimeters to several hundred meters in size. Some of the rings may be made of leftover pieces of an object that got too close to Saturn and was ripped apart by gravity.

© Houghton Mifflin Harcourt Publishing Company • Image Credits: ©NASA/ESA/Space Telescope Science Institute/Science Source/Photo Researchers, Inc

### Statistics Table for Saturn

| | |
|---|---|
| Distance from the sun | 9.58 AU |
| Period of rotation | 10 h 39 min |
| Period of revolution | 29.5 y |
| Tilt of axis | 26.73° |
| Diameter | 120,536 km |
| Density | 0.69 g/cm³ |
| Mean surface temperature | −180 °C |
| Surface gravity | 106% of Earth's gravity |
| Number of satellites | 62 |

Saturn's rings

Saturn's southern aurora

## Saturn's Moon Enceladus Has Water Geysers

In the inner solar system, liquid rock erupts from volcanoes. In some parts of the outer solar system, liquid water erupts from volcanoes. When NASA's *Cassini* spacecraft explored Saturn's moon Enceladus (en•SEL•uh•duhs), it found an icy surface. Scientists believe that Enceladus has a liquid interior beneath this icy surface. Liquid water flows up through cracks in the moon's surface. It either freezes at the surface or forms spectacular water geysers. These geysers are the largest in the solar system.

## Saturn's Moon Titan Has a Dense Atmosphere

Titan (TYT•n), the largest moon of Saturn, has an atmosphere that is denser than Earth's. The moon's atmosphere is composed mostly of nitrogen and has traces of compounds such as methane and ethane. Methane clouds form in Titan's atmosphere. From these clouds, methane rain may fall. Unlike Earth, Titan has a crust of ice, which is frozen at a temperature of –180 °C.

In 2005, the *Huygens* (HY•guhnz) Titan probe descended through Titan's atmosphere. It took pictures of a surface with lakes and ponds. The liquid that fills these lakes and ponds is mostly methane.

**12 Explain** In your own words, write a caption for this illustration of Saturn's moon Enceladus.

_____

_____

_____

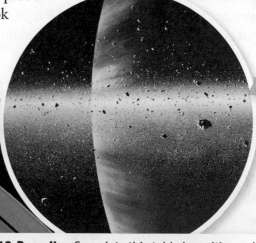

Particles that make up Saturn's ring system

Cassini Division in Saturn's ring system

**13 Describe** Complete this table by writing a description of each structure in Saturn's ring system.

| Structure | Description |
|---|---|
| ring | |
| gap | |
| ring particles | |

# Just Rollin' Along

## How is Uranus unique?

**Active Reading** **14 Identify** As you read the text, underline important physical properties of the planet Uranus.

The atmosphere of Uranus (YUR•uh•nuhs) is composed mostly of hydrogen and helium. However, the atmosphere also contains methane. The methane in Uranus's atmosphere absorbs red light, which gives the planet a blue-green color.

## Uranus Is a Tilted World

Uranus's axis of rotation is tilted almost 98°. This means that unlike any other planet in the solar system, Uranus is tilted on its side as it orbits the sun. The planet's 27 moons all orbit Uranus's equator, just like the moons of other planets do. The ring system of Uranus also orbits the equator.

Scientists are not sure what event caused Uranus's odd axial tilt. But computer models of the four gas giant planets as they were forming may offer an explanation. The huge gravities of Jupiter and Saturn may have caused the orbits of Uranus and Neptune to change. There may also have been many close encounters between Uranus and Neptune that could have tilted the axis of Uranus.

### Statistics Table for Uranus

| | |
|---|---|
| Distance from the sun | 19.2 AU |
| Period of rotation | 17 h 24 min (retrograde) |
| Period of revolution | 84 y |
| Tilt of axis | 97.8° |
| Diameter | 51,118 km |
| Density | 1.27 g/cm³ |
| Mean surface temperature | −220 °C |
| Surface gravity | 91% of Earth's gravity |
| Number of satellites | 27 |

© Houghton Mifflin Harcourt Publishing Company • Image Credits: (bkgd) ©NASA/ESA/STScI/E.Karkoschka/U.Arizona/Photo Researchers, Inc.

**15 Predict** Earth has an axial tilt of 23.5°, whereas Uranus has an axial tilt of almost 98°. If Earth had the same axial tilt as Uranus, how would the conditions be different at Earth's North and South Poles?

_____

_____

_____

_____

_____

_____

_____

_____

_____

_____

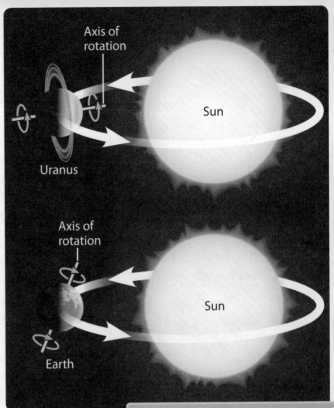

Axis of rotation

Uranus

Sun

Axis of rotation

Sun

Earth

**Think Outside the Book**

**16 Research** Astronomers are discovering planets orbiting stars in other solar systems. Find out what kinds of planets astronomers are discovering in these solar systems.

## Seasons on Uranus Last 21 Years

It takes Uranus 84 years to make a single revolution around the sun. For about 21 years of that 84-year period, the north pole faces the sun, and the south pole is in darkness. About halfway through that 84-year period, the poles are reversed. For 21 years, the south pole faces the sun, and the north pole is in darkness. So what are seasons like on Uranus? Except for a small band near the equator, every place on Uranus has winter periods of constant darkness and summer periods of constant daylight. But during spring and fall, Uranus has periods of both daytime and nighttime just like on Earth.

## Uranus's Moon Miranda Is Active

Miranda (muh•RAN•duh) is Uranus's fifth-largest moon. It is about 470 km in diameter. NASA's *Voyager 2* spacecraft visited Miranda in 1989. Data from *Voyager 2* showed that the moon is covered by different types of icy crust. What is the explanation for this patchwork surface? The gravitational forces of Uranus pull on Miranda's interior. This causes material from the moon's interior to rise to its surface. What we see on the surface is evidence of the moon turning itself inside out.

The surface of Uranus's moon Miranda

# A Blue, Windy Giant

## What is known about Neptune?

Neptune (NEP•toon) is the most distant planet from the sun. It is located 30 times farther from the sun than Earth is. So sunlight on Neptune is 900 times fainter than sunlight on Earth is. High noon on Neptune may look much like twilight on Earth.

## Neptune Is a Blue Ice Giant

Neptune is practically a twin to Uranus. Neptune is almost the same size as Uranus. It also has an atmosphere that is composed mostly of hydrogen and helium, with some methane. The planet's bluish color is caused by the absorption of red light by methane. But because Neptune does not have an atmospheric haze like Uranus does, we can see deeper into the atmosphere. So Neptune appears blue, whereas Uranus is blue-green.

When *Voyager 2* flew by Neptune in 1989, there was a huge, dark area as large as Earth in the planet's atmosphere. This storm, which was located in Neptune's southern hemisphere, was named the *Great Dark Spot*. However, in 1994, the Hubble Space Telescope found no trace of this storm. Meanwhile, other spots that may grow larger with time have been sighted in the atmosphere.

| Statistics Table for Neptune | |
|---|---|
| Distance from the sun | 30.1 AU |
| Period of rotation | 16 h 7 min |
| Period of revolution | 164.8 y |
| Tilt of axis | 28.3° |
| Diameter | 49,528 km |
| Density | 1.64 g/cm³ |
| Mean surface temperature | −210 °C |
| Surface Gravity | 114% of Earth's gravity |
| Number of satellites | 14 |

Great Dark Spot

### Visualize It!

**17 Predict** The wind speeds recorded in Neptune's Great Dark Spot reached 2,000 km/h. Predict what kind of destruction might result on Earth if wind speeds in hurricanes approached 2,000 km/h.

_____

_____

_____

## Neptune Has the Strongest Winds

Winds on Neptune have reached speeds of 2,000 km/h, the strongest winds measured in the solar system. Neptune has a warm interior that produces more energy than the planet receives from sunlight. Some scientists believe that Neptune's weather is controlled from inside the planet and not from outside the planet, as is Earth's weather.

Triton

## Neptune's Moon Triton Has a Different Orbit Than Neptune's Other Moons

Triton (TRYT•n) is the largest moon of Neptune. Unlike the other moons of Neptune, Triton orbits Neptune in the opposite direction from the direction in which Neptune orbits the sun. One explanation for this oddity is that, long ago, there were several large moons that orbited Neptune. These moons came so close together that one moon was ejected. The other moon, Triton, remained behind but began traveling in the opposite direction.

Triton's days are numbered. The moon is slowly spiraling inward toward Neptune. When Triton is a certain distance from Neptune, the planet's gravitational pull will begin pulling Triton apart. Triton will then break into pieces.

### Inquiry

**18 Conclude** Complete the cause-and-effect chart below.

Triton spirals inward toward Neptune.

↓

The gravitational pull of Neptune causes Triton to pull apart.

↓

Triton breaks into pieces.

↓

**What do you think will happen next?**

A category 5 hurricane on Earth has sustained wind speeds of 250 km/h. Some effects of the winds of a category 5 hurricane can be seen in this image.

# Visual Summary

To complete this summary, write the answers to the questions on the lines. Then, use the key below to check your answers. You can use this page to review the main concepts of the lesson.

## Properties
### of Gas Giant Planets

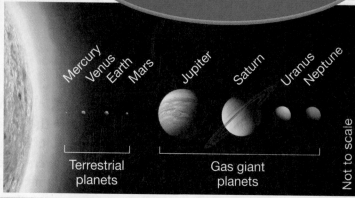

Mercury  Venus  Earth  Mars  Jupiter  Saturn  Uranus  Neptune

Terrestrial planets

Gas giant planets

Not to scale

**Jupiter has cloud bands.**

**19** What causes cloud bands to form on Jupiter?

_____

_____

**Saturn has a complex ring system.**

**20** What are Saturn's rings made up of?

_____

_____

**Uranus is tilted on its side.**

**21** What is the tilt of Uranus's axis of rotation?

_____

_____

**Neptune is a blue planet.**

**22** What gives Neptune its bluish color?

_____

_____

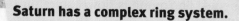

**Answers: 19** high winds that circle the planet; **20** trillions of small, icy bodies; **21** almost 98° (97.8°); **22** the absorption of red light by methane in Neptune's atmosphere

**23 Summarize** Describe the locations and major physical properties of the gas giant planets.

# Lesson Review

## Vocabulary

Fill in the blank with the term that best completes the following sentences.

**1** A large planet that has a deep, massive atmosphere is called a _____

**2** A _____ is a disk of matter that circles a planet and consists of numerous particles in orbit that range in size from a few millimeters to several hundred meters.

## Key Concepts

In the following table, write the name of the correct planet next to the property of that planet.

| Properties | Planet |
|---|---|
| **3 Identify** Which planet has a density that is less than that of water? | |
| **4 Identify** Which planet has the strongest winds in the solar system? | |
| **5 Identify** Which planet is tilted on its side as it orbits the sun? | |
| **6 Identify** Which planet is the largest planet in the solar system? | |

**7 Compare** How do the properties and location of Callisto differ from those of the other Galilean moons?

_____

_____

_____

**8 Compare** How do the periods of rotation and revolution for the gas giant planets differ from those of Earth?

_____

_____

_____

## Critical Thinking

Use this diagram to answer the following questions.

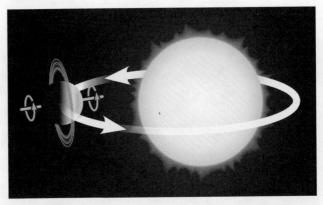

**9 Identify** Which planet is shown in the diagram? How do you know?

_____

_____

**10 Analyze** How does the axial tilt of this planet affect its seasons?

_____

_____

_____

_____

**11 Explain** The period of rotation of each Galilean moon equals its period of revolution around Jupiter. How do the periods of rotation of Io, Europa, and Ganymede compare?

_____

_____

_____

**12 Analyze** List Earth and the gas giant planets in order from the hottest to the coldest planet. How does the temperature of each planet relate to its distance from the sun?

_____

_____

_____

_____

# My Notes

# Small Bodies in the Solar System

## ESSENTIAL QUESTION

## What is found in the solar system besides the sun, planets, and moons?

By the end of this lesson, you should be able to compare and contrast the properties of small bodies in the solar system.

Comet Hale-Bopp was discovered in 1995 and was visible from Earth for 18 months. It is a long-period comet that is thought to take about 2,400 years to orbit the sun.

**TEKS** **6.11A** describe the physical properties, locations, and movements of the Sun, planets, Galilean moons, meteors, asteroids, and comets

## Engage Your Brain

**1 Predict** Check T or F to show whether you think each statement is true or false.

| T | F | |
|---|---|---|
| ☐ | ☐ | Pluto is a planet. |
| ☐ | ☐ | The Kuiper Belt is located beyond the orbit of Neptune. |
| ☐ | ☐ | Comets are made of ice, rock, and dust. |
| ☐ | ☐ | All asteroids have the same composition. |
| ☐ | ☐ | Most meteoroids that enter Earth's atmosphere burn up completely. |

**2 Identify** Can you identify the object that is streaking through the sky in the photograph? What do you think makes this object glow?

_____

_____

_____

_____

_____

## Active Reading

**3 Apply** Many scientific words, such as *belt*, also have everyday meanings. Use context clues to write your own definition for each meaning of the word *belt*.

**Example sentence**
I found a <u>belt</u> to go with my new pants.

belt:

_____

_____

_____

**Example sentence**
Short-term comets originate in the Kuiper <u>Belt</u>.

belt:

_____

_____

_____

_____

### Vocabulary Terms

- dwarf planet
- Kuiper Belt
- Kuiper Belt object
- comet
- Oort cloud
- asteroid
- meteoroid
- meteor
- meteorite

**4 Apply** As you learn the definition of each vocabulary term in this lesson, create your own definition or sketch to help you remember the meaning of the term.

# Bigger is not better

## Where are small bodies in the solar system?

📝 **Active Reading**

**5 Identify** As you read the text, underline the names of different kinds of small bodies that are found in the solar system.

The sun, planets, and moons are not the only objects in the solar system. Scientists estimate that there are up to a trillion small bodies in the solar system. These bodies lack atmospheres and have weak surface gravity. The largest of the small bodies, the dwarf planets, are found in regions known as the *asteroid belt* and the *Kuiper Belt*. The Kuiper (KAHY•per) Belt is located beyond the orbit of Neptune. Kuiper Belt objects, as you might guess, are located in the Kuiper Belt. Comets, too, are found in the Kuiper Belt. However, comets are also located in the Oort cloud. The Oort (OHRT) cloud is a region that surrounds the solar system and extends almost halfway to the nearest star. Two other types of small bodies, asteroids and meteoroids, are located mostly between the orbits of Venus and Neptune.

Sizes and distances are not to scale.

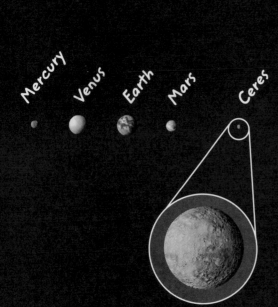

Mercury Venus Earth Mars Ceres

Jupiter

# What are dwarf planets?

In 2006, astronomers decided that Pluto would no longer be considered a planet. It became the first member of a new group of solar system bodies called *dwarf planets*. Like planets, a **dwarf planet** is a celestial body that orbits the sun and is round because of its own gravity. However, a dwarf planet does not have the mass to have cleared other bodies out of its orbit around the sun.

Five dwarf planets, made of ice and rock, have been identified. Ceres (SIR•eez), located between the orbits of Mars and Jupiter, is about 950 km in diameter and travels at around 18 km/s. Pluto, Eris (IR•is), Haumea (HOW•may•uh), and Makemake (MAH•kay•MAH•kay) are located beyond the orbit of Neptune. They range in size from about 1,500 km (Haumea) to about 2,400 km (Eris). Their orbital periods around the sun range from 250 to 560 years. All travel at speeds of between 3 km/s and 5 km/s.

**6 Describe** Describe two properties of dwarf planets.

_____

_____

_____

_____

_____

_____

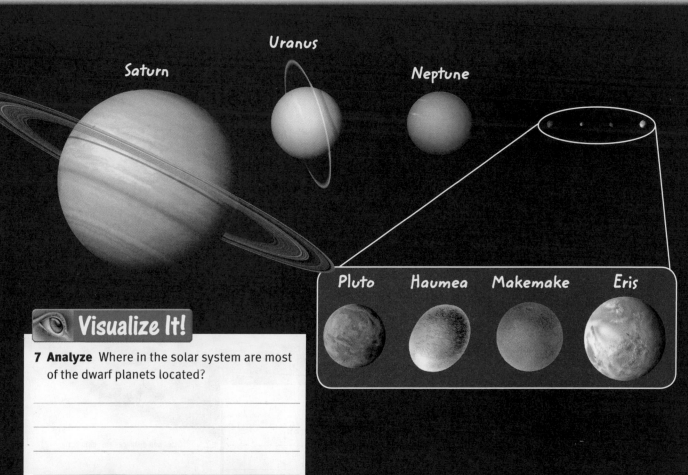

Saturn

Uranus

Neptune

Pluto    Haumea    Makemake    Eris

## Visualize It!

**7 Analyze** Where in the solar system are most of the dwarf planets located?

_____

_____

_____

# KBOs

## What are Kuiper Belt objects?

The **Kuiper Belt** is a region of the solar system that begins just beyond the orbit of Neptune and contains small bodies made mostly of ice. It extends outward to about twice the orbit of Neptune, a distance of about 55 astronomical units (AU). An AU is a unit of length that is equal to the average distance between Earth and the sun, or about 150,000,000 km. The Kuiper Belt is thought to contain matter that was left over from the formation of the solar system. This matter formed small bodies instead of planets.

A **Kuiper Belt object (KBO)** is any of the minor bodies in the Kuiper Belt outside the orbit of Neptune. Kuiper Belt objects are made of methane ice, ammonia ice, and water ice. They have average orbital speeds of between 1 km/s and 5 km/s. The first Kuiper Belt object was not discovered until 1992. Now, about 1,300 KBOs are known. Scientists estimate that there are at least 70,000 objects in the Kuiper Belt that have diameters larger than 100 km.

Quaoar is a KBO that orbits 43 AU from the sun. It is around 1,260 km in diameter and has one satellite.

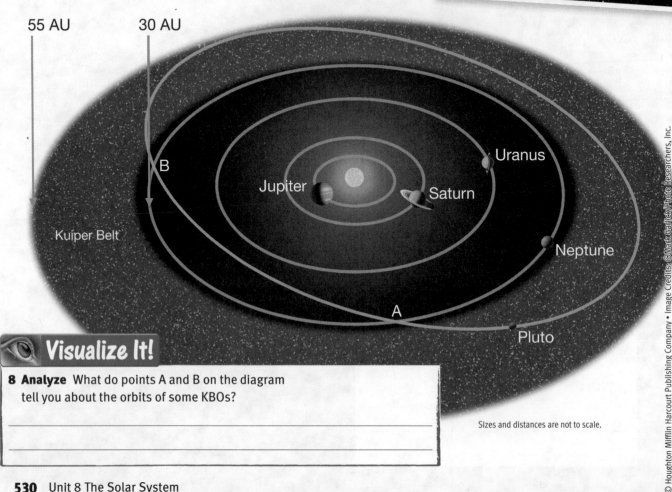

Sizes and distances are not to scale.

© Houghton Mifflin Harcourt Publishing Company • Image Credits: ©Mark Garlick/Photo Researchers, Inc.

### Visualize It!

**8 Analyze** What do points A and B on the diagram tell you about the orbits of some KBOs?

_____

_____

# Pluto: From Planet to KBO

From its discovery in 1930 until 2006, Pluto was considered to be the ninth planet in the solar system. However, beginning in 1992, a new group of small bodies called *Kuiper Belt objects*, or simply KBOs, began to be discovered beyond the orbit of Neptune. Not only are some of the KBOs close to Pluto in size, but some have a similar composition of rock and ice. Astronomers recognized that Pluto was, in fact, a large KBO and not the ninth planet. In 2006, Pluto was redefined as a "dwarf planet" by the International Astronomical Union (IAU).

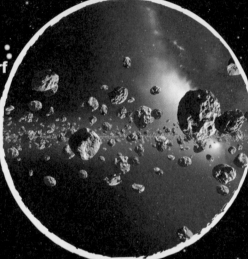

Charon

Pluto

## Pluto and Charon

At 2,306 km in diameter, Pluto is the second largest KBO. It is shown in this artist's rendition with Charon (KAIR•uhn), its largest satellite. Many large KBOs have satellites. Some KBOs and their satellites, such as Pluto and Charon, orbit each other.

## The Kuiper Belt

The Kuiper Belt is located between 30 AU (the orbit of Neptune) and approximately 55 AU. However, most KBOs have been discovered between 42 and 48 AU, where their orbits are not disturbed by the gravitational attraction of Neptune.

## Extend

Inquiry

**9 Explain** Why is Pluto no longer considered a planet?

**10 Research** Astronomer Clyde Tombaugh discovered Pluto in 1930. Research why Tombaugh was searching beyond Neptune for "Planet X" and how he discovered Pluto.

**11 Debate** Research the 2006 IAU decision to redefine Pluto as a "dwarf planet." Combine this research with your research on Pluto. With your classmates, debate whether Pluto should be considered a "dwarf planet" or return to being called the ninth planet in the solar system.

# What do we know about comets?

 **Active Reading** **12 Identify** As you read the text, underline the different parts of a comet and their properties.

A **comet** is a small body of ice, rock, and dust that follows a highly elliptical orbit around the sun. As a comet passes close to the sun, it gives off gas and dust in the form of a coma and a tail.

The speed of a comet will vary depending on how far from or how close to the sun it is. Far from the sun, a comet may travel at speeds as low as 0.32 km/s. Close to the sun, a comet may travel as fast as 445 km/s.

## Comets Are Made of a Nucleus and a Tail

All comets have a *nucleus* that is composed of ice and rock. Most comet nuclei are between 1 km and 10 km in diameter. If a comet approaches the sun, solar radiation and heating cause the comet's ice to change to gas. A *coma* is a spherical cloud of gas and dust that comes off of the nucleus. The *ion tail* of a comet is gas that has been ionized, or stripped of electrons, by the sun. The solar wind—electrically charged particles expanding away from the sun—pushes the gas away from the comet's head. So, regardless of the direction a comet is traveling, its ion tail points away from the sun. A second tail made of dust and gas curves backward along the comet's orbit. This *dust tail* can be millions of kilometers long.

 **Visualize It!**

**13 Identify** Use the write-on lines in the diagram to identify the structures of a comet.

Dust tail

 A

 B

C

# Comets Come from the Kuiper Belt and the Oort Cloud

There are two regions of the solar system where comets come from. The first region is the Kuiper Belt, which is where short-period comets originate. The second region is the Oort cloud, which is where long-period comets originate.

Collisions between objects in the Kuiper Belt produce fragments that become comets. These comets are known as *short-period comets*. Short-period comets take less than 200 years to orbit the sun. Therefore, they return to the inner solar system quite frequently, perhaps every few decades or centuries. Short-period comets also have short life spans. Every time a comet passes the sun, it may lose a layer as much as 1 m thick.

Some comets originate in the Oort cloud. The **Oort cloud** is a spherical region that surrounds the solar system and extends almost halfway to the nearest star. Comets can form in the Oort cloud when two objects collide. Comets can also form when an object in the Oort cloud is disturbed by the gravity of a nearby star and is sent into the inner solar system. Comets that originate in the Oort cloud are called *long-period comets*. Long-period comets may take up to hundreds of thousands of years to orbit the sun.

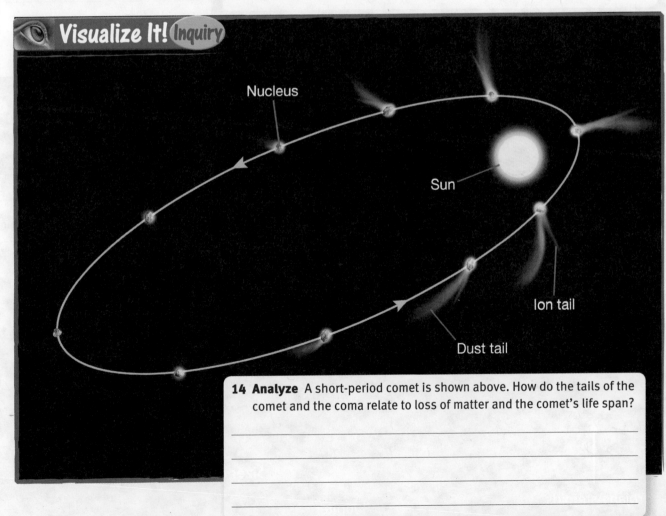

## Visualize It! Inquiry

Nucleus

Sun

Ion tail

Dust tail

**14 Analyze** A short-period comet is shown above. How do the tails of the comet and the coma relate to loss of matter and the comet's life span?

# On the rocks

## What do we know about asteroids?

**Active Reading** **15 Identify** As you read the text, underline those places in the solar system where asteroids are located.

An **asteroid** is a small, irregularly shaped, rocky object that orbits the sun. Most asteroids are located between the orbits of Mars and Jupiter. This 300 million–km–wide region is known as the *asteroid belt*. The asteroid belt contains hundreds of thousands of asteroids, called *main-belt asteroids*. The largest main-belt asteroid by diameter is Pallas, which has a diameter of 570 km. The smallest asteroid is 4 m in diameter. Groups of asteroids are also located in the orbits of Jupiter and Neptune (called *Trojan asteroids*) and in the Kuiper Belt. Still other asteroids are called *near-Earth asteroids*. Some of these asteroids cross the orbits of Earth and Venus.

Asteroids in the asteroid belt orbit the sun at about 18 km/s and have orbital periods of 3 to 8 years. Although most asteroids rotate around their axis, some tumble end over end through space.

## Visualize It!

**16 Analyze** Where is the asteroid belt located?

_____
_____
_____
_____
_____
_____

Asteroid Belt

Mars

Trojan Asteroids

Trojan Asteroids

Jupiter

*Sizes and distances are not to scale.*

## Asteroids Have Different Compositions

The composition of asteroids varies. Many asteroids have dark surfaces. Scientists think that these asteroids are rich in carbon. Other asteroids are thought to be rocky and to have a core made of iron and nickel. Still other asteroids may have a rocky core surrounded largely by ice. Small, rocky asteroids have perhaps the strangest composition of all. They appear to be piles of rock loosely held together by gravity. Asteroid Itokawa (ee•TOH•kah•wah), shown below, is a rocky asteroid known as a "rubble-pile" asteroid.

Some asteroids contain economic minerals like those mined on Earth. Economic minerals that are found in asteroids include gold, iron, nickel, manganese, cobalt, and platinum. Scientists are now investigating the potential for mining near-Earth asteroids.

Itokawa is a rubble-pile asteroid. Astronomers think that the 500 m-long asteroid may be composed of two asteroids that are joined.

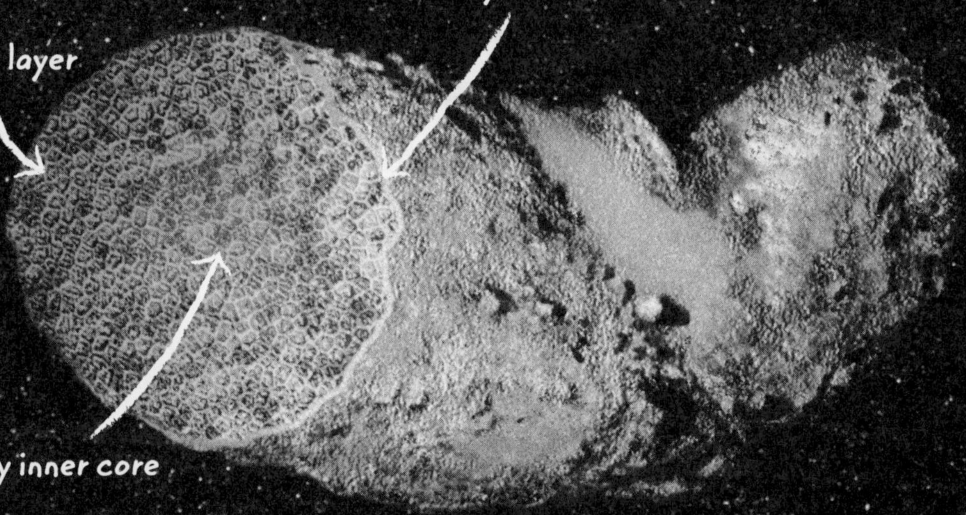

Thin, dusty outer core

Water-ice layer

Rocky inner core

*Greetings from Eros!*

### Think Outside the Book

**17 Describe** Eros is a near-Earth asteroid that tumbles through space. Imagine that you are the first human to explore Eros. Write a postcard that describes what you found on Eros. Then research the asteroid and find out how close your description came to reality.

# Burned Out

## What do we know about meteoroids, meteors, and meteorites?

A sand grain- to boulder-sized, rocky body that travels through space is a **meteoroid**. Meteoroids that enter Earth's atmosphere travel at about 52 km/s, as measured by radar on Earth. Friction heats these meteoroids to thousands of degrees Celsius, which causes them to glow. The atmosphere around a meteoroid's path also gets hotter and glows because of friction between the meteoroid and air molecules. A bright streak of light that results when a meteoroid burns up in Earth's atmosphere is called a **meteor**. A **meteorite** is a meteoroid that reaches Earth's surface without burning up.

**18 Identify** Use the write-on lines below to identify the three objects that are shown.

**A** A small, rocky body that travels through space is a
_____

**B** The glowing trail of a body that is burning up in Earth's atmosphere is a _____

**C** A body that reaches Earth's surface without burning up is a _____

A meteorite 45 m across produced kilometer-wide Barringer Crater in Arizona about 50,000 years ago.

## Meteorites Reach Earth

Meteoroids come from the asteroid belt, Mars, the moon, and comets. Most of the meteoroids that enter Earth's atmosphere do not reach Earth's surface. Many meteoroids explode in the upper atmosphere. These explosions are often recorded by military satellites in orbit around Earth. Other meteoroids skip back into space after briefly crossing the upper atmosphere. However, some large meteoroids that enter Earth's lower atmosphere or strike Earth's surface can be destructive. Scientists estimate that a destructive meteorite impact occurs every 300 to 400 years.

## Meteorites Have Different Compositions

Meteorites can be divided into three general groups. The first group of meteorites are the stony meteorites. They are the most common form of meteorite. Stony meteorites are made of silicate minerals, just like rocks on Earth. Some stony meteorites also contain small amounts of organic matter. A much smaller group of meteorites are the iron meteorites. Iron meteorites are composed of iron and nickel. The rarest group of meteorites are stony-iron meteorites. Stony-iron meteorites are composed of both silicate minerals and iron and nickel. All three groups of meteorites can originate from asteroids. However, some stony meteorites come from the moon and Mars.

**Visualize It!**

**19 Describe** In the boxes below, describe the composition and origin of each group of meteorite. Also, indicate how common each group of meteorite is.

**Stony meteorite**

_____
_____
_____
_____
_____

**Iron meteorite**

_____
_____
_____
_____
_____

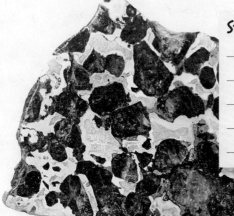

**Stony-iron meteorite**

_____
_____
_____
_____
_____

# Visual Summary

To complete this summary, answer the questions below. Then, use the key below to check your answers. You can use this page to review the main concepts of the lesson.

## Small Bodies in the Solar System

**Small bodies are found throughout the solar system.**

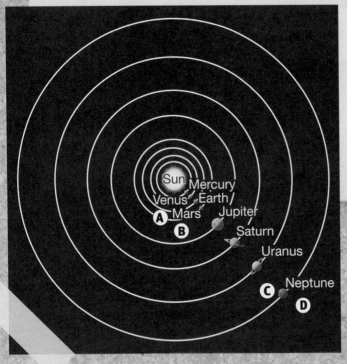

20 Enter the correct letter or letters that indicate a location for each small body in the solar system.

| Asteroids | |
|---|---|
| **Dwarf planets** | |
| **Kuiper Belt objects** | |

Answers: 20 asteroids A, B, C, D; dwarf planets B, D; KBOs C, D; 21 F, F, T

21 Check true or false to answer the questions below.

| T | F | |
|---|---|---|
| ☐ | ☐ | Comets originate in the asteroid belt and the Kuiper Belt. |
| ☐ | ☐ | Three groups of asteroids are stony, iron, and stony-iron. |
| ☐ | ☐ | Most meteoroids that enter Earth's atmosphere burn up. |

22 **Compare** Make a table in which you compare and contrast comets and asteroids in terms of composition, location in the solar system, and size.

# Lesson Review

## Vocabulary

Fill in the blank with the term that best completes the following sentences.

**1** The _____ is a spherical region that surrounds the solar system and extends almost halfway to the nearest star.

**2** A region of the solar system that extends from the orbit of Neptune to about twice the orbit of Neptune is the _____.

**3** Most _____ are located between the orbits of Mars and Jupiter.

**4** A meteoroid that reaches Earth's surface without burning up is a _____.

## Key Concepts

In the following table, write the name of the correct body next to the property of that body.

| Property | Body |
|---|---|
| **5 Identify** What is a minor body that orbits outside the orbit of Neptune? | |
| **6 Identify** What is a small body that follows a highly elliptical orbit around the sun? | |
| **7 Identify** What is the largest of the small bodies that are found in the solar system? | |
| **8 Identify** What is the glowing trail that results when a meteoroid burns up in Earth's atmosphere? | |

## Critical Thinking

Use this table to answer the following questions.

| Comet | Orbital Period (years) |
|---|---|
| Borrelly | 6.9 |
| Halley | 76 |
| Hale-Bopp | 2,400 |
| Hyakutake | 100,000 |

**9 Apply** Which of the comets in the table are short-period comets?

_____

_____

**10 Apply** Which of the comets in the table most likely originated in the Oort cloud?

_____

_____

**11 Infer** Why do you think that the speeds of comets increase as they near the sun?

_____

_____

_____

_____

**12 Predict** Why do you think that some asteroids tumble end over end through space while other asteroids rotate around their axis?

_____

_____

_____

_____

_____

_____

# My Notes

© Houghton Mifflin Harcourt Publishing Company

# Unit 8 Planets and a variety of other bodies form a system of objects orbiting the sun.

### Lesson 1
**ESSENTIAL QUESTION**
**How have people modeled the solar system?**

Compare various historical models of the solar system.

### Lesson 2
**ESSENTIAL QUESTION**
**Why is gravity important in the solar system?**

Explain the role that gravity played in the formation of the solar system and in determining the motion of the planets.

### Lesson 3
**ESSENTIAL QUESTION**
**What are the properties of the sun?**

Describe the structure and rotation of the sun, energy production and energy transport in the sun, and solar activity on the sun.

### Lesson 4
**ESSENTIAL QUESTION**
**What is known about the terrestrial planets?**

Describe some of the properties of the terrestrial planets and how the properties of Mercury, Venus, and Mars differ from the properties of Earth.

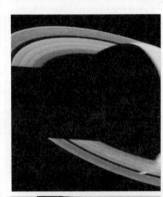

### Lesson 5
**ESSENTIAL QUESTION**
**What is known about the gas giant planets?**

Describe some of the properties of the gas giant planets and how these properties differ from the physical properties of Earth.

### Lesson 6
**ESSENTIAL QUESTION**
**What is found in the solar system besides the sun, planets, and moons?**

Compare and contrast the properties of small bodies in the solar system.

## Connect ESSENTIAL QUESTIONS
Lessons 4 and 5

**1 Synthesize** Explain why the planet Jupiter has more moons than the planet Mars.

_____

_____

_____

_____

## Think Outside the Book

**2 Synthesize** Choose one of these activities to help synthesize what you have learned in this unit.

☐ Using what you learned in lessons 4 and 5, write a short essay explaining where in the solar system besides Earth life could exist.

☐ Using what you learned in lessons 2, 3, and 4, make a poster presentation showing why comets are the fastest-moving bodies in the solar system.

Name _____

## Vocabulary

Fill in the blank with the term that best completes the sentence.

**TEKS** 6.11A, 6.11B

**1** _____ is the process in which energy is released as the nuclei of small atoms combine to form a larger nucleus.

**TEKS** 6.11A, 6.11B

**2** The solar system formed from a _____, which is a rotating cloud of gas and dust.

**TEKS** 6.11A

**3** Earth, Venus, Mars, and Mercury are _____, which are very dense planets nearest the sun.

**TEKS** 6.11A

**4** A(n) _____ is a small, rocky object that orbits the sun; many of these objects are located in a band between the orbits of Mars and Jupiter.

**TEKS** 6.11A

**5** The sun, all of the planets that orbit the sun, and other bodies orbiting around the sun make up the _____.

## Key Concepts

Choose the letter of the best answer.

**TEKS** 6.11A

**6** A satellite took x-ray pictures of a solar flare. How did the solar flare most likely appear on the x-ray pictures? (Hint: Step 1. Recall what a solar flare is. Step 2: Based on the characteristics of a solar flare, determine what it might look like on an x-ray picture.)

**A** as a dark spot

**B** as a swirl of red flames

**C** as an orange glow

**D** as an area of bright white light

TEKS 6.11A, 6.3B

**7** The diagram below shows the different layers of the sun. The sun can be divided into six layers that are different from each other based on certain characteristics, such as temperature and composition.

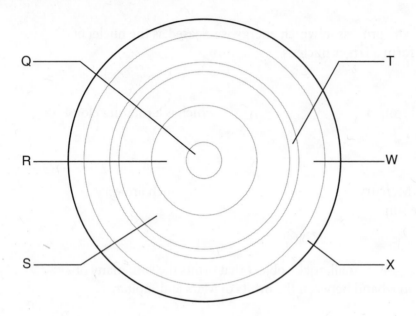

Which layer of the sun is represented by the letter T?

**A** chromosphere

**B** corona

**C** photosphere

**D** radiative zone

TEKS 6.11A, 6.11B

**8** What does Kepler's first law of planetary motion state?

**A** The orbit of a planet around the sun is an ellipse with the sun at one focus.

**B** The orbit of a planet is dependent on heat.

**C** Centripetal force and elliptical force are different.

**D** The orbital period of a planet is infinite.

**TEKS** 6.11A, 6.11B, 6.3B

**9** Venus and Earth have similar surface gravities. Mercury and Mars also have similar surface gravities, even though Mercury is much smaller. Density is related to the force of gravity. The figure shows the densities of the four planets.

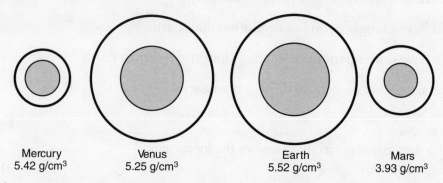

Mercury
5.42 g/cm³

Venus
5.25 g/cm³

Earth
5.52 g/cm³

Mars
3.93 g/cm³

Which of these statements explains the similar surface gravities on Mars and Mercury? (Hint: Step 1. Compare the densities of Mercury and Mars. Step 2. Relate the densities to the surface gravity of the planets.)

**A** Mars is denser than Mercury.

**B** Mars is smaller than Mercury.

**C** Mars is less dense than Mercury.

**D** Mars is less rocky than Mercury.·

**TEKS** 6.11A, 6.2E, 6.3A

**10** The table gives information about the terrestrial planets.

| Planet | Surface temperature (range in °C) | Atmospheric pressure (kg/cm³) |
|---|---|---|
| Earth | −89 to 58 | 1 |
| Mars | −133 to 27 | 0.007 |
| Mercury | −183 to 427 | $2 \times 10^{-12}$ |
| Venus | 467 (average temp.) | 90 |

How does atmospheric pressure appear to relate to surface temperatures on these planets? (Hint: Step 1. Decide which planets have higher pressures and which have lower pressures. Step 2. Determine what the temperature variation is like for the planets with lower pressures and the planets with higher pressures.)

**A** There is no temperature variation for planets with lower pressures.

**B** There is the least temperature variation for planets with lower pressures.

**C** There is the least temperature variation for planets with higher pressures.

**D** There is the most temperature variation for planets with higher pressures.

TEKS 6.11A

11  Earth, Mercury, and Venus are all classified as terrestrial planets. When compared to Earth, which of the following is true of Mercury and Venus?

   **A** Mercury and Venus have a higher surface gravity than Earth.

   **B** Mercury and Venus have a longer period of revolution than Earth.

   **C** Mercury and Venus have slower periods of rotation (longer days) than Earth.

   **D** Mercury and Venus are farther away from the sun than Earth.

TEKS 6.11A

12  Which of the following statements correctly describes the location and movement of the Gallilean moons?

   **A** The Gallilean moons orbit Jupiter.

   **B** The Gallilean moons orbit Saturn.

   **C** The Gallilean moons orbit Uranus.

   **D** The Gallilean moons orbit Neptune.

TEKS 6.11A

13  Which of the following is a list of the gas giant planets?

   **A** Jupiter, Saturn, Uranus, and Neptune

   **B** Earth, Mars, and Venus

   **C** Pluto, Saturn, and Jupiter

   **D** Earth, Jupiter, Neptune, and Saturn

**TEKS** 6.3D, 6.11A

**14** This diagram illustrates a historical model of the solar system.

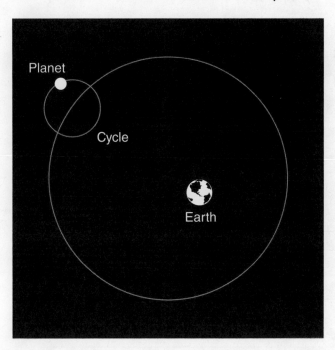

Which type of model is shown?

**A** geocentric model      **C** Copernican model

**B** heliocentric model      **D** Aristarchan model

## Gridded Response

Write your answer in the boxes, then bubble in the corresponding number in the grid below.

**TEKS** 6.11A, 6.2E, 6.3A

**15** The table shows surface temperatures and atmospheric pressures for the terrestrial planets.

| Planet | Surface temperature (range in °C) | Atmospheric pressure (kg/cm³) |
|---|---|---|
| Earth | −89 to 58 | 1 |
| Mars | −133 to 27 | 0.007 |
| Mercury | −183 to 427 | $2 \times 10^{-12}$ |
| Venus | 467 (average temp.) | 90 |

What is the difference in degrees Celsius between the highest temperatures on Earth and Mercury?

# Unit 8 Review continued

## Critical Thinking

Answer the following questions in the space provided.

TEKS 6.11A

**16** Name three characteristics of gas giants that make them different from terrestrial planets.

_____

_____

_____

_____

TEKS 6.11A

**17** Explain the difference between a meteoroid, a meteor, and a meteorite. Which one would you most likely see on the surface of Earth?

_____

_____

_____

_____

_____

_____

## Connect ESSENTIAL QUESTIONS
### Lessons 2, 3, 4, 5, and 6

Answer the following question in the space provided..

TEKS 6.11A, 6.11B

**18** What force controls motion in our solar system? How does this force affect the way the sun produces energy and the way planets, moons, asteroids, comets, and meteoroids move?

_____

_____

_____

_____

_____

_____

_____

**UNIT 9**

# Space Exploration

**Big Idea**

People develop and use technology to explore space.

## What do you think?

Probes send information about the outer solar system back to scientists on Earth. How might humans benefit from space exploration?

# Unit 9
# Space Exploration

## CITIZEN SCIENCE

# Exploring Space!

The exploration of space began in 1957 with the launch of Sputnik I. Since 1957, humans have walked on the moon, rovers have investigated the surface of Mars, and spacecraft have flown by the most distant planets in the solar system.

**Sputnik I, 1957**
On October 4, 1957, the successful launch of the Russian satellite Sputnik I kicked off the race for space.

Sputnik I

Apollo 11

Mars Phoenix

### Apollo 11, 1969
Just 12 years later, on July 16, 1969, Neil Armstrong and Buzz Aldrin became the first humans to walk on the moon.

### International Space Station, 1998
Assembled in Low-Earth Orbit (LEO), the International Space Station is a long-term research laboratory in space. On clear nights, it can be seen without the use of a telescope.

### Mars Phoenix, 2008
On May 25, 2008, the Mars Phoenix landed on the surface of Mars and began to gather data. On May 31, it took pictures of ice beneath the soil.

International Space Station

## Take It Home  New Ideas

Research the X Prize and the technological innovations and discoveries about space exploration that are coming out of private competition. Choose one prizewinner and learn about the project.

**A** What is the project called?

_____

**B** Describe the project. How does it build on earlier knowledge? How is it different?

_____
_____
_____

Lesson **1**

# History of Space Exploration

**ESSENTIAL QUESTION**

## What are some milestones of space exploration?

By the end of this lesson, you should understand some of the achievements of space exploration.

In 1993, astronauts walked in space to repair the damaged Hubble Space Telescope.

**TEKS** **6.11C** describe the history and future of space exploration, including the types of equipment and transportation needed for space travel

##  Engage Your Brain

**1 Describe** Write a word beginning with each letter of the acronym NASA that describes space exploration.

N _____

A _____

S _____

A _____

**2 Describe** Write your own caption to this photo.

Cape Canaveral, 1961

_____

_____

_____

## Active Reading

**3 Apply** Use context clues to write your own definition for the word *challenge*.

**Example sentence:**
Visiting other planets is a <u>challenge</u> for humans given their great distances from Earth.

challenge:

_____

_____

### Vocabulary Terms
- NASA

**4 Identify** As you read, place a question mark next to any words that you don't understand. When you finish reading the lesson, go back and review the text that you marked. If the information is still confusing, consult a classmate or a teacher.

# Space: The Final Frontier

## How did space exploration begin?

### Active Reading

**5 Identify** As you read, underline the four words that make up the acronym NASA.

**6 Infer** Why might people continue to pursue space exploration in the future?

_____

_____

_____

_____

Have you ever looked into the night sky and wondered what exists beyond Earth? If so, you are not alone. People have been curious about space since ancient times. This curiosity and the desire to understand the unknown paved the way for space exploration.

In October of 1957, the Soviet Union launched the first satellite, *Sputnik I*, into low Earth orbit. Though it was a sphere only 585 mm in diameter that contained a 3.5 kg radio transmitter, *Sputnik I* was the first step in space exploration beyond Earth. It was the start of the "Space Age."

The United States clearly understood the advantages of placing technology in space. In response to the Soviet launch of *Sputnik I*, the U.S. launched its first satellite, *Explorer I*, on January 31, 1958. This started what became known as the Space Race between the two nations, which would continue for several decades. In the same year, the National Aeronautics and Space Administration, or **NASA**, was formed. Its purpose was to head up a program of research and development for the "conquest of space."

1950          1960          1970

**1957:** The Space Age began when the Soviet Union launched the first artificial satellite, *Sputnik I*, into low Earth orbit.

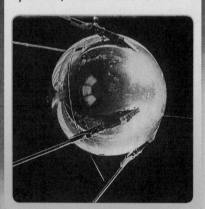

**1961:** The first human to orbit Earth was cosmonaut Yuri A. Gagarin of the Soviet Union, shown below. In the same year, Alan Shepard became the first American in space.

**1961–1966:** Mission control monitors a Gemini space flight below. During this period, projects Mercury and Gemini focused on launching spacecraft that would prepare for journeys to the moon.

The space shuttle **Atlantis** heads into orbit around Earth.

2010

**1998–present:** Numerous countries have participated in the construction and use of the *International Space Station*, a long-term research laboratory that orbits Earth.

2000

1990

1980

**1981:** Shuttle flights began in 1981. The space shuttle launched and retrieved satellites from Earth orbit. The space shuttle later flew to the *International Space Station*.

**1971:** *Salyut 1*, the world's first space station, was launched into orbit by the Soviet Union. Its first crew arrived in the *Soyuz 11* spacecraft and remained on board for 24 days.

**1968–1972:** Six missions to the moon carried three astronauts each. The first moon landing was *Apollo 11* in 1969. The last moon landing was *Apollo 17* in 1972. A total of 12 astronauts walked on the moon.

👁 **Visualize It!**

**7 Interpret** How has space exploration changed over time?

_____

_____

_____

_____

# From Earth to the Moon

## How have people explored space?

It was not until the 1960s that the first rockets capable of launching space capsules were built and tested. All that was needed to explore space was to place astronauts inside these capsules.

### By Using Suborbital Crewed Exploration

*Suborbital* crewed spacecraft do not orbit Earth because they do not reach the required speed and altitude. So, these flights spend only a very short time in space. The first crewed suborbital spaceflight missions were NASA's Mercury project in 1961. On May 5, 1961, a Redstone rocket launched astronaut Alan B. Shepard, Jr., aboard a capsule called *Freedom 7*. Shepard flew safely for 15 minutes before returning to Earth. The second suborbital flight, which took place on July 21, 1961, was that of astronaut Virgil I. Grissom. Although the capsule sank shortly after splashdown in the Atlantic Ocean, Grissom was rescued safely.

### By Using Orbital Crewed Exploration

*Orbital* crewed spacecraft completely orbit Earth. The first crewed orbital space flight was made on April 12, 1961, by Soviet air force pilot Yuri A. Gagarin (guh•GAR•in) aboard *Vostok 1*. Gagarin orbited Earth for 108 minutes before parachuting safely to Earth. On July 21, 1961, John H. Glenn, Jr., observed Earth from space as he became the first American to orbit Earth. Glenn completed three orbits of Earth in a little less than five hours. On June 16, 1963, cosmonaut Valentina V. Tereshkova became the first woman in space. She orbited Earth 48 times over a three-day period.

Meanwhile, the United States was developing plans for a two-person, crewed Gemini program. Ten crewed Gemini missions would follow. One goal of the Gemini program was to see if astronauts could spend longer periods of time in space. The Soviet Union responded with their own multiperson spaceflights as part of their existing Vostok program. Another milestone took place on March 18, 1965, when Soviet cosmonaut Alexei A. Leonov performed the first walk in space. The first American to walk in space was Edward H. White II on June 3, 1965.

**8 Compare** How are suborbital and orbital space exploration alike and different?

_____

_____

_____

Alan Shepard prepares for launch in 1961.

Astronauts emerge from the **Gemini 8** capsule after splashdown in 1966.

Valentina Tereshkova of the Soviet Union became the first woman in space in 1963.

## By Landing on the Moon

The race to the moon began in the 1960s. On September 12, 1962, President John F. Kennedy committed the United States to "landing a man on the moon and returning him safely to Earth" before the decade ended. The key requirement for a successful moon landing is to travel fast enough to escape Earth's gravity and slow enough to land safely on the moon's surface.

The United States would be the only nation to send astronauts to the moon. Six moon landings took place during the Apollo program of the late 1960s and early 1970s. In 1969, the *Apollo 11* spacecraft took astronauts Neil Armstrong, Edwin "Buzz" Aldrin, and Michael Collins to the moon. While Collins orbited the moon in the lunar spacecraft, Armstrong and Aldrin descended to the moon's surface in the lunar module, named the *Eagle*. The *Eagle* landed in the Sea of Tranquility on July 20, 1969. Millions of people heard Armstrong's breathtaking transmission from the lunar surface, "Tranquility Base here. The *Eagle* has landed." Soon after, Neil Armstrong became the first person to set foot on the moon's surface. Six of the 11 Apollo missions landed on the moon. In total, 12 astronauts walked on the moon.

**9 Infer** Why was landing on the moon such an important moment in American history?

______________________________

______________________________

______________________________

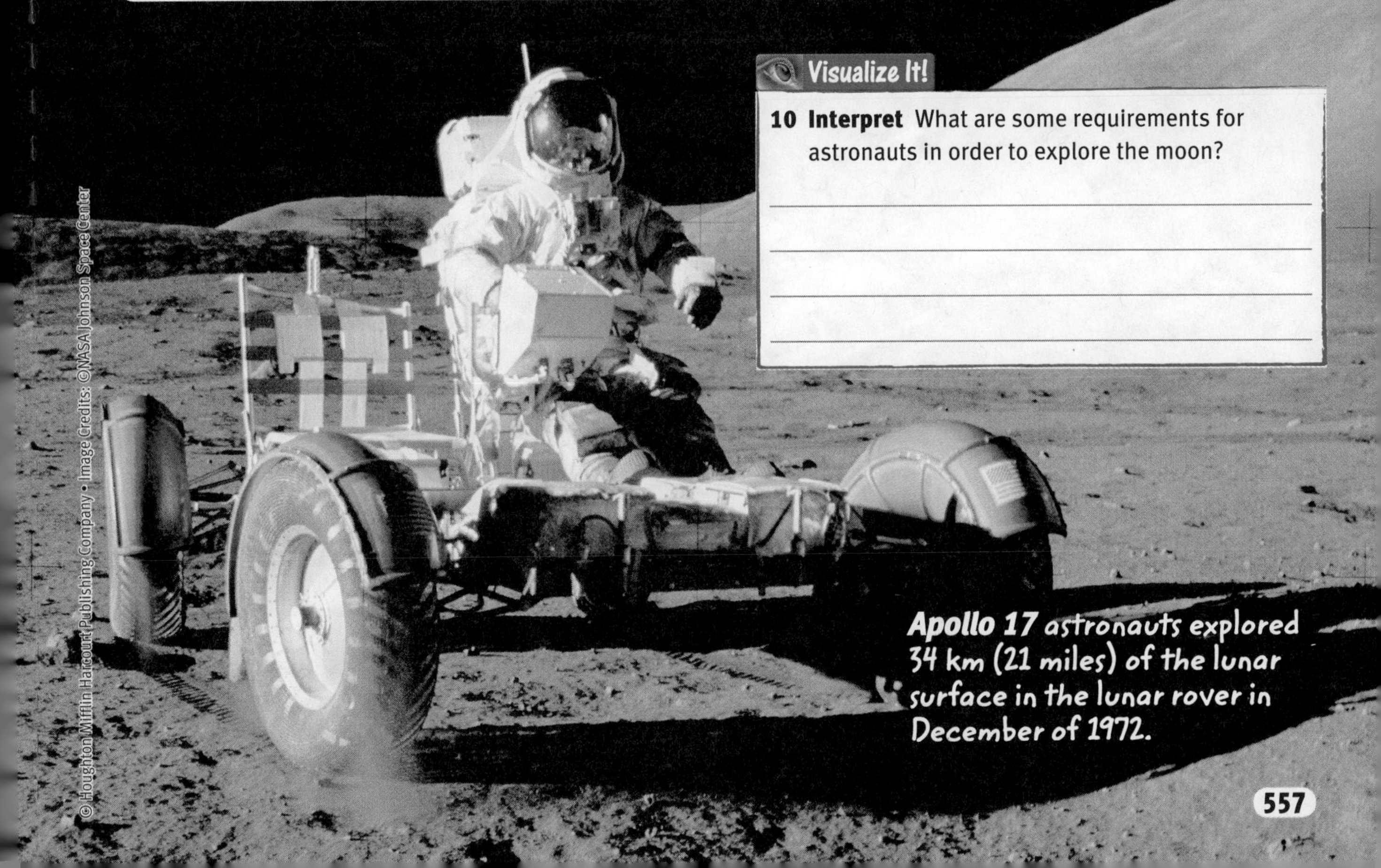

**Visualize It!**

**10 Interpret** What are some requirements for astronauts in order to explore the moon?

______________________________

______________________________

______________________________

______________________________

***Apollo 17*** astronauts explored 34 km (21 miles) of the lunar surface in the lunar rover in December of 1972.

# Where have people lived and worked in space?

**Active Reading** 11 **Assess** As you read, underline different uses of space shuttle technology.

As you might imagine, rocket technology is potentially dangerous. Rockets are also expensive, considering that they cannot be reused. Beginning in the 1970s, NASA made plans to build spacecraft that were not only habitable but also reusable.

## In Space Shuttles

A *space shuttle* is a crewed space vehicle that lifts off with the aid of rocket boosters and liquid fuel. These spacecraft glide to a landing on Earth like airplanes, using parachutes to slow them down. Both the space shuttle and its rocket boosters are reusable. Space shuttles orbit Earth while in space.

Missions using space shuttles began with the launch of the shuttle *Columbia* in 1981. Between 1981 and 2011, six shuttles—*Enterprise, Columbia, Challenger, Discovery, Atlantis,* and *Endeavour*—completed more than 100 missions. Missions aboard shuttles were an important way to gather data, launch satellites, and transport materials. Space shuttles also docked with the *International Space Station.*

Space shuttles carrying supplies traveled to and docked with the **International Space Station.**

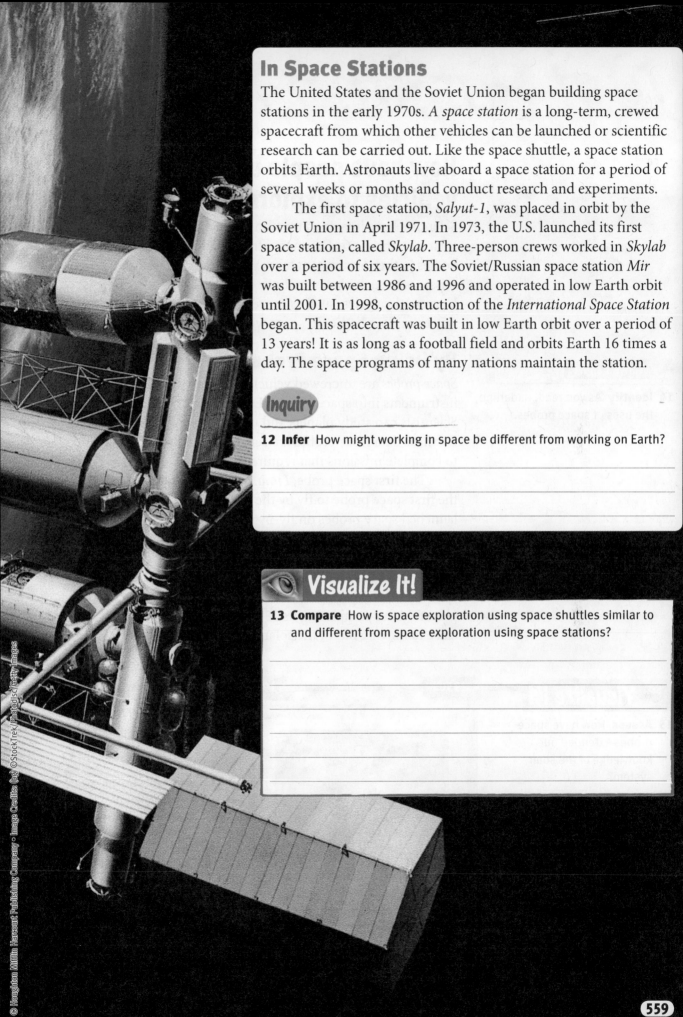

## In Space Stations

The United States and the Soviet Union began building space stations in the early 1970s. *A space station* is a long-term, crewed spacecraft from which other vehicles can be launched or scientific research can be carried out. Like the space shuttle, a space station orbits Earth. Astronauts live aboard a space station for a period of several weeks or months and conduct research and experiments.

The first space station, *Salyut-1*, was placed in orbit by the Soviet Union in April 1971. In 1973, the U.S. launched its first space station, called *Skylab*. Three-person crews worked in *Skylab* over a period of six years. The Soviet/Russian space station *Mir* was built between 1986 and 1996 and operated in low Earth orbit until 2001. In 1998, construction of the *International Space Station* began. This spacecraft was built in low Earth orbit over a period of 13 years! It is as long as a football field and orbits Earth 16 times a day. The space programs of many nations maintain the station.

### Inquiry

**12 Infer** How might working in space be different from working on Earth?

_____

_____

_____

### Visualize It!

**13 Compare** How is space exploration using space shuttles similar to and different from space exploration using space stations?

_____

_____

_____

_____

_____

_____

# Just Passing By

## How have people used uncrewed vehicles to explore space?

Scientists have imagined traveling to planets, moons, and even solar systems at great distances from Earth. But reaching other bodies in the solar system takes years or even decades. Crewed missions to such places are both difficult and dangerous. Uncrewed vehicles, such as space probes and orbiters, are a safe way to explore bodies in space without using people.

## By Using Space Probes

*Space probes* are uncrewed vehicles that carry scientific instruments into space beyond Earth's orbit to collect data. Scientists can study planets and moons at great distances from Earth, as data from probes are sent to Earth. Space probes are used to complete missions that require years of travel time in space.

The first space probe, *Luna 1*, was launched in 1959. It was the first space probe to fly by the moon. Since then, scientists have launched space probes on fly-by missions to Mercury and Venus. Some space probes were designed to land on distant planets, such as the landings of *Viking 1* and *Viking 2* on Mars in 1976. Other space probes have been used to explore the far reaches of the solar system. In 1977, *Voyager 2* was launched to explore the gas giant planets. After completing its 33-year mission, the probe is now close to moving out of the solar system and into interstellar space.

**Active Reading**

**14 Identify** As you read, underline the uses of space probes.

**Visualize It!**

**15 Assess** How have space probes extended our knowledge of the solar system?

_____

_____

_____

_____

_____

_____

_____

1950      1960      1970

In 1962, *Mariner 2* successfully passed within 35,000 km of Venus and returned data from the planet. Here, technicians attach solar panels that powered the probe.

In 1972, *Pioneer 10* was the first space probe to travel through the asteroid belt and make observations of Jupiter.

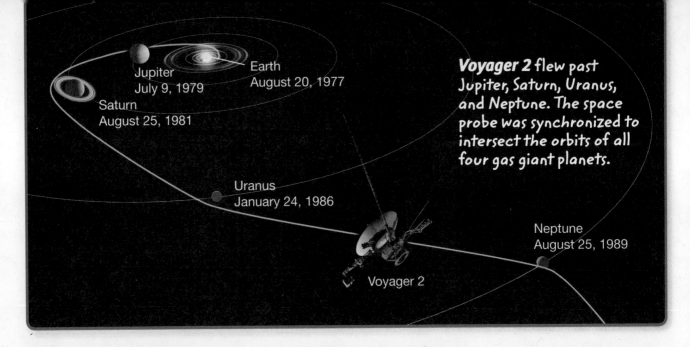

Jupiter
July 9, 1979

Earth
August 20, 1977

Saturn
August 25, 1981

*Voyager 2* flew past Jupiter, Saturn, Uranus, and Neptune. The space probe was synchronized to intersect the orbits of all four gas giant planets.

Uranus
January 24, 1986

Neptune
August 25, 1989

Voyager 2

## By Using Orbiters

An *orbiter* is a spacecraft that travels to a planet and goes into orbit around it. Several orbiters have explored the planetary features of Mars. The first of these orbiters, *Mars Odyssey* (AHD•ih•see), was launched in 2001. It entered the orbit of Mars after a seven-month journey through space. Two of the missions of the *Mars Odyssey* are to make maps of the Martian surface and to collect data about the chemical makeup of the planet. It was still in service as of 2011.

Launched in 2003, the European Space Agency's *Mars Express* is being used to look for signs of water on Mars. It has also played a role in mapping the surface of Mars and studying the composition of the planet's atmosphere. In 2006, NASA's *Mars Reconnaissance Orbiter* arrived at Mars. It has the most powerful camera ever sent to view another planet. The camera can be used to guide future spacecraft to make precise landings on the Martian surface.

### Think Outside the Book

**16 Research** Investigate a particular space probe or orbiter and its mission. What did it discover?

1980　　　1990　　　2000　　　2010

Space probe *Galileo* was deployed from the space shuttle *Atlantis* in 1989 to study Jupiter and its moons. It flew by Jupiter in 1995.

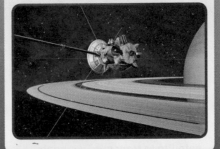

In 1997, the *Cassini-Huygens* space probe was launched to study the planet Saturn and its moons, including Enceladus and Titan.

Comet Temple 1 was the target of the *Deep Impact* space probe, which released an impactor into the comet in 2005 to study the composition of its interior.

This photograph from 1958 shows scientists examining the prototype for *Explorer I*, the first United States satellite in space.

© Houghton Mifflin Harcourt Publishing Company • Image Credits: (t) ©Phil Burchman/Archive Photos/Getty Images; (bl) ©Keystone/Getty Images; (br) ©NASA/Science Photo Library

**17 List** As you read, underline the advantages of using landers and rovers in the exploration of a planet's surface.

## By Using Landers and Rovers

Imagine being able to view a planet's surface from Earth. Robotic exploration on the surface of planets and other bodies in space is done by using landers. A *lander* is designed to land on the surface of a planet and send data back to Earth. A *rover* is a mobile vehicle that is used to physically explore the surface by moving about. The chief advantage of landers and rovers is that they can conduct experiments on soil and rocks. They can also directly record surface conditions, such as temperature and wind flow.

The *Mars Pathfinder*, a lander launched in 1996, placed the Mars rover called *Sojourner* on the planet's surface in 1997. In 2003, NASA sent two more rovers, called *Spirit* and *Opportunity*, to explore Mars. The rovers searched the Martian surface for water and evidence of environments that could possibly support life.

## Visualize It!

**18 Assess** How have we learned about Mars from landers and rovers?

_____

_____

_____

_____

_____

_____

_____

_____

1950    1960    1970

In 1962, technicians joined the *Telstar* satellite to a Delta rocket for launch. *Telstar* was the first satellite to transmit TV signals.

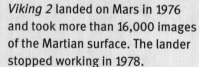

*Viking 2* landed on Mars in 1976 and took more than 16,000 images of the Martian surface. The lander stopped working in 1978.

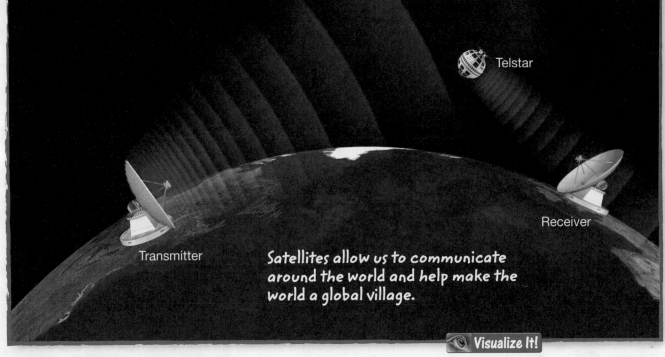

Telstar

Transmitter

Receiver

*Satellites allow us to communicate around the world and help make the world a global village.*

## With Artificial Satellites

When you turn on a TV or a cell phone, a satellite high in the atmosphere often makes this communication possible. An *artificial satellite* is any human-made object placed in orbit around a body in space. Satellites orbit Earth at high speeds. Each satellite has a unique function such as collecting weather data, relaying TV and radio signals, assisting in navigation, and studying Earth's surface.

The *Echo I* satellite was one of the very first communication satellites. It was launched by the United States in 1960. In that same year, the first weather satellite was launched. It carried a video camera to record observations of Earth's atmosphere. A system of orbiting global navigation satellites has been operated by the U.S. since 1978. These satellite systems are used to determine precise locations on Earth. Hundreds of active satellites orbit Earth.

**Visualize It!**

**19 Infer** How do satellites transmit data to Earth?

_____

_____

_____

_____

_____

_____

---

1980        1990        2000        2010

The *Mars Sojourner* lander used an x-ray spectrometer to analyze the Martian surface in 1996.

The *Mars Exploration Rovers Spirit* and *Opportunity* explored opposite sides of the Martian surface in 2004.

NOAA (National Oceanic and Atmospheric Administration) prepared for the launch of a polar orbiter weather satellite in 2009.

# Visual Summary

To complete this summary, check the box that indicates true or false. Then, use the key below to check your answers. You can use this page to review the main concepts of the lesson.

**History of Space Exploration**

Crewed orbital space exploration takes place in a piloted spacecraft that orbits Earth or travels to the moon.

T F
20 ☐ ☐  The first crewed orbital spaceflight mission took place aboard NASA's project Gemini in 1961.

Space probes are uncrewed vehicles that carry scientific instruments into space beyond Earth's orbit to collect data.

T F
21 ☐ ☐  Space probes can travel on the surface of a planet.

A space station is a long-term orbiting crewed spacecraft from which other vehicles can be launched or scientific research can be carried out.

T F
22 ☐ ☐  Space stations are a place where humans can live their daily lives, such as eating, sleeping, and working.

Answers: 20 F; 21 F; 22 T

---

**23 Compare** What are some advantages and disadvantages of crewed and uncrewed missions?

# Lesson Review

## Vocabulary

Fill in the blank with the term that best completes the following sentences.

**1** A/An _____ is a human-made object that is placed in orbit around a body in space.

**2** _____ is a government agency that runs the space program in the United States.

**3** A vehicle that is designed to move about and collect data from the surface of a planet is called a _____ .

## Key Concepts

**4 List** Identify four ways in which people can directly explore space.

_____

_____

_____

**5 Identify** What are five ways in which people can explore and study space without physically going there?

_____

_____

_____

_____

**6 Summarize** Describe three achievements in space exploration that involved the United States.

_____

_____

_____

_____

_____

_____

## Critical Thinking

Use the image to answer the following question.

**7 Infer** Is this an image of an orbiter or a rover? How do you know?

_____

_____

_____

**8 Relate** How is preparing for a space mission similar to planning for a camping trip? How is it different?

_____

_____

_____

_____

_____

_____

_____

**9 Assess** What type of technology would you want to use to study the gas giant plants?

_____

_____

_____

# My Notes

# Think Science

# Making a Presentation

TEKS 6.3D relate the impact of research on scientific thought and society, including the history of science and contributions of scientists as related to the content

6.11C describe the history and future of space exploration, including the types of equipment and transportation needed for space travel

Good communication is important to sharing ideas. Scientists may present their research in front of hundreds of people at a conference, or you may have to present a science project to your class. Like scientists, you too must be able to communicate your ideas in an interesting and effective way.

## Tutorial

**The following steps are guidelines to help in preparing and making a presentation**

**1 Choose your media type** Will your presentation be on paper or be electronic? The purpose of your presentation and the media available to you will often guide your decision.

**2 Prepare for your audience** Your presentation should tell a story, and the story should keep your audience engaged. The less the audience knows about the topic, the simpler the layout should be.

**3 Less is more** Presenting and explaining a few ideas clearly will make your presentation easier to understand than filling it with several ideas and images.

**4 Practice your talk** The best way to remember your presentation and the points you want to make is to take time to create it and then practice it.

**5 Cite your sources** Remember to add your sources. Also thank the people who helped you create your presentation. Plagiarism is the act of presenting someone else's work as your own. Plagiarism is never acceptable.

# You Try It!

Examine this poster presentation. It presents two different NASA space probes that were launched to collect information about the outer solar system and deep space. Identify what elements are good in the presentation, and identify how or why the presentation could be changed to suit the audience you will present it to.

*Your audience should be able to understand your presentation.*

**NASA Missions to Collect Data from the Outer Solar System and Beyond**

**Voyager 2**

Launched: August 1977

Purpose: to study Jupiter, Saturn, and Neptune

**IBEX (Interstellar Boundary Explorer)**

Launched: October 2008

Purpose: to map the boundary between the solar system and interstellar space

**1** This poster is an uncluttered presentation, but it gives limited information about each mission. If you were to focus in depth on one of these missions, which one would you choose? What information would you add to your presentation?

**2** What sources do you think are the most reliable for the information you need for your presentation?

**3** if you were to present the poster shown here to a class of kindergartners, would you change it in any way? Explain your answer.

**4** Could you use this presentation in a science fair? Explain your answer.

**5** What other media types could make this information more interesting for an audience?

### Take It Home

Both Voyager space probes (Voyager 1 and Voyager 2) carry gold-plated disks containing information about Earth. Research what the contents of those records are, and outline how the information is presented and explained on the disks.

# Technology for Space Exploration

**ESSENTIAL QUESTION**

## How do we explore space?

By the end of this lesson, you should be able to analyze the role of technology in the exploration of space.

Space probes, like the artist's conception shown here, visit distant planets in our solar system and transmit data back to Earth.

**TEKS** **6.11C** describe the history and future of space exploration, including the types of equipment and transportation needed for space travel

## Lesson Labs

**Quick Labs**
- Analyzing Satellite Images
- Design a Spacecraft

**S.T.E.M. Lab**
- Build a Rocket

## Engage Your Brain

**1 Predict** Check T or F to show whether you think each statement is true or false.

| T | F | |
|---|---|---|
| ☐ | ☐ | Astronauts can travel to distant planets in the solar system. |
| ☐ | ☐ | The space shuttle orbits the moon. |
| ☐ | ☐ | Artificial satellites in space can help you find locations on Earth. |
| ☐ | ☐ | Rovers explore the surfaces of planets and moons. |

**2 Describe** Write your own caption to this photo.

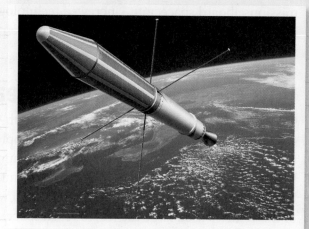

_____
_____
_____

**3 Apply** Use context clues to write your own definition for the words *analyze* and *transmit*.

**Example sentence**
Some spacecraft carry technology that can <u>analyze</u> soil and rock samples from objects in space.

analyze:

_____

_____

**Example sentence**
Satellites <u>transmit</u> data back to Earth.

transmit:

_____

_____

### Vocabulary Terms

- space shuttle
- space station
- probe
- orbiter
- lander
- rover
- artificial satellite

**4 Identify** As you read, place a question mark next to any words that you don't understand. When you finish reading the lesson, go back and review the text that you marked. If the information is still confusing, consult a classmate or a teacher.

# Beyond the Clouds

## What are two types of technology that people use to explore space?

Both crewed and uncrewed technologies are used to explore space. Crewed technologies, such as spacecraft, have astronauts on board. Astronauts are people who pilot spacecraft or complete missions aboard spacecraft. Uncrewed technologies carry scientific instruments that collect data. These data are sent back to Earth, where scientists analyze them.

## How do crewed vehicles reach space?

On April 12, 1961, Yuri Gagarin (YOOR·ee guh·GAR·in) became the first human to orbit Earth. Since then, people have continued to travel into space. The first vehicles to take humans into space had very little room for the crew. The space shuttle was developed later and allowed people more time to live and work in space. All of the vehicles used large rockets to reach space.

### With Rockets

To travel away from Earth, large rockets must overcome Earth's gravitational attraction. A *rocket* is a machine that uses gas, often from burning fuel, to escape Earth's gravitational pull. Rockets launch both crewed and uncrewed vehicles into space. During early space missions, the capsules that contained the crews separated from the rockets. The rockets themselves burned up. The capsules "splashed down" in the ocean and were recovered. But, they were not reused.

### With Space Shuttles

A **space shuttle** is a reusable spacecraft that launches using rocket boosters and liquid fuel, and glides to a landing on Earth like an airplane. The U.S. space shuttle program carried astronauts and supplies back and forth into orbit around Earth. *Columbia*, the first shuttle in a fleet of six, was launched by NASA in 1981. Between 1981 and 2011, more than 100 shuttle missions were completed. Two white, reusable solid rocket boosters (SRBs) helped the shuttle reach orbit. These booster rockets separated from the shuttle.

**Active Reading** 5 **Explain** What is the purpose of SRBs?

_____

_____

Booster rockets launched the space shuttle. Following launch, they detached and fell into the ocean. They were retrieved for reuse.

# What are some technologies that allow people to live in space?

Astronauts have traveled to the moon. Yet, no human has traveled to more distant objects in the solar system. This is because there are many technological challenges. For example, enough fuel is needed for a long return voyage. Other challenges include having enough air, food, and water for a long journey. In addition, the spacecraft must be insulated from the intense cold of space. They must also be protected from harmful radiation from the sun.

Spacesuits protect astronauts when they work outside a spacecraft. But astronauts still face challenges inside a spacecraft. In space, everything seems weightless. Simple tasks like eating and drinking become difficult. The human body also experiences problems in a weightless environment. Bones and muscles weaken. So, astronauts must exercise daily to strengthen their bodies.

People can live and work in space on space stations. A **space station** is a long-term crewed spacecraft on which scientific research can be carried out. Currently, the *International Space Station* (ISS) is the only space station in Earth orbit.

## Active Reading

**6 List** What are challenges humans face when traveling in space?

_____

_____

_____

_____

_____

_____

## Visualize It!

Spacesuits protect astronauts from extreme temperatures and from micrometeoroid strikes in space. They provide oxygen to astronauts and remove excess carbon dioxide.

A life support pack supplies oxygen and removes carbon dioxide.

Pressurized suits protect the astronaut from the vacuum of space.

The astronaut is tethered to the shuttle at the waist.

The helmet contains communication gear and a protective visor.

**7 Identify** What are some technologies humans use to survive outside in space?

_____

_____

_____

_____

_____

_____

The Hubble Space Telescope took this amazing image of Supernova SN1987A in the Large Magellanic Cloud and transmitted the image back to Earth.

# Looking Up

## What uncrewed technologies do people use to explore space?

Most objects in space are too far away for astronauts to visit. Scientists and engineers have developed uncrewed technologies to gather information about those objects. These technologies include space telescopes, probes, orbiters, landers, and rovers.

## Telescopes in Space

Earth's atmosphere blocks some types of light. It also distorts light that passes through it. This makes it difficult to obtain clear images of objects in deep space. So, some telescopes are placed in Earth orbit to obtain clearer images. Computers in the telescopes gather data and transmit them back to Earth. For example, the Hubble Space Telescope is a reflecting telescope that was placed in orbit in 1990. It detects visible light, and ultraviolet and infrared radiation as well. It has greatly expanded our knowledge of the universe.

Other space telescopes collect data using different types of electromagnetic radiation. The *Chandra X-Ray Observatory* and *Compton Gamma-Ray Observatory* were placed in space because Earth's atmosphere blocks most x-rays and gamma rays.

**Active Reading** **8 Relate** What is one advantage of placing a telescope in space?

_____

_____

_____

## Space Probes

A space **probe** is an uncrewed vehicle that carries scientific instruments to distant objects in space. Probes carry a variety of data-collecting instruments. Computers on board handle data, which are sent back to Earth.

Some probes can collect and return materials to Earth. In 2004, NASA's *Stardust* probe collected dust samples as it flew by a comet. The particles were returned to Earth for analysis two years later. It was the first time samples from beyond the moon were brought back to Earth!

Probes have been especially useful for studying the atmospheres of the gas giant planets. An atmospheric entry probe is dropped from a spacecraft into a planet's atmosphere. These probes send atmospheric data back to the spacecraft for a short period of time before they are crushed in the planet's atmosphere. Remember, the gas giant planets do not have solid surfaces on which to land. The pressure within their atmospheres is much greater than the atmospheric pressure on Earth.

© Houghton Mifflin Harcourt Publishing Company • Image Credits: (t) ©SSPL/Getty Images; (b) ©NASA Johnson Space Center

The **Mars Pathfinder** lander touched down on Mars in 1997. It found evidence that water once flowed on the surface of the planet.

This artist's rendition shows the encounter of the space probe **Stardust** with Comet Wild 2 in 2004.

## Visualize It!

**10 Compare** How are probes and landers alike? How are they different?

_____

_____

_____

## Orbiters

An **orbiter** is an uncrewed spacecraft that is designed to enter into orbit around another object in space. As an orbiter approaches its target, rocket engines are fired to slow down the spacecraft so it can go into orbit. Controllers on Earth can place a spacecraft into orbit around a distant planet or its moons.

Orbiters can study a planet for long periods of time. Cameras and other equipment on board are used to monitor atmospheric or surface changes. Instruments are also used to make measurements of temperature and to determine the altitudes of surface features. Orbiters can photograph an entire planet's surface. The data allow scientists to create detailed maps of bodies in the solar system.

**Active Reading** **9 Describe** What information can scientists obtain from orbiters?

_____

_____

## Landers and Rovers

Orbiters allow astronomers to create detailed maps of planets. They do not touch down on a planet or moon, however. That task is accomplished by landers that are controlled by scientists on Earth. A **lander** is a craft designed to land on the surface of a body in space. Landers have been placed successfully on the moon, on Venus, on Mars, and on Saturn's moon Titan. Some, such as the *Mars Pathfinder*, have sent data for years. The images taken by a lander are more detailed than those taken by an orbiter.

In addition, a lander may carry a rover. A **rover** is a small vehicle that comes out of the lander. It explores the surface of a planet or moon beyond the landing site. Both landers and rovers may have mechanical arms for gathering rock, dust, and soil samples.

One of the most successful space missions was the Mars Exploration Rover mission. During this mission, twin rovers landed on Mars in 2004. The rovers, *Spirit* and *Opportunity*, took amazing photos of the surface of Mars. They also found evidence of water below the Martian surface.

# Looking Down

## How are satellites used to observe Earth?

A satellite is any object in space that orbits another object. An **artificial satellite** is any human-made object placed in orbit around a body in space. Artificial satellites orbit Earth and send back data about our planet to ground stations. Some examples of artificial satellites include remote-sensing satellites, navigation satellites, weather satellites, and communications satellites.

Have you ever seen images of a large tropical storm on a weather report? These images are sent to Earth from weather satellites. They help scientists track storms and issue advance weather warnings. Weather satellites also monitor environmental conditions, such as changes in ocean temperatures. Remote-sensing satellites help scientists study Earth from space. They are used to map the ocean floor, identify sources of pollution, determine the size of ice caps, and even map the types of forests around the world. Astronauts in the *International Space Station* have photographed volcanoes during different stages of eruption.

The Global Positioning System (GPS) includes navigation satellites that can help pinpoint a user's exact location on Earth. Scientists use GPS to track wildlife. People use it to find locations on electronic maps. Communications satellites transmit television and telephone signals over long distances.

 Active Reading

**11 Identify** As you read, underline examples of four different kinds of satellites.

Inquiry

**12 Apply** List two different features on Earth's surface, which are not given as an example here, that might be studied from space.

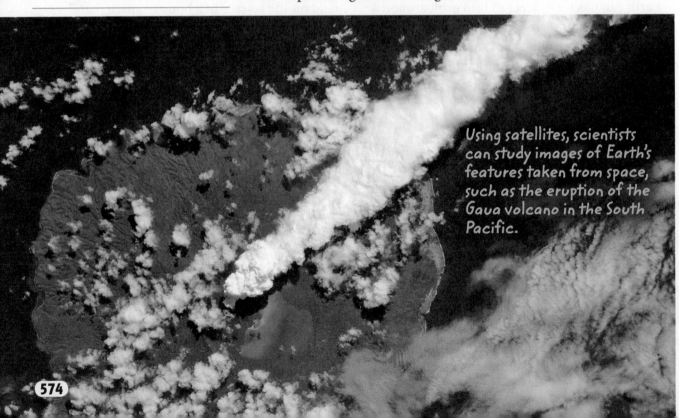

Using satellites, scientists can study images of Earth's features taken from space, such as the eruption of the Gaua volcano in the South Pacific.

# Exploring the Ocean

NEW FRONTIERS

They may not seem related, but deep-sea exploration and space exploration have something in common. Both use advanced technologies to observe locations that are difficult or dangerous for humans to explore.

## Ocean Submersibles

Both marine scientists and space scientists investigate areas most humans will never visit. Ocean submersibles can be crewed or uncrewed.

## Black Smokers

Hydrothermal vents are on the ocean floor where humans cannot withstand the high pressure.

## Tube Worms

In the 1970s, scientists aboard a submersible discovered giant tube worms living near an ocean vent. Similarly, NASA scientists examine the extreme conditions of Mars and other planets for any signs of life.

## Extend

Inquiry

**13 Identify** List two similarities between deep-sea exploration and space exploration.

**14 Research and Record** List some features of an ocean submersible, for example, *Alvin*. How is the submersible's structure similar to that of spacecraft?

**15 Recommend** Support more funding for deep-sea exploration by doing one of the following:
• write a letter
• design an ad for a science magazine
• write a script for a radio commercial

# Space Trips

## What are some goals of crewed space exploration?

Spacecraft have explored distant parts of our solar system. Because of technological limitations, these missions have been uncrewed. No human has traveled beyond the moon. But people may soon travel back to the moon. They may even go beyond the moon. NASA's plans for crewed space exploration include missions to the moon, to near-Earth asteroids, and to Mars.

### To Explore Cis-Lunar Space

*Cis-lunar space* is the region of space between Earth's atmosphere and the moon's orbit. Crewed missions into cis-lunar space can add to our knowledge about the effects of long-term space exploration on the human body. NASA is developing plans for a facility in this space. It would be placed where the gravitational forces of Earth and the moon balance each other out. At such a place, a space facility can "park" for long periods of time. Places in cis-lunar space can be staging posts for crewed and uncrewed missions to Mars and other places that are even farther away. Large spacecraft and exploration equipment could also be assembled there.

### To Explore the Moon

Several countries are developing plans to set up a crewed research base on the moon. A lunar base would allow astronauts to live and work for long periods of time on the moon's surface.

Scientists are eager to return to the moon for several reasons. Data about lunar soil gathered by rovers and crewed space missions indicate that the soil can unlock information about early Earth. Lunar soil also contains valuable resources, such as oxygen, water, silicon, aluminum, and titanium. These resources can be used to produce rocket propellant, drinking water, and the construction materials needed for a lunar base.

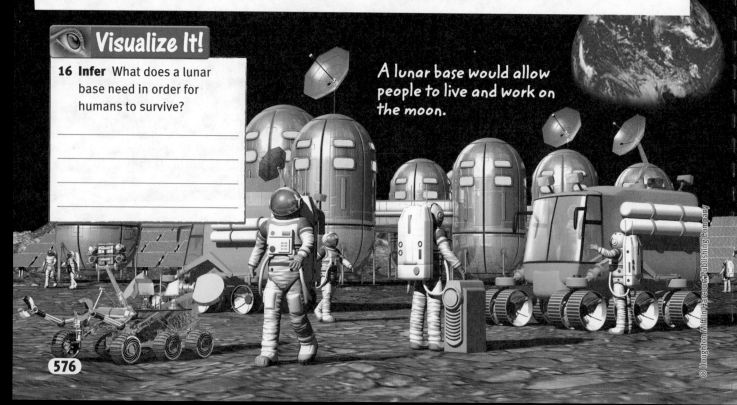

### Visualize It!

**16 Infer** What does a lunar base need in order for humans to survive?

_____

_____

_____

_____

A lunar base would allow people to live and work on the moon.

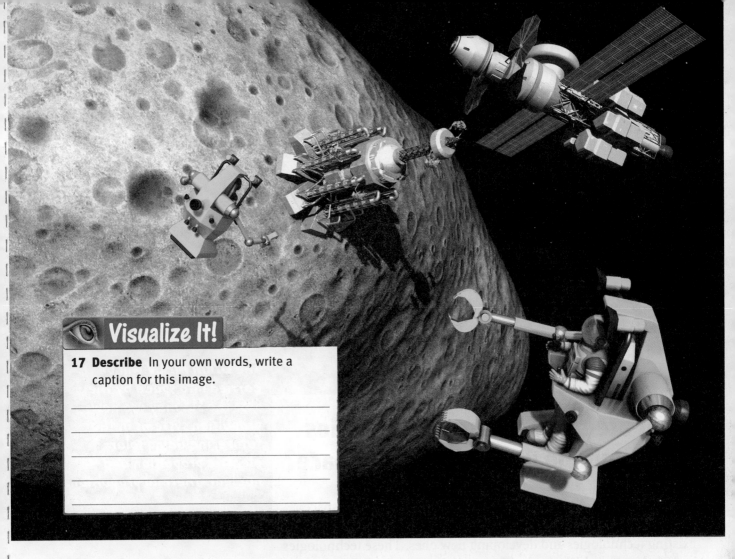

**17 Describe** In your own words, write a caption for this image.

_____

_____

_____

_____

## To Explore Near-Earth Asteroids

Asteroids are small, rocky bodies in space. They are debris that is left over from the period during which the solar system formed. Therefore, asteroids that orbit near Earth, or *near-Earth asteroids*, provide clues about the early history of the solar system. They may also provide information about our own planet. Many asteroids struck ancient Earth. They may have been responsible for bringing the ingredients of life to our planet.

Scientists also want to explore near-Earth asteroids for safety reasons. They can test ways of deflecting near-Earth asteroids. This would prevent possible collisions of asteroids with Earth. In addition, near-Earth asteroids may contain minerals that can be mined.

Crewed missions to asteroids will be tricky. Asteroids have little or no gravity, different rates of rotation, and can be structurally unstable. So, they are going to be challenging places to explore.

## To Explore Mars and Its Moons

NASA's biggest plans for crewed missions involve Mars and its moons. The red planet is one of the main goals of all crewed missions. Missions in cis-lunar space and on the surface of the moon will provide scientists and engineers with data they can use to plan a trip to Mars. Once on Mars, astronauts would search for water. They would also search for signs of life or for signs of the remains of ancient life. They would study the surface and the atmosphere.

Astronauts would have many challenges. For example, they would have to deal with the fine, red Martian dust and changing temperatures. However, they may be able to rely on Mars for water and other resources they need.

**Active Reading 18 Identify** What would astronauts look for on Mars?

_____

_____

# Tools in Space

The **Orion MPCV** will be carried into space by the SLS. The SLS may use new propulsion systems in the future, including solar-electric propulsion and nuclear-thermal propulsion.

## What are some future technologies that might be used to explore space?

To support both crewed and uncrewed missions, new transportation and equipment must be developed. NASA, space agencies of other countries, and private companies are improving existing technologies and developing new ones. These technologies include launch vehicles and capsules, deep-space habitats, space-exploration vehicles, destination systems, and robotic systems.

### Launch Vehicles and Capsules

The Space Launch System (SLS) is a new type of launch vehicle planned by NASA. It will replace the space shuttle and carry the *Orion MPCV*. The *Orion MPCV* is a capsule. It can take a crew of two to four astronauts to places in cis-lunar space. At first, the SLS will use liquid hydrogen and liquid oxygen propulsion systems and solid rocket boosters. Later propulsion systems may use solar panels to collect energy from the sun. The collected energy would be converted into electricity to power thrusters. Nuclear power can also be used to power electric thrusters.

**Active Reading** **19 Identify** What new launch vehicle is planned to transport humans into space?

### Places to Live

To stay on the moon or Mars for long periods of time, humans will need a safe place to live. The systems that are made for humans to live on the moon or Mars are called *deep-space habitats*. Deep-space habitats must have reliable life-support systems that give astronauts clean air and water. Habitats must protect humans from radiation and extreme temperatures. Resources are likely to be limited. Therefore, habitats must have ways to reduce both the use and waste of resources. Materials that are reusable, recyclable, or that can be repurposed for other uses would be used. These habitats must be able to meet the needs of crews in space for long periods of time. Therefore, they need to have medical technologies. They must also have ways of growing and storing food.

## Space-Exploration Vehicles

Astronauts will need vehicles to travel from place to place on the surface of a planet or moon. New space-exploration vehicles will have pressurized cabins that can be adjusted for both high and low gravity. On crewed missions, astronauts in spacesuits may exit pressurized cabins through ports. Some vehicles may be able to hover over the surface of a planet or moon. They may also anchor to a near-Earth asteroid or a Martian moon. Other space-exploration vehicles may have robotic arms to collect soil or rocks.

## Destination Systems

Destination systems include technologies that make it possible for astronauts to remain far away from the resources on Earth. For example, landers would take crews and cargo to and from a destination site, such as on the moon or Mars. At the destination, equipment would be needed to extract resources from the surface, to generate power, and to explore the surface. Destination systems would also include equipment to construct and maintain exploration vehicles.

## Robots and Robotic Systems

Robotic systems and robots have already been used to explore space. They are also part of future space-exploration plans. Robots can withstand the harsh conditions in space better than humans can. They can work with astronauts. Robots can be programmed to do dangerous tasks. They can also do repetitive tasks, which allows astronauts to do more complex work.

Robotic systems can be used to image and map the destination. They can test the conditions before astronauts arrive to determine if the place is habitable. They can also test landing techniques and collect samples, such as soil and rocks.

### Think Outside the Book

20 **Research** Future space exploration will involve using new types of transportation, including propulsion systems. Research these systems to find out the advantages and disadvantages of each. Create a poster that shows each type of system and its advantages and disadvantages.

### Visualize It!

21 **Identify** What are some types of equipment that are shown below?

_____

_____

_____

_____

Space-exploration vehicles and deep-space habitats may be used in the future to explore Mars.

# Visual Summary

To complete this summary, fill in the blanks with the correct word or phrase. Then, use the key below to check your answers. You can use this page to review the main concepts of the lesson.

**Humans use crewed technology to travel to and from space.**

**22** To escape from Earth's gravity, the space shuttle used liquid fuel and

_____

**Uncrewed spacecraft can explore distant planets.**

**23** To obtain clearer images, space telescopes orbit above

_____

**New equipment and transportation will support future space exploration.**

**24** On Mars, astronauts would use equipment to search for signs of life and

_____

Answers: 22 solid rocket boosters; 23 Earth's atmosphere; 24 water

**25 Provide** Give examples of the kind of information scientists can obtain from each type of uncrewed spacecraft.

# Lesson Review

## Vocabulary

Circle the term that best completes the following sentences.

**1** A *rocket / space shuttle* is a reusable crewed spacecraft.

**2** A(n) *lander / orbiter* is a kind of artificial satellite.

**3** A(n) *orbiter / rover* often has mechanical arms to gather rock samples.

**4** A(n) *orbiter / probe* is more suited to the long-term study of a planet or moon.

**5** A *rocket / space shuttle* had detachable capsules that contained the crew.

## Key Concepts

**6 List** Give an example of how weather satellites are used to observe Earth.

_____

_____

**7 Explain** Why is most space exploration accomplished with spacecraft that do not have crews on board?

_____

_____

_____

_____

**8 Summarize** What are four future goals of crewed space travel?

_____

_____

_____

**9 Explain** What is one advantage of using an orbiter to study objects in space?

_____

_____

_____

## Critical Thinking

Use the diagram to answer the following questions.

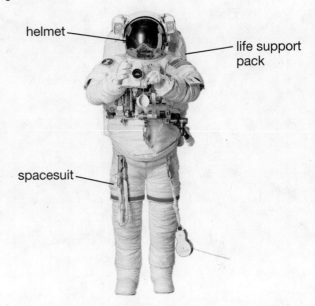

helmet — life support pack

spacesuit

**10 Identify** Which spacesuit feature provides oxygen to an astronaut?

_____

**11 Infer** How is the spacesuit designed to protect the astronaut outside of a spacecraft?

_____

_____

_____

_____

**12 Infer** Why do you think it's important to map a planet's surface before a spacecraft, such as a lander, takes astronauts there?

_____

_____

_____

**13 Analyze** Why will astronauts need equipment to extract resources at future bases in space if they stay for a long time?

_____

_____

_____

# My Notes

People develop and use technology to explore space.

### Lesson 1

**ESSENTIAL QUESTION**
*What are some milestones of space exploration?*

Understand some of the achievements of space exploration.

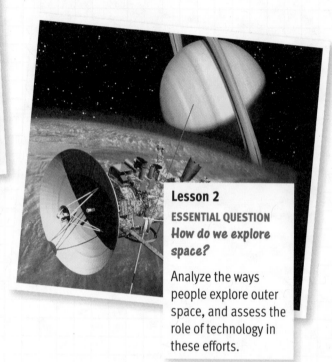

### Lesson 2

**ESSENTIAL QUESTION**
*How do we explore space?*

Analyze the ways people explore outer space, and assess the role of technology in these efforts.

## Connect ESSENTIAL QUESTIONS
Lessons 1 and 2

**1 Synthesize** Choose one specific space vehicle from the past. Explain how this vehicle might be combined with advanced technology for new space exploration programs in the future.

_____
_____
_____
_____
_____
_____
_____
_____

### Think Outside the Book

**2 Synthesize** Choose one of these activities to help synthesize what you have learned in this unit.

☐ Using what you learned in lessons 1 and 2, write a short story about an astronaut, his or her training and space mission experiences, and ways in which technology made the astronaut's journey possible.

☐ Using what you learned in lessons 1 and 2, create a graphic novel to show some of the limitations of human space exploration.

# Unit 9 Review

Name _____

## Vocabulary

Fill in the blank with the term that best completes the sentence.

**TEKS 6.11C**

**1** _____ is the United States agency that explores space through crewed and uncrewed missions.

**TEKS 6.11C**

**2** A machine that uses high-speed escaping gas to move objects into space is called a(n) _____.

**TEKS 6.11C**

**3** An artificial _____ is any human-made object placed in orbit around a body in space, either with or without a crew.

**TEKS 6.11C**

**4** A mobile, uncrewed vehicle that is used to explore the surface of another planet is called a(n) _____.

**5** The _____ was a crewed vehicle used to travel to and from space.

## Key Concepts

Choose the letter of the best answer.

**TEKS 6.11C**

**6** The following diagram shows the path of a spacecraft launched into space in 1977.

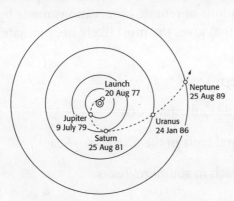

What kind of spacecraft most likely followed this path? (Hint: Step 1. Look at the path of the spacecraft, and decide if the voyage would need a crew. Step 2. Decide if the spacecraft can remain in orbit or if it needs to move through space.)

**A** an uncrewed rover

**C** an uncrewed space probe

**B** a crewed space shuttle

**D** a crewed space station

# Unit 9 Review continued

**TEKS** 6.11C, 6.3D

**7** In 1997, a lander called the *Mars Pathfinder* launched a rover known as *Sojourner*. Which data could have only come from these uncrewed vehicles? (Hint. Step 1. Recall how landers and rovers are used to explore space. Step 2. Think about how they differ from other kinds of space vehicles. Step 3. Choose the example that could have come only from a rover.)

**A** images of stars forming

**C** makeup of soil and rock samples

**B** maps of planetary orbits

**D** distance measurements to far planets

**TEKS** 6.11C

**8** The first space flight was made by Yuri Gagarin aboard the *Vostok 1*. What kind of milestone was this?

**A** crewed, orbital space flight

**C** uncrewed, orbital space flight

**B** crewed, suborbital space flight

**D** uncrewed, suborbital space flight

**TEKS** 6.11C

**9** Which type of spacecraft would best be used to study the long-term effects of life in space on humans?

**A** satellite

**C** space shuttle

**B** space probe

**D** space station

**TEKS** 6.11C, 6.3D

**10** Nikki is designing a project that uses satellites. Which of these observations would best be performed by using satellites that orbit Earth? (Hint: Step 1. Consider both common uses and limitations of remote observations made by satellites. Step 2. Identify the statement that gives the most likely use of a satellite for research.)

**A** composition of a rock layer in northern Texas

**B** summer sea-surface temperature in the Gulf of Mexico

**C** number of different fish species in coral reefs in the Caribbean Sea

**D** height of high tide on one day at a beach in southern Texas

Name _____

TEKS 6.11C

**11** The diagrams below show different types of spacecraft. Which spacecraft has parts that show it can collect and analyze materials from the surface of a planet?

**A**

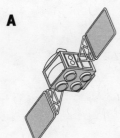

**C**

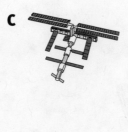

**B**

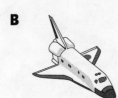

**D**

## Gridded Response

Write your answer in the boxes, then bubble in the corresponding number in the grid below.

TEKS 6.11C

**12** The International Space Station orbits Earth once every 90 minutes. How many times will it orbit Earth in a 12-hour period?

## Critical Thinking

Answer the following questions in the space provided.

TEKS 6.11C, 6.3D

**13** Explain the distinction between astronomy and space exploration.

_____

_____

_____

_____

TEKS 6.11C, 6.3D

**14** Satellites provide us with various forms of communication.

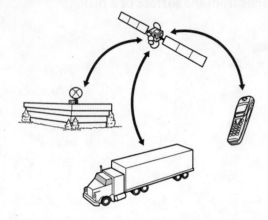

Describe how satellites can aid in communication.

_____

_____

_____

_____

_____

_____

## Connect ESSENTIAL QUESTIONS
Lessons 1 and 2

Answer the following question in the space provided.

TEKS 6.11C, 6.3D

**15** Outline a brief history of space exploration, and discuss some problems humans encounter when they explore space.

_____

_____

_____

_____

_____

_____

_____

_____

# Organisms and Environments

## Big Idea

Scientists classify organisms based on shared characteristics, such as cellular and structural characteristics, and the ways organisms interact with their environment.

Mangroves

Roseate Spoonbill

## What do you think?

Mangroves and Roseate Spoonbills are both found in Florida. How do organisms like these get and use matter and energy?

© Houghton Mifflin Harcourt Publishing Company • Image Credits: (bkgd) ©L. Newman & A. Flowers/Photo Researchers, Inc.; (br) ©Tom Salyer/Photolibrary

# Unit 10
# Organisms and Environments

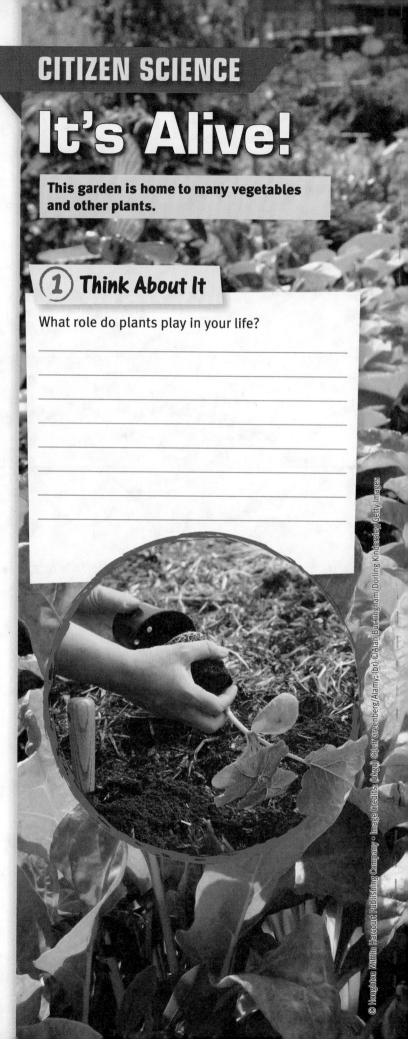

## CITIZEN SCIENCE
# It's Alive!

This garden is home to many vegetables and other plants.

### ① Think About It

What role do plants play in your life?

_____

_____

_____

_____

_____

_____

_____

© Houghton Mifflin Harcourt Publishing Company • Image Credits: (bkgd) ©Jeff Greenberg/Alamy; (br) ©Alan Buckingham/Dorling Kindersley/Getty Images

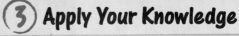

## ② Ask A Question

### How do plants use matter and energy?

As a class, design a plan for a garden plot or window box garden in which the class can grow a variety of plants. Remember that plants have different growing periods and requirements.

### Sketch It!

Draw your plan to show where each plant will be placed.

## ③ Apply Your Knowledge

**A** What do your plants need in order to grow?

_____

_____

_____

**B** Which of the things you listed above are examples of matter? Which are examples of energy?

_____

_____

_____

_____

**C** Create and care for your classroom garden and observe the plant growth.

Describe an area in your community that is used for growing food. If there is no such area, initiate a plan to plant in an area that you think could be used.

591

# The Characteristics of Cells

## ESSENTIAL QUESTION

## What are living things made of?

By the end of this lesson, you should be able to explain the components of the scientific theory of cells.

People communicate to others through talking, signing, body language, and other methods. Inside your body, cells communicate too. Brain cells, like the ones shown here, control balance, posture, and muscle coordination.

**TEKS** **6.3D** relate the impact of research on scientific thought and society, including the history of science and contributions of scientists as related to the content

**TEKS** **6.12A** understand that all organisms are composed of one or more cells

**TEKS** **6.12B** recognize that the presence of a nucleus determines whether a cell is prokaryotic or eukaryotic

**TEKS** **6.12D** identify the basic characteristics of organisms, including prokaryotic or eukaryotic, unicellular or multicellular, autotrophic or heterotrophic, and mode of reproduction, that further classify them in the currently recognized Kingdoms

## Lesson Labs

**Quick Labs**
- How Do Tools that Magnify Help Us Study Cells?
- Investigating Cell Size

**Exploration Lab**
- Using a Microscope to Explore Cells

## Engage Your Brain

**1 Predict** Check T or F to show whether you think each statement is true or false.

T   F

☐   ☐   All living things are made up of one or more cells.

☐   ☐   Rocks are made up of cells.

☐   ☐   All cells are the same size.

☐   ☐   Cells perform life functions for living things.

**2 Describe** Sketch your idea of what a cell looks like. Label any parts you include in your sketch.

## Active Reading

**3 Synthesize** Many English words have their roots in other languages. Use the Greek words below to make an educated guess about the meanings of the words *prokaryote* and *eukaryote*. Here *kernel* refers to the nucleus where genetic material is contained in some cells.

| Word part | Meaning |
|-----------|---------|
| pro- | before |
| eu- | true |
| karyon | kernel |

### Vocabulary Terms

- cell
- organism
- cell membrane
- cytoplasm
- organelle
- nucleus
- prokaryote
- eukaryote

**4 Apply** As you learn the definition of each vocabulary term in this lesson, create your own sketches of a prokaryotic cell and a eukaryotic cell and label the parts in each cell.

prokaryote:

_____

_____

eukaryote:

_____

_____

# Cell-ebrate!

## What is a cell?

Like all living things, you are made up of cells. A **cell** is the smallest functional and structural unit of all living organisms. An **organism** is any living thing. All organisms are made up of cells. Some organisms are just one cell. Others, like humans, contain trillions of cells. An organism carries out all of its own life processes.

Robert Hooke was the first person to describe cells as they appear under a microscope. In 1665, he published a book that described his observations. He looked at a thin slice of cork from tree bark. The cork looked as if it was made of little boxes. Hooke named these boxes *cells*, which means "little rooms" in Latin.

**Visualize It!**

**6 Compare** Looking at the photos of the three different cells, what do the cells have in common?

_____

_____

_____

_____

_____

### Bacterial cell

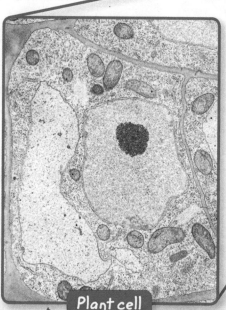

Plant cells range in size from 10 μm to 100 μm. They can be much larger than animal cells.

Plant cell

Bacterial cells are up to 1000 times smaller than human cells.

The average size of a human cell is 10 μm. It would take about 50 average human cells to cover the dot on this letter i.

### Human skin cell

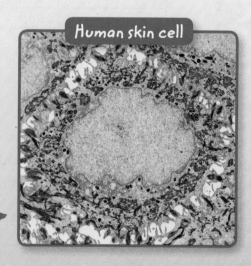

# Why are most cells small?

Most cells are too small to be seen without a microscope. Cells are small because their size is limited by their outer surface area. Cells take in food and get rid of wastes through their outer surface. As a cell grows, it needs more food and produces more waste. Therefore, more materials pass through its outer surface. However, as a cell grows, the cell's volume increases faster than the surface area. If a cell gets too large, the cell's surface area will not be large enough to take in enough nutrients or pump out enough wastes. The ratio of the cell's outer surface area to the cell's volume is called the *surface area-to-volume ratio*. Smaller cells have a greater surface area-to-volume ratio than larger cells.

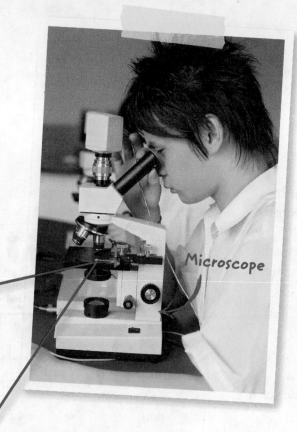

Microscope

## Do the Math

Here's an example of how to calculate the surface area-to-volume ratio of the cube shown at the right.

### Sample Problem

**A** Calculate the surface area.

surface area of cube =

number of faces × area of one face

surface area of cube = $6(2 \text{ cm} \times 2 \text{ cm})$

surface area of cube = $24 \text{ cm}^2$

**B** Calculate the volume.

volume of cube = side × side × side

volume of cube = $2 \text{ cm} \times 2 \text{ cm} \times 2 \text{ cm}$

volume of cube = $8 \text{ cm}^3$

**C** Calculate the surface area-to-volume ratio. A ratio is a comparison between numbers. It can be written by placing a colon between the numbers being compared.

surface area : volume = $24 \text{ cm}^2 : 8 \text{ cm}^3$

surface area : volume = $3 \text{ cm}^2 : 1 \text{ cm}^3$

### You Try It

**7 Calculate** What is the surface area-to-volume ratio of a cube whose sides are 3 cm long?

**A** Calculate the surface area.

**B** Calculate the volume.

**C** Calculate the surface area-to-volume ratio.

# Cell *Hall of* Fame

## What is the cell theory?

Scientific knowledge often results from combining the work of several scientists. For example, the discoveries of Matthias Schleiden (muh•THY•uhs SHLY•duhn), Theodor Schwann (THEE•oh•dohr SHVAHN), Robert Remak, and Rudolf Virchow (ROO•dawlf VIR•koh) led to one very important theory called the *cell theory*. The cell theory lists three basic characteristics of all cells and organisms:

- All organisms are made up of one or more cells.
- The cell is the basic unit of all organisms.
- All cells come from existing cells.

The cell theory is fundamental to the study of organisms, medicine, heredity, evolution, and all other aspects of life science.

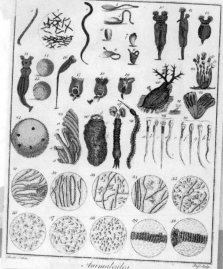

### Visualize It!

**8 Provide** As you read, fill in the missing events on the timeline.

Model of Hooke's microscope

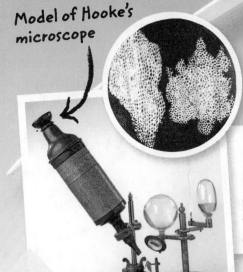

**1673**
Anton van Leeuwenhoek made careful drawings of the organisms he observed.

**1665**
Robert Hooke sees tiny, box-like spaces when using a microscope like this to observe thin slices of cork. He calls these spaces cells.

**1855**
Robert Remak
_____
_____
_____
_____

© Houghton Mifflin Harcourt Publishing Company • Image Credits: (bl) ©Dave King/Getty Images; (tl) ©Dr. Jeremy Burgess/Photo Researchers, Inc.; (tr) ©The Print Collector/Alamy; (br) ©Time & Life Pictures/Getty Images

**9 Relate** When Anton van Leeuwenhoek first reported seeing "tiny animals" in water, other scientists found it hard to believe him! Find out how and why his discoveries were finally accepted by fellow scientists.

**1838**
Matthias Schleiden
_____
_____
_____

Cells of
an iris petal

**1839**
Theodor Schwann
_____
_____
_____
_____
_____

This iris and butterfly are multicellular organisms made up of many cells.

# All Organisms Are Made Up of One or More Cells

Anton van Leeuwenhoek (AN•tahn VAN LAY•vuhn•huk) was the first person to describe actual living cells when he looked at a drop of pond water under a microscope. These studies made other scientists wonder if all living things were made up of cells. In 1838, Matthias Schleiden concluded that plants are made of cells. Then in 1839, Theodor Schwann determined that all animal tissues are made of cells. He concluded that all organisms are made of one or more cells.

Organisms that are made up of just one cell are called *unicellular organisms*. The single cell of a unicellular organism must carry out all of the functions for life. Organisms that are made up of more than one cell are called *multicellular organisms*. The cells of multicellular organism often have specialized functions.

# The Cell Is the Basic Unit of All Organisms

Based on his observations about the cellular make up of organisms, Schwann made another conclusion. He determined that the cell is the basic unit of all living things. Thus, Schwann wrote the first two parts of the cell theory.

# All Cells Come from Existing Cells

In 1855, Robert Remak, a doctor, identified that cells arise from cell division. Remak reported that the cells of chick embryos came from division of the fertilized egg cell. In 1858, Rudolf Virchow supported Remak's discoveries and concluded that all cells come from existing cells.

**Active Reading**

**10 Summarize** What is the cell theory?

_____
_____
_____
_____
_____

# On the Cellular

## What parts do all cells have in common?

Different cells vary in size and shape. However, all cells have some parts in common, including cell membranes, cytoplasm, organelles, and DNA. These different parts help the cell to carry out all the tasks needed for life.

### Cell Membrane

A **cell membrane** is a protective layer that covers a cell's surface and acts as a barrier between the inside of a cell and the cell's environment. It also controls materials, such as water and oxygen, that move into and out of a cell.

### Cytoplasm

The region enclosed by the cell membrane that includes the fluid and all of the *organelles* of the cell is called the **cytoplasm** (SY•tuh•plaz•uhm).

### Organelles

An **organelle** is a small body in a cell's cytoplasm that is specialized to perform a specific function. Cells can have one or more types of organelles. Most, but not all, organelles have a membrane.

### DNA

Deoxyribonucleic acid, or DNA, is genetic material that provides instructions for all cell processes. Organisms inherit DNA from their parent or parents. In some cells, the DNA is contained in a membrane-bound organelle called the **nucleus**. In other types of cells, the DNA is not contained in a nucleus.

# What are the two types of cells?

Although cells have some basic parts in common, there are some important differences. The way that cells store their DNA is the main difference between the two cell types and it is one of the main features by which scientists classify cells.

 **Active Reading**

**12 Define** As you read, underline the differences between prokaryotes and eukaryotes.

## Prokaryotic

A **prokaryote** (proh•KAIR•ee•oht) is a single-celled organism that does not have a nucleus or membrane-bound organelles. Its DNA is located in the cytoplasm. Prokaryotic cells contain organelles called *ribosomes* that do not have a membrane. Some prokaryotic cells have hairlike structures called *flagella* that help them move. Prokaryotes, which include all bacteria and archaea, are smaller than eukaryotes.

## Eukaryotic

A **eukaryote** (yoo•KAIR•ee•oht) is an organism made up of cells that contain their DNA in a nucleus. Eukaryotic cells contain membrane-bound organelles, as well as ribosomes. Not all eukaryotic cells are the same. Animals, plants, protists, and fungi are eukaryotes. All multicellular organisms are eukaryotes. Most eukaryotes are multicellular. Some eukaryotes, such as amoebas and yeasts, are unicellular.

## Visualize It!

**13 Identify** Use the list of terms below to fill in the blanks with the matching cell parts in each cell. Some terms are used twice.

DNA in cytoplasm
DNA in nucleus
Cytoplasm
Cell membrane
Organelles

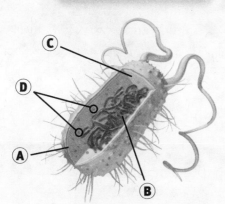

*Prokaryotic*

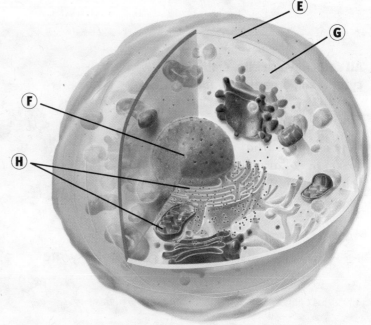

*Eukaryotic*

A _____
B _____
C _____
D _____

E _____
F DNA in nucleus
G _____
H _____

# Visual Summary

To complete this summary, fill in the blanks with the correct word or phrase. Then use the key below to check your answers. You can use this page to review the main concepts of the lesson.

## The Characteristics of Cells

A cell is the smallest unit that can perform all the processes necessary for life.

**14** The cell of a _____ organism must carry out all of its life functions; an organism made up of more than one cell is called a _____ organism.

The cell theory lists three basic principles of all cells and organisms.

**15** All cells come from existing _____

All cells have a cell membrane, cytoplasm, organelles, and DNA.

**16** The organelle that contains DNA in eukaryotic cells is called a _____

Eukaryotic

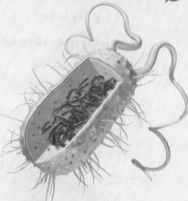

Prokaryotic

Answers: 14 unicellular, multicellular; 15 cells; 16 nucleus

**17 Relate** Choose an organism that you are familiar with, and explain how the three parts of the cell theory relate to that organism.

# Lesson Review

## Vocabulary

Fill in the blank with the term that best completes the following sentences.

**1** The _____ is the smallest functional and structural unit of all living things.

**2** All cells are surrounded by a(n) _____

**3** A living thing is called a(n) _____

## Key Concepts

**4 Describe** Discuss two ways that all cells are alike.

_____

_____

_____

**5 List** What are the main ideas of the cell theory?

_____

_____

_____

_____

_____

**6 Compare** How do prokaryotes differ from eukaryotes? How are they similar?

_____

_____

_____

_____

**7 Relate** People once believed organisms could grow from food or dirt. How might the scientific study of cells have affected this view?

_____

_____

_____

_____

_____

## Critical Thinking

Use this figure to answer the following questions.

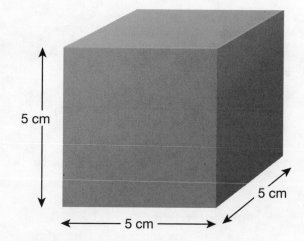

**8 Apply** What is the surface area-to-volume ratio of this cube?

_____

_____

_____

**9 Apply** Cells can not get as large as this cube. Explain why in terms of a cell's surface area-to-volume ratio.

_____

_____

_____

_____

**10 Compare** How is the structure of a unicellular organism different than the structure of a multicellular organism? How does this affect function?

_____

_____

_____

_____

_____

_____

# My Notes

# Classification of Living Things

**ESSENTIAL QUESTION**

## How are organisms classified?

By the end of this lesson, you should be able to describe how people sort living things into groups based on shared characteristics.

Scientists use physical and chemical characteristics to classify organisms. Is that a spider? Look again. It's an ant mimicking a jumping spider!

**TEKS** **6.12C** recognize that the broadest taxonomic classification of living organisms is divided into currently recognized Domains

**TEKS** **6.12D** identify the basic characteristics of organisms, including prokaryotic or eukaryotic, unicellular or multicellular, autotrophic or heterotrophic, and mode of reproduction, that further classify them in the currently recognized Kingdoms

## Lesson Labs

**Quick Labs**
• Using a Dichotomous Key
• Identifying Leaves

**Exploration Lab**
• Developing Scientific Names

## Engage Your Brain

**1 Predict** Check T or F to show whether you think each statement is true or false.

T   F

☐  ☐ The classification system used today has changed very little since it was introduced.

☐  ☐ To be classified as an animal, an organism must have a backbone.

☐  ☐ Organisms can be classified according to whether they have nuclei in their cells.

☐  ☐ Scientists can study genetic material to classify organisms.

☐  ☐ Organisms that have many physical similarities are always related.

**2 Analyze** The flowering plant shown above is called an Indian pipe. It could be mistaken for a fungus. Write down how the plant is similar to and different from other plants you know.

_____

_____

_____

_____

## Active Reading

**3 Word Parts** Many English words have their roots in other languages. Use the Latin suffix below to make an educated guess about the meaning of the word *Plantae*.

| Latin suffix | Meaning |
|---|---|
| -ae | a group of |

**Example sentence**
Maples are part of the kingdom <u>Plantae</u>.

*Plantae:*

_____

_____

### Vocabulary Terms

• species
• genus
• domain
• Bacteria
• Archaea
• Eukarya
• Protista
• Fungi
• Plantae
• Animalia

**4 Apply** As you learn the definition of each vocabulary term in this lesson, write your own definition or make a sketch to help you remember the meaning of each term.

# Sorting Things Out!

## Why do we classify living things?

There are millions of living things on Earth. How do scientists keep all of these living things organized? Scientists *classify* living things based on characteristics that living things share. Classification helps scientists answer questions such as:

- How many kinds of living things are there?
- What characteristics define each kind of living thing?
- What are the relationships among living things?

Sharks have fins and gills.

Dolphins also have fins, but not gills.

 **Visualize It!**

**5 Analyze** The photos show two organisms. In the table, place a check mark in the box for each characteristic that the organisms have.

Yellow pansy butterfly

American goldfinch

|  | Wings | Antennae | Beak | Feathers |
|---|---|---|---|---|
| Yellow pansy butterfly |  |  |  |  |
| American goldfinch |  |  |  |  |

**6 Summarize** What characteristics do yellow pansy butterflies have in common with American goldfinches? How do they differ?

_____

_____

_____

# How do scientists know living things are related?

If two organisms look similar, are they related? To classify organisms, scientists compare physical characteristics. For example, they may look at size or bone structure. Scientists also compare the chemical characteristics of living things.

## Physical Characteristics

How are chickens similar to dinosaurs? If you compare dinosaur fossils and chicken skeletons, you will see that chickens and dinosaurs share many physical characteristics. Scientists look at physical characteristics, such as skeletal structure. They also study how organisms develop from an egg to an adult. For example, animals with similar skeletons and development may be related.

## Chemical Characteristics

Scientists can identify the relationships among organisms by studying genetic material such as DNA and RNA. They study mutations and genetic similarities to find relationships among organisms. Organisms that have very similar gene sequences or have the same mutations are likely related. Other chemicals, such as proteins and hormones, can also be studied to learn how organisms are related.

The two pandas below share habitats and diets. They look alike, but they have different DNA.

Red panda

The red panda is a closer relative to a raccoon than it is to a giant panda.

Raccoon

Giant panda

Spectacled bear

The giant panda is a closer relative to a spectacled bear than it is to a red panda.

**7 List** How does DNA lead scientists to better classify organisms?

_____
_____
_____
_____
_____
_____
_____

# What's in a Name?

## How are living things named?

Early scientists used names as long as 12 words to identify living things, and they also used common names. So, classification was confusing. In the 1700s, a scientist named Carolus Linnaeus (KAR•uh•luhs lih•NEE•uhs) simplified the naming of living things. He gave each kind of living thing a two-part *scientific name*.

### Scientific Names

Each species has its own scientific name. A **species** (SPEE•sheez) is a group of organisms that are very closely related. They can mate and produce fertile offspring. Consider the scientific name for a mountain lion: *Puma concolor*. The first part, *Puma*, is the genus name. A **genus** (JEE•nuhs; plural, *genera*) includes similar species. The second part, *concolor*, is the specific, or species, name. No other species is named *Puma concolor*.

A scientific name always includes the genus name followed by the specific name. The first letter of the genus name is capitalized, and the first letter of the specific name is lowercase. The entire scientific name is written either in italics or underlined.

HELLO
my name is
Carolus Linnaeus

## The A.K.A. Files

Some living things have many common names. Scientific names prevent confusion when people discuss organisms.

Scientific name:
**Puma concolor**

Common names:
Mountain lion
Puma
Cougar
Panther

Scientific name:
**Acer rubrum**

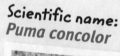

Common names:
Red maple
Swamp maple
Soft maple

**8 Apply** In the scientific names above, circle the genus name and underline the specific name.

# What are the levels of classification?

Linnaeus's ideas became the basis for modern taxonomy (tak•SAHN•uh•mee). *Taxonomy* is the science of describing, classifying, and naming living things. At first, many scientists sorted organisms into two groups: plants and animals. But numerous organisms did not fit into either group.

Today, scientists use an eight-level system to classify living things. Each level gets more specific. Therefore, it contains fewer kinds of living things than the level above it. Living things in the lower levels are more closely related to each other than they are to organisms in the higher levels. From most general to more specific, the levels of classification are domain, kingdom, phylum (plural, *phyla*), class, order, family, genus, and species.

## Classifying Organisms

**Domain** — **Domain Eukarya** includes all protists, fungi, plants, and animals.

**Kingdom** — **Kingdom Animalia** includes all animals.

**Phylum** — Animals in **Phylum Chordata** have a hollow nerve cord in their backs. Some have a backbone.

**Class** — Animals in **Class Mammalia**, or mammals, have a backbone and nurse their young.

**Order** — Animals in **Order Carnivora** are mammals that have special teeth for tearing meat.

**Family** — Animals in **Family Felidae** are cats. They are carnivores that have retractable claws.

**Genus** — Animals in **Genus** *Felis* are cats that cannot roar. They can only purr.

**Species** — The **species** *Felis domesticus*, or the house cat, has unique traits that other members of genus *Felis* do not have.

*From domain to species, each level of classification contains a smaller group of organisms.*

**10 Apply** What is true about the number of organisms as they are classified closer to the species level?

# Triple Play

![Active Reading]
**11 Identify** As you read, underline the shared characteristics of Bacteria and Archaea.

## What are the three domains?

Once, kingdoms were the highest level of classification. Scientists used a six-kingdom system. But scientists noticed that organisms in two of the kingdoms differed greatly from organisms in the other four kingdoms. So scientists added a new classification level: domains. A **domain** represents the largest differences among organisms. The three domains are Bacteria (bak•TIR•ee•uh), Archaea (ar•KEE•uh), and Eukarya (yoo•KAIR•ee•uh).

## Bacteria

Domain Bacteria contains all organisms within Kingdom Bacteria. This domain is made up of prokaryotes that usually have a cell wall and reproduce by cell division. Prokaryotes are single-cell organisms that lack a cell nucleus. Bacteria live in almost any environment—soil, water, and even inside the human body!

## Archaea

Domain Archaea includes all organisms in Kingdom Archaea. This group is also made up of prokaryotes that reproduce by cell division. They differ from bacteria in their genetics and in the makeup of their cell walls. Many Archaea live in harsh environments in which other organisms could not survive. Some Archaea live in the open ocean or soil.

*Bacteria from the genus Streptomyces are commonly found in soil.*

*Archaea from the genus Sulfolobus are found in hot springs.*

## Eukarya

What do algae, mushrooms, trees, and humans have in common? All of these organisms are *eukaryotes*. Eukaryotes are made up of cells that have a nucleus and membrane-bound organelles. The cells of eukaryotes are more complex than the cells of prokaryotes. For this reason, the cells of eukaryotes are usually larger than the cells of prokaryotes. Some eukaryotes, such as many protists and some fungi, are single-celled. Many eukaryotes are multicellular organisms. Some protists and many fungi, plants, and animals are multicellular eukaryotes. Domain **Eukarya** is made up of all eukaryotes.

It may look like a pinecone, but the pangolin is actually an animal from Africa. It is in Domain Eukarya.

**12 Identify** Fill in the blanks with the missing labels.

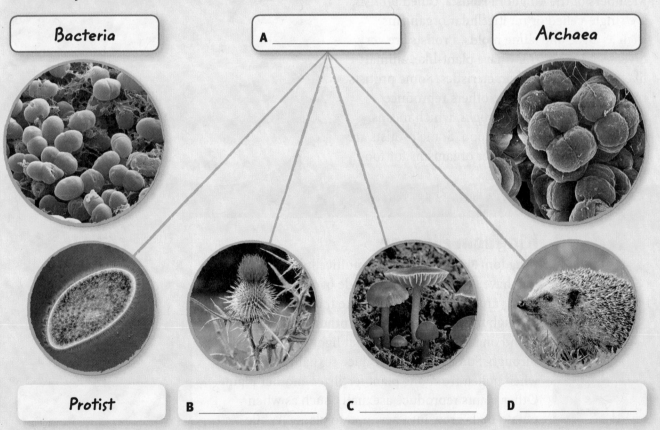

Bacteria

A _____

Archaea

Protist

B _____

C _____

D _____

**13 Compare** What are the differences between Bacteria and Eukarya?

_____

_____

_____

# My Kingdom for a

## What are the four kingdoms in Eukarya?

Scientists have classified four types of Eukarya. They ask questions to decide in which kingdom to classify an organism.

- Is the organism single-celled or multicellular?
- Does it make its food or get it from the environment?
- How does it reproduce?

## Kingdom Protista

Members of the kingdom **Protista**, called *protists*, are single-celled or multicellular organisms such as algae and slime molds. Protists are very diverse. Members may have plant-like, animal-like, or fungus-like characteristics. Some protists reproduce sexually, while others reproduce asexually. Algae are *autotrophs,* which means that they make their own food. Some protists are *heterotrophs.* They eat other organisms for food.

## Kingdom Plantae

Kingdom **Plantae** consists of multicellular organisms that have cell walls, mostly made of cellulose. Most plants are autotrophs; they make their own food through the process of photosynthesis. Plants are found on land and in water that light can pass through. Some plants reproduce sexually, such as when pollen from one plant fertilizes another plant. Other plants reproduce asexually, such as when potato buds grow into new potato plants. While plants can grow, they cannot move by themselves.

**14 Categorize** Name one example organism from each kingdom.

_____

_____

© Houghton Mifflin Harcourt Publishing Company • Image Credits: (bg) ©David Noton Photography/Alamy; (t) ©Ray Simons/Photo Researchers, Inc.; (b) ©John Wright/Photo Researchers, Inc.

# Eukaryote!

## Kingdom Fungi

The members of the kingdom **Fungi** are heterotrophs,and their cell walls contain chitin. Fungal cells do not have chloroplasts. Fungi are single-celled or multicellular and include yeasts, molds, and mushrooms. Fungi use digestive juices to break down materials around them for food. Fungi reproduce sexually, asexually, or in both ways, depending on their type.

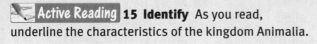 **Active Reading** **15 Identify** As you read, underline the characteristics of the kingdom Animalia.

## Kingdom Animalia

Kingdom **Animalia** contains multicellular organisms that lack cell walls. They do not have chloroplasts like plants and algae, so they must get nutrients by consuming other organisms. Therefore, they are heterotrophic. Animals have specialized sense organs, and most animals are able to move around. Birds, fish, reptiles, amphibians, insects, and mammals are just a few examples of animals. Most animals reproduce sexually, but a few types of animals reproduce asexually, such as by budding.

**16 Classify** Place a check mark in the box for the characteristic that each kingdom displays.

| Kingdom | Cells | | Nutrients | | Reproduction | |
|---|---|---|---|---|---|---|
| | Unicellular | Multicellular | Autotrophic | Heterotrophic | Sexual | Asexual |
| Protista | | | | | | |
| Plantae | | | | | | |
| Fungi | | | | | | |
| Animalia | | | | | | |

# How do classification systems change over time?

Millions of organisms have been identified and classified, but millions have yet to be discovered and named. Not only are scientists still identifying new species, but sometimes these new species do not fit into existing genera or phyla. For example, many scientists argue that protists are so different from one another that they should be classified into several kingdoms instead of one. The number of kingdoms may change as new data are collected. Our classification system changes as we learn more about living things.

# How do branching diagrams show classification relationships?

How do you organize your closet? What about your books? People organize things in many different ways. Linnaeus' two-name system worked for scientists long ago, but the system does not represent what we know about living things today. Scientists use different tools to organize information about classification.

Scientists often use a type of branching diagram called a *cladogram* (KLAD•uh•gram). A cladogram shows relationships among species. Organisms are grouped according to common characteristics. Usually these characteristics are listed along a line. Branches of organisms extend from this line. Organisms on branches above each characteristic have the characteristic. Organisms on branches below lack the characteristic.

**Active Reading**

**17 Predict** How might the classification of protists change in the future?

_____

_____

_____

_____

**Visualize It!**

**18 Apply** How can you use the branching diagram to tell which plants produce seeds?

_____

_____

_____

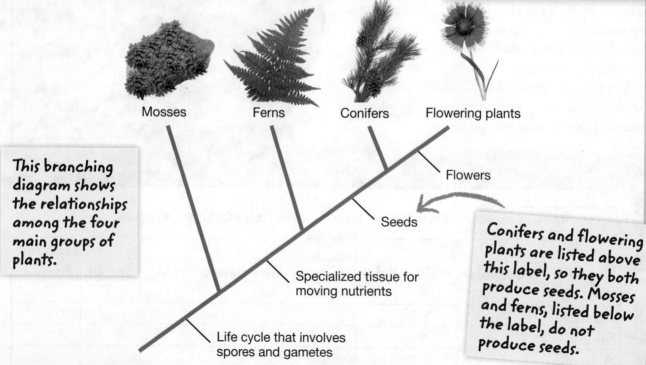

Mosses     Ferns     Conifers     Flowering plants

Flowers

Seeds

Specialized tissue for moving nutrients

Life cycle that involves spores and gametes

This branching diagram shows the relationships among the four main groups of plants.

Conifers and flowering plants are listed above this label, so they both produce seeds. Mosses and ferns, listed below the label, do not produce seeds.

# A Class by Themselves

As scientists find more living things to study, they find that they may not have made enough classifications, or that their classifications may not describe organisms well enough. Some living things have traits that fall under more than one classification. These organisms are very difficult to classify.

*Sea spider*

*Euglena*

## Euglena
Another strange group of creatures is Euglena. Euglena make their own food as plants do. But, like animals, they have no cell walls. They also have a flagellum, a tail-like structure that allows them to move. With this unusual combination of characteristics, Euglena are classified as protists.

## Sea Spider
The sea spider is a difficult-to-classify animal. It is an arthropod because it has body segments and an exoskeleton. The problem is in the sea spider's body structure, which is unlike any known arthropod's. Sea spiders have a straw-like mouth, a tiny abdomen, and portions of their intestines are in their legs! Scientists must decide if they need to make a new classification or change an existing one to account for such unusual body structures.

## Extend

**Inquiry**

19 **Explain** In which domain would the sea spider be classified? Explain your answer.

20 **Research** Investigate how scientists use DNA to help classify organisms such as the sea spider.

21 **Debate** Find more information on Euglena and sea spiders. Hold a class debate on how scientists should classify the organisms.

# Keys to Success

## How can organisms be identified?

Imagine walking through the woods. You see an animal sitting on a rock. It has fur, whiskers, and a large, flat tail. How can you find out what kind of animal it is? You can use a dichotomous key.

## Dichotomous Keys

A *dichotomous key* (dy•KAHT•uh•muhs KEE) uses a series of paired statements to identify organisms. Each pair of statements is numbered. When identifying an organism, read each pair of statements. Then choose the statement that best describes the organism. Either the chosen statement identifies the organism, or you will be directed to another pair of statements. By working through the key, you can eventually identify the organism.

**22 Apply** Use the dichotomous key below to identify the animals shown in the photographs.

### Dichotomous Key to Six Mammals in the Eastern United States

| 1 | A | The mammal has no hair on its tail. | Go to step 2 |
|---|---|---|---|
| | B | The mammal has hair on its tail. | Go to step 3 |
| 2 | A | The mammal has a very short naked tail. | Eastern mole |
| | B | The mammal has a long naked tail. | Go to step 4 |
| 3 | A | The mammal has a black mask. | Raccoon |
| | B | The mammal does not have a black mask. | Go to step 5 |
| 4 | A | The mammal has a flat, paddle-shaped tail. | Beaver |
| | B | The mammal has a round, skinny tail. | Possum |
| 5 | A | The mammal has a long furry tail that is black on the tip. | Long-tailed weasel |
| | B | The mammal has a long tail that has little fur. | White-footed mouse |

A _____

B _____

**23 Apply** Some dichotomous keys are set up as diagrams instead of tables. Work through the key below to identify the unknown plant.

Think Outside the Book **Inquiry**

**24 Summarize** With a partner, choose six plants or animals in a local ecosystem. Then design a dichotomous key that can be used to identify the organisms. When you have finished, trade keys with your classmates and work through their keys with your partner.

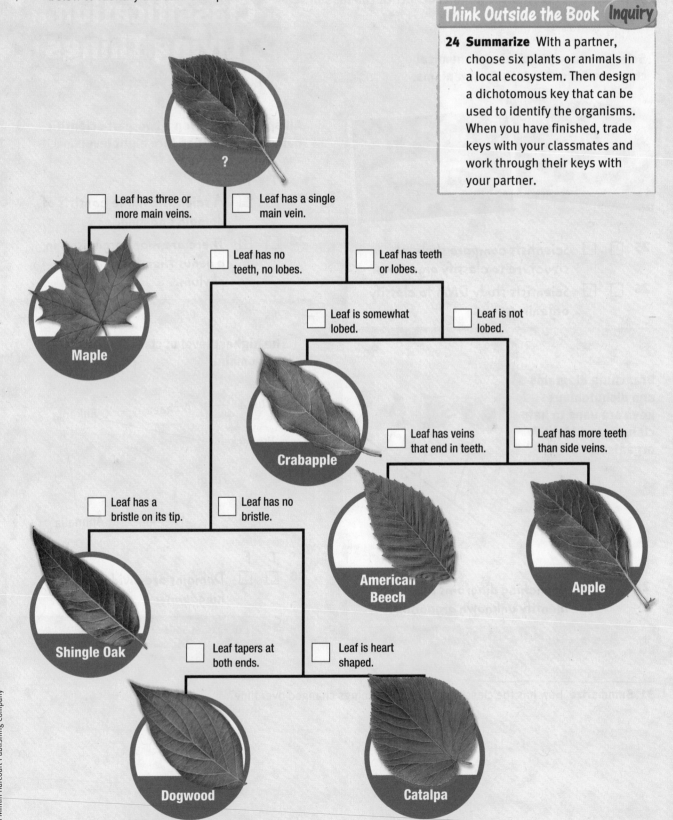

☐ Leaf has three or more main veins.

☐ Leaf has a single main vein.

**Maple**

☐ Leaf has no teeth, no lobes.

☐ Leaf has teeth or lobes.

☐ Leaf is somewhat lobed.

☐ Leaf is not lobed.

**Crabapple**

☐ Leaf has veins that end in teeth.

☐ Leaf has more teeth than side veins.

☐ Leaf has a bristle on its tip.

☐ Leaf has no bristle.

**American Beech**

**Apple**

**Shingle Oak**

☐ Leaf tapers at both ends.

☐ Leaf is heart shaped.

**Dogwood**

**Catalpa**

# Visual Summary

To complete this summary, check the box that indicates true or false. Then, use the key below to check your answers. You can use this page to review the main concepts of the lesson.

## Classification of Living Things

Scientists use physical and chemical characteristics to classify organisms.

T  F
25 ☐ ☐  Scientists compare skeletal structure to classify organisms.
26 ☐ ☐  Scientists study DNA to classify organisms.

All species are given a two-part scientific name and classified into eight levels.

T  F
27 ☐ ☐  A scientific name consists of domain and kingdom.
28 ☐ ☐  There are more organisms in a genus than there are in a phylum.

Branching diagrams and dichotomous keys are used to help classify and identify organisms.

T  F
29 ☐ ☐  Branching diagrams are used to identify unknown organisms.

The highest level of classification is the domain.

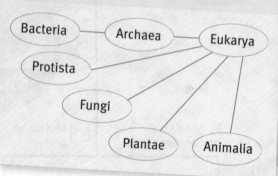

T  F
30 ☐ ☐  Domains are divided into kingdoms.

Answers: 25 T; 26 T; 27 F; 28 F; 29 F; 30 T

31 **Summarize** How has the classification of living things changed over time?

# Lesson Review

## Vocabulary

Fill in the blanks with the term that best completes the following sentences.

**1** A _____ contains paired statements that can be used to identify organisms.

**2** The kingdoms of eukaryotes are _____, Fungi, Plantae, and Animalia.

**3** Domains _____ and _____ are made up of prokaryotes.

## Key Concepts

**4 List** Name the eight levels of classification from most general to most specific.

_____

_____

_____

**5 Explain** Describe how scientists choose the kingdom in which a eukaryote belongs.

_____

_____

_____

_____

**6 Identify** What two types of evidence are used to classify organisms?

_____

_____

**7 Compare** Dichotomous keys and branching diagrams organize different types of information about classification. How are these tools used differently?

_____

_____

_____

_____

## Critical Thinking

Use the figure to answer the following questions.

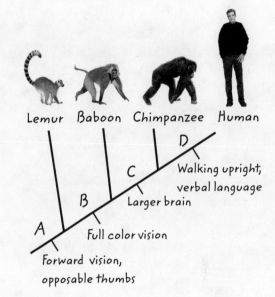

**8 Identify** Which traits do baboons have?

_____

_____

**9 Analyze** Which animal shares the most traits with humans?

_____

**10 Synthesize** Do both lemurs and humans have the trait listed at point D? Explain.

_____

_____

_____

_____

**11 Classify** A scientist finds an organism that cannot move. It has many cells, produces spores, and gets food from its environment. In which kingdom does it belong? Explain.

_____

_____

_____

_____

# My Notes

# Kenneth Krysko

## ECOLOGIST

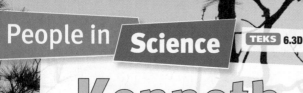

Snakes have fascinated Dr. Kenneth Krysko since he was four years old. Now he is an ecologist specializing in herpetology—the study of snakes. You can often find him in the Florida Everglades looking for Burmese pythons. He tracks these pythons to help limit the effect they have on Florida ecosystems.

Burmese pythons can grow to be 6 meters long. They are native to southeast Asia and were illegally brought to Florida as pets. Many owners released them into the wild when the snakes grew too large. The snakes breed well in Florida's subtropical climate. And they eat just about any animal they can swallow, including many native species. Dr. Krysko tracks down these invasive pythons. Through wildlife management, molecular genetics, and other areas of study, he works with other scientists to search for ways to reduce the python population.

Dr. Krysko studies many other invasive species, that is, nonnative species that can do harm in Florida ecosystems. He shares what he learns, including ways to identify and deal with invasive species with other ecologists. Along with invasion ecology, he has done research in reproduction and conservation biology. Dr. Krysko also works as a collections manager in the herpetology division at the Florida Museum of Natural History.

Dr. Krysko works to get a handle on what to do about the invasive pythons.

# JOB BOARD

## Park Naturalist

**What You'll Do:** Teach visitors at state and national parks about the park's ecology, geology, and landscape. Lead field trips, prepare and deliver lectures with slides, and create educational programs for park visitors. You may participate in research projects and track organisms in the park.

**Where You Might Work:** State and national parks

**Education:** An advanced degree in science and teacher certification

**Other Job Requirements:** You need to be good at communicating and teaching. Having photography and writing skills helps you prepare interesting educational materials.

## Conservation Warden

**What You'll Do:** Patrol an area to enforce rules, and work with communities and groups to help educate the public about conservation and ecology.

**Where You Might Work:** Indoors and outdoors in state and national parks and ecologically sensitive areas

**Education:** A two-year associate's degree or at least 60 fully accredited college-level credits

**Other Job Requirements:** To work in the wild, good wilderness skills, map-reading, hiking, and excellent hearing are useful.

---

**PEOPLE IN SCIENCE NEWS**

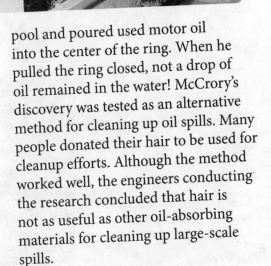

# Phil McCRORY

### Saved by a Hair!

Phil McCrory, a hairdresser in Huntsville, Alabama, asked a brilliant question when he saw an otter whose fur was drenched with oil from the Exxon Valdez oil spill. If the otter's fur soaked up oil, why wouldn't human hair do the same? McCrory gathered hair from the floor of his salon and performed his own experiments. He stuffed hair into a pair of pantyhose and tied the ankles together. McCrory floated this bundle in his son's wading pool and poured used motor oil into the center of the ring. When he pulled the ring closed, not a drop of oil remained in the water! McCrory's discovery was tested as an alternative method for cleaning up oil spills. Many people donated their hair to be used for cleanup efforts. Although the method worked well, the engineers conducting the research concluded that hair is not as useful as other oil-absorbing materials for cleaning up large-scale spills.

# Introduction to Ecology

**ESSENTIAL QUESTION**

## How are parts of the environment connected?

By the end of this lesson, you should be able to describe the parts of the environment and how they are connected.

**TEKS 6.12E** describe biotic and abiotic parts of an ecosystem in which organisms interact

**TEKS 6.12F** diagram the levels of organization within an ecosystem, including organism, population, community, and ecosystem

This rain forest is an ecosystem. Hornbills are organisms in this ecosystem that use the trees for shelter.

## Lesson Labs

**Quick Labs**
• Which Abiotic and Biotic Factors Are Found in an Ecosystem?
• Which Biome?

**Field Lab**
• What's in an Ecosystem?

## Engage Your Brain

**1 Describe** Write a list of living and nonliving things that are in your neighborhood.

_____

_____

_____

_____

_____

_____

_____

_____

**2 Relate** Write a photo caption that compares the ecosystem shown in the picture below with the ecosystem shown on the previous page.

_____

_____

_____

## Active Reading

**3 Synthesize** You can often define an unknown word or term if you know the meaning of its word parts. Use the word parts and sentence below to make an educated guess about the meaning of the term *abiotic factor*.

| Word part | Meaning |
|-----------|---------|
| a- | without |
| bio- | life |

**Example sentence**
In an ecosystem, rocks are an example of an <u>abiotic factor</u> because they are not a living part of the environment.

*abiotic factor:*

_____

_____

### Vocabulary Terms

• ecology          • community
• biotic factor    • ecosystem
• abiotic factor   • biome
• population       • niche
• species          • habitat

**4 Apply** As you learn the definition of each vocabulary term in this lesson, create your own definition or sketch to help you remember the meaning of the term.

# The Web of Life

## How are all living things connected?

Organisms need energy and matter to live. Interactions between organisms cause an exchange of energy and matter. This exchange creates a web of life in which all organisms are connected to each other and to their environment. **Ecology** is the study of how organisms interact with one another and with the environment.

## Through the Living Environment

Every organism is part of the flow of energy and matter. In this way, all organisms are connected to each other. The growth and survival of an organism depends on its interactions with other organisms. **Biotic factors** are the interactions between organisms in an area. Competition is one way that organisms interact. For example, different kinds of plants might compete for water in the desert.

Living and nonliving things are part of this desert. Living things interact with each other and with nonliving things.

This horse is a part of the living environment.

© Houghton Mifflin Harcourt Publishing Company • Image Credits: ©Visions of America/Joe Sohm/The Image Bank/Getty Images

## Through the Nonliving Environment

All organisms depend on the nonliving environment for survival. An **abiotic factor** is a nonliving part of an environment. Water, nutrients, soil, sunlight, and temperature are all abiotic factors. Some of these are *resources*, or materials that organisms need to grow and survive. For example, sunlight, water, and soil nutrients are resources plants use to make food.

Abiotic factors influence where organisms can survive. Air temperature and rainfall are important abiotic factors on land. Water temperature, salt levels, and oxygen levels are important abiotic factors in water. Changes in these basic abiotic factors affect where organisms can live. They also affect how many individuals are able to survive in an environment.

**Active Reading** **5 Infer** How does the environment affect where an organism can survive? Explain your answer.

_____
_____
_____
_____
_____
_____

The rocks and air are parts of the nonliving environment.

## Visualize It!

**6 Categorize** List four abiotic factors that are present in the environment shown in the photo.

_____   _____

_____   _____

**7 Describe** Choose one abiotic factor listed above and describe how the horse interacts with it.

_____
_____
_____
_____

© Houghton Mifflin Harcourt Publishing Company • Image Credits: ©VisionsofAmerica/Joe Sohm/The Image Bank/Getty Images

623

# Stay Organized!

## What are the levels of organization in the environment?

The environment can be organized into different levels. A level can include a single organism. Or it can include all of the organisms and their surroundings in an area. The levels of organization get larger as more of the environment is included.

**Active Reading** **8 Identify** As you read, underline the characteristics of each of the following levels of organization.

### Populations

A **population** is a group of individuals of the same species that live in the same place at the same time. A **species** includes organisms that are closely related and can mate to produce fertile offspring. The alligators that live in the Everglades form a population. Individuals in a population often compete with each other for resources.

Population

Individual

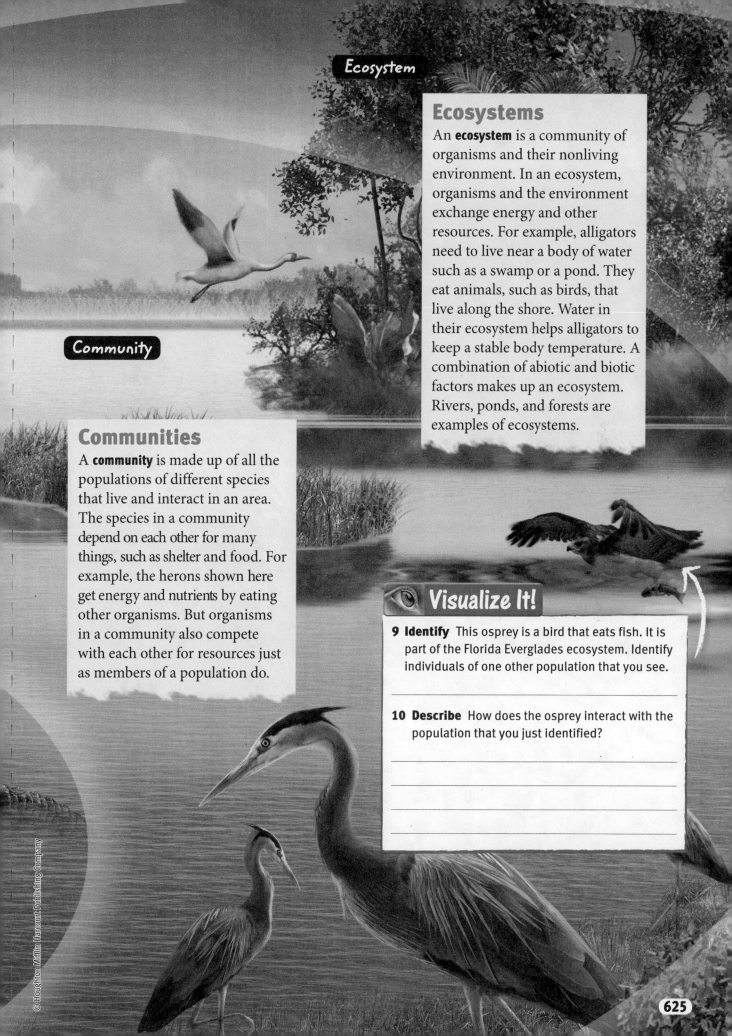

## Ecosystems

An **ecosystem** is a community of organisms and their nonliving environment. In an ecosystem, organisms and the environment exchange energy and other resources. For example, alligators need to live near a body of water such as a swamp or a pond. They eat animals, such as birds, that live along the shore. Water in their ecosystem helps alligators to keep a stable body temperature. A combination of abiotic and biotic factors makes up an ecosystem. Rivers, ponds, and forests are examples of ecosystems.

Community

## Communities

A **community** is made up of all the populations of different species that live and interact in an area. The species in a community depend on each other for many things, such as shelter and food. For example, the herons shown here get energy and nutrients by eating other organisms. But organisms in a community also compete with each other for resources just as members of a population do.

### Visualize It!

**9 Identify** This osprey is a bird that eats fish. It is part of the Florida Everglades ecosystem. Identify individuals of one other population that you see.

_____

**10 Describe** How does the osprey interact with the population that you just identified?

_____

_____

_____

© Houghton Mifflin Harcourt Publishing Company

The picture shows a watering hole in an African savanna. A savanna has wet and dry seasons. Animals gather at watering holes during dry seasons. These animals interact with each other and their nonliving environment.

Tree

Shrub

Elephant

Grass

Giraffe

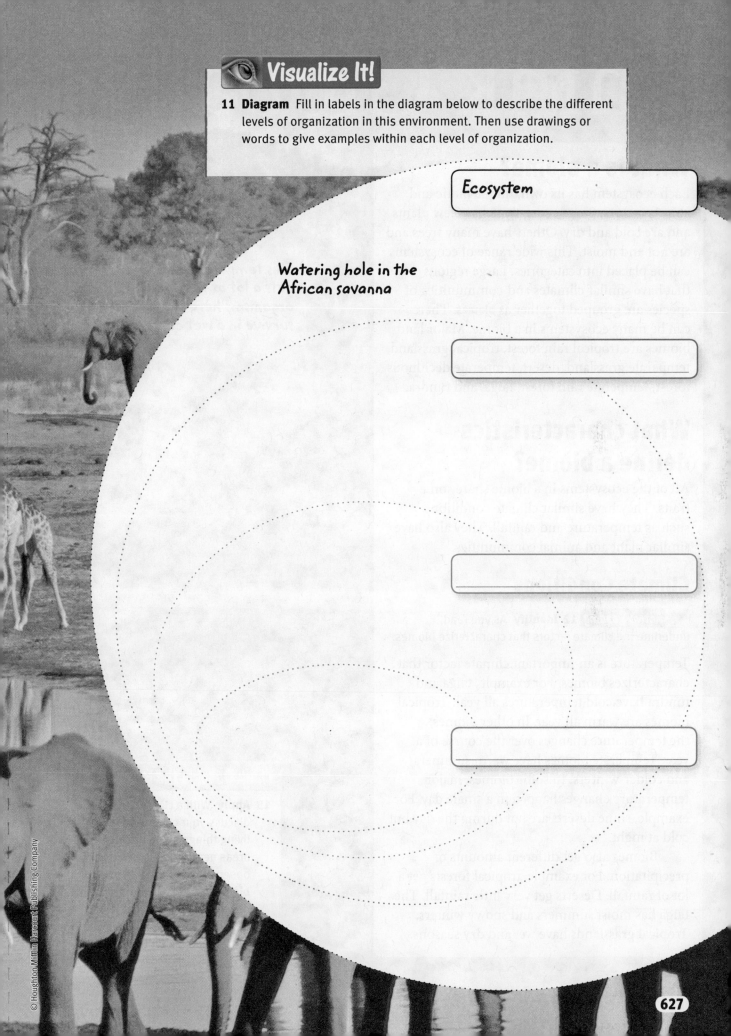

11 **Diagram** Fill in labels in the diagram below to describe the different levels of organization in this environment. Then use drawings or words to give examples within each level of organization.

Ecosystem

Watering hole in the
African savanna

# Think Globally!

## What is a biome?

Each ecosystem has its own unique biotic and abiotic factors. Some ecosystems have few plants and are cold and dry. Others have many trees and are hot and moist. This wide range of ecosystems can be placed into categories. Large regions that have similar climates and communities of species are grouped together as **biomes**. There can be many ecosystems in a biome. Major land biomes are tropical rain forest, tropical grassland, temperate grassland, desert, temperate deciduous forest, temperate rain forest, taiga, and tundra.

## What characteristics define a biome?

All of the ecosystems in a biome share some traits. They have similar climate conditions, such as temperature and rainfall. They also have similar plant and animal communities.

### Climate Conditions

[Active Reading] **12 Identify** As you read, underline the climate factors that characterize biomes.

Temperature is an important climate factor that characterizes biomes. For example, taiga and tundra have cold temperatures all year. Tropical biomes are warm all year. In other biomes, the temperature changes over the course of a year. Temperate biomes have warm summers and colder winters. In some biomes, major temperature changes happen in a single day. For example, some deserts are hot during the day but cold at night.

Biomes also get different amounts of precipitation. For example, tropical forests get a lot of rainfall. Deserts get very little rainfall. The taiga has moist summers and snowy winters. Tropical grasslands have wet and dry seasons.

This temperate rain forest gets a lot of rainfall. The organisms here are able to survive in a wet climate.

**Think Outside the Book** Inquiry

**13 Apply** With a classmate, discuss your climate and the living things found in natural areas nearby. Record your observations. Research which biome has these features. Then, use a biome map to see if your observations match the biome that is mapped for your location.

# Communities of Living Things

The community of living things that can survive in a biome depends on the climate of the region where the biome is found. So similar species are found in each biome around the world. Monkeys, vines, and colorful birds live in hot and moist tropical rain forests. Grasses, large animals that eat grass, and animals that dig underground live in temperate grasslands.

Only certain types of plants and animals can live in extreme climate conditions. For example, caribou, polar bear, and small plants can live in the tundra. However, trees cannot grow there. Cactuses and some animal species have adaptations that let them live in a dry desert climate. Plants with large leaves or animals that need a lot of water cannot live in a desert.

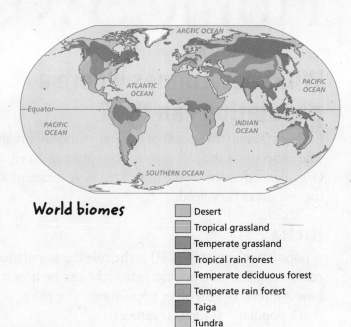

**World biomes**

☐ Desert
☐ Tropical grassland
☐ Temperate grassland
☐ Tropical rain forest
☐ Temperate deciduous forest
☐ Temperate rain forest
☐ Taiga
☐ Tundra

 **Visualize It!**

**14 Compare** The photos below show two different biomes. Use what you learned about the characteristics of biomes to compare these environments. Then explain why they are different biomes. Write your answers in the space provided.

Compare: _____
_____
_____
_____
_____
_____
_____
_____

Explain: _____
_____
_____
_____
_____
_____
_____
_____
_____

# Home Sweet Home

## What determines where a population can live?

Ecologists study the needs of different kinds of organisms. They also study the role each species plays in an environment. Organisms that live in the same area have different ways of getting the resources they need.

### Niche

A population's **niche** (NICH) is the role the population plays in an ecosystem. Part of a population's niche can be how it gets food or how it interacts with other populations. For example, one part of a shark population's niche is eating fish.

A **habitat** is the place where an organism lives. A habitat is part of an organism's niche. The habitat must have all of the resources that an organism needs to grow and survive. Whether a species can live in a certain place often depends on abiotic factors, such as temperature. Biotic factors can also be important. For example, the habitat of a shark must have fish that the shark can eat.

Two populations cannot have exactly the same niche. Even small differences in habitats, roles, and adaptations can let similar species live together in the same ecosystem. For example, different species of sharks can live in the same area of ocean if they eat different species of fish. On land, green and brown anoles sometimes live in the same trees. They avoid competition by living in different parts of the trees.

**15 Relate** How is an organism's habitat like a person's address? How is an organism's niche like a person's job?

_____
_____
_____
_____
_____
_____
_____

**16 Infer** Describe the prairie dog's niche. How does it find shelter and change its environment?

_____
_____
_____
_____
_____
_____

Prairie dogs dig burrows in grasslands. They eat plants and are hunted by animals such as owls and foxes.

© Houghton Mifflin Harcourt Publishing Company • Image Credits: ©Raymond K. Gehman/National Geographic/Getty Images

# Lizard Invasion

Green anole lizards (*Anolis carolinensis*) have been part of ecosystems in the United States for a long time. Recently, a related lizard, the nonnative brown anole (*Anolis sagrei*), moved into the green anoles' habitat. How do they avoid competing with each other for resources?

## Home Base

Green anoles live on branches throughout a tree. Brown anoles live mainly on branches that are close to the ground. If they have to share a tree, green anoles will move away from branches close to the ground. In this way, both kinds of anoles can live in the same tree without competing with each other.

## Dangerous Neighbors

Brown and green anoles can live together by sharing their habitats. However, they do not live together peacefully. For example, brown anoles harm green anoles by eating their young.

## Extend

Inquiry

**17 Describe** How do green and brown anoles avoid competition? Draw a picture of a tree showing both green and brown anoles living in it.

**18 Research** What are other examples of two species that divide up the parts of a habitat?

**19 Relate** Predict what would happen if the niches of the two species overlapped. Take turns describing your ideas with a partner. Use the terms *habitat* and *niche* in your discussion. Present your findings in a story, a music video, a comedy skit, or a play.

# Visual Summary

To complete this summary, circle the correct word. Then use the key below to check your answers. You can use this page to review the main concepts of the lesson.

## Introduction to Ecology

**Ecology is the study of the biotic and abiotic factors in an ecosystem and the relationships between them.**

20 In a desert ecosystem, the sand is a(n) biotic / abiotic factor, and a lizard eating an insect is a(n) biotic / abiotic factor.

**Every organism has a habitat and a niche.**

21 Horses that live in the desert eat other organisms that live there, such as low, dry shrubs. In this example, the desert is a habitat / niche. The horses' feeding behavior is part of a habitat / niche.

**The environment can be organized into different levels, including populations, communities, and ecosystems.**

22 Populations of cacti, together with sand and rocks, are part of a desert community / ecosystem.

**Biomes are characterized by climate conditions and the communities of living things found within them.**

23 Biomes are large / small regions that make up / contain ecosystems.

Answers: 20 abiotic, biotic; 21 habitat, niche; 22 ecosystem; 23 large, contain

24 **Predict** Name a biotic factor that the horses depend on in the desert ecosystem above. Describe the effect on the horses if this factor were removed from the ecosystem.

# Lesson Review

## Vocabulary

**1** Explain how the meanings of the terms *biotic factor* and *abiotic factor* differ.

**2** In your own words, write a definition for *ecology*.

**3** Explain how the meanings of the terms *habitat* and *niche* differ.

## Key Concepts

**4 Compare** What is the relationship between ecosystems and biomes?

**5 List** What are the levels of organization in a biome, from largest to smallest?

**6 Describe** What interactions can happen between two populations in a community?

**7 Identify** What factors influence where a population can live?

## Critical Thinking

**8 Predict** What might happen in a tropical rain forest biome if the area received very little rain for a long period of time?

**9 Infer** Owls and hawks both eat mice. They can also be found in the same habitat. Since no two populations can have exactly the same niche, how do you think owls and hawks can live in the same area?

**10 Demonstrate** Draw a diagram showing the levels of organization for a young deer living in a prairie ecosystem. The other organisms include rabbits, birds, mice, insects, grasses.

# My Notes

# Unit 10

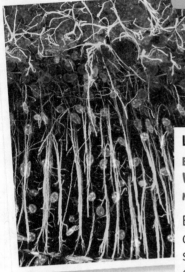

### Lesson 1

**ESSENTIAL QUESTION**
**What are living things made of?**

Explain the components of the scientific theory of cells.

### Lesson 2

**ESSENTIAL QUESTION**
**How are organisms classified?**

Describe how people sort living things into groups based on shared characteristics.

### Lesson 3

**ESSENTIAL QUESTION**
**How are different parts of the environment connected?**

Analyze the parts of an environment.

**Connect** **ESSENTIAL QUESTIONS**
Lessons 1 and 3

**1 Synthesize** How might individual cells affect the ecological balance of an ecosystem?

_____

_____

_____

_____

_____

## Think Outside the Book

**2 Synthesize** Choose one of these activities to help synthesize what you have learned in this unit.

☐ Using what you learned in lessons 2 and 3, choose six organisms that live in an aquatic ecosystem. Make a chart that shows similar and different characteristics of all of these organisms.

☐ Using what you learned in lessons 1, 2, and 3, make a poster that shows the progression of life forms from cells to organisms to ecosystems.

Name _____

## Vocabulary

Check the box to show whether each statement is true or false.

| T | F | |
|---|---|---|
| ☐ | ☐ | **TEKS 6.12B, 6.12D** <br> **1** Each cell of a <u>prokaryote</u> has a nucleus, while each cell of a <u>eukaryote</u> does not. |
| ☐ | ☐ | **TEKS 6.12A** <br> **2** The cells of all living things have a <u>cell membrane</u>, or protective layer, that covers the cell's surface. |
| ☐ | ☐ | **TEKS 6.12C** <br> **3** In the most recent classification system, Bacteria, Archaea, and Eukarya are the three major <u>domains</u> of life. |
| ☐ | ☐ | **4** <u>Biomes</u> are characterized by temperature, precipitation, and the plant and animal communities that live there. |
| ☐ | ☐ | **5** A <u>habitat</u> is the role of a population in its community, including its environment and its relationship with other species. |

## Key Concepts

Choose the letter of the best answer.

**TEKS 6.12A, 6.3A**

**6** Prem finds an unusual object on the forest floor. After he examines it under a microscope and performs several lab tests, he concludes that the object is a living thing. Which of the following observations most likely led to Prem's conclusion? (Hint: Step 1. Recall the characteristics of all living things. Step 2. Consider the lab tests that help determine if an object is a living thing.)

**A** The object contained carbon.

**B** Prem saw cells in the object.

**C** The object had a green color.

**D** Prem saw minerals inside the object.

# Unit 10 Review continued

**7** Unicellular organisms have one cell. Multicellular organisms have many body cells. Which statement correctly tells why these cells of unicellular and multicellular organisms divide?

**A** The cells of unicellular organisms divide to reproduce; those of multicellular organisms divide to replace cells and to grow.

**B** The cells of unicellular organisms divide to replace cells and to grow; those of multicellular organisms divide to reproduce.

**C** The cells of both kinds of organisms divide to reproduce.

**D** The cells of both kinds of organisms divide to replace cells and to grow.

TEKS 6.12D

**8** A branching diagram uses shared characteristics to classify organisms. On a branching diagram that compares the major kingdoms of Domain Eukarya, what label might appear to differentiate animals from organisms in the other kingdoms of Eukarya? (Hint: Step 1. Recall the characteristics of animals. Step 2. Think about how scientists use those characteristics to classify organisms.)

**A** single-celled, make own food

**B** multicellular, make own food

**C** multicellular, move independently

**D** release digestive juices into surroundings

TEKS 6.3D

**9** As Carolus Linnaeus was growing up, he was interested in botany and in the names of plants. His ideas have influenced generations of biologists. How did Carolus Linnaeus contribute to modern classification systems?

**A** He identified the three domains of life.

**B** He developed two-part scientific names.

**C** He standardized common names of organisms.

**D** He used chemical characteristics to classify organisms.

10 The following diagram shows components of an ecosystem. What term should be used to describe the living things in this ecosystem?

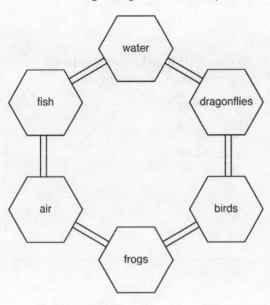

**A** biome

**B** habitat

**C** niche

**D** community

## Gridded Response

Write your answer in the boxes, then bubble in the corresponding number in the grid below.

TEKS 6.12E

11 Water temperature is an abiotic factor that affects the growth of young salmon. The table shows the effects of different temperature ranges on young salmon.

| Water temperature | Effect on young salmon |
|---|---|
| 18 °C to 20 °C | growth stops |
| 10 °C to 15 °C | optimum growth |
| 5 °C to 10 °C | some growth occurs |

The temperature of a river is 18 °C. How many degrees cooler must the river become in order for the young salmon to thrive?

## Critical Thinking

Answer the following questions in the space provided.

TEKS 6.12F

12 In the space below, draw a diagram that shows levels of organization in an ecosystem of your choice. Label and identify each level of organization.

TEKS 6.12A, 6.3D

13 The cell theory describes three basic characteristics of cells and living things. Summarize these characteristics, and identify a scientist associated with each.

_____

_____

_____

_____

_____

_____

Connect ESSENTIAL QUESTIONS

Lessons 1, 2, and 3

Answer the following question in the space provided.

TEKS 6.12C, 6.12D

14 An organism is a prokaryote. Into which domains could you classify the organism? Justify your answer. Explain what additional information you would need to use smaller levels to classify the organism.

_____

_____

_____

_____

_____

# Look It Up!

# References

## Mineral Properties

Here are five steps to take in mineral identification:

1 Determine the color of the mineral. Is it light-colored, dark-colored, or a specific color?

2 Determine the luster of the mineral. Is it metallic or nonmetallic?

3 Determine the color of any powder left by its streak.

4 Determine the hardness of your mineral. Is it soft, hard, or very hard? Using a glass plate, see if the mineral scratches it.

5 Determine whether your sample has cleavage or any special properties.

| TERMS TO KNOW | DEFINITION |
|---|---|
| adamantine | a nonmetallic luster like that of a diamond |
| cleavage | how a mineral breaks when subject to stress on a particular plane |
| luster | the state or quality of shining by reflecting light |
| streak | the color of a mineral when it is powdered |
| submetallic | between metallic and nonmetallic in luster |
| vitreous | glass-like type of luster |

| Silicate Minerals | | | | | |
|---|---|---|---|---|---|
| **Mineral** | **Color** | **Luster** | **Streak** | **Hardness** | **Cleavage and Special Properties** |
| Beryl | deep green, pink, white, bluish green, or yellow | vitreous | white | 7.5–8 | 1 cleavage direction; some varieties fluoresce in ultraviolet light |
| Chlorite | green | vitreous to pearly | pale green | 2–2.5 | 1 cleavage direction |
| Garnet | green, red, brown, black | vitreous | white | 6.5–7.5 | no cleavage |
| Hornblende | dark green, brown, or black | vitreous | none | 5–6 | 2 cleavage directions |
| Muscovite | colorless, silvery white, or brown | vitreous or pearly | white | 2–2.5 | 1 cleavage direction |
| Olivine | olive green, yellow | vitreous | white or none | 6.5–7 | no cleavage |
| Orthoclase | colorless, white, pink, or other colors | vitreous | white or none | 6 | 2 cleavage directions |
| Plagioclase | colorless, white, yellow, pink, green | vitreous | white | 6 | 2 cleavage directions |
| Quartz | colorless or white; any color when not pure | vitreous or waxy | white or none | 7 | no cleavage |

## Nonsilicate Minerals

| Mineral | Color | Luster | Streak | Hardness | Cleavage and Special Properties |
|---------|-------|--------|--------|----------|-------------------------------|
| **Native Elements** | | | | | |
| Copper | copper-red | metallic | copper-red | 2.5–3 | no cleavage |
| Diamond | pale yellow or colorless | adamantine | none | 10 | 4 cleavage directions |
| Graphite | black to gray | submetallic | black | 1–2 | 1 cleavage direction |
| **Carbonates** | | | | | |
| Aragonite | colorless, white, or pale yellow | vitreous | white | 3.5–4 | 2 cleavage directions; reacts with hydrochloric acid |
| Calcite | colorless or white to tan | vitreous | white | 3 | 3 cleavage directions; reacts with weak acid; double refraction |
| **Halides** | | | | | |
| Fluorite | light green, yellow, purple, bluish green, or other colors | vitreous | none | 4 | 4 cleavage directions; some varieties fluoresce |
| Halite | white | vitreous | white | 2.0–2.5 | 3 cleavage directions |
| **Oxides** | | | | | |
| Hematite | reddish brown to black | metallic to earthy | dark red to red-brown | 5.6–6.5 | no cleavage; magnetic when heated |
| Magnetite | iron-black | metallic | black | 5.5–6.5 | no cleavage; magnetic |
| **Sulfates** | | | | | |
| Anhydrite | colorless, bluish, or violet | vitreous to pearly | white | 3–3.5 | 3 cleavage directions |
| Gypsum | white, pink, gray, or colorless | vitreous, pearly, or silky | white | 2.0 | 3 cleavage directions |
| **Sulfides** | | | | | |
| Galena | lead-gray | metallic | lead-gray to black | 2.5–2.8 | 3 cleavage directions |
| Pyrite | brassy yellow | metallic | greenish, brownish, or black | 6–6.5 | no cleavage |

# References

## Geologic Time Scale

Geologists developed the geologic time scale to represent the 4.6 billion years of Earth's history that have passed since Earth formed. This scale divides Earth's history into blocks of time. The boundaries between these time intervals (shown in millions of years ago, or mya, in the table below), represent major changes in Earth's history. Some boundaries are defined by mass extinctions, major changes in Earth's surface, and/or major changes in Earth's climate.

The four major divisions that encompass the history of life on Earth are Precambrian time, the Paleozoic era, the Mesozoic era, and the Cenozoic era. The largest divisions are eons. **Precambrian time** is made up of the first three eons, over 4 billion years of Earth's history.

The **Paleozoic era** lasted from 542 mya to 251 mya. All major plant groups, except flowering plants, appeared during this era. By the end of the era, reptiles, winged insects, and fishes had also appeared. The largest known mass extinction occurred at the end of this era.

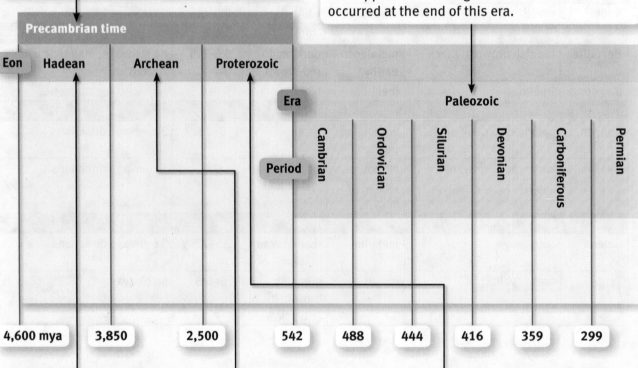

The **Hadean eon** lasted from about 4.6 billion years ago (bya) to 3.85 bya. It is described based on evidence from meteorites and rocks from the moon.

The **Archean eon** lasted from 3.85 bya to 2.5 bya. The earliest rocks from Earth that have been found and dated formed at the start of this eon.

The **Proterozoic eon** lasted from 2.5 bya to 542 mya. The first organisms, which were single-celled organisms, appeared during this eon. These organisms produced so much oxygen that they changed Earth's oceans and Earth's atmosphere.

# Divisions of Time

The divisions of time shown here represent major changes in Earth's surface and when life developed and changed significantly on Earth. As new evidence is found, the boundaries of these divisions may shift. The Phanerozoic eon is divided into three eras. The beginning of each of these eras represents a change in the types of organisms that dominated Earth. And each era is commonly characterized by the types of organisms that dominated the era. These eras are divided into periods, and periods are divided into epochs.

The **Mesozoic era** lasted from 251 mya to 65.5 mya. During this era, many kinds of dinosaurs dominated land, and giant lizards swam in the ocean. The first birds, mammals, and flowering plants also appeared during this time. About two-thirds of all land species went extinct at the end of this era.

The **Phanerozoic eon** began 542 mya. We live in this eon.

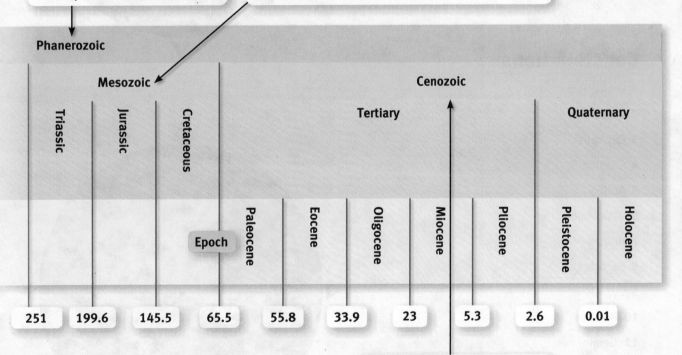

The **Cenozoic era** began 65.5 mya and continues today. Mammals dominate this era. During the Mesozoic era, mammals were small in size but grew much larger during the Cenozoic era. Primates, including humans, appeared during this era.

# References

## Star Charts for the Northern Hemisphere

A star chart is a map of the stars in the night sky. It shows the names and positions of constellations and major stars. Star charts can be used to identify constellations and even to orient yourself using Polaris, the North Star.

Because Earth moves through space, different constellations are visible at different times of the year. The star charts on these pages show the constellations visible during each season in the Northern Hemisphere.

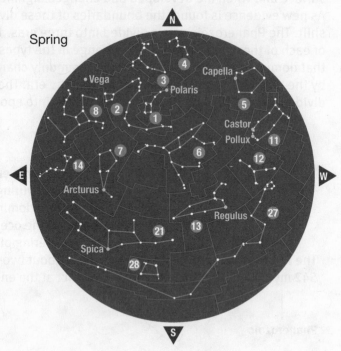

Spring

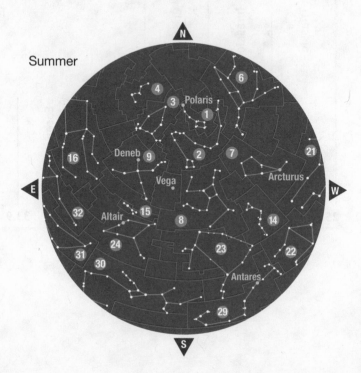

Summer

## Constellations

1  Ursa Minor

2  Draco

3  Cepheus

4  Cassiopeia

5  Auriga

6  Ursa Major

7  Boötes

8  Hercules

9  Cygnus

10  Perseus

11  Gemini

12  Cancer

13  Leo

14  Serpens

15  Sagitta

16  Pegasus

17  Pisces

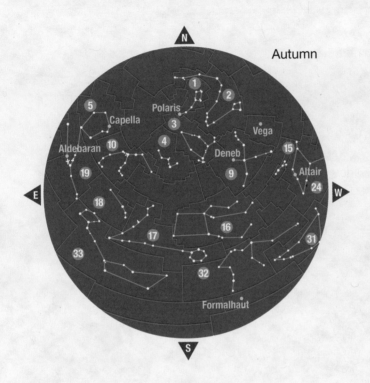

Autumn

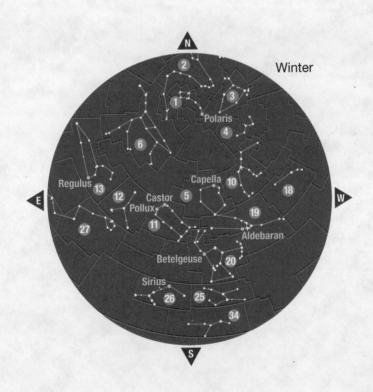

Winter

## Constellations

18 Aries

19 Taurus

20 Orion

21 Virgo

22 Libra

23 Ophiuchus

24 Aquila

25 Lepus

26 Canis Major

27 Hydra

28 Corvus

29 Scorpius

30 Sagittarius

31 Capricornus

32 Aquarius

33 Cetus

34 Columba

# References

## World Map

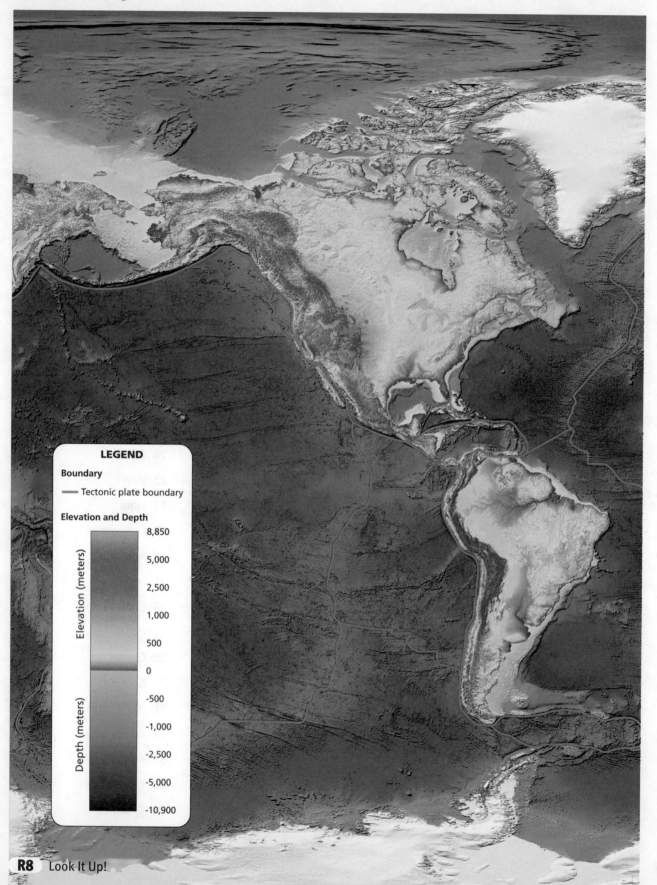

LEGEND

**Boundary**

—— Tectonic plate boundary

**Elevation and Depth**

Elevation (meters)
- 8,850
- 5,000
- 2,500
- 1,000
- 500
- 0

Depth (meters)
- -500
- -1,000
- -2,500
- -5,000
- -10,900

# References

## Classification of Living Things

### Domains and Kingdoms

All organisms belong to one of three domains: Domain Archaea, Domain Bacteria, or Domain Eukarya. Some of the groups within these domains are shown below. (Remember that genus names are italicized.)

#### Domain Archaea

The organisms in this domain are single-celled prokaryotes, many of which live in extreme environments.

| Archaea | | |
|---|---|---|
| **Group** | **Example** | **Characteristics** |
| Methanogens | *Methanococcus* | produce methane gas; can't live in oxygen |
| Thermophiles | *Sulfolobus* | require sulfur; can't live in oxygen |
| Halophiles | *Halococcus* | live in very salty environments; most can live in oxygen |

#### Domain Bacteria

Organisms in this domain are single-celled prokaryotes and are found in almost every environment on Earth.

| Bacteria | | |
|---|---|---|
| **Group** | **Example** | **Characteristics** |
| Bacilli | *Escherichia* | rod shaped; some bacilli fix nitrogen; some cause disease |
| Cocci | *Streptococcus* | spherical shaped; some cause disease; can form spores |
| Spirilla | *Treponema* | spiral shaped; cause diseases such as syphilis and Lyme disease |

#### Domain Eukarya

Organisms in this domain are single-celled or multicellular eukaryotes.

**Kingdom Protista** Many protists resemble fungi, plants, or animals but are smaller and simpler in structure. Most are single celled.

| Protists | | |
|---|---|---|
| **Group** | **Example** | **Characteristics** |
| Sarcodines | *Amoeba* | radiolarians; single-celled consumers |
| Ciliates | *Paramecium* | single-celled consumers |
| Flagellates | *Trypanosoma* | single-celled parasites |
| Sporozoans | *Plasmodium* | single-celled parasites |
| Euglenas | *Euglena* | single celled; photosynthesize |
| Diatoms | *Pinnularia* | most are single celled; photosynthesize |
| Dinoflagellates | *Gymnodinium* | single celled; some photosynthesize |
| Algae | *Volvox* | single celled or multicellular; photosynthesize |
| Slime molds | *Physarum* | single celled or multicellular; consumers or decomposers |
| Water molds | powdery mildew | single celled or multicellular; parasites or decomposers |

**Kingdom Fungi** Most fungi are multicellular. Their cells have thick cell walls. Fungi absorb food from their environment.

| Fungi | | |
|---|---|---|
| **Group** | **Examples** | **Characteristics** |
| Zygote fungi | bread mold | spherical zygote produces spores; decomposers |
| Sac fungi | yeast; morels | saclike spore structure; parasites and decomposers |
| Club fungi | mushrooms; rusts; smuts | club-shaped spore structure; parasites and decomposers |
| Lichens | British soldier | a partnership between a fungus and an alga |

**Kingdom Plantae** Plants are multicellular and have cell walls made of cellulose. Plants make their own food through photosynthesis. Plants are classified into divisions instead of phyla.

| Plants | | |
|---|---|---|
| **Group** | **Examples** | **Characteristics** |
| Bryophytes | mosses; liverworts | no vascular tissue; reproduce by spores |
| Club mosses | *Lycopodium;* ground pine | grow in wooded areas; reproduce by spores |
| Horsetails | rushes | grow in wetland areas; reproduce by spores |
| Ferns | spleenworts; sensitive fern | large leaves called fronds; reproduce by spores |
| Conifers | pines; spruces; firs | needlelike leaves; reproduce by seeds made in cones |
| Cycads | *Zamia* | slow growing; reproduce by seeds made in large cones |
| Gnetophytes | *Welwitschia* | only three living families; reproduce by seeds |
| Ginkgoes | *Ginkgo* | only one living species; reproduce by seeds |
| Angiosperms | all flowering plants | reproduce by seeds made in flowers; fruit |

**Kingdom Animalia** Animals are multicellular. Their cells do not have cell walls. Most animals have specialized tissues and complex organ systems. Animals get food by eating other organisms.

| Animals | | |
|---|---|---|
| **Group** | **Examples** | **Characteristics** |
| Sponges | glass sponges | no symmetry or specialized tissues; aquatic |
| Cnidarians | jellyfish; coral | radial symmetry; aquatic |
| Flatworms | planaria; tapeworms; flukes | bilateral symmetry; organ systems |
| Roundworms | *Trichina;* hookworms | bilateral symmetry; organ systems |
| Annelids | earthworms; leeches | bilateral symmetry; organ systems |
| Mollusks | snails; octopuses | bilateral symmetry; organ systems |
| Echinoderms | sea stars; sand dollars | radial symmetry; organ systems |
| Arthropods | insects; spiders; lobsters | bilateral symmetry; organ systems |
| Chordates | fish; amphibians; reptiles; birds; mammals | bilateral symmetry; complex organ systems |

# References

## Periodic Table of the Elements

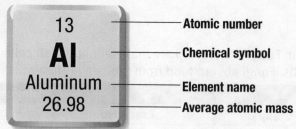

13
**Al**
Aluminum
26.98

— Atomic number
— Chemical symbol
— Element name
— Average atomic mass

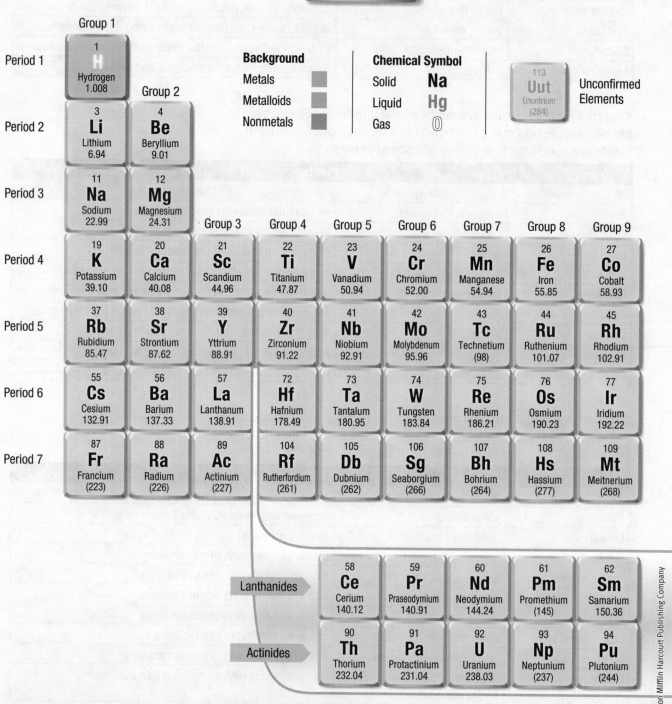

Group 1

Period 1

1
**H**
Hydrogen
1.008

Group 2

**Background**

Metals
Metalloids
Nonmetals

**Chemical Symbol**

Solid **Na**
Liquid **Hg**
Gas ⓞ

113
**Uut**
Ununtrium
(284)

Unconfirmed
Elements

Period 2

3
**Li**
Lithium
6.94

4
**Be**
Beryllium
9.01

Period 3

11
**Na**
Sodium
22.99

12
**Mg**
Magnesium
24.31

| Group 3 | Group 4 | Group 5 | Group 6 | Group 7 | Group 8 | Group 9 |
|---|---|---|---|---|---|---|

Period 4

19
**K**
Potassium
39.10

20
**Ca**
Calcium
40.08

21
**Sc**
Scandium
44.96

22
**Ti**
Titanium
47.87

23
**V**
Vanadium
50.94

24
**Cr**
Chromium
52.00

25
**Mn**
Manganese
54.94

26
**Fe**
Iron
55.85

27
**Co**
Cobalt
58.93

Period 5

37
**Rb**
Rubidium
85.47

38
**Sr**
Strontium
87.62

39
**Y**
Yttrium
88.91

40
**Zr**
Zirconium
91.22

41
**Nb**
Niobium
92.91

42
**Mo**
Molybdenum
95.96

43
**Tc**
Technetium
(98)

44
**Ru**
Ruthenium
101.07

45
**Rh**
Rhodium
102.91

Period 6

55
**Cs**
Cesium
132.91

56
**Ba**
Barium
137.33

57
**La**
Lanthanum
138.91

72
**Hf**
Hafnium
178.49

73
**Ta**
Tantalum
180.95

74
**W**
Tungsten
183.84

75
**Re**
Rhenium
186.21

76
**Os**
Osmium
190.23

77
**Ir**
Iridium
192.22

Period 7

87
**Fr**
Francium
(223)

88
**Ra**
Radium
(226)

89
**Ac**
Actinium
(227)

104
**Rf**
Rutherfordium
(261)

105
**Db**
Dubnium
(262)

106
**Sg**
Seaborgium
(266)

107
**Bh**
Bohrium
(264)

108
**Hs**
Hassium
(277)

109
**Mt**
Meitnerium
(268)

Lanthanides

58
**Ce**
Cerium
140.12

59
**Pr**
Praseodymium
140.91

60
**Nd**
Neodymium
144.24

61
**Pm**
Promethium
(145)

62
**Sm**
Samarium
150.36

Actinides

90
**Th**
Thorium
232.04

91
**Pa**
Protactinium
231.04

92
**U**
Uranium
238.03

93
**Np**
Neptunium
(237)

94
**Pu**
Plutonium
(244)

The International Union of Pure and Applied Chemistry (IUPAC) has determined that, because of isotopic variance, the average atomic mass is best represented by a range of values for each of the following elements: hydrogen, lithium, boron, carbon, nitrogen, oxygen, silicon, sulfur, chlorine, and thallium. However, the values in this table are appropriate for everyday calculations.

| | | | Group 13 | Group 14 | Group 15 | Group 16 | Group 17 | Group 18 |
|---|---|---|---|---|---|---|---|---|
| | | | | | | | | 2<br>**He**<br>Helium<br>4.003 |
| | | | 5<br>**B**<br>Boron<br>10.81 | 6<br>**C**<br>Carbon<br>12.01 | 7<br>**N**<br>Nitrogen<br>14.01 | 8<br>**O**<br>Oxygen<br>16.00 | 9<br>**F**<br>Fluorine<br>19.00 | 10<br>**Ne**<br>Neon<br>20.18 |
| Group 10 | Group 11 | Group 12 | 13<br>**Al**<br>Aluminum<br>26.98 | 14<br>**Si**<br>Silicon<br>28.09 | 15<br>**P**<br>Phosphorus<br>30.97 | 16<br>**S**<br>Sulfur<br>32.06 | 17<br>**Cl**<br>Chlorine<br>35.45 | 18<br>**Ar**<br>Argon<br>39.95 |
| 28<br>**Ni**<br>Nickel<br>58.69 | 29<br>**Cu**<br>Copper<br>63.55 | 30<br>**Zn**<br>Zinc<br>65.38 | 31<br>**Ga**<br>Gallium<br>69.72 | 32<br>**Ge**<br>Germanium<br>72.63 | 33<br>**As**<br>Arsenic<br>74.92 | 34<br>**Se**<br>Selenium<br>78.96 | 35<br>**Br**<br>Bromine<br>79.90 | 36<br>**Kr**<br>Krypton<br>83.80 |
| 46<br>**Pd**<br>Palladium<br>106.42 | 47<br>**Ag**<br>Silver<br>107.87 | 48<br>**Cd**<br>Cadmium<br>112.41 | 49<br>**In**<br>Indium<br>114.82 | 50<br>**Sn**<br>Tin<br>118.71 | 51<br>**Sb**<br>Antimony<br>121.76 | 52<br>**Te**<br>Tellurium<br>127.60 | 53<br>**I**<br>Iodine<br>126.90 | 54<br>**Xe**<br>Xenon<br>131.29 |
| 78<br>**Pt**<br>Platinum<br>195.08 | 79<br>**Au**<br>Gold<br>196.97 | 80<br>**Hg**<br>Mercury<br>200.59 | 81<br>**Tl**<br>Thallium<br>204.38 | 82<br>**Pb**<br>Lead<br>207.2 | 83<br>**Bi**<br>Bismuth<br>208.98 | 84<br>**Po**<br>Polonium<br>(209) | 85<br>**At**<br>Astatine<br>(210) | 86<br>**Rn**<br>Radon<br>(222) |
| 110<br>**Ds**<br>Darmstadtium<br>(271) | 111<br>**Rg**<br>Roentgenium<br>(272) | 112<br>**Cn**<br>Copernicium<br>(285) | 113<br>**Uut**<br>Ununtrium<br>(284) | 114<br>**Fl**<br>Flerovium<br>(289) | 115<br>**Uup**<br>Ununpentium<br>(288) | 116<br>**Lv**<br>Livermorium<br>(293) | 117<br>**Uus**<br>Ununseptium<br>(294) | 118<br>**Uuo**<br>Ununoctium<br>(294) |

| 63<br>**Eu**<br>Europium<br>151.96 | 64<br>**Gd**<br>Gadolinium<br>157.25 | 65<br>**Tb**<br>Terbium<br>158.93 | 66<br>**Dy**<br>Dysprosium<br>162.50 | 67<br>**Ho**<br>Holmium<br>164.93 | 68<br>**Er**<br>Erbium<br>167.26 | 69<br>**Tm**<br>Thulium<br>168.93 | 70<br>**Yb**<br>Ytterbium<br>173.05 | 71<br>**Lu**<br>Lutetium<br>174.97 |
|---|---|---|---|---|---|---|---|---|
| 95<br>**Am**<br>Americium<br>(243) | 96<br>**Cm**<br>Curium<br>(247) | 97<br>**Bk**<br>Berkelium<br>(247) | 98<br>**Cf**<br>Californium<br>(251) | 99<br>**Es**<br>Einsteinium<br>(252) | 100<br>**Fm**<br>Fermium<br>(257) | 101<br>**Md**<br>Mendelevium<br>(258) | 102<br>**No**<br>Nobelium<br>(259) | 103<br>**Lr**<br>Lawrencium<br>(262) |

# References

## Physical Science Refresher

### Atoms and Elements

Every object in the universe is made of matter. **Matter** is anything that takes up space and has mass. All matter is made of atoms. An **atom** is the smallest particle into which an element can be divided and still be the same element. An **element**, in turn, is a substance that cannot be broken down into simpler substances by chemical means. Each element consists of only one kind of atom. An element may be made of many atoms, but they are all the same kind of atom.

### Atomic Structure

Atoms are made of smaller particles called **electrons, protons**, and **neutrons**. Electrons have a negative electric charge, protons have a positive charge, and neutrons have no electric charge. Together, protons and neutrons form the **nucleus**, or small dense center, of an atom. Because protons are positively charged and neutrons are neutral, the nucleus has a positive charge. Electrons move within an area around the nucleus called the **electron cloud**. Electrons move so quickly that scientists cannot determine their exact speeds and positions at the same time.

electron cloud

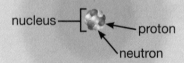
nucleus — proton
neutron

### Atomic Number

To help distinguish one element from another, scientists use the atomic numbers of atoms. The **atomic number** is the number of protons in the nucleus of an atom. The atoms of a certain element always have the same number of protons.

When atoms have an equal number of protons and electrons, they are uncharged, or electrically neutral. The atomic number equals the number of electrons in an uncharged atom. The number of neutrons, however, can vary for a given element. Atoms of the same element that have different numbers of neutrons are called **isotopes**.

### Periodic Table of the Elements

In the periodic table, each element in the table is in a separate box. And the elements are arranged from left to right in order of increasing atomic number. That is, an uncharged atom of each element has one more electron and one more proton than an uncharged atom of the element to its left. Each horizontal row of the table is called a **period**. Changes in chemical properties of elements across a period correspond to changes in the electron arrangements of their atoms.

Each vertical column of the table is known as a **group.** A group lists elements with similar physical and chemical properties. For this reason, a group is also sometimes called a family. The elements in a group have similar properties because their atoms have the same number of electrons in their outer energy level. For example, the elements helium, neon, argon, krypton, xenon, and radon all have similar properties and are known as the noble gases.

## Molecules and Compounds

When two or more elements join chemically, they form a **compound**. A compound is a new substance with properties different from those of the elements that compose it. For example, water, $H_2O$, is a compound formed when hydrogen (H) and oxygen (O) combine. The smallest complete unit of a compound that has the properties of that compound is called a **molecule**. A chemical formula indicates the elements in a compound. It also indicates the relative number of atoms of each element in the compound. The chemical formula for water is $H_2O$. So each water molecule consists of two atoms of hydrogen and one atom of oxygen. The subscript number after the symbol for an element shows how many atoms of that element are in a single molecule of the compound.

## Chemical Equations

A chemical reaction occurs when a chemical change takes place. A chemical equation describes a chemical reaction using chemical formulas. The equation indicates the substances that react and the substances that are produced. For example, when carbon and oxygen combine, they can form carbon dioxide, shown in the following equation: $C + O_2 \longrightarrow CO_2$

## Acids, Bases, and pH

An **ion** is an atom or group of chemically bonded atoms that has an electric charge because it has lost or gained one or more electrons. When an acid, such as hydrochloric acid, HCl, is mixed with water, it separates into ions. An **acid** is a compound that produces hydrogen ions, $H^+$, in water. The hydrogen ions then combine with a water molecule to form a hydronium ion, $H_3O^+$. A **base**, on the other hand, is a substance that produces hydroxide ions, $OH^-$, in water.

To determine whether a solution is acidic or basic, scientists use pH. The **pH** of a solution is a measure of the hydronium ion concentration in a solution. The pH scale ranges from 0 to 14. Acids have a pH that is less than 7. The lower the number, the more acidic the solution. The middle point, pH = 7, is neutral, neither acidic nor basic. Bases have a pH that is greater than 7. The higher the number is, the more basic the solution.

### The pH of Some Common Materials

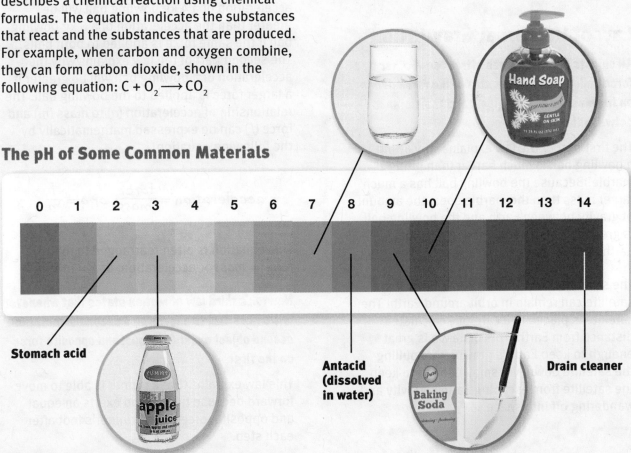

0  1  2  3  4  5  6  7  8  9  10  11  12  13  14

Stomach acid

apple juice

Antacid (dissolved in water)

Baking Soda

Drain cleaner

Hand Soap

# References

## Physical Laws and Useful Equations

### Law of Conservation of Mass

Mass cannot be created or destroyed during ordinary chemical or physical changes.

The total mass in a closed system is always the same no matter how many physical changes or chemical reactions occur.

### Law of Conservation of Energy

Energy can be neither created nor destroyed.

The total amount of energy in a closed system is always the same. Energy can be changed from one form to another, but all of the different forms of energy in a system always add up to the same total amount of energy, no matter how many energy conversions occur.

### Law of Universal Gravitation

All objects in the universe attract each other by a force called gravity. The size of the force depends on the masses of the objects and the distance between the objects.

The first part of the law explains why lifting a bowling ball is much harder than lifting a marble. Because the bowling ball has a much larger mass than the marble does, the amount of gravity between Earth and the bowling ball is greater than the amount of gravity between Earth and the marble.

The second part of the law explains why a satellite can remain in orbit around Earth. The satellite is placed at a carefully calculated distance from Earth. This distance is great enough to keep Earth's gravity from pulling the satellite down, yet small enough to keep the satellite from escaping Earth's gravity and wandering off into space.

### Newton's Laws of Motion

Newton's first law of motion states that an object at rest remains at rest and that an object in motion remains in motion at constant speed and in a straight line unless acted on by an unbalanced force.

The first part of the law explains why a football will remain on a tee until it is kicked off or until a gust of wind blows it off. The second part of the law explains why a bike rider will continue moving forward after the bike comes to an abrupt stop. Gravity and the friction of the sidewalk will eventually stop the rider.

Newton's second law of motion states that the acceleration of an object depends on the mass of the object and the amount of force applied.

The first part of the law explains why the acceleration of a 4 kg bowling ball will be greater than the acceleration of a 6 kg bowling ball if the same force is applied to both balls. The second part of the law explains why the acceleration of a bowling ball will be greater if a larger force is applied to the bowling ball. The relationship of acceleration ($a$) to mass ($m$) and force ($F$) can be expressed mathematically by the following equation:

$$acceleration = \frac{force}{mass}, \text{ or } a = \frac{F}{m}$$

This equation is often rearranged to read $force = mass \times acceleration$, or $F = m \times a$

Newton's third law of motion states that whenever one object exerts a force on a second object, the second object exerts an equal and opposite force on the first.

This law explains that a runner is able to move forward because the ground exerts an equal and opposite force on the runner's foot after each step.

## Average Speed

$$average\ speed = \frac{total\ distance}{total\ time}$$

**Example:**
A bicycle messenger traveled a distance of 136 km in 8 h. What was the messenger's average speed?

$$\frac{136\ km}{8\ h} = 17\ km/h$$

The messenger's average speed was **17 km/h**.

## Average Acceleration

$$average\ acceleration = \frac{final\ velocity - starting\ velocity}{time\ it\ takes\ to\ change\ velocity}$$

**Example:**
Calculate the average acceleration of an Olympic 100 m dash sprinter who reached a velocity of 20 m/s south at the finish line. The race was in a straight line and lasted 10 s.

$$\frac{20\ m/s - 0\ m/s}{10\ s} = 2\ m/s/s$$

The sprinter's average acceleration was **2 m/s/s south**.

## Pressure

**Pressure** is the force exerted over a given area. The SI unit for pressure is the pascal. Its symbol is Pa.

$$pressure = \frac{force}{area}$$

## Net Force
### Forces in the Same Direction

When forces are in the same direction, add the forces together to determine the net force.

**Example:**
Calculate the net force on a stalled car that is being pushed by two people. One person is pushing with a force of 13 N northwest, and the other person is pushing with a force of 8 N in the same direction.

$$13\ N + 8\ N = 21\ N$$

The net force is **21 N northwest**.

### Forces in Opposite Directions

When forces are in opposite directions, subtract the smaller force from the larger force to determine the net force. The net force will be in the direction of the larger force.

**Example:**
Calculate the net force on a rope that is being pulled on each end. One person is pulling on one end of the rope with a force of 12 N south. Another person is pulling on the opposite end of the rope with a force of 7 N north.

$$12\ N - 7\ N = 5\ N$$

The net force is **5 N south**.

**Example:**
Calculate the pressure of the air in a soccer ball if the air exerts a force of 10 N over an area of 0.5 m².

$$pressure = \frac{10\ N}{0.5\ m^2} = \frac{20\ N}{m^2} = 20\ Pa$$

The pressure of the air inside the soccer ball is **20 Pa**.

# Reading and Study Skills

## A How-To Manual for Active Reading

This book belongs to you, and you are invited to write in it. In fact, the book won't be complete until you do. Sometimes you'll answer a question or follow directions to mark up the text. Other times you'll write down your own thoughts. And when you're done reading and writing in the book, the book will be ready to help you review what you learned and prepare for tests.

## Active Reading Annotations

Before you read, you'll often come upon an Active Reading prompt that asks you to underline certain words or number the steps in a process. Here's an example.

> **Active Reading**
>
> **12 Identify** In this paragraph, number the sequence of sentences that describe replication.

Marking the text this way is called **annotating,** and your marks are called **annotations.** Annotating the text can help you identify important concepts while you read.

There are other ways that you can annotate the text. You can draw an asterisk (*) by vocabulary terms, mark unfamiliar or confusing terms and information with a question mark (?), and mark main ideas with a <u>double underline</u>. And you can even invent your own marks to annotate the text!

## Other Annotating Opportunities

Keep your pencil, pen, or highlighter nearby as you read so you can make a note or highlight an important point at any time. Here are a few ideas to get you started.

- Notice the headings in red and blue. The blue headings are questions that point to the main idea of what you're reading. The red headings are answers to the questions in the blue ones. Together these headings outline the content of the lesson. After reading a lesson, you could write your own answers to the questions.

- Notice the bold-faced words that are highlighted in yellow. They are highlighted so that you can easily find them again on the page where they are defined. As you read or as you review, challenge yourself to write your own sentence using the bold-faced term.
- Make a note in the margin at any time. You might
  - Ask a "What if" question
  - Comment on what you read
  - Make a connection to something you read elsewhere
  - Make a logical conclusion from the text

Use your own language and abbreviations. Invent a code, such as using circles and boxes around words to remind you of their importance or relation to each other. Your annotations will help you remember your questions for class discussions, and when you go back to the lesson later, you may be able to fill in what you didn't understand the first time you read it. Like a scientist in the field or in a lab, you will be recording your questions and observations for analysis later.

## Active Reading Questions

After you read, you'll often come upon Active Reading questions that ask you to think about what you've just read. You'll write your answer underneath the question. Here's an example.

 Active Reading

**8 Describe** Where are phosphate groups found in a DNA molecule?

_____

_____

This type of question helps you sum up what you've just read and pull out the most important ideas from the passage. In this case, the question asks you to **describe** the structure of a DNA molecule that you have just read about. Other times you may be asked to do such things as **apply** a concept, **compare** two concepts, **summarize** a process, or **identify a cause-and-effect** relationship. You'll be strengthening those critical thinking skills that you'll use often in learning about science.

# Reading and Study Skills

## Using Graphic Organizers to Take Notes

Graphic organizers help you remember information as you read it for the first time and as you study it later. There are dozens of graphic organizers to choose from, so the first trick is to choose the one that's best suited to your purpose. Following are some graphic organizers to use for different purposes.

| To remember lots of information | To relate a central idea to subordinate details | To describe a process | To make a comparison |
|---|---|---|---|
| • Arrange data in a Content Frame<br><br>• Use Combination Notes to describe a concept in words and pictures | • Show relationships with a Mind Map or a Main Idea Web<br><br>• Sum up relationships among many things with a Concept Map | • Use a Process Diagram to explain a procedure<br><br>• Show a chain of events and results in a Cause-and-Effect Chart | • Compare two or more closely related things in a Venn Diagram |

## Content Frame

1 Make a four-column chart.

2 Fill the first column with categories (e.g., snail, ant, earthworm) and the first row with descriptive information (e.g., group, characteristic, appearance).

3 Fill the chart with details that belong in each row and column.

4 When you finish, you'll have a study aid that helps you compare one category to another.

### Invertebrates

| NAME | GROUP | CHARACTERISTICS | DRAWING |
|---|---|---|---|
| snail | mollusks | mantle | |
| ant | arthropods | six legs, exoskeleton | |
| earthworm | segmented worms | segmented body, circulatory and digestive systems | |
| heartworm | roundworms | digestive system | |
| sea star | echinoderms | spiny skin, tube feet | |
| jellyfish | cnidarians | stinging cells | |

© Houghton Mifflin Harcourt Publishing Company

## Combination Notes

**1** Make a two-column chart.

**2** Write descriptive words and definitions in the first column.

**3** Draw a simple sketch that helps you remember the meaning of the term in the second column.

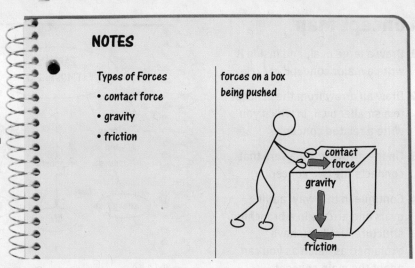

NOTES

Types of Forces
- contact force
- gravity
- friction

forces on a box being pushed

contact force

gravity

friction

## Mind Map

**1** Draw an oval, and inside it write a topic to analyze.

**2** Draw two or more arms extending from the oval. Each arm represents a main idea about the topic.

**3** Draw lines from the arms on which to write details about each of the main ideas.

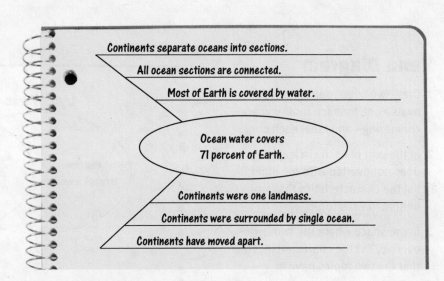

Continents separate oceans into sections.

All ocean sections are connected.

Most of Earth is covered by water.

Ocean water covers 71 percent of Earth.

Continents were one landmass.

Continents were surrounded by single ocean.

Continents have moved apart.

## Main Idea Web

**1** Make a box, and write a concept you want to remember inside it.

**2** Draw boxes around the central box, and label each one with a category of information about the concept (e.g., definition, formula, descriptive details).

**3** Fill in the boxes with relevant details as you read.

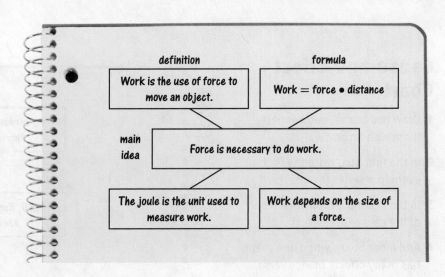

definition

Work is the use of force to move an object.

formula

Work = force • distance

main idea

Force is necessary to do work.

The joule is the unit used to measure work.

Work depends on the size of a force.

# Reading and Study Skills

## Concept Map

1 Draw a large oval, and inside it write a major concept.

2 Draw an arrow from the concept to a smaller oval, in which you write a related concept.

3 On the arrow, write a verb that connects the two concepts.

4 Continue in this way, adding ovals and arrows in a branching structure, until you have explained as much as you can about the main concept.

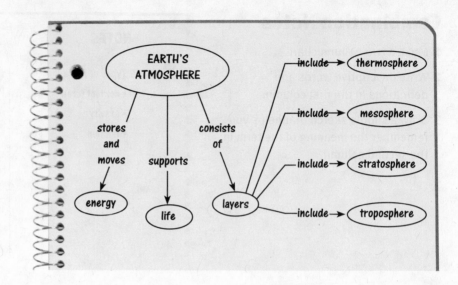

## Venn Diagram

1 Draw two overlapping circles or ovals—one for each topic you are comparing—and label each one.

2 In the part of each circle that does not overlap with the other, list the characteristics that are unique to each topic.

3 In the space where the two circles overlap, list the characteristics that the two topics have in common.

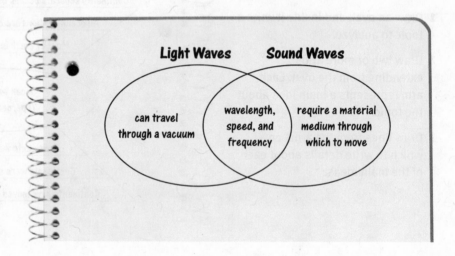

## Cause-and-Effect Chart

1 Draw two boxes, and connect them with an arrow.

2 In the first box, write the first event in a series (a cause).

3 In the second box, write a result of the cause (the effect).

4 Add more boxes when one event has many effects or vice versa.

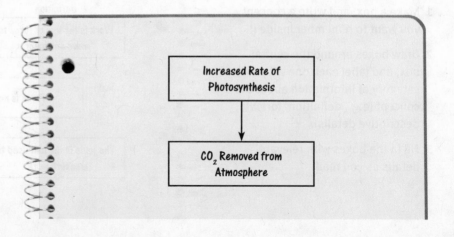

# Process Diagram

A process can be a never-ending cycle. As you can see in this technology design process, engineers may backtrack and repeat steps, they may skip steps entirely, or they may repeat the entire process before a usable design is achieved.

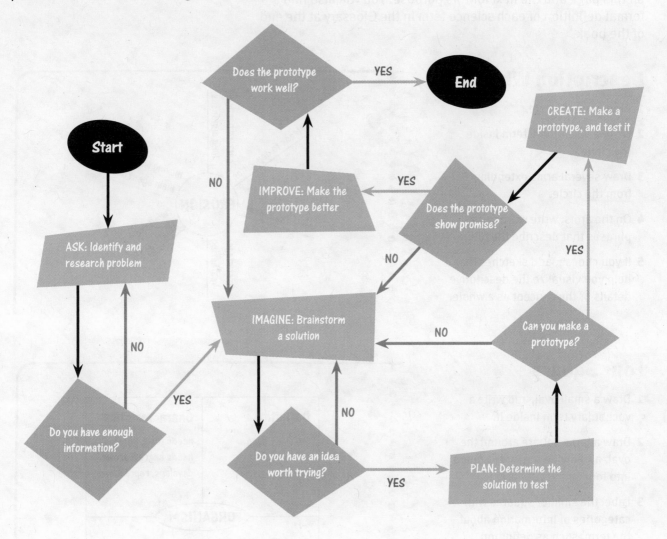

# Reading and Study Skills

## Using Vocabulary Strategies

Important science terms are highlighted where they are first defined in this book. One way to remember these terms is to take notes and make sketches when you come to them. Use the strategies on this page and the next for this purpose. You will also find a formal definition of each science term in the Glossary at the end of the book.

### Description Wheel

**1** Draw a small circle.

**2** Write a vocabulary term inside the circle.

**3** Draw several arms extending from the circle.

**4** On the arms, write words and phrases that describe the term.

**5** If you choose, add sketches that help you visualize the descriptive details or the concept as a whole.

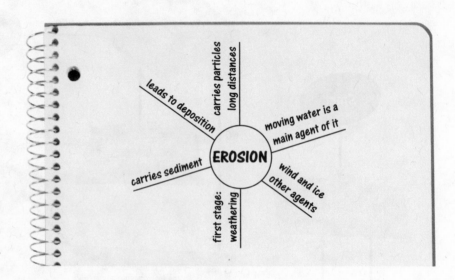

### Four Square

**1** Draw a small oval, and write a vocabulary term inside it.

**2** Draw a large square around the oval, and divide the large square into four smaller squares.

**3** Label the smaller squares with categories of information about the term, such as definition, characteristics, examples, non-examples, appearance, and root words.

**4** Fill the squares with descriptive words and drawings that will help you remember the overall meaning of the term and its essential details.

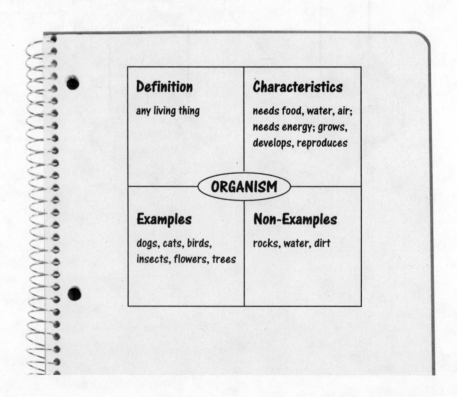

## Frame Game

**1** Draw a small rectangle, and write a vocabulary term inside it.

**2** Draw a larger rectangle around the smaller one. Connect the corners of the larger rectangle to the corners of the smaller one, creating four spaces that frame the word.

**3** In each of the four parts of the frame, draw or write details that help define the term. Consider including a definition, essential characteristics, an equation, examples, and a sentence using the term.

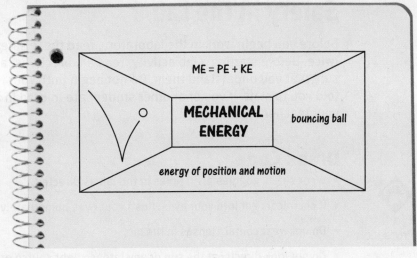

## Magnet Word

**1** Draw horseshoe magnet, and write a vocabulary term inside it.

**2** Add lines that extend from the sides of the magnet.

**3** Brainstorm words and phrases that come to mind when you think about the term.

**4** On the lines, write the words and phrases that describe something essential about the term.

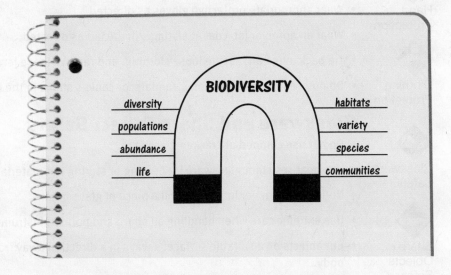

## Word Triangle

**1** Draw a triangle, and add lines to divide it into three parts.

**2** Write a term and its definition in the bottom section of the triangle.

**3** In the middle section, write a sentence in which the term is used correctly.

**4** In the top section, draw a small picture to illustrate the term.

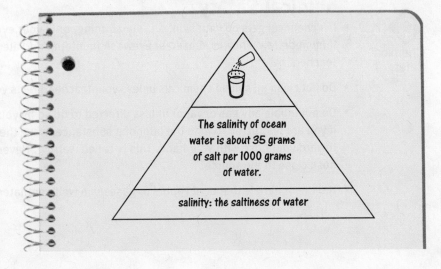

# Science Skills

## Safety in the Lab

Before you begin work in the laboratory, read these safety rules twice. Before starting a lab activity, read all directions, and make sure that you understand them. Do not begin until your teacher has told you to start. If you or another student are injured in any way, tell your teacher immediately.

### Dress Code

Eye Protection

Hand Protection

- Wear safety goggles at all times in the lab as directed.

- If chemicals get into your eyes, flush your eyes immediately.

- Do not wear contact lenses in the lab.

- Do not look directly at the sun or any intense light source or laser.

- Do not cut an object while holding the object in your hand.

- Wear appropriate protective gloves as directed.

- Wear an apron or lab coat at all times in the lab as directed.

- Tie back long hair, secure loose clothing, and remove loose jewelry.

- Do not wear open-toed shoes, sandals, or canvas shoes in the lab.

Clothing Protection

### Glassware and Sharp Object Safety

Glassware Safety

- Do not use chipped or cracked glassware.

- Use heat-resistant glassware for heating or storing hot materials.

- Notify your teacher immediately if a piece of glass breaks.

- Use extreme care when handling all sharp and pointed instruments.

- Cut objects on a suitable surface, always in a direction away from your body.

Sharp Objects Safety

### Chemical Safety

Chemical Safety

- If a chemical gets on your skin, on your clothing, or in your eyes, rinse it immediately (shower, faucet, or eyewash fountain), and alert your teacher.

- Do not clean up spilled chemicals unless your teacher directs you to do so.

- Do not inhale any gas or vapor unless directed to do so by your teacher. If you are instructed to note the odor of a substance, wave the fumes toward your nose with your hand. This is called wafting. Never put your nose close to the source.

- Handle materials that emit vapors or gases in a well-ventilated area.

## Electrical Safety

**Electrical Safety**

- Do not use equipment with frayed electrical cords or loose plugs.
- Do not use electrical equipment near water or when clothing or hands are wet.
- Hold the plug housing when you plug in or unplug equipment.

## Heating and Fire Safety

**Heating Safety**

- Be aware of any source of flames, sparks, or heat (such as flames, heating coils, or hot plates) before working with any flammable substances.
- Know the location of lab fire extinguishers and fire-safety blankets.
- Know your school's fire-evacuation routes.
- If your clothing catches on fire, walk to the lab shower to put out the fire.
- Never leave a hot plate unattended while it is turned on or while it is cooling.
- Use tongs or appropriate insulated holders when handling heated objects.
- Allow all equipment to cool before storing it.

Wafting

## Plant and Animal Safety

**Plant Safety**

- Do not eat any part of a plant.
- Do not pick any wild plants unless your teacher instructs you to do so.

**Animal Safety**

- Handle animals only as your teacher directs.
- Treat animals carefully and respectfully.
- Wash your hands thoroughly after handling any plant or animal.

## Cleanup

**Proper Waste Disposal**

- Clean all work surfaces and protective equipment as directed by your teacher.
- Dispose of hazardous materials or sharp objects only as directed by your teacher.

**Hygienic Care**

- Keep your hands away from your face while you are working on any activity.
- Wash your hands thoroughly before you leave the lab or after any activity.

# Science Skills

## Designing, Conducting, and Reporting an Experiment

An experiment is an organized procedure to study something under specific conditions. Use the following steps of the scientific method when designing or conducting a controlled experiment.

## 1  Identify a Research Problem

Every day, you make observations by using your senses to gather information. Careful observations lead to good questions, and good questions can lead you to an experiment. Imagine, for example, that you pass a pond every day on your way to school, and you notice green scum beginning to form on top of it. You wonder what it is and why it seems to be growing. You list your questions, and then you do a little research to find out what is already known. A good place to start a research project is at the library. A library catalog lists all of the resources available to you at that library and often those found elsewhere. Begin your search by using:

- keywords or main topics.

- words similar to, or synonyms of, your keyword.

The types of resources that will be helpful to you will depend on the kind of information you are interested in. And some resources are more reliable for a given topic than others. Some different kinds of useful resources are:

- magazines and journals (or periodicals)—articles on a topic.

- encyclopedias—a good overview of a topic.

- books on specific subjects—details about a topic.

- newspapers—useful for current events.

The Internet can also be a great place to find information. Some of your library's reference materials may even be online. When using the Internet, however, it is especially important to make sure you are using appropriate and reliable sources. Websites of universities and government agencies are usually more accurate and reliable than websites created by individuals or businesses. Decide which sources are relevant and reliable for your topic. If in doubt, check with your teacher.

Take notes as you read through the information in these resources. You will probably come up with many questions and ideas for which you can do more research as needed. Once you feel you have enough information, think about the questions you have on the topic. Then write down the problem that you want to investigate. Your notes might look like those at the top of the next page.

| Research Questions | Research Problem | Library and Internet Resources |
|---|---|---|
| • How do algae grow?<br>• How do people measure algae?<br>• What kind of fertilizer would affect the growth of algae?<br>• Can fertilizer and algae be used safely in a lab? How? | How does fertilizer affect the algae in a pond? | Pond fertilization: initiating an algal bloom—from University of California Davis website.<br><br>Blue-green algae in Wisconsin waters—from the Department of Natural Resources of Wisconsin website. |

As you gather information from reliable sources, record details about each source, including author name(s), title, date of publication, and/or web address. Make sure to also note the specific information that you use from each source. Staying organized in this way will be important when you write your report and create a bibliography or works cited list. Recording this information and staying organized will help you credit the appropriate author(s) for the information that you have gathered.

Representing someone else's ideas or work as your own (without giving the original author credit) is known as plagiarism. Plagiarism can be intentional or unintentional. The best way to make sure that you do not commit plagiarism is to always do your own work and to always give credit to others when you use their words or ideas.

Current scientific research is built on scientific research and discoveries that have happened in the past. This means that scientists are constantly learning from each other and combining ideas to learn more about the natural world through investigation. But a good scientist always credits the ideas and research gathered from other people to those people. There are more details about crediting sources and creating a bibliography under step 9.

## 2 Make a Prediction

A prediction is a statement of what you expect will happen in your experiment. Before making a prediction, you need to decide in a general way what you will do in your procedure. You may state your prediction in an if-then format.

### Prediction

If the amount of fertilizer in the pond water is increased, then the amount of algae will also increase.

© Houghton Mifflin Harcourt Publishing Company

# Science Skills

## 3 Form a Hypothesis

Many experiments are designed to test a hypothesis. A hypothesis is a tentative explanation for an expected result. You have predicted that additional fertilizer will cause additional algae growth in pond water; your hypothesis should state the connection between fertilizer and algal growth.

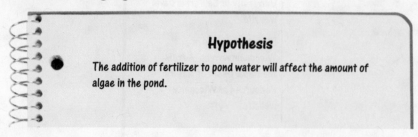

**Hypothesis**

The addition of fertilizer to pond water will affect the amount of algae in the pond.

## 4 Identify Variables to Test the Hypothesis

The next step is to design an experiment to test the hypothesis. The experimental results may or may not support the hypothesis. Either way, the information that results from the experiment may be useful for future investigations.

### Experimental Group and Control Group

An experiment to determine how two factors are related has a control group and an experimental group. The two groups are the same, except that the investigator changes a single factor in the experimental group and does not change it in the control group.

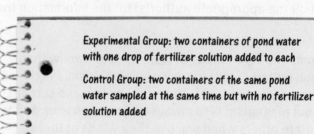

**Experimental Group:** two containers of pond water with one drop of fertilizer solution added to each

**Control Group:** two containers of the same pond water sampled at the same time but with no fertilizer solution added

### Variables and Constants

In a controlled experiment, a variable is any factor that can change. Constants are all of the variables that are kept the same in both the experimental group and the control group.

The independent variable is the factor that is manipulated or changed in order to test the effect of the change on another variable. The dependent variable is the factor the investigator measures to gather data about the effect.

| Independent Variable | Dependent Variable | Constants |
|---|---|---|
| Amount of fertilizer in pond water | Growth of algae in the pond water | • Where and when the pond water is obtained<br>• The type of container used<br>• Light and temperature conditions where the water is stored |

## 5 Write a Procedure

Write each step of your procedure. Start each step with a verb, or action word, and keep the steps short. Your procedure should be clear enough for someone else to use as instructions for repeating your experiment.

### Procedure

1. Use the masking tape and the marker to label the containers with your initials, the date, and the identifiers "Jar 1 with Fertilizer," "Jar 2 with Fertilizer," "Jar 1 without Fertilizer," and "Jar 2 without Fertilizer."

2. Put on your gloves. Use the large container to obtain a sample of pond water.

3. Divide the water sample equally among the four smaller containers.

4. Use the eyedropper to add one drop of fertilizer solution to the two containers labeled "Jar 1 with Fertilizer" and "Jar 2 with Fertilizer."

5. Cover the containers with clear plastic wrap. Use the scissors to punch ten holes in each of the covers.

6. Place all four containers on a window ledge. Make sure that they all receive the same amount of light.

7. Observe the containers every day for one week.

8. Place a ruler over the opening of the jar and measure the diameter of the largest clump of algae in each container. Record your measurements daily.

# Science Skills

## 6 Experiment and Collect Data

Once you have all of your materials and your procedure has been approved, you can begin to experiment and collect data. Record both quantitative data (measurements) and qualitative data (observations), as shown below.

### Algal Growth and Fertilizer

| Date and Time | Experimental Group | | Control Group | | Observations |
| --- | --- | --- | --- | --- | --- |
| | Jar 1 with Fertilizer (diameter of algal clump in mm) | Jar 2 with Fertilizer (diameter of algal clump in mm) | Jar 1 without Fertilizer (diameter of algal clump in mm) | Jar 2 without Fertilizer (diameter of algal clump in mm) | |
| 5/3 4:00 p.m. | 0 | 0 | 0 | 0 | condensation in all containers |
| 5/4 4:00 p.m. | 0 | 3 | 0 | 0 | tiny green blobs in Jar 2 with fertilizer |
| 5/5 4:15 p.m. | 4 | 5 | 0 | 3 | green blobs in Jars 1 and 2 with fertilizer and Jar 2 without fertilizer |
| 5/6 4:00 p.m. | 5 | 6 | 0 | 4 | water light green in Jar 2 with fertilizer |
| 5/7 4:00 p.m. | 8 | 10 | 0 | 6 | water light green in Jars 1 and 2 with fertilizer and Jar 2 without fertilizer |
| 5/8 3:30 p.m. | 10 | 18 | 0 | 6 | cover off of Jar 2 with fertilizer |
| 5/9 3:30 p.m. | 14 | 23 | 0 | 8 | drew sketches of each container |

### Drawings of Samples Viewed Under Microscope on 5/9 at 100x

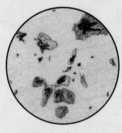

Jar 1 with Fertilizer

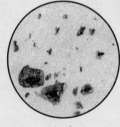

Jar 2 with Fertilizer

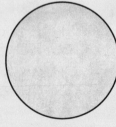

Jar 1 without Fertilizer

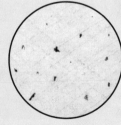

Jar 2 without Fertilizer

# 7 Analyze Data

After you complete your experiment, you must analyze all of the data you have gathered. Tables, statistics, and graphs are often used in this step to organize and analyze both the qualitative and quantitative data. Sometimes, your qualitative data are best used to help explain the relationships you see in your quantitative data.

Computer graphing software is useful for creating a graph from data you have collected. Most graphing software can make line graphs, pie charts, or bar graphs from data that have been organized in a spreadsheet. Graphs are useful for understanding relationships in the data and for communicating the results of your experiment.

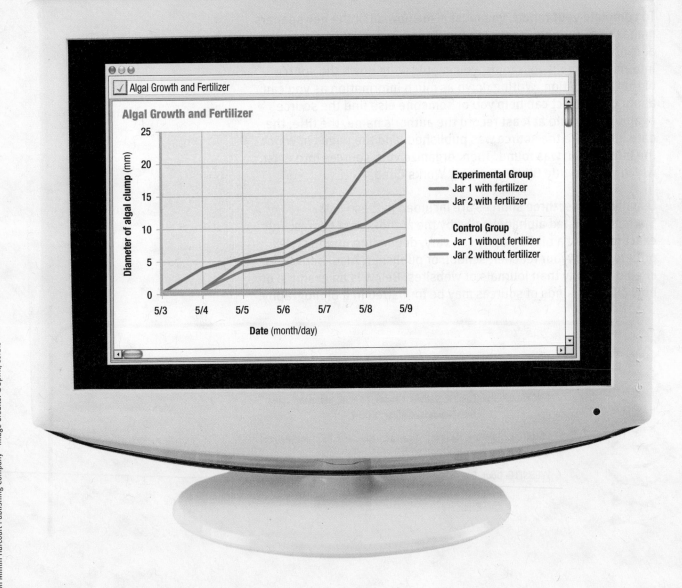

## 8 Make Conclusions

To draw conclusions from your experiment, first, write your results. Then, compare your results with your hypothesis. Do your results support your hypothesis? What have you learned?

**Conclusion**

More algae grew in the pond water to which fertilizer had been added than in the pond water to which fertilizer had not been added. My hypothesis was supported. I conclude that it is possible that the growth of algae in ponds can be influenced by the input of fertilizer.

## 9 Create a Bibliography or Works Cited List

To complete your report, you must also show all of the newspapers, magazines, journals, books, and online sources that you used at every stage of your investigation. Whenever you find useful information about your topic, you should write down the source of that information. Writing down as much information as you can about the subject can help you or someone else find the source again. You should at least record the author's name, the title, the date and where the source was published, and the pages in which the information was found. Then, organize your sources into a list, which you can title Bibliography or Works Cited.

Usually, at least three sources are included in these lists. Sources are listed alphabetically, by the authors' last names. The exact format of a bibliography can vary, depending on the style preferences of your teacher, school, or publisher. Also, books are cited differently than journals or websites. Below is an example of how different kinds of sources may be formatted in a bibliography.

BOOK: Hauschultz, Sara. *Freshwater Algae.* Brainard, Minnesota: Northwoods Publishing, 2011.

ENCYCLOPEDIA: Lasure, Sedona. "Algae is not all just pond scum." *Encyclopedia of Algae.* 2009.

JOURNAL: Johnson, Keagan. "Algae as we know it." *Sci Journal,* vol 64. (September 2010): 201-211.

WEBSITE: Dout, Bill. "Keeping algae scum out of birdbaths." Help Keep Earth Clean. News. January 26, 2011. <www.SaveEarth.org>.

# Using a Microscope

Scientists use microscopes to see very small objects that cannot easily be seen with the eye alone. A microscope magnifies the image of an object so that small details may be observed. A microscope that you may use can magnify an object 400 times—the object will appear 400 times larger than its actual size.

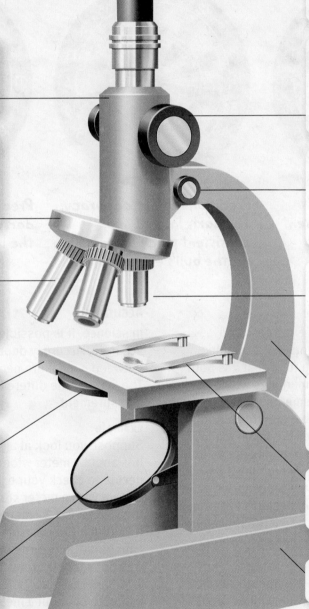

**Eyepiece** Objects are viewed through the eyepiece. The eyepiece contains a lens that commonly magnifies an image 10 times.

**Body** The body separates the lens in the eyepiece from the objective lenses below.

**Coarse Adjustment** This knob is used to focus the image of an object when it is viewed through the low-power lens.

**Nosepiece** The nosepiece holds the objective lenses above the stage and rotates so that all lenses may be used.

**Fine Adjustment** This knob is used to focus the image of an object when it is viewed through the high-power lens.

**High-Power Objective Lens** This is the largest lens on the nosepiece. It magnifies an image approximately 40 times.

**Low-Power Objective Lens** This is the smallest lens on the nosepiece. It magnifies images about 10 times.

**Stage** The stage supports the object being viewed.

**Arm** The arm supports the body above the stage. Always carry a microscope by the arm and base.

**Diaphragm** The diaphragm is used to adjust the amount of light passing through the slide and into an objective lens.

**Stage Clip** The stage clip holds a slide in place on the stage.

**Mirror or Light Source** Some microscopes use light that is reflected through the stage by a mirror. Other microscopes have their own light sources.

**Base** The base supports the microscope.

# Science Skills

## Measuring Accurately

### Precision and Accuracy

When you do a scientific investigation, it is important that your methods, observations, and data be both precise and accurate.

Low precision: The darts did not land in a consistent place on the dartboard.

Precision but not accuracy: The darts landed in a consistent place but did not hit the bull's eye.

Precision and accuracy: The darts landed consistently on the bull's eye.

### Precision

In science, *precision* is the exactness and consistency of measurements. For example, measurements made with a ruler that has both centimeter and millimeter markings would be more precise than measurements made with a ruler that has only centimeter markings. Another indicator of precision is the care taken to make sure that methods and observations are as exact and consistent as possible. Every time a particular experiment is done, the same procedure should be used. Precision is necessary because experiments are repeated several times and if the procedure changes, the results might change.

**Example**

Suppose you are measuring temperatures over a two-week period. Your precision will be greater if you measure each temperature at the same place, at the same time of day, and with the same thermometer than if you change any of these factors from one day to the next.

### Accuracy

In science, it is possible to be precise but not accurate. *Accuracy* depends on the difference between a measurement and an actual value. The smaller the difference, the more accurate the measurement.

**Example**

Suppose you look at a stream and estimate that it is about 1 meter wide at a particular place. You decide to check your estimate by measuring the stream with a meter stick, and you determine that the stream is 1.32 meters wide. However, because it is difficult to measure the width of a stream with a meter stick, it turns out that your measurement was not very accurate. The stream is actually 1.14 meters wide. Therefore, even though your estimate of about 1 meter was less precise than your measurement, your estimate was actually more accurate.

# Graduated Cylinders

## How to Measure the Volume of a Liquid with a Graduated Cylinder

- Be sure that the graduated cylinder is on a flat surface so that your measurement will be accurate.

- When reading the scale on a graduated cylinder, be sure to have your eyes at the level of the surface of the liquid.

- The surface of the liquid will be curved in the graduated cylinder. Read the volume of the liquid at the bottom of the curve, or meniscus (muh•NIHS•kuhs).

- You can use a graduated cylinder to find the volume of a solid object by measuring the increase in a liquid's level after you add the object to the cylinder.

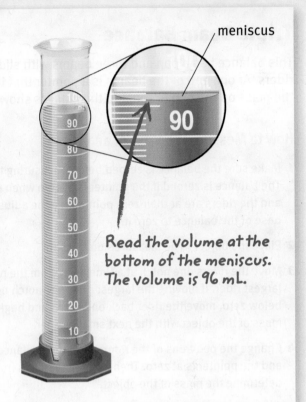

meniscus

Read the volume at the bottom of the meniscus. The volume is 96 mL.

# Metric Rulers

## How to Measure the Length of a Leaf with a Metric Ruler

1. Lay a ruler flat on top of the leaf so that the 1-centimeter mark lines up with one end. Make sure the ruler and the leaf do not move between the time you line them up and the time you take the measurement.

2. Look straight down on the ruler so that you can see exactly how the marks line up with the other end of the leaf.

3. Estimate the length by which the leaf extends beyond a marking. For example, the leaf below extends about halfway between the 4.2-centimeter and 4.3-centimeter marks, so the apparent measurement is about 4.25 centimeters.

4. Remember to subtract 1 centimeter from your apparent measurement, since you started at the 1-centimeter mark on the ruler and not at the end. The leaf is about 3.25 centimeters long (4.25 cm − 1 cm = 3.25 cm).

Not to scale

# Science Skills

## Triple Beam Balance

This balance has a pan and three beams with sliding masses, called riders. At one end of the beams is a pointer that indicates whether the mass on the pan is equal to the masses shown on the beams.

### How to Measure the Mass of an Object

**1** Make sure the balance is zeroed before measuring the mass of an object. The balance is zeroed if the pointer is at zero when nothing is on the pan and the riders are at their zero points. Use the adjustment knob at the base of the balance to zero it.

**2** Place the object to be measured on the pan.

**3** Move the riders one notch at a time away from the pan. Begin with the largest rider. If moving the largest rider one notch brings the pointer below zero, move the rider back one notch and begin measuring the mass of the object with the next smaller rider.

**4** Change the positions of the riders until they balance the mass on the pan and the pointer is at zero. Then add the readings from the three beams to determine the mass of the object.

| | |
|---|---|
| 300 g | position of largest rider |
| 90 g | position of middle rider |
| + 3 g | position of smallest rider |
| 393 g | mass of beaker and water |

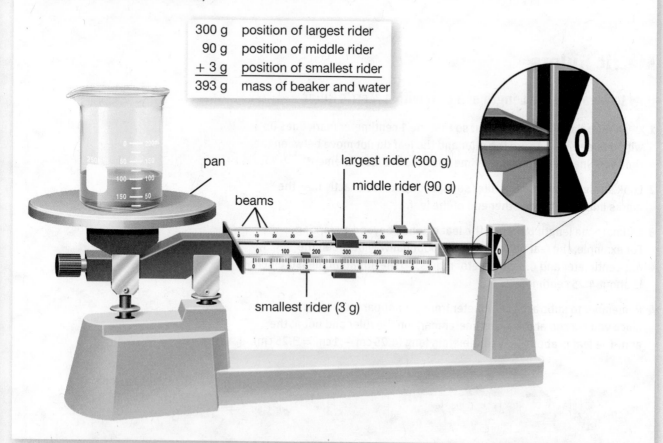

pan

beams

largest rider (300 g)

middle rider (90 g)

smallest rider (3 g)

# Electronic Balance

## How to Measure the Mass of an Object

**1** Be sure the balance is on a flat, stable surface.

**2** Zero, or *tare*, the balance using the appropriate key. If you are measuring a specific quantity of a substance using a weigh boat or other container, place the weigh boat or container on the balance pan before zeroing the balance.

**3** When the readout on the balance is steady and within a few thousandths of zero grams, place the object to be measured on the balance. If you are measuring out chemicals or other substances, wear gloves and use a clean spatula or similar tool to transfer the substance. Do not reach into containers or touch chemicals with your hands.

**4** Record the mass of the object to the nearest milligram (1/1000 of one gram).

Record the mass of an object to the nearest milligram (mg). The mass measured is 5.726 grams.

# Science Skills

## Spring Scale

Spring scales are tools that measure forces, such as weight, or the gravitational force exerted on an object. A spring scale indicates an object's weight by measuring how far the spring stretches when an object is suspended from it. This type of scale is often used in grocery stores or to measure the weights of large loads of crops or industrial products. Spring scales are useful for measuring the weight of larger objects as well.

### How to Measure the Weight of an Object

• Be sure the spring scale is securely suspended and is not touching the ground, wall, or desk. The pointer should be at zero.

• Hang the object to be weighed from the hook at the free end of the spring scale.

• When the object is still—not bouncing, swinging, or otherwise moving—read the object's weight to the nearest 0.5 N.

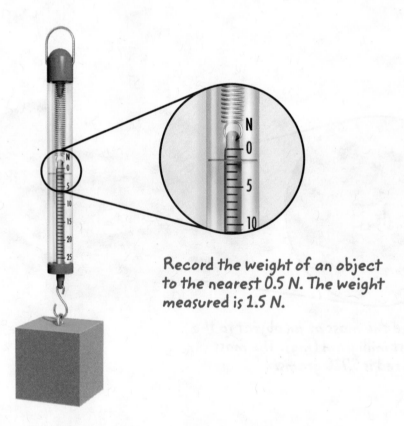

Record the weight of an object to the nearest 0.5 N. The weight measured is 1.5 N.

# Thermometer

Many laboratory thermometers are the bulb type shown below. The sensing bulb of the thermometer is filled with a colored liquid (alcohol) that expands as it is heated. When the liquid expands, it moves up the stem of the thermometer through the capillary tube. Thermometers usually measure temperature in degrees Celsius (°C).

## How to Measure the Temperature of a Substance

**Caution:** Do not hold the thermometer in your hand while measuring the temperature of a heated substance. Never use a thermometer to stir a solution. Always consult your teacher regarding proper laboratory techniques and safety rules when using a thermometer.

- Carefully lower the bulb of the thermometer into the substance. The stem of the thermometer may rest against the side of the container, but the bulb should never rest on the bottom. If the thermometer has an adjustable clip for the side of the container, use the clip to suspend the thermometer in the liquid.

- Watch the colored liquid as it rises in the thermometer's capillary tube. When the liquid stops rising, note the whole-degree increment nearest the top of the liquid column.

- If your thermometer is marked in whole degrees, report temperature to the nearest half degree.

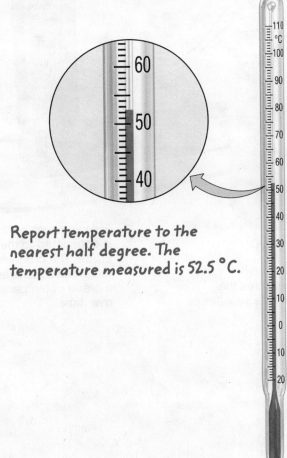

Report temperature to the nearest half degree. The temperature measured is 52.5 °C.

# Introduction to Probeware

*Probeware* is a system of tools that offers a way to measure and analyze various physical properties, such as pressure, pH, temperature, or acceleration. Most probeware systems consist of a sensor, or probe, that is connected to a device such as a computer. As the sensor takes measurements, a computer program records the data. Users can then analyze data using tables, charts, or graphs. Some systems allow you to analyze more than one variable at a time.

## Temperature Probe

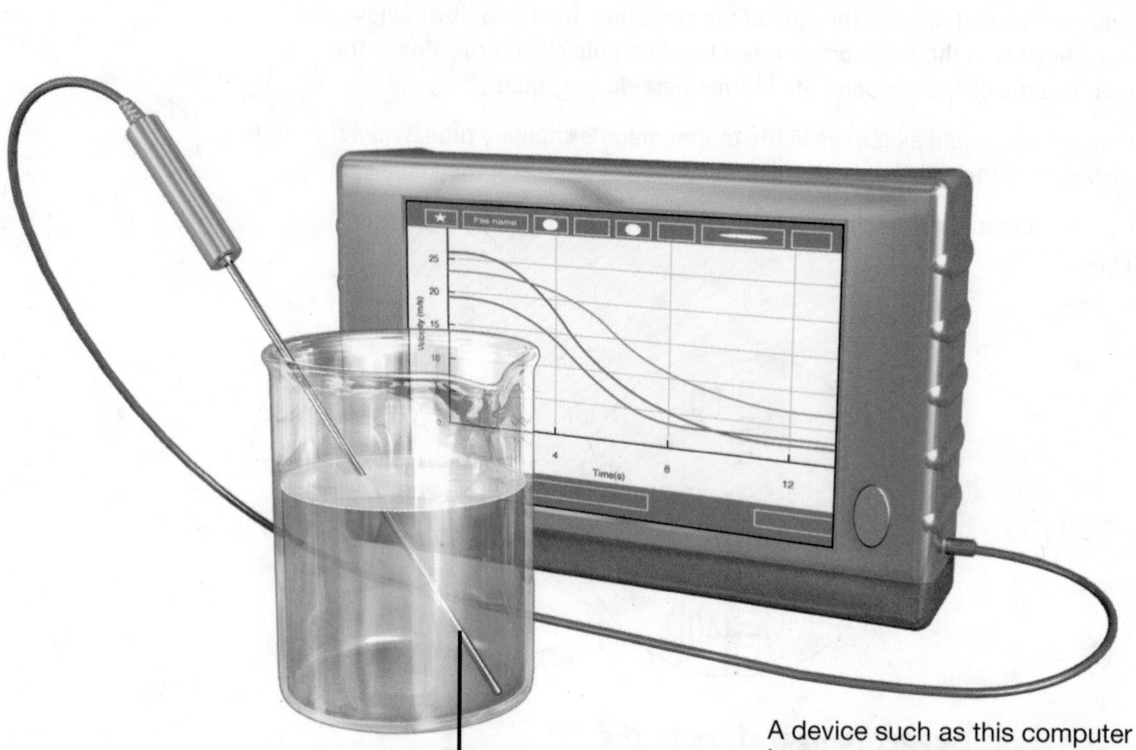


This probe measures the temperature of the substance in the beaker.

A device such as this computer is connected to the temperature probe. The program records temperature data and generates a graph of temperature change over time.



© Houghton Mifflin Harcourt Publishing Company

# Motion Detector

Use a motion detector to gather information about an object's velocity, position, or acceleration.

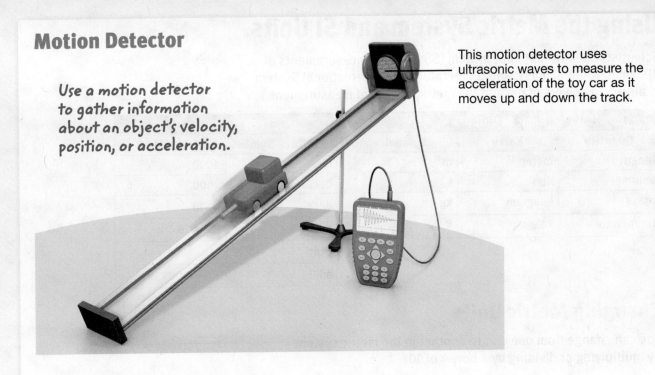

This motion detector uses ultrasonic waves to measure the acceleration of the toy car as it moves up and down the track.

# pH Probe

Use a pH probe to determine whether a substance is acidic, neutral, or basic.

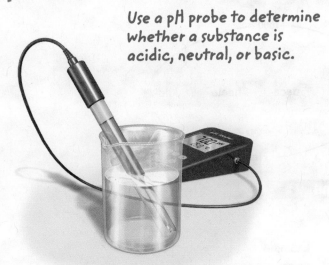

pH probes measure the concentration of hydrogen ions in a liquid, such as the substance in the beaker shown here.

The tip of a pH probe is a thin glass membrane that should not be allowed to dry out. Store pH probes in the appropriate container and solution when you are finished with your investigation.

**Caution:** Probeware equipment should always be handled carefully. Be sure to follow your teacher's instructions regarding the use and storage of all probeware equipment.

# Science Skills

## Using the Metric System and SI Units

Scientists use International System (SI) units for measurements of distance, volume, mass, and temperature. The International System is based on powers of ten and the metric system of measurement.

| Basic SI Units | | |
|---|---|---|
| Quantity | Name | Symbol |
| length | meter | m |
| volume | liter | L |
| mass | kilogram | kg |
| temperature | kelvin | K |

| SI Prefixes | | |
|---|---|---|
| Prefix | Symbol | Power of 10 |
| kilo- | k | 1000 |
| hecto- | h | 100 |
| deca- | da | 10 |
| deci- | d | 0.1 or $\frac{1}{10}$ |
| centi- | c | 0.01 or $\frac{1}{100}$ |
| milli- | m | 0.001 or $\frac{1}{1000}$ |

### Changing Metric Units

You can change from one unit to another in the metric system by multiplying or dividing by a power of 10

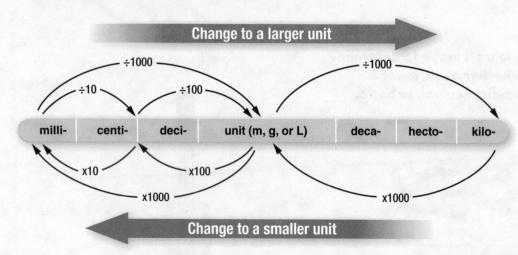

Change to a larger unit

milli-   centi-   deci-   unit (m, g, or L)   deca-   hecto-   kilo-

Change to a smaller unit

---

**Example**

Change 0.64 liters to milliliters.
1  Decide whether to multiply or divide.
2  Select the power of 10.

**Change to a smaller unit by multiplying**

mL ◄──── x 1000 ──── L

0.64 x 1000 = 640.

ANSWER 0.64 L = 640 mL

**Example**

Change 23.6 grams to kilograms.
1  Decide whether to multiply or divide.
2  Select the power of 10.

**Change to a larger unit by dividing**

g ──── ÷ 1000 ────► kg

26.3 ÷ 1000 = 0.0263

ANSWER 23.6 g = 0.0236 kg

# Converting Between SI and U.S. Customary Units

Use the chart below when you need to convert between SI units and U.S. customary units

| SI Unit | From SI to U.S. Customary | | | From U.S. Customary to SI | | |
|---|---|---|---|---|---|---|
| **Length** | **When you know** | **multiply by** | **to find** | **When you know** | **multiply by** | **to find** |
| kilometer (km) = 1000 m | kilometers | 0.62 | miles | miles | 1.61 | kilometers |
| meter (m) = 100 cm | meters | 3.28 | feet | feet | 0.3048 | meters |
| centimeter (cm) = 10 mm | centimeters | 0.39 | inches | inches | 2.54 | centimeters |
| millimeter (mm) = 0.1 cm | millimeters | 0.04 | inches | inches | 25.4 | millimeters |
| **Area** | **When you know** | **multiply by** | **to find** | **When you know** | **multiply by** | **to find** |
| square kilometer (km²) | square kilometers | 0.39 | square miles | square miles | 2.59 | square kilometers |
| square meter (m²) | square meters | 1.2 | square yards | square yards | 0.84 | square meters |
| square centimeter (cm²) | square centimeters | 0.155 | square inches | square inches | 6.45 | square centimeters |
| **Volume** | **When you know** | **multiply by** | **to find** | **When you know** | **multiply by** | **to find** |
| liter (L) = 1000 mL | liters | 1.06 | quarts | quarts | 0.95 | liters |
| | liters | 0.26 | gallons | gallons | 3.79 | liters |
| | liters | 4.23 | cups | cups | 0.24 | liters |
| | liters | 2.12 | pints | pints | 0.47 | liters |
| milliliter (mL) = 0.001 L | milliliters | 0.20 | teaspoons | teaspoons | 4.93 | milliliters |
| | milliliters | 0.07 | tablespoons | tablespoons | 14.79 | milliliters |
| | milliliters | 0.03 | fluid ounces | fluid ounces | 29.57 | milliliters |
| **Mass and Weight** | **When you know** | **multiply by** | **to find** | **When you know** | **multiply by** | **to find** |
| kilogram (kg) = 1000 g | kilograms | 2.2 | pounds | pounds | 0.45 | kilograms |
| gram (g) = 1000 mg | grams | 0.035 | ounces | ounces | 28.35 | grams |

# Temperature Conversions

Even though the kelvin is the SI base unit of temperature, the degree Celsius will be the unit you use most often in your science studies. The formulas below show the relationships between temperatures in degrees Fahrenheit (°F), degrees Celsius (°C), and kelvins (K).

$$°C = \frac{5}{9}\ (°F - 32) \qquad °F = \frac{9}{5}\ °C + 32 \qquad K = °C + 273$$

| Examples of Temperature Conversions | | |
|---|---|---|
| **Condition** | **Degrees Celsius** | **Degrees Fahrenheit** |
| Freezing point of water | 0 | 32 |
| Cool day | 10 | 50 |
| Mild day | 20 | 68 |
| Warm day | 30 | 86 |
| Normal body temperature | 37 | 98.6 |
| Very hot day | 40 | 104 |
| Boiling point of water | 100 | 212 |

# Math Refresher

## Performing Calculations

Science requires an understanding of many math concepts. The following pages will help you review some important math skills.

### Mean

The mean is the sum of all values in a data set divided by the total number of values in the data set. The mean is also called the *average*.

#### Example

Find the mean of the following set of numbers: 5, 4, 7, and 8.

Step 1    Find the sum.

$$5 + 4 + 7 + 8 = 24$$

Step 2    Divide the sum by the number of numbers in your set. Because there are four numbers in this example, divide the sum by 4.

$$24 \div 4 = 6$$

Answer  The average, or mean, is 6.

### Median

The median of a data set is the middle value when the values are written in numerical order. If a data set has an even number of values, the median is the mean of the two middle values.

#### Example

To find the median of a set of measurements, arrange the values in order from least to greatest. The median is the middle value.

13 mm    14 mm    16 mm    21 mm    23 mm

Answer  The median is 16 mm.

### Mode

The mode of a data set is the value that occurs most often.

#### Example

To find the mode of a set of measurements, arrange the values in order from least to greatest, and determine the value that occurs most often.

13 mm, 14 mm, 14 mm, 16 mm,
21 mm, 23 mm, 25 mm

Answer  The mode is 14 mm.

A data set can have more than one mode or no mode. For example, the following data set has modes of 2 mm and 4 mm:

2 mm    2 mm    3 mm    4 mm    4 mm

The data set below has no mode because no value occurs more often than any other.

2 mm    3 mm    4 mm    5 mm

# Ratios

A **ratio** is a comparison between numbers, and it is usually written as a fraction.

**Example**

Find the ratio of thermometers to students if you have 36 thermometers and 48 students in your class.

Step 1  Write the ratio.

$$\frac{36 \text{ thermometers}}{48 \text{ students}}$$

Step 2  Simplify the fraction to its simplest form.

$$\frac{36}{48} = \frac{36 \div 12}{48 \div 12} = \frac{3}{4}$$

The ratio of thermometers to students is 3 to 4 or 3:4. So there are 3 thermometers for every 4 students.

# Proportions

A **proportion** is an equation that states that two ratios are equal.

$$\frac{3}{1} = \frac{12}{4}$$

To solve a proportion, you can use cross-multiplication. If you know three of the quantities in a proportion, you can use cross-multiplication to find the fourth.

**Example**

Imagine that you are making a scale model of the solar system for your science project. The diameter of Jupiter is 11.2 times the diameter of the Earth. If you are using a plastic-foam ball that has a diameter of 2 cm to represent the Earth, what must the diameter of the ball representing Jupiter be?

$$\frac{11.2}{1} = \frac{x}{2 \text{ cm}}$$

Step 1  Cross-multiply.

$$\frac{11.2}{1} = \frac{x}{2}$$

$$11.2 \times 2 = x \times 1$$

Step 2  Multiply.

$$22.4 = x \times 1$$

$$x = 22.4 \text{ cm}$$

You will need to use a ball that has a diameter of 22.4 cm to represent Jupiter.

# Rates

A **rate** is a ratio of two values expressed in different units. A unit rate is a rate with a denominator of 1 unit.

**Example**

A plant grew 6 centimeters in 2 days. The plant's rate of growth was $\frac{6 \text{ cm}}{2 \text{ days}}$.

To describe the plant's growth in centimeters per day, write a unit rate.

Divide numerator and denominator by 2:

$$\frac{6 \text{ cm}}{2 \text{ days}} = \frac{6 \text{ cm} \div 2}{2 \text{ days} \div 2}$$

Simplify:

$$= \frac{3 \text{ cm}}{1 \text{ day}}$$

Answer  The plant's rate of growth is 3 centimeters per day.

# Math Refresher

## Percent

A **percent** is a ratio of a given number to 100. For example, 85% = 85/100. You can use percent to find part of a whole.

**Example**
What is 85% of 40?

**Step 1** Rewrite the percent as a decimal by moving the decimal point two places to the left.

$$0.85$$

**Step 2** Multiply the decimal by the number that you are calculating the percentage of.

$$0.85 \times 40 = 34$$

85% of 40 is 34.

## Decimals

To **add** or **subtract decimals,** line up the digits vertically so that the decimal points line up. Then add or subtract the columns from right to left. Carry or borrow numbers as necessary.

**Example**
Add the following numbers: 3.1415 and 2.96.

**Step 1** Line up the digits vertically so that the decimal points line up.

$$3.1415$$
$$+\ 2.96$$

**Step 2** Add the columns from right to left, and carry when necessary.

$$3.1415$$
$$+\ 2.96$$
$$\overline{6.1015}$$

The sum is 6.1015.

## Fractions

A **fraction** is a ratio of two whole numbers. The top number is the numerator. The bottom number is the denominator. The denominator must not be zero.

**Example**
Your class has 24 plants. Your teacher instructs you to put 5 plants in a shady spot. What fraction of the plants in your class will you put in a shady spot?

**Step 1** In the denominator, write the total number of parts in the whole.

$$\frac{?}{24}$$

**Step 2** In the numerator, write the number of parts of the whole that are being considered.

$$\frac{5}{24}$$

So $\frac{5}{24}$ of the plants will be in the shade.

# Simplifying Fractions

It is usually best to express a fraction in its simplest form. Expressing a fraction in its simplest form is called **simplifying a fraction.**

*Example*

Express the fraction $\frac{30}{45}$ in its simplest form.

Step 1    Find the largest whole number that will divide evenly into both the numerator and denominator. This number is called the greatest common factor (GCF).

Factors of the numerator 30:
1, 2, 3, 5, 6, 10, 15, 30

Factors of the denominator 45:
1, 3, 5, 9, 15, 45

Step 2    Divide both the numerator and the denominator by the GCF, which in this case is 15.

$$\frac{30}{45} = \frac{30 \div 15}{45 \div 15} = \frac{2}{3}$$

Thus, $\frac{30}{45}$ written in its simplest form is $\frac{2}{3}$.

# Adding and Subtracting Fractions

To **add** or **subtract fractions** that have the same denominator, simply add or subtract the numerators.

*Examples*

$\frac{3}{5} + \frac{1}{5} = ?$ and $\frac{3}{4} - \frac{1}{4} = ?$

Step 1    Add or subtract the numerators.
$$\frac{3}{5} + \frac{1}{5} = \frac{4}{5} \text{ and } \frac{3}{4} - \frac{1}{4} = \frac{2}{5}$$

Step 2    Write in the common denominator, which remains the same.
$$\frac{3}{5} + \frac{1}{5} = \frac{4}{5} \text{ and } \frac{3}{4} - \frac{1}{4} = \frac{2}{4}$$

Step 3    If necessary, write the fraction in its simplest form.
$\frac{4}{5}$ cannot be simplified, and $\frac{2}{4} = \frac{1}{2}$.

To **add** or **subtract** fractions that have **different denominators,** first find the least common denominator (LCD).

*Examples*

$\frac{1}{2} + \frac{1}{6} = ?$ and $\frac{3}{4} - \frac{2}{3} = ?$

Step 1    Write the equivalent fractions that have a common denominator.
$$\frac{3}{6} + \frac{1}{6} = ? \text{ and } \frac{9}{12} - \frac{8}{12} = ?$$

Step 2    Add or subtract the fractions.
$$\frac{3}{6} + \frac{1}{6} = \frac{4}{6} \text{ and } \frac{9}{12} - \frac{8}{12} = \frac{1}{12}$$

Step 3    If necessary, write the fraction in its simplest form.
$\frac{4}{6} = \frac{2}{3}$, and $\frac{1}{12}$ cannot be simplified.

# Multiplying Fractions

To **multiply fractions**, multiply the numerators and the denominators together, and then simplify the fraction if necessary.

*Example*

$\frac{5}{9} \times \frac{7}{10} = ?$

Step 1    Multiply the numerators and denominators.
$$\frac{5}{9} \times \frac{7}{10} = \frac{5 \times 7}{9 \times 10} = \frac{35}{90}$$

Step 2    Simplify the fraction.
$$\frac{35}{90} = \frac{35 \div 5}{90 \div 5} = \frac{7}{18}$$

# Math Refresher

## Dividing Fractions

To **divide fractions**, first rewrite the divisor (the number you divide by) upside down. This number is called the reciprocal of the divisor. Then multiply and simplify if necessary.

**Example**

$$\frac{5}{8} \div \frac{3}{2} = ?$$

Step 1   Rewrite the divisor as its reciprocal.

$$\frac{3}{2} \rightarrow \frac{2}{3}$$

Step 2   Multiply the fractions.

$$\frac{5}{8} \times \frac{2}{3} = \frac{5 \times 2}{8 \times 3} = \frac{10}{24}$$

Step 3   Simplify the fraction.

$$\frac{10}{24} = \frac{10 \div 2}{24 \div 2} = \frac{5}{12}$$

## Using Significant Figures

The **significant figures** in a decimal are the digits that are warranted by the accuracy of a measuring device.

When you perform a calculation with measurements, the number of significant figures to include in the result depends in part on the number of significant figures in the measurements. When you multiply or divide measurements, your answer should have only as many significant figures as the measurement with the fewest significant figures.

**Examples**

Using a balance and a graduated cylinder filled with water, you determined that a marble has a mass of 8.0 grams and a volume of 3.5 cubic centimeters. To calculate the density of the marble, divide the mass by the volume.

Write the formula for density: $\text{Density} = \frac{mass}{volume}$

Substitute measurements: $= \frac{8.0 \text{ g}}{3.5 \text{ cm}^3}$

Use a calculator to divide: $\approx 2.285714286 \text{ g/cm}^3$

Answer Because the mass and the volume have two significant figures each, give the density to two significant figures. The marble has a density of 2.3 grams per cubic centimeter.

## Using Scientific Notation

**Scientific notation** is a shorthand way to write very large or very small numbers. For example, 73,500,000,000,000,000,000,000 kg is the mass of the moon. In scientific notation, it is $7.35 \times 10^{22}$ kg. A value written as a number between 1 and 10, times a power of 10, is in scientific notation.

**Examples**

You can convert from standard form to scientific notation.

| Standard Form | Scientific Notation |
|---|---|
| 720,000 | $7.2 \times 10^5$ |
| 5 decimal places left | Exponent is 5. |
| 0.000291 | $2.91 \times 10^{-4}$ |
| 4 decimal places right | Exponent is −4. |

You can convert from scientific notation to standard form.

| Scientific Notation | Standard Form |
|---|---|
| $4.63 \times 10^7$ | 46,300,000 |
| Exponent is 7. | 7 decimal places right |
| $1.08 \times 10^{-6}$ | 0.00000108 |
| Exponent is −6. | 6 decimal places left |

# Making and Interpreting Graphs

## Circle Graph

A circle graph, or pie chart, shows how each group of data relates to all of the data. Each part of the circle represents a category of the data. The entire circle represents all of the data. For example, a biologist studying a hardwood forest in Wisconsin found that there were five different types of trees. The data table at right summarizes the biologist's findings.

| Wisconsin Hardwood Trees | |
|---|---|
| **Type of tree** | **Number found** |
| Oak | 600 |
| Maple | 750 |
| Beech | 300 |
| Birch | 1,200 |
| Hickory | 150 |
| Total | 3,000 |

## How to Make a Circle Graph

**1** To make a circle graph of these data, first find the percentage of each type of tree. Divide the number of trees of each type by the total number of trees, and multiply by 100%.

$$\frac{600 \text{ oak}}{3,000 \text{ trees}} \times 100\% = 20\%$$

$$\frac{750 \text{ maple}}{3,000 \text{ trees}} \times 100\% = 25\%$$

$$\frac{300 \text{ beech}}{3,000 \text{ trees}} \times 100\% = 10\%$$

$$\frac{1,200 \text{ birch}}{3,000 \text{ trees}} \times 100\% = 40\%$$

$$\frac{150 \text{ hickory}}{3,000 \text{ trees}} \times 100\% = 5\%$$

**2** Now, determine the size of the wedges that make up the graph. Multiply each percentage by 360°. Remember that a circle contains 360°.

$20\% \times 360° = 72°$     $25\% \times 360° = 90°$

$10\% \times 360° = 36°$     $40\% \times 360° = 144°$

$5\% \times 360° = 18°$

**3** Check that the sum of the percentages is 100 and the sum of the degrees is 360.

$20\% + 25\% + 10\% + 40\% + 5\% = 100\%$

$72° + 90° + 36° + 144° + 18° = 360°$

**4** Use a compass to draw a circle, and mark the center of the circle.

**5** Then, use a protractor to draw angles of 72°, 90°, 36°, 144°, and 18° in the circle.

**6** Finally, label each part of the graph, and choose an appropriate title.

**A Community of Wisconsin Hardwood Trees**

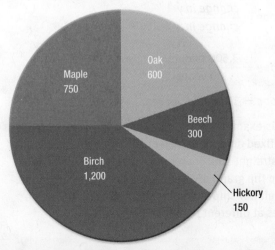

# Math Refresher

## Line Graphs

Line graphs are most often used to demonstrate continuous change. For example, Mr. Smith's students analyzed the population records for their hometown, Appleton, between 1910 and 2010. Examine the data at right.

Because the year and the population change, they are the variables. The population is determined by, or dependent on, the year. Therefore, the population is called the **dependent variable,** and the year is called the **independent variable**. Each year and its population make a **data pair**. To prepare a line graph, you must first organize data pairs into a table like the one at right.

| Population of Appleton, 1910–2010 | |
| --- | --- |
| **Year** | **Population** |
| 1910 | 1,800 |
| 1930 | 2,500 |
| 1950 | 3,200 |
| 1970 | 3,900 |
| 1990 | 4,600 |
| 2010 | 5,300 |

## How to Make a Line Graph

**1** Place the independent variable along the horizontal (*x*) axis. Place the dependent variable along the vertical (*y*) axis.

**2** Label the *x*-axis "Year" and the *y*-axis "Population." Look at your greatest and least values for the population. For the *y*-axis, determine a scale that will provide enough space to show these values. You must use the same scale for the entire length of the axis. Next, find an appropriate scale for the *x*-axis.

**3** Choose reasonable starting points for each axis.

**4** Plot the data pairs as accurately as possible.

**5** Choose a title that accurately represents the data.

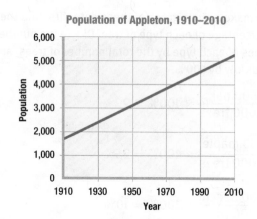

Population of Appleton, 1910–2010

## How to Determine Slope

Slope is the ratio of the change in the *y*-value to the change in the x-value, or "rise over run."

**1** Choose two points on the line graph. For example, the population of Appleton in 2010 was 5,300 people. Therefore, you can define point A as (2010, 5,300). In 1910, the population was 1,800 people. You can define point B as (1910, 1,800).

**2** Find the change in the *y*-value. (*y* at point A) − (*y* at point B) = 5,300 people − 1,800 people = 3,500 people

**3** Find the change in the *x*-value. (*x* at point A) − (*x* at point B) = 2010 − 1910 = 100 years

**4** Calculate the slope of the graph by dividing the change in *y* by the change in *x*.

$$slope = \frac{change\ in\ y}{change\ in\ x}$$

$$slope = \frac{3,500\ people}{100\ years}$$

$$slope = 35\ people\ per\ year$$

In this example, the population in Appleton increased by a fixed amount each year. The graph of these data is a straight line. Therefore, the relationship is **linear**. When the graph of a set of data is not a straight line, the relationship is **nonlinear**. As a result, the slope varies at different points on the graph.

## Bar Graphs

Bar graphs can be used to demonstrate change that is not continuous. These graphs can be used to indicate trends when the data cover a long period of time. A meteorologist gathered the precipitation data shown here for Summerville for April 1–15 and used a bar graph to represent the data.

| Precipitation in Summerville, April 1–15 | | | |
|---|---|---|---|
| Date | Precipitation (cm) | Date | Precipitation (cm) |
| April 1 | 0.5 | April 9 | 0.25 |
| April 2 | 1.25 | April 10 | 0.0 |
| April 3 | 0.0 | April 11 | 1.0 |
| April 4 | 0.0 | April 12 | 0.0 |
| April 5 | 0.0 | April 13 | 0.25 |
| April 6 | 0.0 | April 14 | 0.0 |
| April 7 | 0.0 | April 15 | 6.50 |
| April 8 | 1.75 | | |

## How to Make a Bar Graph

**1** Use an appropriate scale and a reasonable starting point for each axis.

**2** Label the axes, and plot the data.

**3** Choose a title that accurately represents the data.

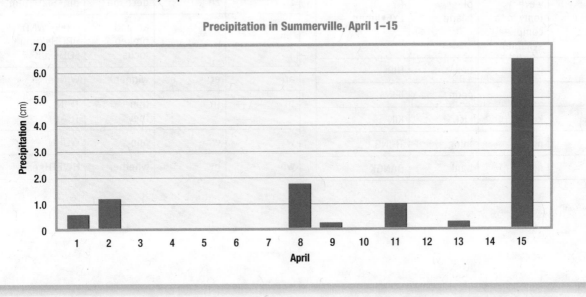

Precipitation in Summerville, April 1–15

# Glossary

| Sound | Symbol | Example | Respelling | Sound | Symbol | Example | Respelling |
|---|---|---|---|---|---|---|---|
| ă | a | pat | PAT | ŏ | ah | bottle | BAHT'l |
| ā | ay | pay | PAY | ō | oh | toe | TOH |
| âr | air | care | KAIR | ô | aw | caught | KAWT |
| ä | ah | father | FAH•ther | ôr | ohr | roar | ROHR |
| är | ar | argue | AR•gyoo | oi | oy | noisy | NOYZ•ee |
| ch | ch | chase | CHAYS | ŏŏ | u | book | BUK |
| ĕ | e | pet | PET | ōō | oo | boot | BOOT |
| ĕ (at end of a syllable) | eh | settee lessee | seh•TEE leh•SEE | ou | ow | pound | POWND |
| ĕr | ehr | merry | MEHR•ee | s | s | center | SEN•ter |
| ē | ee | beach | BEECH | sh | sh | cache | CASH |
| g | g | gas | GAS | ŭ | uh | flood | FLUHD |
| ĭ | i | pit | PIT | ûr | er | bird | BERD |
| ĭ (at end of a syllable) | ih | guitar | gih•TAR | z | z | xylophone | ZY•luh•fohn |
| ī | y eye (only for a complete syllable) | pie island | PY EYE•luhnd | z | z | bags | BAGZ |
| | | | | zh | zh | decision | dih•SIZH•uhn |
| îr | ir | hear | HIR | ə | uh | around broken focus | uh•ROWND BROH•kuhn FOH•kuhs |
| j | j | germ | JERM | ər | er | winner | WIN•er |
| k | k | kick | KIK | th | th | thin they | THIN THAY |
| ng | ng | thing | THING | w | w | one | WUHN |
| ngk | ngk | bank | BANGK | wh | hw | whether | HWETH•er |

# A

**abiotic factor** (ay·by·AHT·ik FAK·ter) an environmental factor that is not associated with the activities of living organisms (623)
**factor abiótico** un factor ambiental que no está asociado con las actividades de los seres vivos

**acceleration** (ak·sel·uh·RAY·shuhn) the rate at which velocity changes over time; an object accelerates if its speed, direction, or both change (238)
**aceleración** la tasa a la que la velocidad cambia con el tiempo; un objeto acelera si su rapidez cambia, si su dirección cambia, o si tanto su rapidez como su dirección cambian

**accuracy** (AK·yer·uh·see) a description of how close a measurement is to the true value of the quantity measured (76)
**exactitud** término que describe qué tanto se aproxima una medición al valor verdadero de la cantidad medida

**Animalia** (an·uh·MAYL·yuh) a kingdom made up of complex, multicellular organisms that lack cell walls, can usually move around, and quickly respond to their environment (611)
**Animalia** un reino formado por organismos pluricelulares complejos que no tienen pared celular, normalmente son capaces de moverse y reaccionan rápidamente a su ambiente

**aphelion** (uh·FEE·lee·uhn) in the orbit of a planet or other body in the solar system, the point that is farthest from the sun (471)
**afelio** en la órbita de un planeta u otros cuerpos en el sistema solar, el punto que está más lejos del Sol

**Archaea** (ar·KEE·uh) a domain made up of prokaryotes most of which are known to live in extreme environments that are distinguished from other prokaryotes by differences in their genetics and in the makeup of their cell wall (608)
**Archaea** un dominio compuesto por procariotes la mayoría de los cuales viven en ambientes extremos que se distinguen de otros procariotes por su genética y por la composición de su pared celular

**artificial satellite** (ar·tuh·FISH·uhl SAT·l·yt) any human-made object placed in orbit around a body in space (574)
**satélite artificial** cualquier objeto hecho por los seres humanos y colocado en órbita alrededor de un cuerpo en el espacio

**asteroid** (AS·tuh·royd) a small, rocky object that orbits the sun; most asteroids are located in a band between the orbits of Mars and Jupiter (534)
**asteroide** un objeto pequeño y rocoso que se encuentra en órbita alrededor del Sol; la mayoría de los asteroides se ubican en una banda entre las órbitas de Marte y Júpiter

**asthenosphere** (as·THEN·uh·sfir) the soft layer of the mantle on which the tectonic plates move (392)
**astenosfera** la capa blanda del manto sobre la que se mueven las placas tectónicas

**astronomical unit** (as·truh·NAHM·ih·kuhl YOO·nit) the average distance between Earth and the sun; approximately 150 million kilometers (symbol, AU) (498)
**unidad astronómica** la distancia promedio entre la Tierra y el Sol; aproximadamente 150 millones de kilómetros (símbolo: UA)

**atom** (AT·uhm) the smallest unit of an element that maintains the properties of that element (154, 168, 338)
**átomo** la unidad más pequeña de un elemento que conserva las propiedades de ese elemento

**atomic number** (uh·TAHM·ik NUM·ber) the number of protons in the nucleus of an atom; the atomic number is the same for all atoms of an element (170)
**número atómico** el número de protones en el núcleo de un átomo; el número atómico es el mismo para todos los átomos de un elemento

# B

**Bacteria** (bak·TIR·ee·uh) a domain made up of prokaryotes that usually have a cell wall and that usually reproduce by cell division (608)
**Bacteria** un dominio compuesto por procariotes que por lo general tienen pared celular y se reproducen por división celular

**biomass** (BY·oh·mas) plant material, manure, or any other organic matter that is used as an energy source (322)
**biomasa** materia vegetal, estiércol o cualquier otra materia orgánica que se usa como fuente de energía

**biome** (BY·ohm) a large region characterized by a specific type of climate and certain types of plant and animal communities (628)
**bioma** una región extensa caracterizada por un tipo de clima específico y ciertos tipos de comunidades de plantas y animales

**biotic factor** (by·AHT·ik FAK·ter) an environmental factor that is associated with or results from the activities of living organisms (622)
**factor biótico** un factor ambiental que está asociado con las actividades de los seres vivos o que resulta de ellas

# C

**calorie** (KAL·uh·ree) the amount of energy needed to raise the temperature of 1 g of water 1 °C; the Calorie used to indicate the energy content of food is a kilocalorie (213)
**caloría** la cantidad de energía que se requiere para aumentar la temperatura de 1 g de agua en 1 °C; la Caloría que se usa para indicar el contenido energético de los alimentos es la kilocaloría

**cell** (SEL) in biology, the smallest unit that can perform all life processes; cells are covered by a membrane and contain DNA and cytoplasm (594)
**célula** en biología, la unidad más pequeña que puede realizar todos los procesos vitales; las células están cubiertas por una membrana y tienen ADN y citoplasma

**cell membrane** (SEL MEM·brayn) a phospholipid layer that covers a cell's surface and acts as a barrier between the inside of a cell and the cell's environment (598)
**membrana celular** una capa de fosfolípidos que cubre la superficie de la célula y funciona como una barrera entre el interior de la célula y el ambiente de la célula

**centripetal acceleration** (sen·TRIP·ih·tl ak·sel·uh·RAY·shuhn) the acceleration directed toward the center of a circular path (241)
**aceleración centrípeta** la aceleración que se dirige hacia el centro de un camino circular

**centripetal force** (sen·TRIP·ih·tl FOHRS) the inward force required to keep a particle or an object moving in a circular path (474)
**fuerza centrípeta** la fuerza hacia adentro que se requiere para mantener en movimiento una partícula o un objeto en un camino circular

**chemical change** (KEM·ih·kuhl CHAYNJ) a change that occurs when one or more substances change into entirely new substances with different properties (142)
**cambio químico** un cambio que ocurre cuando una o más sustancias se transforman en sustancias totalmente nuevas con propiedades diferentes

**chemical property** (KEM·ih·kuhl PRAHP·uhr·tee) a property of matter that describes a substance's ability to participate in chemical reactions (130)
**propiedad química** una propiedad de la materia que describe la capacidad de una sustancia de participar en reacciones químicas

**chemical symbol** (KEM·ih·kuhl SIM·buhl) a one-, two-, or three-letter abbreviation of the name of an element (171)
**símbolo químico** una abreviatura de una, dos o tres letras del nombre de un elemento

**cleavage** (KLEE·vij) in geology, the tendency of a mineral to split along specific planes of weakness to form smooth, flat surfaces (345)
**exfoliación** en geología, la tendencia de un mineral a agrietarse a lo largo de planos débiles específicos y formar superficies lisas y planas

**comet** (KAHM·it) a small body that gives off gas and dust as it passes close to the sun; a typical comet moves in an elliptical orbit around the sun and is made of dust and frozen gases (532)
**cometa** un cuerpo pequeño que libera gas y polvo al pasar cerca del Sol; un cometa típico está formado por polvo y gases congelados y sigue una órbita elíptica alrededor del Sol

**community** (kuh·MYOO·nih·tee) all of the populations of species that live in the same habitat and interact with each other (625)
**comunidad** todas las poblaciones de especies que viven en el mismo hábitat e interactúan entre sí

**composition** (kahm·puh·ZISH·uhn) the chemical makeup of a rock; describes either the minerals or other materials in the rock (352)
**composición** la constitución química de una roca; describe los minerales u otros materiales presentes en ella

**compound** (KAHM·pownd) a substance made up of atoms of two or more different elements joined by chemical bonds (155, 338)
**compuesto** una sustancia formada por átomos de dos o más elementos diferentes unidos por enlaces químicos

**compression** (kuhm·PRESH·uhn) stress that occurs when forces act to squeeze an object (417)
**compresión** estrés que se produce cuando distintas fuerzas actúan para estrechar un objeto

**conceptual model** (kuhn·SEP·choo·uhl MAHD·l) a verbal or graphical explanation for how a system works or is organized (94)
**modelo conceptual** una explicación verbal o gráfica acerca de cómo funciona o está organizado un sistema

**conduction** (kuhn·DUHK·shuhn) the transfer of energy as heat through a material (215)
**conducción** la transferencia de energía en forma de calor a través de un material

**conductor** (kuhn·DUK·ter) a material that transfers energy easily (215)
**conductor** un material a través del cual se transfiere energía

**convection** (kuhn·VEK·shuhn) the movement of matter due to differences in density; the transfer of energy due to the movement of matter (216, 391, 406)
**convección** el movimiento de la materia debido a diferencias en la densidad; la transferencia de energía debido al movimiento de la materia

**convergent boundary** (kuhn·VER·juhnt BOWN·duh·ree) the boundary between tectonic plates that are colliding (404)
**límite convergente** el límite entre placas tectónicas que chocan

**core** (KOHR) the central part of Earth below the mantle (391)
**núcleo** la parte central de la Tierra, debajo del manto

**crust** (KRUHST) the thin and solid outermost layer of Earth above the mantle (391)

**corteza** la capa externa, delgada y sólida de la Tierra, que se encuentra sobre el manto

**crystal** (KRIS·tuhl) a solid whose atoms, ions, or molecules are arranged in a regular, repeating pattern (349)

**cristal** un sólido cuyos átomos, iones o moléculas están ordenados en un patrón regular y repetitivo

**cytoplasm** (SY·toh·plaz·uhm) the region of the cell within the membrane that includes the fluid, the cytoskeleton, and all of the organelles except the nucleus (598)

**citoplasma** la región de la célula dentro de la membrana, que incluye el líquido, el citoesqueleto y los organelos, pero no el núcleo

## D

**data** (DAY·tuh) information gathered by observation or experimentation that can be used in calculating or reasoning (21)

**datos** la información recopilada por medio de la observación o experimentación que puede usarse para hacer cálculos o razonar

**deformation** (dee·fohr·MAY·shuhn) the bending, tilting, and breaking of Earth's crust; the change in the shape of rock in response to stress (414, 439)

**deformación** el proceso de doblar, inclinar y romper la corteza de la Tierra; el cambio en la forma de una roca en respuesta a la tensión

**degree** (dih·GREE) the units of a temperature scale (204)

**grado** la unidad de una escala de temperatura

**density** (DEN·sih·tee) the ratio of the mass of a substance to the volume of the substance (117)

**densidad** la relación entre la masa de una sustancia y su volumen

**dependent variable** (dih·PEN·duhnt VAIR·ee·uh·buhl) in a scientific investigation, the factor that changes as a result of manipulation of one or more independent variables (21)

**variable dependiente** en una investigación científica, el factor que cambia como resultado de la manipulación de una o más variables independientes

**deposition** (dep·uh·ZISH·uhn) in geology, the process in which material is laid down (369)

**sublimación inversa** el proceso por medio del cual un material se deposita

**divergent boundary** (dy·VER·juhnt BOWN·duh·ree) the boundary between two tectonic plates that are moving away from each other (405)

**límite divergente** el límite entre dos placas tectónicas que se están separando una de la otra

**domain** (doh·MAYN) in a taxonomic system, one of the three broad groups that all living things fall into (608)

**dominio** en un sistema taxonómico, uno de los tres amplios grupos al que pertenecen todos los seres vivos

**dwarf planet** (DWOHRF PLAN·it) a celestial body that orbits the sun, is round because of its own gravity, but has not cleared its orbital path (529)

**planeta enano** un cuerpo celeste que orbita alrededor del Sol, es redondo debido a su propia fuerza de gravedad, pero no ha despejado los alrededores de su trayectoria orbitalo

## E

**earthquake** (ERTH·kwayk) a movement or trembling of the ground that is caused by a sudden release of energy when rocks along a fault move (438)

**terremoto** un movimiento o temblor del suelo causado por una liberación súbita de energía que se produce cuando las rocas ubicadas a lo largo de una falla se mueven

**ecology** (ee·KAHL·uh·jee) the study of the interactions of living organisms with one another and with their environment (622)

**ecología** el estudio de las interacciones de los seres vivos entre sí mismos y entre sí mismos y su ambiente

**ecosystem** (EE·koh·sis·tuhm) a community of organisms and their abiotic, or nonliving, environment (625)

**ecosistema** una comunidad de organismos y su ambiente abiótico o no vivo

**elastic rebound** (ee·LAS·tik REE·bownd) the sudden return of elastically deformed rock to its undeformed shape (439)

**rebote elástico** ocurre cuando una roca deformada elásticamente vuelve súbitamente a su forma no deformada

**electron** (ee·LEK·trahn) a subatomic particle that has a negative charge (168)

**electrón** una partícula subatómica que tiene carga negativa

**element** (EL·uh·muhnt) a substance that cannot be separated or broken down into simpler substances by chemical means (155, 170, 338)

**elemento** una sustancia que no se puede separar o descomponer en sustancias más simples por medio de métodos químicos

**empirical evidence** (em·PIR·ih·kuhl EV·ih·duhns) the observations, measurements, and other types of data that people gather and test to support and evaluate scientific explanations (10)

**evidencia empírica** las observaciones, mediciones y demás tipos de datos que se recopilan y examinan para apoyar y evaluar explicaciones científicas

**energy** (EN·er·jee) the ability to cause change (190)
**energía** la capacidad de producir un cambio

**energy resource** (EN·er·jee REE·sohrs) a natural resource that humans use to generate energy (294, 302, 316)
**recurso energético** un recurso natural que utilizan los humanos para generar energía

**energy transformation** (EN·er·jee trans·fohr·MAY·shuhn) the process of energy changing from one form into another (196)
**transformación de energía** el proceso de cambio de un tipo de energía a otro

**epicenter** (EP·ih·sen·ter) the point on Earth's surface directly above an earthquake's starting point, or focus (438)
**epicentro** el punto de la superficie de la Tierra que queda justo arriba del punto de inicio, o foco, de un terremoto

**erosion** (ee·ROH·zhuhn) the process by which wind, water, ice, or gravity transports soil and sediment from one location to another (369)
**erosión** el proceso por medio del cual el viento, el agua, el hielo o la gravedad transporta tierra y sedimentos de un lugar a otro

**Eukarya** (yoo·KAIR·ee·uh) in a modern taxonomic system, a domain made up of all eukaryotes; this domain aligns with the traditional kingdoms Protista, Fungi, Plantae, and Animalia (609)
**Eukarya** en un sistema taxonómico moderno, un dominio compuesto por todos los eucariotes; este dominio coincide con los reinos tradicionales Protista, Fungi, Plantae y Animalia

**eukaryote** (yoo·KAIR·ee·oht) an organism made up of cells that have a nucleus enclosed by a membrane; eukaryotes include protists, animals, plants, and fungi but not archaea or bacteria (599)
**eucariote** un organismo cuyas células tienen un núcleo contenido en una membrana; entre los eucariotes se encuentran protistas, animales, plantas y hongos, pero no arqueas ni bacterias

**experiment** (ek·SPEHR·uh·muhnt) an organized procedure to study something under controlled conditions (18)
**experimento** un procedimiento organizado que se lleva a cabo bajo condiciones controladas para estudiar algo

**fault** (FAWLT) a break in a body of rock along which one block moves relative to another (416, 439)
**falla** una grieta en un cuerpo rocoso a lo largo de la cual un bloque se mueve respecto de otro

**fission** (FISH·uhn) the process by which a nucleus splits into two or more fragments and releases neutrons and energy (307)
**fisión** el proceso por medio del cual un núcleo se divide en dos o más fragmentos y libera neutrones y energía

**focus** (FOH·kuhs) the location within Earth along a fault at which the first motion of an earthquake occurs (438)
**foco** el lugar dentro de la Tierra a lo largo de una falla donde ocurre el primer movimiento de un terremoto

**folding** (FOHLD·ing) the bending of rock layers due to stress (415)
**plegamiento** fenómeno que ocurre cuando las capas de roca se doblan debido a la compresión

**force** (FOHRS) a push or a pull exerted on an object in order to change the motion of the object; force has size and direction (246)
**fuerza** una acción de empuje o atracción que se ejerce sobre un objeto con el fin de cambiar su movimiento; la fuerza tiene magnitud y dirección

**fossil fuel** (FAHS·uhl FYOO·uhl) a nonrenewable energy resource formed from the remains of organisms that lived long ago; examples include oil, coal, and natural gas (291, 302)
**combustible fósil** un recurso energético no renovable formado a partir de los restos de organismos que vivieron hace mucho tiempo; algunos ejemplos incluyen el petróleo, el carbón y el gas natural

**fulcrum** (FUL·kruhm) the point on which a lever pivots (268)
**fulcro** el punto sobre el que pivota una palanca

**Fungi** (FUHN·jy) a kingdom made up of nongreen, eukaryotic organisms that have no means of movement, reproduce by using spores, and get food by breaking down substances in their surroundings and absorbing the nutrients (611)
**Fungi** un reino formado por organismos eucarióticos no verdes que no tienen capacidad de movimiento, se reproducen por esporas y obtienen alimento al descomponer sustancias de su entorno y absorber los nutrientes

# G

**Galilean moons** (gal·uh·LAY·uhn MOONZ)  the four largest moons of Jupiter: Io, Europa, Ganymede, and Callisto (516)
**lunas galileanas**  las cuatro lunas más grandes de Júpiter: Io, Europa, Ganímedes y Calisto

**gas giant** (GAS JY·uhnt)  a planet that has a deep, massive atmosphere, such as Jupiter, Saturn, Uranus, or Neptune (514)
**gigante gaseoso**  un planeta con una atmósfera masiva y profunda, como por ejemplo, Júpiter, Saturno, Urano o Neptuno

**genus** (JEE·nuhs)  the level of classification that comes after family and that contains similar species (606)
**género**  el nivel de clasificación que viene después de la familia y que contiene especies similares

**geocentric** (jee·oh·SEN·trik)  describes something that uses Earth as the reference point (458)
**geocéntrico**  término que describe algo que usa a la Tierra como punto de referencia

**geothermal energy** (jee·oh·THER·muhl EN·er·jee)  the energy produced by heat within Earth (323)
**energía geotérmica**  la energía producida por el calor del interior de la Tierra

**gravity** (GRAV·ih·tee)  a force of attraction between objects that is due to their masses (470)
**gravedad**  una fuerza de atracción entre dos objetos debido a sus masas

**habitat** (HAB·ih·tat)  the place where an organism usually lives (630)
**hábitat**  el lugar donde generalmente vive un organismo

**heat** (HEET)  the energy transferred between objects that are at different temperatures (212)
**calor**  la transferencia de energía entre objetos que están a temperaturas diferentes

**heliocentric** (hee·lee·oh·SEN·trik)  sun-centered (458)
**heliocéntrico**  centrado en el Sol

**heterogeneous** (het·er·uh·JEE·nee·uhs)  describes something that does not have a uniform structure or composition throughout (162)
**heterogéneo**  término que describe algo que no tiene una estructura o composición totalmente uniforme

**homogeneous** (hoh·muh·JEE·nee·uhs)  describes something that has a uniform structure or composition throughout (162)
**homogéneo**  término que describe a algo que tiene una estructura o composición global uniforme

**hot spot** (HAHT SPAHT)  a volcanically active area of Earth's surface, commonly far from a tectonic plate boundary (430)
**mancha caliente**  un área volcánicamente activa de la superficie de la Tierra que comúnmente se encuentra lejos de un límite entre placas tectónicas

**hydroelectric energy** (hy·droh·ee·LEK·trik EN·er·jee)  electrical energy produced by the flow of water (319)
**energía hidroeléctrica**  energía eléctrica producida por el flujo del agua

**hypothesis** (hy·PAHTH·ih·sis)  a testable idea or explanation that leads to scientific investigation (20)
**hipótesis**  una idea o explicación que conlleva a la investigación científica y que se puede probar

# I–J

**igneous rock** (IG·nee·uhs RAHK)  rock that forms when magma cools and solidifies (370)
**roca ígnea**  una roca que se forma cuando el magma se enfría y se solidifica

**inclined plane** (in·KLYND PLAYN)  a simple machine that is a straight, slanted surface, which facilitates the raising of loads; a ramp (272)
**plano inclinado**  una máquina simple que es una superficie recta e inclinada, que facilita el levantamiento de cargas; una rampa

**independent variable** (in·dih·PEN·duhnt VAIR·ee·uh·buhl)  in a scientific investigation, the factor that is deliberately manipulated (21)
**variable independiente**  en una investigación científica, el factor que se manipula deliberadamente

**inertia** (ih·NER·shuh)  the tendency of an object to resist being moved or, if the object is moving, to resist a change in speed or direction (250)
**inercia**  la tendencia de un objeto a resistirse a que lo muevan o, si el objeto está en movimiento, a resistirse a cambiar su velocidad o su dirección

**insulator** (IN·suh·lay·ter)  a material that reduces or prevents the transfer of energy (215)
**aislante**  un material que reduce o evita la transferencia de energía

## K

**kinetic energy** (kih·NET·ik EN·er·jee) the energy of an object that is due to the object's motion (190)
**energía cinética** la energía de un objeto debido al movimiento del objeto

**kinetic theory of matter** (kih·NET·ik THEE·uh·ree UHV MAT·er) a theory that states that all of the particles that make up matter are constantly in motion (202)
**teoría cinética de la materia** una teoría que establece que todas las partículas que forman la materia están en movimiento constante

**Kuiper Belt** (KY·per BELT) a region of the solar system that starts just beyond the orbit of Neptune and that contains dwarf planets and other small bodies made mostly of ice (530)
**cinturón de Kuiper** una región del Sistema Solar que comienza justo después de la órbita de Neptuno y que contiene planetas enanos y otros cuerpos pequeños formados principalmente de hielo

**Kuiper Belt object** (KY·per BELT AHB·jekt) one of the hundreds or thousands of small bodies that orbit the sun in a flat belt beyond Neptune's orbit; also includes dwarf planets located in the Kuiper Belt (530)
**objeto del cinturón de Kuiper** uno de los cientos o miles de cuerpos pequeños que orbitan alrededor del Sol en un cinturón plano, más allá de la órbita de Neptuno; también incluye los planetas enanos ubicados en el cinturón de Kuiper

## L

**lander** (LAN·der) an automated, uncrewed vehicle that is designed to touch down safely on an extraterrestrial body; often carries equipment for exploration of that body (573)
**módulo de aterrizaje** un vehículo automatizado, no tripulado, diseñado para aterrizar sin peligro en un cuerpo extraterrestre; con frecuencia lleva equipos para explorar ese cuerpo

**lava** (LAH·vuh) magma that flows onto Earth's surface; the rock that forms when lava cools and solidifies (424)
**lava** magma que fluye a la superficie terrestre; la roca que se forma cuando la lava se enfría y se solidifica

**law** (LAW) a descriptive statement or equation that reliably predicts events under certain conditions (8)
**ley** una ecuación o afirmación descriptiva que predice sucesos de manera confiable en determinadas condiciones

**law of conservation of energy** (LAW UHV kahn·suhr·VAY·shuhn UHV EN·er·jee) the law that states that energy cannot be created or destroyed but can be changed from one form to another (147, 197)
**ley de la conservación de la energía** la ley que establece que la energía ni se crea ni se destruye, sólo se transforma de una forma a otra

**law of conservation of mass** (LAW UHV kahn·suhr·VAY·shuhn UHV MAS) the law that states that mass cannot be created or destroyed in ordinary chemical and physical changes (146)
**ley de la conservación de la masa** la ley que establece que la masa no se crea ni se destruye por cambios químicos o físicos comunes

**lever** (LEV·er) a simple machine that consists of a bar that pivots at a fixed point called a fulcrum (268)
**palanca** una máquina simple formada por una barra que gira en un punto fijo llamado fulcro

**lithosphere** (LITH·uh·sfir) the solid, outer layer of Earth that consists of the crust and the rigid upper part of the mantle (392)
**litosfera** la capa externa y sólida de la Tierra que está formada por la corteza y la parte superior y rígida del manto

**luster** (LUHS·ter) the way in which a mineral reflects light (345)
**brillo** la forma en que un mineral refleja la luz

## M

**machine** (muh·SHEEN) a device that helps do work by changing the magnitude and/or direction of an applied force (264)
**máquina** un dispositivo que ayuda a realizar trabajos cambiando la magnitud y/o la dirección de una fuerza aplicada

**magma** (MAG·muh) the molten or partially molten rock material containing trapped gases produced under the Earth's surface (424)
**magma** el material rocoso total o parcialmente fundido que contiene gases atrapados que se producen debajo de la superficie terrestre

**mantle** (MAN·tl) the layer of rock between Earth's crust and core (391)
**manto** la capa de roca que se encuentra entre la corteza terrestre y el núcleo

**mass** (MAS) a measure of the amount of matter in an object (111)
**masa** una medida de la cantidad de materia que tiene un objeto

**material resource** (muh·TIR·ee·uhl REE·sohrs) a natural resource that humans use to make objects or to consume as food or drink (292)

**recurso material** un recurso natural que utilizan los seres humanos para fabricar objetos o para consumir como alimento o bebida

**mathematical model** (math·uh·MAT·ih·kuhl MAHD·l) one or more equations that represent the way a system or process works (92)

**modelo matemático** una o más ecuaciones que representan la forma en que funciona un sistema o proceso

**matter** (MAT·er) anything that has mass and takes up space (110, 338)

**materia** cualquier cosa que tiene masa y ocupa un lugar en el espacio

**measurement** (MEZH·uhr·muhnt) a quantitative description of something that includes a number and a unit, such as 42 meters; also, the process of obtaining a quantitative description of something (70)

**medición** una descripción cuantitativa de algo que incluye un número y una unidad, como 42 metros; también, el proceso por el cual se obtiene una descripción cuantitativa de algo

**mechanical advantage** (mih·KAN·ih·kuhl ad·VAN·tij) a number that tells how many times a machine multiplies input force (266)

**ventaja mecánica** un número que indica cuántas veces una máquina multiplica su fuerza de entrada

**mechanical efficiency** (mih·KAN·ih·kuhl ih·FISH·uhn·see) a quantity, usually expressed as a percentage, that measures the ratio of work output to work input in a machine (267)

**eficiencia mecánica** una cantidad, generalmente expresada como un porcentaje, que mide la relación entre el trabajo de entrada y el trabajo de salida en una máquina

**mechanical energy** (mih·KAN·ih·kuhl EN·er·jee) the sum of an object's kinetic energy and potential energy due to gravity or elastic deformation; does not include chemical energy or nuclear energy (192)

**energía mecánica** la suma de las energías cinética y potencial de un objeto debido a la gravedad o a la deformación elástica; no incluye la energía química ni nuclear

**mesosphere** (MEZ·uh·sfir) the strong, lower part of the mantle between the asthenosphere and the outer core (392)

**mesosfera** la parte fuerte e inferior del manto que se encuentra entre la astenosfera y el núcleo externo

**metamorphic rock** (met·uh·MOHR·fik RAHK) a rock that forms from other rocks as a result of intense heat, pressure, or chemical processes (370)

**roca metamórfica** una roca que se forma a partir de otras rocas como resultado de calor intenso, presión o procesos químicos

**meteor** (MEE·tee·er) a bright streak of light that results when a meteoroid burns up in Earth's atmosphere (536)

**meteoro** un rayo de luz brillante que se produce cuando un meteoroide se quema en la atmósfera de la Tierra

**meteorite** (MEE·tee·uh·ryt) a meteoroid that reaches Earth's surface without burning up completely (536)

**meteorito** un meteoroide que llega a la superficie de la Tierra sin quemarse por completo

**meteoroid** (MEE·tee·uh·royd) a relatively small, rocky body that travels through space (536)

**meteoroide** un cuerpo rocoso relativamente pequeño que viaja en el espacio

**mineral** (MIN·er·uhl) a natural, usually inorganic solid that has a characteristic chemical composition and an orderly internal structure (338)

**mineral** un sólido natural, normalmente inorgánico, que tiene una composición química característica y una estructura interna ordenada

**mixture** (MIKS·cher) a combination of two or more substances that are not chemically combined (155)

**mezcla** una combinación de dos o más sustancias que no están combinadas químicamente

**model** (MAHD·l) a pattern, plan, representation, or description designed to show the structure or workings of an object, system, or concept (60, 88)

**modelo** un diseño, plan, representación o descripción cuyo objetivo es mostrar la estructura o funcionamiento de un objeto, sistema o concepto

**motion** (MOH·shuhn) an object's change in position relative to a reference point (224)

**movimiento** el cambio en la posición de un objeto respecto a un punto de referencia

# N

**NASA** (NAS·uh) the National Aeronautics and Space Administration (554)

**NASA** la Administración Nacional de Aeronáutica y del Espacio

**natural resource** (NACH·uh·ruhl REE·sohrs) any natural material that is used by humans, such as water, petroleum, minerals, forests, and animals (290)

**recurso natural** cualquier material natural que es utilizado por los seres humanos, como agua, petróleo, minerales, bosques y animales

**net force** (NET FOHRS) the combination of all of the forces acting on an object (248)

**fuerza neta** la combinación de todas las fuerzas que actúan sobre un objeto

**neutron** (NOO·trahn) a subatomic particle that has no charge and that is located in the nucleus of an atom (168)

**neutrón** una partícula subatómica que no tiene carga y que está ubicada en el núcleo de un átomo

**niche** (NICH) the role of a species in its community, including use of its habitat and its relationships with other species (630)

**nicho** el papel que juega una especie en su comunidad, incluidos el uso de su hábitat y su relación con otras especies

**nonrenewable resource** (nahn·rih·NOO·uh·buhl REE·sohrs) a resource that forms at a rate that is much slower than the rate at which the resource is consumed (291)

**recurso no renovable** un recurso que se forma a una tasa que es mucho más lenta que la tasa a la que se consume

**nuclear energy** (NOO·klee·er EN·er·jee) the energy released by a fission or fusion reaction; the binding energy of the atomic nucleus (302)

**energía nuclear** la energía liberada por una reacción de fisión o fusión; la energía de enlace del núcleo atómico

**nuclear fusion** (NOO·klee·er FYOO·zhuhn) the process by which nuclei of small atoms combine to form a new, more massive nucleus; the process releases energy (488)

**fusión nuclear** el proceso por medio del cual los núcleos de átomos pequeños se combinan y forman un núcleo nuevo con mayor masa; el proceso libera energía

**nucleus** (NOO·klee·uhs) in a eukaryotic cell, a membrane-bound organelle that contains the cell's DNA and that has a role in processes such as growth, metabolism, and reproduction (598)

**núcleo** en una célula eucariótica, un organelo cubierto por una membrana, el cual contiene el ADN de la célula y participa en procesos tales como el crecimiento, metabolismo y reproducción

# O

**observation** (ahb·zer·VAY·shuhn) the process of obtaining information by using the senses (19)

**observación** el proceso de obtener información por medio de los sentidos

**Oort cloud** (OHRT KLOWD) a spherical region that surrounds the solar system, that extends from the Kuiper Belt to almost halfway to the nearest star, and that contains billions of comets (533)

**nube de Oort** una región esférica que rodea al Sistema Solar, que se extiende desde el cinturón de Kuiper hasta la mitad del camino hacia la estrella más cercana y contiene miles de millones de cometas

**orbit** (OHR·bit) the path that a body follows as it travels around another body in space (470)

**órbita** la trayectoria que sigue un cuerpo al desplazarse alrededor de otro cuerpo en el espacio

**orbiter** (OHR·bih·ter) a spacecraft that is designed to orbit a planet, moon, or other body without landing on the body's surface (573)

**orbitador** una nave espacial diseñada para orbitar alrededor de un planeta, luna u otro cuerpo sin aterrizar sobre la superficie de dicho cuerpo

**organelle** (ohr·guhn·EL) one of the small bodies in a cell's cytoplasm that are specialized to perform a specific function (598)

**organelo** uno de los cuerpos pequeños del citoplasma de una célula que están especializados para llevar a cabo una función específica

**organism** (OHR·guh·niz·uhm) a living thing; anything that can carry out life processes independently (594)

**organismo** un ser vivo; cualquier cosa que pueda llevar a cabo procesos vitales independientemente

# P-Q

**Pangaea** (pan·JEE·uh) the supercontinent that formed 300 million years ago and that began to break up 200 million years ago (399)

**Pangea** el supercontinente que se formó hace 300 millones de años y que comenzó a separarse hace 200 millones de años

**parallax** (PAIR·uh·laks) an apparent shift in the position of an object when viewed from different locations (458)

**paralaje** un cambio aparente en la posición de un objeto cuando se ve desde lugares distintos

**perihelion** (pehr·ih·HEE·lee·uhn) in the orbit of a planet or other body in the solar system, the point that is closest to the sun (471)

**perihelio** en la órbita de un planeta u otros cuerpos en el sistema solar, el punto que está más cerca del Sol

**physical change** (FIZ·ih·kuhl CHAYNJ) a change of matter from one form to another without a change in chemical properties (140)
**cambio físico** un cambio de materia de una forma a otra sin que ocurra un cambio en sus propiedades químicas

**physical model** (FIZ·lih·lkuhl MAHD·l) a three-dimensional representation of an object that may be smaller or larger than the object it represents (90)
**modelo físico** una representación tridimensional de un objeto que puede ser más pequeña o más grande que el objeto que representa

**physical property** (FIZ·ih·kuhl PRAHP·er·tee) a characteristic of a substance that does not involve a chemical change, such as density, color, or hardness (126, 172)
**propiedad física** una característica de una sustancia que no implica un cambio químico, tal como la densidad, el color o la dureza

**planetary ring** (PLAN·ih·tehr·ee RING) a disk of matter that encircles a planet that consists of numerous particles in orbit which range in size from dust grains up to objects tens of meters across (518)
**anillo planetario** un disco de materia que rodea un planeta y está compuesto por numerosas partículas en órbita que pueden ser desde motas de polvo hasta objetos de decenas de metros

**planetesimal** (plan·ih·TES·uh·muhl) a small body from which a planet originated in the early stages of development of the solar system (477)
**planetesimal** un cuerpo pequeño a partir del cual se originó un planeta en las primeras etapas de desarrollo del Sistema Solar

**Plantae** (PLAN·tee) a kingdom made up of complex, multicellular organisms that are usually green, have cell walls made of cellulose, cannot move around, and use the sun's energy to make sugar by photosynthesis (610)
**Plantae** un reino formado por organismos pluricelulares complejos que normalmente son verdes, tienen una pared celular de celulosa, no tienen capacidad de movimiento y utilizan la energía del Sol para producir azúcar mediante la fotosíntesis

**plate tectonics** (PLAYT tek·TAHN·iks) the theory that Earth's outer layer is made up of large, moving pieces called tectonic plates; the theory explains how plates interact and how those interactions relate to processes such as earthquakes and mountain building (399)
**tectónica de placas** la teoría de que la capa exterior de la Tierra está formada por grandes bloques que se mueven llamados placas tectónicas; la teoría explica cómo las placas interactúan una con otra y cómo esas interacciones se relacionan con procesos como los terremotos y la formación de montañas

**population** (pahp·yuh·LAY·shuhn) a group of organisms of the same species that live in a specific geographical area (624)
**población** un grupo de organismos de la misma especie que viven en un área geográfica específica

**position** (puh·ZISH·uhn) the location of an object (222)
**posición** la ubicación de un objeto

**potential energy** (puh·TEN·shuhl EN·er·jee) the energy that an object has because of the position, condition, or chemical composition of the object (191)
**energía potencial** la energía que tiene un objeto debido a su posición, condición o composición química

**precision** (prih·SIZH·uhn) the exactness of a measurement (76)
**precisión** la exactitud de una medición

**probe** (PROHB) an uncrewed vehicle that carries scientific instruments into space to collect scientific data (572)
**sonda espacial** en astronomía [O "en exploración espacial"], un vehículo sin tripulación que transporta instrumentos científicos al espacio para recopilar información científica

**prokaryote** (proh·KAIR·ee·oht) a single-celled organism that does not have a nucleus or membrane-bound organelles; examples are archaea and bacteria (599)
**procariote** un organismo unicelular que no tiene núcleo ni organelos cubiertos por una membrana, por ejemplo, las arqueas y las bacterias

**prominence** (PRAHM·uh·nuhns) a loop of relatively cool, incandescent gas that extends above the photosphere and above the sun's edge as seen from Earth (493)
**protuberancia** una espiral de gas incandescente y relativamente frío que, vista desde la Tierra, se extiende por encima de la fotosfera y la superficie del Sol

**Protista** (proh·TIS·tuh) a kingdom of mostly one-celled eukaryotic organisms that are different from plants, animals, archaea, bacteria, and fungi (610)
**Protista** un reino compuesto principalmente por organismos eucarióticos unicelulares que son diferentes de las plantas, animales, arqueas, bacterias y hongos

**proton** (PROH·tahn) a subatomic particle that has a positive charge and that is located in the nucleus of an atom; the number of protons in the nucleus is the atomic number, which determines the identity of an element (168)
**protón** una partícula subatómica que tiene una carga positiva y que está ubicada en el núcleo de un átomo; el número de protones que hay en el núcleo es el número atómico, y éste determina la identidad del elemento

**pulley** (PUL·ee) a simple machine that consists of a wheel over which a rope, chain, or wire passes (271)
**polea** una máquina simple formada por una rueda sobre la cual pasa una cuerda, cadena o cable

**pure substance** (PYOOR SUHB·stuhns) a sample of matter, either a single element or a single compound, that has definite chemical and physical properties (156)
**sustancia pura** una muestra de materia, ya sea un solo elemento o un solo compuesto, que tiene propiedades químicas y físicas definidas

# R

**radiation** (ray·dee·AY·shuhn) the transfer of energy as electromagnetic waves (216)

**radiación** la transferencia de energía en forma de ondas electromagnéticas

**reference point** (REF·er·uhns POYNT) a location to which another location is compared (222)

**punto de referencia** una ubicación con la que se compara otra ubicación

**renewable resource** (rih·NOO·uh·buhl REE·sohrs) a natural resource that can be replaced at the same rate at which the resource is consumed (291)

**recurso renovable** un recurso natural que puede reemplazarse a la misma tasa a la que se consume

**rift zone** (RIFT ZOHN) an area of deep cracks that forms between two tectonic plates that are pulling away from each other (374)

**zona de rift** un área de grietas profundas que se forma entre dos placas tectónicas que se están alejando una de la otra

**rock** (RAHK) a naturally occurring solid mixture of one or more minerals or organic matter (352)

**roca** una mezcla sólida de uno o más minerales o de materia orgánica que se produce de forma natural

**rock cycle** (RAHK SY·kuhl) the series of processes in which rock forms, changes from one type to another, is broken down or melted, and forms again by geologic processes (372)

**ciclo de las rocas** la serie de procesos por medio de los cuales una roca se forma, cambia de un tipo a otro, se destruye o funde y se forma nuevamente por procesos geológicos

**rover** (ROH·ver) a vehicle that is used to explore the surface of an extraterrestrial body (573)

**rover** un vehículo que se usa para explorar la superficie de un cuerpo extraterrestre

# S

**scientific notation** (sy·uhn·TIF·ik noh·TAY·shuhn) a method of expressing a quantity as a number multiplied by 10 to the appropriate power (75)

**notación científica** un método para expresar una cantidad en forma de un número multiplicado por 10 a la potencia adecuada

**sea-floor spreading** (SEE·flohr SPRED·ing) the process by which new oceanic lithosphere (sea floor) forms when magma rises to Earth's surface at mid-ocean ridges and solidifies, as older, existing sea floor moves away from the ridge (400)

**expansión del suelo marino** el proceso por medio del cual se forma nueva litósfera oceánica (suelo marino) cuando el magma sube a la superficie de la Tierra en las dorsales oceánicas y se solidifica, a medida que el antiguo suelo marino existente se aleja de la dorsal oceánica

**sedimentary rock** (sed·uh·MEN·tuh·ree RAHK) a rock that forms from compressed or cemented layers of sediment (370)

**roca sedimentaria** una roca que se forma a partir de capas comprimidas o cementadas de sedimento

**shear stress** (SHIR STRES) stress that occurs when forces act in parallel but opposite directions , pushing parts of a solid in opposite directions (416)

**tensión de corte** el estrés que se produce cuando dos fuerzas actúan en direcciones paralelas pero opuestas, lo que empuja las partes de un sólido en direcciones opuestas

**simulation** (sim·yuh·LAY·shuhn) a method that is used to study and analyze the characteristics of an actual or theoretical system (62, 88)

**simulación** un método que se usa para estudiar y analizar las características de un sistema teórico o real

**solar energy** (SOH·ler EN·er·jee) the energy received by Earth from the sun in the form of radiation (320)

**energía solar** la energía que la Tierra recibe del Sol en forma de radiación

**solar flare** (SOH·ler FLAIR) an explosive release of energy that comes from the sun and that is associated with magnetic disturbances on the sun's surface (493)

**erupción solar** una liberación explosiva de energía que proviene del Sol y que se asocia con disturbios magnéticos en la superficie solar

**solar nebula** (SOH·ler NEB·yuh·luh) a rotating cloud of gas and dust from which the sun and planets formed (475)

**nebulosa solar** una nube de gas y polvo en rotación a partir de la cual se formaron el Sol y los planetas

**solar system** (SOH·ler SIS·tuhm) the sun and all of the planets and other bodies that travel around it (458)

**Sistema Solar** el Sol y todos los planetas y otros cuerpos que se desplazan alrededor de él

© Houghton Mifflin Harcourt Publishing Company • Image Credits:

**space shuttle** (SPAYS SHUHT·l) a reusable space vehicle that takes off like a rocket and lands like an airplane (570)

**transbordador espacial** un vehículo espacial reutilizable que despega como un cohete y aterriza como un avión

**space station** (SPAYS STAY·shuhn) a long-term orbiting platform from which other vehicles can be launched or scientific research can be carried out (571)

**estación espacial** una plataforma orbital de largo plazo desde la cual pueden lanzarse otros vehículos o en la que pueden realizarse investigaciones científicas

**species** (SPEE·sheez) a group of organisms that are closely related and can mate to produce fertile offspring (606, 624)

**especie** un grupo de organismos que tienen un parentesco cercano y que pueden aparearse para producir descendencia fértil

**speed** (SPEED) a measure of how fast something moves; rate of motion (225)

**rapidez** una medida de la celeridad con que se mueve algo; tasa de cambio de la posición por unidad de tiempo

**streak** (STREEK) the color of a mineral in powdered form (344)

**veta** el color de un mineral en forma de polvo

**subsidence** (suhb·SYD·ns) the sinking of regions of the Earth's crust to lower elevations (374)

**hundimiento del terreno** el hundimiento de regiones de la corteza terrestre a elevaciones más bajas

**sunspot** (SUHN·spaht) a dark area of the photosphere of the sun that is cooler than the surrounding areas and that has a strong magnetic field (492)

**mancha solar** un área oscura en la fotosfera del Sol que es más fría que las áreas que la rodean y que tiene un campo magnético fuerte

## T

**tectonic plate** (tek·TAHN·ik PLAYT) a block of lithosphere that consists of the crust and the rigid, outermost part of the mantle (399, 427)

**placa tectónica** un bloque de litosfera formado por la corteza y la parte rígida y más externa del manto

**tectonic plate boundary** (tek·TAHN·ik PLAYT BOWN·duh·ree) the edge between two or more plates classified as divergent, convergent, or transform by the movement taking place between the plates (439)

**límite de placa tectónica** el borde entre dos o más placas clasificado como divergente, convergente o transformante por el movimiento que se produce entre las placas

**temperature** (TEM·per·uh·chur) a measure of how hot (or cold) something is; specifically, a measure of the average kinetic energy of the particles in an object (204)

**temperatura** una medida de qué tan caliente (o frío) está algo; específicamente, una medida de la energía cinética promedio de las partículas de un objeto

**tension** (TEN·shuhn) stress that occurs when forces act to stretch an object (417)

**tensión** estrés que se produce cuando distintas fuerzas actúan para estirar un objeto

**terrestrial planet** (tuh·RES·tree·uhl PLAN·it) one of the highly dense planets nearest to the sun; Mercury, Venus, Mars, and Earth (498)

**planeta terrestre** uno de los planetas muy densos que se encuentran más cerca del Sol; Mercurio, Venus, Marte y la Tierra

**texture** (TEKS·cher) the quality of a rock that is based on the sizes, shapes, and positions of the rock's grains (353)

**textura** la cualidad de una roca que se basa en el tamaño, la forma y la posición de los granos que la forman

**theory** (THEE·uh·ree) a system of ideas that explains many related observations and is supported by a large body of evidence acquired through scientific investigation (9)

**teoría** un sistema de ideas que explica muchas observaciones relacionadas y que está respaldado por una gran cantidad de pruebas obtenidas mediante la investigación científica

**thermal energy** (THER·muhl EN·er·jee) the kinetic energy of a substance's atoms (210)

**energía térmica** la energía cinética de los átomos de una sustancia

**thermometer** (ther·MAHM·ih·ter) an instrument that measures and indicates temperature (204)

**termómetro** un instrumento que mide e indica la temperatura

**transform boundary** (TRANS·fohrm BOWN·duh·ree) the boundary between tectonic plates that are sliding past each other horizontally (405)

**límite de transformación** el límite entre placas tectónicas que se están deslizando horizontalmente una sobre otra

**uplift** (UHP·lift) the rising of regions of Earth's crust to higher elevations (374)

**levantamiento** la elevación de regiones de la corteza terrestre a elevaciones más altas

## V

**vector** (VEK·ter) a quantity that has both size and direction (231)

**vector** una cantidad que tiene tanto magnitud como dirección

**velocity** (vuh·LAHS·ih·tee) the speed of an object in a particular direction (231)

**velocidad** la rapidez de un objeto en una dirección dada

**vent** (VENT) an opening at the surface of the Earth through which volcanic material passes (424)

**chimenea** una abertura en la superficie de la Tierra a través de la cual pasa material volcánico

**volcano** (vahl·KAY·noh) a vent or fissure in Earth's surface through which magma and gases are expelled (424)

**volcán** una chimenea o fisura en la superficie de la Tierra a través de la cual se expulsan magma y gases

**volume** (VAHL·yoom) the amount of space that an object takes up, or occupies (113)

**volumen** la cantidad de espacio que ocupa un objeto

**weathering** (WETH·er·ing) the natural process by which atmospheric and environmental agents, such as wind, rain, and temperature changes, disintegrate and decompose rocks (369)

**meteorización** el proceso natural por medio del cual los agentes atmosféricos o ambientales, como el viento, la lluvia y los cambios de temperatura, desintegran y descomponen las rocas

**weight** (WAYT) a measure of the gravitational force exerted on an object; its value can change with the location of the object in the universe (111)

**peso** una medida de la fuerza gravitacional ejercida sobre un objeto; su valor puede cambiar en función de la ubicación del objeto en el universo

**wheel and axle** (WEEL AND AK suhl) a simple machine consisting of two circular objects of different sizes; the wheel is the larger of the two circular objects, and the axle is attached to the center of the wheel (270)

**rueda y eje** una máquina simple formada por dos objetos circulares de diferentes tamaños; la rueda es el más grande de los dos objetos circulares, y el eje está sujeto al centro de la rueda

**wind energy** (WIND EN·er·jee) the use of the force of moving air to drive an electric generator (318)

**energía eólica** el uso de la fuerza del aire en movimiento para hacer funcionar un generador eléctrico

# Index

**Note:** Italic page numbers represent illustrative material, such as figures, tables, margin elements, photographs, and illustrations. Boldface page numbers represent page numbers for definitions.

communication, of scientific results, 29
community, **625,** *625,* 629
competition, 622
complex system, 88
composite volcano, 425, *425,* 427, 429
composition, **352**
 of asteroids, 535
 chemical, 191
 of Earth's layers, 390–391
 of meteorites, 537
 of mixtures, 162
 of rocks, 352–353
 of the sun, 486
compound, **155, 338,** *338,* R15
 classification of, 159
compression, 417, 441
*Compton Gamma-Ray Observatory,* 572
computer
 computer models, 19, 92–93
 as scientific tools, 37, 61, 79,
  *79, 572*
concept map (graphic organizer),
 R22, *R22*
conceptual model, 60, *60,* **94,** *94*
conchoidal fracture, 345, *345*
conclusion, 23, 24–25, 66–67
conduction, 151, **215**
conductivity, *51, 128,* 172
conductor, **215**
conglomerate, 356
conservation (natural resources), 290
conservation of energy, law of, **147,**
 *147,* **197,** R16
conservation of mass, law of, 146,
 *147,* R16
constant, R30
constellation, *R6–R7*
contact force, 247, *247*
content frame (graphic organizer),
 R20, *R20*
continental crust. *See* crust (Earth).
continental drift, 398–400, *398*
control rod, 307, *307*
convection, **216,** 391
convection cell (sun), 490, *491*
convection current, 216, *216,* 399,
 406, *406*
 in Earth's mantle, 391, *391,*
  406, *406*
 in the sun, 487, *487,* 490, 490–491,
  492
 tectonic plate movement and, 406,
  *406*
convective zone, 487, *487,* 490, *490*
convergent plate boundary, **404**
 collision types at, 404, *404*
 earthquakes at, 441, *441*
 volcanoes at, *404,* 419, 429, *429*
Copernican model, 461, *461*
Copernicus, Nicolaus, 37, *37,* 461,
 *461,* 471, 484
copper, 156, *156, 333*
coquina, 357
core, **391**
 of asteroids, 535, *535*

of Earth, 174, *390, 391, 392,*
 390–393, *393*
of Jupiter, 515
of Mercury, 499, *499*
of the sun, 487, *487,* 488, 490
thickness of, *393*
corona, 487, *487*
corundum, *343*
countermass (balance), 112, *112*
cranberry, *124*
crash test dummy, 251, *251*
crater
 on Mars, *506*
 on Mercury, *498*
 from meteorites, *536*
 on the moon, 503
 on Venus, *501*
 volcanic, 426
cricket, 21
crocodile, *26–27*
crude oil, 303, *303. See also* oil.
crust (Earth), 174, *390,* 390–**391,** *391*
 age of, 402
 continental crust 402, *402*
 at convergent boundaries, 404,
  *404, 429*
 at divergent boundaries, 405, *405*
 minerals in, 342, *342*
 oceanic crust, 402, 429
 tectonic plates and, 374, *374,* 392,
  402, *402*
 thickness of, *390, 393,* 402, *402*
crystal, *336,* **339,** *339*
crystalline structure, 339, *339*
cubic meter, 72
Cunitz, Maria, *501*
Cunitz Crater (Venus), *501*
cytoplasm, **598,** *598*

dam (water), 319, *319*
data, **21**
 analyzing and interpreting, 21, 23,
  58–59, 466, 570
 collected by volunteers, 52–53
 collecting, 23, 471, 485, 507, 551,
  558, 560–562, 570, 572
 describing, 234, 466
 graphing, *57,* 57–59, 234–235
 identifying trends in, 58, 92,
  234, 466
 organizing, 23, 59
 quantitative and qualitative, 21,
  *77, 77*
 recording, 21, 77, *77,* 562, 570
 repeatable, 23, 28–29, 58
 from scientific investigations, 23
 statistics and, 58, 466
 as support for hypotheses, 21, 23
 supporting conclusions with, 471;
  516

data analysis, 21, 23, 58–59
data point, 228, 234
data table, 23, 56, *56*
 analysis of, 466
 constructing, 56
 organizing, 56
*Deep Impact* space probe, *561*
deep-space habitat, 578, *579*
deformation, **414,** *414,* **439**
degree (temperature), **204,** 205, *205*
density, **117**
 calculating, 118–119, 134
 formula, 118
 of gold, 134, 135
 as a physical property, 128, *128*
 substance identification by, *134,*
  134–135, 346
 of water, 118
deoxyribonucleic acid (DNA), 159, *598,*
 598–599, 605
dependent variable, **21,** 23, 59, R30
deposition, **369,** 372, *373*
description wheel (graphic organizer),
 R24, *R24*
desert (biome), 628, 629
 location of, *629*
Designing, Conducting, and Reporting
 an Experiment, R28–R34
destination system, 579
deuterium, 488, *489, 489*
diagram
 branching, 612, *612*
 cladogram, 612, *612*
 as conceptual model, 60, *60,* 202,
  203, *339*
 dichotomous key, 615, *615*
diamond, 340, *346*
dichotomous key, 614, *614, 615*
diesel fuel, 303
differential rotation, 491, *491*
digital camera, 78
digital scale, *111*
diorite, 354, *354*
*Discovery* (space shuttle), 558
displacement
 velocity and, 231
 volume from, 116, *116*
distance measurement, 224, *224*
distance-time graph, *228,* 228–229,
 *229,* 230
divergent plate boundary, **405**
 earthquakes at, 441, *441*
 mid-ocean ridges at, 405, *405,* 427,
  428, 441
 normal faults at, 417, *417*
 volcanoes at, 427, 428, *428, 429*
DNA (deoxyribonucleic acid), 159,
 598–599
 as classification tool, 605
dolomite, 341, *341*
domain, 607, *607, 608,* **608**–609, *609,*
 R10
 Archaea, R10, *R10*
 Bacteria, R10, *R10*
 Eukarya, R10–R11, *R10–R11*

Eukarya, Domain, *609*, **609**, *610*, 610–611, *611*, R10–R11, *R10–R11*
eukaryote, **599**, *599*, 609, *609*
Europa (moon of Jupiter), 516, *516*
European Space Agency, 561
eustachian tube, 8, *8*
evaluation, of scientific information, 29, 122–123
evidence, empirical, *10–11*, **10**–13, *12, 13*
exothermic, 147
experiment, 10–11, **18**, R28–R34. **See *also* scientific investigation.**
*Explorer I* satellite, 554, *562*
exponent, 75, 434–435
exponential growth, 92, *92*
extrusive igneous rock, 355, *355*, 371

**F**

Fahrenheit, Gabriel, 205
Fahrenheit scale, 204, 205, *205*
fairy chimney, *369*
family (classification), 607, *607*
faucet, 270, *270*
fault, **439**. **See *also* fault block; fault plane; normal fault; reverse fault.**
    deformation at, *393*, 439, *439*
    earthquakes at, *438 439*, 438–441, *441*
    normal, 417, *417*
    reverse, 417, *417*, 441, *441*
    strike-slip, 405, 416, *416*, 441, *441*
    tectonic plates and, 441, *441*
fault block, 416, *416*
fault-block mountain, 419, *419*
fault plane, 416, *416*
feet (ft), 224
feldspar, 342
*Felis domesticus*, 607, *607*
Ferris wheel, *262*
fiber analysis, 133, *133*
field observation, 18. **See *also* scientific investigations.**
fieldwork, 10–11, *10–11*
field safety, xxviii
Figueroa, Dijanna, 32, *32*
fine-grained rock, 353, *353*, 355, *355*
fire, chemical change in, 142
fireworks technician, 33
first-class lever, 268, *268*
First Law, Kepler's, 471, *471*
fish ladder, 319
fission. *See* nuclear fission.
fissure, *355*, 426, 427–428, *428*
fixed pulley, 271, *271*
flagellum (plural, *flagella*), 599, 613
flammability, 131, *131*, 142
flashlight, *196–197*
Fleming, Alexander, 18, 21
flight simulator, 91
floating, density and, 118, *118*
fluorite, *343*
flu prevention, 66–67

focus (earthquake), **438**, *438*
folded mountain, 418, *418*
folding, of rock, **415**, *415*
foliated metamorphic rock, 358, *358*
foliation, 358
food, 159, 292
footwall, 416, *417*
force, **246**
    acceleration and, 252
    acting at a distance, 247, *247*
    balanced and unbalanced, 249, *249*
    centripetal, 474, *474*
    contact, 247, *247*
    gravitational, 111–112, 247, 473, 475, *475*, 521
    input and output, 259, *259*, 264–266, 268–273
    magnetic, 247
    net, 248–249, *248–249*, R17
    in Newton's first law of motion, *250*, 250–251, *251*
    in Newton's second law of motion, *252*, 252–253, *253*
    in Newton's third law of motion, *254*, 254–255, *255*
    unit of, 112, 246
force pair, 254, *254–255*, 255
forensic science, 133, *133*
formula
    average acceleration, 239
    average speed, 226
    chemical, 92, 343
    density, 118, 134
fossil, *26–27*, 27, 357, *357*
fossil fuel, **291**, **302**. **See *also* energy resource; nonrenewable resource.**
    advantages and disadvantages of, 309, *309*
    consumption of, *302*
    energy conversion in, 294, *294*, 306, *306*
    formation of, *304*, 304–305, *305*
    fracking, 312–313, *313*
    as nonrenewable energy resource, 291, 302
    in Texas, 286, *287*
    types of, 303, *303*
    uses of, 296, 303, *303*, 306, *306*
fossiliferous limestone, *352*, 357, *357*
four square (graphic organizer), R24, *R24*
fracking, 312–313, *313*
fraction, R48
    addition and subtraction of, R49
    division of, R50
    multiplication of, R49
    simplification of, R49
fracture, of minerals, 345, *345*
fracture zone, 495
frame game (graphic organizer), R25, *R25*
*Freedom 7* capsule, 556
free fall, *253*
freezing point, 204, 205, *205*
frequency, of data, 56

friction, 247
fuel cell, 296, 297, *297*
fuel rod, 307, *307*, 308
fulcrum, *268*, **268**–269, *269*
Fungi, *41*, 609, **611**, *611*
fusion, 476, 488–489, *488–489*

**G**

Gagarin, Yuri, *554*, 556, 570
galaxy, 485, *485*
Galilean moons, 454, 462, 516, **516**–517, *517*
Galileo Galilei, 454, 458, 462, *462*, 463, 516
*Galileo* spacecraft, 463, *463*, 561
Ganymede (moon of Jupiter), 454, 517, *517*
garnet, 340
gas (state of matter)
    Boyle's law and, 8
    chemical changes and, 144, *144*
    kinetic theory of, 9, *9*, 202–203, *203*
gas giant (planet), **514**–523
    formation of, 478, *478*
    Galilean moons of, 462, *516*, 516–517, *517*
    Jupiter, 462, *512*, 514, 514–517, *515, 516*
    Neptune, *512*, 514, *522*, 522–523, *523*
    planetary rings, 518, *518*
    Saturn, *512*, 514, *518*, 518–519, *519, 568*
    temperature on, 514
    Uranus, *512*, 514, *520*, 520–521, *521*
gasohol, 322
gasoline, 159, 303
gasoline engine, 294, *294*
Gaua volcano (Vanuatu), *574*
Gehry, Frank, 347
gelatin, 162, *162*
Gemini program, *554*, 556, *556*
generator, 296, *296*
genes, classification and, 605
genus, **606**, 607, *607*
geocentric (model), **458**, 460, *460*, 471, 484
Geologic Time Scale, R4–R5, *R4–R5*
geologist, 411, 510
geology, 6. **See *also* Earth science.**
geophysicist, 410
geothermal energy, **323**, *323*
giant panda, *605*
Gila Cliff Dwellings (New Mexico), *375*
Gilbert, William, 38
glass, 293
Glenn, John H., Jr., 556
Global Positioning System (GPS), 195, *195*, 574
gneiss, 358, *358*, 371, *371*

© Houghton Mifflin Harcourt Publishing Company

Index  **R71**

**gold**
chemical properties of, 338
chemical symbol of, 171
density of, 135, 346
formation of, *341*
identifying, *134*, 134–135, *135*
physical properties of, 126
smelting, 126–*127*, 127
**Gondwana**, 399, *399*
**GPS (Global Positioning System)**, 195, *195*, 574
**graduated cylinder**, 72, *72*, 116, *116*, R37, *R37*
**gram**, 111
**granite**
as intrusive igneous rock, 354, 371, *371*
minerals in, 340
mining of, 335, *335*
**granule (sun)**, 490, *491*
**graph**
analyzing, 58, *228*, 228–229
axis on, 234, 228
bar, *57*, 57–59, 234, *234*, R53, *R53*
circle, 57, R51, *R51*
constructing, 59, *59*
distance-time, *228*, 228–229, *229*, 230
interpreting, 234–235, R51–R53
line graph, 57, *228*, 228–229, R52, *R52*
making, R51–R53
patterns shown on, 228, *228*, 229–230, *230*
types of, 57, *57*
**graphic organizer**, R20–R23, *R20–R23*
**graphite**, 340
**gravitational force.** *See also* gravity.
on Jupiter, 514
law of universal gravitation, 473
on Miranda, 521, *521*
on the moon, 503
in the solar system formation, *475*, 475
weight and, 111, 112, *112*
**gravitational potential energy**, *190–191*, 191
**gravity, 470**
as force acting at a distance, 247
force pairs in, 255
law of universal gravitation, 473
planetary motion and, 474, *474*
potential energy and, 191
solar system formation and, 475–478, 484
weathering by, 369
weight and, 111
weightlessness and, *470*
**Great Backyard Bird Count**, 52–53
**Great Dark Spot (Neptune)**, 522, *522*
**Great Red Spot (Jupiter)**, *514*, 515
**Great Rift Valley (Africa)**, 428
**Great Sphinx (Egypt)**, *368*
**Griggs, Mount (Alaska)**, 419, *419*
**Grissom, Virgil I.**, 556

**groundwater**, *323*
**group (periodic table)**, R14
**Guggenheim Museum (Spain)**, 347, *347*
**Gula Mons (Venus)**, *501*
**gypsum**, *336*, 341, *341*, *343*

**habitat, 630**
**Hadean eon**, R4
**Hale-Bopp, Comet**, *526*
**halide**, 343, *343*, R3, *R3*
**halite**, 339, *341*, 356, *356*
**Halley, Edmund**, 485
**hammer**, 269
**hand lens**, 78, 353
**hanging wall**, 416, *417*
**hardness**, 129, *129*, 151, 346, *346*
**Haumea (dwarf planet)**, 529, *529*
**Hawaiian Islands**, 425, 430, *430*
**heat, 212.**
conduction, 215
convection, 216, *216*
energy flow from hot to cold, 212, *212–213*, 213
from geothermal energy, 323, *323*
measurement of, 213
radiation, 216, 217, *217*
from solar energy, 320, *320*
states of matter and, 214, *214*
thermal energy and, 194, 213
transfer of, *215*, 215–216, *216*
unit of, 213
**Hebes Chasma (Mars)**, *505*
**heliocentric (model), 458**, 459, 461, *461*
**helium**
fusion and, *316*, 488–489, 489
sun composed of, 486, *486*
**helium-3**, 489, *489*
**helium-4**, 489, *489*
**herpetology**, 618
**Herschel, Sir William**, 455, *455*
**heterogeneous, 162**
**heterotroph**, 610, 611
**hieroglyphic**, 36, *36*
**High Resolution Imaging Science Experiment (HiRISE)**, *1*
**homogeneous, 162**
**Hooke, Robert**, 594, *596*
**hornbill**, *620*
**hot air balloon**, *108*
**hot plate**, 78
**hot spot**, 427, **430**, *430*
**How-to Manual for Active Reading**, R18–R19
**Hubble Space Telescope**, 37, *37*, 522, *572*, 572
**human activity**
climate change and, 67
on the moon, 503, *503*, 551, *555*, *557*, 557, 576, *576*
**hurricane**, *523*

*Huygens* **Titan space probe**, 519
**Hyakutake, Comet**, 455, *455*
**hydraulic fracturing (fracking)**, 312–313, *313*
**hydroelectric energy, 319**, *319*
advantages and disadvantages of, 319
**hydrogen**
on Jupiter, 515
nuclear fusion of, 316, *316*, 488–489, *488–489*
sun composed of, 486, *486*
**hydrogen fuel cell**, 296, 297, *297*
**hydrothermal vent**, *575*
**hypothesis (plural, *hypotheses*)**, 20–21, 22, 26, 150–151, R30

**IAU (International Astronomical Union)**, 531
**ice**
on fruit trees, 107, *107*
on Mars, *504*
as a mineral, 338
in solar system formation, 478, *478*
**iceberg**, *105*
**Iceland, shield volcanoes in**, 428
**ideal mechanical advantage**, 268
**igneous rock**, 354–355, **370**
extrusive, 355, *355*, 371
formation of, 370–371, *371*
intrusive, 354, *354*, 371
in the rock cycle, 372, *372–373*
texture of, 353
**inch (in)**, 224
**inclined plane, 272**, *272*
**independent variable, 21**, 23, R30
**individual**, 624, *624*
**inertia, 250**
**inexhaustible resource**, 291
**inference**, 24–25
**inner core**, *392*, 392–393
**inorganic substance**, 159, 339
**input force**
inclined planes and, 272
levers and, *268*, 268–269, *269*
mechanical advantage and, 259, *259*, 266, *266*
pulleys and, 271, *271*
simple machines and, *264*, 264–265, *265*
wedges and screws and, 273, *273*
wheel and axle and, 270, *270*
**insulation, thermal**, 82–83, *83*
**insulator, thermal, 215**, *215*
**International Astronomical Union (IAU)**, 531
*International Space Station* **(ISS)**
assembly of, 551, *551*
crews of, 558–559, 559, 571, *571*
photographs from, 574
timeline of, 555, *555*
**International System of Units (SI).**
*See* SI units of measurement.

© Houghton Mifflin Harcourt Publishing Company

## M

energy conversion and, *294,*
*294–296, 295*
management of, 290
material resource, *292,* 292–293,
*293*
nonrenewable, 291, *291,* 302–309,
*304, 305, 306, 307, 308, 309*
recycling, 40, *40–41*
renewable, 287, 291, *291, 316,*
316–317, *319,* 319–323, *321*
sun's energy and, 290–291
navigation satellite, 574
Nazca plate, 402
near-Earth asteroid, 534, 535, 577,
*577*
nebula, 475, *475, 479*
negative acceleration, 240, *240*
Neptune
atmosphere of, 522
characteristics of, 514, 522, *522*
discovery of, 455
moons of, 523, *523*
winds on, 523
net force, *248,* **248**–249, *249,* R17
neutron, **168,** *168,* 307, R14
in nuclear fusion, *488,* 488–489,
*489*
newton (N), 112, 246
Newton, Sir Isaac, 473, *473*
Newton's laws of motion, R16
first law, *250,* 250–251, *251*
second law, *252,* 252–253, *253*
third law, *254,* 254–255, *255*
niche, **630**
NOAA (National Oceanic and
Atmospheric Administration),
*563*
nonfoliated metamorphic rock, 359,
*359*
nonmetal, 158
in the periodic table, 172, *172*
nonrenewable resource, **291** *See*
*also* energy resource; fossil fuel;
natural resource.
advantages and disadvantages,
*308,* 308–309, *309*
consumption of, *302*
energy conversion and, 294, *294,*
*306,* 306–307, *307*
fossil fuel, *302,* 303, *303, 304,*
304–305, *305*
material resources as, 292–293,
*293*
two main types of, 302
uranium as, 302, *302*
nonsilicate mineral, 342
classes of, 343, *343,* R3, *R3*
normal fault, 417, *417*
note taking, graphic organizers for,
R20–R23
nuclear energy, 194, **302,** *302, 307,*
307–308
nuclear fission, **307**
advantages and disadvantages of,
308, *308*
energy from, 302, 307, *307*

from interior of Earth, 316, *316*
nuclear wastes from, 208, 307
uranium supply for, 302, *302*
nuclear fusion, 316, *316,* 476,
**488**–489, *488–489*
nuclear waste, 208, 307
nucleic acid, 159
nucleus (atom), 168, *168,* 170
nucleus (cell), **598,** *598*
nucleus (comet), 532, *532*

observation, **19.** *See also* scientific
investigation.
in experiments, 18
in fieldwork, 19, 36, *36*
of physical properties, 127
qualitative data from, 21, 77
obsidian, *118,* 355
ocean, *399*
composition of, *152,* 175
exploration of, 575, *575*
fossil fuels from organisms in, 304,
*304*
sea-floor magnetic properties, 400
trenches in, 401
oceanic crust. *See* crust (Earth).
ocean trench, 401
odor, in chemical change, 144
oil
advantages and disadvantages of,
309, *309*
crude oil, 303, *303*
formation of, *304,* 304–305, *305*
fracking, 312–313, *313*
gasoline, 159, 303
refining of, 303, *303*
in Texas, 286, *287*
uses of, 306
oil spill, 309
olivine, 342
Olympus Mons (Mars), 505, *505*
Oort cloud, 528, **533**
*Opportunity* rover, 507, *507,* 562, *563,*
573
orbit, **470**
eccentricity of, 466
elliptical, *462, 462,* 466, *471,* 471,
*472, 472*
of the Galilean moons, 517, *517*
gravity and, *474, 474*
Kepler's laws and, *462, 462,* 471,
471–472, *472*
in the solar system, 484
of Triton, 523
orbital period, *472, 472*
orbiter, 73, *73,* 561, *561, 563,* **573**
order (classification), 607, *607*
organelle, **598,** *598*
organic compound, 159
organic sedimentary rock, 357, *357*
organism, **594,** 596–597, *596–597*
Orion MPCV capsule, 578, *578*

orrery, *453*
outer core, *392,* 392–393
output force
inclined planes and, 272
levers and, *268,* 268–269, *269*
mechanical advantage and, 259,
*259,* 266, *266*
pulleys and, 271, *271*
simple machines and, 264,
264–265, *265*
wedges and screws and, 273, *273*
wheel and axle and, 270, *270*
oven, electric, 295
oxide, 343, *343,* R3, *R3*

paleontologist, *10–11*
Paleozoic era, R4
Pallas (asteroid), 534
Palouse Falls (Washington state), 426,
*426*
Pangaea, **399,** *399*
pangolin, *609*
Panthalassa, 399, *399*
parallax, **458,** *459*
peat, 305, *305,* 322, *322*
peer review, 29
pegmatite, *340*
penicillin, 18
People in Science
Atekwana, Estella, *410,* 410–411
Figueroa, Dijanna, *32,* 32–33
Krysko, Kenneth, *618,* 618–619
Ward, A. Wesley, *510,* 510–511
percent, R48
Performing Calculations, R46–R50
perihelion, **471,** *471, 472, 472*
period (periodic table), R14
Periodic Table of the Elements, 170,
171, *171,* 172, *172,* 173, *173,*
*R12–R13,* R14
Petra cliff dwellings (Jordan), *375*
petri dish, 78
petroleum. *See* oil.
petroleum technician, 411
pH, 159, R15
Phanerozoic eon, R5
photosphere, 487, *487*
photosynthesis, 322, *322,* 502
photovoltaic cell, 321, *321*
pH probe, R43, *R43*
pH scale, R15, *R15*
phyllite, 358, *358*
phylum, 607, *607*
physical change, **140**–141, *140–141*
conservation of energy in, 147, *147*
conservation of mass in, 146, *146,*
147
mixture separation with, 161, *161*
pure substance and, 157, *157*
physical characteristic (classification),
605, *605*
Physical Laws and Useful Equations,
R16–R17

# R

refining, of crude oil, 303, *303*
refrigerator, *38*
Remak, Robert, 596, 597
renewable resource, **291.** *See also*
    energy resource; natural resource.
repetition, in investigations, 23,
    28–29, *58*
replication, in investigations, 29
research. *See* scientific research.
resource
    advantages and disadvantages,
    *308,* 308–309, *309*
    availability of, 40, 286, 578,
    623–625, 630
    becoming nonrenewable, 317
    biomass, 322, *322*
    conservation of, 290
    energy, 294, 296, 302, 316, 319,
    323
    ethanol, 322, *322*
    geothermal energy, 323, *323*
    heat from Earth's interior, 316, *316*
    heat from the sun, 316, *316*
    hydroelectric energy, 319, *319*
    material, *292,* 292–293, *293*
    natural, 290, 302, 623
    nonrenewable, 286, 291–292, 302,
    308, 317
    photovoltaic cells and, 321, *321*
    recycling of, 40, 362–365, 578
    renewable, 286, 291–292, 302,
    316–317, 323
    reuse of, 40, 297, 570, 578
    solar collectors and, 320–321, *320*
    stewardship of, 290
    trees as, 317
    wind energy, 287, *286–287,* 291,
    296, 318, *318*
retrograde rotation, 500
reverse fault, 417, *417,* 441, *441*
ribosome, 599
ridge push, *406,* 406–407
rift valley, 405, *405,* 410, 428
rift zone, **374,** *374*
Ring of Fire, 419, 427
RNA (ribonucleic acid), 159, 605
robot
    as used in nanotechnology,
    169, *169*
    as used for space exploration, 579
robotic system, as used for space
    exploration, *169,* 579
rock, **352,** 368
    classification of, 352–353,
    370–371, *371*
    cliff dwellings in, 375, *375*
    composition of, 352, *352*
    deformation of, 414, *414,* 439
    folding of, 415, *415*
    formation of, 352–353
    igneous, 352–355, *354, 355,*
    370–372, *371*
    metamorphic, 353, *358,* 358–359,
    *359, 371,* 371–372, *372–373*
    permeable, 304

processes of change, 369, *369*
rock cycle, *94,* 372, *372–373,*
    374, *374*
sedimentary, *356,* 356–357, *357,*
    370, *372,* 372–373
uses of, *290,* 368
rock cycle, *94,* **372,** *372–373*
    tectonic plate motion and, 374, *374*
rocket, 570, *570*
roller coaster, 253, *253*
roseate spoonbill, *589*
rotation
    of Jupiter, 514
    of the moon, 503
    of the sun, 491, *491*
    of Uranus, 520
    of Venus, 500
rover, 507, *507,* 562, *562, 563,* **573**
"rubble-pile" asteroid, 535, *535*
rusting
    as chemical change, *138,* 143
    chemical properties and, 130,
    *130, 132*
rutile, 347
R-value, 83

## S

safety, field, xxviii
safety, lab, xxvii, R26–R27
**Safety in the Lab,** R26–R27
**Safety Preview,** xxvii–xviii
salt, ocean, 175
*Salyut 1* space station, *555,* 559
San Andreas Fault (California), *396,*
    405, *405,* 416
sand, 293
sandstone
    as clastic sedimentary rock, 356,
    *356*
    colors in, 174
    quartzite from, 359, *359*
    sand in, 370, *370*
San Gabriel Mountains (California),
    417
*Sarcosuchus,* 26–27, *27*
satellite. *See* artificial satellite.
Saturn, *512, 513,* 518, *518, 561, 568*
    characteristics of, 518, *518*
    moons of, 519, *519*
    rings of, 518, *518, 519*
savanna environment, *626–627*
scale
    base-ten logarithmic, *434,*
    434–435, *435*
    Celsius, *204,* 205, *205*
    geologic time, R4–R5
    Kelvin, 204, 205, *205*
    linear, 434
    logarithmic, *434,* 434–435, *435*
    Mohs hardness, 346, *346*
scale model, *90,* 90–91
schist, 358, *358*
Schleiden, Matthias, 596, 597

Schwann, Theodor, 596, 597
science, 6
    areas of, 6, 27, 133, 410
    bias in, 29, 122, 312
    careers in, *10–11,* 32, 33, 410, 411,
    510, 511
    changing ideas in, 12–13
    communication in, 29, 566–567
    contributions of scientists to, 18,
    21, 32, 33, 38, 146, 205, 410,
    454, 455, 458, 462–463, 471,
    473, 485, 488, 510, 556, 570,
    594, 596–597, 606
    curiosity in, 10, 22, 36, 554
    empirical evidence in, *10–11,*
    10–13, *12, 13*
    environment and, 312–313
    government and, 29, 71, 312
    history of, 8, 36, 37, 454, 458–459,
    462–463, 473
    journals, 29, 312
    laws in, 8–9, 146–147, 197,
    250–255, 471, 472–473,
    R16–R17
    publication of results and
    conclusions, 312
    societal changes from, *38,* 38–39,
    *39,* 40
    societal needs and, 38–39, 40–41
    as study of natural world, 19, 36, *36*
    technology and, 37, *37,* 79, *79*
    theories in, 7, 9, 12–13, 202–204,
    596–597
    writing, 511
Science Skills, R26–R45
    Designing, Conducting, and
    Reporting an Experiment,
    R28–R34
    Introduction to Probeware, R42–R43
    Measuring Accurately, R36–R41
    Safety in the Lab, R26–R27
    Using a Microscope, R35
    Using the Metric System and SI
    Units, R44–R45
Science, Technology, Engineering, and
    Mathematics. *See* STEM.
science writer, 511
scientific claim, 122–123, 387
scientific debate, 13, 67, 312–313
scientific explanation
    characteristics of, 7, 9, 10, 12
    development of, 12, 24–25
    evaluating, 66
    example of, 506, 520
scientific information
    evaluating, 29, 122–123, 312
    sources of, 312
scientific investigation, 18, 22–23
    analyzing evidence, 23, 66
    characteristics of good, 22–23,
    28–29
    communicating conclusions of,
    23, 29
    conclusions from, 23, 24–25,
    66–67

in the Milky Way, 485, *485*
nuclear fusion in, 316, *316,*
    488–489, *488–489*
physical properties of, 486, *486*
prominences, *482,* 492, 493, *493*
rotation of, 491, *491*
solar flares, 193, 195, 486, 492,
    493, *493*
in the solar system, 484, *484*
structure of, 487, *487*
sunspots, 89, *89,* 492, *492*
sunspot, 89, *89,* **492,** *492*
superconductor, *173*
supercontinent, 399, *399*
SuperCroc, *26–27*
supernova, *572*
surface area-to-volume ratio, 595
surveying and mapping technician,
    411
suspension, 162
swamp, coal formation in, 305, *305*
syncline, 415, *415*

## T

table, data. *See* data table.
taiga, 628
    location of, *629*
Take It Home, 3, 53, 67, 107, 123, 151,
    187, 235, 287, 335, 387, 435,
    455, 551, 567, 591
talc, 339, *346*
tarnishing, 130
taxonomy, 607. *See also*
    classification, of living things.
technology, 22, 95, 169, 297, 302,
    306, 323, 463, 549, 554, 558,
    570. *See also* space exploration,
    crewed technology; space
    exploration, uncrewed technology.
    in laboratories, *78,* 78–79, *79*
    for measurement, 72, *72*
    nanotechnology, 169, *169*
    for ocean exploration, 575, *575*
    scientific research and, 36, 37, *37,*
        79, *79*
    as scientific tools, 79, *79*
    space weather and, 195, *195*
tectonic plate, 6, **399, 427.** *See also*
    plate tectonics; tectonic plate
    boundary.
    deformation of, 414, *414*
    Earth processes and, 401, *401,* 404,
        404–405, *405,* 406–407, 441
    faults and, 396, 416, 416–417,
        *417,* 439, *439,* 441, *441*
    hot spots and, 427
    lithosphere and, *392,* 392–393
    locations of, *402,* 402–403, *403,*
        427, 440
    major plate names, 402, *403*
    motion of, 399
    plate boundary, 404, 404–405,
        *405,* 441
    plate locations, *402, 403*

properties of, 402, *402*
rock cycle and, 372, 374, *374*
tectonic plate boundary, **439,** 441,
    *R8–R9. See also* plate tectonics;
    tectonic plate.
    convergent, 404, *404,* 427, 429,
        *429,* 441, *441*
    divergent, 405, *405,* 427, 428, *428,*
        *429,* 441, *441*
    earthquakes and, 401, 439, *439,*
        441, *441*
    locations of, *403,* 427, 440, 441,
        492
    transform, 405, *405,* 441, *441*
    volcanoes and, 427, 427–430, *428,*
        *429, 430*
telescope
    discoveries made with, 454–455,
        511, 516
    Galileo and, 454, 462–463, *463,*
        516
    Hubble Space Telescope, 37, *37,*
        552, *572*
    space, 37, *37,* 522, 572, *572*
telescope mechanic, 511
*Telstar* satellite, *562, 563*
temperate deciduous forest, *629*
temperate grassland, *629*
temperate rain forest, 628, *628*
    location of, *629*
temperature, **204**
    absolute zero, 204, 205
    of biomes, 628
    chemical change and, 143
    in climate change, 67
    conduction and, 215
    conversions, R45, *R45*
    gases and, 9, *9*
    on gas giants, 514
    kinetic energy and, 204
    measurement of, *51, 71,* 204, *205,*
        R41
    on Mercury, 499
    metamorphic rocks and, 358, 369,
        *373*
    on the moon, 503
    probe, R42, *R42*
    in the protoplanetary disk, 478,
        *478*
    rate of cricket chirping and, 21
    in the rock cycle, 372, *372–373*
    scales, 204, 205, *205*
    in the sun, 487, *487*
    thermal energy and, 210, *210–211*
    thermograms, *83*
    on Venus, 501
Temple 1, Comet, *561*
tensile strength, 151
tension, at divergent boundaries, **417,**
    441
Tereshkova, Valentina, 556, *556*
terrestrial planet, **498.** *See also* Earth.
    Earth, *502,* 502–503, *503*
    formation of, 478, *478*
    Mars, *1,* 504–507, *505, 506, 507,*
        573, *573,* 577

Mercury, *498,* 498–499, *499*
Venus, *500,* 500–501, *501*
tertiary source, 312
Tesla, Nikola, *38*
tesla coil, *38*
test tube, 78, *78*
Teton Mountains (Wyoming), *366,* 419,
    *419*
texture, 353, *353*
theory, scientific, 7, 8–**9.** *See also*
    scientific theory.
thermal conductivity, 128, *128,* 151,
    172
thermal energy, **210**
    conduction, 151, 215
    convection, 216
    heat and, 194, 213
    kinetic energy and, 194
    radiation, 216, 217, *217*
    temperature and, 204, 210,
        *210–211*
    transfer of, 210, 212, 213,
        215–216
    unit of, 210
thermogram, *83*
thermometer, *51, 71,* **204,** *205,* R41,
    *R41*
Think Science
    Evaluating Scientific Evidence,
        122–123
    Forming Hypotheses, 150–151
    Making a Presentation, 566–567
    Making Conclusions from Evidence,
        66–67
    Scientific Debate, 312–313
third-class lever, 269, *269*
Third Law, Kepler's, 472, *472*
tire, 270
Titan (moon of Saturn), 519
titanium, 347, *347*
tool, scientific. *See also* technology.
    computers and technology as, 79,
        *79*
    in laboratories, *78,* 78–79, *79*
    for measurement, 72, *72*
topaz, *339,* 340
transform boundary, **405**
    earthquakes at, 405, 441, *441*
    fracture zones, 405
    strike-slip faults at, 416, *416*
triple-beam balance, 72, *72,* 112, *112,*
    R38, *R38*
Triton (moon of Neptune), 523, *523*
Trojan asteroids, 534, *534*
tropical grassland, 628
    location of, *629*
tsunami, 442–443, *443*
tube worm, *575*
tundra, 628
    location of, *629*
tungsten, 171
turbine, 296, *296*
Tycho Brahe, 471

## U

unbalanced forces, 249, *249*, 252, *252*
unicellular organism, 597, 599, *599*
Unit Review, 47–50, 101–104,
    181–184, 279–284, 329–332,
    381–384, 449–452, 543–548,
    585–588, 637–640
units of measurement. *See also*
    measurement; SI units of
    measurement.
    astronomical unit (AU), 498
    calorie (cal), 213
    centimeter (cm), 114, 224, 228
    cubic centimeter (cm³), 114, 116,
        118, 346
    cubic meter (m³), *71*, 72
    degree, 204, 205, *205*
    feet (ft), 224
    gram (g), *71*, 111, 118, 346
    grams per cubic centimeter (g/cm³),
        *71*, 118, 346
    grams per milliliter (g/mL), *71*, 118
    inch (in), 58, 71, 224
    joule (J), 213
    kelvin (K), *71*, 72, 204, 205
    kilogram (kg), *71*, 72
    kilometer (km), 224, 226, 228, 426,
        518
    kilometers per hour (k/h), 226
    liter (L), 72, 116
    meter (m), 228
    meters per second (m/s), 226, 229,
        239
    meters per second squared (m/s²),
        239
    mile (mi), 224
    miles per hour (mi/h or mph), 226
    milliliter (mL), 72, 116, 118
    millimeter (mm), 74, 518
    newton (N), 112, 246
    pound (lb), 112
    second (s), 72
    SI prefixes, 74, *74*
    watt (W), 151
Unit Summary, 46, 100, 180, 278, 328,
    380, 448, 542, 584, 636
universal gravitation, law of, 473, R16
uplift, **374**, *374*, 418
uranium, 302, 308
Uranus
    axis of rotation, 520, *521*
    characteristics of, 514, 520, *520*
    discovery of, 455
    Miranda and, 521, *521*
    period of revolution, 521
    seasons on, 521
Using a Microscope, R35
Using Graphic Organizers to Take
    Notes, R20–R23
Using the Metric System and SI Units,
    R44–R45
Using Vocabulary Strategies,
    R24–R25

## V

Valhalla crater (Callisto), 517
Valles Marineris (Mars), 505
Valley of Fire State Park (Nevada), *370*
variable, **21**, 23, R30
    controlling, 23
    dependent, 21, 23, 59, R30
    in experiments, 21, 30
    independent, 21, 23, R30
    isolating, 23, 30
    in models and simulations, 61–62,
        91, 93, 95
vector, **231**, 238
velocity, **231**
    acceleration and, 238–241
    average, 231
    force and, 251, 463
    speed and, 231
Venn diagram (graphic organizer), R22,
    *R22*
vent, volcanic, **424**, *424*
Venus, *496*, *500*, 500–501, *501*
    characteristics of, 500, *500*
    phases of, 462
*Viking* space probes, 560, *562*
Virchow, Rudolf, 596, 597
viscosity, 425, 427
Visual Summary, 14, 30, 42, 64, 80,
    96, 120, 136, 148, 164, 176, 198,
    206, 218, 232, 242, 256, 274,
    298, 310, 324, 348, 360, 376,
    394, 408, 420, 432, 444, 464,
    480, 494, 508, 524, 538, 564,
    580, 600, 616, 632
vitreous, R2
vocabulary strategies, R24–R25
volcanic ash, 431, *431*
volcanic glass, 355
volcano, **424**. *See also* magma; lava.
    cinder cones, 425, *425*, 427, 428
    composite volcano, 425, *425*, 427,
        429
    craters and calderas, 426, *426*, 429
    eruptions, *385*, *422*, 424, 431, *431*
    fissures, *355*, 426, 427–428, *428*
    formation of, 369, 424
    on Jupiter's moons, 516
    lava plateau, 426, *426*
    locations of, 401, 419
    magma in, 424, *424*, 429
    on Mars, 505, *505*
    Ring of Fire, 427, *427*
    shield volcano, 425, *425*, 427, 428,
        430
    structure of, 424, *424*
    tectonic plates and, 404, *404*, *427*,
        427–430, *428*, *429*, *430*
    on Venus, 501, *501*
    volcanic mountains, 425, *425*
volume, **113**, 116, 116, 338
    calculating, 114, *114*, *115*
    density and, 117
    formula, 114
    gases and, 9, *9*

water displacement and, 116, *116*
    weight and, 113
*Vostok 1* spacecraft, 556
*Voyager 2* spacecraft, 521, 522,
*Voyager* space probes, 560, *561*, *567*

## W

Ward, A. Wesley, 510, *510*
waste-to-energy plant, *41*
water. *See also* ocean.
    boiling point of, 127
    convection currents in, 216, *216*
    density of, 118
    on Earth, 502
    electrical energy from, 294, 296
    elements in, 175
    on Enceladus, 519, *519*
    on Europa, 516
    hydroelectric energy from, *317*,
        319, *319*
    importance to life, 502
    on Mars, *504*, 506, *506*
    properties of, 106–107
    as a pure substance, 156, *157*
water displacement, volume from, 116,
    *116*
wave
    electromagnetic, 193, 216
    seismic, *438*, 438–439
    tsunami, 442–443, *443*
weathering, **369**, *369*, 372, *373*
weather satellite, *563*, 574, *574*
webpage, evaluating information on,
    29
wedge, 273, *273*
Wegener, Alfred, 398
weight, **111**,
    mass and, 111, 112
    measurement of, 112, *112*
weightlessness, *470*, 571, *571*
Wesley, Anthony, 511
wheel and axle, *262*, **270**, *270*
wheelbarrow, 264, *264*, 269
White, Edward H., II, 556
White Cliffs of Dover (England), *357*
Why It Matters, 73, 133, 169, 195,
    217, 253, 297, 347, 375, 431,
    443, 507, 531, 575, 613, 631
wind
    on Earth, 514
    on Jupiter, 514, 515
    on Mars, 505
    on Neptune, 523
    solar, 505
wind energy, 287, *287*, 291, 296, **318**,
    *318*
    advantages and disadvantages of,
        318
wind farm, 318, *318*
windmill, *318*
wind-powered water pump, *318*
wind tunnel, *91*
wind turbine, 318, *318*
wool processing, 140–141, *140–141*